This air, which, by life's law,
My lung must draw and draw
Now but to breathe its praise,
Minds me in many ways
Of her who not only
Gave God's infinity
Dwindled to infancy
Welcome in womb and breast,
Birth, milk, and all the rest
But mothers each new grace
That does now reach our race.

Gerard Manley Hopkins, S.J. (1844-1889)
"The Blessed Virgin Compared
to the Air We Breathe"

Infinity Dwindled to Infancy

A CATHOLIC AND EVANGELICAL CHRISTOLOGY

Edward T. Oakes, S.J.

WILLIAM B. EERDMANS PUBLISHING COMPANY
GRAND RAPIDS, MICHIGAN / CAMBRIDGE, U.K.

Published 2011 by

Wm. B. Eerdmans Publishing Co.

2140 Oak Industrial Drive N.E., Grand Rapids, Michigan 49505 /

P.O. Box 163, Cambridge CB3 9PU U.K.

www.eerdmans.com

Printed in the United States of America

20 19 18 17 16 15 14   8 7 6 5 4 3 2

Library of Congress Cataloging-in-Publication Data

Oakes, Edward T., S.J.

Infinity dwindled to infancy: a Catholic and evangelical Christology / Edward T. Oakes, S.J.

p.   cm.

Includes bibliographical references and index.

ISBN 978-0-8028-6555-7 (pbk.: alk. paper)

1. Jesus Christ — Person and offices.   2. Incarnation.   I. Title.

BT203.O225   2011

232'.809 — dc22

2010054057

Imprimi potest: V. Rev. Douglas Marcouiller, S.J.

Provincial, Missouri Province of the Society of Jesus

September 9, 2009

Nihil obstat: Rev. Thomas G. Weinandy, O.F.M., Cap.

Secretariat of Doctrine, United States Conference of Catholic Bishops

June 24, 2009

Imprimatur: Francis Cardinal George, O.M.I.

Archbishop of Chicago

July 31, 2009

In accordance with Canon 824, permission to publish was granted on July 31, 2009 by His Eminence, Francis Cardinal George, O.M.I., Archbishop of Chicago. Permission to publish is an official declaration of ecclesiastical authority that the material is free from doctrinal and moral error. No legal responsibility is assumed by the grant of this permission.

Dedicated to the Faculty, Staff, and Students of
The University of St. Mary of the Lake/Mundelein Seminary
and to its Chancellor,
Francis Cardinal George, O.M.I.,
Archbishop of Chicago

and to the members of
Evangelicals and Catholics Together

CONTENTS

Contents

ACKNOWLEDGMENTS

Even if writing a book is mostly a solitary activity, it is also a remarkably collaborative effort, as I discovered time and again in writing this book on Christology. I owe a real debt of gratitude to Lorraine Olley, Dean of the Library at Mundelein Seminary, and to Marian Johnson, in charge of the Interlibrary Loan Desk, both of whom must be at least as glad as I am that the project is finally done.

I twice taught early versions of this book to students at Mundelein in elective seminars, all of whom helped me mightily with their own research papers. (I shamelessly assigned them topics that I had yet to reach in my manuscript, giving them an early lesson in the ways of Hegel's master/slave dialectic.) I can't name them all; but I owe a special debt of thanks to Andrew Liaugminas for his expertise on Jacques Dupuis and the *extra Calvinisticum* (don't ask: it's all explained later); to Shawn Gould for teaching me that Thomas Aquinas's concept of the beatific vision of Christ is compatible with the results of research in the historical Jesus; to Friar Anthony Lajato, OFM Conv., for convincing me to include John Duns Scotus in this book with his fine research paper on the Scot's crucial role in Christology; to Timothy Oudenhoven for researching the Christology of Jon Sobrino; to Fr. Jeffrey Njus for his fine paper on the Christology of John Paul II; to Fr. Gordon Reigle for his expertise on *Dominus Iesus;* and to Christopher Cuddy for his paper on Joseph Ratzinger's theology of the cross. Fr. Thomas Weinandy, O.F.M., Cap. not only graciously provided the *nihil obstat* but proffered many helpful suggestions when he first read the manuscript in its entirety. Fr. Richard Schenk, O.P. helped with the Glossary and encouraged me to be as complete as a Glossary would allow. And of course I must thank Fr. Thomas Cummings, S.J. for suggesting the title for this book (which he did way back in my days as a high school student, when he taught me English literature in my senior year).

Fr. Raymond Webb, Academic Dean, first suggested I teach the manuscript as an elective seminar; and Fr. John Lodge, Ecclesiastical Dean, did the same for the STL summer program, without which this book would be much the poorer.

From the time I began thinking about this book, I kept in mind my friendships — now stretching back many years — with the members of Evangelicals and Catholics Together. What always struck me is how little divides us (at least in my estimation) in matters of Christology. Given that fact, we of course have been concentrating on issues that do divide us, such as justification and Mariology. For that reason, I cannot help but think that a return to the confession that does indeed unite us — the Lordship of Christ — might serve as a lodestar if we hit other doctrinal storms along the way. If at least the general drift of this book meets with their approval, then it will have served its purpose.

Finally, I must thank all those others to whom this book is dedicated: my students in the Christology seminar (including those not named above); my delightful and entirely collegial colleagues on the faculty of Mundelein Seminary; and above all I must thank its Chancellor, Francis Cardinal George, O.M.I. If he had not first offered me a position on the faculty of his seminary seven years ago, I doubt this book would ever have seen the light of day.

EDWARD T. OAKES, S.J.
Feast of the Transfiguration
August 6, 2009

CHAPTER 1

Introduction: The Poets' Incarnation

A key has no logic to its shape. Its logic is: it turns the lock.

G. K. Chesterton, *Orthodoxy*

"Christology," as the two roots "Christ" and "-ology" embedded in the word indicate, means the study (or science) of Jesus Christ, just as "biology" means the science of life, and "psychology" the science of the soul or mind. But the resemblances of these various "-ology" words can be deceptive. For most sciences regard themselves as publicly accessible, accessible precisely because their field of study is recognized by all. Everyone, after all, knows what life is and what a mind is (one's own, if no one else's). To be sure, some people — called materialists — deny that there is anything special about life, which for them results only from the accidental concatenation of chemicals into ever more complex forms (indeed, for them chemicals are themselves just complex arrangements of atoms). Similarly, materialists regard consciousness or mind as but the exhalation of electricity in the brain ("the brain secretes thoughts the way the liver secretes bile," as one materialist put it). But still, even the most hardened materialist recognizes that the very complexity of organisms and of the human mind requires a shift in methodology and of scientific discipline when one studies a frog instead of a stone, or decides to examine the breakdown in a marriage instead of the formation of a galaxy. Here, at least, agreement is both fundamental and universal: biology and psychology are true sciences because their respective fields of investigation are open and accessible to all rational beings.

But not with Jesus Christ. Here the "science" of Christ becomes accessible only to believers, that is, to people who confess that an itinerant rabbi in first-century Galilee was also "God from God, Light from Light, true God from true God." How can that be? Such is the problem set before that branch of theology called "Christology." Even a cursory glance at the history of this branch of theology shows that the fundamental problem running through all christological thought centers on this juxtaposition of the infinite with the finite. But as we have just seen, that problem has a problem of its own: the problem of the infinite-becoming-finite in Jesus of Nazareth is recognized only by Christian believers. In fact, non-Christians stand outside the precincts of Christianity precisely because they deny that Jesus is (at least in any proper, strict sense of the word) the very enfleshment of God.

Let us, however, leave aside (at least for a while) this preliminary, propaedeutic problem of Christology's inaccessibility to the non-Christian. The scientific status of Christology is problematic inside the realm of Christian faith too. This is because, for believers, there still lurks a more fundamental conceptual problem: How could the supposedly unchanging, eternal God become anything else? After all, the word "become" usually denotes change in time.[1] Moreover, what God has "become" in Christian doctrine is not just something else, something conceptually opposite to the infinite and unchanging deity. More crucially, God has become a member of the very race that should be worshiping that changeless God. Among other consequences, this becoming of God "into" a man seems to shift worship away from the eternal God to one of the members of the human race, who as a member of that race should supposedly be worshiping, not being worshiped.

So here is the dilemma: How can the infinite become finite without losing its infinity? Can such a question even be meaningfully asked without lapsing into hopeless contradiction? In other words, how do we develop a Christology without thereby violating the central logical axiom of all sciences

---

1. Just as the verb "to be" has, from the time of Parmenides, been taken to be the main verb denoting *stasis*, so "to become" is the quintessential verb for denoting *change*, of whatever type. Of course there are all kinds of change, from such "weak" types of becoming as when we say, "Socrates is becoming wiser by the day," to such "strong" examples as when the biology textbook says, "the tadpole became a frog" or when the Brothers Grimm tell us that the pumpkin became a carriage. The first type denotes the becoming of *growth* from latent potential to full actuality; the latter is the becoming of *metamorphosis*. But neither sense can apply to God strictly speaking, since first, as Pure Act, God has no potential left to fulfill, and second, because if the Logos of God, as we say, "turned into" a man, he would no longer be God, anymore than a frog is still a tadpole or the carriage has any "pumpkinhood" left in it. Yet the Bible uses that verb explicitly when it says "the Word became flesh" (John 1:14), and so the paradox remains.

without exception, Aristotle's law of noncontradiction? Put even more glar-ingly (to use the striking line of the nineteenth-century Jesuit poet Gerard Manley Hopkins that is both the epigram for this book and the inspiration for its title), what does it mean for God's infinity to "dwindle" to infancy?

Of this baffling paradox at least we can say this: Christian poets have no qualms with the paradoxes of Christology; indeed, they seem to wallow in it. Take, for example, the poem "The Nativity of Our Lord and Saviour Jesus Christ" by Christopher Smart (1722-71):

> God all-bounteous, all-creative,
>> Whom no ills from good dissuade,
> Is incarnate, and a native
>> Of the very world he made.[2]

Or this Christmas poem, "New Prince, New Pomp," from the Jesuit Robert Southwell (1561-95), martyred during the reign of Queen Elizabeth I:

> Behold, a silly tender babe
>> In freezing winter night
> In homely manger trembling lives:
>> Alas! a piteous sight.
> . . . .
> Despise him not for lying there;
>> First what he is inquire:
> An orient pearl is often found
>> In depth of dirty mire.
> . . . .
> This stable is a Prince's court,
>> The crib his chair of state,
> The beasts are parcel of his pomp,
>> The wooden dish his plate.
> . . . .
> With joy approach, O Christian wight, [wight: fellow]
>> Do homage to thy King;
> And highly praise this humble pomp
>> Which he from heaven doth bring.[3]

2. Christopher Smart, "Hymn 32," in *The New Oxford Book of Christian Verse,* ed. Don-ald Davie (Oxford: Oxford University Press, 1981), pp. 182-83.
3. Robert Southwell, "New Prince, New Pomp," in *The New Oxford Book of Christian Verse,* pp. 51-52.

Christmas has often sent Christian poets on these paradoxical flights of fancy, even in modern times, as in John Betjeman's poem "Christmas," the last three stanzas of which speak frankly of the odd juxtaposition of corny gifts around the Yule tree with the real miracle of the Incarnation:

> And is it true? And is it true,
>   This most tremendous tale of all,
> Seen in a stained-glass window's hue,
>   A baby in an ox's stall?
> The Maker of the stars and sea
> Become a Child on earth for me?
>
> And is it true? For if it is,
>   No loving fingers tying strings
> Around those tissued fripperies,
>   The sweet and silly Christmas things,
> Bath salts and inexpensive scent
> And hideous tie so kindly meant,
>
> No love that in a family dwells,
>   No caroling in frosty air,
> Nor all the steeple-shaking bells
>   Can with this single Truth compare —
> That God was Man in Palestine
> And lives to-day in Bread and Wine.[4]

The Metaphysical poets of the seventeenth century made such christological juxtapositions and paradoxes their *métier*, from George Herbert's "The Son" ("For what Christ once in humbleness began / We him in glory call, The Son of Man") to John Donne's "Upon the Annunciation and Passion Falling upon One Day, 1608,"[5] where he calls Mary "at once receiver and the legacy," a paradox that shows that "death and conception in mankind is one."

Even more poignant is his more simply titled poem "Annunciation," a lovely meditation on the paradox of infinity gestating in the womb of the Virgin:

4. John Betjeman, "Christmas," in *Collected Poems* (Cambridge, MA: Riverside Press, 1959), pp. 177-79.

5. In 1608 Good Friday, set by the lunar calendar, occurred on March 25, the annual solar date of the Feast of the Annunciation, a perfect occasion for Donne to reflect on the juxtaposition of these two mysteries.

Salvation to all that will is nigh;
That All, which always is All everywhere,
Which cannot sin, and yet all sins must bear,
Which cannot die, yet cannot choose but die,
So, faithful Virgin, yields himself to lie
In prison, in thy womb . . .

. . . who is thy Son and Brother;
Whom thou conceiv'st, conceiv'd; yea, thou art now
Thy Maker's maker, and thy Father's mother;
Thou hast light in dark, and shut'st in little room
Immensity, cloistered in thy dear womb.[6]

And finally my favorite, an anonymous poem from the fifteenth century, called, appropriately enough, "The Divine Paradox":

A God and yet a man?
A maid and yet a mother?
Wit wonders that wit can
Conceive this or the other.
A God, and can he die?
A dead man, can he live?
What wit can well reply?
What reason reason give?
God, truth itself, does teach it;
Man's wit sinks too far under
By reason's power to reach it.
Believe and leave to wonder.[7]

Ah, but that is just what Christology has refused to do: just believe and wonder. Christology would never have arisen if Christians had decided *only* to wonder and to leave it at that. Both Plato and Aristotle said that philosophy is born in wonder, but the same holds for theology as well. *Reason wants to give reasons for believing what goes beyond reason.* Reason wants to understand. That is its function in the human mind. And if that same mind is a be-

---

6. John Donne, "Annunciation," in *John Donne's Poetry,* selected and edited by Arthur L. Clements (New York: Norton, 1992), pp. 109-10.

7. From *Religious Lyrics of the Fifteenth Century,* ed. Carleton Brown (Oxford: Oxford University Press, 1939), p. 187 (spelling modernized). The poem from Hopkins comes from *Hopkins: Poems and Prose,* Everyman's Library (New York: Alfred A. Knopf, 1995), p. 35.

lieving mind, its reason will want to understand what it itself has been prompted by faith to believe. And so if theology is ultimately faith seeking understanding, what is faith called upon to understand? Nothing less than this: an infinite God who is a finite man, a virgin who is a mother, a God who dies, a dead man who lives, a baby born into the very world it made, a prince who is a pauper, in short, Infinity dwindled to infancy.[8] These are the problems of faith seeking understanding — and for that same reason, these are the problems of Christology too, which come in several guises.

Take, for example, the problem of time. Here I am not just referring to the knotty philosophical problem of the eternal-becoming-temporal. More crucially, the question of time raises the question of salvation-history, indeed of salvation itself: If Jesus came to save the whole world but was born, as all human beings are, in one period of history and not another, how do his saving effects reach out to all those who came before him or to those who could never have heard of him after his birth due to geographical limitations and different civilizational presuppositions? The second-century pagan philosopher Celsus raised this objection just as the Christian religion was beginning to spread throughout the Roman Empire: If Christ came to save all, why was he born in such a backwater province of the Empire and so obscurely known by his contemporaries? So natural and obvious is this objection that missionaries often encounter it. For example, Francis Xavier had to face exactly the same question that Celsus had hurled at Christian apologists like Origen:

> If God was merciful, why had he not revealed himself to the Japanese before the priests came from Tenjiku? And if it was true, as they taught, that those who do not worship God go to hell, God had had no mercy on their ancestors, since he had let them go to hell without granting them a knowledge of himself.[9]

---

8. Thomas Aquinas too tried his hand at poetry from time to time, and we are not surprised to find in his efforts the same chiasmic paradoxes that characterize the best of Christian poetry, as here from the second stanza of his poem *Adora Te Devote, Latens Deitas:* "Visus, tactus, gustus, in te fallitur;/ Sed auditu solo tuto creditur./ Credo quidquid dixit Dei Filius./ Nil hoc verbo veritatis verius." "Sight and touch and taste here fail;/ Hearing only can be believed. I trust what God's own Son has said./ Truth from truth is best received." In *The Aquinas Prayer Book: The Prayers and Hymns of St. Thomas Aquinas,* trans. Robert Anderson and Johann Moser (Manchester, NH: Sophia Institute Press, 2000), p. 68.

9. Georg Schurhammer, *Francis Xavier: His Life and Times* (Rome: Jesuit Historical Institute, 1982), vol. 4, p. 222. As Celsus saw, the temporal particularity of the incarnation also entails spatial particularity, a point addressed by Thomas Aquinas when he took up the

This problem, as we shall discover, is part of what may be called the *soteriological* problem. Another problem that must also be touched on can be called the *psychological* problem, that is, the problem of the mind or consciousness of Jesus: If he is God, does he think God's thoughts? Does he think *only* God's thoughts? That is, has the divine Logos (the Greek word "logos" can in certain contexts mean "mind") replaced the human soul of Jesus, or what would have been the human soul of Jesus had he been conceived in the normal way? What did Jesus know? Could he foretell the future? Did he know all the languages of the world? How did he pray? Did he fear death? Did he know that he would rise from the dead? Was he always aware of his union with God? Did he have a direct vision of God (the "beatific vision") at all times, so that in effect he dwelt in heaven while he was on earth? What kind of awareness did he have of his mission? Was he suffused with a messianic consciousness; and if so, when did it come upon him? Did he plan to found a church, or did he expect the end of the world in his lifetime? What did he think was the purpose of his death? Did he despair? Did he think his death would provoke the end of the world? What did he think of the Judaism of his time? How did he relate to it? Did he expect to found a new religion, or only to reform Judaism from within?

Related to these questions is the *epistemological* or *historical-critical* problem. If the psychological questions about Jesus' self-consciousness have answers (and perhaps they don't), how are we to discover them? Can documents written almost two thousand years ago provide answers to such questions, especially if the authors of those documents did not pose those questions in a modern way? Furthermore, does it distort the answers to these essentially historical questions if faith brings to bear its presuppositions on the question of history, or is faith the only door that can give us true access to the mind and mission of Jesus? And in either case, what role does historical research, whether faith-based or not, have to contribute? Is it a threat? An aid? Or is it more than a mere aid; is it simply downright indispensable, perhaps the only standard at all for answering these questions? In other words, if Christology is, as we have previously asserted, a "science" peculiar to belief, what does history contribute? What if the historian is an

---

question why Jesus was born in Bethlehem: "If He had chosen the great city of Rome, the change in the world would be ascribed to the influence of her citizens. If He had been the son of the Emperor, His benefits would have been attributed to the latter's power. But that we might acknowledge the work of God in the transformation of the whole earth, He chose a poor mother and a birthplace poorer still. 'But the weak things of the world hath God chosen, that He may confound the strong' [1 Cor. 1:27]." *Summa theologiae* III q.35 a.7 ad 3.

atheist, an agnostic, a Jew, a Muslim, a classicist, a Dead Sea Scrolls scholar, a scoffer?

And then of course there is the aforementioned *philosophical* problem, one so beloved of the poets: How can infinite and finite be equated? How can the eternal become the temporal? How can a baby born into the world be worshiped as the Creator of that world? How can the One enter the world of the Many? the Unchanging into the world of change? the Immortal One into the world of death? And finally, how can these paradoxes be protected from the charge of outright contradiction, so that theology does not become a kind of high-grade chatter about square circles and married bachelors? Can paradoxes yield a form of truth that outright contradictions cannot?

Finally, there is the *trinitarian* problem. Gradually, with the increased specialization of theology over the centuries, the theology of the Trinity began to be treated separately from Christology; and indeed there are issues (such as the procession of the Holy Spirit) best dealt with on their own terms, distinct from Christology. But it is a fact of Christian revelation that the church only came to know of the triune God in Christ, and correlatively only knew of Christ's saving work in terms of it being a trinitarian event. The mutuality of Christ and Trinity emerges in the church's consciousness as early as St. Peter's first sermon on Pentecost, when the first apostle speaks of God making Jesus both "Lord and Christ" in the resurrection, who "has received from the Father the Holy Spirit" (Acts 2:36, 33). Although the center of gravity of this book rests more on issues pertaining to the identity of Christ, we will also see how intimately those questions are affected by decisions regarding the Trinity, and how much those decisions will in turn affect later christological debate. For this above all is the basis of Christianity: *Christology is a truth about God, just as the Trinity is a truth about Jesus.*[10]

Indeed, one can rightly say that Christology is a sapiential "science" that

10. "In the 'bad old days' one could write a christological study and largely leave out the Trinity, and — vice versa — one could write a trinitarian study that made little or no reference to Jesus of Nazareth." Gerald O'Collins, S.J., "The Holy Trinity: The State of the Question," in *The Trinity: An Interdisciplinary Symposium on the Trinity,* ed. Stephen T. Davis, Daniel Kendall, S.J., Gerald O'Collins, S.J. (Oxford: Oxford University Press, 1999), pp. 1-25; here 3. This approach is now almost universally regarded as impossible; hence the axiom cited above. For example: "In Bonaventure's thought the Trinity and Christology are inseparably intertwined. It is the mystery of Christ that leads us to the Trinity; and the Trinitarian concept of God is developed as a function of Christology." Zachary Hayes, O.F.M., introduction to *Disputed Questions on the Mystery of the Trinity,* in *Works of Saint Bonaventure,* ed. George Marcil, O.F.M. (New York: Franciscan Institute, 1979), vol. 3, pp. 30-31. What holds true of Bonaventure will prove true of nearly all the theologians treated in this study.

only becomes possible in and by the Holy Spirit: according to Paul, "No one can say 'Jesus is Lord' except by the Holy Spirit" (1 Cor. 12:3). As the Greek Orthodox Metropolitan Ignatius of Latakia said at the Assembly of the World Council of Churches in 1968:

> *Without the Holy Spirit* God is far away, Christ stays in the past, the church is simply an organization, authority a matter of propaganda, the Liturgy no more than an evocation [of events that took place long ago], and Christian loving a slave mentality. But *in the Holy Spirit* the cosmos is resurrected and grows with the birth pangs of the kingdom, the Risen Christ is present to the world, the Gospel becomes the power of life, the church shows forth the life of the Trinity, authority becomes a liberating service, mission is Pentecost, the Liturgy both renewal and anticipation, and human action is deified.[11]

All the problems listed above will be the focus of the rest of the book. But before outlining by anticipation the structure and strategy of the following pages, let me first dispatch this question of paradox, at least provisionally — and once again with the help of poets, who perhaps are those members of each society best endowed to see the value of paradox as a valued avenue to truth. Poetic use of paradox does not of course necessarily justify theological paradoxes; but if the reader can recognize worldly truth lurking in poetic paradox, at least reason will find itself initially open to the possibility of truth embedded in theological paradoxes.

Let us take as our lone example of a nontheological poetic paradox a passage from William Shakespeare's *Romeo and Juliet*, chosen more or less at random (since Shakespeare is so fond of paradoxes, one could choose just about any play or sonnet for an example here). In this passage Friar Lawrence is speaking to Romeo right before he is to marry Juliet. They have been apart for only a few hours after their parting on the balcony, but to both of them it seems an eternity (teenagers in love, and all that), and so when Romeo seems too eager for Juliet's arrival, the good friar issues this warning:

These violent delights have violent ends,
And in their triumph die, like fire and powder,
Which as they kiss, consume. The sweetest honey
Is loathsome in his own deliciousness

---

11. Available online from at http://antiochabouna.blogspot.com/2007/08/orthodoxy-glory-and-shame.html; translation emended. Other sites vary the wording slightly.

And in the taste confounds the appetite.
Therefore, love moderately. Long love doth so.
Too swift arrives as tardy as too slow.

So how can too swift arrive as "tardy" as too slow? "Tardy" means "late" not "early," and the swift arrive too early, not too late. So how can "early" mean "tardy"? How can what is sweet repulse the taste, when "sweet" means what attracts the appetite and is pleasing to the taste?

Pedantic questions surely. The friar is obviously not indulging in word games and confusing the two lovers with logical conundrums about square circles and married bachelors. No, he is using the surface language of opposites to get at something deeper, *more* real than what a flat, stale, and unprofitable use of words in their dictionary meanings can provide. And this is certainly something everyone the world over has recognized and continues to recognize. So it is no wonder that Christian poets glory in the very paradoxes that often intimidate their more pedestrian brethren, the theologians.

Nor will it do to dismiss paradoxes as the indulgence of those who have applied and qualified for a poetic license. Philosophers have long known of paradoxes, from Anaximander and Zeno through Kant and Hegel and down to W. V. O. Quine and our own day. Indeed, in one sense, one may say that paradox has given rise to philosophy in much the same (formal) way it has done for theology.[12] In that history, one encounters a variety of definitions for paradox: riddles like the one given to Oedipus by the Sphinx,[13] or the ones popular on the grade-school playground, like this one recounted by Anaximander: "What has a mouth but never eats, a bed but never sleeps?" (Answer: a river.)

But riddles are theoretically resolvable, even the ever-popular "What came first: the chicken or the egg?" (Evolutionary biology answers that one.) Of greater interest to the philosopher are the truly irresolvable paradoxes, which Gareth Mathews defines as conceptual statements that conflict with other conceptual statements but which still remain true, such as the Stoic claim that those and only those are free who know they are not free.[14] Here

---

12. See Roy Sorensen, *A Brief History of Paradox: Philosophy and the Labyrinths of the Mind* (Oxford: Oxford University Press, 2003), and W. V. O. Quine, *The Ways of Paradox and Other Essays* (Cambridge, MA: Harvard University Press, 1976).

13. Riddle: "What goes on four legs in the morning, two legs in the afternoon, three legs in the evening?" Answer: "Man, who begins life as a baby on all fours; then learns to walk upright on two legs, and finally spends his twilight years using a cane."

14. Gareth Matthews, "Paradoxical Statements," *American Philosophical Quarterly* 11 (1974): 133-39.

the conflict is not seen as an outright contradiction that simply cannot exist (married bachelors, square circles), but as an apparent contradiction that hides a deeper truth (hence the family resemblance between riddles and paradoxes), despite what the dictionary meaning or the rules of logic might say.[15]

Speaking of logic, important developments in that formal science since the Austro-American mathematician Kurt Gödel first proved his two "incompleteness theorems" have also established the cognitive power of paradox. These theorems both, in combination, proved that it is impossible to prove the formal consistency (that is, nonparadoxicality) of mathematics within the mathematical system itself.[16] Prior to Gödel's proofs, this view had seemed absurd to most mathematicians, above all to the German David Hilbert; but all that changed in 1931 when Gödel published his proof, at which point paradox took on a new epistemological sheen, at least according to one of Gödel's keenest interpreters:

> The possibility of paradox, meant to be forever eliminated by Hilbert's program, reasserted itself. And one of the strangest things about the odd and beautiful proof that subverted Hilbert's defense against paradox was the way in which paradox itself was incorporated into the very structure of the proof.[17]

Nor is the paradoxicality of Gödel's proofs an arcane point of use only to mathematicians, for Gödel himself saw its theological relevance: "It [is] something to be expected that sooner or later my proof will be made useful

15. R. M. Sainsbury defines *paradox* as an argument that has acceptable premises and a valid inferential logic but an apparently unacceptable conclusion; see R. M. Sainsbury, *Paradoxes* (Cambridge: Cambridge University Press, 1995). Quine agrees: "May we say in general, then, that a paradox is just any conclusion that at first sounds absurd but that has an argument to sustain it? In the end I think this account stands up pretty well" (Quine, *Ways of Paradox*, p. 1).

16. "What Kurt Gödel proved, in that great paper of 1931, was that no deductive system, with axioms however arbitrary, is capable of embracing among its theorems all the truths of the elementary arithmetic of positive integers unless it discredits itself by letting slip some of the falsehoods too. Gödel showed how, for any given deductive system, he could construct a sentence of elementary number theory that would be true if and only if not provable in that system. Every such system is therefore either incomplete, in that it misses a relevant truth, or else bankrupt, in that it proves a falsehood" (Quine, *Ways of Paradox*, pp. 16-17).

17. Rebecca Goldstein, *Incompleteness: The Proof and Paradox of Kurt Gödel* (New York: W. W. Norton, 2005), p. 164.

for religion, since that is doubtless also justified in a certain sense."[18] As G. K. Chesterton saw so well:

> The real trouble with this world of ours is not that it is an unreasonable world, nor even that it is a reasonable one. The commonest kind of trouble is that it is nearly reasonable, but not quite. Life is not an illogicality; yet it is a trap for logicians. It looks just a little more mathematical and regular than it is; its exactitude is obvious, but its inexactitude is hidden; its wildness lies in wait.[19]

Thus, if Paul Ricoeur is right that "the symbol gives rise to the thought," so too does that hold for the paradoxes of the Christian religion: they are believed because both simple and learned recognize, by a kind of supernatural intuition, as it were, that paradoxes speak the truth.[20] But reason wants to know why and how they can be true, which is why the application of reason to the phenomenon of Jesus Christ in history has given rise to thought, to theology.

Now the application of reason to the data of revelation can be either internally or externally focused: the first shows how various doctrines are interrelated, and goes under the name of systematic theology; while the second attempts to address the objections of outsiders who claim that belief in such a revelation is irrational, and goes under the name of apologetics. As the word "evangelical" in the subtitle indicates, this book means to be systematic, not apologetic. In other words, it uses reason to reflect *from* the faith, not *to* it. In either case, results must perforce be nugatory, as the logician Peter Geach rightly notes:

18. From a letter Gödel wrote to his mother on October 20, 1963, quoted in Goldstein, p. 192.

19. G. K. Chesterton, *Orthodoxy* (San Francisco: Ignatius Press, 1995/1908), p. 87. At least in the formal sense, Quine agrees: "Catastrophe may lurk, therefore, in the most innocent-seeming paradox. More than once in history the discovery of paradox has been the occasion for major reconstruction at the foundations of thought" (Quine, *Ways of Paradox*, p. 1). That Chesterton, himself famous for his fondness for paradoxes, had anticipated these later developments is itself remarkable.

20. Pascal, perhaps Christianity's greatest apologete, agrees: "All these contradictions, which used most to keep me away from the knowledge of any religion, are what have led me soonest to the true religion," Blaise Pascal, *Pensées and Other Writings*, trans. Honor Levi (Oxford: Oxford University Press, 1995), p. 8. Which is why, in Cardinal Newman's famous words, "Ten thousand difficulties do not make one doubt." John Henry Newman, *Apologia pro vita sua* (London: Longmans, 1878), p. 239.

Of course I do not think that natural reason can establish even the non-contradictoriness, let alone the truth, of the Christian belief that a certain human being was and is Almighty God in person. . . . A demand for a strict proof of non-contradictoriness is anyhow often unreasonable — even, as recent logical researches have shown, in pure mathematics. Certainly, if the doctrine of the Incarnation is true, it will not be self-contradictory, and any argument that it is self-contradictory will contain a flaw; but saying this is very different from saying that if the doctrine is true, we ought to be able to see, or prove once for all, that it is non-contradictory.[21]

In other words, the chapters that follow do not claim to have resolved the paradoxes of Christology, nor do they wish to, since, again as we shall see, attempts to resolve Christian paradoxes often lead down heretical trails. Nor do they wish to win over, at least as a direct purpose, the skeptical and the unbelieving. They merely seek to set forth, as simply and as clearly as the subject matter allows, the many ways that Christ has given rise to thought, to theology, to Christology.

The title for this book, *Infinity Dwindled to Infancy: A Catholic and Evangelical Christology,* is meant to set the methodological limits and to determine its operative principles. To work from back to front, the word "evangelical," as we said just above, explicitly avows that, to the extent Christology is scientific, it is so only from inside the confines of a confession of the Lordship of Christ already made.[22] To be sure, secular sciences (above all, history) both impinge upon and influence a scientific account of the identity of Christ. But the New Testament is unanimous in holding that a true knowledge of Christ comes only through faith. "No one knows the Son except the Father, and no one knows the Father except the Son and those to whom the

---

21. P. T. Geach, *God and the Soul* (London: Routledge & Kegan Paul, 1969), pp. 106-7. Thomas Morris adopts the same approach: "[This] book as a whole should be viewed as a defense of the orthodox doctrine of the Incarnation, the two-natures view of Christ, against contemporary philosophical attacks. I do not purport here to show that the doctrine is true; I seek only to answer some contemporary arguments against accepting it as true." Thomas V. Morris, *The Logic of God Incarnate* (Ithaca, NY: Cornell University Press, 1986), p. 16.

22. By "scientific" I am of course referring not to test-tubes, white coats, statistical analysis, and the like, but to that objective method that seeks to conform subjectivity to the reality of the object. But as with all other sciences, matters can sometimes get quite complex. To facilitate the use of this work as a textbook on both undergraduate and graduate classes, I have sequestered the more complex topics inside the *cordon sanitaire* of four *Excursus*, which can be omitted by those less interested in these specialized topics.

Son chooses to reveal him" (Matt. 11:27). For that reason, little attention will be paid to non-Christian critiques of the coherence of Christology except as they prompted a deepening and development of the faith of Christians (just as Celsus did for Origen or Friedrich Nietzsche did for some twentieth-century theologians).

In common parlance, the word "evangelical" has both a more generic meaning, referring to all styles, schools, and denominations of Christianity that are explicitly confessional, and a more specific (and usually American) meaning, which refers to specific churches and denominations that require a confession of Jesus as Lord for church membership. Thus there can be evangelical Anglicans within the Church of England, while other (usually independent) churches are entirely evangelical. My title of course is meant in the generic sense, but not as if only some Catholics confess Jesus as Lord and others don't. The word here is meant in the methodological sense: rather than arguing *to* the possibility of confessing Jesus as Lord (that would be the apologetic approach), I shall begin by presupposing the faith that Jesus is Lord and then seek to understand what that means scientifically (the explicitly confessional approach).

That said, I should also add that my years of involvement in Evangelicals and Catholics Together have taught me how little divides Evangelicals (in the specific sense) from Catholics in matters of Christology. For that reason, especially in the historical sections of this book (Chapters 4 through 10), I shall freely draw on Protestant and Orthodox authors who are themselves evangelical (in the generic sense). In this I will of course be following the directive of the Second Vatican Council, which urged Catholics in these terms:

> Catholics must joyfully acknowledge and esteem the truly Christian endowments from our common heritage which are to be found among our separated brethren. It is right and salutary to recognize the riches of Christ and virtuous works in the lives of others who are bearing witness to Christ, sometimes even to the shedding of their blood. For God is always wonderful in His works and worthy of praise.[23]

As the subtitle indicates, this work will also be frankly and unapologetically Catholic in its outlook, as will emerge especially in Chapter 11, where the developments of modern Christology will find their response in the contemporary Roman magisterium. Throughout the history of Christology the

---

23. Vatican II, *Unitatis redintegratio* (Decree on Ecumenism), §4, in *The Documents of Vatican II,* ed. Walter M. Abbott, S.J. (New York: Guild Press, 1966), p. 349.

reader will notice a dialectic at work in which certain proposals are mooted by individual Christians: when inadequacies are noticed, other writers will respond, often heatedly, but the ultimate resolution of these debates will be found in official responses by magisterial bodies: ecumenical councils primarily but also by individual bishops, very much including the Bishop of Rome; and what was true of the ancient Church holds true for the Roman Church today.

Finally, there is the matter of the title itself, which is meant as no mere nod to the poets, insightful as they are. It will be the fundamental thesis of this book that there can be no getting around the essential paradoxicality of the Christian confession of Christ as Lord. "Take away paradox from a thinker," Søren Kierkegaard once quipped, "and you have a professor." Transposed into Christology, we may paraphrase the line as: "Take away paradox from a theologian, and you have a heretic."[24]

Indeed, long before the poets began to sing the praise of infinity dwindled to infancy, the most important defenders of Christian orthodoxy were adamant that theology would invariably go astray if it did not openly confess the utter strangeness (strange to worldly logic, at least) of the Christian message of salvation. For just that reason, early Christian writers were generally suspicious of Aristotle, not so much for his specific and distinctive philosophical doctrines but because his logic was unsuited, they felt, to the transcendent "logic" of the Logos incarnate, the application of which was bound to lead to heresy. As Harry Wolfson observes:

> Patristic opponents of Arianism as well as Patristic Church historians and heresiographers trace the Arian heresy to Aristotle. . . . But when we study the passages in which Aristotle is mentioned as the source of this heresy, we are surprised to discover that the reference is not to any particular the-

---

24. As we will notice throughout this book, but especially in Chapter 4, denial of the central paradoxes of Christology will inevitably lead to heresy; and pagan critics of Christianity were explicit in their rejection of the Christian message for that same reason: "For the one whom the church was calling God was also the one whose suffering and death on the cross were the burden of the church's witness. . . . The claim that he who was God had suffered called forth some of the earliest doctrinal controversy in the church. Speaking for pagan critics of the gospel, Celsus made this claim the object of his attack, and he contended that 'the body of a god would not have been born . . . nor eat,' . . . and the Gnostic gospels sought to put a screen between the person of the Savior and the pain and suffering described in the canonical Gospels." Jaroslav Pelikan, *The Emergence of the Catholic Tradition (100-600)*, vol. 1 of *The Christian Tradition: A History of the Development of Doctrine* (Chicago: University of Chicago Press, 1971), p. 174.

ory with which the name of Aristotle is generally associated, such, for instance as his denial of Platonic ideas, his belief in the eternity of the world, his conception of God as only a prime mover, or his view that the soul is only a form of the body, but *only to the Aristotelian method of reasoning*. . . . And when we examine these references to the Aristotelian method of reasoning as being the cause of the Arian heresy, we are further surprised to discover that they do not mean reasoning by the Aristotelian method *from premises which are also Aristotelian*, but rather the application of the Aristotelian method of reasoning *to generally accepted Christian premises*.[25]

As we will see in Chapter 4, this is particularly true of the fifth-century Cyril of Alexandria, without whom the Council of Chalcedon — itself the touchstone for all later orthodox Christologies — would never have had available to it the conceptual armory that proved necessary for its teaching. Indeed, Cyril frankly avows that in Christ we find "the strange and rare paradox *(aēthes te kai xenon paradoxon)*" of a master who serves and an abased divine glory.[26] In another work he describes Christ in these terms: "He is filled with wisdom who is himself all wisdom. . . . Rich in poverty; the Most High in humiliation: . . . so thoroughly did God the Word empty himself!"[27]

25. Harry A. Wolfson, "Philosophical Implications of Arianism and Apollinarianism," *Dumbarton Oaks Papers*, Number Twelve (Cambridge, MA: Harvard University Press, 1958), pp. 3-28; here 5; emphases added. Thomas Aquinas of course had a much higher appreciation for Aristotle, as everyone knows. But he too admits the limitations of reason *vis-à-vis* the mysteries of Christology: "Among divine works, this [the incarnation] most especially exceeds reason." *Summa contra Gentiles* IV 27.1, a passage that will be cited at greater length at the end of this chapter and in Chapter 5. Aristotle, by the way, was perfectly aware that logic could not dictate reality but was merely an instrument for its clarification, which was the whole point of his book *Sophistical Refutations:* "By a sophistical refutation and deduction I mean not only a deduction or refutation which appears to be valid but is not, but also one which, though it is valid, only appears to be appropriate to the thing in question." Aristotle, *Sophistical Refutations* 169b20, in *The Complete Works of Aristotle*, ed. Jonathan Barnes (Princeton: Princeton University Press, 1984), vol. 1, p. 287.

26. "We see in Christ the strange and rare paradox of the Lordship in servant's form and divine glory in human abasement." Cyril of Alexandria, *On the Unity of Christ*, trans. John Anthony McGuckin (Crestwood, NY: St. Vladimir's Seminary Press, 1995), p. 101. Earlier in that same work Cyril describes the incarnation of Christ as meaning that ". . . the one who is immaterial could [now] be touched; he who is free in his own nature came in the form of a slave; he who blesses all creation became accursed; he who is all-righteousness was numbered among the transgressors; life itself came in the appearance of death" (p. 61).

27. Cyril of Alexandria, *Commentary on the Gospel of Luke*, trans. R. Payne Smith (New York: Studion, 1983), p. 63.

Such statements could be multiplied at will, both in Cyril's writings and throughout the annals of historical theology. For example, Cyril asks why the Fourth Evangelist said that the Word became *flesh* rather than became *man*. The answer for Cyril was that John wanted to stress the paradox of the incarnation:

> That, in my opinion, is the most probable reason why the holy Evangelist, indicating the whole living being by the part affected, says that the Word of God became flesh. It is so that we might see side by side the wound together with the remedy, the patient together with the physician, what sank towards death together with him who raised it up to life, . . . that which has been mastered by death together with him who conquered death, what was bereft of life with him who was the provider of life. He does not say that the Word came *into* flesh; he says he *became* flesh in order to exclude any idea of a relative indwelling, as in the case of the prophets and the other saints. He really did become flesh, that is to say, a human being.[28]

Going back even further, as early as the second century we read in Ignatius of Antioch: "There is only one physician, who is both flesh and spirit, born and unborn, God in man, true life in death, both from Mary and from God, first subject to suffering and then beyond it, Jesus Christ our Lord."[29] Origen agrees: "He who was in the form of God saw fit to be in the form of a servant; while he who is immortal dies, and the impassible suffers, and the invisible is seen."[30] Athanasius, who would later prove so instrumental in undermining Origen's proto-Arian subordinationist Christology, refused, however, to jettison Origen's paradoxes; indeed, he attacked Origen's Christology for the sake of these same paradoxes:

> For it is a fact that the more unbelievers pour scorn on Him, so much the more does He make His Godhead evident. The things which they, as

28. Cyril of Alexandria, *Commentary on John*, at John 1:14a, in *Cyril of Alexandria*, trans. N. Russell (London: Routledge, 2000), pp. 105-6; emphases added.

29. Ignatius of Antioch, *Epistle to the Ephesians* 7.2, in *The Apostolic Fathers*, trans. Michael W. Holmes, p. 141. A bit later, Melito of Sardis speaks of Christ's crucifixion as predicating Christ both as divine Creator and as the one who suffered a shameful death: "He who hung up the earth is himself hung up; he who fixed the heavens is himself fixed [upon the cross]; he who fastened everything is himself fastened on the wood" (Melito, *On the Pasch*, p. 96).

30. Origen, *In Leviticam Homiliae* 3, 1; *Origen's Homilies on Leviticus 1-16*, trans. W. W. Barkley (Washington, DC: Catholic University of America Press, 1990), p. 52: *qui immortalis est, moritur et impassibilis patitur und invisibilis videtur.*

men, rule out as impossible, He plainly shows to be possible; that which they deride as unfitting, His goodness makes more fit; and things which these wiseacres laugh at as "human" He by His inherent might declares divine.[31]

To be sure, "there is," as Paul Gavrilyuk rightly reminds us, "a thin line between a plain contradiction and a paradox,"[32] and how that line should be drawn will occupy much of the rest of this book. In that regard, we will discover that Paul's use of the concept of the *kenosis* (self-emptying) of the Logos in the second chapter of his letter to the Philippians will prove crucial.[33] But one thing will become clear in the course of the history of Christology: attempts to dissolve the paradox because it is somehow found to be scandalous will invariably run into dead ends, usually heretical.[34] Reason's final task, says Pascal, is to recognize where reason's competence ends; or as Thomas Aquinas says:

It now remains to speak of the mystery of the Incarnation itself. Indeed, among divine works, this most especially exceeds reason. For nothing can be thought of which is more marvelous than this divine accomplishment, that the true God, the Son of God, should become true man. And because among them all it is most marvelous, it follows that toward faith in this particular marvel all other miracles are ordered.[35]

Maximus the Confessor agrees: "For who could know how God takes on flesh, yet remains God? How he, while remaining true God, is yet truly a human being? . . . Only faith understands this, by paying silent homage to the

31. St. Athanasius, *On the Incarnation,* translated by a Member of the C.S.M.V. (Crestwood, NY: St. Vladimir's Seminary Press, 1953), p. 25.

32. Paul L. Gavrilyuk, *The Suffering of the Impassible God: The Dialectics of Patristic Thought,* Oxford Early Christian Studies (Oxford: Oxford University Press, 2004), p. 14.

33. The very fact that Cyril's paradoxes will find their resolution in his interpretation of the kenosis passage in Philippians once again points to the intricate connection of Christology with trinitarian doctrine.

34. As the renowned nineteenth-century theologian Matthias Scheeben says: "Here again the Church proposes two doctrines that seem to contradict each other; yet both have been simultaneously upheld by the Church. . . . With regard to Christian epistemology, the same order is mysterious, that is, it is hidden from natural reason which, by itself and its natural resources, cannot know such an order. It lies above the reach of reason, for it surpasses reason as much as it surpasses nature." Matthias Scheeben, *Nature and Grace,* trans. Cyril Vollert, S.J. (St. Louis: Herder, 1954), pp. 7, 14.

35. Thomas Aquinas, *Summa contra Gentiles* IV, 27.1.

Word of God."[36] John Calvin builds on this tradition and shows how this christological paradox is fundamentally a saving paradox:

> This is the wonderful exchange which, out of his measureless benevolence, he has made with us: that, by his descent on earth, he has prepared an ascent to heaven for us; that, by taking on our mortality, he has conferred his immortality upon us; that, accepting our weakness, he has strengthened us by his power; that, receiving our poverty unto himself, he has transferred his wealth to us; that, taking the weight of our iniquity upon himself that had so sore oppressed us, he has clothed us with his righteousness.[37]

Joseph Ratzinger adopts this same perspective and locates the most fundamental of Christian paradoxes above all in the execution notice that Pontius Pilate placed on the cross: "Jesus of Nazareth, King of the Jews." Pilate spoke more truly than he knew, as the future pope explains: "This execution notice, the death sentence of history, became with paradoxical unity the 'profession of faith,' the real starting point and taproot of the Christian faith, which holds Jesus to be the Christ: *as* the crucified criminal, this Jesus is the Christ, the King. His crucifixion is his coronation; his kingship is his surrender of himself to men, the identification of word, mission, and existence in the yielding up of this very existence."[38]

Such a stress on paradox can lead to some astonishing vistas for apologetics. Even though this book intends to speak within the faith, rather than arguing from skeptical positions to show the reasonability of faith in the manner of apologetics, nevertheless an admission of the paradoxicality of the logic of the incarnation can itself be an entry point for addressing the concerns of the skeptic, even the atheist, a point stressed throughout Chesterton's *Orthodoxy*:

36. Maximus the Confessor, *Ambigua*, PG 91, 1057A. A few pages before, he says: "For the super-essential Word, who took on himself, in that ineffable [virginal] conception, our nature and everything that belongs to it, possessed nothing human, nothing that we might consider 'natural' to him, that was not at the same time divine, negated by the supernatural manner of his existence. The investigation of these things exceeds our reason and our capacity for proof; it is only grasped by the faith of those who reverence the mystery of Christ with upright hearts." *PG* 91, 1053A.

37. John Calvin, *Institutes of the Christian Religion,* trans. Ford Lewis Battles (Philadelphia: Westminster Press, 1960), vol. 2, p. 1362, at 4.17.2.

38. Joseph Ratzinger, *Introduction to Christianity,* trans. J. R. Foster (San Francisco: Ignatius Press, 2004), p. 206; emphasis added.

It is written, "Thou shalt not tempt the Lord thy God." No; but the Lord thy God may tempt Himself; and it seems as if this is what happened in Gethsemane. In a garden Satan tempted man: and in a garden God tempted God. . . . When the world shook and the sun was wiped out of heaven, it was not at the crucifixion, but at the cry from the cross: the cry which confessed that God was forsaken of God. . . . [Let] the atheists themselves choose a god. They will find only one divinity who ever uttered their isolation; only one religion in which God seemed for an instant to be an atheist.[39]

So much, at any rate, for the title and subtitle of the book. As to its structure, the chapters follow in rough chronological order: Chapters 2 and 3 give an overview of the New Testament witness to Christ; they survey the titles applied to Jesus in his lifetime and then in the proclamation by the early church of him risen. Here the question of the historicity of the Gospels will constitute the main focus of treatment. Chapters 4 through 10 then give an overview of the history of christological reflection from the close of the New Testament canon to the present. Finally, Chapters 11 and 12 provide an overview of current magisterial teaching on the identity and work of Christ. (Past magisterial teachings will be taken up as they arise in the course of christological history covered in the earlier chapters.)

Now because contemporary magisterial teaching has taken in, and responded to, the many challenges thrown up by modernity to the Christian gospel, we shall be discussing church teaching not as a kind of reference work that can enable the student to look up "the right answers" and be done with it. Rather we shall see that the teaching of the contemporary church takes place in the same kind of context as did the teaching of the church in the great councils of the first six centuries that will have been treated in Chapter 4: that is, it is a teaching that responds to challenges and speaks definitively from the crises thrown up in each period of church history.

One final point: precisely because Christology is confessional and

---

39. Chesterton, *Orthodoxy*, p. 145. The paradoxes of the Trinity will not be the focus of this work except as they affect Christology proper, probably the most important of which is the one noted by Ratzinger: "[According to Augustine] 'In God there are no accidents, only substance and relation' [quoting *De Trinitate* 5, 5.6]. Therein lies concealed a revolution in man's view of the world: the sole dominion of thinking in terms of substance is ended; relation is discovered as an equally valid primordial mode of reality." Ratzinger, *Introduction to Christianity*, p. 184. See further on this point Francis Cardinal George, "Being through Others in Christ: *esse per* and Ecclesial Communion," *The Difference God Makes: A Catholic Vision of Faith, Communion and Culture* (New York: Crossroad, 2009), pp. 307-26.

ecclesial, it both springs from and returns to worship. Nor should this surprise us. As Abbot Vonier says so marvelously:

> Christ the Son of God could never be man's eternal life, if He were not man's eternal wonder. A Christ whom we could fully comprehend, whom we could understand through and through, could never be our life and our hope because we could not wonder at Him anymore. It is an indispensable condition of all true and lasting admiration that its object should be greater than our knowledge of it; and the growth of knowledge, far from touching the limits of the marvelous, should convince us more and more of their inaccessibility. Love, no doubt, is born from knowledge and understanding; but short-lived and fragile would be the love which would be merely commensurate with knowledge and understanding. Love is actually noblest and strongest when we know enough of a person to realize that there is in him vastly more. . . . We find strong love for Christ the Son of God, a love fresh as a spring morning and unchanging as the eternal hills, only where there is the belief in His divine nature, because there alone the created spirit has scope for endless wonderment. To make of Christ a merely human being is to deprive Him of the attribute of incomprehensibility. Such theology would be the cruelest science, destroying in the soul the most life-giving element of religion — that wonderment which makes it "old yet ever new."[40]

So the paradoxes of Christology not only give rise to theology but, when rightly understood, they also return to worship. In a fascinating collection of early liturgical texts, *The Lenten Triodion*, we find, not surprisingly, the worship of the early church expressed in the most frankly paradoxical terms. For example, in Canticle Five of Good Friday, the early church prayed thus: "I seek Thee early in the morning, Word of God; for in Thy tender mercy towards fallen man, without changing Thou hast emptied Thyself, and impassibly Thou hast submitted to Thy Passion. Grant me Thy peace, O Lord who lovest mankind."[41] And at the moment in the service when the church commemorates the ninth hour, when Jesus gave up his spirit, the congregation sings: "Today He who hung the earth upon the waters is hung upon the

---

40. Abbot Vonier, *The Personality of Christ,* in *The Collected Works of Abbot Vonier,* vol. 1: *The Incarnation and Redemption* (Westminster, MD: Newman Press, no date for publication but *The Personality of Christ* was itself first published in England in 1914), p. 107.

41. *The Lenten Triodion,* translated from the original Greek by Mother Mary and Archimandrite Kallistos Ware (London: Faber & Faber, 1978), p. 593.

Cross. He who is King of the angels is arrayed in a crown of thorns. He who wraps the heavens in clouds is wrapped in the purple of mockery. He who in Jordan set Adam free receives blows upon His face. The Bridegroom of the Church is fixed with nails."[42] And then comes silence. We should expect no less:

> Jesus, we will frequent thy Board,
> And sing the Bounties of our Lord:
> But the rich Food on which we live
> Demands more Praise than Tongues can give.[43]

But that speechless, tongueless praise is still at all points the praise of prayer, where reason finally yields to the light of reason-transcending faith, a point made to brilliant effect in what is probably the most famous English poem of the nineteenth century, Lord Tennyson's *In Memoriam:*

> Strong Son of God, immortal Love
> Whom we, that have not seen thy face,
> By faith, and faith alone, embrace,
> Believing where we cannot prove.
> . . . .
> Thou seemest human and divine,
> The highest, holiest manhood, thou:
> Our wills are ours, we know not how;
> Our wills are ours, to make them thine.
>
> Our little systems have their day;
> They have their day and cease to be:
> They are but broken lights of thee,
> And thou, O Lord, art more than they.
>
> We have but faith: we cannot know;
> For knowledge is of things we see;
> And yet we trust it comes from thee,
> A beam in darkness: let it grow.[44]

42. *The Lenten Triodion,* p. 609.

43. Isaac Watts (1674-1748), "The Church the Garden of Christ," in *The New Oxford Book of Christian Verse,* p. 149.

44. Alfred Lord Tennyson, *In Memoriam,* ed. Erik Gray, A Norton Critical Edition (New York: W. W. Norton, 2004/1850), Prologue, p. 5.

This book, too, is but a "little system" and will someday "cease to be." And even if it speaks the truth, it will do so only as a "broken light of thee," for God-in-Christ is more than all can say.

CHAPTER 2

The Surface Data

No one can say "Jesus is Lord" except by the Holy Spirit.

(1 Cor. 12:3)

The Synchronic Approach

The data for that "science" of Jesus Christ known as Christology come almost entirely from the New Testament. *Almost* entirely. A few pagan authors like Pliny the Younger (c. 61–c. 112) and Suetonius (c. 70–c. 160) make passing reference to Jesus, but their knowledge of his existence stems entirely from their prior knowledge of Christianity, that is, from *Christian* witness to Jesus; so their testimony must be regarded as entirely derivative.[1] The case is somewhat different for the Jewish historian Flavius Josephus, who lived in the generation immediately after Jesus (c. 37–c. 101). He mentions Jesus twice, both times in passing, in his book *The Jewish Antiquities* (his apologetic account of the Jewish religion geared to an educated, non-Jewish reading public); and these references might be based on independent knowledge. The first mention of Jesus is too allusive to be of much value, but the second one is much

---

1. In fact, Suetonius gets the name "Christ" wrong and spells it "Chrestus," which shows how much his knowledge of Christ comes from hearsay; and as governor of Syria Pliny the Younger was dealing with Christians who refused to address the Emperor as *dominus et deus* and explains to the Emperor Trajan their reason: because they worship only their Founder with that title, which clearly indicates that Pliny's knowledge of Christ (whose name he spells correctly) comes from Christian confessions.

more informative. Unfortunately, however, this second brief aside seems to have been doctored by later Christian copyists. But whether the passage is rejected totally as a Christian interpolation, accepted "as is," or taken as basically authentic with a few Christian glosses added, still the passage as a whole tells us little that one would not already have gleaned from the Gospels.[2]

It might seem that the noncanonical gospels (that is, gospels that never made it into the authorized list of New Testament books) would be of use to theologians, for here we have texts that do confess a saving significance to Jesus, even if in terms that will later be judged heretical. However, despite what some scholars like to claim, all these texts without exception stem from the second century at the earliest, and thus are really *reactions* to the faith of first-century Christians.[3] For that reason, informative as they can sometimes

---

2. The second passage about Jesus in the *Jewish Antiquities* reads as follows: "At this time there appeared Jesus, a wise man, if indeed one should call him a man. For he was a doer of startling deeds, a teacher of people who receive the truth with pleasure. And he gained a following both among many Jews and among many of Greek origin. He was the Messiah. And when Pilate, because of an accusation made by the leading men among us, condemned him to the cross, those who had loved him previously did not cease to do so. For he appeared to them on the third day, living again, just as the divine prophets had spoken of these and countless other wondrous things about him. And up until this very day the tribe of Christians, named after him, has not died out" (Flavius Josephus, *Antiquities* 18; 3.3 § 63-64). The translation is that of John Meier in his *A Marginal Jew: Rethinking the Historical Jesus*, vol. 1: *The Roots of the Problem and the Person* (New York: Doubleday, 1991), p. 60. Meier accepts the core of this passage and has the original text written by Josephus to read this way: "At this time there appeared Jesus, a wise man. For he was a doer of startling deeds, a teacher of people who receive the truth with pleasure. And he gained a following both among many Jews and among many of Greek origin. And when Pilate, because of an accusation made by the leading men among us, condemned him to the cross, those who had loved him previously did not cease to do so. And up until this very day the tribe of Christians (named after him) has not died out" (p. 61). Assuming the accuracy of Meier's surgery, the only question becomes how much of this information Josephus gleaned from his own *independent* research. If he got his material solely from the Christian tradition, then we are back where we started, drawing all our data about Jesus solely from the New Testament; if, alternatively, this passage represents independent testimony, then we are given only a few of the barest highpoints about Jesus and his identity: that he was a teacher, gained a following, was condemned to be executed by crucifixion by the Roman governor Pontius Pilate at the instigation of "leading men among us" (presumably above all the Temple authorities), and that the movement he started did not die out after his death. No doubt these are all useful facts for the historian to consider, but if the New Testament is already accepted for its historical reliability on other grounds (a point to be considered later in the next chapter), the utility of Josephus' testimony for the christologian will be minimal.

3. I subscribe here, without further arguing the point, to the conclusion of Joseph

be about the mindset and attitude of later Christians, they really belong in Chapter 4 of this book, treating the history of postbiblical christological controversies.

Accordingly, we may repeat once more: the data for Christology can be found almost exclusively in the New Testament: without these twenty-seven books knowledge of Jesus Christ (as opposed to early Christianity as a religious movement in the Roman Empire) would have likely almost entirely disappeared from history.

This might sound as if Christians now find themselves caught in the precarious position of having little to work with, since the New Testament, despite being made up of twenty-seven "books," is really not all that long; but in fact the New Testament provides them with an abundance of riches, so much so that it takes considerable effort to place the christological teaching of the New Testament into a coherent whole that will make the subsequent history of Christology itself cohere into a meaningful story. The difficulty stems from the two literary genres that the New Testament uses to portray Jesus: the genres comprise either *narratives* or *occasional letters* (in this context "occasional" means writings that were prompted by specific occasions and not necessarily meant as treatises to be read by subsequent generations).

For that reason, the data of the New Testament must be treated under two aspects: the *diachronic* and the *synchronic*. These technical terms come from the science of linguistics and refer, respectively, to the historical (vertical) and the contemporary (horizontal) perspective. For example, linguists often study etymology (the study of the history of the roots of words), and that would form part of the diachronic study of language, because etymology investigates the *history* of words. On the other hand, linguists also study dialects (the regional variations of a standard language), and that contemporary survey of current usage is called the synchronic approach, because the study of dialects looks at the whole range of language use going on *now*. Similarly, semantics studies not the history of the shifting meanings of a word but the range of meaning each word now carries in contemporary usage, and so it too is synchronic in approach.

Because of the complexity of the New Testament data and because of

---

Fitzmyer: "The apocryphal gospels occasionally preserve some primitive tradition about Jesus, but by and large they are merely imaginative outgrowths of the canonical gospel tradition. . . . Despite the contentions of some modern scholars (H. Koester, J. D. Crossan), these apocryphal gospels are scarcely a source of real information about Jesus of Nazareth." Joseph A. Fitzmyer, S.J., *A Christological Catechism: New Testament Answers,* revised and expanded edition (New York: Paulist Press, 1991), pp. 18, 21.

the different literary genres in which that data has been embedded, something similar must be attempted when analyzing the Christology of the New Testament. A diachronic approach would first ask which New Testament books were written in which historical order and then would ask if there is any significant development in christological doctrine as the New Testament itself developed. But it would also look at the narrative of the life of Jesus too, precisely because at least four authors of the New Testament, the Gospel writers, thought the reality of Jesus could best be conveyed through narrative. And finally, a diachronic study of those same Gospels would ask to what extent the narrative progress of christological doctrine inside the church of the first century itself affected the narratives about Jesus, since the Gospels were written for the most part after the epistles were sent out. In other words, because the epistles ("letters") of the New Testament were written before the Gospels (at least those from St. Paul), and because these epistles are more explicit in making doctrinal claims about Jesus, while the Gospels (largely) let the doctrinal claims shine through as implications of their narrative (the Gospel of John is somewhat exceptional in that regard, a point that will be addressed in the next chapter), the question then arises how and to what extent the earlier-embedded doctrinal claims of the epistles influenced the narrative shape of the Gospels.

A synchronic approach, on the other hand, will ignore these historical speculations and simply look across at the whole *range* of the christological teaching of the New Testament, irrespective of when each specific claim about Jesus was "precipitated," so to speak, in the text of the New Testament. It will content itself with merely "cataloguing," as it were, the claims made about Jesus in order to see what the doctrinal import is for each claim made. In other words, like the branch of linguistics known as "semantics" (the study of the meaning of words) irrespective of when these words took on their meaning, a synchronic approach to New Testament Christology will ask about the *meaning* of the titles regardless of when and how the early church began to apply each title to Jesus (thus, this approach will comprise a semantics of the New Testament).

Accordingly, this chapter will first present a survey of the various christological titles given to Jesus by the various authors of the New Testament, regardless of the provenance of the titles or their location in specific New Testament writings — the synchronic approach. Then the following chapter will look at how the New Testament was formed and how that formation itself affected its christological teaching — the diachronic approach. Taking the data in this order will thus allow the various titles applied to Jesus by various New Testament authors to be arranged into a coherent constellation: titles of Jesus that might seem at first to be a matter of individual preference ("Savior" over "Messiah," for example) will then be seen to have a certain inner logic when placed in their historical context, a logic that will then bequeath to subsequent generations the challenge of presenting the identity and work of Jesus Christ to new generations living in new situations and new contexts.

The Titles of Jesus

The major titles the New Testament applies to Jesus are as follows: Prophet, Suffering Servant, High Priest, Messiah, Son of Man, Lord, Savior, Word, Son of God, and God. Far from being a mere litany of honorifics, these titles actually refer to different aspects of his work and identity. The Swiss New Testament scholar Oscar Cullmann, from whom I have drawn this list,[4] usefully clusters these titles under four rubrics: Prophet, Suffering Servant, and High Priest refer to the *earthly* work of Jesus; Messiah and Son of Man refer to the *future* work of Jesus; Lord and Savior to his *present* work; and Word, Son of God, and God to his *preexistence*.[5] Here's how:

Titles That Refer to the Earthly Work of Jesus

Jesus the Prophet   At first glance the title "prophet" seems to be, so to say, a "job description" that anyone — or at least anyone inside the chosen people

4. Oscar Cullmann, *The Christology of the New Testament,* revised edition, trans. Shirley C. Guthrie and Charles A. M. Hall (Philadelphia: Westminster Press, 1963). His headings are of course not hard and fast, and other authors choose other schemas, some of which we will note at the conclusion of this chapter. But Cullmann's are unusually clear, and probably the most influential in contemporary discussion.

5. To be sure, Jesus is also given other titles in the New Testament, such as "rabbi" ("teacher") and "carpenter" but these are not distinctive enough to set Jesus off from other men by specifying in what way he is unique, although both titles do indicate (or at least imply) his full membership in the human race. Similarly, Jesus is also called simply "man," but that specification (in the literal sense of naming his membership in a biological species) can hardly be called a "title," since it pertains to all male human beings and, in some contexts, to all human beings whatsoever. However, in contexts where some early Christians denied the full humanity of Christ, the term "man" could be confessional, as perhaps here: "For there is one God, and there is one mediator between God and men, the *man* Christ Jesus" (1 Tim. 2:5).

of Israel — could fulfill with the right qualifications.[6] Now the reason the title "prophet" can be applied to anyone irrespective of his talents and personality is that, in the Bible, a prophet was someone who experienced the word of God coming to him *from the outside.*[7] Moreover, this divinely vouchsafed word was not given to the prophet for his own benefit but was meant to be handed on to the people in a similarly external, *confrontational* manner (often at great cost to the prophet himself). Thus the title would not seem to convey anything specifically unique about Jesus: "I will raise up for them a prophet like you from among their brethren; and I will put my words in his mouth" (Deut. 18:18). In fact, the New Testament often implies that the title somehow misses the mark: "Others said, 'He is a prophet, *like one of the others*'" (Mark 6:15).

But at the time of Jesus the role of prophet had changed somewhat, and this shift in meaning rendered the title rather less "generic," that is, more amenable for describing the uniqueness of Jesus. First of all, the era of the classical prophets enshrined in the Old Testament — Elijah, Elisha, Amos, Isaiah, Jeremiah, and the like — seems to have died out after the Jews returned from Babylon to Jerusalem in the reign of the Persian king Cyrus. This means that the ascription to Jesus of the title "prophet" would have marked him as at least relatively unusual in his time. In other words, to be called a prophet in the time of Jesus would have implied the dawn of a new era — a restored era, to be sure, but new because it had been so long absent. Second, some of the prophets (Elijah primarily but not exclusively) were expected to return, coming down from heaven or at least reappearing in some mysterious way. This expectation then imbues the term "prophet" at the time of Jesus with a certain eschatological hue: Could this man whom many were calling "prophet" be the very Elijah now come down from heaven whither he had been taken up so many centuries ago?

This expectation clearly affected the kind of reception both Jesus and John the Baptist received from their contemporaries, as we see most clearly

---

6. Actually, the title "prophet" is not exclusive to Israel, for other cultures know of prophets too. Students of Homer and Virgil are already familiar with Cassandra, the Trojan prophetess cursed by Apollo (the god of prophecy to the Greeks) always to be right in her predictions and never to be believed. For a cross-cultural history of prophecy and its relationship to Hebrew prophecy, see Johannes Lindblom, *Prophecy in Ancient Israel* (Philadelphia: Fortress, 1962).

7. Note that the title does not include (necessarily) any notion of being able to foretell the future; indeed the Bible abjures the very concept of soothsaying or fortunetelling (Deut. 18:14; Isa. 44:25).

in the passage from the Gospel of Mark (already partially cited above and which must now be given in full):

> King Herod heard of these things [the miracles of healing and exorcism done by the recently called Twelve], for Jesus' name had become known. Some said, "John the Baptist has been raised from the dead; that is why these powers are at work in him." But others said, "It is Elijah." And others said, "It is a prophet, like one of the prophets of old." But when Herod heard of it he said, "John, whom I beheaded, has been raised." (Mark 6:14-16)

Obviously those of the crowd who thought Jesus was John the Baptist returned from the dead could not have known Jesus during the time of John's active ministry, and perhaps most of them (like King Herod in fact) did not know either one of them directly. But this at least we can say: they connected Jesus and John by their ministerial *behavior*. Neither Jesus himself nor his evangelist Mark is explicitly applying the title "prophet" to Jesus here. Rather, Mark is merely citing the term as it was being used by people who knew Jesus by report or by misinterpretation. Nonetheless both Jesus and the Gospel writers make the behavioral connection with prophecy clear in other contexts, especially when Jesus cleansed the Temple of money-changers, a prophetic gesture clearly alluding to the protests of Jeremiah inside the Temple precincts as recounted in Jeremiah 25. Moreover, Jesus explicitly aligned his own fate at the hands of the chief priests and elders in Jerusalem with the fate of the prophets (Matt. 23:37 = Luke 13:34).[8] But despite these parallels and allusions, reticence on the part of Jesus and the evangelists regarding this title is the key, as Cullmann explains:

> We conclude that according to all four of the Gospels a section of the people expressed their faith in Jesus by the title "the Prophet" and by the associative thoughts which were connected with that term in the Jewish eschatological hope. But Jesus himself did not identify himself in this way. We should repeat here, however, that the prediction of his own return is at least foreshadowed in the conception of the return of the Prophet. Nor did the Synoptic writers express their personal faith in Jesus by means of this conception.[9]

---

8. Ben Witherington III, *Jesus the Seer: The Progress of Prophecy* (Peabody, MA: Hendrickson, 1999).

9. Cullmann, *The Christology of the New Testament*, pp. 36-37; translation silently emended.

Jesus the Suffering Servant   Like the term "prophet," the title "Suffering Servant" refers to an Israelite who fulfills a certain *role* during his life on earth; and since this is a role that anyone (given the disposition and vocation for it) can assume, that disjunction between person and role implies that the *prior* life and identity of the person called to this role are more or less irrelevant to the call (vocations, after all, can come to those whose past life makes them seem quite unsuitable for their new role, like Paul). The term "Suffering Servant," however, is quite ambiguous in the Old Testament, much more so than the term "prophet," for it seems not to have been historically instantiated by any known historical figure, the way the lives of Isaiah and Jeremiah tell us about what a prophet is by their activity.[10] Indeed, some commentators hold that the relatively few descriptions of the Suffering Servant in the second half of the book of Isaiah are meant as a personalized description of a collective reality: that is, that Israel *as a nation* is the real subject of the hymns in Isaiah.

But much more important than this question of identification remains the central fact, undisputed by all commentators, that the Suffering Servant Songs in Isaiah introduce a new motif in Old Testament prophecy: that of *vicarious* suffering. To be sure, the prophets suffered too, but their suffering was regarded as simply a byproduct or consequence of their mission, so much so that many prophets, upon first hearing the call, shirked from their mission precisely because of the suffering that would be entailed by their obedience to it. But the Suffering Servant suffers as the very *essence* of his mission. One of these Songs is especially relevant for the New Testament, whose key passage needs to be quoted here in full (the italicized words highlight the inherent necessity of the Servant's suffering if he is to fulfill his vicarious role):

> He had no form or comeliness that we should look at him, and no beauty that we should desire him. He was despised and rejected by men; a man of sorrows, and acquainted with grief; and as one from whom men hide

10. In fact the *title* "Suffering Servant" is a modern scholarly invention, referring to a figure sketchily portrayed in the second half of the book of Isaiah, where he is called simply "servant" or "servant of the Lord" (in Hebrew, *'ebed YHWH*). But because this anonymous and rather vaguely described servant is characterized primarily by his suffering, modern scholars use the term (usually capitalized as Suffering Servant) as a shorthand reference to the four songs devoted to this figure in Isaiah. But one must be clear that this title, as such, was unknown in the time of Jesus, although the figure himself assumes a significant role in New Testament Christology.

their faces he was despised, and we esteemed him not. Surely he has borne
our griefs and carried our sorrows; yet we esteemed him stricken, smitten
by God, and afflicted. But he was wounded *for* our transgressions, he was
bruised *for* our iniquities; upon him was the chastisement *that made us
whole,* and with his stripes were we healed. All we, like sheep, have gone
astray; and we have turned, every one to his own way; and *the Lord has
laid on him the iniquity of us all.* He was oppressed, and he was afflicted,
yet he opened not his mouth; like a lamb that is led to the slaughter, and
like a sheep that before its shearers is dumb, so he opened not his mouth.
By oppression and judgment he was taken away. . . . By his knowledge
shall the righteous one, my servant, *make many to be accounted righteous;*
and he shall bear their iniquities. . . . *Because* he poured out his soul to
death, and was numbered with the transgressors, yet *he bore the sin of
many,* and made intercession for the transgressors. (Isa. 53:2-12)

These passages of extraordinary beauty, the culmination of the Bible's
Hebrew lyricism, clearly affected the narrative structure of the portrayal of
Jesus in the Gospels (see Matt. 12:15-21), especially in the Passion narratives.
Moreover, we know from Acts of the Apostles that Jesus' fulfillment of these
passages was a crucial factor in the preaching of the earliest church, for these
were the very Songs that the Ethiopian eunuch was reading when the apostle
Philip came upon him and whose explanations prompted the man to convert to Christianity (see Acts 8:26-40). Finally, a comparison of the four
Songs with the accounts of the Passion in all four Gospels shows how much
the evangelists shaped their narrative in terms of the vocabulary and ca-
dences of the Songs.

The question becomes how much Jesus saw himself in those terms, a
complicated question that cannot be fully resolved until we come to the next
chapter dealing with the diachronic, historical development of the New Testament and the historicity of the Gospel accounts. But this at least can be
said: the notion of *vicarious* suffering is the most distinctive semantic implication of the Suffering Servant Songs. In much of the rest of the Old Testament, suffering is seen as either just punishment inflicted upon Israel for its
sins or as the inevitable, if regrettable, consequence of obedience to a call.
Job's suffering is somewhat exceptional here, as he did nothing to merit his
suffering, nor did his suffering come as the consequence of a prophetic call;
but even Job is not understood to suffer vicariously, only innocently.

This means that the real question about Jesus and the Suffering Servant
revolves not so much around his explicit and conscious assumption of the

title (the Gospels do not record him speaking of himself in those terms), but what his attitude was toward his own suffering as explicitly a vicarious suffering. And this we do know: that in all of the accounts of the Last Supper and the institution of the Eucharist by Jesus on the night before he died, he saw his suffering and death as a vicarious act meant to atone for the sins of "the many," an interpretation made even more solemn by its validation in the Eucharist itself. Even so, however, a puzzle remains: as Cullmann says, "The 'Servant of God' is one of the oldest titles used by the first Christians to define their faith in the person and work of Christ. [But] like that of the Prophet, this title disappeared quite early."[11] Why that happened will emerge as the analysis of the titles applied to Jesus proceeds. But this at least we can say at this point: the fact that the title of Suffering Servant fell into disuse by the time the Gospels were composed says something significant about the Gospel depiction of the Last Supper:

> Thus when Jesus took the last meal with his disciples, he announced what he would accomplish the next day on the cross. . . . By the time the Synoptic Gospels were written, [the term Suffering Servant] as a title for Jesus was no longer common in the early Church. The Gospels prefer other titles for him, above all "Christ." It is thus all the more remarkable that not only Paul but also all three Synoptics in relating the story of the Last Supper recall that Jesus at this decisive moment ascribed to himself the role of [Suffering] "Servant of God."[12]

Jesus the High Priest   At first glance the title High Priest would seem to be, of all the titles applied to Jesus, singularly inappropriate, since it was the High Priest at the time who actively colluded in the death of Jesus. Moreover, the institution of the priesthood in Judaism was completely fused to the Temple in Jerusalem, whose cult the High Priest oversaw; and charges swirled around Jesus that his witness and ministry were a threat to the Temple: "We heard him say, 'I will destroy this temple made with hands and in three days will build another not made with hands'" (Mark 14:58).

But it is just that link that provides the key to the basis for this title as applied to Jesus. From the Dead Sea Scrolls we already know that some Jews, presumably the same group Josephus identified as the Essenes, had already made rejection of the current regime of the high priesthood compatible

---

11. Cullmann, *The Christology of the New Testament*, p. 51.
12. Cullmann, *The Christology of the New Testament*, p. 65.

with an idealization of Temple worship in a future millennial reign inaugurated by God. In addition, the concept of priesthood always entails a recognized need for a *mediator;* otherwise a society would not have recognized an institutional need for priesthood,[13] which makes inevitable the linkage between High Priest and the mission of Jesus, especially given Jesus' own supersessionist identification of himself with the Temple: "Something greater than the temple is here" (Matt. 12:6). As Cullmann rightly summarizes:

> We conclude that Judaism knew of an ideal priest who, as the one true priest, would fulfill in the last days all the elements of the Jewish priestly office. The Jewish conception of priest was bound sooner or later to lead to this expectation. Because of his office, the High Priest is *the* proper mediator between God and his people, and as such assumes from the very beginning a position of divine eminence. Judaism had in the High Priest a man who could satisfy already in the present the need of the people for divine mediation in a cultic framework. But the weaker became the correspondence between the reality of the empirical priesthood and their high expectation, the stronger became the Jews' hope for the end when all things would be fulfilled. This hope included also the concept of priest, so that the figure of a perfect High Priest of the end time moved ever nearer to that of Messiah.[14]

This background to the title High Priest goes far to explain the great innovation introduced by the Letter to the Hebrews. At first glance, the title High Priest seems an exalted one, as the word "high" already implies. But the whole point of the Letter to the Hebrews seeks to show that, by virtue of Jesus' sacrifice and his identification with the Temple, the *Mediator also became the victim,* so much so that Hebrews even identifies Jesus the High Priest with Jesus the Suffering Servant: Christ was offered once and for all "to bear the sins of many" (Heb. 9:28), a direct reference to the fourth Suffering Servant Song (at Isa. 53:12). But this linkage works both ways, for now the Suffering Servant is no longer seen merely as victim, a pathetic figure whose suffering is otherwise inexplicable except as somehow being mysteriously redemptive; rather, now the Suffering Servant is transfigured by the voluntary and representative mediatorship of the High Priest, or in Cullmann's words:

---

13. Anthropologically considered, priests always serve as mediators between heaven and earth.

14. Cullmann, *The Christology of the New Testament,* p. 86.

"A new and valuable element is introduced into Christology with the Jewish concept of high priesthood. It is the idea that in his very self-sacrifice Christ manifests his high priestly *majesty*."[15]

Titles That Refer to the Future Work of Jesus

Jesus the Messiah   As a participial passive adjective in Hebrew, "messiah" means "anointed" and as an adjectival noun it means "the anointed one," which translates in Greek as "christos." Originally, the title gained its significance from the ritual of anointing in a coronation ceremony (priests were also anointed, which gives the title a sacerdotal connotation as well). The anointing was done by smearing oil on the head or hands of a king to mark out the monarch (or priest) as having entered a new and permanent status.[16] The reason for oil as the symbolic instrument for anointing stems from its viscosity against water: oil covers the surface in a way that seems to "seal" the watery, less viscous contents below. In other words, anointing is used in ceremonies to denote a *definitive* change in status from one state of life to another (which is also why those undergoing baptism and confirmation, and not just priests and monarchs, are sealed with oil to denote their new, and *irrevocable*, status as Christians entering a new state of life).

The Hebrew concept of Messiah, however, added an additional element: because the institution of kingship was understood as divinely instituted, the real anointer was held to be God, who alone granted the federation of the twelve tribes of Israel the concession of having a monarch in place of the loose confederation of chieftains (or "judges" as they are known in traditional translations of the Bible). In fact, the concession was granted reluctantly: "But the thing displeased Samuel when they said, 'Give us a king to govern us.' And Samuel prayed to the Lord. And the Lord said to Samuel, 'Hearken to the voice of the people in all that they say to you; for they have not rejected you, but they have rejected me as king over them'" (1 Sam. 8:6-7).

At all events, because of the association of Messiah with kingship and with divine election, any monarch, even a pagan one, could be designated Messiah provided he were of royal status and had been set apart by God to

---

15. Cullmann, *The Christology of the New Testament*, p. 91 (Cullmann's emphasis).

16. This ritual has continued on to modern times in the anointing of monarchs, as the world saw when Queen Elizabeth II was crowned in 1953, the first to be televised; and of course priests continue to be anointed in modern times too.

accomplish God's own providential purposes; this we know because Isaiah calls the Persian king Cyrus "Messiah" for his role in allowing the Jews to return from Babylon to Jerusalem in 538 B.C.: "Thus says the Lord to his messiah, to Cyrus whom, the Lord says, I have grasped by his right hand, to make the nations bow down before him, . . . though you do not know me" (Isa. 45:1, 5).

For that reason, Messiah would seem to denote a title pertaining to Christ's present work, for a king is meant to reign on earth *now* and is a role to be filled by human beings currently living. After all, when the king dies, a new one takes over ("The king is dead. Long live the king!"). Nonetheless, this title aptly belongs in that category denoting the future work of Jesus for this reason above all: from the time of the Babylonian captivity Israel had lost its political independence, and thus also the monarchy, and lived, except for brief intervals, under systems of overbearing oppression, especially under the Hellenistic heirs of Alexander the Great (called the Seleucids), and even more under the harsh rod of Rome, whose taxation policies were deeply resented.

Hopes for liberation from such oppression thus had to be focused on the future, when a new king would, like King David of old, expel the oppressors and set up a new kingdom, with foreigners driven out and the Jews free to worship God without fear or favor. Taken in this sense, the title "messiah" would seem to entail a merely political hope. But by the time of Jesus' birth, messianic hopes had begun to take on a new and more extreme coloration, one that looked forward to a deeper transformation of conditions, a transformation so radical that only God, and not a mere human and earthly king, could inaugurate it. In this scenario the messianic agent would not be some chosen young shepherd (as David was), who stepped forth to lead his people because of his natural powers of leadership, piety, and military prowess. Now the Messiah would have to be God's viceroy in a more direct, eschatological sense. In other words, the future work of this Messiah would have to be much more radical than mere military conquest and political liberation — it would have to transform the very conditions of world history that made oppression possible in the first place.

But precisely because the title of Messiah was primarily a Jewish *political* one (whether in its merely royal or in its more extreme eschatological coloration), this meant that the title could not have the same purchase on the hearers of the gospel in a pagan setting. This makes the title "Christ" somewhat unique among the other titles applied to Jesus, for it soon stopped sounding like a title and began to seem more like part of his name. This is partly because the institution of king had lost much of its significance in the Roman Empire. The Roman emperors might well have acted like kings, but they continued to maintain the fiction that they were ruling in continuity with the outmoded forms of the Roman Republic, which had no kings (the word "emperor" comes from the Latin word for a military commander, *imperator*). But more crucially, "messiah" remained a true *title* for the Jews of first-century Palestine because, under Roman oppression, they looked forward to a restoration of the kingdom first established by King David. The title "messiah," in other words, was highly charged politically; indeed it was the title for which the Romans executed Jesus (which we know because the Roman governor of Judea at the time, Pontius Pilate, ordered the charge to be posted on the cross justifying the Nazarene's execution: "Jesus Christ, King of the Jews").

For that reason the translation of the Hebrew title Messiah into the Greek term Christos began a process that finally made the term Christ virtually a proper name for Jesus. Such is often the fate of names. For example, someone in the past might well have been known in his village as "James the Baker," but no one assumes that a James Baker now is especially skilled as a pastry chef, anymore than one assumes that a Geoffrey Wainwright knows how to make wagons. Similarly with the title Christ: it was never a term that had much cachet in a pagan setting, and so in Greek it soon took on the connotations of a proper name. For one thing, the Roman emperors were never anointed upon assuming office, since they wished to maintain republican fictions. For another, anointing with oil was quite a common practice in the Roman Empire for both medicinal and athletic reasons, especially in the gymnasia and baths of the time. The upshot is that once Jesus became known in the pagan world for his work by other terms more meaningful in a pagan setting, like "Savior," the title "Christ" gradually became a kind of last name for him.[17] In fact, so much had the name "Christ" become virtually his last name that some pagan authors could not be bothered to get it right: as we saw at the outset of this chapter, with Suetonius complaining about the followers of "Chrestus." And we are not surprised to learn that the term "Christian" to denote the followers of Christ was first coined in a pagan town, Antioch (see Acts 11:26).

Despite this easily discernible move from title to proper name, however,

---

17. Even today, some library card catalogues will give at the entry for "Jesus" a directional note saying "see Christ," the way some libraries will say at the entry for Napoleon "see Bonaparte."

the New Testament recognizes the title "Christ" (or its Hebrew equivalent "Messiah") as one of the most significant confessional titles assigned to Jesus. The Gospel of John, for example, concludes with this line: "[This book is] written that you may believe that Jesus is the Christ, the Son of God, and that believing you may have life in his name" (John 20:31).[18] Paul, too, clearly means Christ as a title, for although he often uses the expression "Jesus Christ," he also interchangeably will say "Christ Jesus" or, more tellingly, "Jesus the Christ." In other words, the New Testament is saturated in the conviction that Jesus is the Messiah, specifically "anointed" (that is, set apart) by God for redemptive purposes.

Complicating the issue, however, is the most remarkable fact about this title: the apparent diffidence, almost downright reluctance, on the part of Jesus to accept this title. So remarkable is this diffidence that this motif has earned its own moniker in the scholarly community: the so-called "Messianic secret." Only twice in the entire New Testament is Jesus depicted as accepting the title (and even the second instance is ambiguous): In the first episode, during his interrogation before the High Priest Caiaphas, Jesus is directly asked, "Are you the Christ, the Son of the Blessed?" to which Jesus replied simply, "I am" (Mark 14:62). The second episode deals with Peter's profession of faith in Jesus at Caesarea Philippi when Jesus asked his disciples what the people were saying about him, to which Peter finally replied with his own confession: "You are the Christ" (Mark 8:29; see the parallels in Luke 9:20, where the confession reads "the Christ of God"; and in Matt. 16:16, where the confession goes: "You are the Christ, the Son of the Living God"). At this point accounts begin to diverge, for in both Mark and Luke, Jesus' response is only this: "He gave them strict orders not to tell anyone about him." In Matthew, however, Jesus seems to accept the appellation, for he then praises Peter for confessing what only the eyes of faith can see; nonetheless, he goes on, after apparently accepting the title, to warn the disciples still to tell no one outside of their select circle about his real identity.[19]

18. This verse concludes chapter 20, with another chapter following, but that seems to have been an Epilogue, which perhaps was written after the "first edition," so to speak, of the Fourth Gospel had already been initially distributed among the community of the Beloved Disciple, which was then supplemented with chapter 21 before it was sent out for the edification of the other churches in the Mediterranean.

19. In the Gospel of John there is a scene vaguely similar to the Synoptic depiction of the confession at Caesarea Philippi, when many disciples abandon the cause when they find the obligation to eat the flesh and drink the blood of Christ too much for their faith, and Jesus asks the twelve if they too wish to go away, to which Peter replies: "Lord, to whom else

Outside of these two instances, Jesus is consistently depicted as deflecting the title of Messiah as somehow inappropriate, despite its clear relevance to his mission and despite the enthusiastic use of the term by the early church (to such an extent that it became the title by which he is best known, albeit in a way that conflates the title with its use as a proper name). The situation is thus most peculiar: the very title that the early church felt best described Jesus is the very one that he seems to have deflected. Why? In short, because of the context: words have not only a certain denotative meaning (the so-called "dictionary meaning") but also have definite *rhetorical implications* depending on the life-situation in which they are uttered (the connotative meaning). The noted scholar C. H. Dodd perhaps summarizes best of all the import of the Messianic secret in this lapidary formulation:

> The office of Messiah was conceived in various ways, but always it was bound up with the special calling and destiny of Israel as the people of God. From the gospels we gather that Jesus set himself to constitute the new Israel under his own leadership; he nominated its founding members, and admitted them into the new "covenant," and he laid down its new law. That was his mission. If it did not entirely agree with any of the contemporary ideas of what the Messiah should do, there was no other term available which came near to covering it. He could not deny his mission; he could not disavow the authority that went with it; and therefore, if the question was posed, he could not simply repudiate the title "Messiah." But it was an embarrassment to him, and he preferred that it should not be used publicly, until at least his hand was forced. In the popular mind Messiahship was associated with the political and military role of the "Son of David." To play that part was the last thing Jesus desired. Any suggestion that he proposed to do so was a hindrance to his true work and a danger to his cause. His appeal to his people must rest on something other than a debatable claim to Messiahship.[20]

And yet Mark depicts Jesus as finally and unambiguously accepting the title before Caiaphas. Why? Surely we may at least say this: a title that he would not deny to save his life, and for which he was indeed executed, can-

---

shall we go? You have the words of eternal life, and we have believed and have come to see that you are the Holy One of God" (John 6:66-71). But as this passage does not use the specific term "Christ" it is not strictly relevant here.

20. C. H. Dodd, *The Founder of Christianity* (London and New York: Macmillan, 1970), pp. 102-3.

not have been without personal significance for him. But the real question then becomes not the ultimately bootless one, "Did Jesus ever claim in his earthly ministry to be the Messiah?" but rather "What kind of Messiah did he think he was?" For that reason Mark has Jesus adding to his famous "I am" (his admission that he was the Messiah) the additional line, "You will see the Son of Man seated at the right hand of Power and coming with the clouds of heaven" (Mark 14:62b). Similarly, when the twelve apostles acknowledge Jesus' Messiahship at Caesarea Philippi, he goes on to instruct them in these words: "And he began to teach them that the Son of Man must suffer many things, and be rejected by the elders and the chief priests and the scribes, and be killed, and after three days rise again" (Mark 8:31). In other words, in order to understand what Jesus meant by Messiah and how he understood his mission to be characterized by that title, one must first investigate that title by which he most forthrightly designated himself: Son of Man.

Jesus the Son of Man With two exceptions the title "Son of Man" is never used by others in the New Testament to designate Jesus, only by Jesus himself. Except for those two instances (Acts 7:56; Rev. 1:13),[21] the term is exclusively Jesus' own self-designation. We are thus faced with a paradox that is almost the mirror-image of the paradox of the title Messiah: whereas Jesus acknowledged his identity as Messiah only in the most exceptional of circumstances and otherwise deflected its ready and too-easy use by his followers, even as the New Testament makes "Christ" (meaning "Messiah") the most frequently cited title for him, so here, in contrast, Jesus regularly referred to himself as Son of Man, but the early Christians almost never so designated him by that title: Jesus largely deflects the title "Christ" while the church calls him that constantly; but the term he uses of himself most of all, "Son of Man," almost never appears on the lips of Christians as a confessional term.

Complicating the issue even further, the term Son of Man encompasses a wide range of semantic implications. In some contexts the term could mean only a polite way for a male speaker of Aramaic to say "I" (the way some authors write their autobiographies in the third person, to avoid

21. The first occurs on the lips of Stephen just before his death by stoning, and the other is from John the Divine (the author of Revelation); both passages are actually but allusions to Daniel 7:13 and thus not confessions of faith by either Stephen or John the Divine but are silent quotations drawn from Daniel's vision, discussed below.

sounding egotistical by using the first person pronoun too often). Thus when Jesus says "the Son of Man has nowhere to lay his head," this could be merely a periphrastic way of saying "I have nowhere to lay my head."

Another common usage in Aramaic is the generic one, to refer to the human race at large, the way speakers of English will say "man must eat."[22] Thus when Jesus says, "Man was not made for the Sabbath but the Sabbath was meant for man, for the Son of Man is lord even of the Sabbath" (Mark 2:27-28), that could mean (although the verse is hotly disputed among exegetes) that Jesus is referring in the second half of the sentence not to himself but to man in general.

It is of course the third meaning that counts for Christology. Here "Son of Man" becomes a genuinely theological title, for when used in this sense it refers to that eschatological figure from heaven who will come as God's celestial designate to inaugurate the end of the world and to bring about the final reign of God in a *definitive* kingdom, where evil will no longer hold sway and where God will reign utterly unopposed by either earthly powers or by evil supernal principalities. Now why did so generic a term as "Son of Man" (which in some contexts, as we have seen, can refer to humanity at large) come to be associated with so vivid a scenario as the end of the world? The answer simply is: because of an accident of apocalyptic literature.

Readers in our civilization who encounter apocalyptic literature for the first time enter upon a world filled with phantasmagoric imagery, lurid depictions of the end-times, bizarre vocabulary — in short, a world utterly removed from the quotidian display of journalism and the historical sobriety of the typical "just the facts" narrative of modernity. But everything about the apocalyptic genre makes sense when the reader sees the situation that gave birth to that literature: a fusion of extreme tribulation with irrepressible hope.

Consider the worldview of the Jews in the centuries after the Babylonian exile: at all times they knew that history was in God's control and under the sway of his all-seeing providence, so much so that even the unsuspecting Persian king Cyrus was prompted to "let God's people go" without even having a glimmer of a notion of that God's existence. But then again, neither did

---

22. This contemporary usage is less common now because of the critique of feminist grammarians; but the generic use of "man" to refer to all human beings is deeply embedded in the structure of English ("man" comes from the same Indo-European root as "mental" and functions in the way *sapiens* does in the description of our species as *Homo sapiens*) and is still common enough that the generic use highlights the same for the Aramaic, Hebrew, and Greek usage.

Alexander the Great have any inkling that he was acting out in history according to God's set purposes; he conquered the later Persian kings, the very heirs of the same king Cyrus whom Isaiah had called "Messiah" (Isa. 45:1). Nor did Alexander's Seleucid successors have any idea that they were operating out of the laws of providence set forth ahead of time by the God of the Jews; nor did the Roman conquerors, *all of whom were oppressors of God's chosen ones.* But for the strictly monotheistic and prophecy-saturated Jews this oppression, too, had to have taken place under God's suzerainty and by his direction. Why? What could be the answer to this reason-bewildering and soul-confusing cry? If God chose — anointed even! — Cyrus to liberate God's chosen people, why did God allow the Romans to conquer the Promised Land?

Previously, the answer had been that God was punishing the people for their sins, and to some extent that answer still held sway; but the pattern of sin, repentance, restoration of land, sin again, loss of land, repentance, restoration of land, and so on, was starting to lose its prophetic force (not least because of the absence of further prophecy). Something about the current situation under the Romans was pushing the explanation of God's purposes to new extremes. For one thing, the lesson that the Jews had to be strictly faithful to the Mosaic Law, both written and oral, had sunk in with large tracts of the population (later called "Pharisees"), who took obedience to the Law with great seriousness and religious devotion. For another, oppression under the Romans assumed a harshness not previously known, especially because of its taxation system, which allowed licensed "tax farmers" (the hated "tax collectors" of the New Testament) to squeeze as much money out of the Jews as they could for their own use provided they turned in the required amount to the Roman treasury on time. So a new answer had to be given.

Clearly God was deliberately letting evil *run its course.* Like a latent cancer, evil would be allowed to gestate until it would burst forth in full bloom; and then God, like a wise surgeon, could intervene and cut out the canker and restore creation to its originally intended splendor, but only after evil had fully manifested itself. And for that task, as he had done with many of his other works, God would send one of his celestial delegates, that is, one of his angels. Such a scene we find depicted in the Book of Daniel, where we read how the outcome of the end of history will take place:

> I saw in my vision by night, and behold, the four winds of heaven were stirring up the great sea. And four great beasts came out of the sea, differ-

ent from one another.[23] . . . And as I looked, thrones were placed, and the Ancient of Days [meaning God] took his seat. . . . A stream of fire issued and came forth from before him. A thousand thousands served him, and ten thousand times ten thousand [angels] stood before him. The court sat in judgment, and the books were opened. . . . I saw in the night a vision, and behold, with the clouds of heaven there came *one like a son of man,* and he came before the Ancient of Days and was presented before him. And to him was given dominion and glory and kingdom, that all peoples, nations, and languages should serve him. His dominion is an everlasting dominion, which shall not pass away, and his kingdom one that shall not be destroyed. (Dan. 7:2-14)

Notice that in this translation (RSV) the term "son of man" is not capitalized. Granted, the distinction between capital and small letters did not enter Western orthography until the eighth century A.D.; still the translators chose wisely, for here the term "son of man" is not yet a title, but merely the typical Aramaic indication for a human being, or rather in this passage, for someone *like* a son of man, meaning one who amidst the heavenly court has taken on human *appearance.* But this clearly is no angel chosen at random, but some more significant being; for his task will entail that, upon its completion, he will be given "everlasting dominion" so that "all peoples, nations, and languages should serve him."

For that reason, the expression that Daniel used to mean solely the human form or appearance of this divine agent came to take on the connotations of a specific title for that expected figure. It came to be, so to speak, "capitalized" (in the mind, if not in the manuscripts). "Son of Man," in other words, came to designate a specific figure who would come from heaven to "set things right," to give God's final verdict upon the course of world history, to put an end to this seemingly endless series of bestial empires, and to give final definition to God's intentions when he created the world in the first place.

Jesus' awareness of this connotation of the title "Son of Man" is made most evident when he speaks specifically of the Son of Man "coming on the clouds" (as in Mark 14:62, as we have already seen), a clear allusion to this passage in the book of Daniel. Many commentators, especially those of skeptical bent, hold that, insofar as these passages represent the authentic words of the

---

23. These four beasts represent the empires of the Babylonians, Persians, Seleucids, and Romans, respectively.

historical Jesus, Jesus is referring to someone else whom *he too* is expecting. The trouble (apart from the plausibility or implausibility of the exegesis involved) is that when Jesus speaks of the Son of Man in contexts where he is clearly not using the term generically but is being specifically theological, for the most part he describes the Son of Man *in terms that Isaiah uses to describe the Suffering Servant.* We see this most clearly in the very passage where Peter confesses that Jesus is the Christ and where Jesus then admonishes him and the rest of the Twelve not to divulge such dangerous news: "And he began to teach them that the Son of Man must suffer many things, and be rejected by the elders and the chief priests and the scribes, and be killed, and after three days rise again. And he said this plainly" (Mark 8:31-32a). No Messianic secret here at least: for here Jesus openly describes the Son of Man not in his exultant role but in his suffering on behalf of the people.[24]

Again we are forced to ask why. Why did Jesus not use Isaiah's language of the Suffering Servant when he spoke thus? Why use Son-of-Man language when he is intent on describing *not* his exaltation, the end of the world, or receiving dominion, but instead his humiliation and fated execution? Clearly, the association of suffering with the Son of Man meant that *Jesus was linking his suffering with the definitive inauguration of God's kingdom,* something that not even the Suffering Servant Songs had done (that is, for Isaiah the Suffering Servant suffered on behalf of the people, but in an atoning way, and not necessarily to provoke the end of history). In other words, by speaking this way Jesus is signaling his acceptance of a divine vocation, one, moreover, that will transform God's relationship to history in a definitive way: *Jesus' suffering and the end of the world are in some mysterious way linked.*

Moreover, by using Son of Man as the title to express Jesus' suffering, the stress is put on Jesus' own control over his destiny, a feature of Christology that is strongly present in John but is also implied in the Synoptic use of Son of Man, as Heinz Tödt rightly sees:

> How is Jesus seen when in his suffering he is designated as Son of Man? He is not seen as the one who is utterly devoid of power; . . . instead he is

---

24. That Jesus' audience would have understood that eschatological connection is a point made by Craig Evans: "Interpreters of Daniel 7 in late antiquity almost always understood the 'son of man' figure as referring to an individual, often to the Messiah (as in the Gospels, 1 Enoch, and 4 Ezra)." Craig A. Evans, "Jesus' Self-Designation 'The Son of Man,'" in *The Trinity: An Interdisciplinary Symposium on the Trinity,* ed. Stephen T. Davis, Daniel Kendall, S.J., and Gerald O'Collins, S.J. (Oxford: Oxford University Press, 1999), pp. 29-47; here 35-36.

always seen as the one who is marvelously aware of his course beforehand. . . . The one in whom the sovereignty is inherent accepts his rejection by and deliverance to men. . . . His authority on earth is confirmed by his resurrection power.[25]

Titles That Refer to the Present Work of Jesus

Jesus the Lord   Because Jesus was executed as "King of the Jews" and because the title "Messiah" carried inevitable royal connotations, it might seem that no more dangerous title could be given to Jesus than that of "Christ"; but in the Hellenistic setting of the Roman Empire, the truly dangerous title was that of *Lord*. One sign of that danger, a kind of "distant early warning" foreboding a future conflict between Christianity and the Roman Empire, can be seen in a telling decree issued by the Emperor Tiberius in the year A.D. 16 forbidding the prediction of the coming of a new king or a new kingdom within the confines of the Empire.[26] But this is precisely what a confession of Jesus as Lord entailed: by raising him from the dead, said Peter on Pentecost, "God has made this Jesus . . . both Lord and Christ" (Acts 2:36). This title "Lord" was therefore no empty honorific. Rather it meant that a new king has ascended the throne, a new kingdom has been established in history, which means as well that the days of all earthly authority are numbered: "We believe that Jesus died and rose again. . . . For the Lord himself will come down from heaven, with a loud command; . . . Then the lawless one will be revealed, whom the Lord Jesus will overthrow with the breath of his mouth and destroy by the splendor of his coming" (1 Thess. 4:14, 16; 2 Thess. 2:8).

These passages would seem to imply that the title "Lord" would be better placed in the section dealing with Christ's future work; and the prayer often on the lips of the early Christians, "Marana-tha" ("Come, Lord"), also surely indicates that in confessing Jesus as Lord, the early Christians simultaneously looked forward to his imminent coming again. All this is true, and surely one does not want to be too hard and fast in the use of the categories; but I think Cullmann is right in assigning the primary meaning of this term

<hr>

25. H. E. Tödt, *The Son of Man in the Synoptic Tradition*, trans. Dorothea M. Barton (Philadelphia: Westminster Press, 1965), pp. 220-21.

26. See Ben Witherington III, *New Testament History: A Narrative Account* (Grand Rapids: Baker Academic, 2001), p. 262 for details.

to Christ's present work in the church now rather than just to his future in bringing about the end of the world. As he rightly says, "This designation expresses as does no other the thought that Christ is exalted to God's right hand, glorified, and *now* intercedes for men before the Father."[27]

Probably no title given to Jesus is more significant than Lord. Paul even says that no one can confess Jesus as Lord except in the Holy Spirit (1 Cor. 12:3). Furthermore, he makes the confession of Jesus as Lord the very hinge of the Christian's salvation: "If you declare with your mouth that Jesus is Lord, and if you believe with your heart that God raised him from the dead, then you will be saved" (Rom. 10:9).

But why does so much hinge on that title "Lord"? At first glance the title might not seem all that significant, for the title was (and to some extent still is) quite common. Its basic meaning denotes anyone who has a higher position in society over another. For that reason barons and the like are still officially addressed as "lord" in contemporary Britain. Even the almost empty honorific "sir" is etymologically rooted in the word for "lord" in the Romance languages.[28]

The same holds true of the Greek *kyrios:* in some contexts it is best translated as "sir" (an honorific) but at other times as "lord" (or when referring to God, "Lord"). Because Greek, German, and most Romance languages use the same term, but English distinguishes "lord" from "sir," English translations of the Bible can often obscure an important point in the Gospels when they depict someone approaching Jesus with the title *kyrios.* No doubt these curious onlookers might have meant the title merely as a polite way of showing respect for a noted teacher, but the evangelists also want to point out that, perhaps unbeknownst to the speakers, they are confessing Jesus as the true Lord.

But that still does not explain why such an ordinary term could come to be so significant to the Christians who made so much of their confession of Jesus as Lord. Part of the reason for that comes from a development in Jewish piety after the Babylonian exile. The Old Testament records that God had revealed to Moses his personal name, YHWH (perhaps pronounced "Yahweh," although that is disputed because ancient Hebrew did not indi-

---

27. Cullmann, *The Christology of the New Testament,* p. 195; emphasis added.

28. For example the word for "mister" in French is *monsieur,* literally meaning "my lord," just as the Italian *monsignore* means the same thing; and the German for "mister" is *Herr,* the German word for "Lord." Note also that the English "mister" is related to "master," which means roughly the same thing as "lord," inasmuch as it refers to anyone whose social position makes him more powerful than the one addressing him with these terms of respect.

cate vowels). The name is drawn from the Hebrew word for "to be," which is why God also reveals his name as "I AM WHO I AM." But after the return of the Jews during the reign of king Cyrus, pious practice forbade the pronunciation of the divine name except by the High Priest on the feast of Yom Kippur, and then only in the Holy of Holies, the inner chamber of the Temple in Jerusalem.

For that reason, whenever the divine name appeared in the text, the Hebrew word for "Lord," *Adonai,* was substituted when the text was being read aloud; so when the Jews living in Alexandria two to three centuries before Christ commissioned a translation of the Hebrew Bible into Greek (called the Septuagint), the word *kyrios* was always used whenever the Hebrew text read YHWH. In other words, for the Jews of Alexandria, the title "Lord" became the divine name *par excellence,* a connotation of the title that then started to hold true for all the Greek-speaking Jews of the Roman Empire, given the enormous prestige of the Septuagint for them.[29] Little wonder, then, that the Christians were persecuted by the Romans specifically because they refused to address the Roman emperor by the title "lord" in the civic rites required of all "patriotic" members of the Empire.[30] This the Christians could not do, because their confession of Jesus as Lord meant that he was the only one before whom "every knee should bend" (Phil. 2:10). Obeisance offered to any other reputed or putative "lord" would thereby represent a denial of the very faith that was their salvation.

Only one other point needs to be stressed about this title: the ambiguity in this word — that is, whether "Lord" (when applied to Jesus) means mere respect ("sir") or is a confession of his divine status ("one Lord") — only applies to his earthly life. *After* Easter, Jesus is confessed as Lord *exclusively* in its religious meaning. Indeed, it is *because* of Easter that he *becomes* Lord. Such is the testimony of the earliest strata of the New Testament. Peter, in his first sermon on Pentecost, says, "God raised this Jesus to life. . . . Therefore let all Israel be assured of this: God has *made* this Jesus, whom you crucified, both Lord and Christ" (Acts 2:32, 36); and Paul says that Jesus was "*estab-*

29. This linguistic substitution also made sense against the background of the non-monotheistic religions of the Greek-speaking parts of the Roman Empire, where the gods and goddesses (Serapis, Osiris, Isis, and so forth) were addressed as *kyrios* or *kyria.* See Cullmann, *The Christology of the New Testament,* pp. 196-97 for details and bibliography.

30. The Roman emperors might well have maintained republican fictions in Rome and in those lands absorbed by Rome before the fall of the Republic; but in the East they became increasingly insistent that the populace honor the emperor by more religiously exalted titles that implied divinity in the pagan pantheon.

lished with power to be the Son of God by his resurrection from the dead, Jesus Christ our Lord" (Rom. 1:4).

The significance of the resurrection for Christology can only be discussed in the next chapter, but here we can at least note that it is because of the resurrection that the title of "Lord" refers primarily to Jesus' present work in the church, as Cullmann explains so well:

> We must above all ask why, after the death of Christ, a particular community was founded at all. If the very early Church really had *only* a future expectation, if only the *coming* Son of Man was christologically significant for it, then it would be impossible to explain the impulse to form a Church in which enthusiasm ruled and the working of the Spirit determined the whole of life. . . . On the basis of the conviction that with Christ's resurrection the end had already begun, the first Christians could no longer think of him only as the coming Son of Man. He must mean something also for the present, for time already fulfilled. The intense hope that the end is near is thus not the foundation but the consequence of the Easter faith. . . . He has died and is risen, and he will come again. But he must have a task to fulfill also between these two salvation-events. His work cannot simply cease in the meantime.[31]

The present activity of the Lord Jesus in these "between times" comes through most clearly in a passage from Paul dealing with the tricky issue of eating meat from animals that had first been sacrificed to idols, to which question Paul replies with this answer: since the "gods" the pagans worship do not in fact exist, no harm is done provided the Christian not get seduced by appearances. At this point, Paul adds this crucial justification:

> So then, about eating food sacrificed to idols: We know that an idol is nothing at all in the world and that there is no God but one. For even if there are so-called gods, whether in heaven or on earth (as indeed there are many "gods" and many "lords" [in pagan religions]), yet for us there is but *one God, the Father,* from whom all things came and for whom we live; and there is but *one Lord, Jesus Christ,* through whom all things came and through whom we live. (1 Cor. 8:4-6)

As the renowned New Testament scholar N. T. Wright points out, this passage could not possibly be more revolutionary for later doctrinal devel-

---

31. Cullmann, *The Christology of the New Testament,* p. 207.

opment, for its rhetorical parallelism rests on an allusion to the most basic Jewish confession of faith, called the *Shema:* "Hear, O Israel: the Lord our God, the Lord is One" (Deut. 6:4). Paul uses the same structure but *now incorporates Jesus himself into the confession:*

The Lord our God = One God — the Father . . .
The Lord is One = One Lord — Jesus Christ . . .

The reason this parallelism is so revolutionary is that it shows that Paul was already establishing the basis for later doctrinal development, as Wright so lucidly sees:

> Faced with that astonishing statement, one would have to say that if the early Fathers of the church hadn't existed it would be necessary to invent them. Paul has redefined the very meaning of the words that Jews used, every day in their regular prayers, to denote the one true God. The whole argument of the chapter hinges precisely on his being a Jewish-style monotheist, over against pagan polytheism, and, as the lynchpin of the argument, he has quoted the most central and holy confession of that monotheism *and has placed Jesus firmly in the middle of it.* Lots of Pauline scholars have tried to edge their way round this one, but it can't be done. The nettle must be grasped. Somehow, Paul believes, the one and only God is now known in terms, at least, of "father" and "lord." All things are made by the one; all things are made through the other.[32]

In other words, when Christians confessed Jesus as Lord, they confessed his divinity, yet without abandoning their monotheism.

Jesus the Savior/Redeemer Billboards in the Bible Belt of the United States often proclaim "Jesus saves," and some evangelicals and/or fundamentalists still approach the unchurched with the question, "Are you saved?" For that reason it might come as some surprise to learn that "Savior" does not figure prominently in the New Testament as a title for Jesus; and when it does occur, it comes from relatively late strata (the significance of that will be dealt with more fully in the next chapter, on the historical development of New

---

32. N. T. Wright, *What Saint Paul Really Said: Was Paul of Tarsus the Real Founder of Christianity?* (Grand Rapids: Eerdmans, 1997), pp. 66-67; emphasis in the original. Wright goes on to show that Paul does the same with the Spirit; but as that is not relevant to the question of the titles of Jesus, nothing need be said on that score until Chapter 4.

Testament Christology). But the term still functions as an important confession, for what the title points to is not only a present work of Jesus but a work of his that is correlative to a *plight* of ours. No one needs to be saved who is not already in some situation of desperation, who is in some sense "lost." Only someone who is drowning needs a life-saver; and only those who feel lost on this earth, orphaned from their true home, will be on the lookout for a savior.

So the question becomes, what did Jesus save us from? In other words, in what does salvation consist? The answer is simple: Jesus is Savior because he saves people from their sins and from the death that has swept into the world as a consequence of sin (Rom. 5:12). For that reason the title "Savior" accomplishes something that the title "Lord" on its own does not: it stresses Jesus' role as the one who has atoned for our sins. "Lord" after all is applied not just to God, who, so to speak, "owns" the name most of all; but it can also be applied (legitimately and illegitimately) to any number of others who have assumed a social role of power and domination ("domination" comes from the Latin word *dominus,* for "lord"), and so in that sense can be ambiguous. But "Savior" stresses something much more specific, a unique *work* of Jesus: his atoning death on the cross.[33] That said, "Savior" still shares an important feature with "Lord": just as the Lordship of Jesus is universal, so too does the salvation effected by Jesus extend to the whole world, a point stressed most of all in the First Letter of John: "He is the atoning sacrifice for our sins, and not only for ours but also for the sins of the whole world. . . . And we have seen and testify that the Father has sent his Son to be the Savior of the world" (1 John 2:2; 4:14).

The Greek word for "savior" *(sōtēr)* is sometimes translated as "redeemer," but the two words in English bring out different features of the word not available in Greek (just as "sir" and "lord" bring out different meanings not available when translating the single Greek term *kyrios*). Redemption is primarily an economic concept (as in redeeming coupons for the purchase of goods) and implies an exchange or purchase. The religious application of that word in the New Testament is due to the institution of slavery, where an owner could purchase a slave from the slave-market and then set him free if

33. The New Testament does in fact once call God (rather than Jesus specifically) "Savior" but only in the rarely quoted Letter of Jude: "To him who is able to keep you from falling and to present you before his glorious presence without fault and with great joy — to the only God our Savior be glory, majesty, power and authority, through Jesus Christ our Lord, before all ages, now and forevermore" (Jude 24-25). But even here God is "Savior" *through* Christ, that is, through his work of atonement.

he so chose. For Paul the slavery from which we have been purchased was the slavery of sin (Rom. 6:19-23), and the purchase price was the blood of Christ (Rom. 3:25). But because the Greek *sōtēr* does not make that distinction,[34] "redeemer" and "savior" cover the same semantic range for the most part, differing only slightly in their (English) connotations.

Finally, one must recall that the name "Jesus" itself in Hebrew means "the Lord saves," which perhaps accounts for the late appearance of the title "Savior" in the New Testament and for its more prevalent usage in Christianity later on, when the name "Jesus" would sound purely as a proper noun (analogous to the way the name "Christ" became attached as a kind of last name).[35]

Titles That Refer to the Preexistence of Jesus

Jesus the Word   It would be very difficult indeed to overestimate the impact of the title "Word" (Greek, *logos*) to the Christology of the first six centuries of the church. For many church fathers the title was considered crucial, for it marked the great point of contact with the philosophical speculations of the educated pagan mind. That said, the use of this term to describe Jesus in the New Testament can be found *only* in the Johannine writings, and even there it occurs in just a few passages: the Prologue to the Gospel of John (John 1:1-4), in 1 John 1:1, and in Revelation 19:13.

What accounts for this discrepancy between New Testament paucity and patristic favoritism? First of all, as Cullmann points out, "the point at which the author of John makes use of the Logos concept shows that the title is indispensable for him when he wishes to speak of *the relationship between the divine revelation in the life of Jesus and the preexistence of Jesus.*"[36] No wonder, then, that the patristic writers themselves found the concept indispensable too, for questions of the preexistence of the divine Son dominated

34. Except in the verb forms, where the distinction applies: *sōzō* means "to save" (from a plight, like drowning) while *hilaskomai* means "to redeem" (in the Pauline sense of redeem from the slavery of sin by the atoning blood of Christ). But *hilaskomai* has no nominal form in the New Testament, so "Redeemer" as distinct from "Savior" could never become one of the titles of Jesus in New Testament Greek.

35. One example of the favored use of the term "Savior" later on to describe Jesus can be seen in the image of a fish as a symbol for Christianity. The word for fish in Greek is *ichthus*, which can also form a Greek anagram, *Iesous **Christos** **Theou** 'Uios Soter:* "Jesus Christ, God's Son, Savior."

36. Cullmann, *The Christology of the New Testament,* p. 249; emphasis added.

discussion at that time, for reasons to be explained in Chapter 4. (Plus, the Logos concept proved a godsend, so to speak, for Christian apologists trying to justify Christianity to educated Gentiles raised in Platonic and Stoic concepts of *logos*.)

But before touching on these essentially theological issues, we must first outline the (very large) semantic range of the term *logos*, which in Greek happens to have far more meanings attached to it than the English term "word" and includes, among others, these meanings: reason, account, narrative, essence, verbalization, and, of course, the spoken word as such. But because the noun *logos* is the nominative form of the verb *legō, legomai* ("to speak"), we must first concentrate on its primary meaning as spoken word.

As speech-acts, words communicate thoughts, which themselves are the products of minds. Furthermore, words are received by ears and then understood by other minds. This basically *mental* feature in all words surely accounts for the rich and powerful religious symbolism that surrounds the concept of word. For unlike the other senses, which perceive objects in their brute physicality, hearing picks up something much more "spiritual," even evanescent. Tellingly, objects that are seen, touched, smelled, and tasted can be grasped; but words stay ever elusive and disappear as soon as they are heard. For that same reason, a hearer of a word has no control over what is being heard, and this too must surely be religiously significant, as the Swiss Catholic theologian Hans Urs von Balthasar notes in this insightful passage:

> Hearing is different [from the other senses], almost the opposite mode of the revelation of reality. It lacks the fundamental characteristic of material relevance. It is not objects we hear but their utterances and communications. Therefore it is not we ourselves who determine on our part what is heard and place it before us as an object in order to turn our attention to it when it pleases us. No, what is heard comes upon us without our being informed of its coming in advance. It lays hold of us without our being asked. . . . It is in the highest degree symbolic that only our eyes, and not our ears, have lids. . . . The basic relationship between the one who hears and that which is heard is thus one of defenselessness on the one side and of communication on the other. . . . Even in a dialogue between equals in rank, the one who is at the moment hearing is in the subordinate position of humble receiving. The hearer belongs to the other for as long as he is listening and to that extent is "obeying" him.[37]

37. Hans Urs von Balthasar, "Seeing, Hearing, and Reading within the Church," in *Ex-*

The religious implications of this description are clear and hold true even for the nonreligious: listeners have no choice but to receive what is heard. Moreover, what they receive is not so much the object of the speaker but his thoughts, that is, his mental life. In that regard it is telling that Aristotle defines man as the *zōon logikon*, usually translated as "rational animal" but which could just as accurately be given as the "verbal" or "word-using" animal.

Both in pre-Christian Greek and Jewish thought the concept of *logos* became more and more "hypostasized," meaning that Greek and Jewish thought moved more and more away from the concept of word as evanescent, disappearing as soon as it entered the ear, and toward a notion of word as somehow *substantial* (*hypostasis* being the Greek word for "substance"). For example, the Stoics identified the Logos with the cosmic law that governs the universe and is at the same time operative in the human intellect. But that notion of logos as law is still only an abstraction (roughly equivalent to Newton's Law of Gravity). The situation is different in Platonism, but crucially it is the Idea or Form *(eidos)* that is hypostasized, not the Word *(logos)*; in other words it is the mental concept that takes on the contours of substance, not that which is communicated from one mind to the other.[38] But as Platonism developed, the Logos too became more and more "personal," acting as an agent or go-between, an intermediary between the inaccessible One and the finite world.

Nowhere is that personalization made more explicit than in the writings of Philo of Alexandria, a Jewish contemporary of Jesus whose thought was heavily influenced by what scholars now called Middle Platonism. In a remarkable passage, Philo describes the mediatorial role of the Logos in this way:

---

plorations in Theology, vol. 2: *Spouse of the Word,* trans. Brian McNeil, C.R.V. (San Francisco: Ignatius Press, 1991), pp. 473-90; here 475-76; translation silently emended.

38. "A major difficulty in the interpretation of *logos* is determining when this common and amorphous Greek word is being used in a technical, specialized sense. Thus Heraclitus, in whom it first plays a major role, frequently employs it in its common usage, but he also has a peculiar doctrine that centers around *logos* in a more technical sense: for him *logos* is an underlying organizational principle of the universe. . . . Plato also used the term *logos* in a variety of ways, including the opposition between *mythos* (tale) and *logos,* where the latter signifies a true, analytical account. . . . [He also] describes the dialectician as one who can give an account *(logos)* of the true being (or essence, *ousia*) of something. . . . The Stoic point of departure on *logos* is Heraclitus' doctrine of an all-pervasive formula of organization, which the Stoics considered divine." F. E. Peters, *Greek Philosophical Terms* (New York: New York University Press, 1967), pp. 110-12, at *logos.*

To his Logos, his chief messenger, highest in age and honor, the Father of all has given the special prerogative to stand on the border and separate the creature from the Creator. This same Logos both pleads with the Immortal as suppliant for afflicted mortality and acts as ambassador of the ruler to the subject. He glories in this prerogative and proudly describes it in these words: "I stood between the Lord and you."[39]

This passage certainly marks a watershed in the development of the concept of the Logos (capitalized here to show its personal, substantial nature); but it would be an error to think that Philo is influenced here solely by Middle Platonism, for he is also building on developments in the Jewish Bible.[40] In the earlier books of the Bible God speaks his word *efficaciously*. God says, "Let there be light," and light comes to be. The word of God (Hebrew, *debar YHWH*) is thus creative of what it speaks. As Cullmann says, "every creative self-revelation of God to the world happens through his word. *His word is the side of God turned toward the world.*"[41]

What then happened is that *this efficacious word is made the object of independent consideration, precisely because it is so powerful.* The Psalmist says, "By the word of the Lord the heavens were made" (Ps. 33:6); crucially, this powerful word continues its activities after creation: "He sent forth his word and healed them" (Ps. 107:20) and "He sends forth his command to the earth; his word runs swiftly" (Ps. 147:15). The phrase "his word runs swiftly" might be poetic license; but if so, that license in turn licensed further extensions of the image, and with Isaiah we get close to the word acting as an independent agent: "For as the rain and the snow come down from heaven, and return not but water the earth, . . . so shall my word be that goes forth from my mouth; it shall not return to me empty but shall accomplish what I purpose" (Isa. 55:10-11).

Finally, all that is needed now is for this hypostasized Word or Wisdom to speak on its own as an independent agent: "The Lord created me at the beginning of his work, the first of his acts of old. Ages ago I was set up, at the

39. Philo, *Quis rerum divinarum heres* 42.205.
40. One might be tempted to follow contemporary fashion and say "Hebrew Bible" here; but Philo used the Greek translation (called Septuagint), which is significant, because that translation includes books not found in the Hebrew canon; and it is these books above all where certain aspects of God, such as his Wisdom and his Word, are hypostasized. But it is also crucial to note that some Hebrew books included in the Hebrew canon also hypostasize these divine qualities, especially the book of Proverbs.
41. Cullmann, *The Christology of the New Testament*, p. 255; Cullmann's emphasis.

first, before the beginnings of the earth. Where there were no depths I was brought forth, when there were no springs abounding with water" (Prov. 8:22-24).[42]

How much the Fourth Evangelist was influenced by these various trends has become a matter of enormous controversy in biblical scholarship, especially as it pertains to the influence of Greek sources in general, and Philo specifically.[43] But if we concentrate not on the historical antecedents of the

42. Admittedly, Proverbs speaks of Wisdom (*Sophia,* a feminine word in Greek), not Word (*logos,* a masculine word), which raises a host of issues pertaining to the feminine in God. Cullmann rightly says that "*Logos* and *Sophia* are almost interchangeable" (p. 257) in the respective theologies of the Book of Wisdom and the Gospel of John. Certainly, both authors see their favored terms in equally hypostatic ways, which is the main point of this paragraph. Plus, it should be recalled that the terms "masculine," "feminine," and "neuter" for the gender of nouns are terms of convenience invented by the Greek grammarians in Alexandria because most males are described by nouns in the masculine gender and most females by the feminine gender (for example, *hippos* can mean either "stallion" or "mare," depending on the gender of the preceding article); but things, concepts, abstractions, and so forth, can be described by words in any gender. At all events, either Cullmann is right and Wisdom and Word are interchangeable, which means that the question of gender is irrelevant; or the gender of the noun is theologically significant, which means that the Fourth Evangelist must have deliberately chosen *Logos* instead of *Sophia* for theological reasons. But semantically considered (which is the focus of this chapter), I would say that Wisdom refers more to the internal mind of God prior to creating, whereas Word is an inherently expressive concept, which is why Cullmann can say, rightly again, that in the Old Testament the "word of God" always refers (no matter how early or late the text) to the side of God that is turned toward the world. What Wisdom stresses is that when God creates the world, or relates to it thereafter, he always does so in ways that manifest his providence, his governance, his beneficence. Creation, in other words, is not ill-considered but is aboriginally "well thought out." In other words, God's outward and expressive Word is always a Wise Word, expressive of God's internally well-ordered mind.

43. The influence of Gnosticism on the Fourth Gospel should be mentioned here as well, albeit briefly. Speaking very broadly, Gnosticism is a "moralization," so to speak, of Plato's theory of the Divided Line. Plato divided his world into two separate realms, Reality and Appearance, with Reality above the dividing line and Appearance below it. Above the line is static Being as such, the realm of the Ideal, of stasis, and finally of the One. Below the line were matter, division, change, copies of the Ideas, and so forth, in short the realm of Becoming. Because Plato also called the One the Good, Gnostics extended the contrast by calling the realm of matter *evil.* At a stroke this made evil an independent principle. (For Plato what appeared below the line had but a shadowy claim on being, in contrast to the "really real" realm of true Being; but that did not make Appearance "evil," only less "real.") For the Gnostics, then, salvation had to be interpreted as a complete escape from the realm of matter. The anthropological correlate of this view meant that the soul of man inhabited the body like "gold in the mud." And salvation could only be effected by a divine hypostasized

Fourth Gospel (already taking for granted the same trend of hypostatization in both Greek and Jewish sources) but on the meaning of Logos in the text itself, two points emerge immediately. First, Jesus was addressed as *Kyrios* (in the "high," divine sense of that word) in Christian worship, whereas the Logos designation must have arisen as a result of theological reflection (even today, Christians do not address Jesus in their worship as "Word"). Second, prior developments in the intellectual history of Jewish and Greek thought would later make the concept of Jesus as the divine Logos perfectly suited for Christianity's apologetic purposes, as we shall see in later chapters (and this will account for the greater stress in patristic times of the Logos-concept than is found in the New Testament itself).

"In the beginning was the Word, and the Word was with God, and the Word was God. . . . The Word became flesh and dwelt among us" (John 1:1, 14). Leaving aside all questions of historical antecedents, these verses drive home one essential point that is the key to the whole of the Fourth Gospel: in Cullmann's words, "Jesus not only *brings* revelation, but in his person *is* revelation. He brings light, and at the same time he is Light; he bestows life, and he is Life; he proclaims truth, and he is Truth. More properly expressed, he brings light, life and truth just because he himself is Light, Life, and Truth. So it is also with the Logos: he brings the word, because he is the Word."[44]

Finally, we must note that John both *distinguishes* the Logos from God, yet also *identifies* that Logos with God. In other words, God and the Logos are not two beings, and yet they are also not simply identical. This blunt juxtaposition of two seemingly contradictory statements brings us back once again to the inherently paradoxical character of Christian doctrine, a paradoxicality that will prove immensely provocative for later Christian thought ("The paradox gives rise to theology," as we said in the Introduction). Here again the key will be to let theology arise out of paradox without thereby resolving the paradox in a way that would make thought control the doctrine, or theology determine revelation. As Cullmann rightly says:

---

being coming down from heaven merely clothed in the flesh. It would seem rather obvious, judging by the surface of the text, that the Gospel of John polemicizes against this view and thus John must have known of this worldview beforehand. The only trouble is, our sources for Gnostic beliefs all come from documents written after the New Testament was in circulation. In any case, we are concentrating in this chapter on the concept of Logos for its semantic import solely and only later in the next chapters on its role in determining christological doctrine, so these points need not be stressed further.

44. Cullmann, *The Christology of the New Testament*, p. 259. Emphasis in the original.

We must allow this paradox of all Christology to stand. The New Testament does not resolve it, but sets the two statements alongside each other: on the one hand, the Logos *was* God; on the other hand, he was *with* God. The same paradox occurs again in the Gospel of John with regard to the "Son of God" concept. We hear on the one hand, "I and the Father are one" (John 10:30); and on the other hand, "The Father is greater than I" (John 14:28).[45]

Jesus the Son of God   "Son of God" is like "Son of Man" in this sense: it has both a generic meaning that could, at least theoretically, apply to any male human being (or by metonymy, to human beings of both sexes), especially if he is of a pious disposition; and it has a specific meaning with a specific theological connotation, especially when applied to Jesus. But in that regard, the role of these two terms is somewhat reversed. In patristic times, as we shall see, "Son of God" was the term that was taken to apply to Jesus' divine status, while "Son of Man" was seen to refer to his humanity. However, as we saw above, "Son of Man," at least in some contexts, referred to a heavenly, eschatological figure who would come down on the clouds to inaugurate a new age. Conversely, in Hebrew usage "son of God," again in some contexts, could be an honorific title given to any pious Israelite, or even to the whole nation of Israel itself. "Son of God" is also unusual in contrast to "Son of Man" in that Jesus rarely uses the former term to describe himself, whereas the latter is constantly on his lips as self-description.

Similarly, in a pagan setting "son of (the) god"[46] did not necessarily imply that a human being so called had some kind of Olympian genealogy: the usual term in Greek for such a person (like Achilles) would be *theios anēr* (divine man) rather than *'uios tou theou* (son of the god). In any case, such ambiguity would not obtain in Israel, where "son of God" would clearly be understood as an honorific title by virtue of the fact that God was confessed as Israel's Father. Given the fact that the God of Israel is without pedigree, the sonship that binds Israel to God was clearly one not of biological lineage in the pagan manner but of *obedience*.

This linkage of the concepts of sonship and obedience explains why the

---

45. Cullmann, *The Christology of the New Testament,* p. 266. Emphasis in the original.

46. Greek syntax requires the article "the" in front of the word "god" irrespective of whether the reference is to a pagan god or the God of monotheism. Also, small letters were not invented for Greek until about the eighth century of the Christian era, so no *orthographic* distinction could have been drawn in the ancient world between the monotheistic "God" and a polytheistic "god."

Old Testament can apply the term "son of God" to the people of Israel as a whole, to Israel's kings, and to persons specially commissioned by God, including angels. For example, Moses is commanded by God to say to Pharaoh, "Israel is my first-born son" (Exod. 4:22), and God speaks through Hosea saying "Out of Egypt I called my son" (Hos. 11:1); and even when Israel strays, the people are called "faithless sons" (Jer. 3:22), implying that even in disobedience God is still calling the people to repentance, lest the bond between God and Israel be irrevocably broken. Kings, too, are called "sons" by God: "I will be his father, and he shall be my son" (2 Sam. 7:14), says God of David; and in a royal coronation psalm much quoted by the early church we read: "You are my son, today I have begotten you" (Ps. 2:7). Angels too are called "sons of God" (Job 1:6; Ps. 29:1; Dan. 3:25, 28).

This wide range of usage in the Old Testament can create problems in the interpretation of Jesus as Son of God, because clearly the New Testament wants to link the idea of obedience and sonship in Jesus but also wants to insist that he is Son of God in a manner unique to him and unprecedented in Israel. A further complication comes from the fact that Jesus is called "Son of God" by both God (at Jesus' baptism) and by Satan (during his temptations), making it apparently the appellation of choice for the "supernatural" actors in Jesus' life. When Jesus emerges from the River Jordan after being baptized by John, a voice resounds from heaven saying, "This is my Son, my Beloved" (Matt. 3:17) or "You are my Son, my Beloved" (Mark 1:11; Luke 3:22).[47] Then Jesus is driven out by the Spirit into the desert to pray and fast for forty days and forty nights, at the end of which the devil comes to him with temptations that begin, "If you are the Son of God . . ." (Matt. 4:3, 6; Luke 4:3, 9). Both scenes stress the obedience of the Son, with the baptism suggesting a unique sonship and the temptations stressing Jesus' refusal to see his sonship purely in terms of miraculous power but solely in terms of his mission.[48] Moreover, when Peter confesses at Caesarea Philippi that Jesus

47. The voice from heaven repeats (more or less) these same words at the Transfiguration (including in Mark, who does not narrate in any detail the temptations): Matthew 17:5; Mark 9:7; Luke 9:35 (where the voice from heaven says "my Chosen One" instead of "my Beloved").

48. "The most important passages of the Synoptic Gospels in which Jesus appears as the Son of God show him precisely not as a miracle worker and savior like many others, but as one radically and uniquely distinguished from all other men. He knows that he is sent to all other men to fulfill his task in complete unity with the Father. This distinction, this isolation, means to Jesus not primarily miraculous power, but the absolute obedience of a son in the execution of a divine commission" (Cullmann, *The Christology of the New Testament*, p. 276).

is "the Christ, the Son of the living God" (Matt. 16:16), Jesus explicitly says to him that "Flesh and blood has not revealed this to you, but only my Father in heaven" (16:17), once again showing how Jesus' unique sonship is a reality accessible only from a supernatural, not natural, perspective, a point Jesus stresses even more forcefully when he says, "All things have been delivered to me by my Father; and no one knows the Son except the Father, and no one knows the Father except the Son and any one to whom the Son chooses to reveal him" (Matt. 11:27; with slight variations in wording in Luke 10:22).

The linkage between sonship and mission is consistently held throughout the New Testament, but there are variations of emphasis. One point to note as we look at these variations: as we already saw, in the Synoptic Gospels "Son of Man" is the favored self-designation of Jesus whereas "Lord" and "Christ" are the favored titles for Jesus by the confessing, post-Easter church. "Son of God," however, is both a term that Jesus uses to refer to himself *and* is a confessional term of the church. In fact Mark defines the entire purpose of his Gospel as one that wants to bring his readers to a faith in Jesus as Son of God: "The beginning of the good news of Jesus Christ, Son of God" (Mark 1:1), and culminates his narration of the death of Jesus with the centurion's confession at the cross: "Truly this was God's Son" (Mark 15:39). The Johannine literature makes this confessional use of "Son of God" even more explicit: "No one who denies the Son has the Father. He who confesses the Son has the Father also" (1 John 2:23). Paul too sees the Son-title as explicitly confessional in a passage we have already seen: "Paul, a servant of Christ Jesus, called to be an apostle and set apart for the gospel of God — the gospel he promised beforehand through his prophets in the Holy Scriptures regarding his Son, who was a descendant of David according to the flesh and who through the Spirit of holiness was designated with power to be the Son of God by his resurrection from the dead" (Rom. 1:1-4).

Another point to note: whereas Paul generally prefers "Lord" as his confessional term, John highlights "Son" above all other titles: for him it is the key to Jesus' identity and mission. This term more than any other expresses Jesus' unique relation to his Father and his unique mission, a mission to which he is totally obedient: "I do nothing on my own authority; . . . I seek not my own will but the will of the one who sent me" (John 5:30). Just like the Synoptic evangelists, John stresses that this unique relationship of Jesus to his Father cannot be perceived except by God's revelation, as Cullmann deftly explains:

> While witnesses can and must be produced to support other assertions, there can be no question of human witness for Jesus' claim to be the Son

of God. God himself is the only possible competent witness. Only he can validate this claim of oneness with himself. The claim to be the Son of God so bursts all human bonds that only this circular explanation is possible: the Father himself must attest that Jesus is the Son; on the other hand, this divine testimony must be given precisely in the Son.[49]

Jesus as God There can be no question that the New Testament is quite reticent about calling Jesus "God" outright, without further ado. Such reticence is understandable, for an explicit and unqualified designation of Jesus as God could sound polytheistic and mythological; or if "God" is meant monotheistically, to whom then is Jesus praying if he is already God *simpliciter?* On the other hand, a *refusal* to countenance calling Jesus "God" would lead to its own problems, underplaying and undercutting the unique bond that Jesus has with his Father, denigrating his divine status in favor of an excessive stress on his humanity.

We have already seen that the Fourth Evangelist has dealt with that theological dilemma in his prologue when he used Logos terminology: the Word was both *with* God and yet also *was* God (John 1:1). Furthermore, the obvious reticence of the New Testament in calling Jesus "God" can be exaggerated, for, as we have already seen, the title "Lord" was a specifically liturgical confession by which Christians addressed Jesus *in worship*. Still, passages that directly and without further ado designate Jesus as "God" are relatively rare, but no less significant for New Testament Christology on that account.

Outside of John 1:1 the most important passage would be the confession of doubting Thomas to Jesus on the Sunday after Easter, "My Lord and my God" (John 20:28), a passage that "frames" the Fourth Gospel in just the way the centurion's confession "This was truly the Son of God" (Mark 15:39) framed Mark's Gospel about the Son of God.[50] Paul too speaks of Jesus as "God": "Put on the mind of Christ Jesus, who, being the very form of God, did not consider *equality* with God something to be grasped" (Phil. 2:5-6); and he unambiguously asserts: "In him [Christ] the entire fullness of the Deity dwells in bodily form" (Col. 2:9). In the Letter to Titus Paul speaks of waiting "for that

---

49. Cullmann, *The Christology of the New Testament,* p. 302.

50. The fact that the centurion's confession hearkens back to the opening line of Mark's Gospel just as Thomas's confession hearkens back to the opening line of John's Gospel shows how desperate Arius was in the third century when he claimed that Thomas's confession "My Lord and my God" was really only an expostulation on his part, expressing a surprised prayer, rather in the manner of an American teenager crying out "Ohmigod!" Arius's exegesis is clearly a case of special pleading.

blessed hope, the glorious appearing of our great God and Savior, Jesus Christ" (Titus 2:13).[51] Finally we may mention these perhaps ambiguous lines: "Of their race [the Jews] come the patriarchs, and from them comes Christ according to the flesh, who is God over all, forever praised! Amen" (Rom. 9:5).[52] Another potentially ambiguous passage from Paul speaks of "the mystery of God, namely Christ, in whom are hidden all the treasures of wisdom and knowledge" (Col. 2:2).[53] Even more ambiguous is the line from Revelation: "He [Jesus] has a name written on him that no one knows but he himself" (Rev. 19:12), which may or may not be the sacred name of God.[54]

The very ambiguity of these latter passages, together with their relative sparseness, points to one of the central problems that will beset the church's later christological thought: a too-close identification of Jesus with God will render both his obedience to the Father and his outward mission to the world inexplicable; but an excessive reticence, not to say cowardice, about worshiping Jesus as God will undercut the efficacy of his work of redemption and undermine a belief in his uniqueness that it is the whole point of every book in the New Testament to convey.

Conclusion

Our survey of the titles of Jesus was meant to be just that: a survey.[55] The focus was solely on the semantics (referring both to the denotative and conno-

---

51. An almost identical phrase appears in the Petrine corpus too: "From Simon Peter, a servant and apostle of Jesus Christ, to those who through the righteousness of our God and Savior Jesus Christ have received a faith as precious as ours" (2 Pet. 1:1).

52. The ambiguity arises from the possibility that the word translated as "who" (referring to Christ) could instead mean "he" (referring to God), which would result in this translation: "Theirs are the patriarchs, and from them comes Christ according to the flesh, who is over all. God be praised!"

53. The grammar of the Greek allows for the word "Christ" to modify either "mystery" or "God."

54. Finally, mention should be made of two papyrus manuscripts 𝔭66 (published in 1956) and 𝔭75 (published in 1961). Both manuscripts give a variant reading for John 1:18, which most manuscripts read this way: "No one has ever seen God; the only Son, who is in the bosom of the Father, has made him known" (RSV). But these two papyri reproduce the verse to say: "No one has ever seen God, but God the One and Only, who is at the Father's side, has made him known" (NIV), or "No one has ever seen God. It is God the only Son, who is close to the Father's heart, who has made him known" (NRSV).

55. As we said in footnote 4, other schemas are possible. See, for example, Leopold Sabourin, *The Names and Titles of Jesus: Themes of Biblical Theology*, trans. Maurice Carroll

tative meaning) of each of the significant christological titles, at least as they could be gleaned from their context inside Christian narratives and confessions. Still to be treated is a more central enigma, one that perhaps does not emerge, at least in any direct and immediately obvious way, from this purely synchronic survey: Why exactly did *all* of these titles get applied to Jesus? After all, there is nothing initially obvious about linking Suffering Servant with Messiah, nor does High Priest imply by its literal meaning the notion of preexistence; and when was a prophet ever addressed as "savior" or the Son of Man as "Logos" in the Old Testament?

This enigma is further heightened by a fact we have yet to treat: not only did the figure of Jesus cluster about himself the most varied — and at first glance apparently contradictory — titles, he also recapitulated the roles of historical figures like Isaac, David, Moses, and Jeremiah that had never previously been seen as linked to some future redeemer. How can someone be both Isaac *and* David, Moses *and* Jeremiah?[56]

Only a diachronic, historical approach to both the life of Jesus and to the development of Christology as it can be traced during the formation of the New Testament documents will be able, I believe, to answer that question. Only when we take the assemblage of terms and titles as outlined in this chapter and see how they came to be applied to Jesus *and why* will our somewhat two-dimensional overview of Christology as presented in this essentially schematic, semantic, synchronic chapter gain that extra third dimension that will flesh out the figure of Jesus and show how Jesus can be simultaneously called Prophet, Suffering Servant, High Priest, Messiah, Son of Man, Lord, Savior, Word, Son of God — and God.

(New York: Macmillan, 1967), who divides the titles into "Simple Messianic Titles" (He-Who-Comes, Christ, Davidic King, Prophet, and Just and Holy One), "Communal Messianic Titles" (Good Shepherd, Door, Light, Head, Vine, Bread of Life, and Rock/Cornerstone), "Soteriological Titles" (Savior, Servant, Lamb, Expiation, High Priest, Resurrection), and "Properly Christological Titles" (Son of Man, Firstborn of Creation, Last Adam, Alpha and Omega, Judge, Son of God, Lord, Logos, Image of the Invisible God, and God). But the schema of what counts as a "proper" christological title strikes me as arbitrary. Ferdinand Hahn, *The Titles of Jesus in Christology: Their History in Early Christianity,* trans. Harold Knight and George Ogg (New York: World Publishing, 1969) provides, as the title and subtitle say, a history of the names, which will be the topic of the next chapter (although there the concentration will be not so much on the history of each specific name separately as on the confessional history as a totality, embracing all the names).

56. Perhaps this is the underlying reason Judaism and Christianity parted ways: one side took each biblical text and historical figure on its own terms, while the other side saw the whole biblical witness holistically, through the lens of Christ.

CHAPTER 3

The History of the Data

God made him who knew no sin to be sin for us, so that in him we might become the righteousness of God.

(2 Cor. 5:21)

The Diachronic Approach

Anyone who has taught an introductory course in the New Testament to undergraduates knows how difficult it can be to teach a history of these twenty-seven books. For one thing, the books are not arranged in historical order, that is, by the date of their composition or publication. (It is also telling that not a single book of the New Testament provides any indication of when it was written.) Occasionally, one author will show clear reliance on another book in the New Testament (or seem to), as Matthew and Luke seem to know Mark (or Mark's source?), since the parallel texts between Matthew and Mark or between Mark and Luke are often too exact in their word-for-word identity to be coincidental. But for the most part, New Testament authors draw on a common fund of oral tradition or on other documents now lost to us, which makes it difficult to rank the books we now have in a "family tree" of dependence.[1]

---

1. There is, however, one document now lost to us that can be reconstructed, or so say the majority of New Testament scholars. There are several passages in Matthew and Luke that are not found in Mark but which are reproduced in Matthew and Luke in almost word-for-word congruence. Provided one assumes that Matthew and Luke both wrote their Gospels independently of one another, which is plausible on other grounds, their mutual con-

Complicating the issue even further is the fact that those books that present the life and ministry of Jesus as historical narratives were not written to satisfy the historical curiosity of their readers. Normally, works that narrate the life of an individual in historical sequence are called "biographies." The narratives of the life of Jesus, however, are called not biographies but *gospels,* which differ from biographies in this crucial point: they are not meant to entertain, inform, or admonish their readers but to *convert* them. Moreover as the name indicates ("gospel" is derived from the Anglo-Saxon word *godspel,* meaning "good news"), the gospel writers are more than willing to give away the ending by asserting at the outset that they will be narrating a story of *good* news. In other words, the ending — resurrection — will determine the shape of the narrative from its outset.

Now news of great import in the ancient world was spread primarily by oral proclamation, and the news proclaimed by the town crier had to be accepted or rejected according to the trustworthiness of the herald. Even more crucially in the Christian case, the news proclaimed was primarily news about the action of God, for God was the one who, the New Testament consistently maintains, raised Jesus from the dead. Furthermore, acceptance of that news meant eternal life for the hearer: "If you declare with your mouth that Jesus is Lord, and if you believe with your heart that God raised him from the dead, then you will be saved" (Rom. 10:9).

This Pauline nugget-formulation of the proclamation (or *kerygma,* to use the Greek word meaning "proclamation") states the matter only in terms of the ending of the story, the resurrection; but St. Paul can also formulate the proclamation in a short, pithy narrative form that includes the central moment of Christ's earthly life, his death on a cross: "For what I received I passed on to you as of first importance: that Christ died for our sins, that he was buried, that he was raised on the third day according to the Scriptures, and that he appeared to Peter, and then to the Twelve" (1 Cor. 15:3-5). This passage constitutes the essence of the gospel, and its one-sentence brevity determined the entire narrative shape of the four Gospels as we have them today.

Among its other implications, this means that the evangelists wrote not as neutral historians but as, well, *evangelists,* that is, as missionaries, as seekers of converts, whose mission was to bring their hearers/readers into the sphere of salvation: "Since we have now been justified by his blood, how much more shall we be saved from God's wrath through him!" (Rom. 5:9).

---

gruence means that they are both relying on another written source, conventionally called "Q" (a symbol based on the German word for "source," *Quelle*).

For that reason, the evangelists selected the material for their narratives solely with that converting, missionary purpose in mind and not according to the rules of scientific historiography in either the ancient or modern understanding of that term. Thus, one evangelist will place Jesus' Sermon on the Mount early in his ministry, while another will place it a bit later on and describe it as being preached not on a mount but on a plain; three evangelists will place the cleansing of the Temple at the end of Jesus' ministry, while the fourth will put it near the beginning.

These transpositions have often troubled Christians, but that only means that they are importing modern standards of historical curiosity (which can only be assuaged by neutral research) into books not written with that purpose in mind. But the freedom of the evangelists to shape their historical narratives for missionary purposes does complicate the issue for theologians who want to see what light can be thrown on New Testament Christology by looking at the history of its development.

Basically, we must keep in mind two different levels of history here. First, there is the most basic narrative, the objective history as enacted by historical actors. By that we mean the actual, historical events, starting with Jesus' conception, birth, and early childhood; then the onset of his public ministry, his movement from Galilee to Jerusalem, his execution there, his appearances as the Risen One to the first disciples; at which point the narrative shifts into a new key to describe the movement of nascent Christianity from its cradle in Jerusalem, on to its traverse through the eastern portions of the Roman Empire until it finally reaches Rome itself. Let us call this the *event* history of early Christianity: from Galilee, through Jerusalem, and then finally to Rome.

Now *inside* that history Christians would not just be living out that history but will also start to *recount* it, first orally, in their preaching, and then in written form, by their penning various documents for various purposes. Then, some of these documents began to be regarded as valuable and nourishing enough by these early Christians that they would be copied and preserved, eventually forming the New Testament we know today. This we shall call the New Testament's *narrative* history, composed of two elements, *oral* and *documentary* history: meaning the history of how, when, and where Christians recounted the history they were living out.

Now in terms of documentary history, here is the key point: those books that make up the first five books in the New Testament (Matthew through Acts) were written *after* the epistles, at least those written by Paul, even though they come first in the order we now have them (and the epistles themselves are not placed in the order of their composition either). Given that fact, the question arises to what extent the doctrine located in the epistles affected the narrative shape of the Gospels themselves, which are our main source for knowledge of the history of Jesus. Here is how the Second Vatican Council puts the matter, with admirable concision:

> The sacred authors wrote the four Gospels, *selecting* some things from the many which had been handed on *by word of mouth or in writing,* reducing some of them to a synthesis, explicating some things in view of the situation of the churches, and *preserving the form of proclamation,* but always in such fashion that they told us the honest truth about Jesus.[2]

This book purports to be a textbook introduction to Christology, not to New Testament history, still less to the historical Jesus. But I believe one gets a distorted view of New Testament Christology if one is content merely to list the titles given to Jesus, analyzing their semantic range alone, valuable though that exercise is in its own right. For after that valuable work has been done, another crucial question remains: What can the basic event history, both of Jesus and the early church, and the documentary history, teach us about how each of these titles got applied to Jesus? In other words, what new light is thrown on the data by looking at New Testament Christology in a diachronic light? It will be the task of this chapter to set forth answers to those questions.

First, however, we must ask: How does the more basic event history relate to documentary history? Because one can hardly discuss the actual events of the ministry of Jesus and the growth of the early church without first seeing how the documents recounting that history relate to each other as sources or as background inspiration, we must take up the question of the documentary history before outlining the event history. (Moreover, as we saw in the last chapter, our knowledge of the history of Jesus and the early church comes almost entirely from the New Testament documents themselves.) By that same token, one can hardly examine the history and interrelationship of the documents without first seeing how the authors of those documents drew from a common fund of oral preaching ("selecting some things from the many which had been handed on by word of mouth," as Vatican II succinctly puts it). So for methodological reasons, the approach of this chapter will be to start with the common *narrative strategy* found in all

---

2. *Dei verbum,* The Dogmatic Constitution on Divine Revelation, § 19, ed. Walter M. Abbott, S.J., translation editor, V. Rev. Msgr. Joseph Gallagher (New York: Guild Press, 1966), p. 124; emphasis added.

New Testament preaching (both oral and written); then we will move to *documentary history*, that is, to the specific features and unique stresses in the christological teaching of each of the major New Testament authors, considered on their own terms; and then we will conclude with an overview of the *basic event history* of Jesus and his mission and the connection of that mission with New Testament Christology.

Retrospective Narrative as Evangelization: The Structure of Oral Proclamation

Only five of the books of the New Testament — Matthew, Mark, Luke, John, and Acts of the Apostles — can be called, in the strict sense of the term, *narratives* from start to finish. And only the first four of them, the Gospels, imply that Jesus' identity emerges best when told in narrative terms. The other documents that we have, while they contain within their confines some narrative nuggets (as we have seen), tend to convey the meaning and reality of the Christ event in more abstract and doctrinal terms. The Gospels, though, have all chosen narrative as their preferred genre.

Not even the Gospels, though, would claim that narrative *alone* suffices. Actually, no historical account of any event, if that event has any significance at all, can really succeed if told *solely* in narrative terms. What is needed, as one author, John Boyle, succinctly puts it, are "categories of intelligibility":

> The facts of history occur in a temporal sequence and, for this reason, history is in part a temporal narrative. The historian, however, wants to do more than tell a good story; he wants to explain it. He therefore seeks those categories of intelligibility that will explain why certain events happen in the way they do: the role terrain plays in a successful military strategy, for example, or the motives (economic, psychological, or social) that move men to action. Through an abundant number of such categories, the historian tries to make sense of history. In this lies his problem. The categories that interpret what happens have their own principles and rules of exposition, which may not be wholly compatible with a narrative sequence. For this reason, the historian is torn between two masters in his work: the narrative sequence and the categories of intelligibility.[3]

3. John F. Boyle, "The Twofold Division of St. Thomas's Christology in the *Tertia Pars*," *The Thomist* 60, no. 3 (July 1996): 439-40.

Of course the canon of intelligibility for the New Testament differs radically from what a secular historian would accept (which is why the "science" of Christology is accessible as a truth-claim only to believers, although there is no reason why a nonbeliever should balk at a scientific presentation of what Christians in fact accept as true based on their faith in the Christian proclamation). But let us stay for a moment with the formal similarities between secular and New Testament history. Secular histories are under no obligation to present *everything* in their histories in chronological order. For example, if the bend of a river is crucial to an army's victory in a battle, the historian rarely feels obliged to start his history of a particular battle with a history of the earth's geology.[4] Moreover, some causes of historical events belong to the basic constituents of human nature that are not easily described in historical terms, such as psychological motivations (resentment, fear, ambition, and the like). For that reason, the historian is entirely free in deciding when and how to bring these wider and essentially nonchronological factors into play when it comes time to describe the larger causes of the events he is attempting both to narrate and to explain.

Speaking still only formally, the same dilemma of deciding how to "fold in" the categories of intelligibility into the historical narrative of the events of Jesus' life confronts both the evangelist as well as the theologian who is trying to present New Testament Christology as a coherent totality, as Professor Boyle again lucidly explains:

> The theologian, in considering the life and mission of Christ, confronts much the same problem. He has before him both the temporal narrative of that life and the need to understand and explain it, albeit far more profoundly than the historian can. For his information on the life of Christ, the theologian is dependent upon Scripture; the fourfold Gospel narrates the story of Christ's life. For his primary categories of intelligibility, the theologian is also dependent upon Scripture. For example, the Gospel proclaims that Christ is the Word made flesh and thereby understands the import of Christ's life, passion, death, and resurrection. The epistles provide a great number of decisive categories that interpret the mission of Christ: Christ the redeemer of a fallen humanity; Christ the true mediator between God and man; Christ the great high priest; Christ the head of the Church. The theologian must make sense of the life and mission of Christ

---

4. Admittedly, the novelist James Michener, who liked to start most of his historical novels around the time the earth's crust was first beginning to cool, is an exception to this rule. But he was a novelist, and even there decidedly eccentric in his narrative strategies.

in such a way as to account for the varied themes and categories already provided by Scripture.[5]

No wonder, then, that professors teaching introductory courses in the New Testament find the task so challenging, for there are so many factors to keep in mind at the same time: the three levels of history discussed above (the events themselves, initial oral accounts, and finally the documents), the doctrinal (and therefore more notional) categories of understanding without which the history of Christ makes no sense, the different narrative strategies adopted by each evangelist, and their varying reliance on sources both known and unknown to us. But what most complicates the issue is this often forgotten feature of the Gospels: they wish to bring their readers into a view of history that is meant to *overthrow, not confirm,* the contrary view, one that naïvely assumes that all events of history are explicable within the overarching category of history itself. In other words, the New Testament's own categories for understanding Jesus *and history* must be allowed to speak on their own terms. In the case of Christ, to make sense of history means to be governed by the Bible's own theology of history.[6]

These observations make the task of this chapter sound very daunting indeed; but the situation can be clarified by considering one motif of the Gospels that is often overlooked in treatments of Christology: the theme of the incomprehension of the disciples of Jesus during his earthly ministry. Not only did the disciples for the most part not "get it," they are *described* as not getting it.

This motif points up once again that the Gospels are *retrospective* narratives, that is, narratives told with the end already in view. Most histories are in fact written retrospectively, since, after all, most readers of history books already know how World War II ended, how and when Julius Caesar met his

---

5. Boyle, "Twofold Division," p. 440. Further: "In a temporal narrative of Christ's life, there is no obvious place for the treatment of His mediatorship, priesthood, or headship. Each extends throughout, and even beyond, His earthly life, although each is intimately bound to particular aspects of that life" (p. 440). In other words, we can now realize why most of the epistles in the New Testament were written before the Gospels: until the categories for truly understanding the identity of Christ were accepted in faith, a true narrative of his life could not be told. Might this not be the reason Q was not preserved after its valuable material had been incorporated into Matthew and Luke, since it consisted (so far as we can tell) of sayings of Jesus only?

6. "The problem is thus one in which both the narrative and its primary categories of intelligibility are in Scripture. [Theologians are] not simply making sense of history, [they are] making sense of Scripture" (Boyle, "Twofold Division," p. 440).

end, and so forth. This retrospective outlook is often called the "benefit of hindsight," and no historian fails to take advantage of it. This benefit of hindsight primarily (and most obviously) affects the *selection of the material to be treated.*[7]

Augustine says we all know that we must die, but not when. Similarly, as actors on the stage of history, few of us see how things are going to turn out, except those rare seers among us. So, are we surprised that the Gospels portray the disciples of Jesus not understanding who he was except in retrospect? Similarly, are we surprised that the evangelists have written their narratives of the life and identity of Jesus with the benefit of hindsight? Why bother keeping the reader in the same suspense of clueless bafflement that afflicted the disciples until they retrospectively "saw the light"? Especially when one's salvation depends on confessing the truth of the ending of this startling narrative, that Jesus was raised from the dead for our salvation?

Perhaps the most fascinating aspect of the Gospels' strategy is that this history of the disciples not "getting it" did not end with the appearances of the risen Jesus, however much retrospective light that event threw on their minds to make them realize (finally!) who he really is. On the contrary, they still had a lot to learn, or so it seems from accounts we read in the New Testament. For example, after the resurrection and just before Jesus is to ascend into heaven, his disciples ask, "Now has the time come for you to restore the kingdom to Israel?" (Acts 1:6). In other words, they had been following Jesus all along because in some way they saw *their* Messianic hopes being realized in him. But when he died, their hopes were dashed (what king can die and still be a king?), and so they began to slink away

7. For example, I once saw a Masterpiece Theater dramatization of the life of Winston Churchill during the 1930s called "Winston Churchill: The Wilderness Years," about his years as a backbencher in Parliament during the time that Hitler was rearming Germany, obviously with the intent of starting a new war to assuage the bitterness of the Germans at having lost World War I. Because that first global war had been so devastating to the civilization of Europe, very few people — except Churchill and a few likeminded souls — wanted to admit the truth about Hitler's intentions, for that would mean another war was looming. The rest, including the leading lights of the Labour, Liberal, and Conservative parties, all denied the evidence staring them in the face. I only mention this by-now almost universally acknowledged fact of Churchill's foresight to stress that no one would be interested in watching a multi-week presentation of Churchill's fight to get Britain to see the dangers facing it except in the retrospective light of subsequent events that tell us that history has *vindicated* Churchill. All of us, when we look at the historical record, operate from this benefit of hindsight; but only the prophets among us live by the benefit of foresight. And that show on Churchill in his wilderness years confirmed his wisdom, and our folly.

home dejected (Luke 24:13-35). But when they saw him risen from the dead, their hopes in him as their Messiah were restored; but crucially, it was still largely *their* hopes that were restored, at least to the extent that they now expected their Messiah to do what the Old Testament had foreseen as the chief work of Messiah — to drive out the foreigners and restore the kingdom of the Promised Land to Israel.

So the resurrection confirmed for the disciples that Jesus really was Messiah, but they still continued to carry over from their past upbringing a "schedule of expectations," so to speak, about what the long-promised Messiah was meant to accomplish, expectations that still required further reformation and adjustment. Other implications drawn from the event of the resurrection also required adjustment. The Old Testament speaks of resurrection only rarely, and then exclusively in terms of the end of the world (Dan. 12). Based on this learned "script," the earliest Christians took resurrection to mean the imminent end of the world (Acts 2:20-21; 1 Thess. 4:17). This expectation, too, had to be unlearned, chastened by new experience.

Perhaps the most fascinating part of this story is the crisis that this chastening did *not* provoke, a crisis of faith in the resurrection itself, which surely means that the resurrection interpreted the expectations, not the other way around, with the expectations determining the experience of resurrection. As Paula Fredriksen explains:

> The disciples' experience of Jesus' resurrection stands at the heart of the early Christian movement. . . . That Jesus' followers perceived Jesus to have been so raised and so vindicated tells us, further, the degree to which he had forged his followers into a committed community and prepared them for an eschatological event. The one *they* all expected when they went up to Jerusalem was the arrival of the Kingdom, the fulfillment of Jesus' message. Instead, abruptly and brutally, this message was disconfirmed, their leader killed by the enemy who incarnated the ungodly powers of the present order. But shortly thereafter, Jesus' followers experienced an *unexpected* eschatological event: Jesus was raised. The community could continue: disconfirmation became confirmation.[8]

This, I believe, is the pattern that runs through the history of the New Testament (in all three senses) and explains the basic dynamism of early

---

8. Paula Fredriksen, *From Jesus to Christ: The Origins of the New Testament Images of Jesus* (New Haven: Yale University Press, 1999), pp. 133-34; first italics added, second in the original.

Christianity: *all theological problems and puzzles were referred back to the resurrection and found their resolution there.* Early in his missionary career, Paul might well have concluded that Jesus would return soon. Resurrection, after all, represented a radical in-breaking and irruption of God's power into the course of history, so doesn't it stand to reason there is little left to history but some concluding *dénouement?*[9] But when that end was "delayed," Paul felt no crisis of faith, for he always knew that his primary experience was of the risen Lord; whereas the expectation of an imminent end was just that, a conclusion, an expectation, drawn from his reading of Old Testament apocalyptic, which itself must now be reinterpreted in the light of the resurrection. In other words, resurrection determines how the Old Testament is to be interpreted, rather than the Old Testament determining how resurrection is to be interpreted.

And this holds true for all the rest of those titles and historical analogues that the evangelists drew from the Old Testament to portray Jesus: all the traditional titles of Jesus were *reconstituted* by the resurrection, and the Gospel writers wrote their narratives from that point of view. Just as Paul did not (eventually) allow the implicit assumption within the account of the Son of Man in the book of Daniel (namely, that the resurrection of the dead signaled, indeed inaugurated, the end of the world) to determine his experience of the risen Jesus, so too the Evangelists did not use Old Testament prophecies and titles to *determine* the identity of Jesus. Rather, the totality of the figure of Jesus — life, death, and resurrection — *reconstituted* the cluster of images, figures, and titles made available by the Hebrew Scriptures. In other words, once the disciples realized who Jesus really was by virtue of the resurrection, they were able to see *retrospectively* where, how, and why they continued to misunderstand him during his earthly ministry; and the evangelists, sharing that same benefit of hindsight, were able to apply that same benefit to the witness of the Old Testament.

As we have already seen, this is a narrative strategy adopted by all historians, since they already know the outcome of the events they are describing.

---

9. Oscar Cullmann used the analogy of D-Day leading to VE (Victory in Europe) Day: once the Allies had managed to land on the beaches of Normandy and then created successful beachheads, Germany's fate was sealed, and defeat was now a sure thing, however long it might take, and however much the advance of the Allies might be occasionally upset by setbacks like the Battle of the Bulge. Similarly, once God broke into the world of sin and death and currently under the sway of the powers and dominions, history might have to continue on for a while in its petty pace, but the final victory is assured. The implications of this insight will be discussed in Chapter 12.

An example of the reverse narrative strategy will bring out the difference. The whole point of fiction is to put the reader in a "you were there" setting: *not* knowing the outcome is part of what makes the narrative entertaining. But when readers come to the end of the novel, they can look back and see the significance of some events that had eluded them earlier.[10] But the Gospels are not novels. For the Evangelists could look back over the vast history of the Jews and see the significance of certain passages (especially the Suffering Servant songs in Isaiah) for explaining the meaning of Jesus that *had not been seen in their true significance until the resurrection of Jesus;* and they incorporated that insight into the warp and woof of their narrative, as the noted New Testament scholar C. H. Dodd explains:

> All the variations of plot are applied by New Testament writers to the interpretation of the same series of facts. . . . The richness and depth of their interpretation of what happened "under Pontius Pilate" results largely from bringing together these apparently inconsistent features [of Old Testament prophecy] and superimposing them to form a single composite picture.[11]

10. Formally speaking, this retrospective insight that comes only at the end, not the beginning, of the story is clearest in the case of detective fiction, when the detective explains in the last chapter why certain clues, which seemed trivial at the time, were crucial to solving the case.

11. C. H. Dodd, *The Old Testament in the New* (Philadelphia: Fortress Press, 1963), p. 28. Note as well that it is not only the identity of Jesus that receives new illumination and meaning by the way the New Testament reconstitutes the titles of the Old Testament into a new configuration; the church too is explained: "Again, the New Testament doctrine of the person of Christ depends for its richness and depth, almost for its intelligibility, upon the inseparable fusion of two figures of prophecy: the *leader and sovereign* over God's people [the Davidic figure of Messiah], and the *'inclusive representative,'* or *embodiment,* of that people, and indeed, in the last resort, of redeemed humanity as a whole [the Suffering Servant image]. All the ideal attributes of the church are assigned to it in the New Testament solely insofar as it is comprehended 'in Christ'. . . . All that is said about the significance of the work of Christ presupposes that he includes in himself the whole people of God, or redeemed humanity. His death and resurrection are not to be understood if they are thought of as no more than the death and miraculous resurrection of an individual, but only if they are seen as the fulfillment of the whole purpose of God to raise up for himself, through suffering, tribulation, and disaster, a people made wholly one in him and devoted to his righteous purpose. Christ 'rose the third day,' says the ancient formula quoted by Paul in his first epistle to the Corinthians, 'according to the scriptures.' But in the scriptures . . . it is Israel whom God will raise on the third day. The bold application of that prophecy to the resurrection of Christ in the earliest Christian confession of faith known to us lies behind the Pauline doctrine of the church as dead and risen with Christ" (pp. 29-30; emphases added).

This is the fundamental redactional strategy of all four Evangelists. The use of the term "redactor" (a fancy term for "editor") to explain the specific contribution of each Evangelist is perhaps unfortunate, as it might imply that they are merely compiling previously available documents, making no more contribution to their respective Gospels than a newspaper editor makes to a reporter's filed copy. But a comparison of the four Gospels shows that each evangelist wanted to stress certain features in his portrait of Jesus that were unique to him: Mark stresses the unique Messiahship of Jesus as fused to the quite different figure of Son of Man (and accordingly the misunderstanding of the disciples about the real meaning of that Messiahship), Matthew foregrounds the reality of Jesus as the new Moses, Luke highlights Jesus as Healer, and John stresses Jesus as Light of the world.

But beyond those differences (which we will explain in the next section), the key point to see here is the commonality behind the differences in emphasis: *all the elements of past history are reshaped and given a new pattern as determined by the resurrection,* both in the earliest fragments of the oral tradition and in every book of the New Testament. Not surprisingly, therefore, this redactional strategy is precisely the one adopted by Peter in his preaching on Pentecost Sunday, who begins his sermon by quoting appropriate passages from the prophet Joel before he goes on to explain their culminating fulfillment in God's great deed of raising Jesus from the dead and sending the Holy Spirit down on the Apostles that very morning (Acts 2). The continuity of missionary strategy is direct and unbroken — what Peter did orally, Paul did in his written epistles and the evangelists did in their Gospels, as again Dodd explains:

> In its most summary form the *kerygma* consists of the announcement of certain historical events in a setting which displays the significance of those events. The events in question are those of the appearance of Jesus in history — His ministry, sufferings and death and His subsequent manifestation of Himself to His followers as risen from the dead and invested with the glory of another world. . . . The significance attached to these events is mainly indicated by references to the Old Testament.[12]

---

12. C. H. Dodd, *According to the Scriptures: The Sub-Structure of New Testament Theology* (New York: Charles Scribner's Sons, 1953), pp. 11-12. The Scriptures were even able to illuminate the structural reason for the disciples' incomprehension, a fact of history that could otherwise have caused acute embarrassment: "It seems that the apostles saw themselves in a situation somewhat parallel to that of Isaiah at the beginning of his prophetic ministry and included the classic text on unbelief (Isaiah 6:9ff) in the intellectual armory at

This retrospective selection of Old Testament passages (which had become newly meaningful in light of the resurrection) does not mean, however, as is often asserted, that the prophecies of the suffering of an unnamed servant *determined* the narratives, as if historical-*seeming* events were devised to illuminate Old Testament passages.[13] Rather, the core events of death on a cross and subsequent resurrection made select passages singularly appropriate for explaining the *significance* of these events, a significance that had been quite unsuspected by the Jews up until that time (very much including the Jewish disciples of Jesus during his earthly life). According to Ben Witherington:

> It was the startling things that happened to Jesus at the close of his earthly career — his shocking crucifixion and then his equally astonishing resurrection — that caused the earliest Christians to race back to their sacred Scriptures to help them interpret the significance of these events. They did not first find these events in the Old Testament prophecies and then create new narratives out of the old prophecies. This is shown most clearly by the fact that many of the texts used to interpret the key final events of Jesus' life, in their original contexts in the Hebrew Scriptures, would not have suggested such things to a reader who had not heard of Jesus' life, death, and resurrection. I know of no evidence that non-Christian early Jews were looking for a resurrected messiah, and in fact, the evidence that they were looking for a crucified one is also very doubtful.[14]

---

an early date." Barnabas Lindars, *New Testament Apologetic: The Doctrinal Significance of Old Testament Quotations* (Philadelphia: Westminster Press, 1961), p. 253. See as well Donald Juel, *Messianic Exegesis: Christological Interpretation of the Old Testament in Early Christianity* (Philadelphia: Fortress, 1988).

13. "There is no messianism in the New Testament which is derived from the Old Testament. . . . The Old Testament in no way predicts or leads one to expect the historical reality of Jesus proclaimed as accomplished in him." J. L. McKenzie, *A Theology of the Old Testament* (Garden City, NY: Doubleday, 1976), pp. 278, 279. When these words were first penned by this famous Catholic scholar of the Hebrew Bible, they provoked considerable controversy, as they seemed to deny the doctrine of prophetic inspiration, on which so much prior apologetics had rested, Protestant and Catholic (and it certainly gave impetus to interpreting the Hebrew Bible/Old Testament on its own terms, not just in light of the New). But ironically, this insight only proves the startling innovation of Jesus and the later preaching church, as will become clear immediately below.

14. Ben Witherington III, *New Testament History: A Narrative Account* (Grand Rapids: Baker Academic, 2001), p. 169. This point is seconded by another scholar: "Attempts to find in Israel's history a 'suffering Messiah' figure have thus far proven fruitless, yet this does not preclude the possibility that Jesus could have pioneered this combination of images. . . . [T]he

In other words, each of the evangelists followed the same strategy as the earliest preachers of the oral gospel: the event of Jesus determines how the story of God's deeds for his Chosen People up to that moment will be interpreted. It is as if the resurrection had thrown on a light-switch that cast retrospective light on all that went before, so that what happened last shaped the narrative of all previous events; indeed it determined the interpretation of the whole of salvation history, from the creation of Adam (Rom. 5:12-21) to the end of the world (Acts 2:17-21; Rev. 21:1-8). As another scholar puts it:

> The disciples did not stand by Jesus; they fled, denied him and broke the fellowship which he had bestowed on them. But the Easter event forged anew the bond which had been broken. So this event caused a new understanding of the word and the person of Jesus to appear amongst the disciples. Instead of the general breaking in of the kingdom of God, there took place a particular action of God towards the one who had been executed. By the Easter event a new light was thrown both on what was to be expected in the future and on what the significance of Jesus had been. While in the pre-Easter situation there had merely been Jesus' sovereign promise of the salvation to come, given without adducing any support from existing authorities, the post-Easter faith realized that Jesus was vindicated by God himself, who thus had invalidated all contradiction by men and all that men had been able to see. Jesus was now recognized as possessing full authority. From this, then, resulted what we will call a Christological understanding.[15]

New Testament Christology in Formation: Documentary History

So far we have merely established a continuity of strategy adopted by both oral preaching and written documents, stressing above all the common features of narrative structuring present throughout all forms of New Testament evangelization. Yet to be established is the significance for Christology

---

gospels repeatedly witness the obtuseness of Jesus' followers in grasping the connection between divine mission and shameful demise. This suggests that, even if the raw materials had been readily available, such a connection would not have been easy even for his closest followers." Joel B. Green, "Crucifixion," in *The Cambridge Companion to Jesus*, ed. Markus Bockmuehl (Cambridge: Cambridge University Press, 2001), pp. 87-101; here 99.

15. H. E. Tödt, *The Son of Man in the Synoptic Tradition,* trans. Dorothea M. Barton (Philadelphia: Westminster Press, 1965), p. 293.

of the individual documents that make up the New Testament and their unique way of presenting the life and meaning of Jesus.

This chapter obviously does not intend to be a work in the historical criticism of the New Testament. Nonetheless, many of the results of this school of scholarship are extremely important for Christology: above all the well-established fact that all of Paul's epistles without exception were written before the first Gospel was set down in writing. From this fact alone we may deduce several crucial points: first, the Gospels were written for already well-established Christian communities; second, simple proclamation and ethical instruction took precedence over a need to set down in writing a narrative account of the life of Jesus; and third, narrative accounts had to be primarily drawn from an oral tradition that was itself handed on for its edifying impact on the Christian community, and therefore *not* to satisfy some idle curiosity.

But more to the point, these three consequences that can be drawn from the priority of the Pauline epistles lead to a more startling conclusion: *the essentials of the christological thinking of the early church were already complete before the composition of the first Gospel.* This is because the church was forced to think through the implications of the resurrection well before the narratives of the life of Jesus took shape in written form.

This insight represents an overthrow of previous New Testament scholarship that was conducted under a kind of Hegelian hammerlock, which implicitly assumed that any "development" of New Testament Christology had to take place according to the laws of intellectual development set forth in G. W. F. Hegel's *Phenomenology of Spirit,* whereby a more simple thesis generates obvious objections (the "antithesis"), a clash that then leads to a more overarching and reconciling "synthesis." Or, in contemporary terms, the early church gradually progressed, in this schema, from a "low" to a "high" Christology; or, to put it in less abstract terms, the church started with a Palestinian rabbi and ended up with a divine Lord synthesized from an encounter with various Hellenistic savior-cults.

The terminology of "low" and "high" Christology was first coined, to the best of my knowledge, by the German Lutheran theologian Wolfhart Pannenberg in his influential work *Jesus — God and Man.*[16] According to Pannenberg, the distinction is meant to be purely methodological: Does one start "from above" with a consideration of Jesus' divinity (that would be a "high" Christology) or does one begin "from below" by considering Jesus' hu-

---

16. Wolfhart Pannenberg, *Jesus — God and Man,* trans. Lewis L. Wilkins and Duane A. Priebe (Philadelphia: Westminster Press, 1977); cited henceforth as Pannenberg, *Jesus.*

manity (a "low" Christology)? One might well end up with identical conclusions (in fact, for Pannenberg one *should* end up at the same place), but the starting point is crucial: "For Christology that begins 'from above,' from the divinity of Jesus," says Pannenberg, "the concept of the incarnation stands in the center. A Christology 'from below,' rising from the historical man Jesus to the *recognition* of his divinity, is concerned first of all with Jesus' message and fate and arrives only at the end at the concept of incarnation."[17]

Complaints are occasionally voiced that such a schema is conceptually unworkable, both as an analysis of New Testament data and as an aid for understanding the identity of Jesus in contemporary terms.[18] I happen to agree with that assessment.[19] But my point here is that, even if one were to grant (as I do not) its conceptual validity as an early attempt to categorize the data synchronically, the distinction between high and low does violence to the New Testament data *when it is later diachronically placed inside a Hegelian framework that assumes that "low" comes first and only results later in a "high" Christology.* This view gained plausibility after it had been established that the Gospels of Matthew and Luke relied on Mark (with its allegedly "low" Christology) and that the Gospel of John (with its allegedly "high" Christology) was written last of all.

Whatever the legitimacy of this view of the interrelationship of the Gos-

17. Pannenberg, *Jesus*, p. 33.

18. The most rhetorically effective demolition of Pannenberg's schema comes from Nicholas Lash: "There is no clear moment at which once illuminating maxims, models and metaphors become, through overuse, obfuscatory rather than clarificatory, narcotics rather than 'aids to reflection.' Nevertheless, there does come a time when that moment can be seen to have long passed. In this paper, I wish to plead for a moratorium on recommendations to do christology 'from above' or 'from below'" (Nicholas Lash, "Up and Down in Christology," in *New Studies in Theology I*, ed. Stephen Sykes and Derek Holmes [London: Duckworth, 1980], p. 31).

19. Among other reasons, such a schema implies that the contemporary believer has a *choice* in the matter, since according to this distinction, the New Testament itself presents a variety of Christolog*ies,* and since the New Testament validates pluralism, one is justified in choosing which Christology one finds more compatible, or meaningful, or "relevant." Then the "choice" gets politicized in terms of the Culture Wars now raging through the church, with "liberals" preferring a "low" Christology and "conservatives" a "high" one, a move that then gives *de facto* legitimation to divisions in the church. Plus, despite Pannenberg's protestations, one rarely finds Christologies that start "from above" able to do justice to the humanity of Jesus, or, correlatively, Christologies that start "from below" able to do justice to his divinity. Whether this textbook will prove any more successful than previous efforts remains for the reader to decide. All I can say is that, in my opinion, the schema of "high" and "low" distorts the data from the outset.

pels, the thesis as applied to the New Testament generally will not stand scrutiny, for the Pauline epistles provide evidence for a "high" Christology of unimpeachable pedigree, as can be seen especially in the second chapter of the letter to the Philippians, where Paul (quoting an even earlier Christian liturgical hymn) speaks of Christ not clinging to his *equality* with God but emptying himself to become a man (Phil. 2:6-7).[20] So significant, in fact, is Pauline Christology for later doctrinal development that one noted New Testament scholar insists that "*more happened in christology within these few years* [between the resurrection and the epistle to the Philippians] *than in the whole subsequent seven hundred years of church history.*"[21]

In a way, even this stretch of time might be considered too long. For do we not read, in the second chapter of Acts, of Peter telling the assembly on Pentecost how "God made this Jesus, whom you crucified, both Lord and Christ" (Acts 2:36)? And is not "Lord" the very name that is "above every other name" that God gave Jesus when he "raised him high" (Phil. 2:9)?[22] So

20. "The earliest datable parts of the New Testament [the Pauline epistles] . . . indicate nothing short of divine status for Jesus." C. F. D. Moule, *The Origins of Christology* (Cambridge: Cambridge University Press, 1977), p. 6. Gordon Fee agrees: "Although this might be considered an oversimplification, the ultimate issue has to do with the Son's preexistence; that is, does an author consider Christ to have had existence as (or with) God before coming into our history for the purpose of redemption, which included at the end his resurrection and subsequent exaltation to 'the right hand of God' in 'fulfillment' of Ps. 110:1? If the answer to that question is yes, then one speaks of an author (e.g., the Gospel of John, the author of Hebrews) as having a high Christology. If the answer is either no or ambiguous at best, then the author . . . is credited with a low Christology. The ultimate question of Pauline Christology, therefore, is where Paul fits on this spectrum; and my conviction after a careful analysis of all the texts is that he fits at the high end, along with John and the author of Hebrews." Gordon D. Fee, *Pauline Christology: An Exegetical-Theological Study* (Peabody, MA: Hendrickson, 2007), pp. 9-10.

21. Martin Hengel, "Christology and New Testament Chronology," *Between Jesus and Paul: Studies in the Earliest History of Christianity,* trans. John Bowden (Philadelphia: Fortress, 1983), pp. 39-40; Hengel's emphasis. The span of "these few years," by the way, Hengel estimates at being a mere eighteen years.

22. A guardhouse lawyer could, I presume, argue that Peter's sermon on Pentecost is embedded in the second volume of Luke's two-volume work on the history of Jesus and the early church (Luke/Acts) and thus is found in a document that postdates Paul. But an analysis of that sermon shows its roots in a Petrine tradition not otherwise cited or used by Luke. For example, only here and in the first letter of Peter can one find reference to the descent of Jesus into a specifically named Hades (Acts 2:24; 1 Peter 3:18-19). Also, in this sermon Peter describes Jesus entirely in passive terms, never as an independent actor; and the Old Testament passages cited by Peter are not significant for Luke elsewhere. On the ancient Palestinian and Petrine provenance of this Pentecost sermon see C. H. Dodd, *The Apostolic*

clearly, the schema of "high" and "low" Christology fails on both conceptual and historical grounds.

For that reason, and also because both the earliest preaching of the first Christians and the Pauline epistles follow the same retrospective strategy of interpreting the whole of the Old Testament witness in terms of the death and resurrection of Jesus, the specific details of the dating of the New Testament documents (was Galatians written before or after Philippians?) are not all that relevant for the question of the development of New Testament Christology (of course much more rides on that issue for the historical criticism of the New Testament).

But even though the priority of the Pauline epistles is of great significance both for exploding the jejune schema of "low" and "high" Christology and for getting a better picture of New Testament Christology in its true contours, that still leaves open the question of the documentary history of the four Gospels themselves. Here, because nearly all scholars now grant priority to Mark and claim that the Gospel of John was written last, and because Mark allegedly purveys a "low" Christology and John a "high" one, Pannenberg's distinction seems much more plausible when applied to the Gospels alone, as opposed to the development of New Testament Christology as a whole.

Still, even in the case of the interrelationship of the four Gospels, I think one must approach each Gospel on its own terms without putting them into some artificial straitjacket that has already done enough damage in other areas. This is particularly true of Mark, whose Christology is quite literally "from above," since he stresses more than any other Evangelist Jesus' identity as Son of Man, who is described by Jesus himself, in one of the great climactic moments of Mark's Gospel, in these "from above" terms: "and you will see the Son of Man seated at the right hand of Power *coming down* with the clouds of heaven" (Mark 14:62). And as for the Fourth Gospel, far from representing the quintessence of "high" Christology, much of the polemical effort of this Gospel is to insist (against the proto-Gnostics, who denied the humanity of Jesus) that Jesus was fully a man of flesh (John 1:14; 1 John 1:1-3), supposedly the main concern of those who like their Christology "low."

Clearly, what is required is a careful examination of the Christology of each of the major authors of the books of the New Testament on their own terms, an examination in which phenomenological sobriety will trump any artificial schematization, no matter how initially plausible.

Preaching and Its Development (New York: Harper & Row, 1951) and Martin Hengel, *Acts and the History of Early Christianity* (Philadelphia: Fortress, 1980).

The Christology of Paul

One sure sign of the significance of Paul for Christology is that the most important titles for the church's christological confession and orthodox creeds — Christ, Lord, and Son of God — occur with extraordinary frequency in his letters. Interestingly, some of the terms in his thought for which he is most famous, such as reconciliation and justification, are limited to individual letters (or even mere segments of them). But the christological titles saturate his letters with astonishing frequency and density. Thus, of the 531 occurrences of "Christ" or "Christ Jesus" in the whole New Testament, 270 are found in the undisputed letters of Paul.[23] "Lord" is found 719 times in the New Testament as a whole, 189 of them in Paul (more than a fourth!).[24] Finally, while the title "Son of God" appears relatively infrequently in Paul (15 times), they all occur in significant passages.[25]

But a mere list can never convey how astonishingly *dynamic* Paul's Christology is. Mark's Gospel has often been characterized as a passion narrative with a lengthy prologue attached; and the other three Gospels certainly culminate whatever extra drama they add to Mark's account with their own dramatically described passion narratives. So in contrast, Paul's Christology strikes many readers as that much more abstract, colored as it is by such heady concepts as justification, reconciliation, atonement, complicated accounts of the Law and the flesh, which require careful exegetical labors to explain. But from another perspective, Paul's account of God's action in Christ is even more powerfully dramatic than the Gospels', for he sees, more than any other New Testament writer, how *the whole cosmos is involved in the death of Christ,* a point succinctly captured by Paula Fredriksen:

> The Jesus who is the focus of Paul's fierce commitment is the divine and preexistent Son of God, the agent of creation "through whom all things are" (1 Cor. 8:6), who came to earth, died by crucifixion, was raised and exalted, and is about to return. This pattern of descent, ascent, and approaching return is the essential content of Paul's gospel — or, as he sees

23. The statistics for "Christ" or "Christ Jesus" are: 10 times in 1 Thessalonians; 64 times in 1 Corinthians; 47 times in 2 Corinthians; 38 times in Galatians; 66 times in Romans, 37 times in Philippians; and a remarkable 8 times in the very brief Philemon.

24. 24 times in 1 Thessalonians; 66 in 1 Corinthians; 29 in 2 Corinthians; 6 in Galatians; 44 in Romans; 15 in Philippians; and 5 in Philemon.

25. I have drawn these statistics from Udo Schnelle, *Apostle Paul: His Life and Theology,* trans. M. Eugene Boring (Grand Rapids: Baker Academic, 2005), p. 438.

it, of *the* Gospel, the secret and hidden wisdom of God decreed before the *aiōnes* (ages) for the glorification of the believer (1 Cor. 2:7).[26]

But *how* exactly did Paul see this pattern of descent, ascent, and future return bringing about salvation and the defeat of the powers of this age, under the thrall of evil (Gal. 1:4)? Here Paul's Christology is central, for had Christ come *only* in the flesh, or *only* died on the cross, the evil powers and principalities of this age would still be reigning supreme and unopposed (1 Cor. 15:20). But they have been defeated for two reasons: first, by coming in the flesh *as* the Son of God — or rather and more specifically, by coming to earth in the likeness of *sinful* flesh (Rom. 8:3) — Jesus "became sin" (2 Cor. 5:21) and thereby nailed sin itself to the cross; and second, once sin had been nailed to the cross, the ruling powers and sovereignties of this age were stripped of their sway, so that Christ could "parade them in public behind him in his triumphal procession" (Col. 2:15).

Of course, Paul would never claim that the cross — the Roman Empire's most degrading and humiliating form of capital punishment — could alone effect such a dramatic, *cosmic* reversal: only by the power of the resurrection have sin and death been defeated, which will then culminate in the final act of the "script," when God will be all in all. Here in just a few, brief lines, Paul manages to capture the essential drama of the end of the world in terms of the *epistrophe* (reversal) of the resurrection:

> Just as all die in Adam, so in Christ all will be brought to life, but all of them in their proper order: Christ the first fruits, and next, at his coming, those who belong to him. After that will come the end, when he will hand over the kingdom to God the Father, having abolished every principality, every ruling force and power. For he must reign until he has made his enemies his footstool, and the last of the enemies to be done away with is death. . . . When all things are then subjected to him, then the Son himself will also be subject to him who put all things under him, that God may be all in all. (1 Cor. 15:22-28)

26. Fredriksen, *From Jesus to Christ,* p. 56. Seconded by another scholar here: "Through often independent, often brief statements, Paul provides a surprisingly full portrait of Jesus Christ in the assortment of christological comments throughout his letters. When the elements of his christological teaching are pieced together in a plausible chronological series, the predominantly independent statements generally cohere." Marion L. Soards, "The Christology of the Pauline Epistles," *Who Do You Say That I Am? Essays on Christology,* ed. Mark Allan Powell and David R. Bauer (Louisville: Westminster/John Knox, 1999), pp. 88-109; here 104.

The Christology of Mark

To move from the cosmic drama of Paul to the more human drama of Mark can seem at first glance quite a lurch; but again I think we should be wary of imposing modern schemas on these obvious contrasts. For Mark's central drama is one of *recognition*. As we saw in Chapter 2, the title "Christ" or "Messiah" refers, at least in its explicit "dictionary meaning," to a descendant of David who will act as a *political* king by reestablishing independence to the kingdom of Israel, while "Son of Man" refers to a *celestial* being who will descend from on high to inaugurate a more definitive defeat of evil.[27] Now here is the point: while many of Jesus' contemporaries, very much including his disciples, continued to see him in terms of being (possibly) the earthly Messiah, for Mark his real identity was both Son of God and Son of Man — a point that is seen during Jesus' earthly ministry only by the celestial actors, God (Mark 1:11; 9:7) and the demons (1:24; 3:11; 5:7); while during his Passion only the High Priest (14:61), and a Roman centurion (15:39) guess at his true identity.

In contrast to this diverse list, the disciples are uniformly depicted as slow of understanding (4:33; 9:32), trapped by their worldly expectation of Jesus' Messiahship (9:33-37; 10:35-40), to such an extent that whenever their own expectations are awakened after Jesus performs a miracle, especially a healing miracle or an exorcism, he must order them to keep secret his messianic identity (3:12; 7:36; 9:30). This contrast between his real identity as Son of God/Son of Man and the messianic misunderstanding of the disciples culminates in the first (pre-Passion) climax of the Gospel, when Jesus asks his disciples how others are describing him, upon which he then puts the question to them, "and who do you say I am?" to which Peter replies, "You are the *Christ*." Tellingly, in Mark's account Jesus neither accepts nor denies the title but moves immediately to speak of himself as the *Son of Man,* and one moreover who was destined to suffer and die, a part of his identity that never entered into the Old Testament version of *either* title (8:27-33).

There is, however, one passage where Jesus clearly accepts the title of "Christ," very much including its political implications: at the next great cli-

27. Granted, because both terms denote a figure of expectation born out of a time and situation of great plight for the Jews of Jesus' day, a vaguely imagined figure in the future could be posited using both terms, especially since anyone, including a pagan, specifically set apart for some purpose by God, could be designated by the term "anointed," as even King Cyrus of Persia himself was (Isa. 45:1).

max of Mark's Gospel, his trial-scene before the Sanhedrin, where acceptance of the title will mean his certain execution: "Then the High Priest put a
second question to him, saying, 'Are you the *Christ,* the Son of the Blessed
One?' *'I am,'* said Jesus, 'and you will see the Son of Man seated at the right
hand of Power coming down from the clouds of heaven'" (14:61-62). But
here the context makes clear that Jesus only asserts his claim to the title when
it will immediately lead to the fulfillment of his earlier predictions of his
death; furthermore, no sooner has he finally affirmed the title of Christ for
himself, than he goes on to describe his triumph in death by speaking of
himself once again as the Son of Man.

One often overlooked example of Mark's insistence that Jesus be understood as "Christ" only in a heavenly (and therefore not purely Davidic) sense
comes from his use of Psalm 110:1: "The Lord said to my lord." This opening
verse from Psalm 110 is in fact the most frequently cited single passage from
the Old Testament cited in the New.[28] But Mark's version is especially strong
in contrasting the earthliness of a scion of the house of David with the most
important feature of the *real* Messiah — his descent from God. Thus Mark
reports Jesus as asking:

> How can the scribes say that the Christ is David's son? For David himself,
> moved by the Holy Spirit, said:
>
>> *The Lord* [God] *said unto my lord* [the Messiah],
>> *Take your seat at my right hand*
>> *Until I have made your enemies your footstool.*
>
> David himself [the author of the Psalm] calls him [the Messiah] "lord." So
> how is he [the Messiah] David's son [merely]? (Mark 12:35-37)

The use of this Psalm neatly captures how the New Testament looks on
the event of Jesus as fulfilling — in a sense hitherto unexpected — the
meaning of the Old, which is another reason why Psalm 110 was so frequently cited: *it is Jesus' reality as the Son of God that throws retrospective light
on the meaning of who the long-awaited Messiah will be:* namely, a heavenly,
preexisting figure whom David himself addresses by the divine title *par excellence,* "Lord."

In other words, the Gospel of Mark is structured around an interplay
between hiddenness and recognition, specifically a recognition of Jesus'
heavenly identity, one that only certain (primarily cosmic) actors per-

---

28. Matthew 22:44-45; Luke 20:41-44; Acts 2:34-35; Hebrews 1:13; 1 Peter 3:22.

ceive.[29] So, like Paul's Christology, Mark's too is set in a cosmic framework of warring spirits; his too is, quite literally, a Christology "from above." In fact the whole point of his Gospel is to contrast Jesus' true *celestial* identity against the more worldly and uncomprehending understanding of Jesus "from below" that keeps the disciples from seeing who Jesus really is. If one were forced to use the schema of "high" and "low" Christology, one could almost say that the whole point of Mark's Gospel is that those with a "low" understanding of Jesus (as a purely Davidic Messiah) miss the point, whereas all those who are really in the know about Jesus' true identity see him as coming "from above."

The Christology of Matthew

If Mark saw that Jesus finally gave Psalm 110 its true meaning, Matthew extends that insight by showing how Jesus fulfilled the rest of the Old Testament. Hence the frequency in this Gospel of the phrase "This took place to fulfill what the Lord had spoken through the prophets." Thus where Mark simply relates the historical information that Jesus performed cures and exorcisms, Matthew will enhance the account by contextualizing the cure as the fulfillment of a prophecy: "That evening they brought him many who were possessed by demons. He drove out these spirits with a command and cured all who were sick. This was to fulfill what was spoken by the prophet Isaiah: *he himself bore our sicknesses and healed our infirmities*" (Matt. 8:16-17).

This fulfillment, however, is not seamless, for in Matthew Jesus — even more explicitly than in Mark — fulfills the Law precisely by superseding it. In fact, one of the most crucial aspects of Matthew's Christology is his emphasis on Jesus as the new Moses: the flight into Egypt, the Sermon on the Mount (an allusion to Mount Sinai), Jesus' sovereign authority to radicalize the Law, and so forth. More than any other Gospel, Matthew stresses Jesus' role as *Judge*. An extraordinarily large number of parables recounted in Matthew deal with the final judgment. The return of the Son of Man is described not just as the conclusion to the final act of God's drama of salvation, but

---

29. True, the Roman centurion recognizes Jesus as the Son of God (Mark 15:39), but he is only able to do so *after* Jesus' death. In other words, he serves as the actor who gives voice to what Mark saw all along as Jesus' true identity: "The beginning of the Gospel of Jesus Christ, the *Son of God*" (Mark 1:1).

even more as that time when Christ will return to separate the wicked from the righteous, the weeds from the "wheat that springeth green" (13:24-43), the good fish from the rotten (13:47-50); a time when, Jesus solemnly warns, men will have to render an account for every careless word they ever uttered (12:36-37; see also 5:22 and 7:21-23). When the Son of Man returns in glory, it will be to execute judgment, to sentence the whole human race either to eternal life or to eternal perdition (25:31-46); a task that will be shared by the Twelve, enthroned beside the Son of Man, who will co-judge the tribes of Israel "when everything is made new again" (19:28).

Such a promise must have represented a certain comfort to the Twelve, for Matthew too represents them as blind to the real significance of Jesus until after the resurrection. In fact, in some ways the disciples are portrayed in Matthew in an even worse light than in Mark, for Jesus censures their cowardly behavior during the Passion along with their lack of understanding during his earthly ministry. True, prior to the Passion, the disciples, particularly Peter, are presented as models for Jesus' church: he commissions them to preach, teach, heal, and even to raise the dead (10:1-25); and Peter is explicitly praised for his confession at Caesarea Philippi and given remarkable responsibilities on that account.[30]

But against that heightened commission of responsibility, Matthew refuses to mitigate Mark's portrait of the pre-resurrection obtuseness of the disciples and even extends their lack of understanding to the resurrection narratives, perhaps as a way of indicating that the resurrection alone will not guarantee the faithful exercise of ecclesiastical leadership: only the women are depicted as encountering the risen Christ in Jerusalem (28:9-10), just as they were the only ones who stood by him at the cross (27:55-56). Even worse, in Galilee some of the men who are being commissioned in the last scene of the Gospel to go out and preach to all nations doubt Jesus even as they worship him: "When they saw him they worshiped him, though some hesitated" (28:17). So the theme is maintained: only in the light of the resurrection do we truly know the identity of Jesus; and even there growth of understanding is always indicated. What is true of the man who cried out to Jesus in Mark, "Lord, I do believe, help thou my unbelief!" (Mark 9:24) is true for Matthew of the post-resurrection church.

30. "Blessed are you, Simon Bar-Jonah! For *flesh and blood has not revealed this to you,* but my Father who is in heaven. Amen I tell you, you are Peter, and upon this rock I shall build my church, and the powers of death shall not prevail against it. I will give you the keys of the kingdom of heaven, and whatever you bind on earth shall be bound in heaven, and whatever you loose on earth shall be loosed in heaven" (16:13-19).

The Christology of Luke

Dante famously called Luke "the Gospel of mercy," a sure sign that, well before the advent of modern historical criticism of the Bible, Christians were alert to the different emphases that each of the four Evangelists stressed in their portrait of Jesus.[31] Dante is surely on to something when he spots Luke's stress on mercy; but what most distinguishes Luke's Christology from that of the other Evangelists is the altered *setting* for his Gospel. He never denies, of course, the cosmic drama of the incarnate Son of God entering into history, for Satan plays a significant role during the temptations and during the Passion. But it is surely significant that, after the temptations are over, Luke pushes Satan off stage until the more exigent temptations in the Garden of Gethsemane (Luke 4:13; 22:3; see 10:18). The reason for this relative "sidelining" of Satan is that Luke also wishes to place the event of Jesus inside the chronology of secular history: for that reason he imitates those rolling periodic sentences so redolent of Thucydides in his prologue (1:1-4), and regularly specifies key moments in the life of Christ by their relation to secular dates: "In the days of Herod, king of Judea" (1:5); "a decree went out from Caesar Augustus . . . when Quirinius was governor of Syria" (2:1-2), "in the fifteenth year of the reign of Tiberius Caesar, Pontius Pilate then being governor of Judea, and Herod [son of the earlier mentioned Herod] being tetrarch of Galilee" (3:1).

The reason for this shift of setting is ultimately christological: for Luke's Jesus is, above all, the Messiah for the Gentiles too, a point he conveys most obviously in his theology of history, lucidly described by Paula Fredriksen in these terms:

> Jesus' time on earth is a unique sacred period in its own right. Luke presents it as such by dividing his history of salvation into three periods. The first is the time of Israel, from the promise to Abraham through the mission of John the Baptist (Luke 7:28; 16:16). The second is the time of the earthly Jesus, during which Satan is banished (4:14–22:3). The third period, the time of the church, begins at Pentecost, after Jesus' ascension (Acts 2:1ff.), and continues indefinitely. Thus time past and time present are both oriented around the central and unique event of Jesus' ministry.[32]

---

31. On that same point, many early fathers of the church called John the most "theological" of the Gospels, showing that Christians have, almost from the beginning, been aware of how each Evangelist shaped the story of Jesus for his own specific evangelizing purposes.

32. Fredriksen, *From Jesus to Christ,* p. 32.

One sign of this shift in historical setting, made in order to highlight Jesus' identity as Savior of the Gentiles, is that Luke treats Jesus as the Son of Man only in those passages that he has directly taken over from Mark (especially Luke 21:27). In passages that are unique to him, however, the stress falls elsewhere. For example, in the infancy narratives in the first two chapters of his Gospel, Luke describes Jesus by using all of the titles he will later stress in the rest of Luke-Acts: Savior, Lord, Christ, Son of David (=Messiah), and Son of God. As we have seen, "Son of Man" stresses above all the eschatological role of Jesus, whereas Luke wishes to stress the *longue durée* of history more than the imminence of an unexpected end. For similar reasons, he also, in his accounts of Jesus' teaching, makes sure that the term "Christ" is divested of its political associations of purely Davidic sonship (David, after all, was king because of his prowess as a leader in battles). This is also the significance of Luke's scene along the road to Emmaus after Jesus is risen from the dead: two of his disciples are shown as dejected precisely because they had hoped "he would have been the one to redeem Israel," at which point the risen Christ (still unknown as such to these two men traveling away from Jerusalem and from the events that crushed their hopes) teaches them (at 24:21-27) that, as Fredriksen says, "the redemption of Israel is spiritual, not political; the messiah triumphs not over armies, but over death."[33] And when the disciples as a whole group *still* don't understand the point just before his ascension into heaven by asking, "Lord, has the time come for you to restore the kingdom to Israel?" (Acts 1:6), Jesus replies by framing his redemption in the setting of the long stretch of history: "It is not for you to know times or dates that the Father has decided by his own authority; but you will receive the power of the Holy Spirit, who will come on you, and then you will be my witnesses not only in Jerusalem but throughout Judea and Samaria, and indeed to the very ends of the earth" (Acts 1:7-8). For Luke, the vast stretches of geography and of historical time are the crucial framework, one that determines which christological titles he will stress.

The Christology of John

Even the most naïve and untutored reader catches the remarkable difference between the Jesus of the first three Gospels (called "Synoptics," because they

---

33. Fredriksen, *From Jesus to Christ*, p. 35.

can so easily be set out in synoptically arranged parallel columns) and the Gospel of John. To be sure, the contrast can be exaggerated, as I believe happens with the overused schema of so-called "high" and "low" Christologies. For one thing, the basic teaching of John — that the incarnate Son fully reveals the Father — is hardly unknown to the Synoptics. Both Matthew and Luke report Jesus as saying, "I bless you, Father, Lord of heaven and earth, for hiding these things from the learned and the clever and revealing them to little children. Yes, Father, for that is what it pleased you to do. Everything has been entrusted to me by my Father, and no one knows the Son except the Father, just as no one knows the Father except the Son and those to whom the Father chooses to reveal him" (Matt. 11:25-27; Luke 10:21-22), a line that has often been called "a bolt from the Johannine heaven," so similar is it to the central theme of John's Gospel.[34]

Nor can it be confidently stated anymore that John is a decidedly *late* Gospel (even if it might well have been published in its final form after the Synoptics). Research into the Gospel of John in the last century, especially since the discovery of the Dead Sea Scrolls (whose language of light vs. darkness, flesh vs. spirit, and so forth uncannily adumbrates typical Johannine vocabulary), has brought to the fore the specifically Palestinian provenance of the Fourth Gospel. Archeological work has also shown John's descriptive accuracy of Palestinian geography and monumental sites.[35] Then, manuscript

---

34. The fact that Matthew and Luke both reproduce the line indicates that it came from their common source, Q, which dates the tradition of that theme very early. In other words, Q's Christology, in its fundamentals, is just as "high" as John's (assuming Q actually existed). Conversely, John contains many elements that would have to be considered "low" in the normal acceptation of that term, as D. Moody Smith rightly points out: "There is also a low side [to Johannine Christology]: The Jews protest, 'Is this not Jesus the son of Joseph, whose father and mother we know?' How does he now say 'I have come down from heaven?' (6:42). This same Jesus also gets tired at midday, sits down by a well in Samaria, and strikes up a conversation with a Samaritan who happens to be a woman (4:1-42), much to the astonishment of his disciples (4:27)." See D. Moody Smith, "John: A Source for Jesus Research?" in *John, Jesus and History,* vol. 1: *Critical Appraisals of Critical Views,* ed. Paul N. Anderson, Felix Just, S.J., and Tom Thatcher (Leiden: Brill, 2007), pp. 165-78; here 166.

35. "Today there is a growing tendency to take very seriously the historical, social, and geographical details peculiar to narratives found only in the Fourth Gospel. . . . John's references to the Samaritans, their theology, their practice of worshiping on Gerizim, and the location of Jacob's well all seem to be accurate. . . . The very precise information about the pool of Bethesda is perfectly accurate as to name, location, and construction. The theological themes brought up in relation to Passover and the Feast of Tabernacles reflect an accurate knowledge of the festal ceremonies and of the synagogue readings associated with the feasts. . . . From such accuracy we may say that the Fourth Gospel reflects a knowledge of

discoveries of fragments of that Gospel deep into upper Egypt, which are judged on paleographic grounds to stem from early in the second century, have pushed the date of the composition of the Gospel back into the first century. This discovery came as a blow to much of German scholarship in the nineteenth century, which had speculated that the Fourth Gospel was written in the second century specifically to counteract a flourishing Gnosticism of that era (to be defined in the next chapter).[36] Finally, more and more scholars are beginning to see that, at least as regards the Passion narratives, where John differs from the Synoptics, the weight of evidence from other sources seems to indicate the historicity of John over the Synoptics.[37]

But beyond these essentially historical points, one must ask: Is the Christology of John really all that different from the Synoptics or from Paul? Consider John's prologue, which announces the central themes of his Gospel, and then look at their obvious parallels elsewhere in the New Testament: According to that prologue, Jesus comes from God and descends into hu-

Palestine as it was before its destruction in AD 70, when some of these landmarks perished." Raymond E. Brown, *The Gospel According to John I-XII,* Anchor Bible Commentary (Garden City, NY: Doubleday, 1966), vol. 29, p. xlii.

36. This point is argued with great verve by John A. T. Robinson in his last book, post-humously published, called *The Priority of John* (London: SCM Press, 1985). Robinson marshals an amazing amount of material to show not that the Fourth Gospel necessarily had priority in the sense of date of composition or publication but that its traditions go back to the historical memory of John of Zebedee, founder of the community of the Beloved Disciple. It is unfortunate that this book did not find the echo it deserved among Johannine scholars, for in the words of one of them, it "accumulates important evidence which has not always been sufficiently recognized by other scholars." David Wenham, "The Enigma of the Fourth Gospel: Another Look," in *Understanding, Studying, Reading: New Testament Essays in Honour of John Ashton,* ed. Christopher Rowland and Crispin H. T. Fletcher-Louis (Sheffield, UK: Sheffield Academic Press, 1998), p. 105.

37. For example: "On balance, John's account [of the Passion] seems more credible" (Fredriksen, *From Jesus to Christ,* p. 119). Fredriksen relies here on Brown: "In our opinion, as shall be seen in the commentary, a defense can be made for every one of these Johannine details, and in some of them the Johannine picture is almost certainly more correct than the Synoptic picture" (Brown, Anchor Commentary, p. xliii). Brown here is speaking specifically of the three-year public ministry of Jesus, but he extends the same analysis to John's Passion narrative too. John Meier holds that John's dating of the crucifixion (Nisan 14) is to be preferred to the Synoptics' (Nisan 15). And Brown, Meier, and Fredriksen all hold that John's account of the trial of Jesus in John (no full meeting of the Sanhedrin on the eve of Passover) is to be preferred to the Synoptic accounts; see Paula Fredriksen, *Jesus of Nazareth, King of the Jews: A Jewish Life and the Emergence of Christianity* (New York: Knopf, 2000), pp. 223-24; John Meier, *A Marginal Jew:* vol. 1, *The Roots of the Problem and the Person* (New York: Doubleday, 1991), pp. 390-41, both drawing on and agreeing with Brown.

man history by becoming flesh. But that theme can also be found elsewhere in the New Testament (Phil. 2). According to John's prologue, Jesus supersedes both John the Baptist (affirmed by Luke) and Moses (one of the key themes of Matthew). In John's prologue Jesus is rejected by his own people (similarly asserted in 1 Thess. 2:14-16 and Rom. 9–11); and finally for John access to the Father is exclusively through Jesus, since only the Son has seen the Father (said also by Matt. 11:25-27; Luke 10:21-22).[38]

Moreover, John shares with the Synoptics and Paul the *cosmic context* that explains both the incomprehension of Jesus' contemporaries (believing and unbelieving alike) and the reason why his death is an atoning death:

> [John's] gospel has a double context. The first is that of the narrative's ostensible historical setting, the dramatic situation of the characters in this world. But this is dwarfed by the gospel's "true" context, the divine realm of light beyond, whence Jesus came. Those who are of this cosmos, namely Jesus' opponents, cannot see past the context of this world. Limited to it and by it, they are blind to the meaning of the events before their eyes. But *for those in the know, this cosmos becomes transparent;* one can look through it to see Jesus' true point of origin with and in the Father, and this knowledge puts everything in a radically different perspective.[39]

As I hope the reader will have noticed by now, nothing in this description differs in any substantial way from the worldview of the other New Testa-

---

38. The significance of these parallels increases if one holds, with R. Schnackenburg, that the Fourth Gospel was written without knowledge of the Synoptics: "A direct literary dependence of John on the Synoptics is improbable. The occasional verbal agreements with Mark could suggest knowledge of this Gospel, but they may perhaps be explained by oral tradition. . . . The Johannine tradition is on the whole independent, and even where it deals with matters also found in the Synoptics, it does not seem to pass any judgment on them. The fourth evangelist has his own style of narration and formulation, and does not show any tendency to correct or replace the Synoptics." Rudolf Schnackenburg, *The Gospel According to St. John,* trans. Kevin Smyth (New York: Herder & Herder, 1967), vol. 1, pp. 41-42. This is now the majority view: the Fourth Gospel "is substantially independent of the other three. . . . In this, then, the [Fourth Gospel] may well faithfully preserve an aspect of Jesus's ministry that we would not have known had we only had the other Gospels. In other respects also John may help us to form a truer picture of Jesus' ministry and his teaching." J. N. Sanders, *A Commentary on the Gospel According to St. John* (London: Adam & Charles Black, 1968), pp. 12, 15. The definitive study (which has so heavily influenced all of the studies cited in this section) is C. H. Dodd, *Historical Tradition in the Fourth Gospel* (Cambridge: Cambridge University Press, 1963).

39. Fredriksen, *From Jesus to Christ,* p. 20; emphasis added.

ment authors, as all of them describe Jesus in one way or another in terms of a cosmic drama of recognition.

Granted, the surface impression left by the portrait of Jesus in John and in the other Gospels, especially Mark, seems quite stark: in Mark Jesus always seems to be in a *hurry:* the Gospel begins *in medias res* and quickly hurtles forward, carried along by Mark's staccato style, interrupted by the constant use of the adverb "immediately."[40] In John, however, Jesus moves serenely and untroubled to and from Jerusalem and conveys his teaching in lengthy discourses, weaving the same theme through a series of subtle variations.[41]

But these surface contrasts can obscure the central structural similarities held by all New Testament authors. What John's Gospel shares with his peers is this central kerygmatic theme: the drama between those who cannot see Jesus' true identity because of their lack of faith and those who recognize that true identity because they are given to see. To be sure, John has introduced a stress in his Christology that will prove utterly determinative for later debate, especially in the next six centuries of the church: for John makes clear more than any other New Testament writer the *unprecedented relationship of intimacy,* even to the point of *ontological equality,* between Father and Son. Yes, that same theme is adumbrated, however briefly and allusively, in Philippians 2 and in Matthew 11; but nowhere else in the New Testament is that equality, even to the point of outright identification, more stressed than in John: "and the Word *was* God" (1:1); "I and the Father are one" (10:30). Even here, however, the outright identification is qualified, for "the Word was also *with* God."[42] How the subtle distinctions and unique Logos language in this most "theological" of the Gospels affected later debate will emerge in the next chapter.

---

40. In 1964 the Italian director Pier Paolo Passolini brought out his film *The Gospel According to St. Matthew,* which, in its cinematic rush (Jesus, for example, preached his sermons while hurrying toward Jerusalem, not as a standing, stationary figure), reminded me more of Mark's Gospel than Matthew's, although the presence of the Sermon on the Mount in the film dictated the title Passolini gave it.

41. In John's Gospel Jesus moves several times toward Jerusalem for Passover; meaning that the earthly ministry of Jesus took up roughly three years compared to the one year implied by the Synoptics.

42. Moreover, John is able to stop short of full equivalence because of his omission of the Greek definite article before "God" and "one," a nuance impossible to catch in English, a point stressed in Chapter 2.

The Historical Jesus and His Christology: Event History

The Christology of Jesus

We now come to the question of *event history,* meaning the events them-selves: granted that each New Testament author had his own perspective to convey, and granted that each author followed certain basic kerygmatic strategies for the evangelization of the Roman world, what do the documents they wrote reveal about Jesus himself, about his own self-understanding? That is, can we now treat the books of the New Testament not just on their own terms or under the rubric of their mutual interrelationship and structural similarities, but as genuinely historical documents telling the same story, a story that later historians can seamlessly narrate from beginning to conclusion?

In other words, we must now take up the topic of the "historical Jesus." Not, to be sure, that this section of this chapter wishes to be read as an independent, free-standing monograph on this controversial theme, but only insofar as questions of history affect the truth of Christology. Any religion that makes historical claims must, after all, be open to the investigation of historians. The question is admittedly extremely knotty and complex, and a textbook with many other issues in mind besides this one can only present these complexities in summary form. But surely the results of historical scholarship into the life of Jesus and the early church's view of Jesus must have some bearing on christological teaching and truth.[43] Here, at any rate, is how the Second Vatican Council puts the matter, in a passage that is placed just before the one we noticed at the outset of this chapter:

> Holy Mother Church has firmly and with absolute constancy held, and continues to hold, that the four Gospels just named, *whose historical character the Church unhesitatingly asserts,* faithfully hand on what Jesus Christ, while living among men, really did and taught for their eternal salvation until the day He was taken up into heaven. . . . The sacred authors wrote the four Gospels, selecting some things from the many which had been handed on by word of mouth or in writing, reducing some of them

43. As Moule rightly says: "A Gospel which cares only for the apostolic proclamation and denies that it either can or should be tested for its historical antecedents, is really only a thinly veiled gnosticism or docetism and, however much it may continue to move by a borrowed momentum, will prove ultimately to be no Gospel." C. F. D. Moule, *The Phenomenon of the New Testament* (London: SCM Press, 1967), p. 80.

to a synthesis, explicating some things in view of the situation of the churches, and preserving the form of proclamation, *but always in such fashion that they told us the honest truth about Jesus.*[44]

As we have already seen, the lines "reducing some of them to a synthesis, explicating some things in view of the situation of the churches, and preserving the form of proclamation" were carefully chosen by the Council fathers and clearly result from the scientifically irrefutable conclusion of historical critics that the Gospels were written for purposes different from, but hardly opposed to, those that animate documentary historians. For example, the line "reducing some of them to a synthesis" refers to the redactional perspective of each evangelist; and "preserving the form of proclamation" refers both to the evangelizing interest of each Gospel (that is, that they were not written to satisfy the idle curiosity of neutral historians), and to the reliance of all the Gospels on a previously handed-down oral tradition.

To reach that teaching, however, took considerable confidence by the fathers of the Council, for the history of Protestant scholarship roughly from the middle of the eighteenth century to the middle of the twentieth, so dominated as it was by the historical-critical method, might well have given the assembled bishops pause. For once it was admitted that the evangelists were not providing tape-recorded transcriptions of the words of Jesus, but meant to arrange the events of his life (such as the cleansing of the Temple) not (necessarily) in chronological order but to suit their own redactional purposes, the way was open for hypercritical historians to dismiss the entirety of the Gospels as historically unreliable, since they were clearly written for apologetic, and not historical, purposes.[45]

This realization led to two extreme reactions: on the one hand, the German Lutherans Albert Schweitzer (1875-1965) and Rudolf Bultmann (1884-1976) insisted that we can know nothing *historically* reliable (in the hypercritical sense) about Jesus except that he lived and was executed by the

44. *Dei verbum*, The Dogmatic Constitution on Divine Revelation, § 19, ed. Walter M. Abbott, S.J., translation editor, V. Rev. Msgr. Joseph Gallagher (New York: Guild Press, 1966), p. 124; italics added.

45. The operative word here in the term "the historical-critical method" is *critical*, for what critical historians criticize are the documents themselves, treating them like hostile witnesses in a courtroom, whose accounts must be independently verified through archeological and numismatic relics, other (often conflicting) accounts, etc. For a full account of this fascinating story, see Stephen Neill and Tom Wright, *The Interpretation of the New Testament: 1861-1986* (Oxford: Oxford University Press, 1988).

Romans on a cross. (The fact that Bultmann felt he could gain theological mileage out of that dismissal of the historicity of the Gospels because of his Lutheran theology of the Word is irrelevant here.) The other extreme countered the historical-critical method with a theology of biblical inspiration that now goes under the name of "fundamentalism," a term that arose from a manifesto published by some professors at Princeton Theological Seminary defending the "five fundamentals" of Christianity, one of which was the factual inerrancy of Scripture.[46]

From the passage I have just quoted, the reader can clearly see that Vatican II rejects both extremes, Bultmannianism and "fundamentalism." But that still leaves open the question: If the four Gospels "faithfully hand on what Jesus Christ, while living among men, really did and taught" and yet if they *also* did that handing on for their own wider religious purposes, then which parts of the story that the New Testament recounts are elements of what Jesus Christ "really did and taught" and which are more explicitly theological, rather than historical, in character? (For example, when did Jesus cleanse the Temple, at the outset of his earthly ministry, as in John, or the week before he died, as in the Synoptics?)

For Bultmann, as we saw, the issue was moot, because for him the New Testament was entirely theological. He came to that radical position not to be perverse but because an earlier scholar, Albert Schweitzer (the famous physician who won a Nobel Peace Prize for his humanitarian work as a doctor in Africa), had shown that previous views on the historical Jesus were naïve: all portraits of the so-called "historical" Jesus were, Schweitzer showed, really idealized portraits of a nineteenth-century liberal Protestant, with all of Jesus' radical preaching about the end of the world carefully airbrushed from these portraits. The English translation of his book setting out his scathing analysis of this naïveté (a *liberal* naïveté, by the way) was called *The Quest of the Historical Jesus,* and it seemed to foreclose any further attempts to construct a picture of the so-called "historical Jesus."[47] This lesson Bultmann took to heart, and built the entire edifice of his exegetical labors on its foundation.

The fascinating part of this story, however, is that within a few years of

46. Except when referring to those churches that explicitly subscribe to these five fundamentals, the term should be retired for reasons of journalistic overuse, for now it scarcely means more than religious beliefs that are firmly held by believers of any religion over the objections of those who subscribe to norms of secular rationality.

47. Albert Schweitzer, *The Quest of the Historical Jesus: A Critical Study of Its Progress from Reimarus to Wrede,* trans. W. Montgomery (New York: Macmillan, 1906).

Bultmann's greatest influence, even his own former graduate students came to reject his position: there were just too many incidents recounted in the Synoptics (and John!), they showed, that seemed to go against the grain of the Evangelists' own evangelizing purposes, too many odd fragments and disconcerting statements lurking in the Gospels that seemed to have no other explanation than that the Gospel writers preserved certain traditions *because the memory of them in the early Christian communities, however disconcerting it must have been for them, was so strong.*[48] This realization led to what was called the "Second Quest" for the historical Jesus, whose up-and-down vicissitudes·eventually led to a "Third Quest."

Again it must be stressed that this book is not the place to rehearse this oft-told tale.[49] Still, a few highlights of the story are crucial for our purposes, and so some of its key episodes will have to be noted. Christianity is simply too historical in its origins for the church to want to foreclose all knowledge of the historical Jesus. To operate on Bultmannian grounds would radically affect the kind of Christology that could be reliably taught to believers today.

Speaking very generally, the Second Quest was conducted on what might be called Cartesian principles: doubt everything you can about the historical Jesus, and then keep only what survives this bath of Cartesian acid. This too was Bultmann's method, with his disciples only disagreeing with their master on what survived the doubt. For example, Norman Perrin would only accept those sayings of Jesus that were multiply attested (in more than one Gospel, and preferably in Paul too, like the institution of the Eucharist), went against the grain of the needs of the early church (like the saying about paying the Temple tax), and could not be attributed to Jesus' Jewish background, as presumably those teachings could have been drawn from the Palestinian church (such as Jesus' prediction of the imminent end of the world).[50]

---

48. For reasons of space, one example only will have to suffice: Jesus' table-fellowship with sinners and his disregard for the distinction between righteous and unrighteous has no parallel in the early church and would seem to undercut Paul's concern that no one approach the Eucharistic table unworthily (1 Cor. 11:27-30).

49. It is ably told in Ben Witherington III, in *The Jesus Quest: The Third Search for the Jew of Nazareth*, 2nd ed. (Downers Grove, IL: InterVarsity Press, 1997).

50. Norman Perrin, *Rediscovering the Teaching of Jesus* (New York: Harper & Row, 1975); as in this telling sentence of Cartesian doubt: "Certainly [!], every single parable in the tradition has to be approached with the basic assumption that, as it now stands, it represents the teaching of the early Church: that the voice is the voice of the risen Lord to the evangelist, and of the evangelist to the Church, not that of the historical Jesus to a group gathered by the sea of Galilee" (pp. 21-22). Perrin seems unaware of the irony in his use of the adverb "certainly" in the context of his doubt-driven methodology.

Needless to say, the results of such a method did not leave that much material to work with. More to the point, however, it went against a trend that was becoming more and more influential as the Third Quest was beginning to dawn: the stress on Jesus' thoroughgoing Jewishness. This trend, along with a number of other technical features of historical scholarship that cannot be discussed here (such as attempts to provide "back-translations" of the Greek of the New Testament into the Aramaic of Jesus), led to a more robust appraisal of the historicity of the Gospels, the so-called Third Quest.

Even to begin to outline the conclusions drawn from this Third Quest would easily explode the confines of this book, let alone this chapter. But what is most significant for our purposes is that for some scholars of the Second Quest (such as Bultmann's student Günther Bornkamm) and for most of those of the Third Quest, *Jesus had his own Christology.* One of the more obvious contrasts between the Jesus of Mark and the Jesus of John is that in Mark Jesus continues to deflect titles from himself (except, of course, Son of Man), whereas in John Jesus' teaching is remarkably, even startlingly, self-referential (the famous "I am" statements).

In an influential book that heralded the onset of the Second Quest, Bornkamm showed that in his *behavior* Jesus had an implied Christology, for he speaks and acts with an authority that is clearly *sui generis.*[51] Nor can the portrait of Jesus' authoritative behavior be attributed, as Schweitzer concluded, to the "enthusiasm" of the early disciples in the wake of their encounters with the risen Jesus. On the contrary, as Larry Hurtado points out, "a key factor that must be taken into account in understanding the rise of early Christian devotion to Jesus is the pre-Easter ministry of Jesus and its effects upon his followers."[52] Common sense dictates this, as another scholar notes:

51. Günther Bornkamm, *Jesus of Nazareth* (New York: Harper & Row, 1960), especially here: "Jesus belongs to this world. Yet in the midst of it he is of unmistakable otherness. This is the secret of his influence and of his rejection. . . . There is nothing in contemporary Judaism which corresponds to the immediacy with which he teaches. This is true to such a degree that he even dares to confront the literal text of the law with the immediately present will of God. . . . This directness . . . is part of the picture of the historical Jesus. He bears the stamp of this directness right from the very beginning. The immediate present is the hallmark of all the words of Jesus, of his appearance and his actions, in a world which, as we said, had lost the present, because it lived between the past and the future, . . . conscious of its own rights or under sentence for its own lawlessness" (pp. 56-58).

52. Larry W. Hurtado, *One God, One Lord: Early Christian Devotion and Ancient Jewish Monotheism* (Philadelphia: Fortress Press, 1988), p. 116.

Jesus is at the center of all early (and later) Christology. This presupposes some degree of continuity between what he said and did and people's reactions. It also presupposes some continuity between the situation of his followers before Jesus' cross and resurrection and their situation after those events.[53]

Of course, as Ben Witherington, one of the leading figures in the Third Quest, points out: "It is one thing, however, to say Christian faith is based on the facts of Jesus' life and quite another to maintain that faith is based on our ability to establish, much less prove, the reality of those facts by the historical-critical method."[54] Such a warning is welcome in a book such as this, not least because it absolves its author from having to digress at monograph-length to establish the historicity of individual scenes and pericopes. Sufficient for our purposes is the commonsense observation of C. F. D. Moule that we must allow for what he rightly calls the "sheer originality of Jesus," including not only "the originality of what Jesus may have said, but also of what he was."[55]

A perfect example of this originality is Jesus' view of himself as shown forth in his behavior from Palm Sunday until his death on Good Friday. As one of the leaders of the Third Quest, N. T. Wright (whose work on the resurrection we will treat immediately below) says in an extremely important passage:

> *Jesus was conscious of a deeper vocation even than that of Messiah.* Israel's greatest hope was that YHWH, her God, would return to her *in person,* coming to Zion as judge and redeemer. In Jesus' last great journey to Jerusalem, in his action in the Temple and the Upper Room, he dramatically symbolized that return. It looks as though he intended to enact and embody that which, in Israel's scriptures, YHWH had said he would do in person. There could be no greater claim; yet the claim, though stupendous, only made sense within, could only be made from within, the context of the first-century Jewish world that bounded all Jesus' thoughts and

53. M. de Jonge, *Christology in Context: The Earliest Christian Response to Jesus* (Philadelphia: Westminster Press, 1988), p. 21.

54. Ben Witherington III, *The Christology of Jesus* (Minneapolis: Fortress Press, 1990), p. 2. In the opening sentence of the book, Witherington says: "Strange as it may seem, the question whether Jesus himself had a Christology has not been explored in a systematic way" (p. 1), which certainly says a lot about the institutional biases and inertia of contemporary New Testament scholarship.

55. C. F. D. Moule, *Origins of Christology,* p. 8.

actions. He went to his death believing that the hopes and fears of Israel and the world would thereby be drawn together once and for all. This would be the great event, the culmination of Israel's history, the redemption, the new exodus. This is how the kingdom would come.[56]

The Historicity of the Resurrection

But the sheer originality of Jesus in his earthly ministry pales into insignificance before the peerless originality of the resurrection, which is *so* original that some will claim that it breaks down the very category of history, for both skeptic and believer. As for the skeptic, at first glance the accounts of the resurrection seem to be tailor-made for David Hume's critique of miracles. According to this famous eighteenth-century Enlightenment philosopher, the more unlikely the miracle, the more convincing and indubitable must be the witnesses. That is, it is much more economical for the naturalist historian to assume credulity or mendacity on the part of the witnesses (who can no longer be interrogated) than to credit their reports of a miracle.

And sure enough, discrepancies in the resurrection narratives abound, which seem to call into question the veracity of the witnesses to Christianity's most important miracle: in Mark the women who approach the tomb on Easter Sunday to anoint the body of Jesus meet a "young man" already *inside* the tomb (Mark 16:5); in Luke "*two* men in brilliant clothes" suddenly appear at their side *after* the women had entered the tomb (Luke 24:4); and in Matthew the women witness *one* "angel of the Lord" rolling away the stone blocking the entrance to the tomb (Matt. 28:1-4). In Matthew the risen Jesus directs the women to tell the other disciples to go to *Galilee* where he commissions them to fan out to all the nations baptizing in the name of the Father, the Son, and the Holy Spirit (Matt. 28:16-20). In Luke, however, Jesus appears to the disciples in *Jerusalem* (Luke 24:36-43) and orders them to *stay* there (v. 49) from which he ascends into heaven (Acts 1:9-12).

Besides these obvious discrepancies, other historians have called into question the historicity of the resurrection on grounds that it violates the norms for the establishment of historical truth by analogy with other histor-

---

56. N. T. Wright, *What Saint Paul Really Said: Was Paul the Real Founder of Christianity?* (Grand Rapids: Eerdmans, 1997), p. 180; emphases added. Jesus' call of the Twelve fits into this same pattern; see Martin Hengel, *The Charismatic Leader and His Followers,* trans. James C. G. Greig (Edinburgh: T. & T. Clark, 1981).

ical events. Thus, one can plausibly assert the assassination of Julius Caesar in 44 B.C., not only because that event is so well attested in extant documents and because its consequences are so obvious in subsequent Roman history, but also because it can be "slotted into" other episodes of political assassinations. But in the case of the resurrection, it is claimed, analogy fails, for the event is without precedent. Therefore, the only option left is to interpret the event in naturalistic categories, which in essence means attributing the *reports* of the resurrection to the effects of mass psychology, where analogies abound.

Unfortunately for such skeptics, the search for these analogies in naturalistic categories implies repetitions and replications elsewhere (political assassinations, after all, occur with dismaying frequency in world history). But no other religion makes the claims that the New Testament makes, so the search for analogies comes up short. Moreover, such a method ends up forcing the New Testament witness onto a Procrustean bed rather than letting its witness speak for itself. Not only that, it should also be recalled that Hume's standard has itself been called into question on its own terms, quite independently of its serviceability for anti-Christian skeptics.[57]

As for the believer, some Christian theologians see the lack of analogy as the whole point of the resurrection and insist that the resurrection *should not* be subjected to the norms of historical verification. After all, they say, the resurrection describes God's ultimate intervention in history, which is by

---

57. I am thinking here above all of John Earman, *Hume's Abject Failure: The Argument Against Miracles* (Oxford: Oxford University Press, 2000), which argues on the basis of Bayesian probability theory that Hume promulgated standards that depend more on confident, sarcastic rhetoric than sound scientific reasoning: "In 'On Miracles,' Hume pretends to stand on philosophical high ground, hurling down thunderbolts against miracle stories. The thunderbolts are supposed to issue from general principles about inductive inference and the credibility of eyewitness testimony. But when these principles are made explicit and examined under the lens of Bayesianism, they are found to be either vapid, specious, or at variance with actual scientific practice. When Hume leaves the philosophical high ground to evaluate particular miracle stories, his discussion is superficial and certainly does not do justice to the extensive and vigorous debate about miracles that had been raging for several decades in Britain. He was able to create the illusion of a powerful argument by maintaining ambiguities in his claims against miracles, by the use of forceful prose and confident pronouncements, and by liberal doses of sarcasm and irony. Early in Part 2, Hume warns us that 'Eloquence, when at its highest pitch, leaves little room for reason and reflection; but addressing itself entirely to the fancy or the affections, captivates the willing hearers, and subdues their understanding.' I find it ironic that so many readers of Hume's essay have been subdued by its eloquence. And I find it astonishing how well posterity has treated 'On Miracles,' given how completely the confection collapses under a little probing" (pp. 70-71).

definition inaccessible to the historian's methodology. Moreover, the New Testament itself insists that the response to its Good News of Christ's victory over death cannot be mere neutral assent (as one, for example, assents to the statement that Julius Caesar was assassinated in 44 B.C.) but must result in a commitment of faith. Since acceptance of the kerygma means accepting God's overthrow of history embedded in its claim, historians by definition have no access to methods that would allow them to adjudicate the claim.[58]

While true enough, theologians can take this insistence too far, as if the New Testament were making no historical claims whatsoever and the reality of Christ risen could only be located in the proclamation itself. So what exactly about the reality of the resurrection is strictly historical and what is accessible only to faith? The renowned New Testament scholar N. T. Wright illuminates the problem with a folktale about a king who commanded his archers to shoot at the sun. Try as they might, their arrows always fell short, angering the king, until finally the youngest archer saw the reflection of the sun in the still waters of the garden pool in the palace courtyard: "With a single shot the lad pierced it at its heart. The sun splintered into a thousand glittering fragments."[59]

Of course, this tale only explains the *dilemma,* not the solution: on the one hand, no arrow (the world-bound methods of historical scholarship) can reach the sun (God's action in Christ); but when the arrow hits only the water's reflection of the sun (the early church's belief in the resurrection), it only fragments the holistic vision of Christ presented in the New Testament, all the while missing its real target.

So is there, then, another alternative? It is the opinion of this writer that Wright is correct in his historical analysis: Because an assent to the proclamation of the Good News that Jesus was raised by God from the dead is not just self-involving but also self-*committing,* therefore all that historical scholarship can establish (and even that on solely probabilistic grounds) is that the negators of the bodily resurrection are wrong.[60]

58. Hans Frei, for example, argues that we cannot investigate the historicity of the resurrection because it is the ground of Christian epistemology; see Hans Frei, *Theology and Narrative: Selected Essays* (New York: Oxford University Press, 1993).

59. N. T. Wright, *The Resurrection of the Son of God* (Minneapolis: Fortress Press, 2003), p. 11.

60. "I have, I think, demolished [in my book *The Resurrection of the Son of God*] the central thesis . . . that the early Christian experience of the risen Jesus was an experience of some kind of luminosity which could be interpreted as what we would call an essentially private religious experience rather than evidence for an occurrence in the public world and

We can start with one certainty here: there is no way that a belief in the resurrection of Jesus could be a mythical retrojection based on the presuppositions of the Greek-speaking pagan world of the Roman Empire, for pagan beliefs about the afterlife had no place for a resurrection. This we know because pagan authors, in the rare moments they even consider the possibility, rejected it out of hand. For example, Homer has Achilles say to the grief-stricken Priam (king of Troy and father of the Trojan hero Hector, whom Achilles has just slain): "Lamenting for your son will do no good at all. You will be dead yourself before you bring him back to life."[61] Aeschylus is even more emphatic: "Once a man has died, and the dust has soaked up his blood, there is no resurrection."[62] Nor will it do to point to Socrates' and Plato's belief in an afterlife, for their belief presupposed that the body is a prison from which death brings a welcome release, so that a resurrected body after death would be a repugnant throwback into this imprisoning vale of tears, a repugnance that Paul himself encountered in Athens on the Areopagus: "At this mention of rising from the dead, some of them burst out laughing" (Acts 17:32).

But since resurrection was indeed a duly established belief in the Judaism of Jesus' day (with the exception of the Temple party, the Sadducees, who denied the doctrine), can one claim stories of the resurrection arose

---

which developed rather slowly into a belief in bodily resurrection, on the one hand, and into gnostic theology, on the other. I've shown that we can't account for early Christian faith by suggesting that stories about appearances and stories about an empty tomb have nothing whatever to do with one another. I have shown that the idea of resurrection faith being generated by some kind of cognitive dissonance simply doesn't work. And I believe I've shown against [John Dominic Crossan] and others that the early Christian belief in the resurrection of Jesus could not have been generated from the combination of their previous knowledge of Jesus and their study of particular biblical texts, however much both of those things contributed to their interpretation of the event *once it happened.* Now the point to all this negative exercise, I stress, is not first and foremost to prove the resurrection by modernist or supposedly naturalistic historiography. The point is rather to force the question back where it ought to be rather than allowing yet another generation of students to be taught that the Easter stories and the Gospels are simply mythical back projections of early Christian consciousness rather than accounts of something exceedingly strange and unprecedented in the real world." N. T. Wright, "The Resurrection: Historical Event or Theological Explanation? A Dialogue," in *The Resurrection of Jesus: John Dominic Crossan and N. T. Wright in Dialogue,* ed. Robert B. Stewart (Minneapolis: Fortress Press, 2006), pp. 17-18; emphasis added.

61. Homer, *Iliad,* Book 24, lines 549-51, Rieu translation. The line translated as "before you bring him back to life" used the Greek word for "resurrection," which, translated literally, reads: "You will not resurrect him [*oude min anasteseis*]."

62. Aeschylus, *Eumenides,* line 647.

solely from the Jewish background of the Palestinian church? No, because here again the Christians quite transformed the prior Jewish background belief based on their experience of the fact of Jesus' own resurrection. First they moved a doctrine of the resurrection from the circumference of belief to the center. Further, they treated it no longer as a single event at the end of history but split it chronologically into two moments, the first of which has already happened to Jesus, with the general resurrection to follow for those baptized into his death. And finally, they insisted that now resurrection no longer refers to the national restoration of Israel but to the present sacramental reality: a new life bestowed in baptism, nourished by the Eucharist, and manifesting itself in a holy life.

Even when all that is granted, however, one must still insist that the most crucial feature of the resurrection remains inaccessible but to faith. For one thing, the body into which Jesus was raised is no longer available for "investigation" inside the confines of historical time, for now the very meaning of "body" is quite transformed, a point made by Paul here:

> But someone may ask: "How are the dead raised? With what kind of body will they come?" How foolish! What you sow does not come to life unless it dies. And what you sow is not the body which is to be, but a bare kernel. . . . So it is with the resurrection of the dead. What is sown is perishable, what is raised is imperishable. It is sown in dishonor, it is raised in glory. It is sown in weakness, it is raised in power. It is sown a physical body, it is raised a spiritual body. If there is a physical body, there is also a spiritual body. . . . But it is not the spiritual which is first but the physical, and then the spiritual. The first man was from the earth, a man of dust; the second man is from heaven. As was the man of dust, so are those who are of the dust; and as is the man of heaven, so are those who are of heaven. . . . I tell you this, brethren, flesh and blood cannot inherit the kingdom of God, nor does the perishable inherit the imperishable. (1 Cor. 15:35-37a; 42-44; 46-47; 50)[63]

---

63. On this passage see Fredriksen, *From Jesus to Christ*, p. 59: "But the dead will not be raised with physical bodies, nor could the living faithful join Christ in the air if they still had theirs. No: the raised body will not be fleshly, but spiritual, as Christ's was at the resurrection. Thus the body of the living believer will also be transformed, 'in the twinkling of an eye, at the last trumpet. For the trumpet shall sound, the dead will be raised imperishable, and we shall all be changed' (1 Cor. 15:52). This transformation is necessary, because 'flesh and blood cannot inherit the kingdom' (15:50)." In other words, a belief in the resurrection also entails an overthrow of a person's usual anthropology of the body. As J. A. T. Robinson

In other words, the consistent meaning of the impact of the resurrection on the early church is the *reconstitution of all prior beliefs, presuppositions, and Old Testament expectations into a new pattern and a new worldview.* Elements of the past were not so much jettisoned, except when clearly wrong, but were, so to speak, rearranged into a new configuration, like iron filings atop a sheet of paper when a magnet is placed under them. This reconfiguring power of the resurrection to reconstitute prior expectations into a new pattern also explains why so many titles and historical antecedents, which refer to so many disparate roles (as outlined in the previous chapter), could all be applied to Jesus. As long as history was proceeding apace, moving forward into the future, there would be no reason to associate Isaac with David, or Jeremiah with Moses (especially with Moses, whose revelation received on Mount Sinai was regarded as definitive and unsupersedable), because their roles were so obviously various and irreplaceable. Similarly, with the Son of Man and Suffering Servant, or king and prophet. But in the retrospective light of the cross and resurrection, it all finally made sense. True, each author of the New Testament had his own editorial preferences, his own way of stressing the uniqueness of Christ, his own range of colors from the Old Testament palette to prefer.[64] But nothing true in the fore-types of the past was left out:

---

points out, only with a right understanding of the body will we come to understand what resurrection means for the New Testament, especially for Paul: "One could say without exaggeration that the concept of the body forms the keystone of Paul's theology. In its closely interconnected meanings, the word *soma* [body] knits together all his great themes. It is from the body of sin and death that we are delivered; it is through the body of Christ on the Cross that we are saved; it is into His body the Church that we are incorporated; it is by His body in the Eucharist that this Community is sustained; it is in our body that its new life has to be manifested; it is to a resurrection of this body to the likeness of His glorious body that we are destined. Here, with the exception of the doctrine of God, are represented all the main tenets of the Christian Faith — the doctrines of Man, Sin, the Incarnation and Atonement, the Church, the Sacraments, Sanctification, and Eschatology. To trace the subtle links and interaction between the different senses of this word *soma* is to grasp the thread that leads through the maze of Pauline thought." J. A. T. Robinson, *The Body: A Study in Pauline Theology* (Philadelphia: Westminster Press, 1952), p. 9.

64. For example, we have already noted Matthew's stress on Jesus as the new Moses, but that does not stop him from seeing Jesus as the new Jeremiah as well: "As Jesus walked in the typological footsteps of Moses, so does he also walk in the footsteps and teaching of Jeremiah. Similarly, as he transcends Moses' role in the giving of the Law, so it is clear from the final words in the Gospel of Matthew that Jesus both fulfills Jeremiah's role and far transcends him by taking the place of the divine covenant maker." Mark F. Whitters, "Jesus in the Footsteps of Jeremiah," *Catholic Biblical Quarterly* 68 (April 2006): 229-47; here 247. In other words, the church's Old Testament Christology is entirely a resurrection Christology.

For he is the image of the unseen God, the first-born of all creation, for in him were created all things, in heaven and on earth. He exists before all things, and in him all things hold together, and he is the Head of the Body, his Church. He is the Beginning, the first-born from the dead, so that he should be supreme in every way, because God wanted all fullness to be found in him and through him to reconcile all things to him, everything in heaven and everything on earth, by making peace through his death on the cross. (Col. 1:15-20)

For that reason, the *essence* of the doctrine of Christ's resurrection must remain inaccessible to the critical methods of historians, for resurrection means, first of all, a specifically divine action that raised Jesus from the dead; secondly, the proclamation of the resurrection entails the transformation of the meaning of body to include a spiritualized, sacramentalized reality that anticipates (because it shares in) the age to come.

Consider this counterfactual argument: suppose everything related in the New Testament could be independently verified using neutral, secular norms of the historical-critical method. So what? As Herbert Butterfield rightly points out, even then unbelief can make a stand (and belief would have been robbed of its freedom):

If we remember as a solemn fact that those who saw Christ and heard Him were still divided in opinion about Him, we might doubt whether anything in the written Gospels or anything that historical science may discover will overcome such obstructions as exist or obliterate those factors which made possible so great a difference of opinion amongst those who saw the historical Jesus in the flesh. . . . If instead of the present narratives we had an undoubted autobiography of Christ; if He instead of St. Paul had left us great Epistles of unchallenged authenticity; if we had state documents concerning the public events of His life, I am not clear that the differences of judgement to-day would be a whit less sharp than they are, or the distribution of opinion very different. For the truth is that the essential question is not one of scholarship at all.[65]

In other words, the resurrection both belongs and does not belong to history. Fascinatingly, Matthew himself admits that the skeptic can always resort to the hypothesis that Jesus' body was stolen to account for the empty tomb (Matt. 28:11-15). Moreover, Paul openly avows that the risen Jesus appeared

---

65. Herbert Butterfield, *Christianity and History* (New York: Scribner's, 1950), pp. 125-26.

only to his followers, and even then to not very many of them (1 Cor. 15:5-7). In other words, *no nonbeliever was ever vouchsafed a vision of the risen Jesus, and this fact is theologically significant.* Here is how Jean Guitton puts it:

> If an *historical* event is one that is verifiable universally, the apparitions do not belong to history. Though their object was one who had been known before his death by a vast number of contemporaries, the risen Christ never presented himself publicly to all, as he had done during his trial and Passion. History, in the strict sense, knows only events that are verifiable by any normal man and call for no privileged means of knowledge. . . . It would seem to me that if Tiberius or Tacitus, if Philo or Pilate or Josephus had happened to be present in that room where Jesus appeared, none of these would have seen anything at all.[66]

Perhaps that last sentence poses a false alternative; I think a better way of phrasing it might be to say that Jesus specifically chose to appear in settings where only his followers were assembled (although, in Guitton's favor, Luke's account of Paul's conversion on the road to Damascus gives some credence to the notion that only the recipient of the vision of the risen Lord was allowed to perceive him directly, while onlookers could only guess what was really going on, despite the clearly extraordinary event taking place right before them).

This essential inaccessibility of the risen Jesus to those not vouchsafed a vision of him, however, does not mean that historians' *denials* of the resurrection can withstand the scrutiny of the historical-critical method, when properly carried out with due skepticism toward the naturalistic assumptions of Humean historians, a point effectively made by Avery Dulles:

> [T]he New Testament doctrine about Christ is utterly novel. Nothing in the Jewish tradition — the tradition in which Peter and Andrew, James and John, Stephen and Paul and Barnabas were reared — would have predisposed them to accept what they now proclaim. Before they became Christians they would have shrunk in horror at the very thought of paying divine honors to a man. How can one explain, if not through a revelation, that they now so confidently and unanimously look upon this Galilean carpenter as Lord of the universe?[67]

66. Jean Guitton, *The Problem of Jesus* (New York: Kenedy, 1955), p. 214.

67. Avery Dulles, S.J., *Apologetics and the Biblical Christ* (Westminster, MD: Newman Press, 1966), p. 38.

In other words, a properly sober historian, who sticks to the texts as they present themselves, will be able, at a minimum, to negate the negators and affirm these key facts about the historical dimension of the resurrection.[68] Or as Wright puts it: "The two things which must be regarded as historically secure when we talk about the first Easter are the emptiness of the tomb and the meetings with the risen Jesus."[69]

The Historicity of the Virgin Birth

Nothing has more obscured the question of the historicity of the virginal conception of Jesus than the assumption that early Christians took isolated passages from the Old Testament and then invented stories out of them whole-cloth.[70] We have already shown above how that same assumption when applied to the resurrection collapses under the glare of a more careful analysis of New Testament data; and when a similar light is thrown on the

---

68. "Quite what happened on that third day after the crucifixion is of course a complex problem, in part no doubt beyond the remit of 'secular' historians. Nevertheless, it is a matter of historical record that *something* happened — and that this changed the course of world history like no other event before or since. . . . The New Testament writers affirm of the resurrection of Jesus both (1) that *it is an event in historical time and space,* and (2) that *it cannot be straightforwardly understood as an event in historical space and time.*" Markus Bockmuehl, "Resurrection," in *The Cambridge Companion to Jesus,* pp. 102-18; here, 103, 109.

69. Wright, *Resurrection of the Son of God,* p. 686. Wright justifies this assertion with an analysis of the data that leads him to these results: "To sum up where we have got so far: 1. The world of second-Temple Judaism supplied the concept of resurrection, but the striking and consistent Christian mutations within Jewish resurrection belief rule out any possibility that the belief could have [been] generated spontaneously from within its Jewish context. . . . 2. Neither the empty tomb by itself, however, nor the appearances by themselves, could have generated the early Christian belief. The empty tomb alone would be a puzzle and a tragedy. Sightings of an apparently alive Jesus, by themselves, would have been classified as visions or hallucinations, which were well enough known in the ancient world. 3. However, an empty tomb and appearances of a living Jesus, taken together, would have presented a powerful reason for the emergence of the belief. 4. The meaning of resurrection within second-Temple Judaism makes it impossible to conceive of this reshaped resurrection belief emerging without it being known that a body had disappeared, and that the person had been discovered to be thoroughly alive again. 5. The other explanations sometimes offered for the emergence of the belief do not possess the same explanatory power" (p. 686).

70. The more technically correct term is "virginal conception," since Matthew and Luke both speak of Mary's conception of Jesus without aid of a human father; but, as we shall see in the next chapter, the more usual term "Virgin Birth" carries a special theological weight of its own.

question of Jesus' parentage, the historicity of his conception and birth "by the Holy Spirit of the Virgin Mary" (to borrow from the Nicene Creed) comes into a new and unexpected focus.

According to liberal Protestant scholarship, the story of Jesus' virginal conception arose in the Christian community because of a mistranslation of Isaiah 7:14, which in Hebrew translates as "a *young woman* shall conceive and bear a son" (NRSV) but was translated by the Jews of Alexandria several centuries before the birth of Christ into the Greek as "a *virgin* shall conceive." Since this Greek translation (known as the Septuagint and abbreviated as LXX) was the one commonly used by Gentile Christians in their worship, the thesis goes that a notion of the Virgin Birth was unknown to Palestinian Christians and only arose later on in a Greek-speaking environment under the influence of the LXX.

The fact that Luke also asserts the Virgin Birth without using this verse is an obvious problem for this thesis; but let us stay for a moment with Matthew's use of Isaiah 7:14. What is ignored here is the fact that the Hebrew for "young woman," *'almah*, while not a technical term for "virgin" (that would be *bethulah*) but instead a term for a young woman of marriageable age, certainly implies virginity. For in Semitic cultures even up to today, a demonstrated status of *not* being a virgin would render the young woman *un*marriageable, which explains why the Septuagint so readily translates *'almah* with the Greek term for "virgin," *parthenos*. Furthermore, there is no notion in either the Hebrew or the Greek text of Isaiah 7:14 that the young woman would *remain* a virgin from the time of her marriage vows. (Pre-Christian interpretation of the text saw its fulfillment in the birth of King Hezekiah, son and successor of Ahaz.) And that is how other texts, when speaking of the imminent marriage of a young woman, mean that word to be taken. In other words, no one had ever taken that text, or any other in the Old Testament, to be predicting the birth of a virginally conceived Messiah, which completely undercuts the notion that Christians took a prevalent interpretation of Isaiah 7:14 and invented a story to go along with it. As Ben Witherington rightly says:

> What one can say on the basis of the linguistic evidence is that it is improbable that Matthew deduced the notion of a virginal conception on the basis of his meditation on the Isaianic prophecy either in the Hebrew or in the Greek. To say "a virgin shall conceive and give birth" need imply no more to an early Jew than that a woman who had not previously had intercourse did so and thereby got pregnant. The notion of the virginal

conception seems already to have existed prior to Matthew's connection of the idea with this Isaianic text, as its independent attestation in Luke without such a scriptural connection confirms.[71]

Nor can it be maintained that Mary's virginal conception of Jesus finds parallels in Greek mythology, where gods are frequently depicted as coming down in the guise of a man and mating with human women. "But this is not at all what Matthew or Luke suggests happened in the case of Mary, which is about miraculous conception without any form of intercourse and without the aid of any male figure, divine or otherwise."[72] Nor could the story have been invented to counter charges of Jesus' illegitimacy (John 8:41; Mark 6:3), for if they were in the inventing mood, it would have been simpler to assert that Joseph was Jesus' biological father, and that Jesus was born after Joseph's marriage to Mary (who could prove otherwise?). Furthermore, the extreme awkwardness of including the story of Jesus' virginal conception inside the framework of genealogies in both Matthew and Luke that terminate with Joseph shows again that the evangelists are trying to incorporate a tradition whose historical reality they cannot deny but needed to explain:

> When all is said and done, it is easier to explain the Gospel evidence on the assumption that the virginal conception was a historical event that the Gospel writers tried to explain, albeit somewhat awkwardly, than to assume that this is a theological idea dreamed up by some early pious Christian. . . . The sort of apologetics and adjustments in genealogies we find in Matthew and Luke suggest writers struggling to come to grips with an idea whose historical reality they could not doubt, but had to explain.[73]

Under the assaults of skeptics, some theologians try to argue that the Virgin Birth has no inherent connection to the Incarnation, meaning that

---

71. Witherington, *New Testament History,* p. 68.

72. Witherington, p. 68. Seconded by another Protestant New Testament exegete here: "Appeal is made to the existence of a great many alleged parallels: stories of the births of Greek mythological heroes such as Heracles and Perseus. . . . But none of these alleged parallels is a real parallel. In none of them is there any question of a truly virginal conception: rather is it a matter of physical intercourse between a god and a mortal woman from which a birth results. In fact, the more closely these parallels are examined, the starker becomes the contrast between them and the narratives of Matthew and Luke. What is attested in the Gospels is a divine act of creation." C. E. B. Cranfield, "Some Reflections on the Subject of the Virgin Birth," *Scottish Journal of Theology* 41 (1988): 177-89; here 181ff.

73. Witherington, p. 70. Cranfield again: "it [is] virtually certain that Joseph was not biologically the father of Jesus." Cranfield, "Some Reflections," p. 185.

Jesus could just as well be the incarnate Son of God yet have Joseph for his biological father. As a matter of mere conceptual distinction, Virgin Birth and Incarnation are indeed different *doctrines*, but that does not mean they are congruently *unrelated*, a point the church fathers in the next several centuries all recognized, and whose thoughts on the issue we will encounter in the next chapter.[74] Moreover, the idea that the Virgin Birth can be cordoned off from the Incarnation so easily hearkens back, oddly enough, to the view of the medieval nominalists, who liked to speculate on such jejune topics as whether God could become incarnate in the form of a donkey or a rock to prove his absolute power. Fortunately, the New Testament writers and the early church fathers show no predilection for such speculative decadence and simply proclaim a doctrine that will become the central preoccupation of the next chapter, that Jesus had only one Father, the one from whom all paternity takes its name (Eph. 3:15). As Abbot Vonier rightly says:

> The mode of Our Lord's formation in the womb of His Blessed Mother was such that the result had to be human nature with divine existence. She conceived by the Holy Ghost, and conception by the Holy Ghost is necessarily the origin of a nature that must have divinity. . . . In the Hypostatic Union, therefore, the human nature is as divine as divine can be, not only because it always has been divine, but because, through the laws of its conception it had to be divine. "The grace of Union is natural to Christ in regard to His humanity on account of the propriety of His birth, as He was conceived by the Holy Ghost, so that He might be the natural Son of God, and of Man."[75]

---

74. See Oliver D. Crisp, "On the 'Fittingness' of the Virgin Birth," *Heythrop Journal* 49 (2008): 197-221; here 197.

75. Abbot Vonier, *The Collected Works of Abbot Vonier,* vol. 1, *The Incarnation and Redemption* (Westminster, MD: Newman Press, no date), pp. 123-24. Vonier is here quoting Thomas Aquinas, *Summa theologiae* III q.2 a.12 ad 3. The doctrine is also compatible with the Protestant stress on *sola gratia:* "The Virginal Conception attests the fact that God's redemption of his creation was by grace alone. The *sola* of *sola gratia* is seriously meant and must be seriously acknowledged. Our humanity, represented by Mary, here does nothing more than just accept — and even that acceptance is God's gracious gift. . . . The male sex, which has been characteristically the dominant, powerful, aggressive element of humanity, is altogether excluded from this action." Cranfield, "Some Reflections," p. 189.

CHAPTER 4

Patristic Christology

The One incapable of suffering did suffer.

Cyril of Alexandria

Philosophy, the New Ally

This chapter will survey the Christology of those theologians who came to be called "church fathers," a title bestowed on them by subsequent generations to indicate their authoritative status for all later developments. So when does this so-called "patristic" period begin and end? As to the endpoint, the transition from the patristic to the medieval era cannot be exactly demarcated and depends to some extent on one's point of view. At all events, we shall bring this chapter to a conclusion around the year 700.

As to its beginning, a much clearer demarcation separates the New Testament from patristic concerns. Granted, a few (a very few) of what are now included among the patristic documents might have been written during the New Testament period.[1] Nonetheless, when one looks at the New Testament

---

1. So, for example, if the *Didache* is a first-century document, it might have been composed while some of the later New Testament books were being written (on the assumption of a late dating for 2 Peter, for example). But since, as we saw in the last chapter, none of these documents (or the *Didache* for that matter) bears a date of composition or publication, the issue remains controversial. Johannes Quasten gives as possible dates for the *Didache* as between 100 and 150: Johannes Quasten, *Patrology,* vol. 1, *The Beginnings of Patristic Literature: From the Apostles' Creed to Irenaeus* (Westminster, MD: Christian Classics, 1985), p. 37.

as a whole and compares it with the totality of the patristic corpus, one cannot help but notice a decided shift in emphasis.

For the church fathers were forced to ask a set of questions that had only rarely registered with the authors of the New Testament, such as: Does philosophy have a role to play in theology? Can logic help to illuminate the central mystery of the person of Christ? Or are the central premises of Christology so paradoxical that logic is overthrown? Is reason boon or bane for theology? And prescinding from philosophy's utility when used by specifically Christian thinkers, what about its past? Might Socrates' execution at the hands of his fellow Athenians, and precisely for his criticism of the Greek gods, be seen, if not as a foretype, at least as an adumbration, of Christ's death on the cross? Did Plato's monotheism (such as it was) help or hinder the spread of the gospel? In other words, did Greek philosophy serve to "prepare the way" of the gospel for pagans in a way analogous to the role that the Hebrew prophets had for making the story of Jesus intelligible to his contemporaries in Israel?

What makes this patristic period so distinctive is that most (but not all) of the great theologians in the early church answered Yes to this question of philosophy's admissibility into the theologians' debating halls. This might strike the untutored student as surprising, because, at first glance anyway, the New Testament seems — at least on the rare occasions when it considers the matter at all — to give the opposite answer. For do we not read in St. Paul this seeming condemnation of philosophy?

> The word of the cross is folly to those who are perishing, but to us who are being saved it is the power of God. For it is written: "I will destroy the wisdom of the wise, and the cleverness of the clever I will thwart." Where is the wise man? Where is the scribe? Where is the debater of this age? Has not God made foolish the wisdom of the world? For since, in the wisdom of God, the world did not know God through wisdom, it pleased God through the folly of what we preach to save those who believe. For Jews demand signs and Greeks seek wisdom, but we preach Christ crucified, a stumbling block to Jews and folly to Gentiles, but to those who are called, both Jews and Greeks, Christ is the power of God and the wisdom of God. For the foolishness of God is wiser than men, and the weakness of God is stronger than men. (1 Cor. 1:18-25)

Given Paul's clarity here, why did most church fathers admit the usefulness of philosophy in their work? But this passage is not the whole story, even for Paul himself, as we learn from Acts of the Apostles, where Luke records a fascinating scene when Paul tried to preach the gospel to the Athenians on the Areopagus, the hill overlooking Athens crowded with temples, shrines, and altars to the gods, including one altar to "the unknown god." Taking his cue from that inscription, Paul preached that the real God had indeed been unknown to the Athenians all this time but had now made himself known to the nations by raising his Son from the dead. What is intriguing for our purposes is Luke's aside that "some Epicurean and Stoic philosophers met him" (Acts 17:18) and his report that Paul used language specifically drawn from Stoic philosophy in his preaching: "Even some of your own poets have said, 'For we are all his children'" (17:28b).[2] Nor can this be considered merely Luke's pro-Gentile spin on Paul's original hostility to Greek "wisdom," for in his own words Paul also seems to give warrant for philosophy: "Ever since the creation of the world [God's] invisible nature, namely, his eternal power and deity, has been clearly perceived in the things that have been made" (Rom. 1:20). Because Paul explicitly attributes this ability to come to a knowledge of God *to creation,* that is, to nature, and claims that man, *ever since the creation of the world* (that is, not in the wake of some supervening revelation), could have *clearly* perceived God's invisible nature but for the sin of rebellion, this passage has often been taken as the prooftext warrant for natural theology, usually defined as that branch of theology that operates from strict philosophical principles without the aid of a special act of new revelation.[3]

On the basis of these scriptural precedents, as well as because of the exigencies of the apologetic task in the patristic period (when Christians had to defend their faith against attacks by pagan authors), most early Christian writers from the second century on admitted the utility of Greek philosophy into their proceedings, not least because so many Greek philosophers, above all Socrates, had already so thoroughly criticized the Greek mythological system, making the preaching of a monotheistic God that much easier.[4]

---

2. The line comes from the *Phainomena* of Aratus, a poet of the third century B.C., echoed in almost identical words by his contemporary, Cleanthes the Stoic.

3. Attempts by Karl Barth to make Romans say the opposite of what it says because of his antecedent hostility to natural theology have failed, at least according to James Barr: "What he [Barth] offers has not the slightest likeness to a serious exegesis of the text." James Barr, *Biblical Faith and Natural Theology,* the Gifford Lectures for 1991 Delivered in the University of Edinburgh (Oxford: Clarendon Press, 1993). The book is a ringing defense of natural theology for Protestants as validated in the Bible.

4. Ironically, the situation has now reversed itself for liberal theology, a point noted by G. Ernest Wright: "The Bible definitely and consciously repudiates the gods of the nations

The Protestant Reformers changed that evaluation. First of all, their more radical theology of original sin compelled them, correlatively, to denigrate the ability of reason to know the things of God independently of revelation. Further, their principle of *sola scriptura* (the Protestant compensation for the weakness of reason) also made philosophy suspect. Finally, their suspicion of later, post-scriptural traditions carried with it the clear implication that the more primitive the church was, the purer was its Christian life; so that philosophy was bound to seem an adulteration (in both senses of the word), not a handmaid. These Reformed presuppositions had an enormous influence on much of German patristic scholarship of the nineteenth century, especially in the work done by the historian of dogma Adolf von Harnack, who argued that "Hellenization" (the adaptation of the gospel message to Greek culture) ruined the Semitic simplicity and rural directness of the teachings of Jesus and transformed a religion of peasants and the lower classes into a hierarchical cult for an intellectual elite.

So from Harnack's day to ours, a prejudice has taken hold that claims that Greek philosophy did more harm than good to the christological debates of the first six or seven centuries of the church's existence. Admittedly, this view gains a certain plausibility from a superficial glance at certain christological tracts by the church fathers when compared to the more existentially powerful and more limpidly presented portrait of Jesus in the Gospels, who himself taught that the simple and unlettered would understand his identity more clearly than the clever and learned ever would (Matt. 11:25). In contrast, even a brief survey of patristic Christology leads one into a forest of technical terms and arcane heresies: hypostasis, substance, essence, consubstantial, adoptionism, modalism, subordinationism, Arianism, monophysitism, monothelitism, and so forth. Does it really all have to be so complicated? And given the abstract difficulties of the issues involved, why does it seem so easy to fall into heresy, the penalty for which was excommunication from the church of orthodox believers? Even granted the need to get things right, do the polemics hurled at authors of differing views have to be so cutthroat and heated, with the consequences for the "wrong answer" being expulsion from the church?

---

together with their mythology and their magic. To worship the God of Israel and the Father of Jesus Christ meant the discarding of nature myths of immanent gods. . . . Consequently, in the early Church 'science' and theology were allied against mythology. Today this alliance has become a problem. Either we keep it and demythologize Biblical theology, or else we discard it and ally theology and mythology against science." G. Ernest Wright, *God Who Acts: Biblical Theology as Recital* (London: SCM Press, 1952), p. 119.

Theology and Worship

Accusations of prejudice by one age against an earlier one, especially ones made over a long stretch of time, are always tricky, for as the historical theologian Henri de Lubac once pointed out, no one is more prejudiced than someone who thinks he is without prejudices.[5] While it would be foolhardy to attempt to excuse every jot and tittle of every sentence that came from the pens of every single church father, nonetheless one can never gain an understanding of their thought until one first understands what motivated them, what animated their thinking and writing, and why they were so passionate about dogma. And that animating motivation can be put into one word: *worship*. Unless we start there, where theology meets liturgy, we will never understand the significance of their legacy, a point admirably caught by the patristic scholar Robert Louis Wilken in this passage from his survey of early Christian theologians:

> All the figures portrayed in this book prayed regularly, and their thinking was never far removed from the church's worship. Whether the task at hand was the defense of Christian belief to an outsider, the refutation of the views of a heretic, or the exposition of a passage from the Bible, their intellectual work was always in service of praise and adoration of the one God. "This is the Catholic faith," begins an ancient creed, "that we *worship* one God in Trinity and Trinity in Unity." Often their treatises ended with a doxology to God, as in Augustine's *On the Spirit and the Letter:* "to whom be glory forever. Amen." They wished not only to understand and express the dazzling truth they had seen in Christ, by thinking and writing they sought to know God more intimately and love him more ardently. The intellectual task was a spiritual undertaking. In the oft-cited words of the desert monk Evagrius: "A theologian is one who prays, and one who prays is a theologian."[6]

More to the point, the one they prayed *to* was Jesus, in whom "all the fullness of the Godhead was pleased to dwell" (Col. 1:19). To be sure, early Christians did not pray to Jesus exclusively, but to him under a trinitarian

5. "We think that we can affirm tolerance is making progress. What we don't realize is that a new intolerance has taken the place of the old one." Henri de Lubac, *Paradoxes of Faith,* trans. Ernest Beaumont (San Francisco: Ignatius Press, 1987), p. 161.

6. Robert Louis Wilken, *The Spirit of Early Christian Thought: Seeking the Face of God* (New Haven: Yale University Press, 2003), pp. 25-26; Wilken's emphasis.

rubric most succinctly summed up by Paul: "There is one body and *one Spirit,* just as you were called to the one hope that belongs to your call, *one Lord,* one faith, one baptism, *one God and Father* of us all, who is above all and through all and in all" (Eph. 4:4-6). Admittedly, working out how the *fullness* of the Godhead could dwell in Jesus while the Spirit and the Father yet remain one and yet also distinct would take centuries to work out, and will be the task of this chapter to narrate. But the crucial point to stress at the outset of our reflections is that *theology followed worship.* Wilken again:

> On page after page the reader senses what they [the fathers] believe is anchored in regular, indeed habitual, participation in the church's worship, and what they teach is confirmed by how they pray. At one point in his work against the Gnostics, Irenaeus observed, . . . "Our teaching is consonant with what we do in the Eucharist, and the celebration of the Eucharist establishes what we teach."[7]

The Two Axioms of Patristic Christology

Granted all this, still it would represent a distorted picture of patristic Christology to claim that the fathers were purely doxological in their theology, perpetually "lost in wonder, love, and praise." For as we said in the Introduction, just as symbol gives rise to thought, so too do the paradoxes of the Christian message give rise to theology. Under that rubric, the church had no choice but to confront what it meant for Paul to say that there was only one God, Father of us all, and *yet also* one Lord and one Spirit.

What will immediately strike the reader in this statement is how intimately questions of the identity of Jesus are tied up with questions of the identity of God, "one in Trinity and triune in unity." To put the matter in

7. Wilken, *Spirit,* pp. 26-27. This point does not gainsay, of course, the difference in tone and rhetoric of the fathers from that of the New Testament, but for Wilken the contrast between both of them and the pagan authors is even more striking: "More often than not the church fathers have been interpreted as solitary intellectuals, each working out his own system, beholden chiefly to the world of ideas and arguments, as though they are clandestine members of an ancient philosophical guild. To be sure, many of the best minds in the early church were philosophically astute and moved comfortably within the intellectual traditions of the ancient world. They knew the argot of philosophy, and their books and ideas were taken seriously by Greek and Roman intellectuals. But if one picks up a treatise of Origen or Basil of Caesarea and compares it with the writings of the philosopher Alcinous or the neo-Platonist Plotinus, it is apparent at once that something else is at work" (p. 26).

crude mathematical terms, the church had two fundamental questions to answer at the theoretical level: How can God be, at the same time and in full reality, both *one and three* (1=3) and how could Jesus represent the *fullness* of the Godhead and yet be the "man of tears" as he is represented in the Gospels (infinite=finite)? The two questions are obviously related, because if Christ is divine, then the question immediately arises: What is his relation to the Father and the Spirit? And if Christ is both human and divine, how are humanity and divinity related in him? Brian Daley deftly captures the dilemma in this pithy summary of the fundamental problem of patristic Christology:

> The more ancient authors emphasize the complex personal *unity* of Christ as the agent of salvation, the more they are forced to acknowledge the irreducible *threeness* of God, even to the point of having to conceive of the Father, Son, and Holy Spirit as in some way ontologically ranked or subordinated, as sharing in the divine reality in differing degrees of fullness. Conversely, the more ancient authors emphasize the radical *unity* of the divine Mystery and see the threeness of Father, Son, and Holy Spirit in what we might call perspectival rather than ontological terms, as a threeness of manifestation in history, . . . the more they are forced to see Jesus, the Savior, as subjectively *double* and to understand his saving role in terms of God's dwelling in a human being or acting in ways parallel to his human actions, rather than in terms of God's personal identity with him. . . . The real issue of both Trinitarian theology and Christology [is this]: how can we understand God as radically one and eternally transcendent with respect to creation and still understand Jesus as a genuinely divine savior, who genuinely acts in our history as a human being like ourselves?[8]

Putting it this way obviously makes it sound as if theology is only a matter of pure logic or a theoretical brainteaser. But of course behind the sheer paradoxicality of the problem lurks the more existential problem: *only because the death of Jesus was regarded as a saving death did the problem of Christology arise in the first place.*[9] This becomes evident even as early as Pen-

8. Brian E. Daley, S.J., "'One Thing and Another': The Persons in God and the Person of Christ in Patristic Theology," *Pro Ecclesia* 15, no. 1 (Winter 2006): 17-46; here 21-22.

9. In other words, I take to heart Khaled Anatolios's warning: "my fundamental discomfort has to do precisely with the prioritizing of what I have called the mathematics of tri-unity over the presentation of a holistic vision of Christian life in which a particular reading of Scripture is appropriated and performed." Khaled Anatolios, "Final Reflections," *Harvard Theological Review* 100, no. 2 (2007): 174.

tecost, when Peter (not one whose subsequent behavior showed any indication that he was inclined to abandon the traditions of Judaism) found himself forced to speak a proto-trinitarian language to the polyglot Jews assembled for Pentecost if he was going to be able to explain just how the death of Jesus was a saving death. We have already briefly touched on this passage in the previous chapter, but its specifically trinitarian focus requires a more exact exegesis here because it will show both how foundational a theology of the Trinity is for Christology and how far back in the tradition the patristic problematic reaches:

> "Men of Israel, listen to this: Jesus of Nazareth was *a man* accredited by God to you by miracles, wonders and signs, which *God* did among you *through* him, as you yourselves know. This *man* was handed over to you by *God's* set purpose and foreknowledge, and you — with the help of wicked men — put him to death by nailing him to the cross. But *God* raised him from the dead, freeing him from the torments of Hades, because it was impossible for death to keep its hold on him. . . . *God* raised this Jesus to life, and we are all witnesses of the fact. Exalted to God's right hand, he has *received* from the *Father* the promised *Holy Spirit* and has poured out what you now see and hear. . . . Therefore let all Israel be assured of this: *God* has *made* this Jesus, whom you crucified, both *Lord* and *Christ*. . . . *Save* yourselves from this perverse generation." They accepted what he said and were *baptized*. (Acts 2:22-24, 32-33, 36, 40-41)

Exegetically, this passage is fascinating in many regards, most of which I have tried to highlight through the added italics. Notice that Jesus is not only consistently called "a man" but is also described entirely in passive terms.[10] Even when he performs miracles, he is described not as his own agent; rather, it is God who is acting through him, almost as if he were merely a template or conduit for God's action. Throughout this passage God is the ultimate agent, who has foreordained matters so that Jesus is handed over by *God's* set purpose and foreknowledge. Finally, of course, it is God, and God alone, who *raises* Jesus from the dead.[11] But suddenly, in the middle of this

10. The only time Jesus is the grammatical subject of an active, transitive verb is when he is the subject of the verb "receive," which of course is passive in meaning.

11. In other words, Jesus does not "rise" from the dead the way someone "rises" in the morning out of bed. Unfortunately, English translations often obscure the point by translating the Greek aorist passive *ēgerthē* ("he was raised") as "he rose," which can imply that he rose on his own power, whereas New Testament verbal forms for the most part imply that he was the object of God's action upon him.

consistently passive description comes the strange statement that something about Jesus' *identity* prevents him from staying in Hades ("for it was *impossible* for death to keep its hold on him"), which then leads Peter to begin to speak of Jesus in proto-trinitarian terms, proclaiming him to be "Lord" (a divine title, as we saw in Chapter 2) and "Christ" who receives the "Holy Spirit." Obviously Peter is not giving a theological lecture here, but is speaking of Jesus in these terms as the only way available to him for explaining how Christ's death is a *redemptive* death, the response to which on the part of Peter's listeners must be baptism if they are to be saved.

These points need to be rehearsed not just to point out how early comes the church's trinitarian language but more crucially to show *how impossible it was, even for the earliest strata of the Palestinian community, to speak of Jesus' death as saving except in trinitarian terms.* This inexorable connection between the saving death of Jesus and trinitarian language highlights a point we will notice throughout this chapter: questions of the identity of Jesus are *always* connected both to questions of salvation and to questions of the Trinity, that is, to questions that treat the true identity of God and his saving purposes in history.

Now because these questions are obviously not easy to answer at a first attempt, we must also mention the role of heresy in the development of later orthodox solutions. To speak schematically once again, when faced with the logical conundrum of God being both one and three, or Jesus being both human and divine, it will occur to some early Christian writers that the solution is obvious: let God be regarded as *fundamentally* one, with his *manifestations* in history "coming across" as three; or let us regard Jesus as *fundamentally* human, who has been, as it were, "adopted" as divine. As we will later see, these solutions will be rejected, *but for reasons internal to the problem itself.* In other words, even though ecclesiastical politics will obviously play a role, what will eventually be called heretical solutions will ultimately be rejected, after much back-and-forth debate, because other writers will have shown that these so-called "solutions" *dis*solved, rather than *re*solved, the problem *already given.*

In other words, given the axiomatic nature of trinitarian and christological language going all the way back to Pentecost (the very birthday of the church), the theological problems attendant upon that language could not be wished away by superficial proposals. But while the failure of these heretical tracts might be obvious to us in retrospect, in the context of their time they could seem quite plausible. So the upshot is that heresies ended up forcing other theologians, operating within the received axioms of a three-in-one God and a human-divine Jesus, to hone the reasons why earlier proposals had to be rejected. As St. Augustine pointed out, in the long run heretics serve the cause of orthodoxy by forcing orthodox Christians to think through and to come to terms with the faith they have received from the apostles.[12] At all events, solutions to these very knotty issues were bound to be proposed; and when they struck their listeners as superficial, thought (and therefore theology) was bound to arise, the story of which it is now our task to tell.

Gnosticism and the Three Rules of Adjudication

This story, as it is normally told, speaks of three operative norms for adjudicating the debate, the "rules of the game," as it were, for winning the argument, which one historian of dogma summarizes this way:

> 1. *Do not contradict the Bible.* Christians [in the early centuries] continued to debate just which books belonged in the New Testament, but they recognized the general authority of Scripture and tended to reject theories that seemed to contradict it.
>
> 2. *Do not interfere with the liturgy.* Christians will generally leave theologians alone, considering them harmless enough, but theologians who tell them to stop praying as their parents taught them risk instant unpopularity.
>
> 3. *Do not threaten the means of salvation.* As already noted, early

12. "Only because of the heretics in her midst could the Catholic Church find a more exact way to express herself in words, and the orthodox were preserved in their right-thinking because of the false thinkers among them. . . . For example, was any complete account of the Trinity available before the Arians began to bay at it? . . . Nor had the unity of Christ's body [the Church] been discussed in such a developed, explicit way until [the Donatist] division began to trouble the weaker brethren." Augustine, *Exposition of the Psalms: 51–72*, at Psalm 54:22, trans. Maria Boulding, O.S.B. (Hyde Park, NY: New City Press, 2001), pp. 74-75. Further: "For you are not to suppose, brethren, that heresies could be produced through any little souls. None save great men have been the authors of heresies." *Expositions of the Psalms* at Psalm 124:5; cited in *An Augustine Synthesis*, ed. Erich Przywara, S.J. (New York: Sheed & Ward, 1936), p. 272. Modern observers, of course, agree: "Orthodoxy — the accepted truth — is established and articulated against a background of heresy. Paradoxically, more often than not dogmas are crystallized in the struggle against their rejection." Leszek Kolakowski, "Heresy," in *The Two Eyes of Spinoza & Other Essays on Philosophers*, trans. Agnieszka Kolakowska (South Bend, IN: St. Augustine's Press, 2004), pp. 263-88; here 267.

Christians affirmed Christ's divinity and humanity in part because saying that Christ had only seemed to be human, or had not been truly divine, had threatened their confidence in their salvation. That concern continued to shape subsequent debates.[13]

All of this is true enough, but one should not get the impression that these "rules" were arbitrarily chosen, like some theological version of *Robert's Rules of Order*. Rather, they arose organically, like theology itself, out of the presuppositions of Christian worship. Moreover, they arose not just organically but also in a historical context, in a process, that is, as determined by the crucible of the second century. In other words, the "rules" were themselves in the process of coming to be. First of all, the canon of the New Testament was still assuming the standard of twenty-seven books that we know today. This does not mean, as some people erroneously think, that the *documents* of the New Testament were composed in the second or third century, only that the decision of what documents to include was still being debated. Obviously the documents had to be written before the *canon* could be decided.[14]

But the crucial point to stress here is that the need for a rule or a standard would never have been felt in the first place if the original twenty-seven books were the only ones that had been written. In other words, there were competing gospels, competing accounts of the deeds and actions of the apostles, and competing doctrinal treatises, the swirl of which competition forced the issue of the canon. With this cacophony of voices competing for attention, the church was forced to confront a new question: Which documents that spoke of Jesus and the apostles were reliable, both historically and theologically; and which did not, so to speak, "ring true" in the context of the church's worship?[15]

Closely allied to this issue is the ideological ground out of which so many of the competing (and eventually noncanonical) writings grew to fru-

13. William C. Placher, *A History of Christian Theology: An Introduction* (Philadelphia: Westminster Press, 1983), pp. 69-70.

14. "Canon" is the Greek word for "spine," including the spine of a codex book, which then took on the extended meaning of "ruler" or "measuring rod," and then came to mean the rule or standard that determined what books would be included, and which excluded, from the New Testament. At Galatians 6:16, Paul speaks of a "canon" of faith in an even wider sense, referring to his gospel of justification by faith.

15. Because the minute details of this process of canonization are not directly relevant to the specific issues of Christology, the reader is referred to the comprehensive study of Hans von Campenhausen, *The Formation of the Christian Bible*, trans. J. A. Baker (Minneapolis: Augsburg/Fortress, 1977).

ition: Gnosticism. We have already taken brief note of Gnosticism in Chapter 2 (in the section on "Jesus the Word"), but now more must be said about this peculiar worldview because of its influence (a negative influence, to be sure) on the formation of the church's christological doctrines.

Basically, Gnosticism is, with the possible exception of Zoroastrianism (a pre-Christian form of dualism that arose in Persia), the most thoroughgoing form of religious dualism known to history.[16] In Gnosticism everything is equipoised: there is light, and there is darkness; there is good, and there is evil; there is spirit, and there is matter; and, most crucially, there are two gods, one the good god of light and the other the evil god of darkness and matter.

When the Christian religion began to make headway in the Roman world, a Christian variant of Gnosticism arose that was able to add some twists to the story.[17] In a Christian context the evil god of matter could now be identified with the creator of that matter, as recounted in the book of Genesis. At a stroke, the monotheistic God of the Jews, the same God worshiped by the Christians (Luke 24:52), became the evil counter-god of darkness and matter — the very element that the Gnostics found to be such a baneful prison, the source of all our woes. Therefore, to be saved for the Gnostics meant, by definition, that one had to be saved *from* matter. Thus, if Jesus were to be truly a "savior" in their understanding of the term, he would have had to have been sent *from a different god than the one worshiped by the Jews,* sent, that is, from the good god of light and spirit. Moreover, he could have assumed, at best, only a *seeming* matter, a kind of diaphanous body,

---

16. Some scholars hold in fact that Gnosticism was imported from Persian Zoroastrianism, at least in its basic outlook, so that they constitute, in their essentials, the same worldview: "Moreover, we know from some sources, e.g. from Plutarch, that the concepts of Mazdaean [Iranian] dualism also were so widespread in this period that Zarathustra had become one of the most acclaimed 'prophets of the Orient.' According to his teachings, the evil present in the world is attributable to the existence *ab aeterno* of two opposing principles: good and evil; and the world is merely the stage upon which the struggle between Ahura Mazda, the Lord of Good, and Angra Manyu, the Lord of Evil, is played out in periods that are varied and complex." Giovanni Filoramo, *A History of Gnosticism*, trans. Anthony Alcock (Oxford: Basil Blackwell, 1990), p. 54.

17. The majority of scholars hold that Gnosticism was a well-formed religion prior to the advent of Christianity, which influenced Christianity only when it entered the Hellenized world, although a minority holds that it sprang into being only as a Christian heresy. For a survey of this problem and its literature, see Luke Timothy Johnson, *Among the Gentiles: Greco-Roman Religion and Christianity* (New Haven: Yale University Press, 2009), pp. 337-79, endnotes 2 and 3.

rather like what the gods of Greek mythology assumed when they took on disguises to walk among mortal men.[18]

One of the earliest proponents of this Christian variant of Gnosticism was a Roman priest by the name of Marcion (dates unknown, but he died around A.D. 160), whose central thesis was that the Christian evangel was solely a message of love in absolute contrast to law, which led him to reject the Old Testament in its entirety. But as we saw in the last chapter, the New Testament is tissued throughout with quotes from the Bible of the Jews, which forced Marcion, with the relentless logic that will mark so many heretics, to expunge not just the whole of the Old Testament but numerous books from the New Testament as well. According to this wealthy shipowner (for such he was before immigrating to Rome), only Paul fully understood this contrast between the lawgiving counter-god of the Hebrews and the good god of love. So he accepted ten of Paul's letters (heavily bowdlerized, to be sure) and rejected all the other books of the New Testament except an expurgated version of Luke.[19]

Marcion was excommunicated from the Roman church in the year 144, which shows that even at this early date Roman Christians had accepted as inspired Scripture most of the books that now make up our New Testament, precisely because Marcion felt they had to be deliberately expunged from the canon. That is, unless the Gospels expunged by Marcion had already been serving as authoritative texts, he would never have needed to attack them. To be sure, the Gospels and epistles that Marcion rejected might not have been explicitly seen as belonging to an officially promulgated canon yet. For it was not until Marcion began a deliberate campaign to remove them that steps had to be taken to give them a more official status. But they were clearly operating as inspired and authoritative texts already, used both in liturgical worship and in theological argumentation; otherwise Marcion would not have found them so threatening to his views.

Marcion's heresies are a perfect example of the interlocking factors that converged to crystallize the church's defense of her doctrine. First, because

---

18. From this assertion that Jesus assumed only an apparent, not a real, body comes the name for that heresy, "docetism," from the Greek word *dokeō*, "to seem."

19. The refusal to admit the other Gospels shows, at a minimum, that Marcion wasn't stupid, for at least *he* knew how thoroughly Jewish was the provenance of the Gospels, unlike some later historical critics of the nineteenth century who place them so late and so far from their originating Jewish matrix. Interesting too that Marcion recognized the Jewish character of John's Gospel whereas so many later critics, Rudolf Bultmann especially, could see only a Hellenistic Savior-myth in its Christology.

of Marcion's surgical efforts to amputate the New Testament and extirpate the Old Testament entirely, the church had to come to a more explicit recognition of what books do and do not belong to her Bible, very much including the Old Testament. Second, because the doctrinal system of Gnosticism was so radically at odds with the monotheistic presuppositions of Jesus' resurrection as *God's* action (an action that culminated all his previous saving deeds to Israel), creeds began to be formulated with phrases explicitly aimed to counter Gnosticism's heretical propositions. Finally, bishops (whose chief role was to preside at the community's Eucharist) recognized that their role as heirs to the apostles required them to guard the rule of faith as encapsulated in the creeds from the assaults of the heretics. In other words, the church needed not just an officially recognized canon of scripture; she also needed *a canon of interpretation* to go along with it, a point elegantly made by the patristic scholar G. L. Prestige:

> When both sides are appealing to the same Scriptures and both claim to be rendering a true interpretation of their meaning, how can the common man judge between the conflicting conclusions? He must go to the churches of the apostolic succession, because they alone possess the creed that expresses the faith to which the Scriptures belong. . . . [There was a] common need for some canon of interpretation, and also the duty of placing Scripture in its right historical context of creed and bishop.[20]

Thus there is an interlocking relationship between the formation of the biblical canon, the apostolic succession of bishops, their role in presiding at the Eucharist, and the baptismal creed as prerequisite for admission to the Eucharist. In the second century all of this will converge to create the "norms for adjudication" to bring resolution to theological debate in the next seven centuries, the story of orthodoxy we are about to unfold in this chapter. But in the interactions between these various levels of adjudication, *the Bible still trumped all other authorities,* even if the church recognized that it was her decision that determined the canon:

> But since [the church fathers] recognized in the Bible itself something which the Church had instituted — at any rate, before the New Testament could begin to shape the thought of the Church, it had itself had to be put into shape by the Church — it is wholly to their credit that they also recognized the need for comparing its witness with that of the other great

20. G. L. Prestige, *Fathers and Heretics* (London: SPCK, 1940), p. 17.

formative contributions of the apostolic and sub-apostolic Church to spiritual order and discipline — that is, in particular, the sacraments, the creeds, and the episcopate. . . . If it is the duty of the Church to teach, it is the privilege of the Bible to prove.[21]

Early Christological and Trinitarian Heresies

So with the axioms in place and the rules for adjudicating the debate emerging into view, how did the debate proceed? What will become clear as this story proceeds is that any attempt to abolish the basic axioms of a one-in-three God or a human-and-divine Jesus will be rapidly rejected, which is what justifies us in calling them axioms. Just as the alteration of any of the six axioms of Euclidian geometry destroys it as a specifically Euclidian system, so too the church discovered that to abolish either prong of the two axioms, God-as-both-one-and-three and Jesus-as-human-and-divine, would be to undercut the very presuppositions that make the Christian religion Christian.

Adoptionism

It was the fundamental task and the most significant legacy of the second-century church to discover these axioms *as* axioms. We have already seen how quickly the church came to reject the docetism of Marcion. But there was also another heresy on the opposite end of the spectrum, adoptionism, which claimed that Jesus was only given the status of divine Son by a kind of legal fiction. This was apparently the view of a rump group of Jewish Christians from Palestine who had to flee to the hills of Judea after the Romans had destroyed the Temple in A.D. 70 and who lived an exiguous life of extreme poverty there, until finally dying out after the Romans expelled all Jews from Palestine in A.D. 135.[22] This group was too small and too isolated

---

21. Prestige, *Fathers and Heretics,* pp. 15-16. In other words, the whole point of coming to determine a canon was not so that the church could "lord it over Scripture" but rather so that the church could recognize in precisely those documents and no others the ultimate norm that she above all was obliged to obey, a point explicitly affirmed in the decree of the Second Vatican Council on divine revelation, *Dei Verbum* §10. Orthodoxy gains its tensile strength from this organically formed whole.

22. It is from their poverty that these Jewish Christians got the name "Ebionites," from the Hebrew word *'ebionim,* meaning "poor men."

to affect the debate elsewhere, but this heresy cropped up later (independently of the Ebionites, it would seem) in Theodotus the Cobbler (second century, dates otherwise unknown), a Roman lay Christian who claimed that, after living a life of perfect virtue, Jesus received the Holy Spirit at his baptism, enabling him to perform miracles.[23] Finally, Paul of Samosata (third century), a bishop of Antioch, was deposed from his see for holding that the Logos came upon the man Jesus, who for that reason was called, honorifically, Son of God.

This heresy is sometimes called *psilanthropism,* from the Greek *psilos anthrōpos,* meaning "mere man." As the careers of Theodotus and Paul of Samosata clearly show, this option found little traction in the church, having been quickly condemned even before Christianity had been legally recognized by Rome; but this heresy has found new resonance in modern times with the post-Enlightenment rejection of the supernatural. As a broadly conceived theoretical possibility, adoptionism crops up anytime a theologian claims that Jesus was merely human, who can be denominated God only because Christian faith recognizes him as but a "symbol" of God.[24]

23. Citing Deuteronomy in justification: "The Lord your God will raise up for you a prophet like me from among you" (Deut. 18:15). He was condemned by Pope Victor (r. 189-98). Details in J. N. D. Kelly, *Early Christian Doctrines* (New York: Harper & Row, 1960), p. 116.

24. Adoptionism was even held by two bishops in eighth-century Spain, Elipandus, the Archbishop of Toledo, and Felix, Bishop of Urgel. Elipandus never recanted, but Felix did after a synod in Ratisbon condemned him in 792. But when he relapsed into his old views, Charlemagne's chancellor, the monk Alcuin, wrote a seven-book tract *Contra Felicem,* which prompted Pope Leo III to call a synod in Rome in 798 to anathematize Felix, who then recanted his views a second time. It might seem bizarre that such an unworkable heresy would crop up in, of all places, eighth-century Spain. But in fact this Spanish heresy differs from that of the Ebionites in this respect: Elipandus and Felix admitted the divine nature of the hypostatic union but said that *in his humanity* Jesus could only be considered the adopted Son of God. The Franciscan John Duns Scotus and the Jesuit Francisco Suarez were sympathetic to this technical point; but because these views come so close to the adoptionism of the Ebionites, they have generally been rejected as undermining sound Christology. See John C. Cavadini, *The Last Christology of the West: Adoptionism in Spain and Gaul, 785-820* (Philadelphia: University of Pennsylvania Press, 1993), who rightly says of this strain of theology: "'Adoptionism' is a word without a fixed historical reference, as there have been several theologies, historically unrelated, which have been given this name" (p. 1). He also raises the possibility that the Spanish version of this heresy was due to, or at least influenced by, the Muslim conquests of Spain in the years 710-712, the result of which was Arab suzerainty over almost the whole of the Iberian peninsula, a period called Mozarabic, which lasted until the fifteenth century.

Modalism

Similarly with issues of the Trinity: the simplest solution would be to hold that God is one fundamentally but "comes across" in salvation-history in the "modes" of Father, Son, and Spirit — hence the name "modalism" for this heresy. It was first propounded in Rome by three priests, Noetus, Praxeas, and Sabellius (thus the name "Sabellianism" is sometimes given to this heresy).[25] But despite its superficial simplicity, the proposal had to fail: for it meant that the whole of the Godhead *without distinction* had to be present in Jesus; but Scripture depicts Jesus praying *to* the Father throughout his earthly life and has the Father saying *to* Jesus, "This is my beloved Son in whom I am well pleased" (Matt. 3:17). Plus, on a more abstract level, who is governing and sustaining the universe in being if the whole of the Godhead is incarnate in Jesus? Finally, because the whole of the Godhead would have to be incarnate in Jesus, and since Jesus suffered, this heresy also goes under the name of "patripassianism," meaning the assertion that the Father suffered, a name that stuck because of this line from Noetus: "If I acknowledge Christ to be God, [then] He is the Father himself, if He is indeed God; and Christ suffered, being Himself God; and consequently the Father suffered, for He was the Father Himself."[26] This lapidary summary of the modalist position was taken as self-evidently absurd, not just on Platonic grounds that suffering is incompatible with deity but also because suffering is what we are supposed to be saved from, and a God who shares our plight can hardly be in a position to rescue us from it.[27]

25. Exact dates for these three men are unknown, but they all flourished around the year 200.

26. Quoted by Hippolytus of Rome, *Contra Noetum* 2.3, trans. R. Butterworth (London: Heythrop College, 1977); note the rigorous (and flat-footed) use of syllogistic logic here, always a sure sign of trouble when dealing with the paradoxes of Christology. This heresy also is known as "monarchism" because of its refusal to draw a distinction between Father and Son, meaning that there is only one *archē* (principle) in God.

27. The opposite heresy to modalism would of course be "tritheism," which would hold that God is fundamentally three separate, independently acting gods who are united only because they share the one divine nature. But in point of fact, tritheism is a paper heresy. Not one single theologian in the history of the church has ever subscribed to tritheism. Of course, some attempts to explain the Trinity, such as speaking of the Persons of the Trinity on analogy with human persons who share one human nature, can prove to be misleading. But not one of those who, perhaps unhelpfully, adopted that imagery ever used it to defend an explicit tritheism. So accusations of tritheism can only serve as a scare tactic, at best to ward off potential tendencies in certain styles of thinking or types of imagery, at worst to

Subordinationism (Arianism)

But if the Son cannot be identical with the Father, then how can he be divine without there being two gods? The solution seemed obvious to many at the time and now goes under the name of "subordinationism": since a son is obviously subordinate to his father while sharing in the same nature, one can draw all kinds of analogies (speaker/word, sun/ray, root/tree and so forth) based on the primary father-son analogue to show unity-in-subordination, as Tertullian (c. 160–c. 225) did in his polemic against modalism:

> God sent forth the Word . . . just as the root puts forth the tree, and the fountain the river, and the sun the ray. . . . For root and tree are distinctly two things, but correlatively joined; fountain and river are also two forms, but indivisible; so likewise sun and ray are two forms, but coherent ones. Everything which proceeds from something else must needs be second to that from which it proceeds, without being on that account separated.[28]

We know of the obviousness of these metaphors because most of the theologians in the third century speak in these same frankly subordinationist terms, especially Origen (c. 185–c. 254). Not only did subordinationism seem perfectly orthodox from the very terminology of Father and Son (what son is not subordinate to his father?), but Scripture records Jesus himself as saying "The Father is greater than I" (John 14:28). The seeming obviousness and simplicity of these metaphors concealed, however, a lurking problem.[29] This latent difficulty came most vividly to the fore when Arius (born c. 260-80, died 360), a priest from Alexandria, wanted to make it absolutely clear, against the modalists, that the Son is not identical with the Father. Such an assertion entailed for Arius the conclusion that only the Father is eternal, while the subordinate Son was a part of creation, even if "the *firstborn* of creation" (Col. 1:15).

---

force Christians to defend a position they never held in the first place. No Christian *ever* subscribed to an assertion that there are three gods, despite what outsiders (Jews, Moslems, skeptics) and insiders (Unitarians) will later say in the future. The accusation might work as an attempt to throw orthodox Christians on the defensive, but the accusation itself shows a fundamental misunderstanding of Christianity from the ground up.

28. Tertullian, *Against Praxeas,* Book XIII, trans. Peter Holmes, in *The Ante-Nicene Fathers,* vol. 3 (Grand Rapids: Eerdmans, 1963), p. 603.

29. And sometimes not so lurking, for Tertullian frankly avows: "For the Father is the whole substance, while the Son is an outflow and assignment of the whole." *Tertullian's Treatise Against Praxeas,* trans. Ernest Evans (London: SPCK, 1948), p. 140.

This phrase from Paul, quoted incessantly by the Arians, shows how plausible the Arian system must have seemed to many in the third- and fourth-century church. If one was going to ascribe a place to the divine Christ within the Godhead in a way consistent with monotheism yet without falling into the modalist heresy, then both Scripture and logic seemed to point to giving the Son a secondary status, where he could assume his rightful place, one step lower from the supreme Father.[30] Arius stood within this broad tradition and hotly disputed accusations of his deviations from orthodoxy. Perhaps if he had been born fifty years earlier and had not been so insistent on the specifically created status of the Son, no one would have noticed. Consider Origen, who spoke in ways that the later church would judge as clearly unacceptable, yet who was never condemned in his lifetime.[31] As the scholar Maurice Wiles explains:

> Despite the spirit of personal devotion to Jesus which shines through so much of his preaching, Origen insists that strictly speaking prayer can be offered only to the Father. When we offer our prayers to the Son, what we are really doing is asking him to convey them to the Father, the supreme God, the ultimate recipient of all true prayer. But in the long run the verdict of the Church was clear. Praying to Christ was not to be explained away in this manner. It was not enough to dub him "god" in some secondary sense. The Christian trinity was not to be identified with the three-tiered hierarchical trinity of Neo-platonic speculation.[32]

30. The neo-Platonic schema of the pagan philosopher Plotinus (c. 205-270) also lent subordinationism an added plausibility, because he had proposed an account of God as the One and the Good, who as the Good, that is, with the goodness of an overflowing generosity, first emanated Mind (Greek: *Nous*), from which then came Spirit *(Pneuma)*, from which later arose the rest of the world, first the world of archetypal Ideas and then that of formed matter, terminating in unformed (prime) matter. The point is that, precisely as an emanation (and in Plotinus, an *unwilled* emanation at that), Mind and Spirit were subordinate to the One.

31. Heavily reliant on the neo-Platonist doctrine of the Mind-transcending One, Origen held that God the Father is God in the absolute sense of the word and thus is above Mind *(Logos)* and even above being. For that reason he distinguished in his exegesis of John's Gospel between "the" God and the Logos of God, who is God without the article: "*The* God, therefore, is the true God." Origen, *Commentary on the Gospel According to John,* trans. Ronald E. Heine, *The Fathers of the Church: A New Translation,* vol. 80 (Washington, DC: Catholic University of America Press, 1989), bk. 2.17. Origen also held that Jesus himself confessed his subordinate status here: "And this is eternal life, that they know you the only true God, and Jesus Christ whom you have sent" (John 17:3).

32. Maurice Wiles, *The Christian Fathers* (New York: Oxford University Press, 1982), p. 37. In Origen's own words: "We should not pray to any generate being, not even to Christ,

Origen managed to skirt condemnation during his life for these views, partly because he was writing while the imperial persecutions against the Christian religion were still proceeding apace, which made it difficult for structures to be put in place that could enforce doctrinal orthodoxy.[33] But Origen was also no Arian, at least in this regard: unlike Arius he saw the problems in his views and tried to mitigate them by insisting on the *eternal* generation of the Son from the Father. Moreover, he insisted that the Son was the *perfect* reflection of all the Father's divine attributes, including the divine essence.

This *essential* connection between Father and Son from all eternity, which Origen strove to maintain (however awkwardly), Arius was prepared to deny outright. To revert to the Greek that Arius used, there was for him a definite difference in *ousia* ("essence") between them. Thus the Son was not essentially God but only secondarily divine by virtue of his proximity to God as the *first*-born of *creation*. So rather than being of the *same* essence (Greek: *homoousios*), the Son was only of *similar* essence *(homoiousios):* in Greek a matter of a mere iota, but conceptually of enormous import, as in this paraphrase from Wiles:

> The Son was not eternal, for there could not be two eternals. Must one therefore say that he was temporal, brought into being at some specific point in time? Arius had no wish to say that and tried to steer a middle course. He was not eternal but nor was his coming into being a temporal event. It was necessary to say that "there was when he was not" to guard against the false view of his co-eternity with the Father; but it would be misleading to say that "there was [a] time when he was not" for his being is prior to all notions of time.[34]

Using the same logic, Arius also had no desire to say that the Son was of the same essence as creation either, only that he was in some way genuinely created. To say that he was generated directly from the Father, either as begotten or even as emanated, would for Arius destroy the divine unity; but to call him created without further ado would be equally misleading. Thus he says:

---

but only to the one God and Father of the universe, to Whom our Savior Himself prayed." Cited in Kelly, *Early Christian Doctrines*, p. 132, quoting Origen, *On Prayer*, 15.1.

33. Origen was indeed condemned two centuries after his death, but not so much for his subordinationist Christology as for his neo-Platonic cosmology and anthropology (the eternal existence of souls before birth, the souls of the bad angels located in the bodies of men, etc.).

34. Wiles, *Christian Fathers*, p. 39.

What have we taught and what do we teach? That the Son is not unbegotten or a portion of the unbegotten in any manner or from any substratum, but that by the will and counsel of the Father he subsisted before times and ages, full of grace and truth, God, only-begotten, unchangeable. And before he was begotten or created or defined or established, he was not. For he was not unbegotten.[35]

So the Son was both placed within the world of creation, yet established apart from and above creation because of his uniquely proximate relation to his Father, a place of proximation that to Arius seemed sanctioned by tradition, reason, and Scripture.

The Orthodox Synthesis: Nicea

Athanasius

Not, however, to Athanasius (c. 296-373), bishop of Alexandria. It fell to this extremely tenacious theologian to see the underlying tensions and problems in the previous century's subordinationist assumptions and to fight for their extirpation root and branch from the life of the church. For, according to Athanasius, the problem wasn't just Arius's tendency to put the most extreme formulations to an otherwise orthodox subordinationism. No, the whole subordinationist paradigm had to be completely rethought, for until that happened, the whole doctrinal point of the Christian religion was at stake:

To Athanasius, Arianism was not a misleading interpretation of Christianity; it was not Christianity at all. It could be Judaism with its solitary God; it could be Greek philosophy with its "unbegotten" replacing the Father God of the Bible; it could be Greek polytheism with its gods of different rank. The one thing it could not be was Christianity. Every Christian

---

35. Arius, *Letter to Eusebius of Nicomedia* in *The Trinitarian Controversy*, ed. and trans. William G. Rusch (Philadelphia: Fortress Press, 1980), pp. 29-30. Arius is even more apodictic here: "God being the cause of all is without beginning, most alone; but the Son, begotten by the Father, created and founded before the ages, was not before he was begotten. Rather, the Son begotten timelessly before everything, alone was caused to subsist by the Father. For he is not everlasting or co-everlasting or unbegotten with the Father." Arius, *Letter to Alexander of Alexandria* in Rusch, *Trinitarian Controversy*, p. 31. Note how Arius throughout equates the state of being begotten with the state of having been created, an equation the Nicene Creed will reject by calling the Son "begotten not made."

was baptized "in the name of the Father and of the Son and of the Holy Ghost"; was that one name a conjunction of beings of different orders of existence? Christian worship was offered to that same Trinity and prayer was regularly made to the Son; were Christians then guilty of worshipping a being of the created realm? Most important of all Christ was the Christian's Savior. Only a truly divine savior could save; only one who was divine absolutely and in his own right could impart to man a share in his own divine nature, could make them "partakers of the divine nature" (2 Peter 1:4) which was the essence of their salvation. Arianism spelt doom to all the religious values of Christianity; it was the death of the Christian religion. No true progress could be made unless it were absolutely and unequivocally rejected.[36]

And rejected it was. It was Arius's misfortune that he had to confront not only the adamantine opposition of Athanasius but, as well, the imperial opposition of the recently converted emperor, Constantine I (born c. 273-88; died 337). The polemical tracts hurled by Arius and Athanasius against each other were written in the early years of Constantine's reign. One of his main motivations in first legalizing the Christian religion and then making it the official religion of the realm was to bring unity and cohesion to a fractious and increasingly disintegrating empire, and so he did not appreciate the theological wrangling and attendant disunity that Arianism brought in its wake. This meant that the emperor saw concerted action by the church as a matter of state interest, which prompted him to convoke a council of bishops, the first so-called "ecumenical" (meaning "worldwide") council of the church, to meet in Nicea, a suburb of Constantinople. As expected, it condemned Arianism by promulgating a creed, the key lines of which are the statements that the Son is "one in substance" *(homoousios)* with the Father, that he is "true God from true God" (and therefore not a secondary kind of god), and finally was "begotten not made," thereby rejecting Arius's conflation of those two terms.[37]

Because Arianism grew out of, and indeed drew much of its plausibility from, the condemnation of modalism,[38] the condemnation of Arius left the

36. Wiles, *Christian Fathers,* pp. 40-41.

37. The Nicene Creed recited at Mass on Sunday actually comes from the later Council of Constantinople in 381, but this version retains all the key anti-Arian phrases of Nicea and so is aptly named the Nicene Creed.

38. "It was natural that in reaction to Sabellianism the theological pendulum would swing in the opposite direction. Those who saw the inadequacy of Patripassianism tried to

church with an unresolved problem: Nicea said that both Father and Son are God in the full sense of that word, but there still must be only one God. How could that be done without slipping back into modalism, which said that Father and Son are just different aspects or modes of one substantial deity?[39] In other words, was Nicea silently conceding that the modalists had a point? (No wonder, then, that Arianism lasted so long after Nicea and why it took so long for *homoousios* to win out.[40])

The Cappadocians

It was largely left to the so-called Cappadocian fathers — Basil of Caesarea (c. 330-379), his brother Gregory of Nyssa (c. 330–c. 395), and their mutual friend Gregory of Nazianzus (329/30–389/90) — to work out this problem. Because this chapter intends to give a survey of patristic Christology, while touching on trinitarian issues only insofar as they affect Christology, the exact contours of Cappadocian trinitarian theology need not detain us here. But because the Cappadocians made some important terminological distinctions that became absolutely essential in later christological teaching, a brief account of their terminological innovations must be mentioned here, even if space prevents giving a full account of their reasoning.

They first began by realizing that the controversies surrounding the sameness in essence between Father and Son had to apply to the Holy Spirit as well. After all, each believer was baptized in the name of Father, Son, and

bring out as sharply as possible the distinctions between the Father and the Son, to the point of either separating the divine hypostases . . . or of diminishing the Son's divine status before that of the Father." Paul L. Gavrilyuk, *The Suffering of the Impassible God: The Dialectics of Patristic Thought* (Oxford: Oxford University Press, 2004), p. 101.

39. "The fact that anti-Nicene literature is full of polemical references to Sabellianism indicates that these theologians worked out their subordinationist views in conscious opposition to the Monarchian extreme. Arius believed that one of the strongest sides of their position was that it successfully avoided the self-evidently heretical Sabellianism. By implication, they regarded their pro-Nicene opponents as failing to offer a serious logical alternative either to Sabellianism or to tritheism." Gavrilyuk, *Impassible God*, p. 102.

40. Jerome (c. 345-420), looking back on these debates three quarters of a century later, made a famous remark: "The whole world groaned and marveled to find itself Arian" (*Dialogue against the Luciferians*, 19). The classical treatment of the pervasiveness and seeming plausibility of Arianism and the difficulties of the orthodox party to root it out in this period is John Henry Newman's *The Arians of the Fourth Century* (Notre Dame: University of Notre Dame Press, 2001/1833).

Spirit equally; so the Spirit had a saving function too, which implied his full divinity. For his work of sanctification was nothing less than the imparting of Christ's divine life into the human life of the believer, so that if the Spirit were divine in a secondary (or worse, in a tertiary) sense in the manner of the Arians, our sanctification would be threatened, just as our salvation had been in Arianism proper. But if modalism was to be avoided, a way had to be found to establish a legitimate *distinction* within the Godhead *without lapsing into Arianism.*

It was Basil who saw the way out by distinguishing between *ousia* and *hypostasis.* The trouble is, *hypostasis* literally means that-which-stands-under, or in other words, sub-stance. Unfortunately, the Latin word for sub-stance, *substantia,* was the word usually chosen to translate the Greek *ousia,* as in the Latin version of the Nicene Creed, which translates *homoousios* as "consubstantial."[41]

Conversely, through Tertullian the preferred Latin term for the Basilian *hypostasis* was *persona,* a theatrical term meaning "mask," which carries a certain vaguely modalistic connotation (since a mask can be donned and doffed at will) and is in any event far from what is conveyed by the word "substance."[42] This terminological confusion began a process of divergent emphases between Greek and Latin trinitarian theologies that would eventually, much later, become church-dividing.[43]

41. See the Glossary of Technical Terms for further details.

42. Although too much can be read into these translation issues because of later history. In fact the Cappadocians used *hypostasis* and *prosōpon* interchangeably, especially Basil: "Because of his synthesis, Basil is often credited with having enshrined a Trinitarian formula that would be the hallmark of orthodoxy for Greek speakers for ages to come, but his accomplishment is more complicated than that. . . . [His] use of *prosōpon* and *hypostasis* . . . prevents us from considering Basil's thought inflexible." Stephen M. Hildebrand, *The Trinitarian Theology of Basil of Caesarea* (Washington, DC: Catholic University of America Press, 2007), p. 99. Moreover, as is often recognized, the concept of person changed because of this terminological interchangeability and eventually took on the more "substantial" meaning we know today: "[T]he ancients did not have a notion of person before the Cappadocians." Lucian Turescu, *Gregory of Nyssa and the Concept of Divine Persons* (Oxford: Oxford University Press, 2005), p. 7.

43. That said, the reader must take most seriously the charge of Lewis Ayres that the differences in trinitarian theology between the Cappadocians and Augustine have been way overdrawn by later historians: ". . . the use of an extended social analogy (by which I mean the use of three human persons as an analogy for the Trinity . . .) is extremely rare [among Eastern theologians] and — to be provocative — is as common in Augustine as it is in any of the Cappadocians." Lewis Ayres, "*Nicea and Its Legacy:* An Introduction," *Harvard Theological Review* 100, no. 2 (2007): 143. This counterintuitive, revisionist thesis is fully set out in his

But none of these issues were part of the Cappadocians' problematic. Their concern was to maintain the unity of the Godhead while granting a proper distinctiveness in the Persons, and this they did through their distinction between essence and hypostasis.[44] Again, the arguments adduced to make legitimate this distinction cannot detain us, but its import for Christology should now be clear: *insofar as Jesus was worshiped as divine, his divinity could no longer be conceived in lesser terms than the Father's divinity.* For in Athanasian and Cappadocian theology, the Father begot the Son without stint, bestowing upon the Son the entirety of the divine essence. Jesus' divinity was henceforth to be understood as a *substantial* divinity, differing not in the slightest (literally not even by one iota!) from the divinity of God the Father.[45]

---

book *Nicea and Its Legacy: An Approach to Fourth-Century Trinitarian Theology* (Oxford: Oxford University Press, 2004).

44. Wiles effectively refutes charges of Cappadocian "tritheism" here: "The different persons are never to be thought of in separation from one another. None ever acts apart from the others. We ought not to think of a Father who made us, a Son who redeemed us and a Holy Spirit who sanctifies us, for every act of God is an act of the whole and undivided Trinity. So after a time it may come to seem that far from being tritheists they are really unitarians or Sabellians denying the reality of the distinctions between the persons. Like many another thinker since, the Cappadocians rejoiced in the fact that they were attacked from both sides. They saw in it confirmation that the path they were following was the right one. The Christian view was the mean between Judaism and Hellenism; between monotheism on the one hand and popular polytheism on the other. If they were accused of underemphasizing the unity of God and also of destroying the distinctions of the persons, it was a sure sign that they had found the true *via media.*" Wiles, *Christian Fathers,* p. 47.

45. One reliable sign that a contemporary Christian is orthodox would be his ability to see the continued relevance of the Athanasian/Cappadocian achievement, something that G. K. Chesterton showed with his characteristic brilliance in this marvelous passage: "If there is one question which the enlightened and liberal have the habit of deriding and holding up as a dreadful example of barren dogmas and senseless sectarian strife, it is this Athanasian question of the Co-Eternity of the Divine Son. On the other hand, if there is one thing that the same liberals always offer us as a piece of pure and simple Christianity, untroubled by doctrinal disputes, it is this single sentence, 'God is love.' Yet the two statements are almost identical; at least one is very nearly nonsense without the other. The barren dogma is only the logical way of stating the beautiful sentiment. For if there be a being without beginning, existing before all things, was He loving when there was nothing to be loved? If through that unthinkable eternity He is lonely, what is the meaning of saying He is love? The only justification of such a mystery is the mystical conception that in His own nature there was something analogous to self-expression; something of what begets and beholds what it has begotten. Without some such idea, it is really illogical to complicate the ultimate essence of deity with an idea like love. If moderns really want a simple religion of love, they must look for it in the Athanasian Creed. The truth is that the trumpet of true Christianity,

Post-Nicene Christological Heresies

Logos-Sarx Christology (Apollinarianism)

It was inevitable that the Nicene Creed would reopen the question of Christology. For now, inasmuch as the divinity of Jesus had to be understood as fully divine, new questions were bound to arise as to how *that* kind of divinity, *full* divinity, related to the humanity of Jesus. In a sense, the subordinationists could deal with the simultaneous humanity and divinity in Jesus more easily, since by their lights his "divinity" (such as it was) was of a lower status than the Father's. But after Nicea that way was blocked.

One solution was what became known as Logos-Sarx ("Word-Flesh") Christology, which like subordinationism can sound orthodox, given its scriptural resonances ("The Word became flesh and dwelt among us": John 1:14). But a bishop of Laodicea by the name of Apollinaris (c. 310–c. 390) took this biblical terminology in a direction that proved unworkable, and therefore heretical. As we saw in Chapter 2, the Greek word *logos* cuts a very wide semantic swath and can mean not just "word" but "reason" and "rationality" as well. Since those latter meanings define the very essence of man,[46] Apollinaris held that the divine Logos *replaced* what would otherwise have been Christ's rational (human) soul.[47] But it is precisely the import of Nicea that the Logos could in no way differ essentially from all that appertains to the divinity of God as God, which would have to include immutability, omniscience, and impassivity. Yet do we not read in the Gospels that Jesus grew in age, *wisdom*, and grace (Luke 2:52)? And did not Jesus himself aver that

---

the challenge of the charities and simplicities of Bethlehem on Christmas Day, never rang out more arrestingly and unmistakably than in the defiance of Athanasius to the cold compromise of the Arians." G. K. Chesterton, *The Everlasting Man* (San Francisco: Ignatius Press, 1993/1925), pp. 227-28.

46. Aristotle's definition of man as "the rational animal" uses for "rational" the Greek word *logikos*.

47. "Therefore, the human race is saved not by [Christ's] assumption of an intellect and of a whole human being but by the assumption of flesh, whose nature is to be ruled. . . . In their irrational body, people are coessential with irrational animals, but insofar as they are rational [*logikoi*], they are of a different essence. So also God, who is coessential with men in his flesh, is of a different essence insofar as he is Logos and God." Apollinaris of Laodicea, *On the Union in Christ of the Body with the Godhead* in *The Christological Controversies*, trans. Richard A. Norris, Jr. (Philadelphia: Fortress, 1980), pp. 109, 111. Tellingly, Apollinaris claims that "it is inconceivable that the same person should be both God and entire man" (p. 108), another indication that the denial of christological paradox will lead to heresy.

"of that day or that hour [of final judgment] no one knows, not even the angels in heaven, *nor the Son,* but only the Father" (Mark 13:32)?

Apollinaris responded by invoking a distinction inherited from Platonic psychology, one that posited a three-tiered hierarchy of the soul: the appetitive, the emotional, and the rational. With that distinction in mind, he conceded that Christ had assumed the lower parts of the soul (which would allow him to feel his sufferings), but that the highest, rational part was replaced by the Logos.[48] Gregory of Nazianzus, however, responded that this schema would threaten the means of salvation. Previously that rubric had been invoked by Athanasius against Arius to defend the full divinity of Jesus; but now it was being invoked to defend Christ's full humanity: if Christ lacked a full human reason, then precisely the highest part of the human soul (the very faculty by which Adam and Eve had sinned) has not been united with God — and therefore has not been saved. As Gregory put it in words that have since become a standard for all subsequent Christologies that seek to defend the full humanity of Christ: "For what he has not assumed he has not healed; but what is united to his Godhead is thereby saved."[49] This argument won the day, and Apollinaris was condemned in the First Council of Constantinople in 381.

Two-Natures Christology (Nestorianism)

The Council's decree perforce shifted the debate to a new level, because now it seemed that, with a fully human and rational soul ascribed to him, Christ possessed two self-subsistent centers of subjectivity, two "consciousnesses," so to speak.[50] The problem was further exacerbated by the radically disjunctive differences between the two natures, human and divine: God is immuta-

48. "He is not a human being but is like a human being, since he is not coessential with humanity in his highest part." Apollinaris, *On the Union in Christ,* in Norris, p. 109. Note the similarity with docetism on this point that Christ is only "like" a human but not really one (although, of course, Apollinaris accepted the reality of Christ's flesh).

49. Gregory of Nazianzus, *Letter 101* (to Cledonius the priest against Apollinaris), trans. Charles Gordon Browne and James Edward Swallow, in *A Select Library of the Nicene and Post-Nicene Fathers,* 2nd series, vol. 7 (London: Christian Literature Co., 1894), p. 440.

50. Of course that begs the question whether it is appropriate to speak of God having a "consciousness" at all, since that word implies a certain discursiveness across a span of time, which cannot apply to God. But prayer to God clearly implies a personal addressee, so the conceptual problem still remains, however analogously one treats God's personhood — or "consciousness."

ble, humanity is mutable; God is immortal, man is mortal; God is free from passivity and suffering, while it is man's lot to suffer and to endure the onslaughts of his environment. In other words, only certain predicates can be legitimately applied to God, while their opposite terms belong to humanity.

Thus began the school known as Two-Natures Christology, which soon led to the heresy known as Nestorianism, named after the patriarch of Constantinople, Nestorius (born after 351, died after 451).[51] An earlier opponent of Apollinaris, Theodore of Mopsuestia (c. 350-428), had initiated the Two-Natures theory in a way hardly distinguishable from Nestorius's views; but it was Nestorius who provoked the controversy and subsequently merited condemnation when he refused to countenance the title given to Mary in the church's worship, *Theotokos* ("God-bearer" or "Mother of God").[52]

---

51. Notice how names of earlier heresies have both an abstract name (like "modalism") and a proper name derived from their main advocates ("Sabellianism"). But as things proceed the abstract name need not *necessarily* imply heresy, only the proper name. Thus there can be an orthodox version of subordinationism ("The Father is greater than I") and a heretical one, which goes by the proper name ("Arianism"). *Pari passu,* there can be an orthodox Logos-Sarx Christology ("The Word was made flesh") and a heretical one, as advocated by Apollinaris. Similarly, there is an orthodox Two-Natures Christology (the one validated by the Council of Chalcedon) and a heretical one, as advocated by Nestorius. One should therefore use the proper name when speaking of these specifically condemned heresies. To add to the terminological mix, followers, both orthodox and heretical, of Logos-Sarx Christology are called Alexandrians (or Alexandrines) because that is where that school was most popular, while followers of a more Nestorian bent were called Antiochenes (or Antiochians) for similar reasons. But since Apollinaris was bishop of Laodicea (in Asia Minor) and Nestorius was most active as a controversialist in Constantinople, these terms should not imply any sense of geographical determinism. Plus, as Cyril of Alexandria proves, one can be "Alexandrian" and fully orthodox, just as the "Antiochene" advocates of Chalcedon's two-natures terminology were orthodox, even if the Nestorian rejecters of Chalcedon were not. Recall here the wise words of John O'Keefe: "Indeed, for decades students of patristic exegesis have distinguished sharply between the historically-minded Antiochenes and the 'allegorizing' Alexandrians. . . . Fortunately this way of understanding ancient exegesis has been seriously challenged. Not only is it misleading to distinguish rigidly between Antioch and Alexandria, but it is anachronistic." John J. O'Keefe, "Introduction," in *Cyril of Alexandria: The Festal Letters 1-12,* trans. Philip R. Amidon, S.J., edited with introduction and notes by John J. O'Keefe (Washington, DC: Catholic University of America Press, 2009), pp. 3-32, here 9.

52. Modern scholarship of course properly wants to ask if the historical Theodore (or even the historical Nestorius, for that matter) was a true "Nestorian" and thus merited his condemnation by the Fifth Ecumenical Council (Constantinople II meeting in 553). Some accuse him of making Christ a fit Savior for Pelagian man, while others see him as the forerunner of Maximus the Confessor (treated at the end of this chapter): "Christ, for Theodore,

According to Theodore, predicates pertaining to the divinity could only be applied to the divinity, and predicates pertaining to the humanity could only be applied to the humanity. Thus, for example, when Christ wept or feared his imminent death, that was his human nature at work; but when he performed miracles or forgave sinners, that was his divine nature at work. But taken to extremes, Theodore's exegesis of scriptural passages could prove bizarre: Thus when Jesus said "I come from the Father," that was his divinity speaking; but when he said "I return to the Father," that was his humanity speaking:

> The expression *I have gone out from the Father,* as I have said, can be understood of the Divinity . . . but plainly can in no way be taken of the assumed Man. On the other hand, the expression *I leave and return to the Father* can in no wise be said of the Divinity. But it can be said of the Man. Therefore, it is impossible for both of the expressions at once to be taken of one of the natures; the two together fit neither God the Word nor the Man. But according to the sense we have set forth, the first befits the Divinity, the other the assumed Man.[53]

The obvious trouble with these views is that the Gospels in no way give the impression that Jesus speaks out of anything less than a fully integrated center of personality or consciousness. True, Theodore recognized the problem; and like his near-contemporaries, the Cappadocians, he developed a distinctive terminology to resolve his difficulties: Christ, he said, had two na-

---

is the one in whom God the Word achieves the redemption of humanity in the free activity of a perfectly obedient Man. . . . What is done in Christ must, for him, be the work of the free human will; and therefore he must emphasize the 'personal' character of Christ's manhood, the reality of his human soul, which is the subject of the obedience by which the world is redeemed." R. A. Norris, *Manhood and Christ: A Study in the Christology of Theodore of Mopsuestia* (Oxford: Clarendon Press, 1963), p. 237.

53. Theodore of Mopsuestia, *Commentary on the Gospel of John,* at John 16:28; in J. M. Vosté, *Theodori Mopsuesteni Commentarius in Evangelium Johannis Apostoli.* Corpus Scriptorum Christianorum Orientalium, series 4, vol. 3 (Louvain, 1940), p. 217, cited with translation in Norris, *Manhood and Christ,* p. 199. Theodore also ran aground at John 10:30 ("I and the Father are one"). As one scholar points out: "Theodore must have been perplexed by such a clear statement, as well as others in John's Gospel, particularly that 'the Word became flesh' (John 1:14), suggesting a substantial unity between Jesus' humanity and the Father. This ran counter to his theological conviction that the Infinite God cannot be joined to a finite creature. His reply illustrates how his mindset affected his exegesis." Frederick G. McLeod, S.J., "Theodore of Mopsuestia Revisited," *Theological Studies* 61 (September 2000): 447-80; here 467.

tures (Greek: *physeis;* singular: *physis*) in one person *(prosōpon)*. This would prove, with modifications, to be the terminology that would be adopted at the Council of Chalcedon several decades later (451).[54] But by no means did that Council mean to affirm Theodore's Christology, something that Nestorius would ensure with his attack on Mary's divine motherhood.

Nestorius of course was doing no more to Mary than Theodore had done to Christ: carefully dividing up the activities of Christ into their appropriate divine or human boxes. Unfortunately for Nestorius, he applied his basic methodology to a title that had entered liturgical practice for at least a century. That did not matter to him, for the logic was clear: Since Mary cannot give birth to a god (that for Nestorius would be pure paganism) but only to a human nature, she cannot be called the Mother of God. And so, in a notorious sermon, delivered on Christmas Day (!) no less in the Basilica of Constantinople, where he had just been installed as patriarch, he forbade the use of the title.

The patriarch's attack, besides understandably upsetting the devout, uncovered the basic untenability of Theodore's views. The problem here is: natures are abstractions that don't exist outside of individuals having that nature (no lionhood, in other words, without lions). As a moment's reflection will demonstrate, predicates don't apply to natures but to *things,* as Aristotle taught.[55] At a stroke, this insight undercuts Theodore's exegetical method

54. And with good reason: "The Arians attributed all the human frailties of Christ to the nature of the Logos and thereby tried to prove His created and inferior status. St. Athanasius attacked the Arians by maintaining on the one hand the traditional attribution of all human properties and activities to the Logos, but on the other hand he made a clear distinction [as would Chalcedon later] between the Word in His uncreated nature and the Same Word united to humanity by means of His Birth from the Virgin." John S. Romanides, "Highlights in the Debate over Theodore of Mopsuestia's Christology and Some Suggestions for a Fresh Approach," *The Greek Orthodox Historical Review* 5, no. 1 (Summer 1959): 140-85; here 144.

55. As here: "*White* signifies nothing but a qualification." Aristotle, *Categories* 3b1. In other words, natures (in that abstract sense) are just a description of the range of predicates that are possible for an individual of that particular form to have. In modern terms: "There is no special realm where redness resides: it exists in the here and now, and consists in the redness of particular things. . . . Aristotle's point . . . is to remind us that general terms acquire their meaning in the description of particular things. If we learned them by applying them in the abstract realm, then our thoughts would stay in that realm, and never descend to earth. But it is only in their concrete application that terms like 'red' can be understood, [a] role quite different from the one implied by Plato." Roger Scruton, *Modern Philosophy: An Introduction and Survey* (New York: Penguin Books USA, 1994), pp. 89-90. Perhaps, once again, it was the overweening influence of Plato that was jimmying the debate here, as it did with Origen earlier.

utterly. One cannot predicate weeping to the humanity of Jesus, because it is not Jesus' humanness that is weeping — *he* is. Humanhood can't weep anymore than lionhood can roar.

No wonder Nestorius got into such trouble. For it wasn't just piety, but logic too, that was offended when he said Mary could not be called *Theotokos* ("God-bearer" or "Mother of God"), since for him Mary was really only the Mother of Christ's human nature.[56] But no human mother gives birth to a human *nature*, only to a human *baby*. No wonder Jesus said the simple and unlettered would understand his true identity better than the learned and the clever, since they were the ones who instinctively knew this elementary truth, whereas the patriarch of Constantinople was in the meantime trying to show why the term "Mother of God" was pagan, since the gods too had mothers!

Cyril of Alexandria and the Road to Chalcedon

As Arius met his match, and more, in Athanasius, Nestorius more than found his in Cyril, patriarch of Alexandria (c. 378-444), an unbending opponent whose very tenacity on behalf of true doctrine often lapsed into tyrannical irascibility, at least according to his enemies.[57] Nor has Cyril ever quite

56. Origen's problem, as we have already seen, was that he had a *wrong* metaphysics, Plato's; Nestorius's that he had *no* metaphysics, a point noticed to devastating effect by Aloys Grillmeier: "Nestorius would seem not to see fully the metaphysical structure of this word 'Christ.' He does not show that the Logos is subject as the bearer of both the divinity and humanity. Instead, he regards 'Christ' superficially only as the sum of the two natures and sees these in turn merely as a collection of qualitative expressions. . . . He thus reduces the subject 'Christ' to the sum of the two natures and only rarely leaves room to consider the bearer, the subject of these natures. This preference of Nestorius for 'nature' instead of 'subject' or 'person' seems to be decisive. . . . But at this very point, just where we seem [most to need from him] an ontological analysis, Nestorius explicitly remarks that he is concerned with semantics and does not mean to make ontological statements." Aloys Grillmeier, S.J., *Christ in Christian Tradition*, vol. 1: *From the Apostolic Age to Chalcedon (451)*, 2nd revised ed., trans. John Bowden (Atlanta: John Knox Press, 1975), pp. 454-55. Thus Nestorius proves that philosophy is *necessary*, while Origen proves that only the *right* philosophy will do.

57. Prestige offers an amusing example: "Cyril . . . was one of those active and strong characters that excite the animosity of less successful controversialists. When his death was announced, in the year 444, one of his critics wrote a letter to a friend, from which the following sentences are quoted: 'At last with a final struggle the villain has passed away. . . . His departure delights the survivors, but possibly disheartens the dead; there is some fear that under the provocation of his company they may send him back again to us. . . . Care must

managed to live down the reputation bequeathed to him by no less a light than Edward Gibbon, who wrote of Cyril's ecclesiastical ruthlessness in these unflattering but typically elegant terms (he is speaking here of Cyril's campaign to drive the Jews out of his diocese):

> Without any legal sentence, without any royal mandate, the patriarch, at the dawn of day, led a seditious multitude to the attack of the synagogues. Unarmed and unprepared, the Jews were incapable of resistance; their houses of prayer were leveled with the ground, and the episcopal warrior, after rewarding his troops with the plunder of their goods, expelled from the city the remnant of the unbelieving nation. Perhaps he might plead the insolence of their prosperity, and their deadly hatred of the Christians, whose blood they had recently shed in a malicious or accidental tumult. Such crimes would have deserved the animadversion of the magistrate; but in this promiscuous outrage, the innocent were confounded with the guilty, and Alexandria was impoverished by the loss of a wealthy and industrious colony.[58]

The author of this book has no wish to exonerate Cyril from these charges of fanaticism, except perhaps to recall the wise words of Cyril's most astute biographer, John McGuckin:

> Nestorius was no less "dogmatic," uncompromising, and ready to use the full extent of his powers, both political and canonical, than Cyril or any of the other leading hierarchs of this period.[59] . . . To cast the ancient hierarchs in the mould of twentieth-century western European gentlemanly churchmanship is a peculiarly misinformed canon of judgment.[60]

---

therefore be taken to order the guild of undertakers to place a very big and heavy stone on his grave to stop him coming back here'. . . . [This letter] offers striking testimony to Cyril's greatness. Small men do not earn such heartfelt obituaries, even from deeply indignant men." Prestige, *Fathers and Heretics*, p. 150.

58. Edward Gibbon, *The History of the Decline and Fall of the Roman Empire*, vol. 2, ed. David Womersley (London: Allen Lane/Penguin Press, 1994), p. 944. For those with other editions, the passage occurs in the fourth volume of the original edition (1788), ch. xlvii.

59. Gibbon would certainly agree with *that* part of McGuckin's assessment of Nestorius: "Humanity may drop a tear on the fate of Nestorius: yet justice must observe, that he suffered the persecution which he had approved and inflicted" (p. 956).

60. John McGuckin, *Saint Cyril of Alexandria and the Christological Controversy: Its History, Theology, and Texts* (Crestwood, NY: St. Vladimir's Seminary Press, 2004), p. 21. And in a passage that recalls Henri de Lubac's line about the intolerance of those who keep congratulating themselves on their tolerance, McGuckin adds this crucial point: "The contexts

Much more to the point is this crucial difference between Cyril and Nestorius: Cyril saw his theology in terms of its service to liturgical piety, while Nestorius, as we noted above, thought theology (and a singularly inept and metaphysically obtuse theology at that) should dictate to the People of God proper liturgical practice:

> [Cyril] was determined to draw water from the deep wells of popular Christian piety, wishing to communicate a sense of the immediacy of the presence and power of his divine Lord, whose presence, as for example in the eucharistic mysteries, or in the healing virtues of the sacred relics of the martyrs, depended first and foremost on the immediacy and validity of the divine presence in the Incarnate One. For Cyril, the elevated intellectual argument about christology and the validity and security of a simple Christian life were ultimately one.[61]

But back to the specifics of the christological debate: after Apollinarianism was condemned in 381, the way seemed clear for the Antiochenes to posit both a human mind and a divine Logos in the constitution of Jesus, both of which were sitting juxtaposed behind a kind of "mask" (the original meaning of *prosōpon*). But who then was the "I" that spoke the words "I thirst"? Was it a different "I" from the one that said "Before Abraham was, I am"? Clearly some way out had to be found to avoid Nestorian schizophrenia.

It was the great merit of Cyril, often in the heat of battle with Nestorius, to point the way to a solution to this great riddle. Cyril's first move was to deny the symmetry of the contrary theses of Apollinaris and Nestorius.

---

and agendas of liberal ecumenism do not accurately convey the realities of fifth-century Alexandria. It is a matter of some debate whether, in the face of innumerable examples [of religiously motivated violence today], ranging from Israel to Northern Ireland, Yugoslavia, Sri Lanka, Russia, Cambodia (the list is endless), whether those contexts can even be said accurately to describe the realities of religions and politics in the late twentieth century either" (p. 9).

61. McGuckin, *Cyril*, p. 19. Recall Chesterton's remarks about the connection between the Nicene Creed and Christian piety. Moreover, Cyril was first and foremost an exegete of the Bible before he was a theologian: "Cyril was not only a controversial theologian, he was also a biblical commentator, one of the greatest in Christian antiquity. This Cyril, the exegete, has been largely neglected. In his commentaries on the Bible one discovers a man whose mind and soul were shaped by the rhythms of biblical narrative, and whose thinking was permeated with the Bible's language and imagery. . . . Cyril's works filled ten volumes of the [*Patrologia Graeca*], volumes 68-77. The first seven volumes are all exegetical." Robert L. Wilken, "St. Cyril of Alexandria: The Mystery of Christ in the Bible," *Pro Ecclesia* 4 (Fall 1995): 454-78; here 455.

Rather he saw Apollinaris as someone who started with the right presupposition ("Christ" referred to a single subject) but fell into error later because of a false view of the human soul, whereas Nestorius was utterly confused from the beginning.[62] As he pointed out to those who accused him at every turn of being Apollinarist: "Not everything a heretic says is necessarily heretical."[63] Secondly, he focused not so much on the philosophical conundrum entailed by the incarnation but on God's purpose in sending his Son to die in our place. As McGuckin lucidly summarizes Cyril here:

> This is the way he answers two key questions about the incarnation: "Why did it happen?", and, "How did it happen?" To both queries he replies: "As an economy of salvation." To say that the Logos was born is, for Cyril, not the nonsense Nestorius thought it to be, any more than to say the Logos suffered or died, because the apparent paradox brings home to the believer the constantly presumed context — that these things, birth, suffering, death, and resurrection, took place "economically," that is, as a practical exercise of the Logos who assumed a human bodily life not pointlessly but in order to work out the salvation of the human race in and through that bodily condition.[64]

Cyril, in other words, introduced a distinction that has continued to play a crucial role in theology down to the present: between what would later come to be called the "immanent" and the "economic" Trinity, a distinction that allows for the Son to be both fully consubstantial with the Father and yet also hypostatically united to the human nature without his divine identity lapsing into modalism and thereby patripassianism. Nestorius had agreed that Christ's suffering and death on the cross were salvific; but ac-

62. One thinks here of Athanasius' crucial insight that everything about the subordinationist system had to be undone before progress could be made on the trinitarian front: better modalism than subordinationism, although both were wrong, if in different ways.

63. Cyril, *Letter to Eulogius*, paragraph 1. The letter is translated in full in McGuckin, *Cyril*, pp. 349-51.

64. McGuckin, *Cyril*, p. 184. This stress is on soteriology is a consistent Alexandrine motif and emerges already in Athanasius: "The Word perceived that corruption could not be got rid of otherwise than through death; yet He Himself, as the Word, being immortal and the Father's Son, was such as could not die. For this reason, therefore, He assumed a body capable of death, in order that it, because it belongs to the Word who is above all, might become in dying a sufficient exchange for all, and, itself remaining incorruptible through his indwelling, might thereafter put an end to corruption for all others as well, by the grace of the resurrection." Athanasius, *On the Incarnation*, translated by a Religious of the C.S.M.V. (Crestwood, NY: St. Vladimir's Seminary Press, 1953), p. 35.

cording to his presuppositions and methodology, that suffering and death could only apply to the human nature and not to the divinity. But what is saving about that? It is after all part of the nature of man to die (1 Cor. 15:42-50); and so it can never be the office of a mere man to bring salvation from sin and death. But nor can God suffer or die. God's inherent impassibility was the central axiom that spelled ruin for Apollinaris: if the sole locus of the inner life of the incarnate Christ was the divine Logos, then it seemed one either has to affirm that the "true God from true God" feared death, admitted ignorance, and wept for his friend Lazarus *or* one has to concede that Arius was right, that the Logos was not divine in the fullest sense of the word.

The dilemma that needed addressing, then, was first that, against the extreme position of Apollinaris, the Word had to assume not just flesh, the material "stuff" of humanity, but in doing so had to become a full man.[65] In other words, "becoming" meant that the Son of God must actually come to exist as a man. On the other hand, to ward off Nestorian objections that he was mixing and confusing the natures by positing a fusion of humanity and divinity, Cyril had to insist that the Word was not *transformed* into flesh the way, for example, a caterpillar changes into a butterfly, a metamorphosis whereby the caterpillar ceases to exist. "Rather," as Thomas Weinandy explains, "the 'becoming' established an *ontological* union but one that did not involve any change in the Word, for the Word can actually be said, after the 'becoming,' to dwell among us as a man."[66]

65. So why didn't John say "the Word became *man*" instead of "the Word became *flesh*"? That was the crux of Apollinaris's argument, which Cyril answered by insisting that John meant "man" in that verse but was emphasizing the weakness, vulnerability, and woundedness of the fallen human race and that it was precisely this fallen humanity that the Word needed to assume if he were to heal those wounds and weaknesses: "That, in my opinion, is the most probable reason why the holy Evangelist, indicating the whole living being by the part affected, says that the Word of God became flesh. It is so that we might see side by side the wound together with the remedy, the patient together with the physician, what sank towards death together with him who raised it up to life, . . . that which has been mastered by death together with him who conquered death, what was bereft of life with him who was the provider of life. He does not say that the Word *came into* flesh; he says he *became* flesh in order to exclude any idea of a relative indwelling, as in the case of the prophets and the other saints. He really did become flesh, that is to say, a human being." Cyril of Alexandria, *Commentary on John*, at John 1:14a, in *Cyril of Alexandria*, trans. N. Russell (London: Routledge, 2000), pp. 105-6; italics added.

66. Thomas Weinandy, OFM, Cap, "Cyril and the Mystery of the Incarnation," in *The Theology of St Cyril of Alexandria: A Critical Appreciation,* ed. Thomas G. Weinandy, OFM, Cap., and Daniel A. Keating (London: T. & T. Clark, 2003), p. 28; emphasis added.

By an inexorable logic this leads Cyril to the other great innovation for which he is known: the "interchange of predicates" (Latin: *communicatio idiomatum*). The logic goes as follows: because the Logos *became* man without having been *transformed* into a man, the Logos remains as the *subject* ("hypostasis") of the Incarnation. But since the Son genuinely *became* man rather than merely *assumed flesh* as an outer vesture, we can ascribe the properties, attributes, and predicates appropriate to the humanity of Jesus (including of course the elements that make up the essence of a human soul) to the hypostasis of the Son (hence the term "hypostatic union"). So when Jesus died, we can say God the Son died; and conversely, all the properties, attributes, and predicates of the divine Logos could be ascribed to the man Jesus, so that one can truly say that Jesus is God and therefore Mary is the Mother of God.[67]

Cyril had actually already worked out these concepts in his commentary on John's Gospel, that is, before he began tussling with Nestorius; but these exegetical efforts, worked out in a nonpolemical framework in more serene times, later served him admirably in his debates with the Nestorians and gave him the conceptual armory necessary to secure Nestorius's condemnation at the Council of Ephesus in 431, which declared Mary to be the Mother of God.

---

67. Everyone admits that the decree of Ephesus declaring Mary to be the Mother of God was meant to refute a christological heresy, not to define mariological doctrine, but of course its influence on the latter was immense, and properly so. The same connection between piety, simplicity, and conciliar decrees can also be seen in the unanimity of church teaching that Mary remained a virgin after giving birth to Jesus virginally (the Councils regularly refer to Mary as *ever*-Virgin). Although not technically a part of Christology, the doctrine of Mary's perpetual virginity does create a lovely symmetry with the Annunciation (when Christ first became flesh), as Tertullian saw: "God recovered His own image and likeness, of which He had been robbed by the devil. For it was while Eve was yet a virgin that the ensnaring word had crept into her ear which was to build the edifice of death. Into a virgin's soul, in like manner, must be introduced that Word of God which was to raise the fabric of life; so that what had been reduced to ruin by the female sex might by the selfsame sex be recovered to salvation. As Eve had believed the serpent, so Mary believed the angel. The delinquency which the one occasioned by believing [the serpent], the other by believing [the angel] effaced." Tertullian, *On the Flesh of Christ,* chapter 17; quoted in *The Teachings of the Church Fathers,* ed. John R. Willis, S.J. (San Francisco: Ignatius Press, 2002), p. 357. Augustine too holds that Mary's freedom to say Yes to the angel entailed her perpetual virginity: "Thus Christ, by being born of a virgin — who, before she knew who was to be born of her, had determined to continue a virgin — chose rather to approve, than to command, holy virginity. And so even in the woman herself, in whose womb he took the form of a servant, he willed that virginity should be free." Augustine, *On Holy Virginity,* Chapter 4:4; quoted in Willis, p. 361.

At that crucial moment in the history of the church, Cyril's Christology was assured in all its essential contours as fully orthodox. Not only was Nestorius refuted, but the paradoxes of Cyrillian Christology were given a specifically dogmatic and philosophical foundation, again as McGuckin explains:

> Cyril insists that while of itself human nature is not powerful but passible, in its union with the Godhead, as in the dynamic act of incarnation, the human nature of the Logos thereby becomes an instrument of omnipotent power and thus, in a real though paradoxical sense, an "omnipotent instrument." It is at once powerful and fragile, majestic and humble. Cyril loved to press the force of this economy by the use of strong paradoxes. One of his favorites was "The Logos suffered impassibly."[68]

For this reason, Cyril's Christology is often called "theopaschism," meaning that God suffered. But wasn't that precisely the heresy condemned earlier as patripassianism? No, because now the suffering of the Logos is understood paradoxically, not univocally, and that by virtue of the hypostatic union: because Jesus suffered, who is not two subjects but one, and that subject is the hypostasis of the Second Person of the Blessed Trinity, the Subject may be said to have suffered even if the Logos by nature cannot suffer. Hence: "The Logos suffered impassibly." Gavrilyuk agrees: "Thus, according to Cyril, the statements 'God wept' or 'God was crucified' were theologically legitimate, as long as it was added that the subject was God-in-the-flesh, and not God outside the framework of the incarnation."[69] Or, as another scholar puts it:

> [In Cyril] the fully divine Nicene Son seemed to suffer. It is not a very large step to overt theopaschite language, yet Cyril avoided that. Nonetheless he leaned in the direction of the narrative and gave it a privileged place in his thought. The narrative of the Incarnation, not the notion of impassibility, drove his Christology. This put Cyril in the awkward position of having to resort to paradoxical language to express how God the Son could both suffer and not suffer. According to Cyril, the only way to articulate this mystery was to say that the Son "suffered impassibly."[70]

68. McGuckin, *Cyril*, p. 185.

69. Gavrilyuk, *Suffering of the Impassible God*, p. 156.

70. John J. O'Keefe, "Impassible Suffering? Divine Passion and Fifth-Century Christology," *Theological Studies* 58 (1997): 39-60; here 51. O'Keefe stresses a further paradox (at least as far as the reception-history of Cyril against the Nestorians is concerned): *Cyril* ended up defending the humanity of Christ better than the Nestorians! "Nestorius [was] not inter-

If theopaschism sounds odd in the wake of the condemnation of modalism, one should recall that Paul too preached a kind of theopaschism: "None of the rulers of this age understood this; for if they had, they would not have *crucified the Lord of glory*" (1 Cor. 2:8).

Monophysitism

Unfortunately, certain ambiguities in his thought, as well as his death in 444, led to an exaggerated version of Cyril's position, which goes under the rather lumpy name of "monophysitism," meaning One-Nature Christology.[71] In some of his writings, Cyril so wanted to stress the oneness of Christ as a person that he would admit that Christ was not just one individual *(hypostasis)* yet also had, *after* the Incarnation, one nature *(physis)* only. But under the onslaughts of Nestorian polemic (which continued on, of course, as these things always do, after the Council of Ephesus), Cyril gradually came to see that he had to speak of Christ as having two natures if the word "incarnation" was to have any meaning at all. But that concession began to rankle many of Cyril's less subtle supporters, both in Constantinople and in Alexandria — especially Eutyches (c. 378-454), the head of a monastery in the capital, and Dioscorus (died 454), Cyril's successor as patriarch in Alexandria.

These two hierarchs grew increasingly obstreperous, so that eventually Eutyches found himself deposed by the patriarch of Constantinople (after synodal action, which seems to indicate his unpopularity in the capital). But with support from the emperor, Theodosius II, the patriarch Dioscorus secured Eutyches' retrial and acquittal at the so-called Robber Council in Ephesus, in 449, which, besides vindicating Eutyches, also forbade any refer-

---

ested in history and the human Jesus. . . . Reflecting on the mystery of suffering, Annie Dillard asks the question, 'Does God touch the world at all?' Were Cyril to respond to this question, he would have to say yes. Nestorius, however, [was] not so sure. And many moderns would answer yes but not specify where God does touch the world" (pp. 59-60). The same can be said of Cyril's supposed rival, Leo the Great. See Geoffrey D. Dunn, "Divine Impassibility and Christology in the Christmas Homilies of Leo the Great," *Theological Studies* 62 (March 2001): 71-85. Notice again how the more orthodox the theologian, the better able he is to defend the notion of God's involvement in the world.

71. The term "monophysitism" represents an exception to the previous warning above that generic names do not necessarily represent heresies. There are no One-Nature theologians who are also orthodox. The proper name for this heresy is Eutychianism, from its chief exponent, Eutyches. The same applies to the heresy of monothelitism, taken up in the Excursus to this chapter.

ence to the two natures of Christ after the Incarnation.[72] So outrageous were the shenanigans of this Robber Council (Dioscorus had refused to let opposing speakers address the assembly, and Pope Leo's delegates had to flee Ephesus for their lives) that it provoked the orthodox party into action, helped by the fact that Theodosius died in 450 after a timely fall from his horse.[73]

The Council of Chalcedon

The new emperor, Marcian (392-457) by name, enjoyed excellent relations with Pope Leo, whose representatives had been so manhandled at Ephesus the year before, and so he lost no time in convoking another council, to convene in 451, this time at Chalcedon, a suburb of Constantinople in Asia Minor almost directly across from Byzantium.[74] The decree proved to be epochal in every way, setting the standard and the foundation for all subsequent christological teaching and theology. The relevant passages are:

> Following therefore the holy fathers, we confess one and the same our Lord Jesus Christ ["one and the same" guarantees the hypostatic union], and we all teach harmoniously [that he is] the same perfect in godhead, the same perfect in manhood, truly God and truly man, the same of a reasonable soul and body [thus condemning Apollinarianism], one in substance with the Father in godhead [against the Arians], and the same one in substance with us in humanity [against the docetists and monophysites], like us in all things except sin; begotten before the ages of the Father in godhead; the same in the last days and for our salvation of Mary the Virgin God-bearer [against Nestorius], in manhood, one and the same Christ, Son, Lord, only begotten; acknowledged *in* two natures [against Eutyches and the monophysites], which undergo no confusion, no

72. Convoked by the emperor Theodosius II, the same ruler who had convoked the Ephesian Council of 431, but he had by that time fallen under the influence of Eutyches. The term "Robber Council" comes from a line in one of Leo's letters (*Epistle 95*, to the next emperor's wife Pulcheria), in which he described this council as *non judicium, sed latrocinium:* "not a legal assembly, but a band of thieves."

73. Everything about the story of monophysitism is gripping and is told with appropriately dramatic flair in W. H. C. Frend, *The Rise of the Monophysite Movement: Chapters in the History of the Church in the Fifth and Sixth Centuries* (Cambridge: Cambridge University Press, 1972).

74. Marcian's interest can be seen in the fact that he appeared personally in the sixth session of the Council.

change, no division, no separation — the difference between the two natures being by no means taken away because of the union, but rather the distinctive character of each nature being preserved, combining in one person and hypostasis — not divided or separated into two persons [against Nestorius again], but one and the same Son and only-begotten God, Logos, Lord Jesus Christ.[75]

One reason for the vast influence of this decree is that it was assembled, as Jaroslav Pelikan rightly says, "almost entirely from stones that were already available," specifically from two letters of Cyril to the Nestorians and from the *Tome* of Leo, the very one that that great pope had sent to the earlier Robber Council. As to the relative weight that must be given to their respective contributions, again Pelikan gets it right when he says:

> Even though it may be statistically accurate to say that "the majority of the quotations comes from the letters of St. Cyril," the contributions of Leo's *Tome* were the decisive ones. . . . The formula [of the Council], like the *Tome*, condemned any notion of hypostatic union that would jeopardize "the differences of the natures" or would violate the rule that the union was accomplished "without confusion." At the same time it insisted that Christ not be "divided or separated into two persons," setting itself apart from any theology of the indwelling Logos that would make the Logos one person and the man assumed by him another person.[76]

But prescinding from the question of who contributed how much to what more significant line of the formula, the more crucial question is: Did Chalcedon resolve the debate? To which the answer must be: Yes and No.[77]

---

75. *Decrees of the Ecumenical Councils*, ed. Norman Tanner, S.J. (Washington, DC: Georgetown University Press, 1990), vol. 1, p. 86.

76. Jaroslav Pelikan, *The Emergence of the Catholic Tradition (100-600)*, vol. 1 of *The Christian Tradition: A History of the Development of Doctrine* (Chicago: University of Chicago Press, 1971), pp. 263-64. McGuckin denies this and claims that Cyril's was the more decisive contribution and that the Council only agreed with Leo because he agreed with Cyril; but this thesis is belied by the later behavior of the Alexandrine monophysites: if Chalcedon had been merely an exegesis of Cyril's theology, why did they object to Chalcedon so vociferously as to reject its teachings so strongly? Plus, Cyril did not like the term "person" (*prosōpon*) for specifying the subject of the unity of human and divine in Christ and preferred *hypostasis*; but Chalcedon used both. And Cyril usually spoke of the unity of Christ coming *from* the two natures, while the Antiochenes preferred to say Christ was united *in* two natures; and Chalcedon used "in," not "from."

77. And sometimes both at the same time: "It is not that the opponents of the Council

Yes, in the sense that it became the touchstone for orthodox reflection on the question of Christ's identity from then on out. No, in the sense that both Nestorians and monophysites knew themselves to be the target of the decree; and they both accordingly rejected it.[78] (Churches representing both traditions live on to this day.[79])

But what of the decree itself? What does it mean, what has it solved, and how does it still serve as the platform for all subsequent christological reflection? Does, for example, the fact that it was rejected by the extreme sides of the debate mean anything about the tenability of the decree?[80] As has been noted more than once by dogmatic historians, the purpose of the decree was

---

deny the reality of the properties of the Logos and the flesh in one Person of Jesus Christ, or that they do not recognize the difference of these two elements. Their point is that in these passages Leo so separates, and personalizes, what is divine and what is human in Christ that the hypostatic union is dissolved, and its place taken by a mere conjunction of the divine Logos and a Man." R. V. Sellers, *The Council of Chalcedon: A Historical and Doctrinal Survey* (London: SPCK, 1953), p. 266.

78. The Orthodox theologian John Meyendorff captures the ambiguous legacy of Chalcedon in these words: "The Council of Chalcedon opened a new era in the history of Eastern Christian thought. By its representative character, by the number of its participants, and by the scope of its debates, this assembly offered all the aspects that could be expected at that time from a true ecumenical council. Yet it caused within the Eastern Church a schism that endures to our own day." John Meyendorff, *Christ in Eastern Christian Thought* (Washington, DC: Corpus Books, 1969), p. 3.

79. Because Marcian and subsequent emperors enforced the decree by compulsion, the claim is often made that this imperial *force majeure* alienated the Nestorian and monophysite churches so much from the imperial sway that it made them less hostile toward (or even open to) the invading and allegedly more "tolerant" Islamic armies of the seventh century. If so, it was a blunder of the first order on the part of the regime in Constantinople, and even more on the part of the supposedly "welcoming" churches, who have paid a heavy price indeed for such a welcome, right down to today's headlines. One should always beware of those, especially invading foreign armies, that come under the banner of "tolerance" and "liberation."

80. Wiles points out how Chalcedon's need to condemn simultaneously two opposite extremes influenced the "reception-history," so to speak, of the decree: "The Alexandrians had traditionally protested that to describe the unity of Christ as one of 'prosopon' was to use so loose a term as to suggest it was not a real unity at all. The Antiochenes had similarly objected that to describe it as one of 'hypostasis' was to use so tight a term as to leave no room for the continuing distinction of natures. The difference is solved by treating the two terms as simple equivalents. Like all such compromises it failed to satisfy the extremists of either party. Political and nationalist factors may have been the primary causes, but doctrinal discontent contributed its share to the breakaway of the Nestorian churches of Persia and the Monophysite churches of Egypt and Ethiopia after the Council of Chalcedon." Wiles, *Christian Fathers*, p. 80.

more negative than positive, meaning that the Council wanted to exclude *wrong* proposals rather than to set forth a binding account of Christ's identity that would foreclose all further reflection.

This necessity for further reflection becomes immediately obvious when we compare, against one another, the famous four adverbs in the decree that are usually translated into English as four prepositional phrases: "without confusion, without change, without division, without separation." The first two adverbs are a clear concession to the worries of the Antiochenes that the human nature of Jesus might get so "absorbed" into his divinity that his humanity vanishes and gets completely changed into the divinity. But then again, the natures cannot just sit there simply juxtaposed (although such a schema would certainly prevent *confusion*!). So the Council also had to insist that, distinct and unchanging as the natures were, they also had to subsist in Christ as a subject, that is, without division or separation either.

So — and we are not surprised to learn this — the essential paradox of all Christology remains, and is proclaimed as such. Although Cyril died seven years before the Council at Chalcedon, he surely would have been pleased with this final resolution, whereby the paradox of Christ remains in all its integrity (even if he would probably have disliked some of Chalcedon's more Antiochene phraseology). For no one more gloried in the paradox of Christ than Cyril: the Impassible One suffered, the Immortal One died, the wounded patient was the physician, the victim was the priest, the one mastered by death has conquered it — and Mary is the Mother of God. That title could hardly be of more significance for Cyril than if he had invented it himself (which he most certainly did not). For what Nestorius took to be a term expressing the ignorant mythological imagination of insufficiently catechized simple believers, Cyril knew encapsulated the very essence of the Christian faith, which is the very reason it must be (and remain) paradoxical, as McGuckin explains:

> For Nestorius the phrase "God wrapped in swaddling bands" was at worst blasphemous nonsense, or at best evidence of simple-mindedness and theological ineptitude. If such a phrase implied that the Logos was the direct "personal" subject of the God-Man's human sufferings, then it involved the impassible Logos directly in passibility and thus was heretical. . . . On Cyril's part such language was a natural progression from belief in the incarnation. He presumed that the context for all such statements (including the *Theotokos*) was self-evidently the incarnate state of God the

Word and to have to labor the point every time, as Nestorius seemed to be insisting, by such a rigid scheme of language rules, was simply not necessary, in fact it was detrimental to belief precisely because it weakened the sense of the paradox such language-crossing evoked, the paradox which enshrined the church's sense of the single subjectivity of Christ.[81]

Maximus the Confessor

That language-crossing paradox of course continued to give rise to new issues in theology — meaning controversies continued to boil, above all centered on McGuckin's closing phrase above, "the church's sense of the single subjectivity of Christ." Because the monophysites resisted Chalcedon (a resistance that was causing increasing problems for the government), the imperial palace was eager to find a way to bring them back into the fold.[82] And since the monophysites' central concern had always been to maintain the single divine subject as the hypostasis upon which all the human and divine attributes could be ascribed, there seemed to be a way out: by asserting that Christ had only one (exclusively divine) will.

That proposal — again in line with most other heretical proposals — had a certain plausibility; and even today, among those who don't know this history, if they are asked how many "wills" Christ has, some would spontaneously answer "only one." For as we have already seen, the Gospels never imply an ontological schizophrenia in Jesus. And since it was always the concern of the Alexandrines, both orthodox and monophysite, to preserve the teaching of the single subjectivity of Christ, and since single subjectivity must surely include the notion of a single will, the emperors saw monothelitism as an easy expedient for uniting the anti-Chalcedonians under the imperial flag once more.[83]

81. McGuckin, *Cyril*, p. 154.

82. "The circumstances following the councils of Ephesus and Chalcedon placed Constantinople in the position of an arbiter between East and West and led it to elaborate a theology of conciliation and synthesis. This type of theology was favored by the emperors who were seeking a reconciliation between the Chalcedonian and anti-Chalcedonian parts of their empire: such was the first task of the specifically 'Byzantine' theology. The christological problems of the fifth and sixth centuries thus can be said basically to have shaped the Byzantine theological mentality and to have provided its main theme until about the ninth century." Meyendorff, *Christ in Eastern Thought*, p. 3.

83. Monothelitism is the heresy that says Christ has only one will. It comes from the Greek word for "will," *thelēma*, which means that the more technically correct term should

New resolutions to the perennial dilemmas concerning Christ's identity always seem, at least in the patristic era, to require some figure of remarkable tenacity to ensure that the orthodox solution will win out, which is certainly one more indication of the initial plausibility of heretical views. So just as Nicea needed Athanasius, and Ephesus and Chalcedon needed Cyril, the orthodox cause in the seventh century needed Maximus the Confessor (c. 580-662). But Maximus' role was not simply to stamp out the last remaining vestiges of monophysite presuppositions and thus wrap up the story of patristic orthodoxy. If his only claim to fame had been to defeat monothelitism, he would be but a footnote to dogmatic history. For this issue of the two wills of Christ (for which he fought so valiantly, even to the point of a martyr's death) strikes contemporary ears as too arcane to be worth bothering about, even if they can bring themselves to see what is at stake and why the Third Council of Constantinople (680-681) condemned monothelitism as a heresy.[84]

But again, as with so much else of patristic theology, superficial judgments can be highly misleading. "In fact," as John Meyendorff rightly notes, "Maximus can be called the real father of Byzantine theology. Only through his system, in which the valid traditions of the past found their legitimate place, were the ideas of Origen, Evagrius, the Cappadocians, Cyril, and Pseudo-Dionysius preserved within Eastern Christianity."[85]

---

be "monothel*e*tism." But while used by some authors, it has gradually been replaced by "monothel*i*tism," presumably a back-formation on the word for the adherents of this heresy, monothel*i*tes. The orthodox counterposition is of course called dyothelitism, sometimes spelled duothelitism.

84. This was the sixth Ecumenical Council. The fifth, the Second Council of Constantinople (553), met to give retroactive condemnation to Origen, Theodore of Mopsuestia, and others of a Nestorian bent, a move that the pope at the time, Vigilius (died 555), resented because the Antiochene targets had not been condemned by Ephesus and Chalcedon while they were alive; and thus it made no sense to excommunicate the dead (although he had no objections to condemning certain propositions from these authors). Vigilius refused to attend this Council for fear of violence against his person and refused to sign the decree, thereby prompting the emperor to exile him. But the emperor's efforts on behalf of this council eventually succeeded: he prevailed upon Vigilius to accept the Council. See the appendix on the First Seven Ecumenical Councils for the relevant decrees.

85. Meyendorff, *Christ in Eastern Thought*, p. 99. The influential Swiss theologian Hans Urs von Balthasar, who did so much to bring Maximus back into the contemporary discussion in his remarkable monograph on the Confessor, *Cosmic Liturgy*, heartily agrees with Meyendorff: "Maximus had undoubtedly read a great deal. But, despite his vast erudition, he built his spiritual house on just a few well-chosen pillars: those that permitted him to look beyond all the spectacular cross-beams and trellises, past the distracting façade of the past, and win back once more the true form of the living tradition. Maximus' genius was that he was

Maximus was able to represent both the capstone of the past and the hinge to the future because, more than any other patristic writer, he let his Christology dominate and determine all the rest of his theology. As Hans Urs von Balthasar aptly put it, "The figure of the redeemer stands in the center of Maximus' theology."[86]

One can gain at least an initial glimpse into Maximus' achievement by first recognizing that the problems raised by the divine-human christological axiom had yet to be resolved in any fully satisfactory way (otherwise the Nestorians and monophysites would not have resisted Chalcedon). Clearly, there must be something at work; some hidden, implicit, but powerfully operative presupposition that was hampering a solution; one that could not only satisfy the alienated but, more importantly, actually bring the issue to closure by resolving the fundamental problem.

So what was the lurking but so influential unconscious presupposition operative in patristic theology that Maximus spotted? Actually, it wasn't so much of an unconscious presupposition as a *missing* one. Like the dog that didn't bark in the Sherlock Holmes story, there was a missing term lacking in the patristic lexicon: *existence*.[87] In a remarkable anticipation of Thomas

---

able to open up five or six spiritual worlds that apparently had come to seem irreconcilable and to interrelate them. Moreover, he was then able, from within each of these worlds, to find an inner light to illuminate all the others and to set them in a new relationship with one another, from which the most unexpected reflections and relations would arise." Hans Urs von Balthasar, "Mittler zwischen Ost und West: Zur 1300. Jahrfeier Maximus' des Bekenners (580-662)," *Sein und Sendung* 8 (1962): 358-61; here 358-59; my translation.

86. Hans Urs von Balthasar, *Cosmic Liturgy: The Universe according to Maximus the Confessor,* trans. Brian E. Daley, S.J. (San Francisco: Ignatius Press, 2003), p. 207. This verdict is universal among Maximus scholars and even adorns the title of one study, Torstein Theodor Tollefsen's *The Christocentric Cosmology of St. Maximus the Confessor* (Oxford: Oxford University Press, 2008). Amid this remarkable flourishing of scholarship on this difficult theologian, the best overall account of Maximus' thought is Lars Thunberg, *Microcosm and Mediator: The Theological Anthropology of Maximus the Confessor* (La Salle, IL: Open Court, 1995).

87. It is odd that Greek does not have an exact analogue to the Latin *existentia.* To be sure, it has the verb "to be" *(einai)* from which is formed the participle "being", meaning *a being (on),* and the noun "essence" *(ousia,* formed from the feminine form of the participle *on).* But it has nothing for "beingness," so to speak, meaning the *fact* that something exists, which we denote through the Latinate word "existence." At all events, there was the Greek verb *hyparchō,* basically meaning to initiate or to be the beginning of something. Aristotle used that word to mean *to exist really* in contrast to "only appear" (Aristotle, *Metaphysics* 1046b10). From that usage came the noun *hyparxis,* meaning "existence, reality." Except for the ancient Greek mathematicians, though, who used the term to mean "positive number," it

Aquinas's distinction between essence and existence (the famous "real" distinction of medieval philosophy), Maximus insisted that *hyparxis* (existence) must be distinguished from *ousia* (essence), *physis* (nature), and *hypostasis* (substance). This passage from Maximus is very dense but is crucial for understanding how he managed to reconcile Antiochene and Alexandrian emphases:

> The fact that there is no nature without hypostasis does not make nature into a hypostasis but rather into something hypostatized. Nature should not be conceived simply as a property that can only be distinguished [from the hypostasis] *in thought,* but rather is recognized as a form *(eidos) in actual fact.* Even so, *the fact that a hypostasis is not without its essence does not make the hypostasis into an essence,* but shows it to be essential; hypostasis should not be thought of as a mere quality [of a nature], but must be seen as truly existing together with that in which the qualities are grounded.[88]

The upshot and relevance of this distinction for Christology can be seen by recalling Cyril's objections to Nestorius. Cyril realized that "nature" is an abstraction that only draws its meaning from the "substance" or "thing" that has that nature: so lionhood doesn't roar, lions do. But equally the roar never gets roared just because it is part of the *essence* of a lion to roar. For that you need an actually existing lion who is doing that roaring at the moment. Perfectly obvious, one might say, and so it is. But the refusal to acknowledge so elementary an insight throughout the career of Greek philosophy had its consequences for theology too; and with Maximus we finally get to the point of seeing that connection.[89]

---

is remarkable how rarely the word is used in the extant literature. Citations for these different usages can be found in *The Greek-English Lexicon* compiled by Henry George Liddell and Robert Scott, revised and augmented throughout by Sir Henry Stuart Jones (Oxford: Clarendon Press, 1968), p. 1853.

88. Maximus, *Opuscula*, PG 91, 205AB; italics added.

89. As Mark McIntosh puts it: "[One] of the most significant contributions the Confessor had made was his nurturing and employment of a growing philosophical distinction between the order of being *(einai)* or essence *(ousia)* on one hand, and the order of actual existence *(hypostasis)* or personal existence *(hyparxis)* on the other. . . . Maximus was pushing towards a crucial new dimension beyond the fixed philosophical categories of nature and essence. For Maximus this was a dimension of reality revealed in the free relationship of God to the radically contingent world. Beyond the necessary *natures* of things there is the gratuitous fact that they *exist.* Maximus sees a polarity between the true unchanging essence, on

Without this "real distinction" between essence and existence, the Alexandrines and Antiochenes only ended up talking at cross-purposes to each other: the theologians from Plato-saturated Egypt thought the Nestorians were undermining the unity of Christ by making each nature too self-subsistent; while the ones from Syriac-speaking Antioch thought the Alexandrine monophysites were undercutting the integrity of the self-subsisting human nature by uniting Christ to the divinity too much.

But the real problem was that they were *both* seeking to establish the unity of Christ on the level of nature. For as long as nature *(physis)* and substance *(hypostasis)* were not sufficiently distinguished from each other but were being used more or less interchangeably, then the union of the two natures in Christ could never be secured. Either the two self-subsistent natures would be conceived in terms of juxtaposition and as a mere moral union by the Nestorians; or one nature would have to trump the other and be the "real" locus of the unity, the position of the aptly named mono*phys*ites.[90]

Chalcedon, as we saw, had defined the union of the two natures of Christ in terms of the single subject of *hypostasis* <u>and</u> *prosōpon.* But that "compromise" had bequeathed an ambiguity that both Nestorian and monophysite exploited. So a term had to be found that would incorporate both of them while simultaneously transcending their respective weaknesses: and that for Maximus was *hyparxis,* actual existence. The change in terminology is by no means insignificant or hairsplitting. For now both natures can be preserved in their integrity and fullness once the union is placed at the level of existence:

> [The] divine and human in Christ are united in enacting together their particular pattern of self-surrender, obedience, and love which is the

---

one side, and personal, actual, free-acting existence on the other side." Mark A. McIntosh, *Christology from Within: Spirituality and Incarnation in Hans Urs von Balthasar* (Notre Dame: University of Notre Dame Press, 2000), p. 39.

90. The dilemma is nicely captured by Demetrios Bathrellos here: "On the level of the humanity of Christ, for Theodore and Nestorius the word 'hypostasis' is identical with the word 'nature' and not with the word 'person,' which implies that they placed the real ontology of a being on the side of nature rather than on that of person. . . . The condemnation of Nestorianism, however, should not blind us to the positive elements of the Christology of the school of Antioch. To assert the fullness of the humanity of Christ at a time when different forms of at least latent monophysitism held sway in various parts of the Empire should not pass unnoticed." Demetrios Bathrellos, *The Byzantine Christ: Person, Nature, and Will in the Christology of St. Maximus the Confessor* (Oxford: Oxford University Press, 2004), pp. 19, 23.

mode of existence of the eternal Son, the pattern which distinguishes the Son from the Father and the Spirit. A human being living according to this pattern would be existing in every respect as a fully human *person*, in the modern sense of that term; but this very same pattern of life would identify this human being as the Person of the Trinity.[91]

What this resolves, especially in light of modern concerns, is that this perspective preserves the full *human* personhood of Christ: meaning someone with his own mind and soul, which Chalcedon explicitly affirms. Of course, this does not make this "personhood" self-subsistent, but rather should be conceived as roughly what we mean by "personality." The technical term for this is the *anhypostasis* of Christ's humanity, meaning that the humanity of Christ lacks its own subsistence but subsists in the Person of the Logos.

To be sure, this doctrine (defined as such by the Fifth Ecumenical Council, Constantinople II in 553) must be paired with its correlative doctrine, *enhypostasis*, a coinage of Leontius of Byzantium (died 543) and taken up by John of Damascus (c. 655-750), to counteract any impression that Christ's manhood lacked anything at all appertaining to being entirely human. While not defined by a council, the orthodox pedigree of the term brought the coinage into the writings of the advocates of Chalcedon against the monophysites.[92]

But the doctrine of the *anhypostasis*, even when tempered by the *enhypostasis*, contained a lurking problem, as Bathrellos explains:

> The post-Chalcedonian theologians constantly argued that Chalcedon had attributed a human nature to Christ without thereby introducing into Christology a human person/hypostasis alongside the Logos. Admittedly, by attributing a human nature but not a second — human — person/hypostasis to Christ, Chalcedon had drawn a distinction between person/hypostasis and nature/essence at the level of economy; but the inevitable question as to what this distinction consists in remained. Un-

---

91. McIntosh, *Christology from Within*, pp. 40-41; McIntosh's emphasis.

92. Karl Barth usefully defines the two terms as asserting the negative and positive poles of the same reality: "*Anhypostasis* asserts the negative . . . meaning the human nature does not possess its mode of being in and for itself, *in abstracto*. . . . *Enhypostasis* asserts the positive. . . . The divine mode of being gives the human nature existence . . . and in this way has a concrete existence of its own." Karl Barth, *Church Dogmatics* I/2: *The Doctrine of the Word of God*, trans. G. T. Thomson and Harold Knight (Edinburgh: T. & T. Clark, 1956), p. 163.

doubtedly, the orthodoxy of Chalcedon was conditional upon a satisfactory response to this question.[93]

Because of the terminology that had been chosen to explain the union of Christ (either in Cyrillian terms, the *hypostasis* of the Logos uniting with the human *nature* of the man Jesus; or in Latin and Antiochene terms, the *persona* of the Second Person of the Trinity uniting with the human nature of Christ), the impression would constantly arise that somehow the human personality of Christ had been "crowded out," so to speak. This was clearly not the intention of Chalcedon, otherwise monophysitism and monothelitism would not have been declared heresies. But the fact that these various heresies kept cropping up anyway shows that somehow theologians were not quite sure how Jesus could be a fully human *person* (in the modern sense of that term, meaning with a fully functioning mind, soul, emotions, and will) while simultaneously being the hypostatically united Person of the Son.[94]

It would hardly do to say there are two "persons" united in the way the two natures are united, for the Second Person is precisely the subject of the union of the two natures. So the Person of the Logos cannot be both subject and principle of the union while also being one of its components. This is why Maximus is so significant a hinge from patristic to medieval Christology, and why the Fifth and Sixth Ecumenical Councils (Constantinople II and III) must be read through his achievement, as John Meyendorff explains:

> Byzantine Christology as defined in Justinian's time is criticized, however, for leaving too much in the dark the reality of the psychological life of the Savior's soul and for modifying the properties of human nature as such. And since it is obvious that all the subsequent destiny of Eastern Christianity is implicated in this judgment, the question is of some importance. In order to solve it one must remember that the decisions of the fifth

93. Bathrellos, *Byzantine Christ*, pp. 34-35.

94. As an indication of how often the word "person" is used of Christ in its modern acceptation and therefore in reference to his humanity, I cite Joseph Ratzinger: "Since the center of the person of Jesus is prayer, it is essential to participate in his prayer if we are to know and understand him." Joseph Ratzinger, *Behold the Pierced One: An Approach to a Spiritual Christology*, trans. Graham Harrison (San Francisco: Ignatius Press, 1986), p. 25. Also he uses the word "personality" of Jesus unproblematically: "[This book] sees Jesus in the light of his communion with the Father, which is the true center of his personality; without it, we cannot understand him at all, and it is from this center that he makes himself present to us today." Pope Benedict XVI/Joseph Ratzinger, *Jesus of Nazareth: From the Baptism in the Jordan to the Transfiguration*, trans. Adrian J. Walker (New York: Doubleday, 2007), p. xiv.

council do not constitute a final conclusion but only a stage in the development of Christology. The dogmatic content must be considered in the light of latter stages, and especially of St. Maximus' doctrine of the two wills and his conception of deification.[95]

The voice of Jesus, his call to the lost sheep, his admission of meekness and humility of heart, his tears at the death of Lazarus, the homeliness of his parables, and above all his cry of dereliction on the cross, all resonate as coming from a truly human (but hauntingly mysterious) being. As Hans Urs von Balthasar says in describing Maximus' Christology:

> Are we not invited to a kind of phenomenological glimpsing of the appearance of Christ, who shows us a being whose whole bearing — down to the last word, the least gesture — reveals a human nature, yet a human nature transposed in its entirety into a wholly different manner of existing?[96]

This surely is the experience of every believer: the Jesus who comes across in the Gospels always seems completely human, yet strangely not, as if he came from another world (Luke 2:49) — not in the manner, to be sure, of a visitor from another planet, but as one truly like us yet still so strangely different. How can this be? Well, according to Maximus, the answer is simply this: *the humanity of Christ reveals the divine precisely by being so human.*

Part of the problem, as Maximus saw, was that, although the terms were used interchangeably by Chalcedon, *hypostasis* (self-subsisting substance) and *prosōpon* (person) were beginning to drift apart semantically, with the former more and more referring to the *ontological* subject underneath change and the latter meaning a purely *psychological* subjectivity. But for Maximus, unity of consciousness is not the foundation of hypostatic unity. Otherwise, he would have to posit only one will in Christ to go along with that one consciousness. Indeed, his very refutation of monothelitism required that he distinguish (divine) hypostasis from (human) person, a complex argument which is the subject of the *Excursus* immediately below.

---

95. John Meyendorff, *Christ in Eastern Christian Thought*, pp. 85-86.
96. Balthasar, *Cosmic Liturgy*, p. 214.

Monothelitism vs. Dyothelitism

The philosophical and theological principles that allowed Maximus to conclude that Christ had two wills were discussed in the section above on the Confessor's broader thought. But because the refutation of the heresy of monothelitism involves considerable technicalities in philosophical psychology and the ontology of *hypostasis* and *physis*, the topic merits a separate, more technical discussion here.

There is no question that the doctrine that Christ had two wills seems to many modern theologians to represent a reversion to a Nestorian duality in Christ. Wolfhart Pannenberg, for example, openly asserts that "with the doctrine of Christ's two wills . . . the perception of the concrete vital unity of Jesus was basically lost."[97] However plausible such a position might sound initially, it was the great merit of Maximus to show that the assertion of one will in Christ leads to intolerable antinomies.

For one thing, to say that Jesus had only a divine will would make a hash of his confession: "I have come down from heaven not to do my own will but the will of the one who sent me" (John 6:38); otherwise, one would have to attribute a plurality of wills in the Trinity, something no church father would countenance, very much including Maximus.[98] Second, to identify

97. Wolfhart Pannenberg, *Jesus: God and Man,* trans. Lewis L. Wilkens and Duane A. Priebe (London: SCM Press, 1968), p. 294.

98. As here: "The godhead is beyond all division and composition and part and whole." Maximus, *Ambigua, PG* 91, 1185D. John of Damascus is even more explicit: "We believe, then, in one God: one principle without source, uncreated, unbegotten, indestructible and immortal, eternal, unlimited, uncircumscribed, unbounded, infinite in power, simple, uncompounded, incorporeal, never diminishing, . . . one substance, one godhead, one power, *one*

Christ's will solely with his divine will renders incoherent the episode in the Garden of Olives on the night before he died, when he prayed: "Father, if it be your will, take this cup from me; yet not my will, but yours be done" (Luke 22:42). Tellingly, Luke makes sure the reader knows the cost of Jesus' human struggle to conform his will to the Father's by noting that "in his anguish, he prayed more earnestly, and his sweat was like drops of blood falling to the ground" (22:44).

Third, explicitly relying on the axiom first formulated by Gregory of Nazianzus that what has not been assumed has not been saved, the Confessor insisted that, unless Jesus had a fully human will, then our will too had not been saved. In fact, since will is the very seat of sin, its *fons et origo*, we are still left in our plight if Christ did not have a human will, a point he drives home with special force here:

> If Adam ate [from the Tree] willingly, then the will is the first thing in us that became subject to passion. And since the will is the first thing in us that became subject to passion, if, according to them [the monothelites], the Word did not assume that selfsame will along with the [rest of] human nature when he became incarnate, then I have not been made free from sin. And if I have not become free from sin, I was not saved, since whatever is not assumed is not saved.[99]

Part of the Confessor's challenge is that, in order to refute monothelitism, he first had to undermine the Socratic view that the will was subordinate to the intellect, which had the effect of diminishing the role of will in the drama of salvation. According to Socrates, doing wrong resulted merely from ignorance of the right choices. This tradition culminated in the neo-Platonic doctrine that "all movement towards the inferior is involuntary."[100] But Maximus saw that Christian anthropology required making

---

will, one operation, one principality, one power, one domination, one kingdom." John of Damascus, *Exposition of the Orthodox Faith* 8 in *John of Damascus: Writings*, trans. Frederic P. Chase (New York: Fathers of the Church, 1958).

99. Maximus, *Disputatio*, PG 91, 325A.

100. Plotinus, *Enneads* IV 8, 5. Richard Norris points out how Plotinus (a third-century neo-Platonist) found himself caught in a dilemma: "Plotinus is committed to the classical Socratic view that no rational agent can be thought to go wrong knowingly or voluntarily: that vice, in fact, if it does not proceed from some obvious compulsion, must stem from error. . . . The philosopher wants to maintain the soul's responsibility for its vices and distractions; yet he is also committed to the idea that the reasonable soul cannot willingly or knowingly sin." R. A. Norris, *Manhood and Christ: A Study in the Christology of Theodore of*

the will *its own faculty independent of the intellect,* fully able to choose either good or evil, even though one already knows *what* the good or evil choice should be.[101]

To be sure, Augustine preceded Maximus with these insights, but with a crucial difference: the bishop of Hippo placed the dilemma of a free will which was created good but which chooses evil anyway inside his nature/grace dialectic, whereas the Confessor saw the problem primarily inside his Christology; for, as we have seen in the previous section, Christology dominates Maximus' thought far more than it does in Augustine, with fateful consequences in the West.[102]

But despite the real advantages that come from the Confessor's Christocentric analysis of the role of will in the human constitution, the problem with his dyothelitism for modern Christians does not come from any excessive Socratic valuation of intellect over will *we* might have. The experience of the abattoir of twentieth-century history, with its genocide and total wars, blocks any naïveté about the mind's ability to govern the will and keep it from committing evil when it so chooses. Rather, it comes from the opposite error: moderns tend to identify person with the person's will;[103] and in that context, dyothelitism will inevitably sound Nestorian.

This was basically the error of Apollinarius, who likewise identified *mind* with *person,* and thus could see no way to affirm that Jesus had a truly human mind without jeopardizing his ontological unity, which is why Aloys Grillmeier sees monothelitism as merely a continuation of the Logos-Sarx

---

Mopsuestia (Oxford: Clarendon Press, 1963), pp. 45, 48-49. This dilemma is a direct result of the neo-Platonic doctrine of the preexistence of souls and their "fall" into bodies. Now, was that fall voluntary or involuntary? "If the soul's descent is not voluntary, then the evils consequent upon embodiment stand as a cosmic injustice: if it is not involuntary, then one must suppose that the intellectual soul can freely elect to be false to its own nature." Norris, p. 49.

101. This is perfectly captured in John Milton giving Satan the line "Evil, be thou my good" in *Paradise Lost.*

102. "Richard Sorabji argued that Augustine was the first to raise the will to the stage of a full-fledged faculty in the West, whereas the first to do so in the East was Maximus. But Augustine's treatment of the will was perhaps not sufficiently shaped by *Christology,* but rather fell under the wider topic of the relationship between nature and grace, which has much bewildered Western theology up to our times, partly on account of the very treatment of the issue which Augustine bequeathed." Demetrios Bathrellos, *The Byzantine Christ: Person, Nature, and Will in the Christology of St. Maximus the Confessor* (Oxford: Oxford University Press, 2004), p. 128, footnote 161; emphasis in the original.

103. As in ethical voluntarism and "pro-choice" rhetoric, which assumes choice is automatically good and self-justifying simply by being a free choice.

Christology of Apollinarius.[104] This too is a deeply held presupposition (and error) of modernity, which tends to identify personhood with both consciousness (mind) and will. When personhood is identified without further ado with mind or consciousness, then the concept of eternal life after death becomes well-nigh incredible, since consciousness is so obviously tied to the continued metabolism of the brain; and when personhood is identified without further ado with the will, then the cult of will in Friedrich Nietzsche and his postmodern successors inevitably follows.[105]

But the whole point of Chalcedon is that it forced orthodox theologians to make just that distinction, showing once again how other problems, including purely philosophical ones, can be resolved in terms of Christology, as Bathrellos notes here:

> Post-Chalcedonian Christology proved capable of employing the distinction between person and nature in a helpful way. At the level of divinity, by distinguishing the Logos from his divine nature, post-Chalcedonian Christology was able to affirm, following Cyril, that God the Logos was born of the Virgin and suffered on the cross. However, this did not mean for the proponents of such a Christology that *the divine nature* was born of the Virgin or that the divine nature suffered on the cross; it means that the person who redeemed us was not a human person, but God himself as man.[106]

This insight forms the operative principle governing the Confessor's Christology, as can be seen in this important manifesto from his pen:

> He who does not accept equally and appropriately both [the unity and duality of Christ], applying the former to the union and the latter to the

104. "The Apollinarian system is rather a monergetic or monothelitic creation and exerted its great influence in this form." Aloys Grillmeier, S.J., *Christ in Christian Tradition*, vol. 1: *From the Apostolic Age to Chalcedon,* trans. John Bowden (Atlanta: John Knox Press, 1975), p. 339.

105. Bathrellos makes the extremely thought-provoking observation that so many of the ethical outrages of today can be traced to the Apollinarian error of identifying nature with person: "The tendency to identify personhood with nature or natural qualities and especially with the mind, which characterized Apollinarianism, seems to occur quite often in the history of human thought. It is remarkable that in our own day some philosophers of ethics give a definition of 'person' based on mental and volitional capacities, and in doing so make it possible to justify, for example, abortion and even infanticide; see, for example, Peter Singer, *Practical Ethics.*" Bathrellos, *Byzantine Christ,* p. 14, footnote 29.

106. Bathrellos, *Byzantine Christ,* p. 57; emphasis in the original.

natural difference, falls inevitably, as is normal, into either division or confusion. . . . For although the flesh became one with the Logos according to hypostasis and acquired the richness of his energy, it in no way ceased to be created according to essence.[107]

Maximus is of course still left with the task of showing how the assertion of Christ's fully human will does not lead to Nestorianism, which he does with an acute exegesis of the scene in Gethsemane when Jesus pleads that the cup of suffering might pass from him. As Bathrellos demonstrates, the Confessor "was really the first to point out in an unambiguous way that it is the Logos *as a man* who addressed the Father in Gethsemane."[108] Christ's prayer, he explained, can hardly be *God's* prayer, for that would imply that Christ as God had a different will from the Father's, an impossibility. Maximus argued instead that Christ wanted to fulfill the will of the Father both as God the Son and as man. "However, he emphasized the fact that in Gethsemane Christ decided as man to obey the divine will, and thus overcame the blameless human instinctive urge to avoid death."[109]

In prior centuries, pagan philosophers often invidiously pointed to Christ's agony in the Garden as a sign of weakness before death, in pointed contrast to Socrates, who faced death serenely. Prior to Maximus, the accusation often stung; but with his more robust and anti-Socratic defense of the independent faculty of the will, the Confessor was able to turn the tables on the Platonists by showing how the human will *by nature* seeks the good of life and thus flinches from death, especially voluntary death.[110] Yet this natural reluctance to die, in the case of Jesus, does not result in disobedience — not because his divine will overwhelmed his human will, but because the human will always sought obedience — and did obey in a constant human act: "Christ's will not to die belongs essentially to his humanity, even though it is overcome by his [human] decision to obey the will of the Father."[111]

---

107. Maximus, *Opusculum 8*, in *PG* 91, 105A.

108. Bathrellos, *Byzantine Christ,* pp. 146-47.

109. Bathrellos, *Byzantine Christ,* p. 147.

110. It would make a fascinating study to compare Maximus here with the modern view of the will, especially in Schopenhauer and Nietzsche, somewhat on the order of Balthasar's *Cosmic Liturgy,* which showed the Confessor's relevance for an engagement with Hegel (to the consternation of some Maximus scholars, to be sure).

111. Bathrellos, *Byzantine Christ,* pp. 141-42. Also: "If we were to say that it is the divinity or the divine will that moves the human will without at the same time stressing that the Logos as man allows his human will to be moved by them in an act of obedience, not only the whole point of the obedience of the Son to the Father, but also the self-determination of

Only such a perspective, Maximus insisted, could explain what Paul meant by his enigmatic line: "For our sake God made him who knew no sin to become sin" (2 Cor. 5:21). The Confessor asks: "How is it that we are said to commit sin and know it [1 John 1:8], while the Lord became sin but did not know it? Is it not more serious to become sin and not realize it, than to commit sin and know it?"[112] His answer must necessarily be complex and thus bears quoting at length, as the paradoxes are subtle:

Having originally been corrupted from its natural design, Adam's free choice corrupted, not just that free choice, but our human nature as well, which forfeited the grace of impassibility. Thus came sin into existence. The first sin, culpable indeed, was the fall of free choice from good into evil; the second, following upon the first, was the innocent transformation of human nature from incorruption into corruption. For our forefather Adam committed two sins by his transgression of God's commandment: the first sin was culpable, when his free choice willfully rejected the good; but the second "sin," occasioned by the first, was innocent, since human nature *unwillingly* put off its incorruption. Therefore our Lord and God, rectifying this reciprocal corruption and alteration of our human nature by taking on the whole of our nature, even had in his assumed nature the liability to passions which, in his own exercise of free choice, he adorned with incorruptibility. And it is by virtue of his assumption of this natural passibility that he "became sin for our sake," though he did not *know* any deliberate sin because of the immutability of his free choice.... For our sake he became a human being *naturally liable to passions* and used the sin that I caused to destroy the sin that I commit. Just as in Adam, with his own act of freely choosing evil, the common glory of human nature, incorruption, was robbed, ... so too in Christ, with his own act of freely choosing the good, the common scourge of our whole nature, corruption, was taken away.[113]

---

the human will of the Son, both of which Maximus insists upon so strongly, would be nullified. On the contrary, by emphasizing that the Logos as God wills by his divine will and as man obeys the divine will by his human will, the self-determination of the human will is secured" (p. 174).

112. Maximus the Confessor, *Ad Thalassium 42* in *On the Cosmic Mystery of Jesus Christ: Selected Writings from St. Maximus the Confessor*, trans. Paul M. Blowers and Robert Louis Wilken (Crestwood, NY: St. Vladimir's Seminary Press, 2003), p. 119; translation amended at minor points.

113. Maximus, in *On the Cosmic Mystery*, pp. 119-20; italics added.

This passage is complex because of its carefully woven paradoxes and complex use of the word "sin," but its import is clear: human nature as such cannot be sinful, including the passions to which human beings are, in his words, "naturally liable." This too represents a real advance on both Alexandrian and Antiochene Christologies, both of which tended to equate passion to sinfulness, which threw their respective Christologies off balance: On the one hand, Apollinarius and the monophysites shied away from confessing Christ's full humanity lest he be identified with sin too closely (this despite Paul's line that Christ became sin for our sake and "came in the likeness of sinful flesh": Rom. 8:3b).[114] On the other hand, the Antiochenes also conceded the inherent sinfulness of the human nature that Christ took on; but for that same reason they wanted to keep the two natures in Christ, divine and human, radically distinct, thereby undermining Christ's unity.[115]

But by showing that Christ had a fully human will naturally liable to passions, but which was nonetheless a will that always obeyed God, even in the face of the (naturally good) instinct for self-preservation, Maximus could finally break with a still-lingering Platonic anthropology that eschewed the flesh in favor of the spirit. Obviously, the incarnation, as the word implies, entails just the opposite evaluation of the flesh. Nonetheless, the flight from bodiliness is a constant motif in human religion, very much including Christianity. But with Maximus, this quasi-Gnosticism finally died a needed death, and that for Christological reasons.[116]

Unfortunately, the Confessor's voice gradually died out in the West when it might have done the most good, largely due to the Islamic conquests in the East and the collapse of the Roman Empire in the West. Christians at that time witnessed these events as horrors and tribulations in their own right, but here I am speaking specifically (if in a much more minor key, of course) of the effect these two events had on the christological teaching of the church. For the upshot was that what Maximus had accomplished lay

114. Or, if his opponents spoke of Jesus assuming a *perfect* humanity, he had another objection: "Apollinarius seems to have fallen prey to the philosophical axiom that two perfect things cannot become one." Bathrellos, *Byzantine Christ,* p. 11.

115. "It seems that not only for Apollinarius, but also for the Antiochenes, full humanity goes hand in hand with sinfulness, which is perhaps why Nestorius and Theodore, who conceived of Christ as a complete man, attributed a kind of sinfulness to him." Bathrellos, *Byzantine Christ,* p. 23, footnote 73.

116. Of course, it would later reappear in Martin Luther's doctrine that temptation is itself a sin and in French Jansenism. But that is another story, and one for which Augustine bears a certain amount of genealogical responsibility.

dormant, without influence in the West; and what influence it achieved in the East (which was considerable) grew more and more restricted in its global impact.[117]

Because this book is meant primarily for Catholic and evangelical students in the English-speaking world, we must now turn to the Occident for the rest of this narrative. But there too one finds stasis, at least in Christology. Part of the problem was that Pope Leo's intervention had proved so successful that, for the West at least, the ensuing controversies that happened in the East found little resonance in the West. Perhaps part of the reason for that is that the Romans never displayed the same kind of philosophical flair that the East always enjoyed (although that never stopped Augustine). But surely the main reason for the quiescence of christological speculation was the collapse of the Roman Empire, recovery from which would prove to be a long and slow business. Thus in the narrative we are recounting here, we will have to move several centuries ahead, when suddenly Christology takes on new accents in Anselm, Bonaventure, Thomas Aquinas, and John Duns Scotus.

---

117. But once the significance of Maximus came into focus in the twentieth century, the implications of his Christology for contemporary debate also became obvious, as this entry in a theological dictionary shows: "[The debate over monothelitism comes] closer than any other of the ancient Christological disputes to raising the question of the human personality of Jesus, in the modern psychological sense, and the decision of 680 [condemning monothelitism] was based on the important principle that union with the divine did not deprive Jesus of any element of true humanity, but perfected it." *Westminster Dictionary of Church History*, ed. Jerald C. Brauer (Philadelphia: Westminster Press, 1971), p. 568, at "Monothelites." Thomas Joseph White makes this insight even more specific: "Translated into the terms of human consciousness, this means that the Son of God made man would deliberate and think like any other historical human being, employing terms and concepts of his epoch." Thomas Joseph White, O.P., "Dyotheletism and the Instrumental Human Consciousness of Jesus," *Pro Ecclesia* 17, no. 4 (Fall 2008): 369-422; here 419.

CHAPTER 5

Medieval Christology

In former times people went into monasteries. Were they stupid or insensitive people? — Well, if people like that found they needed to take such measures in order to be able to go on living, the problem cannot be an easy one!

Ludwig Wittgenstein, *Culture and Value*

The Medieval Context

"A text without a context is a pretext." Or so one of my high school English teachers used to say when our adolescent flights of fancy got out of hand. Under that rubric, it needs to be stressed that whenever historians of dogma discuss the striking differences in style, method, and substance between the patristic, medieval, and modern periods, they are fundamentally talking about a change in context. Consider this datum from the sociology of knowledge: in the patristic era most theologians were bishops; in the medieval period most were monks or friars; while in the modern era most have been professors.[1]

---

1. Periodization of history is always a controversial business because of the difficulty of specifying when the transition from one period to another took place. But by using the bishop-monk-professor rubric we can see with reasonable exactitude when each transition took place: the transition from patristic times to the medieval happened with Augustine, who was both a bishop and a monk (he founded an order of priests that soon became the order of monks called Augustinians); while the transition from the medieval to the modern era took place with Martin Luther, who started off as a monk (indeed an Augustinian

How that shift from monk to professor affected modern Christology will be the task of Chapters 6 through 10 to set forth; but the meaning for Christology of the first shift, from bishop to monk, should be clear: for the most part, *conflicting Christologies in the medieval period were no longer being adjudicated in church councils or synods.* Which is another way of saying that heresy was no longer playing a crucial pedagogical role in fashioning christological doctrine. Rather, differing Christologies were meant to fit in as components of larger personal theological systems created by individual theologians, each of whom had a different vision born out of different contexts and different temperaments. And even there, "conflicting" might be too strong a word. Different the Christologies certainly were, but never conflicting, if by that is meant Christologies that were so contradictory with one another that an ecumenical council was required to adjudicate them.[2]

Nor will it do to insist on a sociological uniformity among the theologians of the Middle Ages, despite what was said just above about the evident contrasts with the patristic and modern eras. For example, I said above that most medieval theologians were "monks or friars." Monks belong in monasteries, that is, to religious orders founded in the tradition of Augustine or (especially) Benedict of Nursia, foundations that were rural-based and insisted on the value of stability (meaning that the monks, for the most part, took a vow not just to the order itself but to the specific monastery they initially joined, where they usually stayed for the rest of their lives). But with the increased urbanization of Europe from about 1200 on, the pastoral needs of cities grew increasingly urgent, to which the mendicant (begging) orders of Dominic (c. 1172-1221) and Francis of Assisi (1181/2-1226) were meant to respond and whose members are usually called "friars," to distinguish them from monks.

The only reason this distinction is important here is that the theology

---

monk), assumed the chair of Old Testament studies at the University of Wittenberg, and then stayed on as a professor for the rest of his life — once he had made his break with Rome definitive by renouncing his monastic vows and getting married.

2. The one great exception to this would be the condemnation of the adoptionist Christology advocated in eighth-century Spain, which was mentioned in the last chapter, a teaching that was condemned "by no less than three councils called by Charlemagne, in 792 (Ratisbon or Regensburg), 795 (Frankfurt), and 799 (Aachen or Aix). Their dossier of denunciations also included a warning in 785 by Pope Hadrian I . . . and a condemnation endorsed by Pope Leo III in Rome in 798, among others." John C. Cavadini, *The Last Christology of the West: Adoptionism in Spain and Gaul, 785-820* (Philadelphia: University of Pennsylvania Press, 1993), p. 1.

pursued in the monasteries was, to a large extent, and for reasons adduced above, monastery-bound — and thus meant to serve the contemplative needs of the monks. But with increased urbanization came the formation of the earliest universities, in which the friars often founded their own chairs of learning. Again, this would not be terribly relevant to the story we are about to tell except as it affected the style of theology being pursued in monastery and school ("scholasticism" gets its name from the fact that it was school-based). Monastic theology was, for obvious reasons, *contemplative* in tone and style, while scholastic theology grew ever more *logical,* more exacting, more precise — in a word, more "scholastic," in both the medieval and modern senses of that word.

This shift from the contemplative to the more scientifically systematic was not due simply to a shift in geography, from monastic *latifundium* to the urban classroom. For more or less simultaneously with the growth of the cities and the foundation of the universities came the influx of the texts of Aristotle into these newborn scholastic centers. "Books have their own fate," said Horace; and never was that more true than of the books of Aristotle, which underwent a series of adventures worthy of inclusion in an Indiana Jones movie: The story is told in antiquity that Aristotle bequeathed his library to his most famous student, Theophrastus,[3] who then passed it on to his nephew Neleus, who took it to a cave near Scepsis, a city in Asia Minor, where it lay gathering dust and mold for two centuries, at which point it was transferred first to Athens and then to Rome, where a professional philosopher by the name of Andronicus prepared an edition of Aristotle's books more or less like the one we know today.

Assuming the story is true (and "it is hard to decide whether to be sceptical about Scepsis," as Jonathan Barnes dryly puns[4]), we do know that the texts that *did* survive were the so-called esoteric texts, meaning those meant for students in Aristotle's classroom in the Lyceum (the school he founded, named after the district in Athens where the school was located). From other sources (including Cicero, who praised them) we know that Aristotle composed exoteric works as well, meaning works meant for a wider public. These latter works did not survive.[5] The point is crucial only because

3. Aristotle's will was reproduced in Diogenes Laertius, *Lives of the Philosophers* V, 11-16, where Theophrastus is indeed named as executor but no mention is made of his library.

4. Jonathan Barnes, "Aristotle: Life and Work," in *The Cambridge Companion to Aristotle,* ed. Jonathan Barnes (Cambridge: Cambridge University Press, 1995), p. 10.

5. The current two-volume English translation of Aristotle's works runs to 2383 pages. On the basis of a list of Aristotle's works provided by Diogenes and reports from Cicero and

of the evident difference in style between his esoteric and exoteric books: the fact that it was only Aristotle's "drier" works that reached the medieval schools would itself have a noticeable impact on scholastic style too.[6]

Further complicating the matter, knowledge of Greek in the Latin-speaking West began to wane precipitously after the collapse of the Roman Empire. Tragically, one philosopher/theologian of the early Middle Ages, Boethius (c. 480-524), had planned to translate all of Plato *and* Aristotle (!) but was executed by order of the Ravenna-based Ostrogothic king Theodoric (c. 455-526) on a charge of high treason. Aristotle's works, however, were sufficiently influential in the Byzantine side of the Empire that they would be translated into Syriac. It was in these Syriac translations that the newly arrived Muslim conquerors first encountered the intimidating genius of Aristotle; and these Syriac texts they had translated into Arabic, translations that eventually made their way into Muslim Spain in the tenth century. In contrast to most of northern Africa (except Egypt), the Muslim conquest of Spain did not entail the extirpation of Christianity on the Iberian peninsula, so that some learned Christians who knew Arabic could now encounter Aristotle's texts for the first time, albeit in a translation at least twice-removed from the original. And finally, by the late twelfth century, via Sicily, Western scholars were gaining access to the original Greek texts of the surviving Stagirite corpus, texts that the Dominican William of Moerbeke (died 1286) translated into Latin for his friend and confrère Thomas Aquinas. It certainly makes for an exciting story; but beyond these vicissitudes of textual fate, Aristotle's revolutionary impact on the West can hardly be exaggerated:

> There is something about these works, or about their conjunction with certain moments in human history, that makes them seem almost indestructible. Time and again, they fade from sight in one civilization only to reappear centuries later in another, often with the most extraordinary im-

---

others of the exoteric works, Barnes estimates that a complete edition of all the works Aristotle wrote would run to about 6000 modern pages, an extraordinary loss for posterity.

6. "The distinction in Aristotle's works between the esoteric and the exoteric is an ancient one. Roughly speaking, the exoteric works were supposed to have been written for a broad public: they were serious, but they were not tough and technical — and they were no doubt written with style and elegance. None of these works has survived, and of them we can form only a partial and frustrating impression from the few fragments which have by chance been preserved. By contrast, the esoteric works were technical things, made for the use of philosophers and for use within the school: they were not 'written up for publication' and they were not given a literary polish — indeed they were not literary texts at all. All Aristotle's surviving works are esoteric in this sense" (Barnes, "Life and Work," p. 12).

pact. "Lost" in Greece, they are later "found" in Rome. Neglected by Byzantine Christians, they inspire a great burst of philosophical creativity in the Islamic world. Unread for centuries in the Latin West, their rediscovery in medieval Spain triggers an intellectual revolution in Europe. The enduring power of this work is all the more remarkable when one considers that Aristotle's most influential books are difficult to follow, do not tell stories like those of Homer or the Bible, and have none of the literary appeal of classical poetry or Plato's dialogues. . . . He does not overwhelm the reader rhetorically, as Plato does by making Socrates the fount of all wisdom and having his dialogue opponents admit the truth of his remarks. The tone of these presentations is that of a well-educated, thoughtful man (in Greek terms, an aristocrat) addressing others who are as well-educated and thoughtful as himself.[7]

The upshot of this strange story of the fluctuating fortunes of the Stagirite corpus is that Aristotle never influenced patristic theology in the way Plato did. For good or ill, the fathers did their thinking largely under the warm (and perhaps glaring?) influence of the Platonic sun. That sun continued to shine in the West largely because of the work of an anonymous sixth-century Syrian monk whom history knows from his pseudonym, Dionysius the Areopagite, and author of the most remarkable texts of neo-Platonic theology in the history of Christian thought. The Areopagite's thought was nothing if not hierarchical, but hardly in the modern sense of bureaucratic flowcharts. Rather, for him earthly hierarchy was but a reflection of the celestial hierarchy, which implied a direct ontological connection between the office of the bishop and his call to be both saint and teacher.

But the question now is: How did the impact of Aristotle's newly discovered and increasingly influential texts change things for theology? Here at least is the thesis of Hans Urs von Balthasar, whose analysis here strives to strike a balance between the legacies of the two phases of medieval theology, pre- and post-Aristotelian: "But as theology increasingly took on a 'scholastic' form, and Aristotelianism burst in like an elemental force, the naïve unity hitherto accepted was gravely shaken."[8] The trouble is, Aristotle was absorbed

7. Richard E. Rubenstein, *Aristotle's Children: How Christians, Muslims, and Jews Rediscovered Ancient Wisdom and Illuminated the Middle Ages* (New York: Harcourt, 2003), pp. 39-40.

8. Hans Urs von Balthasar, "Theology and Sanctity," in *Explorations in Theology*, vol. 1: *The Word Made Flesh*, trans. A. V. Littledale and Alexander Dru (San Francisco: Ignatius Press, 1989), p. 184.

into the medieval lecture hall in a way that had no precedent in patristic times, when Plato influenced the debate (again, for good or ill): this is because most of the church fathers *were already trained* in philosophy from their youth, the Cappadocians and Maximus especially. So when they talked about the legitimacy of using the bounty of Greek philosophy in the same way the ancient Hebrews took the "spoils of Egypt" with them during the Exodus, they were really only taking items already in the household cupboard. But the enthusiasm of some early medieval scholastics for Aristotle took on a much different tone, for here was something entirely new in their experience: "The mood which fastened on Christian thinkers was like the intoxication of victors after battle, at the sight of booty far beyond their expectations."[9]

One should perhaps not gainsay enthusiasm, especially when directed toward Aristotle, whom Dante called the "master of all who know." Yet the enthusiasm for Aristotle created a set of unique problems for theology, ones that would be left ultimately to Thomas Aquinas to resolve. But to speak of the Thomistic solution(s) gets us beyond our story at this juncture of the narrative. What must be stressed here is the overall impact of Aristotle once he arrived in the West:

> The booty in this case was primarily philosophical, and only indirectly theological. Philosophy began to emerge as a special discipline alongside theology, with its own concept of philosophical truth, which was perfectly correct in its own sphere, and could lay no claim to the superior content of revealed truth. . . . [But] philosophy, as a doctrine of natural being and excluding revelation, could not know that the highest mode of interpreting that philosophical definition of truth must be a trinitarian one. . . . There was no danger of misconceiving supernatural truth, so long as philosophical concepts were used as pointers to the final truth, which is supernatural and divine. . . . But the Aristotelianism of the thirteenth century not only enlarged the basis of theology, it was itself the start of the modern sciences of nature and mind as independent disciplines, and rightly so. It gave birth to modern "secularism," and thereby introduced new tensions and set new problems to the Christian.[10]

9. Balthasar, "Theology and Sanctity," p. 185.

10. Balthasar, "Theology and Sanctity," p. 185. Perhaps the introduction of Aristotle into the medieval classroom would have a greater impact on modern times than the Middle Ages, at least according to Balthasar: "Moreover this [enthusiasm for Aristotle] was not without its dangers, especially when the philosophical propaedeutic came to be considered a fixed and unalterable basis, whose concepts, without the necessary transposition, were used

In this chapter we shall treat the highpoints of this story — that is, the move from monastery to classroom, and the move from a Platonically influenced Christology to one cast in a more scholastic, Aristotelian mode — by highlighting the Christology of four of the most influential figures (at least for christological questions) in the Middle Ages: Anselm, Bonaventure, Aquinas, and Scotus. A mere chapter in a textbook can of course make no claim to function as an independent monograph on these four men or on their respective Christologies. We shall be focusing on them because they both represent the highpoints of the story that we have adumbrated above and because they have had the most influence on later discussions, up to and including our own day.

Anselm

Drawing on a famous line from Augustine, Anselm (c. 1033-1109) defined theology as "faith seeking understanding" *(fides quaerens intellectum)*. But what did Anselm mean by *understanding?* To come to an accurate interpretation of his meaning for this crucial word, one cannot overstress the importance of the word *rectitudo* in his thought. Normally one might think that "rectitude" would serve best as a translation of that medieval Latin neologism. But in today's English "rectitude" usually refers to ethical integrity, perhaps even to the point of overdoing it, as when an "upright" person starts to be described as "uptight" as well: "Such unbending *rectitude* that man shows!"

But *rectitudo* (literally "rightness") in Anselm refers more to what we mean in English when we say that someone, a portrait-painter say, has got his painting "just right." When we say "just right" in that context, we are really saying that, from that point on, the artist shouldn't "touch a thing" in the work. And behind *that* implication is the idea that the artist has all along been following some *inner rule of necessity* that leads him along until he has

---

as norms and criteria of the content of faith, and therefore set in judgment over it. Teachers behaved as though man knew from the outset and with some sort of finality, before he had been given revelation, what truth, goodness, being, light, love and faith were. It was as though divine revelation on these realities had to accommodate itself to these fixed philosophical conceptual containers that admitted of no expansion" (p. 186). For all the attacks on Aristotle in the Renaissance and Reformation, without him the secularization of Western civilization from the medieval synthesis would be scarcely conceivable. In other words, no Aristotle, no Enlightenment.

reached his ultimate end — the goal of perfection toward which he had been striving all along. In other words, once he has got his piece "just right," he has reached the point where *necessity meets perfection,* which Anselm defines as *ordinis pulchritudo,* the "beauty of arrangement."[11]

This linkage between *rectitudo* and necessity explains another feature of Anselm's thought that has often puzzled readers from his day to ours: the way he seems to place God under necessary rules, including that all-important rule that God "must" exist. I am referring here of course to Anselm's famous Ontological Argument, which argued that God must exist because by definition (a definition that even atheists presumably accept) God is "that than which nothing greater can be conceived"; and since it is greater to exist in reality than just in the mind, God must exist, because to conceive of God existing only in the mind as mere idea would violate the definition of God previously agreed upon. So by necessity God exists.

The argument fails at numerous levels.[12] First of all, if the argument were valid, it would mean that atheists are merely terminologically confused, like people who think there are married bachelors and who thus simply need to consult their dictionaries to get right with the word. But more crucially, the argument rests on the assumption that ideas control reality rather than the reverse. Finally, it presumes, based on the previous assumption, that

---

11. *Cur Deus Homo* I.15, in *Anselm of Canterbury: The Major Works,* ed. Brian Davies and Gillian Evans (Oxford: Oxford University Press, 1998), p. 289. Because other editions are also available, I shall cite the *Cur Deus Homo* by book and chapter number (a "book" in the manuscript tradition usually corresponds to our "chapter" and a manuscript "chapter" to our "section"). Thus *CDH* II, 8 means *Cur Deus Homo,* book 2, chapter 8.

12. It does not, however, fail because the argument places reason over faith, as if Anselm were a Kantian *avant la lettre,* putting God "within the limits of reason alone." We know this because of his other principle for theology: *si comprehendis, non est Deus* ("if you have grasped something, whatever it is you have got hold of is not God"). David Brown gets the distinction exactly right when he writes: "Already in the preface [to *Why God Became Man*] Anselm had announced his intention to proceed by 'necessary reasons.' 'What is inferred to be true by a necessary reason,' he tells us, 'ought not to be called into doubt, even if the reason why it is true is not understood.' That insistence on the limits of human understanding matches well with his repeated insistence throughout this work that *in offering 'necessary' reasons he does not mean to imply any constraint on God.* It is not a case of reason somehow imposing limits on God; rather, it is a matter of human beings coming to comprehend what follows from the fact that God remains consistent with his nature or else, putting it another way, is self-consistent. So . . . we should not think of God as governed by 'necessity' but rather by His own 'eternal constancy.'" David Brown, "Anselm on Atonement," in *The Cambridge Companion to Anselm,* ed. Brian Davies and Brian Leftow (Cambridge: Cambridge University Press, 2004), p. 284; emphasis added.

ideas are fundamentally indistinguishable from reality because they *are* reality, the ultimate reality of the world, more real than the instantiated things in the current world that just happen to exist. In other words, heavily influenced by Plato and innocent of Aristotle's writings, Anselm lacks that distinction between essence and existence that Maximus was groping toward and that Aquinas formulated with such keen philosophical precision a century and a half later.[13]

I am of course highlighting the logic of this argument not because it is directly relevant to Christology but to show how Anselm habitually argues his case. Of more direct relevance is how Anselm applied his principle of necessary reasoning in his extremely influential tract *Cur Deus Homo,* or *Why God Became Man.*[14] Here we seem to find God once again under the necessity of his definitions, this time the definition that requires that God, in order to be God, must be perfectly just and perfectly merciful. Now to us pathetically finite creatures, justice and mercy often seem to be discrepant and even contradictory virtues, as when a presidential pardon causes outrage among citizens who feel a too-easy pardon has violated the norms of justice.[15]

But in God these qualities must perfectly coincide. That means that God cannot just let "bygones be bygones" by offering a kind of celestial presidential pardon that would violate the norms of justice. God's justice, precisely as *God*'s justice, means that God "must" respond justly to an offense against the very justice of God, which "by definition" (again that key moment in Anselm's logic) represents an *infinite* offense, albeit committed by a finite being, Adam. Therefore the compensation or satisfaction must itself be infinite, an obvious impossibility for man. But it was man who committed this catastrophic act of infinite injustice, so only a man can do the atoning. But if God is to be merciful (which he "must" be, as God), then the only "way out,"

13. Karl Barth tried to defend the ontological argument in his book *Fides Quaerens Intellectum* by pointing out that Anselm put forth this argument in the *Proslogion,* which significantly begins with a *prayer* to God for enlightenment. This means, according to Barth, that Anselm had already begun his argument by assuming that God exists. In this Barth is surely right, given Anselm's principle that faith must seek understanding, rather than understanding working itself toward faith. But Barth's thesis does not address the question of whether the argument works on purely philosophical grounds, which Thomas held it did not, based on his notion of the real distinction between essence and reality.

14. The translation of the *Proslogion* and *Cur Deus Homo* may be found in Davies and Evans, *Anselm of Canterbury: The Major Works,* as previously cited.

15. William Shakespeare's play *The Merchant of Venice* centers on the impossibility of reconciling justice and mercy in purely human terms.

so to speak, is for God, in the Person of his Son, to become incarnate as the God-man, whose freely chosen death can alone atone for the infinite offense.

This is what is known as Anselm's doctrine of atonement, and to call it controversial is to speak mildly.[16] But as we said at the outset of this chapter, a text without a context is a pretext; so let us see if sense can be made of Anselm's christological account of the atonement. Prior theories of the atonement drew from any number of images and metaphors: ransom, conquest of the enemy, penal substitution, sacrifice, one friend standing in for another, and so forth. But one of the favorite theories, especially for Gregory of Nyssa and Augustine, is what might be called with only slight (and facetious) exaggeration the Trick-the-Devil theory.

On the basis of Paul's line that "none of the rulers of this age understood this [Christ's true identity], otherwise they never would have crucified the Lord of glory" (1 Cor. 2:8), Gregory developed that phrase into a full-fledged account that combines frankly mythological motifs with, of all things, imagery drawn from fishing. As William Placher points out, it makes for a riveting, if quite disconcerting story:

> According to one view, Adam had yielded to Satan's trickery and obeyed him rather than God, thereby putting humanity under Satan's lordship. Christ then freed us by defeating Satan. According to some accounts he even used trickery to defeat trickery. Since Adam had voluntarily submitted to Satan [although by Satan's deceptive promise], so the argument went, Satan had legitimate rights over all Adam's descendants. Since God is completely just, he could not simply ignore those rights. But *God* had never submitted to Satan, so Satan had no rights over God. Now Christ looked like a mere human being, and therefore Satan, deceived, tried to seize him. Since Christ was also divine, Satan thereby overreached his rights. Now all deals were off, and God could legitimately punish Satan by freeing humanity from his power. In the vivid words of the fourth-century theologian Gregory of Nyssa, "The Deity was under the veil of

---

16. "Among his critics, Anselm has long been the victim of his own clarity; he cuts a conveniently epochal figure because he is identifiably a peculiar product of the early Western Middle Ages, because in arguing for the 'necessity' of a certain picture of redemption he appears to adumbrate Western, Catholic theological method of the following centuries, and because his is so recognizably a *theory* of atonement and hence so easy to abstract, simplify, formulate, and assess [and attack, one might add]." David Bentley Hart, "A Gift Exceeding Every Debt: An Eastern Orthodox Appreciation of Anselm's *Cur Deus Homo*," *Pro Ecclesia* 7 (Summer 1998): 333-49; here 335-36; Hart's emphasis.

our nature, so that, as with ravenous fish, the hook of the Deity might be gulped down along with the bait of flesh." Augustine later said the same thing: "The cross of the Lord became a trap for the devil; the death of the Lord was the bait by which he was ensnared."[17]

Despite the evident charm of this piscine imagery, the underlying deceit that God had to use, if this theory were right, bothered Anselm, again for reasons that should not surprise us. For Anselm felt that God cannot deceive anyone, since he is Truth itself (once again, "by definition").[18] So as an alternative he proposed a theory of atonement not based on "tricking the devil" but on the "debt" we owe to God for having sinned against him. The argument in *Cur Deus Homo* is quite complex,[19] but in a nutshell it says that since we are already indebted to God for our very existence, we have no wherewithal to pay back the debt we owe to God for sin, for "to sin is nothing other than not to render to God his due" (*CDH* I.1). This means that "none but God can make this satisfaction" (II.6), but this he cannot do simply by "wiping the slate clean" without thereby violating his always self-consistent justice. This means that it is necessary that the one making the satisfaction also be a man, "otherwise neither Adam nor his race would make satisfaction for themselves" (II.8). And this leads to the conclusion of the syllogism:

> If, as is certain, it is therefore necessary that the heavenly community be made up of human beings and this cannot take place unless the aforesaid satisfaction be made, which none but God can make and none but a human being ought to make, it is necessary for a God-man to make it. (II.2)[20]

17. William C. Placher, *A History of Christian Theology: An Introduction* (Philadelphia: Westminster Press, 1983), pp. 70-71; emphasis added. The quote from Gregory comes from his *Great Catechism* 24, and the one from Augustine is from Sermon 263, paragraph 1.

18. How such a view is compatible with the line quoted above from 1 Corinthians 2:8 Anselm does not address; but his view seems to conflict with the plain sense of the line. At all events, the church has never solemnly defined one theory of the atonement as better than another, let alone that a particular version advanced by a theologian is heretical. Why that would be so is itself an interesting question, but perhaps it is due to the fact that the New Testament itself seems willing to draw upon any number of images for the atonement, which, when put into systematic order, do not seem to privilege one image or theory over another.

19. David Brown breaks it down into a syllogism of 26 steps! See Brown, "Anselm on Atonement," pp. 281-82.

20. For an intriguing analysis of the range of this redemption and what kind of human beings the heavenly community "needs" to make up its celestial throng, see F. B. A. Asiedu, "Anselm and the Unbelievers: Pagans, Jews, and Christians in the *Cur Deus Homo*," *Theological Studies* 62 (2001): 530-48.

The argument continues because Anselm needs to prove further that it would be fitting only for the Son, and not the Father or the Spirit, to take on this burden of being the God-man ("for no unfitness, however small, is possible with God" [I.20]). The argument, in all its aspects, has met with tremendous resistance, starting with Anselm's contemporaries, who zeroed in on his most basic premise: that while God operates by no external restraint, he is, in the Anselmian construction, "constrained" by his own self-consistent identity *as God* (meaning that this is a "constraint" that God owes only to himself). While Thomas Aquinas's view of the atonement is largely Anselmian, he also insists, *pace* Anselm, that God could have achieved our redemption in other ways, "for nothing is impossible with God."[21]

But this assertion of divine freedom from self-constraint is not without its difficulties either, at least when taken to the extremes of the late-medieval nominalists. These theologians stressed the absolute power *(potentia absoluta)* of God to do *anything* not inherently self-contradictory, thereby making Anselm's first principle a purely negative one: Anselm said that no unfitness, however small, is possible with God. The nominalists changed that to the axiom that God is free to do anything not logically self-contradictory, even if it seems ugly and unfitting to our eyes.

John Duns Scotus (c. 1265-1308) also objected to Anselm's theory, insisting that the notion of an *infinite* debt to God on the part of finite man made no sense, since only God can hold an infinite "debt," and then only to himself. But by making our debt to God finite, Scotus introduced an element into Anselm's theory that would later prove disastrous for church unity: since our debt to God is now finite, it can (theoretically) be "paid off" through merit. To be sure, Scotus called this merit "supervening merit," which accrues to us based on our identification with the death of Christ. But the move, once made, proved consequential: For once Martin Luther inherited the nominalist assumption of God's absolute (that is, completely arbitrary) power and fused it to the Scot's view of a finite and potentially compensable debt, he found himself trapped inside a theological system that wreaked havoc on his religious psychology, with consequences that live on to this day.

The tragedy of the story is that the minor premise of Anselm's debt-based syllogism could have saved Luther all that pain of feeling reprobated by God without a chance of paying recompense, even though he felt he should theoretically be able to pay off his debts to God — for it is precisely

---

21. Thomas Aquinas, *Summa theologiae* III 46, 2.

Anselm's point in insisting that our debt to God is infinite that *we* can *never* pay off our debt to God, *only Jesus can.* Being infinite, our debt could never be paid off no matter how many pilgrimages we make, Masses we have said for our souls, fastings we perform, or works of charity we do. Only Jesus can save, and we are *entirely* dependent on him for our redemption, effected by his atoning death on the cross — the very same premise that evangelical Christianity uses to win converts and get sinners to "open their hearts to Christ." In other words, it is precisely the import of Anselm's theory of the atonement that Jesus has offered *complete* satisfaction for sins by virtue of his identity as the God-man, *fully* God and *fully* man.[22]

But if the medievals objected to Anselm's theory on more abstract grounds of what is theoretically possible with God, nothing compares to the reactions of some modern theologians, who object to the image of God that they say is required of the theory, a kind of miserly divine landlord who demands that his debts be paid even by his most penurious of tenants. Ironically enough, Protestants are especially critical, even though they ought to be the ones most appreciative of Anselm's premises. Adolf von Harnack called Anselm's theory of the atonement "unevangelical," which it most certainly is not for anyone who knows the least about evangelical preaching (think of the hymn "Amazing Grace" here); and his misunderstanding becomes especially glaring in this passage: "The worst thing in Anselm's theory [is its] mythological conception of God as the mighty private man who is incensed at the injury done to his honor and does not forgo his wrath till he has received an at least adequately great equivalent."[23]

In the face of this distorted view, David Brown usefully points out that Anselm's debt-language actually has the very best biblical pedigree of all theories of the atonement — for it comes from Jesus himself, who, according to Matthew's version of the Our Father, teaches his disciples to pray, "forgive us our *debts* as we forgive those *indebted* to us" (Matt. 6:12), a pedigree quite lost by translating the Greek word for "debt" with the misleading "tres-

22. One should recall here that "satisfaction" literally means "doing enough," precisely what Luther felt he could never do by himself. Anselm could hardly disagree, and his devotional works display a vivid sense of his own sinfulness, not to mention that of humanity's. But that sense of sinfulness never led him to despair, perhaps because he would have found the nominalist theory of God's absolute power repulsive (including aesthetically repulsive). But more crucially, he realized that our debt to God was infinite and therefore never (even theoretically) recompensable.

23. A. von Harnack, *History of Dogma* (London: Williams & Norgate, 1899), vol. 4, pp. 68, 76. I owe this reference to Brown, "Anselm on Atonement," pp. 290, 291.

passes."[24] Nor is the notion of offended honor a nonbiblical feudal throw-back, for in the liturgy we say to God "all honor and glory is yours." But still, "a text without a context is a pretext," and so Brown suggests we transpose Anselm's language into our own with a bit of "dynamic equivalence," as it were. Thus he offers two different translations of a line from the *Cur Deus Homo,* one literal and the other modern:

1) Everyone who sins ought to pay back the honor of which he has robbed God; and this is the satisfaction that everyone owes God. (I.11)
2) Anyone who sins should return to God the respect and worship that he has denied him; in doing this he makes up for sin.[25]

At least you can say this about Anselm: he certainly provokes reactions; and as with Cyril of Alexandria, that probably means he must be onto something. In fact, one of the more fascinating aspects of his legacy is the renais-sance he has enjoyed in the past one hundred years, a renaissance that started with several philosophers, mostly from America, who thought that Anselm might be onto something with his Ontological Argument.[26] But that is not our concern here. Of more relevance will be the revival of Anselm's theory on the atonement in the twentieth century in thinkers as widely dis-parate as the French anthropologist René Girard and the Swiss Catholic Hans Urs von Balthasar, who are not in the least intimidated by Harnack's dismissals or the accusation from liberal Christians that the doctrine of the atonement relies on an image of God as patriarchal child-abuser. Clearly, Anselm will never lose his relevance.[27]

24. Although the translation "sin" has biblical pedigree too, as in Luke's version, even Luke reverts to debt-language in the last part of the verse: "and forgive us our sins, for we ourselves forgive all those indebted to us" (Luke 11:4).

25. Brown, "Anselm on Atonement," p. 291.

26. Placher recounts this amusing anecdote, told by the famous atheist philosopher Bertrand Russell on himself: "One day in 1894, as I was walking along Trinity Lane . . . I saw in a flash (or thought I saw) that the ontological argument is valid. I had gone out to buy a tin of tobacco; on my way back, I suddenly threw it up in the air, and exclaimed as I caught it: 'Great Scott, the ontological argument is sound.'" Bertrand Russell, "My Mental Develop-ment," in *The Philosophy of Bertrand Russell,* ed. Paul Arthur Schilpp (La Salle, IL: Open Court, 1944), p. 10. He obviously recovered, but one must add that this is surely an achieve-ment on Anselm's part to have given Russell, for perhaps the only time in his life, a moment of self-doubt about his atheism.

27. Anselm gave his fellow monks quite a shock when he told them that he would prefer to go to hell innocent than be permitted entrance into heaven while still polluted with the

That relevance, however, has come with a price, for Anselm's theory of the atonement has become so controversial that it tends to obscure his insistence on the sheer beauty of the church's doctrine of Christ. Basing himself on a rhetorical technique called "chiasmus," Anselm arranges the events of salvation-history in a tableau of extraordinary loveliness. Chiasmus refers to a reversal in the syntactic structure of two parallel phrases in a sentence, as in Shakespeare's "I wasted time, and now doth time waste me" (*Richard II*, Act V, scene 5, line 49), or Augustine's line that "every man seeks peace by waging war, but no man seeks war by making peace."[28] In a similar way Anselm shows how Christ reverses Adam as Mary reversed Eve: since Eve came virginally from Adam's side, it befits that Christ take flesh from a virginal womb; and because Eve was taken from a male alone, God performed a fitting reversal by being born from a woman alone (*CDH* II.8). Reversal also dictates the kind of suffering Jesus was called upon to undergo: because the human race was conquered with such ease, it was fitting that Christ would have to conquer that catastrophic sin with difficulty (*CDH* II.11). And finally, in a passage that could have assuaged all of Luther's despair about God's total act of reconciliation in Christ, Anselm asks rhetorically: "Is it not fitting that man, who by sinning removed himself as far as he possibly could away from God, should, as recompense to God, make a gift of himself in an act of the greatest possible self-giving?" (II.11).[29]

One final point can be added here: Anselm's theory is hardly the legalis-

---

stain of sin. But the assertion makes perfect sense when one realizes that heaven means union with the all-holy God, who "by definition" cannot tolerate sin. Perhaps he was also making, however unwittingly, a christological point about Christ's descent into hell, who *did* descend to hell sinless so that *we* might be cleansed of sin before entering heaven.

28. To get technical here for a moment, these citations are more accurately called examples of "epanodos," while "chiasmus" refers to reversals of order on larger blocks of text outside of individual phrases.

29. "Anselm is dealing [in the *CDH*] with a single question [posed by Boso]: If the rights of the devil (who himself is already infinitely indebted to God) over humanity are not really 'rights' (a position of purest patristic pedigree), why must death's overthrow proceed as it does? For God could have reclaimed his creation by force, if all that were at issue were the devil's prerogatives; but, for Anselm, the true issue is God's own righteousness. From which unfolds Anselm's story of the 'necessity' (the inner coherence) of the action of the God-man. And it is explicitly not a story about a substitutionary sacrifice offered as simple restitution for human guilt, but concerns rather the triumph over death, the devil, and sin accomplished in Christ's voluntary self-donation to the Father, which the Father receives (as Gregory the Theologian would say) 'by economy,' so that its benefits might redound to those with whom Christ has assumed solidarity." Hart, "A Gift Exceeding Every Debt," pp. 342-43.

tic innovation it has often been seen to be, nor does it lead (rightly interpreted) to an image of God as an exacting judge demanding his just due, as
so many critics claim.[30] In fact, some early Christian writers sound, in retrospect, remarkably Anselmian, if only *avant la lettre,* especially Athanasius:

> He [the Word of God] saw that corruption held us all the closer, because it
> was the penalty for the transgression. He saw too how unthinkable it
> would be for the law to be repealed before it was fulfilled. He saw how *un-
> seemly* it was that the very things of which He Himself was the Artificer
> should be disappearing. . . . The Word perceived that corruption could
> not be got rid of otherwise than through death. Yet He Himself, as the
> Word, being immortal and the Father's Son, was such as could not die. For
> this reason, therefore, He assumed a body capable of death in order that it,
> by belonging to the Word who is above all, might become in dying a suffi-
> cient exchange for all.[31]

Anselm's Christology will never lose its relevance, precisely because his
thought is so deeply grounded in the tradition, indeed in the Bible's own images and doctrine.

Bonaventure

Bonaventure di Fidanza (c. 1217-74) was a Franciscan, and therefore a spiritual son of Francis of Assisi (1181/2-1226), the author of "A Canticle to the
Sun"; and so it does not surprise us to learn that the concept of *creation* will
play a key role in Bonaventure's theology, and therefore in his Christology.[32]
He was not of course a cultist of creation in the manner of modern-day en-
vironmentalists of extreme views, for his was a view of creation in the literal
sense of the word, meaning that which has been truly created by *God.* Not
for Bonaventure, then, is there any notion of the world considered indepen-

30. Including Joseph Ratzinger: "[T]he perfectly logical divine-*cum*-human legal system erected by Anselm distorts [biblical] perspectives and with its rigid logic can make the
image of God appear in a sinister light." Joseph Ratzinger, *Introduction to Christianity,* trans.
J. R. Foster (San Francisco: Ignatius Press, 2004), p. 233.

31. Athanasius, *On the Incarnation,* translated by a Religious of the C.S.N.V. (Crestwood, NY: St. Vladimir's Seminary Press, 1953), pp. 34, 35.

32. "Just as Francis grasped an integral connection between Christ and Creation, so too
Franciscan Christology is marked by its cosmological context." Ilia Delio, O.S.F., "Revisiting
the Franciscan Doctrine of Christ," *Theological Studies* 64 (2003): 3-23; here 5.

dently of God.[33] But this of course was a view that was shared by all his theological contemporaries, where everything was brought under the rubric of Christian revelation. Whatever their differences, all medieval theologians (and artists) agreed on this fundamental principle: that revelation claimed to judge all other truths.[34]

But inside that common field Bonaventure merits our attention because of several unique accents that come from his Franciscan background. His premier interpreter in the English-speaking world, Zachary Hayes, summarizes the unique contours of Bonaventure's thought in this way:

> Even a cursory reading of Bonaventure reveals certain traits in his theological style that have come to be associated with Franciscan theology, so much so that some interpreters would single out the Seraphic Doctor as the truest embodiment of the Franciscan School. Among those qualities which are pointed out as characteristic of Franciscan thought, we may mention: 1) Its clear relation to biblical imagery, 2) The central place given to Christ, 3) The emphasis on the humanity of Christ, 4) The emphasis on God as the Highest Good.[35]

To that list I would also add two other unique features of Bonaventure's theology: his special appreciation, already mentioned, for creation;[36] and his

33. "Looked at from the rationalist point of view of modern philosophy, St. Bonaventure's doctrine [of creation] does undoubtedly appear as the most medieval of medieval philosophies; and so, in certain aspects, it is. No thirteenth-century thinker set himself more systematically to reduce the sciences to theology and put them entirely at its service." Étienne Gilson, *The Philosophy of St. Bonaventure*, trans. Dom Illtyd Trethowan and F. J. Sheed (London: Sheed & Ward, 1938), p. 481.

34. "Whether or not it was the 'greatest of the centuries,' the thirteenth century does hold a special place in the history of Christendom. It was the age of Pope Innocent III and Emperor Frederick II, of Saint Dominic and Saint Francis of Assisi, of Albertus Magnus and Roger Bacon, of Thomas Aquinas and Bonaventure, of Giotto and Dante, of the Fourth Crusade and the Fourth Lateran Council. . . . Probably never before, and perhaps never again, did the Christian view of the world and of man play so decisive a role in the life of the mind." Jaroslav Pelikan, *The Growth of Medieval Theology (600-1300)*, vol. 3: *The Christian Tradition: A History of the Development of Doctrine* (Chicago: University of Chicago Press, 1978), p. 268.

35. Zachary Hayes, O.F.M., "Introduction" to *What Manner of Man? Sermons on Christ by St. Bonaventure*, trans. Zachary Hayes, O.F.M (Chicago: Franciscan Herald Press, 1974), pp. 5-6.

36. "Here, for the last time within Christian theology, the doctrine of the *world* is considered in very close relationship to the doctrine of scriptural revelation." Hans Urs von Balthasar, "Bonaventure," in *The Glory of the Lord: A Theological Aesthetics*, vol. 2: *Studies in Theological Style: Clerical Styles*, trans. Andrew Louth et al. (San Francisco: Ignatius Press,

theology of the Trinity, which registered certain disagreements with — or at least demurrals of — Augustine's theology of the Trinity.[37] Specifically, one can detect a certain distancing in Bonaventure from the notion that *opera omnia Trinitatis ad extra indivisa sunt* ("all the works of the Trinity directed outward are indivisible"). Bonaventure could hardly deny that maxim outright without threatening monotheism. But an overstress on it can lead to its own distortions too: yes, all the actions of the Trinity in the economy of salvation are common to all the Persons of the Trinity, but Bonaventure reminds us that God, when acting *ad extra,* is still always acting *as the trinitarian God,* traces and vestiges of which can be detected throughout creation. True, it is from Augustine that Bonaventure draws this notion of the "vestiges of the Trinity" in creation, but he takes it further than did Augustine:

> When he speaks of the relationship between the Trinity and the creation of the world, Bonaventure clearly distances himself from Augustine, in favor of the view of the Greek fathers. God behaves externally as he is, that is, as Trinity. Therefore, although all his actions in the dispensation of salvation are common to the Trinity, each expresses the individual position of the Persons: the positions of the Son as expression of God and of the Spirit as the self-giving of God are preserved externally just as much as the inner life of the Trinity. . . . *This means nothing less than the grounding of the act of creation in the act of generation within the Godhead.*[38]

The point might seem arcane, but this slight shift of emphasis actually solves a number of problems that had beset pre-Nicene trinitarian theology:

1984), pp. 309-10; emphasis in the original. The assertion "for the last time" might be an exaggeration, especially when one thinks of Duns Scotus, treated below.

37. As we have already seen often enough, theologies of the Trinity, even at their most abstract, *always* have an impact on a theologian's Christology, but this is especially true of Bonaventure: "Since Bonaventure's entire theology deals with the Triune God and the history of His dealings with the world as that history is focused in the history of Jesus Christ, it is virtually impossible to deal with any aspect of his thought without treating in some way the mystery of the Trinity and the person of Christ. As the Bonaventurian metaphysics is primarily an explication of Trinitarian and Christological reality, so the epistemology involves the explication of the role of God and of Christ in the human cognitive process. Since the principle of being and of knowing is identical, it follows that if the being of things can be clarified only in terms of the Trinity and the Word, so the possibility of knowledge [in humans] must imply the operation of the Triune God and His eternal Word" (Hayes, "Introduction," p. 4).

38. Balthasar, "Bonaventure," p. 291; emphasis added.

To base creation in the Trinity in this way avoids both the danger of sub-ordinationism which is found in the early Greek fathers, because every appearance of locating the purpose of the generation of the Son *in* creation is avoided, and likewise [on the other side] the danger of an absorption of the natural order in the supernatural, because the natural order and reason are unreservedly granted their relative independence.[39]

The advantages of this perspective should be clear. First of all, it finally expels a hidden (or often not so hidden) Platonic presupposition inherited from the Greek fathers:

The old Platonic axiom *bonum diffusivum sui* [the good is diffusive of it-self] now, in the light of Christian revelation, no longer refers simply to God's relationship with the world but to his absolute being itself: and this opens the way for an explanation of the structure that belongs to the natural kinds in the world, makes it possible to trace them back to their origin without absorbing them monistically into the rays of the light that is their source.[40]

---

39. Balthasar, "Bonaventure," pp. 291-92; emphasis added. Because Bonaventure defines intra-trinitarian relations not just in terms of the relativity of the Persons to each other (as when we speak of father and son being "relatives") but also in terms of "Expresser" (the Father) and "Exemplar" (the One Expressed, the Son), he can then add another element: symbol as that-which-is-expressed, as Zachary Hayes explains: "It is clear that exemplarity has a critical role to play in Bonaventure's thought both at the philosophical and at the theological levels, for only exemplarity can unlock the deepest meaning of created reality. It is only when we perceive the world in its symbolic nature as the objectification of the self-knowledge of God that we know it in its true reality. In the most fundamental sense, it is God in His own self-knowledge who is the exemplar of all else; and since God exists only as a trinity, exemplarity refers to the entire trinity. But, writes Bonaventure, the Son proceeds by way of exemplarity. The entire mystery of the trinity is reflected in a particular way in the mystery of the Son. *As the full and total expression of God's primal fruitfulness, He is simultaneously the expression of all that God can be in relation to the finite.* While at one level, the whole of the trinity is exemplary with respect to the world, at another level the mystery of exemplarity is concentrated in a unique way in the Son, for the triune structure of God Himself is expressed in Him. *Since the relation between the Father and the Son is the first and primal relation, it is the real basis for any other relation.*" Zachary Hayes, O.F.M, *The Hidden Center: Spirituality and Speculative Christology in St. Bonaventure* (New York: Paulist Press, 1981), pp. 59-60; emphases added.

40. Balthasar, "Bonaventure," p. 285. For an independent echo of these views together with a defense of Bonaventure's Christ-centered trinitarian metaphysics of creation, see Ilia Delio, O.S.M., "Theology, Metaphysics, and the Centrality of Christ," *Theological Studies* 68 (2007): 254-73, especially here at 272-73: "Bonaventure's Christocentric thought may seem

But secondly, and perhaps more importantly, it throws new light on the meaning of the doctrine of the hypostatic union.[41] In his lectures on the hypostatic union Bonaventure has no trouble dispensing with the ancient heresies of the patristic era. For example, docetism (the doctrine that Christ only appeared in a seeming body) he curtly dismisses as blasphemous since it would imply that God was deceiving us; and so he concludes that Christ's flesh is "in a true sense completely similar in nature to our flesh."[42] Similarly he dismisses monophysitism on Cappadocian grounds, citing one of his favorite texts: "He was made in the likeness of men" (Phil. 2:7), which he interprets to mean a fully realized human nature.[43]

Of even greater import for our purposes is Bonaventure's stress on *congruence* in his Christology, what he calls the *medium congruentiae*. He means for this term to be taken first of all technically, referring first to the congruence of soul and body (an anticipation of Thomas's views) as Hayes explains:

---

stifling, but there is irony within: modernity's search for freedom and plurality has led to fragmentation, individualism, and irreverence for the human person and things of creation. While postmodern Christians may favor retrieving the Trinity of history, they shudder at the idea of Christocentrism, as if the centrality of Christ may quench plurality and freedom. Ironically, the postmodern obsession with freedom and respect for difference has led to rampant individualism, isolation, fragmentation, and the longing for community and relatedness. Bonaventure's 'wisdom' of Christ the center is a union in love that differentiates. The more one is in union with the Word of love, the more one finds oneself bearing the Word of love in one's life and thus [is] related to others in community. . . . Bonaventure's 'center' is not an abstract center of the whole but a personal center; that is, every person bears the center because every person is created through the Word of God."

41. Just as the hypostatic union throws light on the meaning of reality: "Bonaventure's emphasis on Jesus Christ as center is a radical step in a new direction. Since Christ is the One in whom ultimate truth and goodness is found, it is Christ and not the Father who is the metaphysical ground of reality. True knowledge is no longer associated with objective universals; rather, it is now identified on the level of the singular, the person of Jesus Christ. Since the basis of all knowledge is eternally generated by a personal relationship of love between the Father and Son, true knowledge is contingent on love, that is, there is no knowledge without relationship or participation in the other through sharing of the good. In Bonaventure's view, knowledge for the sake of deepening love is the basis of wisdom." Ilia Delio, O.S.F., "Bonaventure's Metaphysics of the Good," *Theological Studies* 60 (1999): 228-46; here 242-43.

42. Bonaventure, *Commentary on the Sentences* III, d.2, a.3, q.1, *respondeo*.

43. "It is, therefore, not an abstract or universal human nature that is assumed, but a concrete, individual nature which includes the same essential elements as does any other concrete, individual human nature." Hayes, *Hidden Center*, p. 67. This insight represents a real advance in the clarification of some ambiguities in the reception-history of Chalcedon.

The soul is a medium or a reality which, in its union with the body as completive form, overcomes the opaqueness of inanimate materiality. The body is not a material being existing as such in isolation from the soul; it exists as a human body only and precisely in union with the soul. But if this is the case, then a human body is not merely matter, but human, living matter. For the soul vivifies the body, and the body shares in the intellectual functions of the soul. Thus, in union with the soul, matter becomes a living, human body which is an apt vessel for receiving immortal life. Living by the power of the soul and ordained to perpetual, incorruptible life in the Spirit, the body is rendered fit or congruous for union with the Word. The Word is united immediately and inseparably both to the body and to the soul of Christ.[44]

But Bonaventure's attraction to the concept of congruence in the Incarnation extends far beyond its utility in refuting heresy or otherwise providing technical explanations for the hypostatic union. Much like Anselm's aesthetic interpretation of *rectitudo*, Bonaventure's use of *congruentia* extends throughout his entire interpretation of the relation of the Trinity to creation, the economy of salvation, and man's destiny as a being of flesh and spirit for union with Christ. For just as the Son is the "center term" of the Trinity, so man is the "center term" of creation, placed by God between the angels and the lower orders of creation.[45] Adam's fall shattered that congruence, which was righted by Christ's role as the second Adam, a key motif in Bonaventure's Christology.[46]

As is well known, Franciscan spirituality introduced a new element of realism in its portrayal of the human nature of Christ: the Christmas crèche, for example, is the innovation of Francis himself, and the Franciscans made the Stations of the Cross a popular devotion. This stress on the human sufferings of Christ during his Passion had an obvious influence on Bonaventure's views of the human soul of Christ, deftly summarized by Marilyn McCord Adams in these words:

44. Hayes, *Hidden Center*, pp. 70-71.

45. Balthasar makes the good point that Bonaventure's placement of man as the midpoint and summit of the world guards against the charge that his doctrine is too one-sidedly spiritual, in the sense of being in flight from the world or one that seeks an ecstatic departure from the body (Balthasar, "Bonaventure," p. 315).

46. C. Colt Anderson rightly points out that "Bonaventure portrays Christ as the fulfillment of the promises and not as a stage of partial fulfillment of God's promises," which had been the gravamen of Joachim of Fiore's view of salvation history: C. Colt Anderson, *A Call to Piety: Saint Bonaventure's Collations on the Six Days* (Quincy, IL: Franciscan Press, 2002), p. 106.

For Bonaventure, the human soul is no aloof pilot directing a ship through rocky shoals. No, the soul hurts when the body hurts; when reason is distressed, the senses cry out. In this discussion, Bonaventure also displays his steadfast commitment to the reality of Christ's human nature, not only of mind but also of passible and pierceable body, not only of its rational but also of its sensory powers. . . . Christ's reason-as-nature is acutely afflicted at the damage to His body and the suffering of His senses, and this suffering is also of very high degree due to the keenness of Christ's sensory powers. That Christ's real human faculties are fully engaged in suffering His passion and death is necessary — Bonaventure thinks — for our salvation.[47]

For Bonaventure *congruence* refers to a constellation of elements that converge upon its proper center: Christ as both the "center term" of the Trinity *and* the redeeming center of a now-restored creation. Christ as the Incarnate Word is thus the midpoint and summit of all things for Bonaventure; and, as Balthasar rightly points out, "there is nothing that Bonaventure declared with greater fondness and detail" than this motif of Christ as the midpoint of creation.[48] As Bonaventure himself puts it: "Christ is the source-principle and the origin of every human science. As the one sun sends out many rays, so the numerous and varied sciences proceed from the one spiritual sun, the one teacher."[49] This stress on this connection between the Logos of creation and the inner logic of science is perhaps that feature of Bonaventure's Christology that has the most relevance for today, a point made by Joseph Ratzinger in his doctoral dissertation of 1959:

[In Bonaventure] Christ is presented as the center of all things. He is, therefore, also the center of all the sciences in as far as we must go on beyond the "literal sense" of the individual sciences to the hidden, deeper meaning. . . . In this vision, it is true to say that Christ, among other things, is the *medium distantiae;* that is, He is [even] that center that is the concern of the mathematician, and He is this *medium* precisely in His crucifixion. . . . [In other words] the lost middle of the circle is found

47. Marilyn McCord Adams, *What Sort of Human Nature? Medieval Philosophy and the Systematics of Christology,* The Aquinas Lecture, 1999 (Milwaukee: Marquette University Press, 1999), p. 47.

48. Balthasar, "Bonaventure," p. 326.

49. From a sermon of Bonaventure's for the 22nd Sunday after Pentecost; cited in Balthasar, p. 326.

again by means of two lines that intersect at right angles, that is, by a cross. This means that by His cross, Christ has definitively solved the geometry-problem of world history. With His cross He has uncovered the lost center of the circle of the world so as to give true direction and meaning to the movement of the individual life and to the history of mankind as such.[50]

Thomas Aquinas

Despite the fact that the influence of the Angelic Doctor Thomas Aquinas (c. 1225-74) has waxed and waned in the course of history, no one has ever really disputed — even in those eras when he exerted the least influence — that he stands as the most significant and even magisterial theologian the Catholic Church has ever produced. Unanimity, however, stops there. Even among those who acknowledge his authority, dispute rages about exactly what he said, how his authority in the church functions, and what his significance should be for today. But no one could possibly dispute his standing, made all the more remarkable by the fact that he produced roughly eight million words in an age when all books were hand-produced in manuscript form; and most astonishing of all, he died at the relatively young age of 49.

In some ways his Christology is the least innovative portion of his legacy.[51] But, however paradoxically, it also represents that part of his teaching that is most disputed today. No other doctrine taught by Thomas in either the philosophical or theological realm, with the possible exception of his teaching on the nature-grace relationship, has caused more neuralgia for contemporary theologians than his Christology. Here is how Roch Kereszty draws the bottom line on his own balance sheet, an assessment widely echoed in the rest of the theological world:

---

50. Ratzinger, *The Theology of History in St. Bonaventure,* trans. Zachary Hayes, O.F.M. (Chicago: Franciscan Herald Press, 1971), p. 146.

51. One sign of Thomas's thoroughly traditional Christology is Jaroslav Pelikan's decision to treat only in passing Thomas's contribution to the *development* of Christian doctrine in his five-volume study of its development: "Although I was, as my earlier publications indicate, better prepared to write about Thomas than about any of the other authors on whom I have drawn in the present volume, the limitations I have imposed on the subject matter of [this work] made a detailed exposition of Thomistic thought unjustifiable, despite its obvious attractions." Jaroslav Pelikan, *The Christian Tradition: A History of the Development of Doctrine,* vol. 3: *The Growth of Medieval Theology (600-1300)* (Chicago: University of Chicago Press, 1978), p. vii.

St. Thomas built a consistent Christological system from elements of the patristic and medieval tradition. He deduced his Christology from one basic principle accepted in faith, that of the hypostatic union. His system shows convincingly the intrinsic unity between Christology proper and soteriology. . . . However, his speculative, metaphysical emphasis resulted in various deficiencies of both structure and content. Structurally, [his] Christology is misplaced in the *Summa*. The final goal of man, the grace offered to fallen man, and man's moral life, all receive their concrete shape and form through Christ. As a consequence, Christology should have preceded the treatise on grace and morality. Moreover, his one-sided deductive method does not do justice to the portrait of Jesus as it emerges from the synoptic gospels. Thomas does not admit ignorance or even limitations in the knowledge of the earthly Jesus, nor does he see any real development in him. According to Thomas, there is no real difference between the earthly and risen Jesus except for the glorification of his body.[52]

In my opinion, this assessment fails in almost all respects and reads rather like the book reviewer who accuses the author of not writing the book the reviewer wished to write. I am referring here specifically to the charge that Thomas should have placed his Christology in the second part of the *Summa*, rather than the third.[53] But this preference reflects the fashion of contemporary systematic theologies, which frequently follow a vaguely trinitarian model, in which treatments of philosophical theology, the divine unity, God's action in the world, and so forth, come in the first part, while salvation history culminating in the coming of Christ is treated in the second part, and ecclesiological issues and moral theology are taken up in the third part, roughly mirroring the distinction between Father, Son, and Spirit.

But that was not Thomas's intention in conceiving the outline of the *Summa theologiae*. Rather than compose his theology in terms of salvation history, he cast everything in terms of the neo-Platonic schema of *exitus-reditus*, that is, of the proceeding-forth of creation out of God's creative act,

52. Roch A. Kereszty, O. Cist., *Jesus Christ: Fundamentals of Christology,* ed. J. Stephen Maddux (Staten Island, NY: Alba House, 1991), 224.

53. "Aquinas' seemingly tardy location of Christ . . . never ceases to raise questions. Should not Jesus appear first in any theology? Is not Christology on a higher level than a Christian psychology of grace? Is he not more important than our lives and stories?" Thomas F. O'Meara, O.P, *Thomas Aquinas Theologian* (Notre Dame: University of Notre Dame Press, 1997), p. 128.

which God had initially done so as finally to bring all things back to himself. One can certainly argue if one likes that casting systematic theology in terms of salvation history is preferable to the schema of *exitus-reditus,* but that preference is itself a product of modern developments unknown to the medievals, who unanimously accepted (at least up to the time Thomas was working) this neo-Platonic assumption.[54] Besides, why not give Thomas the benefit of the doubt by allowing that he managed to "put moral theology in its place," so to speak, by sandwiching it (as Part II of the *Summa*) between Trinity (treated in Part I) and Christology (Part III)?[55]

Of course, the allegedly Procrustean bed of the *exitus-reditus* schema is hardly the only assumption that causes the difficulty so many have with Thomas's Christology. A much more common objection is voiced in Kereszty's last charge: that Thomas's supposed "deductive" method distorts the picture (and therefore the doctrine) of Jesus as presented in the Gospels. I am referring here above all to Thomas's teaching that Jesus enjoyed from the moment of his conception the "beatific vision" of God. At first glance the thesis does sound odd: How can a being who has not yet reached conscious-

54. As one author tartly observes, "If this embarrasses you, then you will find Aquinas embarrassing." M.-D. Chenu, O.P., *Toward Understanding St. Thomas,* trans. A.-M. Landry and D. Hughes (Chicago: Regnery, 1964), p. 9. One might add that Thomas's schema has excellent biblical warrant: "All things were created through Christ [*exitus*] and for him [*reditus*]" (Col. 1:16b). Plus it can be argued both that Thomas is not as reliant on neo-Platonism as is often alleged, and that insofar as Thomas is a neo-Platonist (at least as mediated by Dionysius the Areopagite), that makes him all that much more our contemporary: "Dionysius's authority and ambiguity brought Aquinas many opportunities for further development of his own thought in Christology. As an acutely perceptive theologian, Aquinas gladly borrows much from Dionysius in constructing his teaching on Christ, but uses him with great care so as to clarify both the sacred teaching itself and Dionysius as an authority. . . . When writing his treatise on Christ in the *Summa Theologiae,* Aquinas tellingly begins with a quotation from Dionysius on divine goodness because it is precisely in Christ that one comes to know the infinite love [of Christ] drawing sinners on the way back to the most loving God. Aquinas thus wholeheartedly agrees with the central principle of divine love that guides Dionysian Christology, a principle well worth stressing in their times and ours." Andrew Hofer, O.P., "Dionysian Elements in Thomas Aquinas's Christology: A Case of Authority and Ambiguity of Pseudo-Dionysius," *The Thomist* 72 (2008): 409-42; here 442.

55. "This purposeful design . . . indicates that, for Aquinas, a proper grasp of Christian morality comes only when [it is] put in direct relation both to the Trinity (the *Prima Pars*) and to Christ (the *Tertia Pars*)." Paul Gondreau, *The Passions of Christ's Soul in the Theology of St. Thomas Aquinas* (Münster: Aschendorff, 2002), p. 22. Somewhat the same point is made by Jean-Marc Laporte, S.J., "Christ in Aquinas's *Summa theologiae:* Peripheral or Pervasive?" *The Thomist* 67 (2003): 221-48.

ness, let alone the age of reason, enjoy a *vision* of God, which surely must presuppose consciousness? The problem is compounded by the fact that in contemporary English, "beatific" implies that one is "blissed out" in some kind of mystical or drug-induced stupor, hardly the impression one gets from reading the Gospels, even John's. (Given the technicalities of this issue, discussion of this topic will be prorogued to the *Excursus* following this chapter. The task here will be merely to set forth Thomas's wider Christology in its historical theological context.)

The main body of Thomas's Christology can be found chiefly in two places: in Book IV of the *Summa contra Gentiles* and in Part III of the *Summa theologiae*.[56] One of the more remarkable features of these tractates, especially when viewed against previous medieval Christologies, is their grounding in the christological debates of the patristic era. For along with the influx of Aristotelian texts in their original Greek, the West was also finally beginning to gain access to the writings of the fathers and, most remarkably, to the conciliar documents themselves, so that Thomas was really "the first scholastic of the thirteenth century to quote the texts of Chalcedon and other early councils."[57] He worked on the *Summa contra Gentiles* from 1259 to around 1265 and then began work on the *Summa theologiae* in 1266 and kept at it with Stakhanovite industry until his mental collapse in late 1273.[58] This dating is

56. There are also christological tracts to be found in Thomas's commentaries on the so-called *Sentences* of Peter Lombard. These "sentences" (from the Latin word for "opinions") were a compendium of various theological opinions inherited from the past that became the basis for a neophyte theologian's induction into the guild of theologians, as a way to cut his "eye teeth," as it were, on the tradition so that he might develop his own dialectical skills: "Lecturing on the *Sentences* played an important role in the training of the Scholastic theologian, and was the last major step in qualifying for employment at the university. Through the *Sentences,* one was exposed to major theological topics, as well as pertinent authorities on these topics." Joseph Wawrykow, "Hypostatic Union," in *The Theology of Thomas Aquinas,* ed. Rik van Nieuwenhove and Joseph Wawrykow (Notre Dame: University of Notre Dame Press, 2005), 222-51, here 251, note 44. Given their obvious propaedeutic purpose, Thomas's Christology in his commentaries on these *Sentences* will not be treated here. A good discussion of the influence of Lombard on Thomas's Christology throughout his career can be found in Walter H. Principe, C.S.B, "St. Thomas on the Habitus Theory of the Incarnation," in *St. Thomas Aquinas, 1274-1974: Commemorative Studies,* ed. Etienne Gilson (Toronto: Pontifical Institute of Medieval Studies Press, 1974), vol. 1, pp. 381-418. Thomas of course also wrote commentaries on many books of the New Testament; his commentary on John is especially important for his Christology, and that will be discussed in this section too, where appropriate.

57. J. A. Weisheipl, *Friar Thomas d'Aquino* (New York: Doubleday, 1974), p. 164.

58. Thomas commented on Lombard's *Sentences* in the years of his apprenticeship

important because Thomas spent the years between 1261 and 1265 in Orvieto, an ancient town of Etruscan origins located in Umbria, a region in central Italy. It was there that Thomas made an intensive study of patristic texts, where he composed his famous *Catena aurea*, a compilation of those same texts, including some by authors unknown at the time in the West.

But this *Catena* (a Latin word meaning "chain" or "string" on which pearls or other objects were strung in the manner of a necklace) was no mere compilation, as the name might otherwise imply. As is widely recognized by scholars today, the publication of the *Catena* marked a turning point in Thomas's intellectual development and was an immediate publishing success. And no wonder either, as Jean-Pierre Torrell explains:

> Initially a simple compilation, this work in reality takes on a considerable importance: First, for the quantity and quality of the material assembled, then because Thomas shows here an exceptional knowledge, for his time, of Greek Patristics; thus he cites fifty-seven Greek authors compared with twenty-two Latins, of whom certain ones . . . were unknown in the West before their use in the *Catena*. . . . [It] is even more interesting that the person whom we willingly regard as the archetype of the metaphysician and speculative theologian also occupies a place of the first rank in the history of positive and patristic theology.[59]

The result of this research on the *contra Gentiles* led to what is, in effect, the first history of patristic dogma ever penned in the West, the predecessor, ironically enough, of Harnack's nineteenth-century history of dogma (without, of course, Harnack's tendentious editorializing about the nefarious influence of his pet bugbear, "Hellenization"). Not only was Thomas, therefore, the first historian in the West of christological doctrine, he also narrated that history in terms that have influenced (even if often unwittingly) all subsequent dogmatic histories: for he was the first to give an account of the rise of orthodoxy and its coming to a full expression of itself by means of its encounter with heresies and/or inadequate proposals.[60]

---

from 1252 to 1256 and thus began work on the *contra Gentiles* three years later, and started work on his final *Summa* almost immediately after the first's completion. Henceforth in this text the *Summa contra Gentiles* will be called in the body of the text the *contra Gentiles* and cited in the notes as *ScG*, while the *Summa theologiae* will be called simply the *Summa* and cited in the notes as *ST*. (Peter Lombard wrote his *Sentences* between 1154 and 1158.)

59. Jean-Pierre Torrell, O.P., *Saint Thomas Aquinas*, vol. 1: *The Person and the Work*, trans. Robert Royal (Washington, DC: Catholic University of America Press, 1996), p. 139.

60. "It would appear that readers of Aquinas, whether disciple or foe, were stunningly

Not surprisingly, Thomas leads off his treatment in the *contra Gentiles* with an open avowal of Christology's inherent paradoxicality: "Indeed, among the divine works, this most especially exceeds reason: for nothing can be thought of which is more marvelous than this divine accomplishment: that the true God, the Son of God, should become true man" (*ScG* IV 27.1). Further, those who fail to keep in mind this paradox soon end up in heresy: "Yet this appears foreign to what natural reason experiences, and therefore some later on took a position . . . entirely repugnant to the teaching of the faith" (*ScG* IV 37.1,2).

As we learned in Chapter 4, the fundamental and essential paradox of christological doctrine dissolves whenever a theologian collapses either the divinity or the humanity of Christ for the sake of a conceptual unity not grounded in the reason-transcending hypostatic union. Thomas fully grants the difficulties here and even displays a modified sympathy for the reason why heretics so regularly fall into traps:

> Since . . . there is one and the same person of the Word of God and of the man, a certain difficulty remains in the consideration of this truth. For necessarily the Personhood is determined by the divine nature. But the case seems to be the same for human nature [as well]; for everything which subsists in an intellectual or a rational nature is precisely what is meant by person. Hence, it does not seem possible that there be one Person and two natures, human and divine. (*ScG* IV 35.1)

Hence the "obvious" solutions of adoptionists, Arians, Nestorians, and Eutychians, who from different initial presuppositions all end up tailoring the mystery to their own logic.[61] Eutyches especially comes in for just this criticism. Indeed, Thomas's rejoinder here constitutes an important founda-

---

inattentive to the new Greek documentation that Aquinas had attempted to introduce into Christological discourse, preferring to cite the usual Latin authorities, as transmitted principally through the Lombard's *Sentences*. This makes for a rather impoverished reception of Aquinas' Christology" (Wawrykow, "Hypostatic Union," p. 250, note 33). Indeed, I would add that it makes for an impoverished Christology *tout court*. No Christology can ever be adequate that is not thoroughly grounded in the thinking of the church fathers.

61. "When the heretics heard that in Christ a union of God and man took place, they approached the exposition of this point in contrary ways, but neglected the way of the truth. For some thought of this union after the mode of things united into one nature: so Arius and Apollinaris, holding that the Word stood to the body of Christ as soul or as mind; and so Eutyches, who held that before the Incarnation there were two natures of God and man, but after the Incarnation only one" (*ScG* IV 41.4).

tion for his later, more abstract and metaphysical treatment of the Incarnation in the second *Summa*. Here are the principles he sets forth more briefly in the first *Summa:*

> There was in Christ Jesus a body, a rational soul, and divinity. And clearly, the body of Christ even after the union was not the very divinity of the Word; for the body of Christ even after the union could be touched, could be seen with bodily eyes, and had distinctly outlined members. All of these are foreign to the divinity of the Word. . . . In like fashion the soul of Christ was other than the divinity of the Word, because after the union the soul of Christ was affected by the passions of sadness, of sorrow, and of anger. These too are entirely disproportionate to the divinity of the Word. . . . But a human soul and a human body constitute a human nature. Thus, then, even after the union, the human nature in Christ was other than the divinity of the Word which is the divine nature. Therefore, in Christ, even after the union, there are two natures. (*ScG* IV 35.3)

Another error, on the opposite end, takes place when the integrity of the two natures is conceded but the union is regarded as, in whatever respects, accidental.[62] The only alternative to this implicitly Nestorian heresy is to insist on the integrity of Christ's human nature *across the board,* very much including the human personality that is an inherent aspect of Christ's human soul, as Thomas explains in this often overlooked passage:

> Others wished to avoid this awkwardness [of attributing two persons to Christ, both Word and man]. So, regarding the human nature they introduced a disposition such that personality could not be properly suitable to it. They said that the soul and the body, in which the integrity of human nature consists, were so assumed by the Word that the soul was not united to the body to establish any substance, *lest they be forced to say that the substance so established fulfilled the account of person. . . .* It must [on the contrary] be laid down that the union of the Word and the man was

---

62. "But others, seeing the impossibility of this position, went off on a contrary road. Now, the things which accrue to one having a nature but do not belong to the integrity of that nature, seem either to be accidents — say, whiteness and music; or to stand in an accidental relation — say, a ring, a garment, a house, and the like. Of course, they weighed this: Since the human nature accrues to the Word of God without belonging to the integrity of His nature, it is necessary (so they thought) that the human nature have an accidental union with the Word" (*ScG* IV 41.5). On this issue see J. L. A. West, "Aquinas on the Metaphysics of *Esse* in Christ," *The Thomist* 66 (2002): 231-50.

such that one nature was not breathed together out of two; and that the union of the Word to the human nature was not like that of a substance — a man, say — to those externals which are accidentally related to him, like a house and a garment. But let the Word be set down as subsisting in a human nature as in one made his very own by the incarnation; and in consequence that body is truly the body of the Word of God, and the soul in like manner, and the Word of God is truly man. (*ScG* IV 41.6-7)

This conclusion of the full integrity of the human soul of Jesus will form an important basis for the generally more abstract, metaphysical, and topic-determined Christology of Part III *(tertia pars)* of the *Summa theologiae*.[63] But this characterization can be overdone. The *tertia pars* consists of ninety questions, fully fifty-nine of which are devoted to Christology — a very large number, so large that this section of the *Summa* is conventionally divided into two major sections, the first (qq. 1-26) dealing with the "metaphysics" of the Incarnation, the second (qq. 27-59) with the life and death of the Savior, that is, with what he has done for us — the very reason that God made his Son incarnate in the first place (John 3:16).

In other words, Thomas's treatment of Christ, even in the second *Summa,* is strikingly *biblical* and therefore *narrative* in its approach, at least in the latter section, more so perhaps than is often recognized, at least on the popular level.[64] And because, as we saw in Chapter 3, the Bible never narrates its events except in the highly pitched tones of a cosmic *drama,* Thomas's Christology, too, is often cast in dramatic terms, although the stately pace

63. ". . . patristic discussions of Christ do not, as in the *contra Gentiles,* provide the structure of the account of the hypostatic union in the [second] *Summa.* Aquinas here follows a more purely topical, rather than historical, order in presenting the basic aspects of the union of the two natures in the Person of Christ" (Wawrykow, "Hypostatic Union," p. 234).

64. Some commentators claim that only the second section, treating the mysteries of the life of Christ, can be described as biblically based, the first section being strictly "scientific." For example M. D. Chenu speaks of the "biblical zones" in the *Summa,* meaning the second section comprising questions 27-59. (See M. D. Chenu, *Toward Understanding St. Thomas,* p. 316.) But surely the only reason for the earlier "scientific" section was to provide a foundation for the second section in the *saving intentions of God,* which we saw in the previous chapters can only be done on trinitarian and incarnational grounds. Surely John Boyle is right here when he says: "In [questions 1-26, Thomas] arms his reader with an understanding of who and what Christ is so as to grasp more profoundly [in questions 27-59] the meaning of what Christ does. . . . The complexity of Thomas's analysis of Christ's life is only possible given the fullness of his examination of who and what Christ is in the first part." John Boyle, "The Twofold Division of St. Thomas's Christology in the *Tertia Pars,*" *The Thomist* 60, no. 3 (July 1996): 439-47; here 444, 446-47.

and serene consideration of each question he treats can often obscure the underlying drama he is considering. For example, in treating the question of whether Christ suffered more intensely than any other human being, Thomas points out that Christ took upon himself the sins of everyone and, precisely because of his wisdom and love, he understood the evil nature of sin better than did those who committed the sin, so that his "contrition" exceeded that of any other human being:

> Christ grieved not only over the loss of his own bodily life, but also over the sins of all others. And this grief in Christ surpassed all grief of every contrite heart, both because it flowed from a greater wisdom and charity, by which the pang of contrition is intensified, and because he grieved at the one time for all sins, according to Isaiah [53:4]: *Surely he hath borne our sorrows.* But such was the dignity of Christ's life in the body, especially on account of the Godhead united with it, that its loss, even for one hour, would be a matter of greater grief than the loss of another man's life for howsoever long a time. . . . And in like fashion Christ laid down his most beloved life for the good of charity, according to Jeremiah [12:7]: *I have given my dear soul into the hands of her enemies.* (*ST* III q.46 a.6 obj. 4)

But of course, what makes this suffering specifically salvific is not just that Jesus understood the real meaning of sin better than sinners but that he understood it because of who he was: hence the necessity for Thomas to set forth in Questions 1 through 26 Christ's full divine-human identity. On the one hand, he insists that Christ assumed a human nature, not a hypostasis taken over at the moment of the incarnation.[65] *However,* Thomas will insist on the other hand that *what* is assumed (the human nature) includes a fully human soul (q.5 a.3), a fully human mind (a.4), and a fully human will (q.18 a.18). In sum: "Nothing God planted in our nature is lacking in the human nature assumed by the Word of God" (9.4), very much including the passions: "The passions of the soul were in Christ just as with everything else pertaining to the human nature" (q.15 a.4).[66]

---

65. "Augustine says [*De Fide ad Petrum* ii] that *God assumed the nature, not the person of man.* I reply that a thing is said to be assumed inasmuch as it is taken into another. Hence what is assumed must be presupposed to the assumption, just as what is moved must exist prior to the motion. . . . Hence it follows that the Son of God nowise assumed a human person" (*ST* III q.4 a.2). The argument in other words is chronological: "the individual to whom the human nature is assumed is none other than the Divine Person, who is the term of the assumption" (III q.4 a.3).

66. On this point see the definitive study by Gondreau, *The Passions of Christ's Soul,*

From this flows the requirement that Christ's human soul be both receptive to grace and have that grace in its fullness, both habitual and gratuitous: "because together with the unity of person there remains distinction of natures, the soul of Christ is not essentially divine. Hence it behooves it to be divine by participation, which is grace" (q.7 a.1 ad 1). Further, that grace must be finite, not infinite: "Grace is something created in the soul. But every created thing is finite. . . . Therefore, the grace of Christ is not infinite" (q.7 a.11). From this flows as well the consequence that the human soul of Christ is not omnipotent: "What is proper to God cannot belong to any creature. But it is proper to God to be omnipotent. . . . Therefore the soul of Christ, as being a creature, has not omnipotence" (q.13 a.1); it feels pain and sorrow: "as there could be true pain in Christ, so too could there be true sorrow" (q.15 a.6); it knows fear: "As sorrow is caused by the apprehension of a present evil, so also is fear caused by the apprehension of a future evil, . . . and thus fear was in Christ, even as sorrow" (q.15 a.7); Christ's human soul (or, here, mind) acquires (some of its) knowledge by experience and acquisition (q.9 a.4): "human wisdom is that which is acquired in a human manner, that is, by the light of the active intellect. Therefore Christ advanced in this knowledge" (q.12 a.2).[67] Finally, on the basis of all of the above, Christ had the fullness of the virtues (q.7 a.2).[68]

---

cited above. One implication of Thomas's position on Christ's passion is of course the logical implication that the passions as such cannot be sinful (hence the Council of Trent's later condemnation of Martin Luther's position that concupiscence is itself sinful). In other words, Thomas is far more appreciative in his anthropology of the human passions than is often realized. On this see Paul Gondreau, "The Passions and the Moral Life," *The Thomist* 71 (2007): 419-50.

67. According to Kevin Madigan, "From the third century through the eighth, Christian exegetes (both Greek and Latin) were deeply divided on the issue of whether Jesus in fact progressed in human knowledge. However, from the eighth century to the thirteenth, almost all Latin expositors denied that Jesus truly so progressed. . . . In this context, it is remarkable that Thomas Aquinas was willing to depart, late in his career, from his mendicant contemporaries and teachers, from the majority opinion of the fathers and, interestingly, from his own early interpretation of the text [of Luke 2:40]. . . . Had Christ not progressed in knowledge, it would have been impossible for Thomas to maintain the central Christian conviction that Christ's humanity was consubstantial with ours. For Thomas to state that Christ progressed in knowledge is to affirm that Christ's humanity was indeed complete and utterly consubstantial with ours." Kevin Madigan, *The Passions of Christ in High-Medieval Thought: An Essay on Christological Development*, Oxford Studies in Historical Theology (Oxford: Oxford University Press, 2007), pp. 24, 36.

68. But according to Thomas, Christ did not have the virtues of faith or hope (q.7 aa.2-3); nor for Thomas was Christ ignorant (q.15 a.3). These positions seem at odds with the

These principles, serenely stated, form the foundation for the much more dramatically colored presentation of the mysteries of Christ's life in the second section of the *tertia pars,* questions 27 to 59. The limitations of space prevent this chapter from being able to provide a full account of this section; but its dramatic power comes through perhaps most effectively at question 46, article 5, where Thomas asks if Christ endured all sufferings. Specifically, Thomas answers in the negative, in the sense that no one human being can experience both burning and drowning; but "speaking generically, he did endure every human suffering." And what were those sufferings? Here only a full quotation will suffice to bring out Thomas's portrait of the drama of our salvation during the Passion of Christ:

> First of all, [Christ suffered] on the part of men: for he endured some-thing from Gentiles and from Jews; from men and from women, as is clear from the women servants who accused Peter. He suffered from the rulers, and from servants and from the mob. . . . . He suffered from friends and ac-quaintances, as is manifest from Judas betraying and Peter denying Him. Secondly, the same is evident on the part of the sufferings which a man can endure. For Christ suffered from friends abandoning him; in his rep-utation, from the blasphemies hurled at him; in his honor and glory, from the mockeries and the insults heaped upon him; in things, for he was de-spoiled of his garments; in his soul, from sadness, weariness, and fear; in his body, from wounds and scourgings. Thirdly, it may be considered with regard to his bodily members. In his head he suffered from the crown of piercing thorns; in his hands and feet, from the fastening of the nails; on his face from the blows and spittle; and from the lashes over his entire body. Moreover, he suffered in all his bodily senses: in touch, by being scourged and nailed; in taste, by being given vinegar and gall to drink; in smell, by being fastened to the gibbet in a place reeking with the stench of corpses; in hearing, by being tormented with the cries of blasphemers and scorners; in sight, by beholding the tears of his mother and of the disciple whom he loved. (q.46 a.5)

This extraordinary passage highlights a theme that became increasingly dominant in Western theology: the stress on Christ's sufferings, in all their

---

points made above, and even with his remark on Christ's agony in the Garden of Olives that *erat talis dubitatio in Christo quantum ad sensualitatem* (*Sent.* III 17.4). These tensions come to the fore especially in Thomas's account of Christ's beatific vision, the technicalities of which are reserved for treatment in the *Excursus* following this chapter.

fullness, as inherently atoning, a motif already present in Franciscan spirituality and one that would come to full flower in the mystics, all the way up to modern times. Of course, what makes those sufferings inherently salvific is due to the one on whom they were inflicted (the Roman slave Spartacus was crucified too, but no one attributed release from bondage to this slave's tragic death — quite the opposite in fact). Which brings us back to the central paradox of the incarnation, and more specifically to how Thomas interpreted that paradox: Has Thomas illuminated the paradox through a theology that gives due respect for the essential mystery of the incarnation, or has he dissolved it under a mountain of syllogistic reasoning? The answer in one sense is easy to come by, and can be found in Thomas's own words already cited: "Among the divine works, this [doctrine of the incarnation] most especially exceeds [man's] reason. For nothing can be thought of which is more marvelous than this divine accomplishment: that the true God, the Son of God, should become true man" (*ScG* IV 27, 1).

This judgment, that Thomas has given due priority to the reason-challenging paradox of the incarnation, however, has not always been the judgment of history. According to one influential school of thought, Thomas used Aristotelian logic, with its well-known phobia of self-contradictory statements, to bleach out the essential paradoxicality of the Christian message. For is that not the very purpose of the scholastic method: to juxtapose seemingly contradictory statements in Scripture and tradition in the opening *videtur quod* ("it would *seem* that . . .") and *sed contra* ("on the other hand") sections, only to be resolved in the all-reconciling *respondeo* ("I answer as follows") section? But on closer examination this objection can be shown to be specious. For in fact the scholastic method is the prime example of the principle that pervades our treatment of Christology in this book: that "paradox gives rise to theology." As Denis Janz rightly points out:

> It should be noted that the Scholastic method took as its most basic task the resolution of contradictions. . . . Each article sets up the theological problematic in the initial arguments and the *sed contra* — a yes and no. The mind, ill at ease in the presence of this contradiction, then works to resolve it in the response. The resolution it achieves is more often than not another yes and no which can be held simultaneously because of a distinction Aquinas makes in his response. Still, the fact remains that Aquinas's answer to most questions is a simultaneous yes and no. Whenever this is the case, we are in the proximity of paradox. For is paradox not an

apparent contradiction that the mind suspects is not utter nonsense but points in fact to a hidden truth?[69]

To be sure, one can easily point to passages in Thomas where his method clearly seeks to resolve an apparent paradox by dissolving it, as in his exegesis of this Pauline paradox: "For my power is made perfect in weakness" (2 Cor. 12:9), which Thomas explains (or for some "explains away") by claiming that Paul is referring to the weakness of the lower appetitive powers of the soul, not to its higher rational powers; and thus Paul is encouraging *fortitude* not infirmity, just as the spirit is willing but the flesh weak.[70] Here Paul's paradox becomes but a *seeming* paradox through the introduction of a distinction, which then translates the paradox into a simple assertion. But in this case at least, Thomas has a point, for Paul could hardly be recommending infirmity for its own sake, anymore than Jesus was recommending that someone pluck out his right eye when it becomes the cause of sin (Matt. 5:29). Furthermore, as Janz rightly observes, "does not any attempt to explain a paradox do this to some extent? Which thinker, when faced with a paradox, does not attempt to explain it in some way?"[71]

I would go further and say that a refusal to let paradox give rise to thought harms theology. Compared to Martin Luther, Søren Kierkegaard, and G. K. Chesterton, Thomas is certainly no pure reveler in paradox. But I wonder how far pure indulgence in paradox can take theology, as the example of Karl Barth proves, who began with an almost stroboscopic celebration of paradox in his famous commentary on Romans, but then felt he had to move to a more careful appreciation of the inner rationality of the Christian

69. Denis R. Janz, "Syllogism or Paradox: Aquinas and Luther on Theological Method," *Theological Studies* 59 (1998): 3-21; here 15. I shall be drawing most of my examples to demonstrate Thomas's reliance on Christian paradox from this well-researched and paradigm-altering article.

70. "It seems that fortitude is not a virtue, for the Apostle says 'Virtue is perfected in infirmity.' But fortitude is contrary to infirmity. Therefore fortitude is not a virtue. . . . But I respond . . . that the virtue of the soul is perfect not in the infirmity of the soul but in the infirmity of the body, and such was Paul's meaning" (*ST* II/II q.123 a.1 obj. 1 and ad 1).

71. Janz, "Syllogism or Paradox," p. 18. Notice how the priority of paradox over binary logic also affects Thomas's account of the priority of wisdom over science: "Wisdom is not distinguished from science as something opposed to it but as related to science by adding to it. For wisdom is indeed, as the Philosopher says in Book VI of his *Nicomachean Ethics,* the head of all the sciences, regulating all others." Thomas Aquinas, *The Trinity and the Unicity of the Intellect,* trans. Sister Rose Emmanuella Brennan, S.H.N. (St. Louis: Herder, 1946), p. 53.

message (under the influence of Anselm, not coincidently) in his *Church Dogmatics* period. (Discussions of Luther and Barth are taken up in Chapters 6 and 9, respectively.)

At all events, the crucial point about these observations in relation to Thomas's theology of the incarnation is that he makes no move whatever to resolve *this* central mystery of the Christian religion, the incarnation itself. Here we find no bald assertions that dissolve the mystery itself, a point that shines through magnificently in that portion of the second *Summa* specifically dedicated to the mystery of the Incarnation (III q.16), where he addresses the following great paradoxes: whether God was made man (a.6), whether man was made God (a.7), whether Christ is a creature (a.8), whether this man Christ began to be (a.9), whether Christ *as man* is God (a.11), and so forth. And in these passages time and again the answer rests in the terminal paradox of Christ's true identity: "in the incarnation it was brought about that man is God and God is man; and in this sense both sayings are true" (q.16 a.7 ad 2). Thomas of course admits that by virtue of the incarnation Christians can say "God is man," since the placement of the word "God" as the subject of the sentence and "man" as the predicate implies that the initiative rests with God. But he also says that it is equally true that "man is God," as he explains in this important passage:

> I respond as follows: Granted the reality of both natures, divine and human, and of the union in person and hypostasis, this is true and proper: *Man is God* even as this too is true: *God is man.* For this word "man" may stand for any hypostasis of human nature; and thus it may stand for the Person of the Son of God, *who we say is a hypostasis of human nature.* Now it is manifest that the word "God" is truly and properly predicated of the Person of the Son of God, as was said earlier [in q.39 a.4]. Hence it remains that this is true and proper: *Man is God.* (q.16 a.2)[72]

---

72. Emphases added. Thomas Weinandy glosses this passage to show its full radicality as follows: "The Son of God must *truly* be man. As implied in the above, it is no use upholding either the full divinity or the full humanity, if the divine Son of God does not *actually exist* as an authentic man. The incarnational 'becoming' must terminate in the extraordinary fact that the Son of God now simply *is* man. . . . [It] is this incarnational 'is' that makes the Incarnation, for Aquinas, the most marvellous of all mysteries." Thomas G. Weinandy, "Aquinas: God *IS* Man: The Marvel of the Incarnation," in *Aquinas on Doctrine: A Critical Introduction,* ed. Thomas G. Weinandy, O.F.M. Cap. and John P. Yocum (London: T. & T. Clark, 2004), pp. 67-89; here 69.

Duns Scotus

In the discipline of Christology, the Subtle Doctor John Duns Scotus (c. 1265-1308) is most famous and influential for his teaching that the Second Person of the Trinity, the Logos of God, would have become the incarnate Christ even if Adam had not sinned, technically known as the doctrine of the "absolute priority" of Christ. Scotus is, to be sure, not the first to put forward such a view.[73] But he was the one who most vigorously disputed the majority view that the incarnation was dependent on the sin of Adam. Moreover, he explicitly tied this notion that the incarnate Christ was always intended by the creator God from the start to his defense of Mary's Immaculate Conception, as we shall see below.

But first, it has to be admitted that at the time he was living, he was bucking the consensus of theologians of the past. Writing around the year 180 Irenaeus of Lyons explicitly said that if there were no flesh to save, the Word of God would never have become flesh, an opinion followed by Origen, Athanasius, John Chrysostom, and Augustine.[74] But cracks in that consensus began to appear when another question was asked, one first mooted by Anselm: Did God create human beings to make up for the number of angels who fell? To which Anselm replied: If men exist solely to replenish the lost angels, then humans would not exist if the angels had not fallen, which would make humans rejoice over the very sin to which they owe their existence. So if our existence was not contingent on sin, how could *Christ's* be?

Admittedly, this is not probative, and Anselm does not directly address our question; but his speculations did provoke theologians to ask *why* the bad angels sinned. Pride was the near universal answer, but what provoked their pride? Once it became common teaching that Lucifer and his minions

---

73. Those who object to Scotus here, such as Jeremy Moiser, tend to put the first mention of this *theologoumenon* late, as here: "The first, however, to answer our question explicitly in the affirmative [that Christ would have become man if Adam had not sinned] was Honorius of Autem (died after 1130)." Jeremy Moiser, "Why Did the Son of God Become Man?" *The Thomist* 37, no. 2 (April 1973): 288-305; here 298. However, the strongest defender of Scotus in the twentieth century, Juniper Carol, traces this teaching on the absolute priority of Christ to Isaac of Nineveh (died c. 659), and he includes among the Latin medieval defenders Alcuin of York (died 804) and Bruno the Carthusian (died 1101). See Juniper B. Carol, O.F.M., *Why Jesus Christ? Thomistic, Scotistic and Contemporary Perspectives* (Manassas, VA: Trinity Communications, 1986), p. 255.

74. Citations and bibliography in Moiser, "Why?" pp. 288-89.

were given a prevision of the human Christ to whom they would have to offer worshipful obeisance, then the teaching of the absolute priority of Christ
had its opening.[75]

That gambit, however, was not the argument of Scotus, who focused on
Paul's teaching that "all things were created through him [Christ] and for
him" (Col. 1:16b), which speaks solely of Christ in terms of creation. Thomas
Aquinas is generally held as coming down for the contingency of the incarnation on sin, but his position is rather more nuanced than he is sometimes
given credit for. He admits that the majority position opts for contingency,
but then concedes that Christ's predestination to become man independent
of sin cannot be disproved:

> The truth of this question is known only to God. We can know what de-
> pends solely on the divine will only insofar as we can glean some knowl-
> edge from the writings of the saints to whom God has revealed his pur-
> pose. The canon of Scripture and the quotations from the Fathers
> mentioned above [Augustine, Gregory] assign one cause to the incarna-
> tion: man's redemption from the slavery of sin. . . . Other theologians,
> however, hold that the purpose of the incarnation of the Son of God was
> not only freedom from sin, but also the exaltation of human nature and
> the consummation of the whole universe. It follows that even had there
> been no sin, the incarnation would have taken place for these other rea-
> sons. This opinion is equally probable.[76]

Writing about twenty years later, however, he seems to give the argument,
on balance, to the defenders of contingency: "In Scripture the cause of the incarnation is always given as the sin of the first man. It is therefore more conveniently said that the incarnation is a work ordained by God as a remedy for
sin. Wherefore: no sin, no incarnation. However, God's power is not limited
to this, and even without sin he could have become man" (*ST* III q.1 a.3).[77]

These kinds of speculations often provoke impatience in modern readers, very much including theologians, but more rides on this issue than

---

75. One thinks here of Milton's Satan: he attributes Satan's "fixed mind and high dis-
dain" to his "sense of injured merit" (*Paradise Lost* I, lines 97-98).

76. Thomas Aquinas, *III Sent.* d.1 q.1 a.3. Moiser's translation.

77. Whether the different Christologies of Thomas and Scotus are affected as well by
their different definitions of what it means to be a *person* is addressed by James B.
Reichmann, S.J., "Aquinas, Scotus, and the Christological Mystery: Why Christ Is Not a Human Person," *The Thomist* 71 (2007): 451-74.

might be evident at first glance.[78] This can be seen in the *locus classicus* of the Subtle Doctor's argument, here:

> *Quaero:* I ask, was Christ predestined to be the Son of God?
>
> *Respondeo:* I reply that predestination consists in foreordaining someone, first of all to glory and then to all other things which are ordained to that glory. . . . At this point, however, two doubts arise: *First,* does this predestination depend necessarily upon the fall of human nature? Many authorities seem to say as much when they declare the Son of God would never have become incarnate had man not fallen. Without passing [invidious] judgment [on these authorities], it can be said that so far as priority of the objects intended by God is concerned, *the predestination of anyone to glory is prior by nature to the prevision of sin or damnation of anyone.* . . . So much the more is this true of the predestination of that soul [Christ's] which was destined beforehand to possess the very highest glory possible.[79]

Those familiar with Karl Barth's Christology (to be treated in Chapter 9) will spot an early adumbration of his doctrine that the predestination of Christ to be simultaneously priest and victim means that Christ is both elect and reprobate at the same time, which means that contrary to the teaching of Augustine and Calvin, God's predestination of Christ precedes God's predestination of the elect and reprobate at the end of time. Also related to the absolute priority of Christ would be the role of the church in the cosmic scheme of salvation: the famous Creation/Covenant dialectic. That is, is the church a "sacrament of salvation" for the whole world (the teaching of Vatican II), or is membership in the church necessary for salvation?[80]

Related to this same question is the debate over Mary's Immaculate

78. Thus I disagree with E. M. Mascall, who claims "The controversy is largely an academic one." E. M. Mascall, *The Importance of Being Human* (Oxford: Oxford University Press, 1959), pp. 92-93.

79. John Duns Scotus, *Ordinatio* III, d.7 q.3. The full Latin text with facing English translation can be found in Allan Wolter, "John Duns Scotus on the Primacy and Personality of Christ," in *Franciscan Christology,* ed. Damian McElrath (St. Bonaventure, NY: Franciscan Institute Publications, 1980), pp. 139-82; here 147, 149; italics added.

80. This at least seems to be the point of the rather enigmatic line from Moiser: "*Dato non concesso* [if one grants, although I do not] that only the Son could become incarnate, it would be because there is only one decree of salvation embracing equally creation and redemption." Moiser, p. 303.

Conception. While not technically a part of Christology proper (unlike the Virgin Birth of Jesus, or more properly, his virginal conception), Scotus's insistence on Christ's absolute priority proved determinative not just for his own defense of the doctrine of the Immaculate Conception (again, he was in the minority in the Middle Ages in his defense of that doctrine too) but also for the church's later definition of the doctrine by Pope Pius IX. Pius's 1854 Apostolic Letter *Ineffabilis Deus* infallibly decreeing the truth of Mary's Immaculate Conception is well known, but less well known is his Scotist reasoning. Admittedly, its most famous passage speaks of Christ's role as redeemer when defining the dogma, here:

> We declare, pronounce, and define that the Most Blessed Virgin Mary, at the first instant of her Conception, was preserved immaculate from all stain of original sin, by the singular grace and privilege of the Omnipotent God in virtue of the merits of Jesus Christ, the Savior of mankind.[81]

But earlier in the encyclical, in his exposition of the traditional provenance of the doctrine, he notes how the church's liturgy regularly used passages from the Wisdom writings of the Old Testament on feasts of the Virgin. Tellingly, the Scotists often used passages that speak of Uncreated Wisdom to justify their position that Christ was always intended to assume his role as first-born of creation from all eternity, from which fact Pius draws this conclusion:

> For this reason, the very words by which the Sacred Scriptures speak of Uncreated Wisdom, and by which they represent his eternal origin, the Church has been accustomed to use not only in the ecclesiastical Office [meaning the Liturgy of the Hours or Breviary] but also in the Sacred Liturgy itself [the Mass], applying them to this Virgin's origin. *For her origin was preordained by one and the same decree with the Incarnation of Divine Wisdom.*[82]

In other words, among the important implications of the doctrine is that sin was never part of the original predestining intention of God when he created the world, a point that would come to be increasingly appreciated

---

81. Pius IX, *Ineffabilis Deus,* paragraph 39, text in *Mary Immaculate: The Bull Ineffabilis Dei* [sic] *of Pope Pius IX,* trans. Dominic J. Unger (Paterson, NJ: St. Anthony Guild Press, 1946), p. 21.

82. *Ineffabilis Deus,* paragraph 6, p. 3; emphasis added.

by Catholic theologians in the twentieth century, argued with great force and verve by Jean-François Bonnefoy:

> The place of Mary in the divine plan appears more and more clearly in proportion as the eminence of her grace is grasped by the Christian sense. Here again, the Scotistic school has shown itself to be consistent. If by the fullness of her grace and her divine maternity, the blessed Virgin is situated immediately after Christ in the ontological order, then she must be accorded the same place in the order of predestinations [sic]. *Her destiny was decided even before,* according to our human but quite valid way of thinking, *there was any question of Adam or of the foresight and permission of sin.* There was, then, no real reason to subject her to the law of original sin, and her Immaculate Conception flows logically from the priority of her predestination as it is conceived and propounded by the Scotistic school.[83]

In conclusion, John Duns Scotus gave us in his Christology not only solid grounds for arguing that the incarnation was God's aboriginal intent in creating the universe; but his arguments bring Mariology and Christology into a new and more intimate relationship, a fusion that hearkens back to Cyril of Alexandria's defense of the title of Mary as the Mother of God, and precisely for christological reasons. Splitting Mary off from her Son always does damage both to piety and to theology. But conversely, bringing them into greater relation adds new luster to the development of doctrine and makes even the doctrine of predestination seem not foreboding but consoling.

---

83. Jean-François Bonnefoy, O.F.M., *The Immaculate Conception in the Divine Plan,* trans. Michael D. Meilach, O.F.M. (Paterson, NJ: St. Anthony Guild Press, 1967), p. 13; emphasis added.

EXCURSUS

Thomas and the Beatific Vision of Christ

No christological doctrine of the Angelic Doctor is more controversial or more easily misunderstood than his teaching that Christ enjoyed, from the moment of his conception, all the way up to his death on the cross, and even in his descent into hell, the beatific vision of God his Father. Discontent with Thomas at this point is quite widespread, as we shall see. In this *Excursus,* therefore, I would like to try, as an experiment, to discuss this difficult doctrine in the old medieval manner, by adopting the format of the *disputatio,* which Thomas had made his own throughout the *Summa theologiae,* and which in this case would go as follows:

Did Christ Enjoy the Beatific Vision
Throughout His Earthly Existence?

It would seem that Christ did not enjoy the beatific vision throughout his earthly existence for the following reasons:

Objection 1: For in Scripture we read (at Mark 15:34) that on the cross Jesus cried out in despair "My God, my God, why have you forsaken me?" Clearly it is impossible for anyone directly seeing the glory of the Father to feel abandonment. As Jean Galot says:

> A Jesus whose soul would have been continually immersed in the beatific vision would have only assumed the exterior appearances of our human life. . . . His resemblance to us would only have been a façade. . . . What would become of the sufferings of the passion? . . . Not only does [the

210

doctrine of Christ's beatific vision] put at risk the reality of the incarnation, but also that of the redemptive sacrifice. How can we attribute to a Savior who is filled with heavenly beatitude these words: "My God, my God, why hast thou forsaken me?" . . . The cry of Jesus on the cross makes manifest the depths of a suffering that is incompatible with the beatitude of the vision.[84]

In other words, the concept of the beatific vision of Christ both contradicts Scripture and makes it impossible to see Jesus as a fully human actor on the stage of life.

Objection 2: The concept of the beatific vision of Christ depends on a Nestorian understanding of the relationship between the human soul of Christ and the divine hypostasis of God the Son. Thomas Weinandy is particularly insistent on this point, as it rests on a notion that the consciousness of Christ is different from his identity as the divine Son:

What makes this a "Nestorian" question is that the beatific vision is defined as the immediate vision of God by someone who is not God. It is an objective vision, a "seeing" or "contemplating," of the divine essence that not only stands ontologically distinct from, but also then over against, the one "seeing" or "contemplating." Within a Nestorian Christology, where the Son of God and the man Jesus are not ontologically united within the Incarnation, and so stand over against one another, the question of whether or not Jesus, the man, possessed the beatific vision would make sense, and Nestorius would, in all probability, have answered "Yes" to such a question. Such a vision would have sanctioned the special union he saw between the Son of God and the man Jesus.[85]

Objection 3: In ordinary language, "beatific" carries the connotation of being in a state of bliss, as in radiating a "beatific face," implying the person is in a state of rapture. However, the Gospels regularly show Jesus displaying a full range of emotions, very much including anger, frustration, surprise, and agony. But the notion of beatific vision carries with it the implication that Jesus enjoyed some kind of celestial anesthetic inuring his human soul from the feeling of pain, a clear contradiction of the Gospels.

84. Jean Galot, "Le Christ terrestre et la vision," *Gregorianum* 67 (1986): 429-50; here 434.

85. Thomas G. Weinandy, O.F.M. Cap., "Jesus' Filial Vision of the Father," *Pro Ecclesia* 13, no. 2 (Spring 2004): 189-201; here 190.

On the contrary, Scripture reveals Jesus saying: "You do not know him, but I know him because I have my being from him, and it was he who sent me. . . . The one who sent me is true, and what I declare to the world I have learned from him" (John 7:29; 8:26).[86]

I respond as follows: The essential premise for understanding Thomas's understanding of Christ's beatific vision comes from a principle first enunciated by Augustine: "What belongs by nature to the Son of God belongs by grace to the Son of Man" (*De Trinitate* I, 13).

To understand what Thomas is getting at here we must recall the debate over monothelitism in sixth- and seventh-century Byzantium. Basing himself not only on the assumption that to have a human nature is to have a will, but also on the scene depicted in the Gospels of Jesus' agony in the Garden, when Christ said "Not my will but thine be done" (Mark 14:36), Maximus insisted that Christ had to have two wills; otherwise God would be at war with himself, an impossibility. But this doctrine of two wills would again raise the specter of a duality of subjects in Christ, forbidden by Chalcedon, which means that the two wills have to be seen *as aspects of the two natures* hypostatically united to the divine Second Person.

Thus, to avoid Nestorianism, the two wills must subsist in the single Person of the Logos. According to Thomas the single subject of the divine Person can only act as one subject with two wills if the created soul of Christ has an immediate knowledge *of his own personal identity as the Son of God.* But that does *not* mean that his human soul, even as hypostatically united

---

86. Nor can scriptural references to the beatific vision be found only in John, for there are many passages in the Synoptics that also became important touchstones leading to this teaching. On this see William G. Most, *The Consciousness of Christ* (Front Royal, VA: Christendom Publications, 1980), which explicitly confines itself to the Synoptic tradition in its examination of the biblical evidence: "We will limit our investigation to the Synoptics, omitting St. John's Gospel, not because it has little to offer, but because the problem of its literary genre complicates the presentation of the matter" (p. 74). But that methodological limitation did not prevent Most from providing a full-throated defense of the doctrine of the beatific vision based on Synoptic sources alone. One should recall here the wise words of Raymond Moloney: on the one hand, what was in "the mind and heart of Christ, and how he viewed the world and its history, will always remain shrouded in the mystery which the Son of God is in his very being." On the other hand, "given that we have some objective knowledge about him, in so far as he is both true God and true human being, given also the manifold data of the New Testament about him, it seems that, by combing scripture and tradition, a few statements can be made as to his knowledge and consciousness with some degree of confidence." Raymond Moloney, *The Knowledge of Christ* (London: Continuum, 1999), pp. 5-6.

with the Logos, comprehends the divine essence. That is often the implication people draw from Thomas's theology of Christ's beatific vision. But he denies that implication in this important passage:

> The union of the two natures in the Person of Christ took place in such a way that the properties of both natures remained unconfused, that is, the uncreated remained uncreated, and the created remained within the limits of the creature. Now it is impossible for any creature to comprehend the Divine Essence, seeing that the infinite is not comprehended by the finite. And hence it must be said that *the soul of Christ nowise comprehends the Divine Essence.* (*ST* III q.10 a.1, *respondeo;* emphasis added)

Upon the grounding of that principle Thomas sees the *functional* necessity for Christ to have a *vision* (not comprehension) of the Father; or more specifically, it is a *soteriological* necessity, since Christ came to give us by grace what was his by nature:

> By the union this Man is blessed with the uncreated beatitude, even as by the union He is God; yet besides the uncreated beatitude it was necessary that there should be in the human nature of Christ *a created beatitude,* whereby his soul was established in the last end of human nature. The beatific vision and knowledge are to some extent above the nature of the rational soul, inasmuch as it cannot reach it of its own strength; but *in another way it is in accordance with its nature, inasmuch as it is capable of it by nature, having been made to the likeness of God,* as stated above. But the uncreated knowledge is in every way above the nature of the human soul. (III q.9 a.2 ad 2 & 3; emphases added)

In other words, while Christ's beatific vision is certainly an epistemological correlate of his ontological uniqueness,[87] *what* he enjoys is that very grace that is the destiny of all those saved in Christ: "Anyone who loves me will keep my word, and my Father will love him, and we shall come to him and make a home in him.... Peace I leave with you, *my own* peace I give you, a peace which the world cannot give, this is my gift to you" (John 14:23b, 27).

As to the first objection, no part of Thomas's understanding of the be-

---

87. "For Aquinas, however, the integrity of the human nature of Christ is first understood not in epistemological but in ontological terms, and is seen as guaranteed by a classical scriptural principle: revelation teaches that God assumed in Christ a true and complete human nature." Thomas Joseph White, "The Voluntary Action of the Earthly Christ and the Necessity of the Beatific Vision," *The Thomist* 69, no. 4 (2005): 497-534; here 507.

atific vision renders Jesus in any way less than fully human, as shown above.[88] Still less do Jesus' vision of God and his realization of his divine identity serve to assuage or mitigate his suffering; rather it is what accounts for his realization that his destined suffering will be salvific: "the Son of Man came not to be served but to serve, and to give up his life as a ransom for the many" (Matt. 20:28).

Perhaps the most ideal passage for seeing how suffering, salvation, and Christ's divine identity converge can be found in Thomas's *Exposition of the Apostles' Creed* where the Common Doctor explains just how and why Christ's descent into hell was a saving descent:

> *He descended into hell.* As we say, the death of Christ lies in the separation of the soul from the body, just as in the death of other human beings. But, the divinity was so indissolubly united to the humanity of Christ that, although body and soul were separated from each other, nonetheless that very divinity was always perfectly present both to the soul and the body. Therefore, the Son of God was both in the tomb with the body *and* descended into hell with the soul. And thus the holy apostles said "*he* descended into hell."
>
> There are four reasons why Christ as a soul descended into hell. First: to shoulder [*sustineret*] the *full* punishment of sin, and so to atone for [*expiaret*] *all* of its guilt. The punishment of sin for humanity, however, was not only the death of the body, but also involved the soul, because sin also belonged to the soul. And thus before the coming of Christ, the soul after death descended into hell. In order that Christ *completely* shoulder the entire punishment due to sinners, he wished not only to die, but also to descend into hell as a soul. Thus we read: "I am labeled with those going down into the depths" (Psalm 87:5 [88:5-6]).[89]

---

88. Although in his earlier writings Thomas did seem to imply that the beatific vision served as a kind of celestial anesthetic for Christ's human soul, he changed his mind by the time he began writing the *tertia pars*: "Aquinas' position progressed in some notable ways: whereas in the commentary on the *Sentences* Thomas was unable to affirm passions originating in Christ's soul ('animal' passions, from the Latin *anima* for 'soul,' to use his terminology), since the joy of the blessed vision would have excluded them, in the *Summa* he would henceforth admit of such passions. This view of the mature Aquinas was unique in the writings of his time, as understood by the fact that his master Albert the Great flatly refused to admit the same." Jean-Pierre Torrell, O.P., Preface to Gondreau, *The Passions of Christ's Soul*, p. 12.

89. *The Sermon-Conferences of St. Thomas Aquinas on the Apostles' Creed*, trans. Nicholas Ayo, C.S.C. (Notre Dame: University of Notre Dame Press, 1988), p. 79; emphases added.

The same principles are at work to explain Christ's cry of dereliction on the cross — "My God, my God, why have you forsaken me?" — a line that Jean Galot takes to be the definitive refutation of the viability of the beatific vision. On the contrary, they go together, and intimately, as Pope John Paul II taught in his encyclical *Novo millennio ineunte*, in this crucial and most illuminating passage:

> At the very moment when he identifies with our sin, "abandoned" by the Father, he "abandons" himself into the hands of the Father. His eyes remain fixed on the Father. Precisely because of the knowledge and experience of the Father which *he alone has,* even at the moment of darkness he sees clearly the gravity of sin and suffers *because* of it. He alone, who sees the Father and rejoices fully in him, can understand completely what it means to resist the Father's love by sin. More than an experience of physical pain, his passion is an agonizing suffering of the soul. Theological tradition has not failed to ask how Jesus could possibly experience at one and the same time his profound unity with the Father, by its very nature a source of joy and happiness, and an agony that goes all the way to his final cry of abandonment. The simultaneous presence of these two seemingly irreconcilable aspects is rooted in the fathomless depths of the hypostatic union. (No. 26; emphases added)[90]

As to the second objection, it seems to me that, provided the concept of the beatific vision is properly understood as a human grace granted to the human soul of Christ by virtue of the hypostatic union to bring him to a full realization of his divine identity, then a denial of this vision would rather lead to (or at least imply) a Nestorian Christology. To the best of my knowl-

---

90. Thomas Joseph White defends this paradox with an important distinction between Christ's "economic" state in his earthly life and his exalted state: "Is the beatific vision in the heights of Christ's soul compatible with any form of agony in the soul of Christ during his crucifixion? After all, one might reasonably object that the bliss of the vision excludes any real capacity for suffering. To respond to this difficulty we must first note that according to Aquinas, the 'economic' mode or 'dispensation' of Christ's vision during his earthly life is understood to be very different from that of his vision of the exalted state of glory. In the latter state, his body and emotional psychology participate each in their own way directly in the glory of his resurrected life. . . . In the former state, however, this vision is not the source of any such experience. It does assure his soul of a continual knowledge of his own divine identity and will as the Son of God, but it *in no way* alleviates his 'ordinary' states of human consciousness and sensation." Thomas Joseph White, O.P., "Jesus' Cry on the Cross and His Beatific Vision," *Nova et Vetera,* English Edition 5 (2007): 555-82; here, 573-74; White's emphasis.

edge, Thomas Weinandy is the only theologian who suspects a crypto-Nestorianism in the concept of beatific vision. Most objections tend to see a closet monophysitism or Apollinarianism at work, as if Christ's beatific vision "took over" his human consciousness, virtually replacing anything that Jesus would have learned in the normal process of growing up in his environment.

In that regard one certainly wishes to applaud Weinandy for explaining with great clarity a theological fact often overlooked in this debate: that is, *that whenever Christ uses the pronoun "I" he does so using a grammar in nowise different from anyone else who speaks of his or her "I" as the grammatical subject denoting the human center of self-consciousness:*

> Jesus possessed not only a human body, mind, and will, but also a human center of self-consciousness, a human self-identity. He thought and spoke with the integrity of a thoroughly human "I." He was self-conscious, composed his thoughts, and spoke in an entirely human manner, with the human "I" of a man. When Jesus said, for example, "I have come not to abolish the Law and the prophets, but to fulfill them" (Matt. 5:17), that "I" sprang from and manifested a human self-conscious awareness — a human "I." What the Incarnation demands is that he who embraced a human center of self-consciousness, and thought and spoke with an integral human "I," was the eternal Son. The *identity* of Jesus is the eternal Son. The *mode* of that identity is as a man. Properly understood, then, we can truly say that the divine person of the Son (the who) spoke and acted as a human person (with a human "I").[91]

So far, so good. What remains missing in this analysis is why the full humanity of Jesus' human "I" thereby excludes his beatific vision. Rather, it would seem to be required to *avoid* Nestorianism. Otherwise the *what* of what Jesus would be aware of would be a human self, *groping toward* a gradually dawning awareness of something *odd* about his self. No doubt many moderns, both Christian and the sympathetic non-Christian, suppose something like this, as the Jesus novels of Ann Rice and Nikos Kazantzakis show.[92] But surely the Gospels portray a Jesus far more self-aware and self-assured than that!

---

91. Thomas G. Weinandy, O.F.M., Cap., *In the Likeness of Sinful Flesh: An Essay on the Humanity of Christ* (Edinburgh: T. & T. Clark, 1993), pp. 12-13; emphases added.

92. One author speaks of the plotline of *The Last Temptation of Christ* in this way: "[Jesus] is not at first consciously aware of his own divine status, his mission of salvation or his

As to the third objection: No one disputes that the term *beatific* has changed its meaning from the medieval connotation, where it meant "that which makes blessed or favored," to today's implication of meaning "blissed out." This semantic shift has often led to misinterpretations, by both supposed supporters of the doctrine and its critics, who both often seem to think that Christ's beatific vision has supplied what would normally be missing from Christ's human consciousness as a specifically human mode of awareness. But this cannot be Thomas's own meaning, for he explicitly avows that both Christ's body and soul are "defective" (in the Aristotelian sense). Thus, answering the objection that "as his soul is personally united to the Word of God, so also is his body. And since the soul had every perfection; . . . hence, his body ought to have been in every way perfect" (*ST* III q.14 a.1 obj.1), Thomas replies that "it was fitting for the Son of God to assume flesh subject to human infirmities, in order to suffer and be tempted in it and so bring succor to it" *(sed contra).* Therefore, if he suffered in body, then *a fortiori* he suffered in soul: "For true bodily pain [to occur], there must be both bodily hurt and the sense of hurt. . . . Therefore, no one should doubt but that in Christ there was true pain also" (q.15 a.5). As a consequence, in that same question 15 he asserts that Christ's soul knew fear (a.7), amazement (a.8), anger (a.9), and, above all, sorrow (a.6).[93]

Thomas even asserts that Christ has *acquired knowledge,* since Christ's

---

destiny of crucifixion. He encounters his divinity as something hostile and alien — a possession, a persecution, a haunting. Although messianic hope is second nature to him, . . . he does not initially associate the coming [of the Son of Man] with his own destiny. God comes to him as a dementia, a seizure, or the sensation of claws dug into his skull. This seems less like a perfect hypostatic union than an uneasy affiliation between a weak and fearful human consciousness and a slumbering, latent divinity." Graham Holderness, "'Half God, half man': Kazantzakis, Scorsese, and *The Last Temptation,*" *Harvard Theological Review* 111, no. 1 (2007): 65-96; here 71. The director Martin Scorsese was obviously drawn to film the novel for just this reason: "His divine side doesn't fully comprehend what the human side has to do; how He has to transform Himself and eventually become the sacrifice on the cross — Christ the man only learns this a little at a time." Martin Scorsese, *Scorsese on Scorsese,* ed. David Thompson and Ian Christie (London: Faber & Faber, 1989), pp. 116-17.

93. Thomas is following here a long patristic tradition that emphasized Christ's deep compassion for others that he had *learned* from his own sorrow of personal loss, as when he wept for the dead Lazarus (John 11:35). Here is Cyril on this passage: "He condescends still further, revealing his human nature, and weeps and is troubled, when he sees her [Martha, the sister of Lazarus] weeping and the Jews who came with her also weeping. Now, since Christ was not only God by nature but also man, he suffers in common with the rest that is human." Cyril of Alexandria, *Commentary on the Gospel according to St. John,* vol. 2, *John IX-XXI,* trans. P. E. Pusey (London: Walter Smith, 1885), p. 121.

soul had to have both an active and a passive intellect (in Aristotle, the active or agent intellect must receive phantasms from the passive intellect in order to abstract the intelligible forms from the sensory object, which alone counts as true knowledge): "Thus it is necessary to say that in Christ there were intelligible species received in the passive intellect by the action of the active intellect, which means that there was acquired knowledge in him, which some call empiric" (q.9 a.4). True, this statement sits uneasily with his later assertion that there was no ignorance in Christ's soul (q.15 a.3), which in turn sits uneasily with his insistence that Christ's human soul was *not* omnipotent: "since the soul of Christ is part of human nature, it cannot possibly have omnipotence" (q.13 a.1).

In this latter point of Christ's ignorance of knowledge that he has yet to acquire,[94] Thomas departs from Athanasius, who has no difficulty in admitting ignorance. Speaking of the famous crux of Mark 13:32 ("No one knows that hour, no angel, not even the Son, only the Father"), Athanasius says:

> The Word as man was ignorant [of the last day], for ignorance is proper to man, and especially ignorance of these [eschatological] things. Moreover, this is proper to the Savior's love of man, for since he was made man he was not ashamed — on account of the flesh which is ignorant — to say "I know not," so that he may show that, while knowing as God, he is ignorant according to the flesh.[95]

Clearly there are tensions that run throughout Thomas's account of Christ's beatific vision,[96] a point that particularly exercised the famous

94. And note that Thomas, commenting on Luke 2:52, explicitly says (at *ST* III q.12 a.2) that Christ *grew* in acquired knowledge, which requires advancement from the unknown to the known.

95. Athanasius, *Contra Arianos* 3.43. I am following here the more literal translation in Thomas Weinandy, *Athanasius: A Theological Introduction* (Burlington, VT: Ashgate, 2007), p. 93. Full text in *Nicene and Post-Nicene Fathers*, vol. 4, *Athanasius: Select Works and Letters* (Peabody, MA: Hendrickson, 2004), here at p. 417. Elsewhere, in discussing the need for Christ to ask questions — such as "How many loaves do you have?" (Mark 6:38) or "What do you want me to do for you?" (Matt. 20:32) — Athanasius says: "If they still want to argue because Christ asked questions, let them hear that there is no ignorance in the deity, but that not knowing is, as has been said, proper to the flesh. . . . For the all-holy Logos of God, who endures everything for our sakes, did this also in order that — *just as he bore the burden of our ignorance* — so he might lavish upon us knowledge of his Father." Athanasius, *Contra Arianos* 3.37; emphasis added.

96. For example, Thomas says that the grace given to Christ could not increase (q.7 a.12), but right before that passage he insists that the grace possessed by the human soul of

Thomist of the twentieth century, Jacques Maritain, who claimed that
Thomas had a deficient understanding of the biblical verse that said Christ
"grew in wisdom, age and grace" (Luke 2:52).[97] Another problem for
Maritain concerns Thomas's teaching that Christ enjoyed the beatific vision
from the first moment of his conception, which would seem to entail a fully
self-present consciousness from the beginning of Christ's earthly existence.

Yet far from rejecting the very concept of the beatific vision, or even
Thomas's version of it, Maritain insists that the contradictions lurking in
Thomas's account are of "an accidental order" (p. 53). He holds to this defense by making a distinction unavailable to medieval psychology between
consciousness, the subconscious, and what he calls "supraconsciousness":

> Let there be no misunderstanding: when I speak of a *world of conscious-
> ness,* I am speaking of a world of which consciousness and the conscious
> faculties are the seat and, as it were, the sun — but in this world there is,
> on one hand, *below* consciousness, the vast psycho-somatic unconscious
> of tendencies and of instincts, of sensations not yet elaborated in percep-
> tions, of latent memories etc., and, on the other hand, *above* conscious-
> ness, a preconscious or supraconscious of the spirit, in which are found
> the agent intellect and the sources of the intuitive activities of the spirit.[98]

Christ is finite (a.11). Another tension in his Christology comes from his assertion that
Christ did not have the virtue of faith, for faith believes in things unseen, whereas Christ saw
by virtue of his beatific vision (q.7 a.3). But Thomas also says that the soul of Christ did *not*
comprehend the divine essence (q.10 a.1). Again, Thomas holds that Christ was genuinely
tempted (q.41 a.1) but also insists that he had no *fomes peccati* (St. Augustine's term, meaning "tinderbox" or "powder keg" of sin, the premiere legacy of original sin), since Christ was
born without sin (q.15 a.1). This would imply that Christ knew only external temptations
(q.15 a.2 ad 3); yet he also holds that Christ's soul knew fear (q.15 a.7), a fear that made Jesus
feel dread at the prospect of his death, which tempted him to draw back from his mission
(Matt. 26:39-45).

97. "This is the point which causes difficulty for me, and which I contest: this manner in which St. Thomas treats St. Luke. With St. Augustine and the Fathers of the Church,
one can proceed thus: they have but a human authority. But with the Gospel text it is altogether different, because one has to deal there with revelation itself; and very clearly St.
Luke is not thinking of the effects and of the works produced [by the grace of Christ in his
soul]; he is thinking of the *grace* and of the *wisdom* themselves, it is all the more clear as
he says in the same breath: in wisdom, *in age,* and in grace. The growth in wisdom and in
grace is for him in the same case as the growth *in age.*" Jacques Maritain, *On the Grace and
Humanity of Jesus,* trans. Joseph W. Evans (New York: Herder & Herder, 1969), p. 51; Maritain's emphases.

98. Maritain, *On the Grace and Humanity of Jesus,* p. 55; emphases in the original.

Whether other Thomists agree with this interpretation cannot be our concern here. In my view, Maritain's suggestion is plausible, even as a legitimate development of a purely Thomistic Christology, because of the way he places the psychological distinction within the deeper (and paradoxical) point governing Thomas's account of the incarnation, which made Christ simultaneously *viator* (wayfarer) and *comprehensor* (encompassing principle of creation and redemption).[99] This now allows Maritain to resolve any lingering tension (meaning, an incipient or outright contradiction) in Thomas into the more fundamental paradox of the incarnation:

> [I]t is necessary to say of the consciousness of Christ what we say later on about his grace, namely, that it found itself, like his human nature, at the same time under two different *states:* insofar as he was *comprehensor* it was a divinized supraconsciousness; insofar as he was a *viator* it was a consciousness in the ordinary sense which the word has in our common human life, a consciousness similar to our own as much as this was possible to a man whose person was not human but divine. . . . The latter, however, had of necessity to exist in him because he was not only *comprehensor,* but also *viator.* . . . If one does not admit in the soul of Christ a difference of level, a *heaven* of the soul, but supraconscious, for the state of *comprehensor,* and a *here-below* of the soul, the here-below of consciousness and of the conscious and deliberate operations, for the sake of *viator,* I believe that one is inevitably led to wrong the one or the other of these two states.[100]

So perhaps, if the term "beatific vision" conjures up a feeling that Christ is not really a wayfarer sharing humanity's collective pilgrimage to God, if rather it suggests that Christ knew not suffering, darkness, fear, and anger but was instead always in a state of bliss (as some implicitly monophysite Catholics of an unschooled, pious type seem to hold), it should be retired, *provided that the biblical witness of Christ's unique awareness of his identity is preserved.* Thomas Weinandy, as we have seen, suggests we speak of "Christ's

---

99. "A man is called a wayfarer from *tending to* beatitude and a comprehensor from having *already obtained* beatitude. . . . Now before his passion Christ's mind saw God fully, and thus he had beatitude as far as it regards what is proper to the soul; but *beatitude was wanting* with regard *to all else,* since *his* soul was passible, and his body both passible and mortal. . . . Hence he was at once comprehensor, inasmuch as he had the beatitude proper to the soul, and at the same time wayfaring, inasumuch as he was *tending* toward beatitude, as regards what was wanting to his beatitude" (*ST* III q.15 a.10); emphases added.

100. Maritain, *Grace and Humanity,* pp. 57, 59; all emphases Maritain's.

filial vision of the Father," which sounds plausible, except for two points: first, Christ's beatific vision refers not just to Christ's relation to his Father but also to his own self-reflective awareness of who he is; second, at least according to Weinandy, the phrase is meant to replace not just an outmoded terminology but also the way the problem has been treated in medieval Christology, Thomas Aquinas not at all excepted.[101]

In the above I have tried to show that Thomas's account of the beatific vision is far more subtle than both his critics and some of his (less subtle) defenders seem to think. So maybe, instead of retiring the term for something better, it would be preferable to keep the term but always define it in the way Maritain has done. At all events, we can surely agree with Maritain on at least this methodological point:

> Let us not forget that as dear and venerable as are to us the Fathers and the Doctors, and the greatest among them, a million St. Augustines and a million St. Thomases will never make a St. Paul or a St. Luke. If on a given point St. Luke and St. Thomas are truly and really in conflict, the authority of St. Thomas, however high it may be, is nothing before that of St. Luke.[102]

That point, of course, works both ways: if the Bible speaks of Christ's unique awareness of his mission and his identity, then theologians are obliged to follow and render a plausible account of that unique consciousness.

101. The Jesuit theologian Bernard Lonergan suggests using the term beatific *knowledge* rather than beatific *vision* in order to stress Christ's self-awareness of his identity and mission and not just his awareness of his relationship with his Father: see Bernard Lonergan, S.J., *De Verbo Incarnato* (Rome: Gregorian University Press, 3rd edition, 1964), p. 339.

102. Maritain, *Grace and Humanity*, p. 51, note 4. There is of course an intermediate term here: magisterial teaching, the subject of Chapter 11 of this book.

CHAPTER 6

Reformation Christology, Protestant and Catholic

All these contradictions, which used most to keep me away from the knowledge of any religion, are what have led me soonest to the true religion.

Blaise Pascal, *Pensées*

This chapter will treat the Christologies of the sixteenth and seventeenth centuries in one synoptic overview. Admittedly, most histories of this topic treat Protestant and Catholic theologies in this period as adversarial, for indeed they were. But the view that Catholics were merely reacting to Protestants and not engaging in a reform prompted by their own internal resources has largely been abandoned. For that reason the catch-all term "Counter-Reformation" to denote the Catholic reforms of Teresa of Avila and Ignatius Loyola (among a host of others) is now seen as inapt.[1] In fact,

---

1. Despite its title, this thesis is the gravamen of H. Outram Evennett's *The Spirit of the Counter-Reformation* (Notre Dame: University of Notre Dame Press, 1970). Indeed the first chapter of the book, "Towards a New Definition" (originally a lecture delivered in 1951), is often cited as the opening salvo when historians began to call the Catholic response to the Reformation one of genuine reform and not just a reactive "counter"-reform. Thus, according to Evennett, "The word 'Counter-Reformation,' like the word 'Renaissance,' combines the implication of much that is obviously true with much that is highly misleading. . . . The word has a certain constricting effect upon the evolution of historical thought about its subject-matter, and has perhaps contributed to a certain delay in modernizing the historical treatment of the Catholic Church in the sixteenth and seventeenth centuries" (p. 2). For more on this theme see Hubert Jedin, "Catholic Reformation or Counter-Reformation?" in

222

as this chapter progresses, we shall see in the first two sections that Loyola shared many unacknowledged presuppositions with Martin Luther (including an unacknowledged debt to Anselm); and then in the following two sections we will point out how much Blaise Pascal and John Calvin operated out of a common Augustinian framework. Yes, Catholics and Protestants differed bitterly, even to the point of outright war. But as Pascal himself said, of all the evils in the world, none is greater than civil war, precisely because the warring parties share so much. For without that shared agreement over certain essentials, there would be no bitterness in their disagreement over the implications of those shared commonalities. Thus, if either side had simply been indifferent to the question of God's intentions for the world, then sharp disagreement would never have arisen about how to "get right" with God, that is, how to be regarded as justified in his sight. If Jesus Christ had not been confessed in common as the only way to the Father, disagreements over the church and her sacraments would have lost their point. Only if God matters does theology matter.

Martin Luther

But even when we concede the common debt that all theologians of that period, both Protestant and Catholic, owed to past Christologies (including of course the most recent ones of the immediate medieval past), we still must stress this crucial point: Without the Christology of Martin Luther (1483-1546), in its specific and unique contours, there would have been no Protestant Reformation. Of course I am not saying that Luther first devised a Christology out of some perverse desire to destroy the unity of the church and then purposely fashioned that newly minted Christology into a kind of Samson's rope in order to bring down the edifice of late-medieval Christendom. For, in Luther's case at least, the protest came first, with the Christology following shortly thereafter. Nor would Luther, whether rightly or wrongly, have thought his Christology was anything other than a faithful republication of the New Testament witness and of the decrees of past ecumenical councils (and this despite his insistence that Scripture must be the judge of the councils and not vice versa).

What Luther shared with his medieval predecessors can be seen in his

The Counter-Reformation, ed. David M. Leubke (Oxford: Blackwell, 1999), pp. 19-46, and Michael A. Mullett, *The Catholic Reformation* (London: Routledge, 1999).

early Reformed tract *On the Servility of the Will*, where he affirms one of the most fundamental values of the scholastic method, clarity of doctrine: "It is not the way of a Christian heart to rejoice in unreliable statements. To the contrary, a Christian must take delight in reliable statements, or he would not be a Christian. . . . Take away assertions, and you take away Christianity."[2] To be sure, Luther abhorred much of the scholastic product and never described himself as a scholastic theologian, usually preferring the professional title of Master of Holy Scripture.[3] But even in his distaste for scholasticism he was a child of his time, for by the last half of the fifteenth century scholasticism found itself under heavy assault from numerous quarters of late-medieval university life.[4]

2. Martin Luther, *On the Bondage of the Will*, in *Luther's Works*, ed. Jaroslav Pelikan, Philip S. Watson, and Helmut T. Lehmann (Saint Louis: Concordia, 1972), pp. 19-20, 21; original text: *De servo arbitrio*, in *D. Martin Luthers Werke* (Weimar: H. Böhlau, 1883-1993), vol. 18, p. 603; this edition will be cited henceforth as *WA*. The target of Luther's polemics here is Erasmus, and his objections to the Dutch humanist show that Luther meant to be no liberal theologian: "In short, what you say here seems to mean that it does not matter to you what anyone believes anywhere, so long as the peace of the world is undisturbed. . . . Things that are above us, you would say, are no concern of ours. So, with a view to ending our conflicts, you come forward as a mediator, calling a halt to both sides, and trying to persuade us that we are brandishing our swords about stupid and useless things" (p. 23).

3. Significantly, Luther wrote a "Disputation against Scholastic Theology" several months before he posted his famous ninety-five theses, but that same disputation was motivated, at least in part, by a desire to purge theology of inexact formulations and muddled compromises, which by Luther's lights meant bringing theology back to its Augustinian fountainhead: "To say that Augustine exaggerates in speaking against heretics is to say that Augustine tells lies almost everywhere. This is contrary to common knowledge. This is the same as permitting Pelagians and all heretics to triumph, indeed, the same as conceding victory to them. It is the same as making sport of the authority of all doctors of theology." Martin Luther, "Disputation against Scholastic Theology," in *Selected Writings of Martin Luther*, vol. 1: *1517-1520*, ed. Theodore G. Tappert (Philadelphia: Fortress Press, 1967), p. 35. Luther is here in effect conceding the legitimacy of Aristotle's law of noncontradiction (A cannot be not-A at the same time and in the same respect), even though he says in the same Disputation: "It is an error to say that no one can become a theologian without Aristotle" (p. 38). We will shortly see how this contempt for Aristotle affected his Christology.

4. "Over the course of the late Middle Ages numerous and highly different ways of scholastic thought had developed that denied one another's authorization. . . . In addition, some explicitly anti-scholastic approaches to education and knowledge systems began to gain influence, which made for an ever more diverse and colorful theological landscape toward the end of the late Middle Ages: the diverse movements of humanism and their highly varied proponents in Erfurt; numerous theologies in various [religious] orders that did not draw on Thomas Aquinas and the Dominican scholasticism reliant on him but, for example,

Like so many other cataclysmic events that set history on a new course, the Protestant Reformation did not begin deliberately, as part of some predetermined platform. No, it began with an out-of-the-way incident, in itself relatively trivial: Luther's posting on the cathedral door of Wittenberg ninety-five theses that he planned to debate in the classroom (which, ironically enough, was a common scholastic practice). But, like the rifle shot whose echoing retort touches off an avalanche, Luther's nailing of these debate topics set in motion events long waiting to happen.[5]

But the fact that these ninety-five "debating points" set in motion the Protestant Reformation means that, in his life up to that point (that is, as an Augustinian monk), Luther was already operating with a set of principles and ideas that would only later come to full expression. As his protest against the sale of indulgences grew, he more and more brought to bear the full brunt of his theological armory; and as he did so, he discovered that his theological reasoning was proving to be radically incompatible with the Roman understanding of grace and the sacraments.[6] In other words, once the forces that set the Protestant Reformation into motion had been released to do their work, Luther had to give expression to his ideas, a key element of which was his Christology.

Now whether his Christology was as incompatible with the Catholic understanding of Christ as the Council of Trent declared his theology of grace,

---

on Augustine, who generated many a reform movement or 'theology' during the fourteenth and fifteenth centuries." Markus Wreidt, "Luther's Theology," in *The Cambridge Companion to Martin Luther*, ed. Donald K. McKim (Cambridge: Cambridge University Press, 2003), pp. 115-16, note 13.

5. The assassination of Archduke Ferdinand by a Serbian nationalist in 1914, which ignited World War I, is another example of how a small incident can set off a whole series of events that rapidly become cataclysmic: structural instabilities go on for decades, remain unaddressed, until finally the seismic tension builds to a point where an earthquake in human affairs strikes, touched off by some apparently trivial event.

6. Again, difficult as this might be, we must still try to distinguish the historical Luther from his later effects in history. I do not deny the originality of his theology or its revolutionary impact on history. That said, I agree with this assessment: "But if Luther had a singular power with language, there were bigger forces at work in sixteenth-century life inflating his work with significance far beyond his own intentions. One such force was Northern European Renaissance humanism, . . . [which] shared a historically romantic vision of personal and public reform. The humanists quickly saw Luther's potential for their program and began to spread his Theses. In the process, they made Luther into something he hadn't wanted to be and in fact resisted. They made him a reformer." James Arne Nestingen, "Approaching Luther," in *The Cambridge Companion to Martin Luther*, p. 242. I would even go further and say that Luther was not only hijacked by the humanists, but by history itself.

justification, sacraments, and sanctification to be is itself an important question. After all, Trent condemned the Lutheran doctrine of justification, but his Christology was not the gravamen of its concerns.[7] By pointing out that fact, I am not denying what I said above, that there is an intimate connection between Luther's Christology and the rest of his theology. But the topics must still be kept distinct.

At all events, there can be no doubt that Luther's Christology gave the church new accents and a new perspective, the newness of which surely had something to do with the spread of his ideas and the speed by which the Reformation spread as a program to so many of the lands of Europe. His doctrine of justification was surely the key feature of his theology that seized the imagination of so many of his contemporaries; but, as we shall see, that doctrine is intimately related to his view of the identity and mission of Jesus Christ.

Luther himself summed up the crux, so to speak, of his Christology in this lapidary line: *crux sola est nostra theologia* — "The cross alone is our theology" (*WA* 5:176). Prompted by the uproar caused by his posting of the ninety-five theses, Luther was summoned by his order to defend himself in a theological debate in Heidelberg, which took place one year before the historic Leipzig Disputation with the Dominican theologian Johannes Eck, which sealed his breach with Rome, made irrevocable when Luther flatly declared that Scripture judges the councils and not the reverse. But already by April 1518 (the date of the Heidelberg Disputation) Luther had come to an understanding of the christological basis for his protest; for it was there that he coined the phrase *theologia crucis* ("theology of the cross") as the touchstone of his theology and said, programmatically, *crux probat omnia* — the cross is the test of everything. As Alister McGrath rightly says: "For Luther, Christian thinking about God comes to an abrupt halt at the foot of the cross. The Christian is forced, by the very existence of the crucified Christ, to make a momentous decision. Either he will seek God elsewhere, or he will make the cross itself the foundation and criterion of his thought about God."[8]

---

7. Significantly, the Catholic cardinals and theologians deputized to examine the Augsburg Confession (the touchstone of Lutheran orthodoxy) explicitly approved its christological articles. As Jaroslav Pelikan mentions, "Sporadic efforts by various Roman Catholic opponents to locate heretical tendencies in the christology of Luther on the basis of some of his obiter dicta proved to be basically unsuccessful." Jaroslav Pelikan, *The Christian Tradition: A History of the Development of Doctrine*, vol. 4: *Reformation of Church and Dogma (1300-1700)* (Chicago: University of Chicago Press, 1984), p. 158; cited henceforth as Pelikan, *Reformation*.

8. Alister E. McGrath, *Luther's Theology of the Cross: Martin Luther's Theological Breakthrough* (Oxford: Blackwell, 1985), p. 1.

One suspects that, given the venue — a meeting of the Augustinian order — and his own still-active membership in it at the time, Luther did not suspect what lay ahead for the future of Christianity once he had fully worked out this primal insight; but as the later development of his theology would show, he never shrank from its implications. McGrath again:

> The "crucified God" — to use Luther's daring phrase — is not merely the foundation of the Christian faith, but is also the key to a proper understanding of the nature of God. The Christian can only speak about the glory, the wisdom, the righteousness and the strength of God as they are revealed in the crucified Christ. . . . If God is present in the cross, then he is a God whose presence is hidden from us. As Luther observed, citing Isaiah 45:15, "Truly you are a hidden God."[9]

In other words, this theology of the cross turns everything upside down, as Luther himself puts it in his twenty-first thesis: "A theology of glory calls evil good and good evil. A theology of the cross calls the thing what it actually is."[10] This gives to Luther's theology a wildly paradoxical flair and accounts for everything that is distinctive about his doctrine of Christ's atonement and the justification of the sinner, a point that comes through most vividly in his *Commentary on Galatians* of 1535:

> My flesh distrusts God, is angry with Him, does not rejoice in Him. But God overlooks these sins, and in His sight they are as though they were not sins. This is accomplished by imputation on account of the faith by which I begin to take hold of Christ; and on His account God reckons imperfect righteousness as perfect, and *sin as not sin, even though it really is sin.* . . . Thus a Christian is righteous and a sinner at the same time, holy and profane, an enemy of God and a child of God. None of the sophists

---

9. McGrath, *Luther's Theology,* pp. 1-2. In a sense Luther's theology of justification was the logical outgrowth of his theology of the cross, even if Paul's doctrine of justification gave Luther his first sense of release from his religious torments; and so as McGrath rightly points out: "the unfolding of that hidden presence of God in the scene of dereliction upon the cross holds the key to Luther's protracted search for a gracious God. No one would dream of seeking God in the 'distance, poverty, death and everything else that is shown to us in the suffering Christ' — nevertheless, God is there, hidden and yet revealed, for those who care to seek him. . . . Luther's developing insights into man's justification *coram Deo* [before God] are encapsulated in the concept of the 'theology of the cross'" (p. 2).

10. Martin Luther, "Heidelberg Disputation," in *Selected Writings of Martin Luther,* vol. 1: *1517-1520,* ed. Theodore G. Tappert (Philadelphia: Fortress Press, 1967), p. 79.

will admit this paradox, because they do not understand the meaning of justification.[11]

To be sure, Luther's theology of the cross is not the sheer wallowing in paradox it has often been taken to be; otherwise his defense of Chalcedonian orthodoxy, with its careful resolution of the essential paradox of Christ by the application of important (often philosophical) distinctions, would make no sense. Furthermore, the subsequent history of officially sanctioned Lutheran theology moved in a markedly "scholastic" milieu: for it attempted to set Luther's insights into a systematic array of explicit formulations marshaled into an arrangement determined by logical relations, just as the medieval scholastics had done with the paradoxes of patristic thought.[12]

In sum, then, we must see Luther's Christology as a synthesis (to be sure, an often volatile synthesis) between his late-medieval appreciation for exactitude in theological language and his revolutionary insight that the cross is the only locus of salvation and the only place where we can encounter the God of mercy. In other words, we must ask: What is the relationship between his profession of Chalcedonian orthodoxy and his revolutionary theology of the cross? Certainly the two have to go together if his theology of the cross is not to descend into mere rhetoric. For unless Jesus is in some sense truly divine, there would be no reason to find the hidden God in the cross of Jesus,

11. Martin Luther, *Lectures on Galatians, 1535, Chapters 1-4*, in *Luther's Works*, ed. Jaroslav Pelikan, Hilton C. Oswald, and Helmut T. Lehmann (Saint Louis: Concordia, 1999, c1963), vol. 26, pp. 232-33; original in *WA* vol. 40.1, 378; emphasis added. By the way, the phrase translated as "righteous and sinner at the same time" in Latin is the famous *simul justus et peccator*, which on the basis of this passage rightly came to be seen as the touchstone of all of Luther's theology, including his Christology, as we shall see.

12. The most famous of these efforts to initiate a Lutheran scholasticism was Martin Chemnitz's *De duabus naturis in Christo* of 1570, translated by Jacob Preus as *The Two Natures in Christ* (St. Louis: Concordia, 1971). On the Calvinist side, Johann Heinrich Alsted even called one of his books (published in 1618) *Scholastic Theology*! Later Lutheran theology, especially in the twentieth century, would score this brand of Lutheran scholasticism for its abandonment of Luther's denunciation of the scholastic method because of its dread reliance on Aristotle's "pagan" logic; but the fact that a kind of Lutheran scholasticism emerged so quickly after Luther's death must surely indicate something about his own concerns, as Pelikan rightly notes: "Although the polemical stance of the theologians in the seventeenth century compelled all [theologians, both Protestant and Catholic] to emphasize their theological differences, they did have much in common, both theologically and philosophically. . . . All of them employed a method of presenting Christian doctrine that was principally 'scholastic' (or, perhaps, 'neo-scholastic')." Jaroslav Pelikan, *The Christian Tradition*, vol. 4: *Reformation of Church and Dogma (1300-1700)*, p. 337.

as opposed to that of, say, the good thief or Spartacus, a point Luther himself recognized when he said: "Whoever confesses the two natures in Christ, God and man, must also ascribe the *idiomata* [properties] of both to the person."[13] How else could Luther find the very nature of God revealed in the cross unless Jesus is himself divine?

Unfortunately, the episode of nominalism in the previous two centuries of medieval philosophy would end up hobbling Luther's intent to remain an orthodox Chalcedonian. For it was the central teaching of the nominalists that there are no such things as essences or natures. If one begins theologizing under that assumption, then clearly Chalcedon's teaching of the union of two *natures* in the one Person of Christ will break down into incoherence. In Luther's case this can be seen in another statement in his defense of Chalcedon: on the one hand he says, with perfect orthodoxy, in a sentence already cited, "Whoever confesses the two natures in Christ, God and man, must also ascribe the *idiomata* [properties] of both to the person." But he then confuses the issue completely by claiming in the previous paragraph that Nestorius "does not want to give the *idiomata* of humanity to the divinity of Christ" and Eutyches "does not want to give the *idiomata* of the divinity to the humanity."[14]

But such an assertion represents a thoroughgoing philosophical confusion. The properties of divinity can no more be "given" to the humanity than the properties of infinity can be given to finitude — no more than the essence of bachelorhood can be ascribed to the married state. Luther's philosophical confusion here is not a minor matter. We recall from previous chapters how difficult it can be to maintain the paradoxes of Christology without falling into outright self-contradiction, and the surest way to that declension from provocative paradox to outright absurdity would be to abandon the concept of nature as appertaining to the *essence* of the being that possesses that nature.[15]

13. Martin Luther, "On the Councils and the Church," in *Selected Writings of Martin Luther*, vol. 4: *1529-1546*, ed. Theodore G. Tappert (Philadelphia: Fortress Press, 1967), p. 301.

14. Luther, "On the Councils and the Church," p. 301.

15. Note that Luther seems to equate paradox with contradiction outright in his *Commentary on Galatians* of 1519 (in other words, a year after the Heidelberg Disputation), at Galatians 4:27. Here Paul quotes Isaiah 54:1: "Rejoice, O barren one who bore no children. Break forth and shout, you who are not in travail. For the children of the desolate woman are many more than the children of her who is married." This typical Pauline paradox Luther glosses as follows: "These words are . . . a strange antithesis *and contradiction* [which] gives them *the nature of a paradox*." Martin Luther, *Lectures on Galatians, 1519*, in *Luther's*

This confusion surely accounts for some of Luther's more phantasmagoric statements about the atonement. Drawing on Paul's line that "God made him who knew no sin to become sin" (2 Cor. 5:21), Luther again confuses the nature of Christ's *essential* sinlessness with the *manner* by which he "became" sin. The following passage is no doubt rhetorically powerful, but it remains both theologically and philosophically impossible to maintain: "All the prophets foresaw this, that Christ was to become the greatest thief, murderer, robber, desecrator, blasphemer, and so on, greater than there has ever been in the world." And on the same page he claims that on the cross Christ is "*not* the Son of God, born of the Virgin but a sinner." On the cross Christ is "Paul, the violent and blasphemous persecutor," and "Peter, who denied Christ," and "David, the adulterer."[16]

This remarkable passage neatly encapsulates the same conceptual confusions on a soteriological level that we saw had afflicted Luther's christological interpretation of Chalcedon. As long as Luther holds in mind the Person of Christ as the locus of the unity of humanity and divinity, he interprets Christ's substitutionary atonement in an orthodox manner, just as he does with Chalcedon. For in that same paragraph he says that Christ "has and bears all the sins of all men in His body — not in the sense that He has committed them but in the sense that He took these sins, committed by us, upon His own body, in order to make satisfaction for them with His own blood. Therefore this general Law of Moses included Him, although He was innocent so far as His own Person was concerned; for it found Him among sinners and thieves."[17] But then he confuses the whole point of soteriology by concluding that Christ "bore the *person* of a sinner and a thief — and not of one but of all sinners and thieves."[18] But if that were the case, then Christ would have been justly condemned, and we would not be saved. As Athanasius said in the fourth century: "You cannot put straight in others what is warped in yourself."[19]

In many other respects, though, Luther was quintessentially medieval in

---

Works, trans. Jaroslav Pelikan, ed. Jaroslav Pelikan and Walter A. Hansen (Saint Louis: Concordia, 1999, c1963), vol. 27, p. 319.

16. Martin Luther, *Lectures on Galatians, 1535, Chapters 1-4*, in *Luther's Works*, vol. 26, p. 277; original in *WA* vol. 40.1, 417; emphasis added.

17. Luther, *Lectures on Galatians, 1535, Chapters 1-4*, in *Luther's Works*, vol. 26, p. 277.

18. Luther, *Lectures on Galatians, 1535, Chapters 1-4*, in *Luther's Works*, vol. 26, p. 277; emphasis added.

19. Athanasius, *On the Incarnation*, trans. by a Member of the C.S.M.V. (Crestwood, NY: St. Vladimir's Seminary Press, 1953), p. 42.

his stress on the humanity of Christ as the locus where the mercy of God could most be found, an important theme of Franciscan piety and, closer to Luther's day, of the so-called *devotio moderna* of the German Rhineland. Moreover, he adopted, however unawares, Anselm's notion that God — meaning, of course, God "by definition" — cannot tolerate sin. Before the holiness of God sin can only provoke divine wrath. So what Luther was really trying to do was to unite Anselm's theory of satisfaction with the late-medieval stress on the suffering humanity of Christ in a way that would make the salvation won by Christ's death on the cross *meaningful and applicable* to the believer, as Pelikan rightly sees:

> [Luther's] polemical target . . . was a theological method that [he] attributed to scholasticism, which treated the truths of the Christian faith as objects of intellectual curiosity without reference to the cross and benefits of Christ. Specifically, the dogmas of the Trinity and the person of Christ were not an exercise in logical inquiry or metaphysical speculation. Luther ridiculed the scholastics for investigating the relation between the two natures of Christ and branded such investigation as "sophistic."[20]

Unfortunately, Luther's own conceptual confusions prove the dangers that befall theology when it eschews the ministrations of philosophy, a contempt that can too easily lead to a theology of raw paradox untempered by the Aristotelian logic implicit in all arguments of whatever stripe. For that reason, Luther had no choice but to pose radical contrasts between a theology of glory (all bad) and a theology of the cross (the only legitimate theological option), from which he drew the conclusion that the God who is hidden from the world in his majesty can only be a condemning God, whereas the God hidden in the humanity of Christ reveals himself fully as the merciful God:

> 18. It is certain that man must utterly despair of his own ability before he is prepared to receive the grace of Christ.
>
> 19. That person does not deserve to be called a theologian who looks upon the invisible things of God as though they were clearly perceptible in those things which have actually happened.
>
> 20. He deserves to be called a theologian, however, who comprehends the visible and manifest things of God seen through suffering and the cross.

20. Pelikan, *Reformation*, p. 156.

21. A theology of glory calls evil good and good evil. A theology of the cross calls the thing what it actually is.[21]

It is just this kind of reasoning that drew Luther into statements that even deny that Christ was innocent. Whether his view of justification required him to confuse the meaning of Chalcedon or his nominalism confused his Christology and then led him to his forensic view of imputed justification cannot be settled here. But they are certainly mutually interdependent in the logical order:

> And this is our highest comfort, to clothe and wrap Christ this way in my sins, your sins, and the sins of the entire world, and in this way to behold Him bearing all our sins. When He is beheld this way, He easily removes all the fanatical opinions of our opponents about justification by works. For the papists dream about a kind of faith "formed by love." Through this they want to remove sins and be justified. This is clearly to unwrap Christ and to unclothe Him from our sins, *to make Him innocent*, to burden and overwhelm ourselves with our own sins, and to behold them, not in Christ but in ourselves. This is to abolish Christ and make Him useless.[22]

In other words the comfort that Luther drew from his doctrine of justification is directly linked to the confusions inherent in his soteriology; and these confusions are themselves rooted, logically if not chronologically, in his more basic confusion between the Person and natures of Christ, a point that becomes clearest in this passage:

> This is the most joyous of all doctrines and the one that contains the most comfort. It teaches that we have the indescribable and inestimable mercy and love of God. When the merciful Father saw that we were being oppressed through the Law, that we were being held under a curse, and that we could not be liberated from it by anything, He sent His Son into the world, heaped all the sins of all men upon Him, and said to Him: "*Be* Peter the denier; Paul the persecutor, blasphemer, and assaulter; David the adulterer; the sinner who ate the apple in Paradise; the thief on the cross. In short, *be* the *person* of all men, the one who has

21. Martin Luther, "Heidelberg Disputation," in Tappert, *Selected Writings of Martin Luther*, vol. 1, p. 66.

22. Martin Luther, *Lectures on Galatians*, in *Luther's Works*, vol. 26, p. 279; original in WA 40.1, p. 419; emphasis added.

committed the sins of all men. And see to it that you pay and make satisfaction for them."[23]

Ignatius of Loyola

Nothing shows more the divergent paths taken by Protestant and Catholic
theology in the sixteenth century than the different ways Martin Luther and
Ignatius of Loyola (1491-1556) experienced God, sin, and redemption. To see
this contrast in its starkest form, let us first take up this autobiographical
reminiscence of Luther's, speaking here in retrospect of his experience as an
Augustinian monk:

> At such times God seem[ed] terribly angry, and with him the whole cre-
> ation. At such a time there is no flight, no comfort, within or without, but
> all things accuse. At such a time as that the Psalmist mourns, "I am cut off
> from thy sight" (Psalm 31:22). . . . In this moment, strange to say, the soul
> cannot believe that it can ever be redeemed. . . . All that remains is the
> stark-naked desire for help and a terrible groaning, but it does not know
> where to turn for help.[24]

Consider now a remarkably similar passage, at least in the formal sense,
from the autobiographical dictations of Ignatius. Recall that for Anselm God
and sin are so antithetical that God cannot tolerate sin in his presence. How
then can a sinner approach God and not expect wrath and reprobation?
Ignatius had led, at least by his own post-conversion retrospective lights, the
dissolute life of a soldier, until a wound incurred in 1521 during a siege of
Pamplona, Spain, forced him to a lengthy and extremely painful convales-
cence.[25] To while away the time after he had passed the danger of death, he

23. Luther, *Lectures on Galatians,* vol. 26, p. 280; emphases added.
24. Martin Luther, "Explanation of the Ninety-Five Theses," in *Luther's Works,* ed.
Jaroslav Pelikan (Philadelphia: Fortress Press, 1967), vol. 31, p. 129; *WA* 1:579.
25. Note that this is the same year as the Diet of Worms, when Luther's "Here I stand, I
can do no other" speech made the break with Rome irrevocable. One author draws from
that coincidence this fascinating portrait of the two men: "That the life of Ignatius so closely
parallels that of Luther is surely in the designs of Divine Providence. Ignatius was born eight
years after Luther, and his conversion takes place eight years after Luther's; hence, both Luther and Ignatius are of the same age when they experience the great change in their lives.
For Ignatius it was the year 1521. At the same time, that year became a very decisive one for
Luther and the history of the West. In 1521 Luther stood before the Diet of Worms and won

asked for reading material, thinking to read the romance fiction of knights errant and damsels in distress, the kind of reading material so mercilessly satirized by Miguel Cervantes' *Don Quixote*. His castle, however, had on hand only a life of Christ and a book of the lives of the saints. When he read these works, he began fantasizing in the same kind of romantic way about following the example of Francis of Assisi and Dominic as he had done when reading romance fiction; but after he set aside these edifying works, he also fantasized once again about noble ladies to be won over, as had been his previous wont. Then he began to notice a change in his "mood" after the two different fantasizing visions: The consolations that came to him after dreaming about following Francis and Dominic *lasted,* but fantasies about courtly love began soon enough to pale, leaving him feeling dispirited and listless.

This experience eventually led him, after the recovery of his health in 1522, following two botched operations to repair a broken shin, to renounce his previous life and to begin a life of penance as a lay pilgrim. He had first visited the Benedictine monastery of Our Lady of the Black Madonna, the famous pilgrimage sight in the Montserrat mountain range, where he donated his soldier's armor before the altar of the Black Madonna. Then he moved to a cave near a Dominican priory in Manresa several miles downhill from Montserrat. It was in this cave that his past sins began to torment him. Like Anselm and Luther before him, he knew that God and sin are so antithetical that God cannot tolerate sin before his presence. In that regard it was perhaps fortunate that Ignatius was quite innocent of theology (in fact he was entirely unlettered in Latin), for he did not have to read his sense of sinfulness through the medium of Paul's intricate theology of justification or still less through the scrim of late-medieval nominalism. Even so, the tradi-

---

world popularity for his cause by defying the papal bull of excommunication. This popularity became immediately so strong that it was the driving force of the Reformation. . . . In 1521, during the defense of the fortress of Pamplona, Ignatius was severely wounded, seriously incapacitating him for a very promising officer's career. Furthermore, all hopes were ended of obtaining any of the highly desired positions at court." Friedrich Richter, *Martin Luther and Ignatius Loyola: Spokesmen for Two Worlds of Belief,* trans. Leonard F. Zwinger (Westminster, MD: Newman Press, 1960), p. 55. Provocative as this book is, it is often too sweeping in its judgments and counterintuitive in its conclusions. For example, Richter claims that Luther's "personality merits him a place among the leading figures of the Renaissance" (p. 18). But Ignatius he claims "had his own particular mission. It is in direct opposition to the Renaissance, of which he becomes the chief antagonist" (p. 19). Most historians, though, see much greater connections between Loyola and the Renaissance than Richter grants, and much greater tension between Luther's theology of the cross and Renaissance humanism, as seen in Luther's strong criticisms of Erasmus.

tional balm of the Catholic sacrament of confession availed nothing to soothe his soul in its quasi-Anselmian, quasi-Lutheran agony, even when he went back to his confessor time and again to confess the same sins that had already been absolved. For how could God tolerate even the most minor of yet-unconfessed sins?

In frustration, his Dominican confessor forbade him under pain of sin (!) to confess anything from the past that had already been confessed, which led him to this crisis, as described in his own words, in a passage that merits comparison with Luther's sense of despair before a sinless God who must expel all sin from his presence:

> He found no cure for his scruples. Many months had now passed since they had begun to torment him. Once when he was very upset by them, he began to pray with such fervor that he shouted out loud to God, saying "Help me, Lord, for I find no remedy among men nor in any creature. Yet if I thought I could find it, no labor would be too great for me. Even though I should have to follow a little dog so he could help me, I would do it." While he had these thoughts, the temptation often came over him with great force to throw himself into a large hole in his room next to the place where he was praying. But realizing it was a sin to kill oneself, he shouted again, "Lord, I will do nothing to offend you."[26]

Still there was no respite. Unwilling — or perhaps willing but afraid — to commit suicide, he decided as a penance to forgo solid food entirely, a total fast that lasted a full week, when he was due to go to confession again. But when he told his confessor of the fast, the Dominican priest promptly ordered him to resume eating, where the story comes to its climax:

> His confessor ordered him to break off his abstinence; though he still felt strong, he obeyed his confessor and that day and the next felt free from scruples. But on the third day, which was Tuesday, while at prayer he began to remember his sins one by one, and he went on thinking about one sin after the other out of his past and felt he was required to confess them again. But after these thoughts, disgust for the life he led and the desire to give it up came over him. In this way the Lord wished to awaken him as if from a dream. From the lessons God had given him, he now had some experience of the diversity of spirits, and he began to wonder about the

---

26. From *The Autobiography of St. Ignatius Loyola*, trans. Joseph O'Callaghan (New York: Harper & Row, 1974), p. 35. Throughout, Ignatius speaks of himself in the third person.

means by which that spirit had come. He decided very clearly, therefore, not to confess anything from the past anymore. From that day forward he remained free of those scruples and held it for certain that Our Lord through his mercy had wished to deliver him.[27]

The formal similarities between this scene from 1522 and Luther's discovery in 1517 of Paul's doctrine of justification by faith as the resolution of his own torment over his sinfulness (the famous *Turmerlebnis*, or "experience in the tower") are more than obvious: both men were wracked by a sense of distance from God, an abyss made even more unbridgeable by sin; both felt despair before the presence of God in light of that sin; and both came to a resolution of that conflict in a way that would determine the rest of their lives, not to mention of history itself. But of course the similarities are more formal than material, for in their respective accounts of their conflicts with God we see the key difference: for Luther, despair at his inability to overcome his sinfulness led him, at least partially, to hate God, which he was able to turn into love only by seeing the reversal of God's attitude toward him through faith, defined as that which speaks of God's forensic, imputed acquittal *despite* God's justified wrath at sin:

> Though I lived as a monk without reproach, I felt that I was a sinner before God with an extremely disturbed conscience. I could not believe that he was placated by my satisfaction. I did not love, yes, I hated the righteous God who punishes sinners, and secretly, if not blasphemously, certainly murmuring greatly, I was angry with God. . . . At last, by the mercy of God, meditating day and night, I gave heed to the context of the words, namely, "In it [the gospel] the righteousness of God is revealed, as it is written, 'He who through faith is righteous shall live.'" There I began to understand that the righteousness of God is that by which the righteous lives by a gift of God, namely by faith. . . . Here I felt that I was altogether born again and had entered paradise itself through open gates.[28]

Ignatius, in contrast, always hated *himself* during his struggles, which is no doubt why he kept trying to expunge his sins by extreme fasts to the point of starvation, no matter how trivial those sins were or how scrupulously he

27. *The Autobiography of St. Ignatius Loyola*, p. 36.
28. Martin Luther, "Preface to the Complete Edition of Luther's Latin Writings" (1545), in *Luther's Works*, trans. Lewis W. Spitz, ed. Helmut T. Lehmann (Philadelphia: Fortress Press, 1960), vol. 34, pp. 336-37; WA vol. 54, p. 185.

sought to get rid of them. (He once fell into a fit of scruples after having stepped on two overlapping twigs that had accidentally been formed into the shape of a cross.) But once he came to see that such hatred for his own self was itself contrary to the will of God, he came to this crucial breakthrough:

> He continued to abstain from eating meat and was so firm about it that he would not think of changing it for any reason; but one morning after he arose some meat appeared before him, as if he saw it with his own eyes, though he had not had any desire for it. At the same time he also had a strong inclination of his will to eat meat from that time on. Although he remembered his previous intention, he could not hesitate about this and decided that he ought to eat meat. Later, when telling this to his confessor, the confessor told him to consider whether perhaps this was a temptation; but examining it [the vision] carefully, he could never be in doubt about it [its authenticity].[29]

Although at the time Ignatius had no theological training — indeed, as we saw, he did not even know Latin and would later be thrown into prison three times by the authorities of the Spanish Inquisition for giving advice to souls without the benefit of formal theological training and the validation of clerical status — he found himself coming to important theological insights under God's direct tutelage, as it were:

> God treated him at this time just as a schoolmaster treats a child whom he is teaching. Whether this was on account of his coarseness or his dense intelligence or because he had no one to teach him or because of the strong desire God himself had given him to serve Him, he clearly believed and has always believed that God treated him in this way. Indeed, if he were to doubt this, he thought he would offend His divine majesty. . . . [For example,] at the elevation of the Body of the Lord [at Mass one day in Manresa], he saw with interior eyes something like white rays coming from above. Although he cannot explain this very well after so long a time, nevertheless what he saw clearly with his understanding was how Jesus Christ our Lord was there in that most holy sacrament.[30]

29. *The Autobiography of St. Ignatius Loyola*, p. 37.

30. *The Autobiography of St. Ignatius Loyola*, p. 38. Here too we can see another formal similarity between Luther and Loyola: their insight that the doctrine of the Eucharist and Christology are mutually interdependent: "the controversy between the two major parties of Protestantism, the Lutheran and the Reformed, over the real presence of the body and blood of Christ in the Lord's Supper . . . was responsible for the most detailed Western preoccupa-

It is this passage, above all, that in my opinion justifies giving Ignatius of Loyola a place in this textbook, for — perhaps unbeknownst to himself — he was a genuine theologian. True, his training in theology came only much later, after he realized that his purely experiential approach was not only jeopardizing his ministry of helping souls because of the ever-watchful eye of the Spanish Inquisition, but more importantly because he knew that his mystical gifts needed tempering in the crucible of theological study and obedience to the magisterial hierarchy of the church. In the meantime, however, he was putting together the rudiments of his famous *Spiritual Exercises,* which themselves contain an abundance of theological — and above all of christological — insight.[31]

We have already seen how Luther forged his Christology out of a concern that its technicalities not get in the way of their direct relevance to the believer — however important those refinements are in their own right and however much Luther himself might have misunderstood the careful distinctions forged by Chalcedon. Unfortunately, in Luther's case that drive for relevance (what we now call the "existential" meaning of doctrine) often led him to an excessively one-sided reaction against scholasticism in general and Aristotle in particular. Fortunately for Ignatius, he had so little exposure to school theology that he had nothing to react against. But it is striking how many orthodox Catholics, who had no theoretical objections to and felt no alienation against the scholastic mode, found the Exercises of Ignatius a godsend. Because of Ignatius' past brushes with the Spanish Inquisition, and also because Lutherans also stressed experience over against scholastic dogma, a certain cloud had hung over Ignatius even in Rome, and even when he enjoyed papal favor. So the approval of the publication of the *Spiritual Exercises* was by no means a sure thing. But one influential doctor of theology, Bartholomé Torres, defended them in these glowing terms:

> As God is my witness, for thirty years I have been studying and teaching
> theology, yet in the whole of this time I have not made such progress as
> during the few short days of making the Spiritual Exercises. For they are
> essentially an attempt to taste [*gustar*] and to bring vividly to mind the

---

tion with the intricacies of christology since the ancient church." Jaroslav Pelikan, *Reformation of Church and Dogma (1300-1700),* p. 157.

31. The final published form of the *Exercises,* with approval of the authorities in Rome, did not come until Ignatius had already founded the Society of Jesus; and that version contains many revisions and additions folded into the original text dating from Manresa. There is, in other words, more theology in this small manual than first meets the eye.

things which one already knows as an object of study, but in such a way that one is now also prepared to act on them. There is, after all, a world of difference between the knowledge which one teaches and the knowledge which one puts into practice.[32]

Like Luther, Ignatius sees the spiritual life as intensely dramatic, as a battle between God and Satan over the individual soul, a battle that can only be won when the individual soul takes refuge in the victory over Satan already won by Christ on the cross. So dramatically Christocentric is Ignatius' vision of salvation history that one can even spot an underlying Lutheran-esque *theologia crucis* animating his vision, as Hugo Rahner rightly sees:

> The whole of his theology and mysticism oscillated between the world and the heavenly throne, between renunciation and embrace, between the abandonment of all things and the discovery of God in all things. God is the author of nature and grace alike; but the natural world, which was created by the eternal Word and must be restored through the cross, *has lost all value in its own right* because the incarnate Son drew all things on the circumference of the earth into his own violent death. Thus it was that Ignatius could say: "We must consider all creatures not as beautiful and loveable in themselves, but as bathed in the blood of Christ." . . . All created things, therefore, are meaningful only if seen in relation to Christ.[33]

Although as the founder of the Society of Jesus Ignatius required that Jesuit seminarians be trained according to the school of Thomas, one also can detect in his Christology certain themes adumbrated by John Duns Scotus, who, as we saw in the last chapter, disputed Thomas's explanation for the incarnation. According to Thomas, God sent his Son in the flesh in order to outdo the damage caused by sin, which seems to make the incarnation

32. This testimonial was first published for public scrutiny in *Monumenta Ignatiana, Part II: Exercitia spiritualia S. Ignatii eorumque Directoria* (Madrid and Rome: Jesuit Historical Institute, 1911), I:667; cited in Hugo Rahner, *Ignatius the Theologian,* trans. Michael Barry (New York: Herder & Herder, 1968), pp. 102-3. In a passage somewhat reminiscent of the opening chapter of Paul's letter to the Galatians, an early companion of Ignatius by the name of Father Jerome Nadal speaks of the interplay between Ignatius's experience and his formal theological training at the University of Paris in these terms: "Ignatius also used other books and consulted every branch of theology. Thus all books, all theologians and the whole of Holy Scripture were to serve as confirmation for what he had really [already] learned from spiritual inspiration alone" (quoted in Rahner, *Ignatius the Theologian,* p. 53).

33. Rahner, *Ignatius the Theologian,* p. 65; emphasis added. The affinities with Luther's theology of the cross should be evident here.

somehow contingent upon a historical event. Scotus, however, insists on the incarnation as the culmination of God's aboriginal intent to create the world, irrespective of the fall of Adam. Ignatius in effect reconciles these two views (again, however unintentionally) by showing how, in Rahner's lapidary formulation, "sin is essentially a christological event."[34] He establishes that point in two of the meditations ("exercises"), the one called "The Two Standards" and the other "The Sin of the Angels." The two "standards" refer to the standard (or banner) of Satan and the other of Christ, and Ignatius paints the conflict between these two standards in almost Miltonic intensity:

> Imagine you see the chief of all the enemy in the vast plain about Babylon, seated on a great throne of fire and smoke, his appearance inspiring horror and terror. Consider how he summons innumerable demons and scatters them, some to one city and some to another, throughout the whole world, so that no province, no place, no state of life, no individual is overlooked. Consider the address he makes to them, how he goads them on to lay snares for men and to bind them with chains. First they are to tempt them to covet riches (as Satan himself is accustomed to do in most cases) that they may the more easily attain the empty honors of this world, and then come to overweening pride.[35]

Against this cosmic fiend the retreatant then meditates on "Christ our Lord, standing in a lowly place" near Jerusalem (#144), "choosing so many persons, apostles, disciples, etc., and sending them throughout the whole world to spread His sacred doctrine among all men, no matter what their state or condition" (#145). But where did Satan's enmity come from? For that, we turn to the meditation on the sin of the angels, where Ignatius asks us to recall that the angels, though "created in a state of grace, did not want to make use of the freedom God gave them to reverence and obey their Creator and Lord, and so falling into pride, were changed from grace to hatred of God, and cast out of heaven into hell" (#50).

Hugo Rahner argues that, when we put these two meditations together, we see that Ignatius believed that the pride of the bad angels was provoked by a prevision of the incarnation as the ultimate purpose of God's creation, a

34. Rahner, *Ignatius the Theologian*, p. 67.

35. *The Spiritual Exercises of St. Ignatius*, trans. Louis J. Puhl, S.J. (Chicago: Loyola Press, 1951), #140-42. Citations from the *Exercises* are usually done by the standard paragraph number found in nearly all editions and translations. Subsequent quotations will be cited by that number in the body of the text.

point he makes even more explicit than did John Milton in *Paradise Lost*. Because this prevision was given to the angels prior to their sin, this means that the incarnation had been decided by God *antecedenter ad peccatum praevisum* (independently of God's foresight into later sin). While not stated explicitly in Scripture and never defined as obligatory doctrine by the magisterium, this view has now become generally accepted in Catholic theology, whose authority is described by the dogmatic theologian Matthias Scheeben in these terms:

> According to a fairly general theological opinion, the angels received the revelation of the future incarnation of the Son of God before their fall. The firmest basis for this opinion is the somewhat less widely held view that the incarnate Word who, according to the Apostle, is the "head of all rule and authority" and "the first-born of all creation" (Col. 1:15; 2:10) was predestined from the very inception of God's design to be the Head and King of the angels, and was thus intended to be the source of supernatural grace and glory for them also.[36]

I feel sure that Ignatius held to the same view, however inchoately, because it balances so well with a remark he made about Adam and Eve in a small catechism he penned for the use of Jesuits in their efforts to instruct the unlettered in the rudiments of their faith.[37] In that small work Ignatius depicts the following scene, a kind of Jesuit midrash on the third chapter of Genesis:

> After God our Lord had created heaven, earth and all things, and when the first man was in paradise, it was revealed to him [Adam] how the Son of God had resolved to become man. And *after* Adam and Eve had sinned, they recognized that God had resolved to become man in order to redeem their sin; . . . and then they passed this knowledge down to their children, how the Son of God, our Creator and Lord, proposed to become man.[38]

36. Matthias Scheeben, *The Mysteries of Christianity,* trans. Cyril Vollert, S.J. (St. Louis: Herder, 1946), §42, 268.

37. According to the *Formula of the Institute* (the first papal charter for what would soon become the canonically established order to be called the "Society of Jesus"), one of the purposes of this new band of priests was to catechize the woefully uninstructed Catholic laity, children especially.

38. Ignatius Loyola, *Small Catechism* in *Monumenta Ignatiana*, Part I: *Epistolae et Instructiones S. Ignatii* (Madrid: Jesuit Historical Institute, 1911), vol. 12, p. 668, cited in Hugo Rahner, *Ignatius the Theologian,* p. 78. Note how Luther also penned a *Small Catechism*.

Many of the church fathers and medieval theologians were fond of spotting the rhetorical technique of *chiasmus* in the storyline of the Bible. "Chiasmus," as we already saw in Chapter 5, is technically defined as a grammatical figure by which the order of words in one of two parallel clauses is inverted in the other, as in the Bible's line, "Whoever sheds the blood of man by man shall his blood be shed" (Gen. 9:6), where the order of the words "shed," "blood," and "man" is reversed in the second clause from their order in the first.[39] But chiasmus also takes on a wider meaning in the interpretation of salvation history, starting with Paul's parallelism of Adam and Christ as the second Adam, upon which many patristic writers spoke of Mary as the second Eve, and saw the tree of the cross as the fitting place for atoning the sin of Adam and Eve at the Tree of the Knowledge of Good and Evil, and so forth. For that reason, I hold with Hugo Rahner the plausibility of Ignatius subscribing to the view that the angels were given a prevision of the incarnation as the aboriginal intent of God for all creation independent of sin.[40]

This might seem a trivial point, except that it has a bearing on Ignatius' Christology in important ways. For without it we cannot understand his insight that sin is essentially and at all points a christological event. Because belief in angels, whether good or bad, has declined so much in modern times, and because the concept of evolution has made the account of the first sin of Adam and Eve seem merely "symbolic," this point has been largely lost. But without the idea that sin is essentially connected with the sin of Lucifer and, later, of Adam and Eve, we can never understand why Ignatius directs the retreatant to a meditation on his or her own sins not just in the context of the cosmic sin of the bad angels and the original sin of Adam and Eve but also before Christ on the cross.

39. Other examples, which can be multiplied almost to infinity, would be Shakespeare's "O powerful love, that in some respects makes a beast a man, in some other, a man a beast" (*The Merry Wives of Windsor*), Amy Carmichael's "You can give without loving, but you cannot love without giving," the ancient Greek proverb, "In peace sons bury their fathers, but in war fathers bury their sons," and (my favorite) Ambrose Bierce's "The gambling known as business looks with austere disfavor on the business known as gambling."

40. Support for this view may also be found in the prayer of oblation that concludes the Meditation on the Kingdom of Christ: "Eternal Lord of all things, in the presence of Thy infinite goodness, and of *Thy glorious mother*" (#98). Without a context to indicate otherwise, one would normally expect the phrase "eternal Lord of all things" to refer to God the Father or to God *simpliciter*. But by adding "and of Thy glorious mother," Ignatius shows that he considers Christ (and not just the Son as the preexistent Logos) to be "creator of all things," implying the fore-intention of God the Father to become incarnate prior even to creation, let alone sin.

To put it bluntly, Ignatius seeks to drag the retreatant through the same terrifying experience that he had in the cave of Manresa, that is, to realize "the gravity and malice of sin against our Creator and Lord," to contemplate "how many went to hell because of one mortal sin" and how "countless others have been lost for fewer sins than I have committed," and finally how "because of sin, of acting against the Infinite Goodness, one is justly condemned forever" (#52). In later centuries, this meditation would prove to be the occasion of great trial for many souls because so many Catholics, including retreat directors, had lost sight of its essential christological focus.[41] But Ignatius' thoroughgoing Christocentrism forestalls (or is meant to forestall) that despair, as Rahner explains:

> A yawning abyss opens up between God alone and man alone [in this meditation]. Yet there is a bridge whose soaring span enables us to gain some idea of this frightening gap between God and sin, and the moment we see it we realize, with a certain sweet amazement, that the two ends have, in fact, already been joined: it is the blood-stained cross upon which my Creator and Lord died, so that I, who am no more than a poisonous outcast, might be made whole and sound, restored to new life as part of a vital universe.[42]

For that reason Ignatius does not shirk from requiring the retreatant to put himself in the same situation that seems, at least at first glance, to parallel what Luther felt in his days as an Augustinian monk: "I will consider who God is against whom I have sinned, going through His attributes and comparing them with their contraries in me: His wisdom with my ignorance, His power with my weakness, His justice with my iniquity, His goodness with my wickedness" (#59). As Rahner says so well of the meaning of this meditation, "The dimensions of the divine justice and goodness can only be measured against Christ crucified."[43]

For the most part the rest of the *Exercises* treats of the life of Christ, starting with the decision of the Trinity to send the Son to redeem the human race, sending the angel Gabriel to Mary to announce the birth of the Savior

---

41. The best — and most lurid — example of the revulsion caused by this meditation can be found in James Joyce's *Portrait of the Artist as a Young Man*, where the narrator, Stephen Dedalus, is led to despair, and then to reject the Christian faith, when he is forced to make a so-called "preached retreat" at the Jesuit college of Dublin, where the focus is all on the eternal sufferings of the denizens of hell.

42. Hugo Rahner, *Ignatius the Theologian*, p. 81.

43. Hugo Rahner, *Ignatius the Theologian*, p. 82.

through her, the Nativity, the finding in the Temple, the temptations, the public ministry (this is the matter of the so-called Second Week of a thirty-day retreat), concluding in the passion and death of Jesus (the matter of the Third Week), and then his resurrection and appearance to his mother and the other disciples (the Fourth Week).[44] These meditations are almost all purely scriptural and put the retreatant into various gospel scenes through an almost cinematic exercise of the imagination, and are thus not meant to convey specific points of christological doctrine. Nonetheless they are guided by an important christological presupposition, one best expressed in the biblical doctrine that Christ is the "forerunner" and "pioneer and perfecter of our faith" (Heb. 6:20; 12:2). The retreatant, having already made the decision in the First Week to seek salvation in the cross, now "works through" (hence the stress on spiritual *exercises*) the path of discipleship, always looking to Christ as his pathfinder, forerunner, and pioneer, as again Rahner explains:

> Hence, for anyone trying to understand the christology running through the Exercises, it is vitally important here . . . to bear in mind the redemptive significance of the good and evil angels during the lifetime of Christ on earth. What the Bible brings to the surface for a brief instant is but a fragment of the tremendous struggle between light and darkness during which, in an hour of evil, the power of darkness hastened on the crucifixion, and this struggle will end in the splendor of the second coming, when the King "will slay Satan with the breath of his mouth" (2 Thess. 2:8).[45]

Leaving aside the obvious differences between Luther and Loyola regarding the sinner's experience of God in both mercy and reprobation, there is very little difference, I suspect, in the Christology of the two men when the focus is solely on the life of Christ and his role as pioneer of our faith, and even the First Week has remarkable Lutheran resonances. But the differences, however subtle they seem at first, become remarkably divergent when we look at some of the concluding matter at the back of the *Exercises*, especially the famous (or for some, infamous) "Rules for Thinking with the Church," most of which were clearly formulated with Protestantism in mind,[46] and the

---

44. Although Scripture is silent on the matter, Ignatius strongly insists that Christ must have appeared to his mother first of all (#219, 299).

45. Hugo Rahner, *Ignatius the Theologian*, p. 117.

46. Such as Rule 5: "We should praise vows of religion, obedience, poverty, chastity, and vows to perform other works of supererogation conducive to perfection" (#357) and Rule 6: "We should show our esteem for the relics of the saints by venerating them and praying to

starkest of which surely is Rule 13: "If we wish to proceed securely in all things, we must hold fast to the following principle: What seems to me white I will believe black if the hierarchical Church so defines. For I must be convinced that in Christ our Lord, the bridegroom, and in His spouse the Church, only one Spirit holds sway, which governs and rules for the salvation of souls. For it is by the same Spirit and Lord who gave the Ten Commandments that our holy Mother Church is ruled and governed" (#365).

Here we see the principle once more operative that tells us that small differences in initial presuppositions will lead to vastly different conclusions later on, just as a rocket sent into outer space will diverge wildly from its target if its initial settings are even slightly askew. If one were to ask exactly where the two men differ in their initial presuppositions, we have to consider not only the question of nominalism in Luther or Loyola's background in the intense crusader mentality of sixteenth-century Spain. Determinative also are the accidents of what led each man to come to discover a merciful God despite each one's deep sense of sin: Luther was already a theologian and had been lecturing on Paul and the Psalms for several years, so that he was almost forced to use Paul over against the training that had made him feel so desperate. But Ignatius began his journey away from the vanities of knight errantry by reading not the Bible but a life of Christ and, crucially, the lives of the saints, men already consecrated to the good of the church through their vows.

During the next several centuries these divergences over what are essentially ecclesiastical matters became the obsessive focus of theologians. What became lost in the heat of controversy, however, were the points that Luther and Ignatius most shared, their insistence that all salvation comes from the cross. This insight, too, they bequeathed to their respective communities, Protestant and Catholic, as can best be seen by looking at John Calvin — a Protestant who frequently differed from Luther — and at a Catholic who bitterly opposed the Jesuits and all they stood for: Blaise Pascal.

John Calvin

In one of his letters Paul speaks of distinct ministries in the church as explicit gifts of Christ, "who gave some to be apostles, some to be prophets, some to be evangelists, and some to be pastors and teachers" (Eph. 4:11). The grammar of

---

the saints. We should praise visits to the Station Churches, pilgrimages, indulgences, jubilees, crusade indults, and the lighting of candles in churches" (#358).

this verse implies that for Paul pastors and teachers constituted one single ministry, distinct from apostleship, prophecy, and evangelization. But for John Calvin (1509-64) the ministries of pastor and teacher *("doctor"* in the Latin translation that he used) were distinct — and he very much identified himself as someone who was called to the ministry of teaching theology, that is, of being a *doctor theologiae*. Because of the fame (or notoriety, if you will) of Calvin's role in helping to establish a Reformed theocracy in the city of Geneva, one might also see him as a pastor, and indeed a singularly rigorous one, who banned card-playing, dancing, and the like. But actually his role in Geneva was always strictly advisory; and when he ran afoul of the municipal authorities in Switzerland's most renowned city, he was forced to leave, as he did once when he departed for Strasbourg, although he was eventually invited back.

To be sure, the distinction can be overdrawn, for as one commentator says, "Calvin understood himself to be called to two distinct offices: the office of teacher, and the office of pastor. The teacher has as his audience future pastors of the church, . . . [whereas] the pastor teaches the young the rudiments of the doctrine of piety . . . and applies [Scripture] to the life of the congregation, not only in public worship but also in private visitation."[47] But even here one notices how much Calvin stresses the specific teaching responsibilities of the pastor, a stress that surely reflects the woeful state of clerical and lay instruction in the Christian religion that did so much to contribute to the Reformation in the first place.[48] Indeed, his most famous and influential book, the *Institutes of the Christian Religion*, gets its name from the Latin word for "instruction," *institutio*.

As more than one commentator has pointed out, Calvin had a far more systematic mind than did Luther: Although both men wrote more commentaries on individual books of the Bible than any other genre, Luther never wrote up a systematic account of his theology (unless one counts his two catechisms), while Calvin's *Institutes* became the most influential work of

47. Randall C. Zachman, *John Calvin as Teacher, Pastor, and Theologian: The Shape of His Writings and Thought* (Grand Rapids: Baker Academic, 2006), p. 13.

48. As again Zachman rightly sees: "John Calvin lived during a time when many Christians, both Roman and evangelical, recognized that the ministry of the church was in crisis. It is difficult for us to imagine what the training of ministers must have been like before seminaries were created precisely to address the lack of adequate ministerial formation during this period. John Calvin was well aware of the dire consequences of this lack of ministerial formation. According to Calvin, neither bishops nor priests were skilled in the interpretation of Scripture or particularly adept at teaching the summary of the doctrine that leads to genuine piety" (Zachman, p. 11).

the Protestant Reformation and determined its shape in countries that went far beyond Luther's Germany: France, Scotland, England and its American colonies, and of course Switzerland.

One can even, with due caution, call Calvin a quintessential scholastic theologian, again a point often made by his commentators.[49] Granted, Calvin's references to the "schoolmen" are nearly always critical, to the point of being merely abusive; but even here his targets are mainly those *late* scholastics who deviated from, indeed destroyed, the careful synthesis soldered together so painstakingly by Thomas Aquinas.[50] So strong in fact is this scholastic tincture in Calvin's theology that some scholars speculate that he learned this method from a former Dominican priest, Martin Bucer (1491-1551), who had befriended Calvin during his years in Strasbourg from 1538 to 1541. Bucer had entered the Dominican Order in 1506 at the age of fifteen. Fatefully for history, he was transferred to the Blackfriars cloister in Heidelberg in 1516, where he gained permission to attend Luther's epochal Heidelberg Disputation in April 1518, which so swept him away that he applied for release from his order to work as a parish priest in Landstuhl. His increasingly convinced Lutheranism then forced him to flee to Strasbourg, where he eventually invited Calvin to accept a pastorate.

Such an influence seems unlikely, however, given Bucer's own more pronounced Lutheran views. A more likely source would surely be Calvin's own training as a theology student in Paris in the years before he became a convinced Reformer. Born in 1509 in Noyon in Picardy, Calvin seems to have been destined by his father early on for an ecclesiastical degree, for he was given a benefice and tonsure (denoting clerical status) at the age of 12 and

49. For example: "It is worth recognizing from the outset that the Reformation altered comparatively few of the major *loci* of theology: the doctrines of justification, the sacraments, and the church received the greatest [shift of] emphasis, while the doctrines of God, the trinity, creation, providence, predestination, and the last things were taken over by the magisterial Reformation virtually without alteration. In addition, many of the differences between the theological methods of the Reformation and those of the Middle Ages can be attributed to the development of logic and rhetoric and to their impact on the relatively stable *disputatio*, rather than to a vast rebellion in academic approach." Richard A. Muller, *The Unaccommodated Calvin: Studies in the Foundation of a Theological Tradition* (Oxford: Oxford University Press, 2000), p. 39.

50. Muller points out (p. 50) that in Calvin's own French translation of the *Institutes* (which he originally wrote in Latin), he translates *scholastici* ("schoolmen" or "scholastics") as *théologiens Sorboniques* ("theologians at the Sorbonne"). Furthermore, "Calvin appears to attack as 'scholastic' views not held by the major medieval doctors — and, after his attack, to adopt positions that actually reflect teachings of the medieval scholastics" (p. 46).

then went to study theology at Paris sometime between 1521 and 1523. Apparently, his father had an abrupt change of mind, for he forced his son to abort his studies in Paris in 1528 to study law at Orléans. It was there that Calvin grew increasingly sympathetic to the Reformation; for after getting his doctorate in law, he returned to Paris and helped to ghostwrite an address given by the Rector of the University of Paris, Nicholas Cop by name, which was so openly Lutheran in tone and content that its outcry forced Calvin to flee Paris for Basel, where in 1534 he resigned his benefice and soon wrote, in 1536, the first (Latin) edition of the *Institutes*. Calvin himself describes this change in his convictions in only one passage, a preface to his *Commentary on the Psalms* (1557), that is so laconic that he does not even bother to specify the date of his change of mind:

> At that time I was too obstinately addicted to the superstitions of the papacy to be easily drawn out of such a deep cesspool. But then God, by a sudden conversion, reined in my heart (already more rigid than suited my age) and subdued it to teachableness. . . . Now I was astounded that before one year had passed, all those who felt some desire for pure doctrine came to me to learn, although I was only beginning myself.[51]

The contrast between the religious torments that afflicted Luther and Loyola and the serene reflections on Calvin's change of mind is startling. The phrase "by a sudden conversion" seems to indicate a quick about-face in his views (a moment that scholars date as occurring anytime between 1527 and 1536). But if so, this *volte face* seems to have been the result of *thinking through* issues that were primarily *theological in the abstract, objective sense* more than it was the result of feeling existential despair over God's intentions for Calvin's individual soul.[52]

However frustrating this reticence has proved for Calvin scholars, the

---

51. John Calvin, *Ioannis Calvini opera quae supersunt omnia,* ed. Wilhelm Baum, Edward Cunitz, and Edward Ruess, 59 volumes, *Corpus Reformatorum,* vols. 29-87 (Brunsvigae [Bruhn]: Schwetschke, 1863-60), here vol. 31, p. 21. English translation: *John Calvin's Commentary on the Book of Psalms,* trans. James Anderson (Grand Rapids: Eerdmans, 1963), vol. 1, pp. xl-xlvii.

52. It seems most plausible to date the "sudden conversion" to 1534, when Calvin resigned his benefice and renounced his clerical status. What adds plausibility to this view is the fact that in early 1534 Calvin lived with the cathedral canon of Angoulême, Louie du Tillet by name, whose library contained the complete works of Augustine, which Calvin intensively studied during that period. Significantly, Calvin began writing the *Institutes* in that same town, primarily, he said, to teach himself.

benefit for theologians cannot be downplayed, for with Calvin's theology one has a text that one can take purely on its own terms and judge by its arguments systematically set forth. Of course Calvin had his own unique personality and temperament, which influenced his approach, his rhetoric, and his core convictions, as it does with all other authors without exception. But Calvin's personality was always drawn toward objectivity, from which grew his powers of systematization, as Karl Barth sees:

> Calvin has always been called the born systematician, the great systematician of the older Protestantism and perhaps of all Protestantism. A systematician is not just one who wants order and purity of thinking and has some skill in arranging and structuring his thoughts. . . . The first and very different [requirement], however, is a profound need for synthesis and an ardent desire for it. Synthesis is something original and creative. It precedes all detailed discussion. It is not itself discussion but the subject in every discussion. It is an ability and desire to see antitheses together. . . . It is Calvin the systematician who on his own initiative becomes the educator and apologist.[53]

Given its tightly systematic character, the question has naturally arisen whether the *Institutes* is governed by one single overarching theme that determines the whole. Because of the notoriety of Calvin's doctrine of predestination for later Calvinism, leading eventually to the split of the Arminian branch of Presbyterianism from strict Calvinist orthodoxy, one might suspect that predestination represents the key doctrine that gives Calvin's theology its inner coherence. Telling in that regard is the fact that as Calvin continued to revise and expand on the original 1536 draft, he devoted more and more space to the question of predestination. But even as late as 1556 Calvin himself insisted that the *Institutes* did not take predestination as its touchstone.[54]

Others locate the driving force of Calvin's theology in the doctrine on which predestination depends, the sovereignty of God; while others see it in

53. Karl Barth, *The Theology of John Calvin*, trans. Geoffrey W. Bromiley (Grand Rapids: Eerdmans, 1922/1995), pp. 159-60, 161.

54. "With each subsequent edition of Calvin's *Institutes*, the amount of space devoted to predestination increased, as did the consideration specifically addressed to the problem of the 'reprobate,' those whom God had predestined to damnation. Yet as late as 1556, when this process had already gone almost as far as it ever would (the climax came in 1559, with the final edition of the *Institutes*), Calvin indignantly repudiated the accusation that his exposition of the certainty of salvation took predestination as its starting point." Pelikan, *Reformation*, p. 218.

his unique vision of how we attain union with Christ, which would explain the derivative doctrines of faith, grace, justification, and the sacraments; still others see Calvin as the first dialectical theologian, who tried to mediate between Luther's paradoxes and scholastic clarity; while others see Calvin merely trying to comment on the Apostles' Creed.[55]

In the face of this confusion, surely the safest path is to follow Barth, who insists that we begin with the famous opening sentence of the *Institutes*, which remained the same in every edition: "Nearly all the wisdom we possess, that is to say, true and sound wisdom, consists of two parts: the knowledge of God and of ourselves."[56] This axiom Calvin certainly means as a dialectic, meaning we cannot have the one without the other, as Barth rightly notes: "[Calvin] sets God at once in the light of a full and sufficient knowledge of *man,* and he at once speaks of man [as] the man who is seen and known by *God.*"[57] But because of the fall, man now needs a Mediator, who is revealed to us in the Bible:

> Without the biblical revelation that defines God the Redeemer Calvin sees no real knowledge of God the Creator, and conversely knowledge of God the Redeemer is simply a sharper and clearer seeing of the revelation of God the Creator. Materially the two forms of knowledge are exactly the same. We differentiate them only at once to grasp more truly their essential unity. Hence I think it is wrong to say that Calvin did not gain his insight into God and us from Christ or that he simply forced Christian elements into a general metaphysical, philosophical view. . . . Christ is from the first the key with which he unlocks the whole.[58]

In other words, Calvin's theology is Christocentric to the core. To be sure, he does not assert in the manner of Luther that Christocentrism must be expressed solely in terms of a theology of the cross as opposed to a theol-

---

55. "Previous discussions of the *Institutes* have tended to focus on the theological method pursued by Calvin. Some have argued for a 'central dogma' of Calvin's theology, be it sovereignty, predestination, or union with Christ. Others . . . have claimed that there is no central doctrine, but rather a complex of opposites, creating a dialectical field of tension between two extremes. Other scholars have argued that there is a central structure to the *Institutes,* be it the twofold knowledge of God or the fourfold structure of the Apostles' Creed." Randall Zachman, *John Calvin as Teacher, Pastor, and Theologian,* pp. 77-78.

56. John Calvin, *Institutes of the Christian Religion,* ed. John T. McNeill, trans. Ford Lewis Battles (Philadelphia: Westminster Press, 1960), p. 35; abbreviated henceforth as *ICR.*

57. Barth, *The Theology of John Calvin,* p. 162.

58. Barth, *The Theology of John Calvin,* p. 164.

ogy of glory. For in fact Christ's role as the revealer of God the Creator shows that Calvin concedes a proper role to the perception of God's glory, which even includes granting a proper role to natural law, as Barth sees: "Strictly, says Calvin, God's law is written in our hearts. It is the same thing as conscience. . . . We can none of us make the excuse that we do not know the law or are not under its authority."[59] Furthermore, that ongoing legitimacy to law, both natural and Mosaic, helps give access to Christ:

> Again, we none of us should regard ourselves as lost for not knowing the promise that always accompanies the law. There is no escaping divine judgment, but also no total distance away from divine mercy for those who can and will hear God's voice. Christ once more stands between the contradictions or rather above them, as the principle of knowledge, showing us both the full terror of judgment and the full depth of grace, yet not accepting the fact that these two both are and always will be two things.[60]

So despite disclaimers from other interpreters, Calvin's theology is thoroughly Christocentric.[61] Nonetheless, Calvin does have a distinctive doctrine of the sovereignty of God that is strong enough to affect his Christology in unique ways, an influence that would lead to significant divergences from classical Lutheran formulations and, at least to some extent, can account for their different versions of the presence of Christ in the Eucharist.

Given Calvin's own exposure to (if not training in) scholastic theology while he was a student in Paris in the 1520s, and taking into account his later training in law and his personal predilection for clarity of thought and rigor of conceptual connections, we are not surprised to learn that Calvin never made Luther's elementary philosophical blunder of ascribing the attributes of the divinity to the human *nature* of Christ by virtue of the hypostatic union. Indeed, so strictly does Calvin hold to the conceptual opposition be-

---

59. Barth, *The Theology of John Calvin,* pp. 164-65.

60. Barth, *The Theology of John Calvin,* p. 165.

61. Even among those who concede this point, objections are raised: "[Calvin] never set forth a comprehensive account of Christology in the classical sense of a careful investigation into the ontological constitution of the Mediator." Bruce L. McCormack, *For Us and Our Salvation: Incarnation and Atonement in the Reformed Tradition,* Studies in Reformed Theology and History 1.2 (Princeton: Princeton Theological Seminary Press, 1993), p. 6. Similarly: "For, while Calvin gives great credence to the humanity of Christ in relation to the benefits of Christ, he lacks extended discussion of the ontological claims germane to such benefits." R. Michael Allen, "Calvin's Christ: A Dogmatic Matrix for Discussion of Christ's Human Nature," *International Journal of Systematic Theology* 9 (October 2007): 382-97; here 383.

tween humanity and divinity that Lutheran theologians in turn accused Calvin of a crypto-Nestorianism, perhaps most evident in this passage:

> Surely God does not have blood, does not suffer, cannot be touched with hands. But since Christ, who was true God and also true man, was crucified and shed his blood for us, the things that he carried out in his human nature are transferred *improperly,* although not without reason, to his divinity. (*ICR* II 14, p. 484; emphasis added)

The catchword of Calvinist Christology was always *finitum non capax infiniti,* the finite cannot contain the infinite, which is true enough on the conceptual level but which, when taken too far, would undercut the whole logic of the incarnation. So resolutely did Calvin maintain this axiom (at least by Lutheran lights) that it led to an accusation that goes by the name of the *extra Calvinisticum.* This arcane term was by no means coined by Calvinists, but was a *Schimpfwort* (a sneer-word or term of abuse) invented by Lutherans to describe what they found objectionable in Calvinist Christology. According to Lutheran claims, Calvinists maintained that it was impossible for the *whole* of the Godhead of the Second Person of the Trinity to become incarnate in Jesus; so that the divine Son still reigned in heaven while Christ was on earth. Despite the polemical provenance of the coinage, the term stuck and has now come to mean something more neutral: that feature of Calvin's Christology that differs most markedly from Luther's and later Lutheran "scholastic" Christology, so that even Calvinists not only use it but defend it too, as in this Reformed dictionary of theological terms:

> **Extra calvinisticum:** *the Calvinistic extra;* a term used by the Lutherans to refer to the Reformed insistence on the utter transcendence of the human nature of Christ by the Second Person of the Trinity in and during the incarnation. The Reformed argued that the Word is fully united to but never totally contained within the human nature and, therefore, even in incarnation is to be conceived of as beyond or outside of *(extra)* the human nature. In response to the Calvinistic *extra,* the Lutherans taught the maxim *Logos non extra carnem* [the Word is not outside the flesh]. It is clear . . . that the polarization of Lutheran and Reformed Christologies owed much to the debate over the mode of Christ's presence in the Lord's Supper, in which the Lutherans emphasized the real but illocal [nonlocal] presence of Christ's body and blood by reason of the communicated omnipresence of the Logos and the Reformed emphasized the transcendence of the divine and the heavenly location of Christ's body.

Against the Lutherans, the Reformed interpreted the *extra calvinisticum* in terms of the maxim *finitum non capax infiniti,* the finite is incapable of the infinite. In other words, the finite humanity of Christ is incapable of receiving or grasping infinite attributes such as omnipresence, omnipotence, or omniscience.[62]

Protestant dogmatics was never able to adjudicate the issue, partly because it had no magisterial authority to rule on the matter and partly because of the hardening of confessional lines in the seventeenth century following the Thirty Years' War (1618-48), which is no doubt why that issue never became a central one in Catholic theology either (the Catholic magisterium has never ruled on the matter). However, the fact that it remained such a central touchstone between Lutheran and Calvinist orthodoxy meant that its unresolved tensions would later lead to the Lutheran-inspired "kenotic Christology," a topic for a later chapter.

More crucial for the sixteenth century, though, were the *Eucharistic implications* of the different Christologies, Lutheran and Calvinist. For that reason, I suspect that Catholic theologians at that time, had they joined the debate at this point, would have been more sympathetic to the Lutheran principle *Logos non extra carnem* (the Word is not outside the flesh) than to the *extra Calvinisticum,*[63] a hunch that can perhaps be verified by Pelikan's keen observation here:

> What the [Lutheran] *Augsburg Confession* [of 1530] asserted about the two natures as "so inseparably united in one person that there is one Christ, true God and true man" met with the explicit approval of the appointed [Catholic] critics of the *Confession,* which was in turn acknowledged by its defenders. Sporadic efforts by various Roman Catholic opponents to locate heretical tendencies in the christology of Luther on the basis of some of his obiter dicta proved to be basically unsuccessful. Rather, it was the controversy between the two major parties of Protestantism, the Lutheran and the Reformed, over the real presence of the body and blood of

---

62. Richard A. Muller, *Dictionary of Latin and Greek Theological Terms: Drawn Principally from Protestant Scholastic Theology* (Grand Rapids: Baker Books, 1985), p. 111. This essential reference book testifies yet again to the prevalence of the scholastic method in Protestant theologians after the death of the great Reformers.

63. The doctrine, however, has solid grounding in the tradition, the denial of which can lead to its own antinomies. Because of the extremely technical nature of this debate, I have placed a consideration of the *extra Calvinisticum* in an *excursus* at the end of this chapter, where stress will be placed on its firm roots in the patristic and medieval tradition.

Christ in the Lord's Supper that was responsible for the most detailed Western preoccupation with the intricacies of christology since the ancient church. The confessions of both sides affirmed their loyalty to the orthodox doctrine of the person of Christ as promulgated at the Councils of Ephesus and Chalcedon, while theologians on both sides (as well as on the Roman Catholic) appropriated the anti-Nestorian slogan of the Council of Ephesus in calling the Virgin Mary "Theotokos." Each side, moreover, professed to find in its opponents a parallel to one or the other of the heretical extremes condemned at those councils: Luther took the occasion of a historical examination of Ephesus to brand Ulrich Zwingli a "neo-Nestorian," and Calvin saw it as an unintended implication of the Lutheran doctrine of the real presence "that [Christ's] body was swallowed up by his divinity," which was the "Eutychian" [monophysite] heresy condemned at Chalcedon.[64]

However much intra-Protestant debate in the sixteenth century might seem to hearken back to the antinomies of fifth-century disputes, it was in fact provoked by a factor new to christological dispute: the meaning of the presence of Christ in the Eucharist. Part of what makes Calvin's Christology unique is not just his stress on the sovereignty of God or on the utter transcendence of the Godhead even in the incarnation, but also his special stress on Christ's ascension into heaven. For some Protestants suddenly became aware of a potential problem: If Christ ascended in his body into heaven on Ascension Thursday, how could he be said to be present "body and blood, soul and divinity" under the species of bread and wine in the Eucharist too? So if Christ's body is located solely in heaven, how could that same body be "really" present in the Eucharist except symbolically? Lutherans rejoined that the Reformed denial of the local presence of Christ's body in the Eucharist implied that Christ's body could only be present to believers in their imaginations, which meant, as Zwingli frankly conceded, that believers must bring faith *to* the Eucharist and not find it supported and strengthened by receiving the Eucharist.

Calvin, however, was no Zwinglian, for from the outset he thought that Zwingli was looking at the matter through the wrong end of the telescope, as B. A. Gerrish notes:

From the very first, he was convinced that Zwingli was wrong about the principal agent in both Baptism and the Lord's Supper. A sacrament is

64. Jaroslav Pelikan, *Reformation,* p. 158.

first and foremost an act of God or Christ rather than of the candidate, the communicant, or the church. Zwingli had the priorities wrong. Indeed, he not only put first what can only be secondary but made it the whole sacrament; he imagined that a sacrament is only an act by which we attest our faith and not rather, as it truly is, a sign by which God strengthens our faith. And yet, although he found Zwingli's understanding of a sacrament defective, Calvin thought him right about the meaning of Christ's ascension for what happens in the Lord's Supper: if the Lord's body has been taken up to heaven, it cannot be enclosed down here in the bread. A literal eating of Christ's flesh is impossible; the elements and actions in the Eucharist, as Zwingli held, must be an analogy of a spiritual eating. For all his criticisms of him, Calvin accepted Zwingli's arguments against a local presence, and for this reason he could not lay to rest the Lutherans' doubts about his own position. The interpretation of his eucharistic theology still to this day turns largely around the same doubts: whether, in particular, there really was, for him, a bodily presence of Christ to the communicant. And with the question of the Real Presence goes the second, companion question concerning the instrumental efficacy of sacred objects and actions: whether sacramental signs are genuine means of grace. The suspicion has never quite been laid to rest that even when Calvin's language appears to affirm a real presence and the efficacy of sacred signs, he could not honestly have meant it.[65]

During the patristic period christological debates focused almost entirely on issues relating to the person, nature, and saving work of Jesus and were little affected by the sacramental implications of coming to an exact definition of the meaning of Christ's body. In the Middle Ages there were two brief flare-ups over Eucharistic doctrine, both dealing with trying to draw conceptual clarity over the meaning of Christ's body. In the ninth century a theologian by the name of Paschasius Radbertus (c. 790–c. 860) published a tract *De corpore et sanguine Domini* (the first treatise devoted specifically to the Eucharist in the western church), wherein the author maintained that the Real Presence of Christ in the Eucharist was the very real presence of the very flesh of Christ born of the Virgin Mary miraculously made present in the Eucharist by the omnipotence of God.

His opponent and contemporary, a fellow Benedictine with a vaguely similar name, Ratramnus (ninth century, specific dates unknown), ob-

---

65. B. A. Gerrish, *Grace and Gratitude: The Eucharistic Theology of John Calvin* (Minneapolis: Fortress Press, 1993), pp. 8-9.

jected to these views based on a different notion of the relation of sign to reality. For him "reality" meant empirical reality, based on sense experience, whereas "figure" or "sign" referred to reality, in his words, "under some sort of veil."[66] Obviously, that definition requires that Radbertus was wrong to hold that in the Eucharist nothing was being received figuratively but only in reality without a veil, for that would be to substitute sense experience for faith. Furthermore, Ratramnus held that the historical body of Christ was properly called "the real body of Christ," whereas the Eucharistic body was the signifying sacrament of the flesh and blood of Christ, so that there is a "great difference" between the two bodies, which "are not the same."[67]

These views had no direct influence on Calvin, despite the obvious parallels with his thought.[68] Of more direct relevance was the eleventh-century debate on the meaning of the word *body*, which is applied to the human form of Christ, Paul's definition of the church as the Body of Christ, and the meaning of the Eucharist as the presence of the Body of Christ. In this debate (partly in reaction to the earlier views of Ratramnus), the consensus held that "there are not two bodies, the one received from the altar and the one received from the womb of the Virgin."[69]

Again, Calvin never cited any of the figures in this debate, even if he is clearly reopening the issue all over again with his unique stress on the ascension of Christ into heaven, which had also, as it happens, figured in the medieval debate on the Eucharist.[70] When a theologian by the name of

66. Ratramnus, *De corpore et sanguine Domini*, ed. J. N. Bakhuizen van den Brink (Amsterdam, 1954), pp. 33-34; cited in Jaroslav Pelikan, *The Growth of Medieval Theology (600-1300)*, vol. 3: *The Christian Tradition: A History of the Development of Doctrine* (Chicago: University of Chicago Press, 1978), p. 76.

67. Ratramnus, *De corpore*, cited in Pelikan, *Growth*, p. 77.

68. However, Ratramnus's book was published in 1531, so it is possible Calvin knew of it, although he never cited it. Ratramnus was never condemned in his lifetime, but in the eleventh century his book (wrongly attributed to John Scotus Eriugena) was condemned by Pope Leo IX at the Synod of Vercelli in 1050.

69. Rupert of Deutz, *De divinis Officiis*, 2.2, in *Corpus christianorum, continuatio mediaevalis* (Turnhout, Belgium: Brepols, 1953), pp. 34-35, cited in Pelikan, *Growth*, p. 192.

70. As Pelikan notes: "Yet the flesh and body that Christ had received at birth from his Virgin Mother was the flesh and body that he took into heaven at his ascension. . . . Although theologians repeated the warning of Augustine that speculative inquiry into the state of the ascended body of Christ at the right hand of God in heaven was useless, some answer to this argument seemed necessary; for if Christ could not come down from heaven, then he was not reigning there, but was a prisoner. . . . Because the human nature of Christ, and thus his physical body, was inseparable from his divine nature through the hypostatic union, 'the

Berengar of Tours (c. 1010-88) justified his figural interpretation of the Eucharist on the basis of the locality of Christ's body in heaven, other theologians quickly objected on the basis of the hypostatic union: even in Christ's days on earth, his body transcended the laws of nature by virtue of its union with the divinity; and by virtue of that same — now ascended — ubiquitous divinity, Christ is bodily present in the Eucharist as well. In other words, the controversies of Eucharistic theology are directly related to those of Christology, something all the Reformers recognized, although they seem little aware of the previous debate. But in a sense, they hardly needed to draw on this medieval debate to see the connection, since the connection between Christology and Eucharistic doctrine had already become obvious on its own terms, as Gerrish explains:

> Despite his formally correct assertions of Chalcedonian orthodoxy, Calvin has repeatedly been seen as moving close to the Nestorian limit: that is, as failing to do full justice to the union of the human and divine natures in Christ's person. The issue becomes critical in the debates between Lutherans and Calvinists on the Lord's Supper. The Lutheran view of the Real Presence required belief in the ubiquity of Christ's body, and this the Lutherans defended on the grounds of the intimate personal union of Christ's two natures: by a communication of properties, the unlimited presence of his divinity was communicated to his humanity. Calvin, on the other hand, held that the communication of properties, which he recognized as a very ancient idea, was simply a manner of speaking. To his mind, there was no possibility that the body of Christ might actually become ubiquitous by reason of its union with his divinity. True, the Scriptures do sometimes ascribe to one of Christ's natures what properly belongs only to the other. We are told, for example, that God purchased the church with his blood (Acts 20:28). But God does not have blood, and the assertion is only a bold manner of speaking warranted by the intimacy of personal union. There can be no question of such an actual exchange of properties as the Lutheran doctrine of the ubiquity of Christ's body requires. Clearly, the eucharistic debate between Lutherans and the Reformed was at the same time a christological debate: the Reformed ac-

---

divinity of the Logos of God, which is one and which fills all things and which is everywhere, brings it about . . . that there is one body of Christ, identical with that which he received from the Virgin's womb'. . . . Therefore, if Christ willed it, his body could be present, completely and truly, in heaven and in the Sacrament at one and the same time." Pelikan, *Reformation*, pp. 193-94.

cused their opponents of a Eutychian confusion of Christ's natures, and they were in turn accused of a Nestorian separation.[71]

The debate of course by this time had hardened into separate confessional stances, just as the debate on justification and works had hardened between Protestants and Catholics after the Council of Trent. The ecumenical movement of the twentieth century altered that confessional sclerosis somewhat, as did a renewed understanding of how the New Testament authors understood the meaning of the term "body" when speaking of Christ and his church.

Blaise Pascal

Because Blaise Pascal (1623-62) was a Catholic, his enemies (of which he had many, especially among the Jesuits of France) knew that they could most damage his reputation by accusing him of being a Calvinist. How fair such an accusation was cannot be the burden of this book to decide. Certainly, as a Jansenist, Pascal felt certain "elective affinities" with Calvin (and Luther), but that probably has more to do with their common debt to Augustine.[72] Indeed, when Pascal does mention Reformation views, he often gets them wrong, which suggests little direct acquaintance with the thought of the Reformers.[73]

---

71. B. A. Gerrish, *Grace and Gratitude*, pp. 54-55.

72. As is well known, specific statements from Bishop Cornelius Otto Jansen (or Jansenius, 1585-1638), the founder of the Jansenist school, can be found, almost word for word, in Augustine's own writings. Despite Jansen's complete reliance on Augustine, his book *Augustinus* was declared heretical by several popes after his death. For that reason, in his book *God Owes Us Nothing: A Brief Remark on Pascal's Religion and the Spirit of Jansenism* (Chicago: University of Chicago Press, 1995), Leszek Kolakowski maintained that the condemnation of Jansenism represented the Roman Church's official disengagement from, and even repudiation of, Augustinian orthodoxy on grace and freedom, an intriguing thesis that also cannot be analyzed or criticized here.

73. For example, in the *Pensées* Pascal says, cryptically, "Luther, completely outside the truth, . . . Luther, anything but the truth." Blaise Pascal, *Pensées*, trans. A. J. Krailsheimer (Harmondsworth: Penguin Classics, 1966), p. 331, L954 (the "L" refers to the Lafuma number, one of the standard numbers used for citing the *Pensées* across many editions). But if he is referring to Luther in the following passage, then he has misunderstood Luther's theology of the Eucharist: "Modern heresy, unable to conceive that this sacrament contains at once the presence and the figuration of Jesus Christ . . . believes that one of these truths cannot be admitted without thereby excluding the other" (*Pensées*, p. 253, L733). But that does not describe Luther's position, whose theology of the Eucharist insisted on both the presence and the figuration of Christ.

Nonetheless, perhaps the Jesuit polemicists were not that far off the mark when they accused Pascal of Protestant leanings, for his theology of the cross shows remarkable affinities with the Reformed tradition (I am using "Reformed" here in its generic sense to refer to all the classical Protestant writers, and not in its specific sense to refer to the Calvinist tradition alone). In those polemical times, that accusation was alone regarded as probative, but is it? To be sure, Pascal's views on grace and free will were condemned (although not Pascal himself, who died in the bosom of the church). But his theology of the cross seems more Pauline than specifically Protestant. Speaking of his remarkably poor health, his sister Gilberte Périer mentions in her biography of her brother that "he often used to say . . . that a Christian finds value in everything, and especially in sufferings, because there he comes to know Jesus Christ crucified, who must be the entire sum of a Christian's knowledge and his life's sole glory,"[74] which exactly parallels Paul's assertion, "I resolved to know nothing among you except Jesus Christ and him crucified" (1 Cor. 2:2) and "Far be it from me to glory except in the cross of our Lord Jesus Christ, through whom the world has been crucified to me, and I to the world" (Gal. 6:14).

Much as Paul, Luther, and Calvin (and, ironically, Ignatius Loyola) would no doubt agree with Pascal here, this famous French mathematician also strikes a note unique to him: the stress on our *knowledge* of Christ. For seen in retrospect, he was far less concerned than Luther or Calvin (or even Ignatius) with the question "where can I find a gracious God?" as with Montaigne's and Descartes' question *"que sais-je?"* — what do I know? If the sixteenth century was obsessed with soteriology, the seventeenth century was fixated on epistemology, very much including theological epistemology, which often got intertwined with philosophical issues. One of the remarkable features of early modern philosophy was the frequency with which God would be invoked to get out of a philosophical jam, a kind of *deus ex machina,* so to speak, to resolve the philosophical "plot." For example, Descartes could only resolve his radical doubt with an appeal to the "clear and distinct" idea of God, whom he took to be an existing God via his own version of Anselm's ontological argument.

Pascal had no more use for Descartes than he did for Luther, but that did not stop him from sharing in the same epistemological obsessions that made early modern philosophy so distinctive from its medieval precedents.

---

74. Gilberte Périer, *Vie de Monsieur Pascal,* in Blaise Pascal, *Œuvres Complètes* (Paris: Editions du Seuil, 1963), p. 21.

But far from invoking God at the last moment to shore up a rickety philosophical system, Pascal radically distinguished the god of the philosophers from the God of Abraham, Isaac, and Jacob, to such an extent that, in the manner of Luther (but not Calvin or still less the medievals), he saw little use for natural theology. Relying on an obvious point of psychology, that even proofs for the existence of God that strike the reader as valid wear off within an hour or two, Pascal made that psychological uncertainty the basis for his famous Wager:

> If there is a God, he is infinitely beyond our comprehension, since, being indivisible and without limits, he bears no relation to us. We are therefore incapable of knowing either what he is or whether he is. . . . Who then will condemn Christians for being unable to give rational grounds for their belief, professing as they do a religion for which they cannot give rational grounds? . . . Either God is or he is not. But to which view shall we be inclined? Reason cannot decide the question. . . . How will you wager? Reason cannot make you choose either, reason cannot prove either wrong.[75]

If Pascal had left the matter hanging there, there would be no place for Christ, for the outcome of the Wager only happens after death, whereas life on earth hovers between the fifty-fifty chance of getting it wrong, no matter where the bet is placed. But for Pascal that very uncertainty is precisely the point: it opens the way to a knowledge of Christ:

> The metaphysical proofs for the existence of God are so remote from human reasoning and so involved that they make little impact, and, even if they did help some people, it would only be for the moment during which they watched the demonstration, because an hour later they would be

---

75. *Pensées,* p. 150, L148. These statements are not so much a denial of Thomas Aquinas' "proofs" for the existence of God as an explication of Anselm's insight into the nature of man's mind before the light of God: "Is the eye darkened by its own weakness, or blinded by your light? Without doubt it is darkened in itself and blinded by you. Indeed, it is obscured by its own littleness and overwhelmed by your immensity. Surely it is contracted by its own narrowness and overcome by your greatness" (Anselm, *Proslogion,* 14). Henri de Lubac agrees: "Why is it that the mind which has found God still retains, or constantly reverts to, the feeling of not having found him? . . . Why always a wall or a gaping void? Why do all things, as soon as they have shown him to us, betray us by concealing him again? The temptation is to succumb to this scandal and to despair in proportion as one had formerly thought to have found him: a temptation to deny the light, because the veil becomes opaque once again." Henri de Lubac, *The Discovery of God,* trans. Alexander Dru (Grand Rapids: Eerdmans, 1996), p. 45.

afraid they had made a mistake. "What they gained by curiosity they lost by pride." That is the result of knowing God without Christ, in other words communicating, without a mediator, with a God [also] known without a mediator. Whereas those who have known God through a mediator know their own wretchedness. It is not only impossible but useless to know God without Christ. . . . Knowing God without knowing our own wretchedness makes for pride. Knowing our own wretchedness without knowing God makes for despair. Knowing Jesus Christ strikes the balance because he shows us both God and our own wretchedness.[76]

In other words, Pascal's Christology is intimately linked to his anthropology, which consistently depicts man in all his contradictory misery and glory. He famously defined man as a "thinking reed,"[77] and on that basis saw that only the paradox of Christ could heal the paradox of the human condition. We have already seen how Christology is, in any orthodox version, inherently paradoxical; but Pascal was the first to stress how much Christ's paradoxical identity is crucial to his saving work to help man find healing from his own paradoxical state as a thinking reed. Anticipating by almost three centuries G. K. Chesterton's analysis of heresy as always entailing the denial of one prong of the paradox, Pascal becomes the first to make paradox a *formal* principle of his Christology:

Faith embraces many apparently contradictory truths ("a time to weep and a time to laugh," etc.). *The origin of this is the union of two natures in Christ.* . . . The source of all heresies is the exclusion of certain of these truths. . . . It usually happens that, being unable to imagine the connection between two opposing truths, and thinking that the acceptance of the one entails the exclusion of the other, they hold on to one and exclude the other, and think we are doing just the opposite. Now this exclusion is the cause of their heresy, and ignorance of the fact that we hold the other causes their objection. *First example:* Jesus Christ is God and man. The Arians, unable to combine two things they believe to be incompatible, say

---

76. *Pensées,* pp. 86-87, L190-92.

77. "Man is only a reed, the weakest in nature, but he is a thinking reed. There is no need for the whole universe to take up arms to crush him: a vapor, a drop of water is enough to kill him. But even if the universe were to crush him, man would still be nobler than his slayer, because he knows that he is dying and the advantage the universe has over him. The universe knows none of this. Thus all our dignity consists in thought. It is on thought that we must depend for our recovery, not on space and time, which we could never fill. Let us then strive to think well; that is the basic principle of morality" (*Pensées,* p. 95, L200).

that he is man, and in this are Catholic, but they deny that he is God, and in that they are heretical. They claim that we deny his humanity, and in that they are ignorant.[78]

In these remarks, Pascal is doing more than summing up past history, he is also linking the essential paradoxes of Christology to salvation, a move first adumbrated by Luther but now shorn of the logical confusions that Luther introduced. But Pascal was also a true innovator in another sense: he is also the first Christian to take up explicitly a theme that will become a burning topic in late modernity: the question of pluralism, that is, the question of how Christ relates to other religions and thus to other "founders" of world religions.[79] But while Pascal might be the first adumbrator of a topic that would consume the church in late modernity, he in no way would follow the fashionable assertions of the pluralists who posit different ways to God, all equally valid in their own setting. On the contrary, Pascal insists (we are not surprised to learn) that the plurality of religions is itself a testimony to the pathos of man, and thus to the sole truth of the Christian religion:

> I see a number of religions in conflict, and therefore all false, except one. Each of them wishes to be believed on its own authority and threatens unbelievers. I do not believe them on that account. Anyone can say that. Anyone can call himself a prophet, but I see Christianity, and find its prophecies, which are not something that anyone can come up with.[80]

The secular liberal would immediately object, of course, that Christians have threatened unbelievers down through the ages, which is why the episode of the Inquisition has become so notorious, but that too Pascal would turn to his own account:

78. *Pensées*, p. 253, L73; emphases added. Pascal's analysis is somewhat hampered by the fact that he rarely uses the term "paradox" but rather its definition, "*apparently* contradictory truths." But sometimes he uses the term "contradiction" to mean something else, it would seem, than outright contradiction: "Contradiction is a poor indication of truth. Many things that are certain are contradicted. Many that are false pass without contradiction. Contradiction is no more an indication of falsehood than lack of it is an indication of truth" (*Pensées*, p. 84, L177). His analysis would have been more effective, in my opinion, if he had devoted more thought to the peculiar logic of paradox in reality and in theology and had not used "contradiction" to mean so many other, more exact terms.

79. It is for that reason that I called Pascal "the first modern Christian" in an article for *First Things*: "Makers of the Millennium" series; see Edward T. Oakes, "Pascal: The First Modern Christian," *First Things* 95 (August/September 1999): 41-48.

80. *Pensées*, p. 88, L198, translation slightly altered.

That God wished to hide himself. If there were only one religion, God would be clearly manifest. If there were no martyrs except in our religion, likewise. God being thus hidden, any religion that does not say that God is hidden is not true, and any religion which does not explain why does not instruct. Ours does all this. "Truly you are a hidden God" (Isaiah 45:15).[81]

This position gives Pascal the justification for looking at other religions, Judaism and Islam primarily, and finding them wanting. Thus Pascal points to the tribal limitations of Judaism compared to the universality of Christianity: "Jesus Christ for all, Moses for one people" (*Pensées*, p. 99, L221). True, Jews hoped for a redeemer, while pagans lived without that hope, but the situation is still fundamentally the same: "Carnal Jews and heathen have their miseries, and so have Christians. There is no redeemer for the heathen, for they do not even hope for one. There is no redeemer for the Jews; they hope for one in vain. Only for the Christians is there a redeemer" (*Pensées*, p. 100, L222). And on Islam Pascal is even more pointed:

Difference between Jesus Christ and Mahomet. Mahomet not foretold, Jesus foretold. Mahomet slew, Jesus caused his followers to be slain. Mahomet forbade reading, the Apostles commanded it. In a word, the difference is so great that, if Mahomet followed the path of success, humanly speaking, Jesus followed that of death, humanly speaking, and, instead of concluding that where Mahomet succeeded Jesus could have done so too, we must say that, since Mahomet succeeded, Jesus had to die.[82]

The validity of these tart remarks cannot be treated here, except perhaps to add that Pascal looks on Judaism much more favorably than he does on Islam.[83] More crucial for our purposes is Pascal's finely balanced portrayal of man, whose plight can only be answered by Christ:

81. *Pensées*, p. 103, L242.
82. *Pensées*, p. 97, L209. The line about Muslims being forbidden to read is, of course, a red herring and probably comes from Muslim insistence that Mohammed was illiterate, the better to stress the divine origins of the Koran. Pascal also shows his inadequate knowledge of Muslim theology and texts when he claims that "the Koran says that St Matthew was a good man, so he [Mohammed] was a false prophet either in calling good men evil or in disagreeing with what they said about Christ" (*Pensées*, p. 96, L207).
83. Pascal devotes three sections of the *Pensées* to, respectively, "Advantages of the Jewish People," "Sincerity of Jewish People," and "Perpetuity of the Jewish People," and has another section asserting that "True Jews and True Christians Have the Same Religion." His debt to Judaism is gratefully acknowledged: "These are the facts: while philosophers are all split into different sects, there are in one corner of the world people who are the most an-

If there were no obscurity man would not feel his corruption; if there were no light man could not hope for a cure. Thus it is not only right but useful for us that God should be partly concealed and partly revealed, since it is equally dangerous for man to know God without knowing his own wretchedness as to know his wretchedness without knowing God. . . . Those who go astray only do so for want of seeing one of these two things. It is then perfectly possible to know God but not our own wretchedness, or our own wretchedness but not God. But it is not possible to know Christ without knowing both God and our wretchedness alike.[84]

It remains only to add that such knowledge is obviously scarcely one that reason, or at least reason alone, can reach. Only the heart really knows how wretched the human condition really is. Probably Pascal's most famous line is that the heart has its reasons that reason knows nothing of. In that light Pascal has often struck his readers as being, on the whole, relentlessly grim, or at least unsparing, in his portrayal of the human condition. He certainly seems to be operating with a different definition of what the heart longs for than do later theologians and mystics, notably those saints who spread a devotion to the Sacred Heart of Jesus in Catholicism, and in Protestantism those leaders of German Pietism and English Methodism, whose treatment of the knowledge of the heart will lead Christology in new directions, a treatment of which it will be the task of the next chapter to elucidate.

---

cient in the world, who declare that the whole world is in error, that God has revealed the truth to them, that it will always exist on earth. In fact all the other sects come to an end; this one still exists and for 4,000 years they have been declaring that they have it from their forefathers that man has fallen from communion with God into total estrangement from God, but that he has promised to redeem them, that this doctrine will always be on earth, that their law has a double meaning" (*Pensées*, p. 177, L456). Not surprisingly, he is also drawn to Judaism's great paradox: "Lovingly and faithfully they hand on this book [the Bible] in which Moses declares that they have been ungrateful towards God throughout their lives, that he knows they will be still more so after his death, but that he calls heaven and earth to witness against them that he told them so often enough" (*Pensées*, p. 172, L452).

84. *Pensées*, pp. 167, 169, L446, L449.

The *Extra Calvinisticum*

No topic in Christology, not even Christ's beatific vision during his earthly life, is more arcane than that of the *extra Calvinisticum*. (Not even some doctoral students specializing in Christology have heard the term, I have discovered.) As we saw above, part of the reason for the puzzlement is due to its origins in complicated Reformation debates over the Eucharist. But another reason is grammatical. Although the word *extra* is normally a preposition in Latin, here it is used as a (neuter) noun, as in English when we speak of "a certain extra" or when advertisers promise a free vegetable slicer as an added extra to your purchase of a blender. In other words, Lutherans were claiming that Calvinists were not only adding something extra to the church's traditional Christology but more crucially were saying that, by their lights, Calvinists posited something "left over" in the divinity of Christ during the incarnation.

For that reason, the term is extremely misleading and perhaps should be retired, because it makes no sense to speak of "part" of the divinity of the Logos being "held back" in heaven while the other "part" of the divinity became incarnate. But what Calvin was getting at (of course *he* never used the term, since he was firmly convinced he had tradition on his side) was simply this: Is the Word of God so fully incarnate that he has no existence whatever beyond the flesh he assumed? Calvin was quite sure that the Son of God, after the incarnation, was totally united to the human nature but was not restricted to it; rather the Son existed *etiam extra carnem* ("even beyond the flesh"). That prompted the Lutherans to attack *illud extra Calvinisticum* ("that so-called Calvinistic 'beyond'").[85]

---

85. The Latin word *illud* often connotes a dismissive sneer attached to the term that follows.

Although E. David Willis defends the orthodoxy of the doctrine in his monograph *Calvin's Catholic Christology,* he admits the issue is complicated, especially for Reformed theology:

> The difficulty is this: *if* the "extra Calvinisticum" involves an implicit distinction between the *logos ensarkos* [the enfleshed Word] and the *logos asarkos* [the unfleshed Word], is not God's full revelation of himself exclusively in Jesus Christ menaced, and is not the way opened to a natural theology alongside and complementary to revealed theology?[86]

Perhaps so; but if so, such objections pertain to a branch of Christianity that eschews natural theology entirely, which of course Calvin never did.[87] More to the point for Willis is that the doctrine is fully consonant with the sovereignty of God, indeed is an aspect of it: "The 'extra Calvinisticum' is not a sign of the discontinuity between creation and redemption, but of the fact that by assuming our condition the Eternal Son did not relinquish part of his empire but extended that empire over lost ground."[88]

Lutheran polemics stressed time and again that, with his axiom *finitum non capax infiniti,* Calvin was implying that human nature — ours certainly, but also Christ's, even after the miracle of the incarnation — was by definition incapable of receiving the divine. Not so, replied the Calvinists: they were trying to guard against monophysitism by consistently holding that Christ's finitude *remained* finite:

> Christ was human in all respects like us: sin and not finitude was excepted. Here is one of the ironies continually emerging in the history of

86. E. David Willis, *Calvin's Catholic Christology: The Function of the So-Called Extra Calvinisticum in Calvin's Christology* (Leiden: E. J. Brill, 1966), p. 2.

87. But Karl Barth does. We shall look briefly in this *excursus* at his views on the *extra Calvinisticum* but will consider his views in greater depth in Chapter 9.

88. Willis, *Calvin's Catholic Christology,* p. 7. Willis even goes so far as to redub the *extra Calvinisticum* as the *extra patristicum,* which in effect means therefore that the term should really be known as the *extra Catholicum!* See, for example, this key text from Athanasius: "There is a paradox in this last statement which we must now examine. The Word was not hedged in by His body, nor did His presence in the body prevent His being present elsewhere as well. When He moved His body He did not cease also to direct the universe by His mind and might. No. The marvelous truth is that being the Word, so far from being Himself contained by anything, He actually contained all things Himself. In creation He is present everywhere, yet is distinct in being from it; ordering, directing, giving life to all, containing all, yet is He Himself the Uncontained, existing solely in His Father." St. Athanasius, *On the Incarnation* III, 17, trans. by a Member of the C.S.M.V. (Crestwood, NY: St. Vladimir's Seminary Press, 1953), p. 45.

doctrines. Reformed Christology has been pilloried for refusing to recognize the capacity of the finite for the infinite. . . . [But Calvinists reply], can the finite be related to the infinite in a way not destructive to the finite? Or, can the Word of God be united to the humanity of Jesus Christ so as not to nullify that finitude without which his humanity is only illusory? . . . Although none of the disputants put it this way, the logic of the Reformed position was that the majesty of the humanity of Christ consisted in the very fact that it remained finite and creaturely even when hypostatically joined to the Creator.[89]

Phrased in this way, the *extra Calvinisticum* emerges unscathed. So grounded is the doctrine in the tradition that Calvin does not scruple to quote that fount of scholastic theology, Peter Lombard (c. 1100-1160), who solved the problem by drawing a distinction between *totus* (a masculine form of the adjective meaning "whole") applied to the Person and *totum* (the neuter form of the same adjective) to refer to the nature.[90] Thomas Aquinas knew of that distinction of course from his own commentary on Peter's *Sentences* and put it to his own use in his last *Summa* here:

> Not even in the hypostatic union is the Word of God or the divine nature comprehended by the human nature. Although that divine nature was wholly united to the human nature in the one Person of the Son, nevertheless the whole power of the divinity was not, as it were, circumscribed. (*ST* III q.10 a.1 ad 2)

To justify this position Thomas quotes from one of Augustine's letters that also happened to be Calvin's chief defense of his own views:

> I would have you know that it is not Christian doctrine that God was so poured into the flesh in which he was born of the Virgin that he either abandoned or lost the care of the government of the universe or that he transferred this care into that small body as into a gathered and contracted material.[91]

---

89. Willis, *Calvin's Catholic Christology,* p. 18. This dovetails with Thomas Aquinas's insistence that the human soul of Christ was finite in its powers, as seen in Chapter 5.

90. The distinction is made in Lombard's *Sententiarum Liber III, distinctio* 22,3. Although Calvin does not refer to Lombard by name in his *Institutes,* he does cite him as his authority in his *Final Admonition to Westphal,* written in 1557. Full references to both Lombard and Calvin in Willis, *Calvin's Catholic Christology,* pp. 30-35.

91. Augustine, *Epistle 137 ad Volusianum,* 2 in *PL* 33, 517; cited in Willis, *Calvin's Catholic Christology,* p. 46.

In other words, one function of this *etiam extra carnem* doctrine for Augustine was both to avoid modalism and yet also to identify the incarnate Lord with him who never ceases to provide for the world.

What then of Lutheran worries that what they called the *extra Calvinisticum* represents a diminution of divine commitment in the incarnation or of modern worries by some Barthians that it provides an end-run that will legitimize natural theology? It might surprise some to hear this, but for the most part Barth defends the doctrine. This can be seen not only in his statement that the Word of God "without becoming unlike Himself assumed His likeness to us,"[92] but also in his own *excursus* on the doctrine:

> Luther could quite well say: "I will know of no other Son of God except Him who was born of the Virgin Mary and has suffered." . . . The problems raised by this idea may be plainly reduced to the following questions. Does it take such account of the freedom, majesty and glory of the Word of God that they are in no way merged and submerged in His becoming flesh?[93]

This question for Barth is clearly meant to be rhetorical, for he goes on to defend the *extra Calvinisticum* in these terms:

> From this concern there resulted a protest on the part of Reformed theology . . . against the crowning assertion of Luther and the Lutherans about the existence of the Word solely in the human existence of Christ. The "solely" was contested, and it was asserted in reply that since the Word is flesh, He also is and continues to be what He is in Himself. He also exists beyond *(extra)* the flesh. . . . "Because the divinity is inconceivably and everywhere present, it must follow that it is indeed beyond its adopted humanity and yet none the less also in the same and remains in personal union with it" (*Heidelberg Catechism*, question 48). To understand this protest we must keep constantly in mind that the Reformed theologians maintained this not as a theological innovation, but in continuation of all early Christology. The description *extra Calvinisticum* which was given to their doctrine by the Lutherans was apt only to the extent that it actually was Calvinists who reverted to this tradition to meet the innovation introduced by Luther and the Lutherans. . . . Even Luther has given

92. Karl Barth, *Church Dogmatics* I/2: *The Doctrine of the Word of God*, trans. G. T. Thomson and Harold Knight (Edinburgh: T. & T. Clark, 1956), p. 165.

93. Barth, *Church Dogmatics* I/2, pp. 166-67.

the *extra* its due and proper form in his "Children's Christmas Hymn" when he sings:

> And were the wide world e'er so great
> With gold and precious stones ornate,
> Yet were it far too small to be
> A narrow cradle, Lord, for Thee.[94]

The debate on the *extra Calvinisticum* was, as the name implies, mostly an intra-Reformation debate; but it cropped up in Catholic debate when the Jesuit theologian Jacques Dupuis met with the Congregation for the Doctrine of the Faith (CDF) from 1999 to 2000. Before that conversation had reached its resolution, the Vatican had, in the summer of 2000, released a document *Dominus Iesus*, condemning various trends in Catholic Christology since Vatican II, which contained this key passage:

> It is likewise contrary to the Catholic faith to introduce a separation between the salvific actions of the Word as such and that of the Word made man. With the incarnation, all the salvific actions of the Word of God are always done in unity with the human nature that he has assumed for the salvation of all people. The one subject which operates in the two natures, human and divine, is the single person of the Word.
>
> Therefore, the theory which would attribute, after the incarnation as well, a salvific activity to the Logos as such in his divinity, exercised "in addition to" or "beyond" the humanity of Christ, is not compatible with the Catholic faith. (*DI* §10)

That Dupuis (along with others no doubt) was clearly the target here can be seen in a document he signed that was approved by Pope John Paul II on November 24, 2000, but which contained this key change in wording: "It is therefore contrary to the Catholic faith not only to posit a separation between the Word and Jesus, or between the Word's salvific activity and that of Jesus, but also to maintain that there is a salvific activity of the Word as such in his divinity, *independent* of the humanity of the Incarnate Word."[95] Chapter 11 will deal with this issue in more detail. Here I only wish to point out that the *extra Calvinisticum,* this seemingly arcane and esoteric topic of

---

94. Barth, *Church Dogmatics* I/2, pp. 168-69; translation emended.

95. *Notification on the book* Toward a Christian Theology of Religions *by Jacques Dupuis,* §I.2; emphasis added; available at the Vatican website here: http://www.vatican.va/roman _curia/congregations/cfaith/documents/rc_con_cfaith_doc_20010124_dupuis_en.html.

Christology, actually has a lot riding on it. Not only does it seem to validate natural theology, although Barth might disagree here (an issue treated in Chapter 9), but it also has implications for interreligious dialogue. For if the eternal Son of God also has his existence *etiam extra carnem,* does that mean we must also concede that his salvific activity also ranges *etiam extra Ecclesiam?* Such will be the concerns of Chapters 8 through 12. But in the meantime, it would be well to bear in mind that the debate over the *extra Calvinisticum,* despite its redolence of the odors of the scholar's musty *scriptorium,* is directly relevant. It is why the debate arose in the first place — because it matters: by attributing a ubiquity to Christ's divinity that was in no way diminished by the incarnation, Calvinists were (however unawares) opening the way to a greater openness to the activity of Christ in the world after the incarnation.

CHAPTER 7

Christologies of the Heart

Jesu, thou art all compassion,
Pure, unbounded love thou art;
Visit us with thy salvation!
Enter every trembling heart.

John Wesley, "Hymn 374"

People are religious to the extent that they believe themselves to be not
so much imperfect, as ill. Any man who is half-way decent will think
himself extremely imperfect, but a religious man thinks himself
wretched.

Ludwig Wittgenstein, *Culture and Value*

It is useless to state what one's heart does not feel.

Alexander Solzhenitsyn, "1970 Nobel Prize Lecture"

Science is cold, the heart is warm. Paul tells us that knowledge puffs up but love endures: "For we know in part and we prophesy in part, but when perfection comes, the imperfect disappears" (1 Cor. 13:9-10). Such a line has always been the occasion for an examination of conscience by theologians and pastors: Do not the complexities of christological doctrine too often lead to hairsplitting distinctions, pointless controversies, and even irreparable splits

271

in the one church of Christ? Why not let the gospel speak for itself, from heart to heart?

Although these questions have often been raised throughout the history of theology, they became truly exigent in the seventeenth and eighteenth centuries, especially in Germany, England, and France, where — in different cultures and in different denominational forms, to be sure — a new stress on *feeling* was privileged as the best locale for gaining access to the saving effects of Christ. For that reason, it might seem pointless to devote much time to Christian writers of that time, most of whom seemed to eschew the very doctrines that are the focus of this book. But in fact, these "feeling Christologies," so to speak, are much richer in theological content than is often assumed. True, the representatives of Pietism in Germany, the founders and leaders of Methodism in England, and the devotees of the Sacred Heart in France from time to time made statements that seemed to dismiss academic theology entirely. But a closer look at some of the most significant figures in these three movements shows that the insights they had into the person and work of Christ were of lasting value and of greater theological significance than they themselves may perhaps have suspected.

German Pietism

As a general term used by church historians, *Pietism* most often refers to that Protestant (generally Lutheran) movement in German-speaking lands from the late seventeenth to the late eighteenth century which sought to supplement — and occasionally (though rarely) to supplant — the heavy emphasis on institutional membership and subscription to dogma in orthodox Protestant circles with something more devotional. Generally speaking, they valued the practice of personal piety — rooted in inner experience but also expressing itself in a life of intense outer commitment — over mere credal orthodoxy. The word *Pietism* came into currency in the late seventeenth century, first it would seem as a term of abuse and derision, then as a nickname, and finally as a full-fledged descriptive noun.[1] But even when defanged of its

1. "Puritans and Pietists did not choose these labels for themselves. They became [so] labeled, as part of a social process of mockery and abuse, and as part of a set of political processes." Mary Fulbrook, *Piety and Politics: Religion and the Rise of Absolutism in England, Württemberg, and Prussia* (Cambridge: Cambridge University Press, 1984), p. 27. The Jesuits, Quakers, and Shakers also suffered from the same fate, and eventually adopted the names given to them by their scoffers, thereby removing the sting from the earlier intended derision.

insulting bite, the term is remarkably protean, since it depends on a prior definition of the meaning of piety.[2]

But even to try to define an abstract standard of piety in the Socratic manner before proceeding to the matter at hand implies that Pietism started with an abstraction and then built upon that. In fact Pietism grew spontaneously out of certain felt deficiencies in Lutheran orthodoxy. Hence, in this chapter, the term will denote a certain historical period in German Lutheranism that both depended upon, yet also rejected, key christological motifs of orthodox Lutheranism; and the term will be used here only in that strictly historical sense.[3]

Broadly considered, Pietism arose because of the difficulties Lutherans had in living out the Christian life in the wake of the Thirty Years' War (1618-48), after which each Christian body — Lutherans, Calvinists, Catholics — could settle down into more-or-less secure boundaries and live their religious lives relatively unmolested. Only then did the inherited tensions *within* each theological system come to the fore: what might work in a polemical setting against another Christian body might not prove nourishing — or even meaningful — within the setting of an internally cohesive community. Admittedly, for the most part the pastors and theologians who adopted the name of Pietist for themselves did not depart in any explicit way from Lutheran orthodoxy, as can be seen in the figure widely regarded as, if not the "founder," at least the catalyst for the movement that soon became known as Pietism: Philipp Jakob Spener (1630-1705). His book *Pia Desideria*

---

2. The difficulty of defining piety first appeared in Western literature in Plato's dialogue, the *Euthyphro*. Socrates' eponymous interlocutor, the supposed religious "expert" Euthyphro, had claimed that hauling his father to court on a dubious charge of murder was the "pious" thing to do, since Zeus after all had overthrown *his* father. (A slave on his father's farm had died in custody while the father was in Athens, and Euthyphro decided he should file charges against his father on that flimsy basis.) This justification prompted Socrates to ask if the pious was such because it was approved by the gods — or did the gods approve of something because it really was the pious thing to do? Meaning: Did the gods determine the pious arbitrarily, or did they too have to recognize standards independent of themselves? Euthyphro was unable to answer the question, and so Socrates lost another vote at his trial later that week for "atheism." The confusion lives on to this day in the dispute whether the ethics of revealed religion is based, at least in part, in natural law (promulgated by God, to be sure, but also inherent in the goodness of human nature itself and *per se*), or is something other ("heteronomous"). Then there is also the confusion between pious behavior (which can be mimicked) and a pious heart (known to God alone). No wonder the term Pietism is so protean.

3. "Enlightenment" is another example of a term that should be used only in the chronological, and not in the descriptive or still less honorific, sense.

(1675) effectively launched the movement with its call for devotional groups to study the Bible and pray in common. In this work he stressed the universal priesthood of all believers (as did of course Luther) and the role of personal piety in Christian discipleship, but he never left the Lutheran Church.[4] To be sure, other, more radical groups stressed the work of the Holy Spirit in the hearts of the faithful, and they often broke away from the established religion of their homeland. In other words, the relationship of the Pietists (however defined) with orthodox, clerical Lutheranism is quite complicated, a complex situation perhaps best described by Andrew Weeks here:

> It should be noted that the image of orthodox German Protestantism that emerges when one focuses on its dissenters is slanted. The boundaries between orthodoxy and Pietism were not altogether rigid. Nor was mainstream Lutheranism as petrified, as close-minded, or even as hostile to mysticism as it appears from the invectives of the dissenters. The Lutheran pastorate nurtured much of the intellectual culture of Germany. . . . Still, both the fervor of Pietism and the cooler light of the *Aufklärung* [Enlightenment] at some point defined themselves through their opposition to a rigid tradition based on the outer or literal word of the Bible. Viewed retrospectively, there was a powerful rationale for the multiform rebellion against the shallowness and narrowness of religious life, and against a clerical establishment that rested its case on the authority of the Bible. Scriptural authority had served to fan the flames of Germany's destruction and was now quite powerless to surmount her continued division.[5]

Given this incapacity of Scripture "alone" to address this crisis, let alone adjudicate it, an appeal to experience had in retrospect become inevitable, which altered not only the religious history of western Europe, but to some

4. Spener was indeed accused of heresy in 1695; although vigorously defended by other theologians, he finally grew weary of the battle and retired to pastoral work in 1698 — without, however, leaving the Lutheran Church.

5. Andrew Weeks, *German Mysticism from Hildegard of Bingen to Ludwig Wittgenstein* (Albany: State University of New York Press, 1993), pp. 193-94. Albert Outler agrees: "Neither the Protestant Reformation nor the Roman Catholic Church achieved its spiritual aim. Born in bitterness and hardened by controversy and an ensuing century of wars of religion, they had torn Western Christendom asunder and had reaffirmed the Constantinian doctrine of a necessary reliance of churches upon the civil states in which they dwelled." Albert C. Outler, "Pietism and Enlightenment: Alternatives to Tradition," in *Christian Spirituality: Post-Reformation and Modern*, ed. Louis Dupré and Don E. Saliers (New York: Crossroad, 1989), pp. 240-56; here 240.

extent the contours of christological debate. At all events, the two most significant theologians for later specifically christological development were Johanna Petersen and Nicholas Zinzendorf, an account of whose teaching here follows.

Johanna Petersen

Although little read after her death, Johanna Eleonora Petersen (1644-1724) not only exerted an unusual influence in her day — made all the more remarkable by the fact that women rarely were given a theological hearing then — but she also anticipates themes that would become increasingly important in the twentieth century.

Perhaps the most notable feature of her Christology is her heavy stress on the preexistence of Christ. The preexistence of the Logos is of course rooted in Scripture (John 1:1-3) and forms the central doctrinal basis for the *extra Calvinisticum.* But as a Lutheran, Petersen was born into a tradition that denied that *theologoumenon,* creating a tension in her mind that led to the innovation for which she is most known: her doctrine of the preexistence of the heavenly God-*humanity* of Jesus Christ. While the prologue to the Gospel of John speaks solely of the preexistence of the Logos and only at verse 14 says that that Word became flesh, for Petersen it is significant that in his letter to the Philippians Paul makes the subject of the preexistence *Christ Jesus:* "Put on the mind of Christ Jesus, who being in the very form of God did not consider equality with God something to be grasped but emptied himself" (Phil. 2:5-7a). Further, she placed heavy emphasis on the line in Hebrews that "Jesus Christ is the same yesterday and today and forever" (13:8) and the verse in Revelation that the Lamb "was slain before the foundation of the world" (13:8).[6]

According to Petersen, her doctrine was not only well grounded in Scripture but also had the advantage of resolving the lingering dispute between Lutherans and Calvinists on the real presence of Christ in the elements of the Lord's Supper, as Martin Jung explains:

6. On more dubious exegetical grounds (at least judging by contemporary standards), she also relied on Proverbs 8:22-23 ("The Lord created me at the beginning of his work, the first of his acts of old. Ages ago I was established, at the first, before the beginnings of the earth") and Micah 5:2 ("But you, O Bethlehem, . . . from you shall come forth from me one who is to be ruler in Israel, whose origin is from of old, from ancient days"). Tellingly, these were also the favored prooftexts of the Arians.

She thought her Christology would make understandable and clarify the Lutheran concept of the Real Presence of Christ's human nature with or even in the elements [of bread and wine]. Namely, Christ is personally present at the Lord's Supper in "His heavenly God-humanity," and his flesh and blood that "is poured out and received among the community" is not that which "He received from Mary," but rather that [which had been] raised to the right hand of God and had originally become flesh and blood in heaven, as John 6:51-56 testifies. ["I am the living bread that *came down* from heaven. If anyone eats of *this* bread, he will live forever. This bread is my *flesh,* which I will give for the life of the world."] The partaking of this heavenly flesh and blood gives — as the Lutherans taught — life and close communion with Christ. Petersen granted that in spite of her distinctly formulated doctrine of the Real Presence, those who knew nothing of the heavenly God-man could hardly accept the Lutheran doctrine, and — like the Reformed — had to interpret the elements of the Lord's Supper in a "manner of speaking," thus symbolically.[7]

In a way, Petersen's logic makes perfect sense, provided one had first rejected the Calvinist axiom *finitum non capax infiniti* (the finite cannot contain the infinite). While that axiom certainly led to a symbolic interpretation of the real presence in later Calvinist theology, and while the rejection of that axiom made it easier for Lutherans to admit the real presence (since now the Eucharistic elements *can* contain the infinite), the Lutheran solution founders, as we saw in Chapter 6, on the confusion between the two natures, divine and human, in Christ, which only gets compounded in Petersen's solution. For if she is right that the solution to the problem of the real presence is to be found in the preexistent heavenly flesh of Christ, then she is caught in a dilemma: either she has made matter eternal with God (thus denying creation *ex nihilo*), or she has lapsed into Arianism (by making the heavenly Christ a creature, however exalted). Either Christ's flesh, however "heavenly," must preexist the universe (thereby making matter somehow coterminous with God's eternity), or else Christ's preexistence must be a part of creation, which is Arianism.

Whether she was aware of these difficulties does not emerge from her

7. Martin H. Jung, "Johanna Eleonora Petersen," in *The Pietist Theologians: An Introduction to Theology in the Seventeenth and Eighteenth Centuries,* ed. Carter Lindberg (Oxford: Blackwell, 2005), pp. 147-60; here 154; emphases added. The internal quotations are drawn from Petersen's works, *Leben Frauen Johanna Eleonora Petersen,* 2nd ed. (Frankfurt: Müller, 1719) and *Das Geheimniss des Erst-Geborenen* (Frankfurt: Heyl & Liebezeit, 1711).

writings; but she pressed these views for another reason, one that would become increasingly exigent in the nineteenth and twentieth centuries: Only a stress on the preexistence of Christ could resolve, she felt, the problem of pluralism and God's universal will to save. As she recounted in her autobiography, nothing more alienated her from orthodox, clerical Lutheranism than this issue: from her early youth, she struggled because she "could not comprehend how God, who is essentially love, should damn so many in eternal damnation."[8] For that reason, she of course rejected out of hand Calvinism's doctrine of double predestination; nor could she countenance orthodox Lutheran doctrine, which did indeed (unlike Calvinism) begin with God's universal will to save but still envisioned the end of time resulting in only a small number of the saved.

The problem obviously had to be solved christologically, and she found her solution not just in the priority of the heavenly flesh of Christ before creation, but also in the enigmatic phrase in the first letter of Peter that Christ, after his death, went to preach to those spirits in "prison who *disobeyed* God long ago" (1 Pet. 3:19-20). Her problem was how to take seriously the words in Mark, "Whoever believes and is baptized will be saved, but whoever does not believe will be condemned" (Mark 16:16). While the verse does not explicitly say that those who are not *baptized* will be condemned, yet it does imply that unbelief in and of itself counts unto reprobation. For Petersen, though, that applies only to life on earth, that is, to life in the body; but Christ's descent to the underworld gave an opportunity for redemption in the spirit, justification for which view she found again in the same Petrine epistle: "For this reason the gospel was preached even to those who are now dead, so that they might be judged in the flesh like men, but live according to God in the spirit" (1 Pet. 4:6). Only by reexamining these verses from 1 Peter could one begin, Petersen felt, to reconcile Lutheran and Calvinist theories of predestination while simultaneously doing justice to God's universal will to save over against the common opinion of the day (shared by most Lutherans, Calvinists, and Catholics) that only a few will be saved.

Though read widely in her day, her influence rapidly waned after her death, and she is not much read today.[9] Even Karl Barth, whose views on predestination and the descent bear remarkable "elective affinities" with

8. Petersen, *Leben*, p. 49; cited in Jung, p. 154.

9. For example, her books (to the best of my knowledge) have never been reprinted or translated.

Petersen's,[10] never cites her. But perhaps for that very reason, one must salute her untutored eye for spotting unresolved antinomies in orthodox Lutheranism and realizing that they could only be resolved by a fresh look at the Bible, viewed christologically. No doubt her proposals lack a certain maturity and often collapse on further reflection, which perhaps accounts for her lack of influence after her death. But her suggestions would prove highly stimulating in the nineteenth and twentieth centuries.

Count Zinzendorf

Nicholas Ludwig von Zinzendorf (1700-1760) probably ranks as the most significant and influential of the German Pietists. Born in Dresden (Saxony) of Austrian Protestant nobility, he was raised by his maternal grandmother after the early death of his father. An enthusiast for Lutheran Pietism (and learned in her own right), this benign matriarch sent her grandson to an *Adelspädagogium* (a secondary school for the nobility) in Halle noted for its strict Pietist principles. The education must have taken hold, for Zinzendorf resisted the idea of next attending the University of Wittenberg, at that time the center, for obvious reasons, of Lutheran orthodoxy. As it happens, his family, despite their Pietism, wanted him to study law there, not theology, to prepare for a career in government. But before establishing himself in a career, he went on the customary "Grand Tour" of Europe that most wealthy young men made at the time (Netherlands and France, in his case, but not Italy), during which he met, among others, Louis Cardinal de Noailles (1651-1729), with whom he felt certain elective affinities because of their mutual proclivity for "heart religion."

But the decisive moment in his life came when Protestant refugees from Moravia arrived on his estates in 1722. These were the lineal descendants of the so-called *Unitas Fratrum*, known more popularly as the Bohemian Brethren, who were sprung from a pre-Reformation Czech group inspired

---

10. As here: "It is a serious matter to be a Pharaoh, a Saul, a Judas, an Alexander or a Hymenaeus. It is a serious matter to be threatened by hell, sentenced to hell, worthy of hell, and already on the road to hell. On the other hand, we must not minimize the fact that we actually know of only one certain triumph of hell — the handing-over of Jesus — and that this triumph of hell took place in order that it would never again be able to triumph over anyone." Karl Barth, *Church Dogmatics* II/2: *The Doctrine of God*, trans. G. W. Bromiley et al. (Edinburgh: T. & T. Clark, 1957), p. 496. On this theme see David Lauber, *Barth on the Descent into Hell: God, Atonement and the Christian Life* (Burlington, VT: Ashgate, 2004).

by Jan Hus (c. 1372-1415) that had demanded communion under both species.[11] As time went on, these breakaway Brethren went further, rejecting oaths and military service, shunning cities and private property, and organizing communal life around the ideals of the Sermon on the Mount. By the time of the Reformation they had dropped the demand for communion under both species (and were persecuted by the Utraquists accordingly). But their efforts to affiliate with Lutherans were frustrated by their refusal to abandon a celibate priesthood and the seven sacraments. However, with the death of their leader in 1528, they accepted justification by faith alone but got to keep their practice of private confession of sins. A series of Holy Roman Emperors persecuted them, with some fleeing to Poland (where they affiliated with the Calvinists) and others to Moravia; and in 1721 some accepted an offer from Zinzendorf for refuge at his own foundation, the village of Herrnhut ("Under the Lord's Watch"), some forty miles east of Dresden.

This community, now known more generally as the Moravian Church or Moravian Brethren, brought with them their views that each member was to live out the Sermon on the Mount (in tension with Luther, who held the Sermon on the Mount was impossible of fulfillment) and that the efficacy of the sacraments depended on the virtue of the minister and the faith of the recipient. The community experienced rapid growth in Herrnhut, drawing disaffected Lutherans throughout Germany. But internal doctrinal tensions soon led to dissension, compelling Zinzendorf to quit his government post in 1727 and to devote himself entirely to the welfare, material and spiritual, of the community. His move paid off, as Peter Vogt vividly describes: "On August 13, 1727, the new covenant was powerfully brought to life by the overwhelming experience of a spiritual renewal during a Holy Communion service at the local Lutheran parish church. The Herrnhut congregation now had a new sense of unity and purpose, and Zinzendorf's career would henceforth be closely intertwined with its transformation into an interdenominational renewal movement and mission church."[12]

The crucible of these events proved determinative for Zinzendorf's theol-

11. Technically known as "Utraquists," from the Latin *sub utraque specie* ("under the other species [as well]." Communion under both kinds was permitted the Bohemians in 1433 but was later canceled by Pope Pius II in 1462. That edict, however, remained without writ by the order of the Bohemian Diet until 1567, although authorities continued to turn a blind eye to the practice until the defeat of the Bohemian revolt in 1620.

12. Peter Vogt, "Nicholas Ludwig von Zinzendorf," in *The Pietist Theologians: An Introduction to Theology in the Seventeenth and Eighteenth Centuries* (Malden, MA: Blackwell, 2005), pp. 207-23; here 208.

ogy, out of which he fashioned his *Tropenlehre*. The term means literally "doc-trine of tropes," from the opening verse in the letter to the Hebrews that in the past God spoke in many and various ways *(polutropōs)*. Of course the next verse says that now "in these last days" God finally spoke through his Son, im-plying that the "many ways" (of the past) have now been superseded and ful-filled by the advent of the definitive Christ. Precisely Zinzendorf's point. But then he added a twist: he saw possibilities for unifying the "tropes" in the many and various doctrinal fragments and theological shards *of his day* (and the Bo-hemian/Moravian Brethren were nothing if not eclectic in their doctrine[13]) under the rubric of what we now call Christocentrism. Underneath these vari-ants, in other words, Zinzendorf looked for the "one thing necessary" and forged a theology that continues to influence evangelical Christianity down to our own day, a living and salvation-focused Christocentrism. Vogt again:

> The most prominent feature of Zinzendorf's theology is its focus on Jesus Christ as the Savior, who suffered and died on the cross for the salvation of sinful human beings. The person of the incarnate Christ and the benefit of his atoning death form, according to Zinzendorf, the center of the Gospel and the core subject of genuine theology. To know nothing except Jesus Christ and him crucified (1 Cor. 2:2) summarizes the essence of the Chris-tian faith. For Zinzendorf, Christology is thus not simply one area of Christian doctrine among others, it is the beginning and end of *all* theol-ogy. Zinzendorf does not recognize any true knowledge of God apart from the crucified Christ. God the Father is accessible only through God the Son: "Whoever does not have the Son, has no God." Any general concep-tions of a divine being based on nature or reason are false and deceptive.[14]

The parallels with Karl Barth's theology are evident.[15] But in a way, that might be just the problem. In a famous accusation, Hans Urs von Balthasar

---

13. "Moravians have always emphasized fellowship and service rather than credal state-ments. They accept the Apostles', Athanasian, and Nicene Creeds and the main Reformation statements of faith (including the Augsburg Confession, the shorter Catechism of Luther and the Thirty-Nine Articles of the Church of England) as helpful in formulating Christian truth, but they do not make adherence to any of them a requirement for membership." *The Oxford Dictionary of the Christian Church*, ed. F. L. Cross and E. A. Livingstone, 3rd ed. (Ox-ford: Oxford University Press, 1997), p. 1112.

14. Vogt, "Zinzendorf," in *Pietist Theologians*, p. 211, quoting Zinzendorf's *Berliner Reden an die Männer* (Vogt's emphasis).

15. As Barth himself acknowledged: "Obedience to God always means that we become and are continually obedient to Jesus. The concentration and intensity with which this was

once charged Barth with constructing a "christological bottleneck" (*Engführung*); and in reading Zinzendorf one finds the bottleneck has become virtually a christological torque, strangling all the rest of his theology. He arrived at his Christocentrism from an earlier crisis, when he felt he could never reach, through rational reflection, the transcendent God, who without the revelation of Christ remained for Zinzendorf a hidden God, an abyss of incomprehensible mystery. Hence his huge relief when he came to believe that the incomprehensible God had revealed himself fully in the incarnate Christ, as the opening verses of Hebrews taught. But after 1740 his Christocentrism became even more radical, as Vogt explains:

> Now he looked at Christ as the full manifestation of God to humanity. Although he did not reject the doctrine of the Trinity, Zinzendorf stated clearly that the common God with whom human beings were concerned was no one other than the Son. . . . Christ is the "concentrated God," the "compendium" and "sum" in which the whole Godhead of the Trinity is present. Moreover, the God attested in Holy Scripture is everywhere the Son. Accordingly, Zinzendorf affirmed that Christ is the Creator, the "Jehova" of the Old Testament, and that even the appellation "Father" refers properly to him. This complete identification of God with the person of Christ led Zinzendorf to believe that there was only one choice: either believing in Jesus or becoming an atheist.[16]

These flirtations with modalism should not obscure Zinzendorf's other great contribution to Christology, for he is also responsible for stressing the atoning work of Christ on the cross as the correlate of his Christocentrism.

---

continually said by Nicholas von Zinzendorf was amply justified. He said it in opposition not only to a secularized orthodoxy, and not only to the Enlightenment, but also to the moral and mystical ambiguities of the Pietism of his time. In so doing, he reestablished not merely a Reformation but a New Testament insight. We may be astonished at baroque features in the way in which he said it. And we may argue that, entangled in certain Lutheran ideas, he did not say it universally enough. But we must give him credit that he was one of the few not only of his own time but of all times who have said it so definitely and loudly and impressively. To become obedient to Jesus is actually to become obedient to God, not a conceived and imaginary God, but to God as He is in His inmost essence, the gracious God, the God in whom we may believe." Karl Barth, *Church Dogmatics* II/2, pp. 568-69.

16. Vogt, *Pietist Theologians*, p. 211, quoting from Zinzendorf's *Apologetische Schluss Schrift*. In the nineteenth century Ludwig Feuerbach called Zinzendorf a nascent "Christian atheist," which — however unfair the charge — should alert us all to the dangers of eschewing natural theology in all its forms or of stressing the divinity of Christ so much that his relation to the Father recedes: that way lies atheism.

Like all forms of evangelical Christianity after him, he insisted that the preaching of that atoning work be the main task of evangelization; and in a remarkable parallel with the devotion to the Sacred Heart just beginning in France at that time, he promoted a devotion to the "Five Wounds" of Christ: "Particularly prominent is Zinzendorf's interest in Christ's woundedness. The wounds of Jesus, especially the 'Side Wound,' represent for him the most tangible manifestation of Christ's saving work and the place where his deliverance is most accessible to the believers."[17]

In the nineteenth century John Henry Newman lamented this evangelical stress on the atoning work of Christ because he felt that it keyed up the emotions too much, which would inevitably lead to a slackening off of the hard work of daily fidelity. But Zinzendorf would surely have been surprised at the charge. For he was careful to craft his sermons and devotional works so that they led to a confident relationship of believers with their Savior, a relationship that could and should be nourished *daily*, as Vogt rightly sees:

> Thus an important part of the preaching of the Gospel is to "paint" the crucified Christ before the people so that Christ may be received by all hearts that are open and receptive. . . . [This] emphasis on Christ's immediate presence led Zinzendorf eventually to speak about the religious life in terms of an intimate personal "connection" with the Savior. The believers can converse and walk with the Savior as with an invisible friend. They should daily assure themselves individually of his presence in prayer and meditation. The personal acquaintance with Christ represents for Zinzendorf the core of Moravian spirituality.[18]

Parallels with the Catholic devotion to the Sacred Heart leap immediately to mind; and they are real, as we shall see at the end of this chapter. But for the most part these parallels arose more from the common need of the age to get beyond sterile and endless debate over theological abstractions like justification and church membership. The parallels with Methodism, however, are more direct and historically caused; for John Wesley visited

17. Vogt, *Pietist Theologians*, p. 212. Nor is Zinzendorf's devotion without parallels in the Middle Ages: "In allegorical language borrowed from the Song of Songs [a common medieval trope], Zinzendorf describes the wounds as a place of refuge, where human souls find protection, rest, and nourishment. *He insists that Christ will bear his wounds in all eternity* and that these wounds form the sign by which he will be recognized at his second coming" (p. 212, emphasis added). As we will see, the revelations of the Sacred Heart also stress this eternal woundedness.

18. Vogt, *Pietist Theologians*, pp. 213-14.

Herrnhut, and Zinzendorf spent time in both London and the American colonies during the Methodist revivals in both places, to a consideration of which we now turn.

John Wesley and Methodist Christology

John Wesley (1703-91), the founder of Methodism, must be any biographer's dream-come-true. The man was a bundle of contradictions — and what biographer does not love to portray a human life torn asunder from within, at inner conflict with itself, thrashing about on the stage of history? As Stephen Tomkins explains at the conclusion of his almost novelistic biography, Wesley fascinates because he marshaled so many of the conflicts of his age and fused them into a life of remarkable achievement:

> He combined a Catholic devotion to the sacraments of the Church with a Pentecostal welcoming of healings, ecstasies and Low Church spontaneity. He had an evangelical horror of trying to satisfy God by good works, but an even greater horror of trying to satisfy God without good works. He was a founding father of evangelicalism, but for his last twenty years, he consistently retreated from its stark certainties.[19]

These tensions clearly worked creatively, for out of them Wesley became one of the most zealous and effective evangelists in the history of Christianity. "At fairly sober estimates," Tomkins writes, Wesley himself "rode 250,000 miles, gave away £30,000, . . . and preached more than 40,000 sermons," while the published version of his *Journal* ran to over twenty volumes. Moreover, under his influence England finally became, for the first and perhaps only time in its history, in all its classes and throughout the land, a thoroughly Christian nation, so much so that nonconformists grew from 6 percent of churchgoers in Wesley's youth to 45.5 percent by 1851.[20]

---

19. Stephen Tomkins, *John Wesley: A Biography* (Grand Rapids: Eerdmans, 2003), p. 196.

20. Tomkins, *John Wesley*, p. 199. His disastrously bad marriage probably also contributed to his zeal, as relations with his wife were so bad he had little motivation to stay at home. One time, arriving for a Methodist conference in Bristol, he heard that his wife had taken dangerously ill, at which news he headed back to London to attend her. But upon arriving at their apartment at the ungodly hour of one o'clock the following morning, he discovered that her fever had by then abated — and so he turned round and headed back to Bristol an hour later! When he suspected his wife of reading his private mail, he had his desk

At first·this zeal was entirely directed at revivifying a nearly moribund Church of England, in which Wesley had been ordained a priest. But in travels to the British colony of Georgia in 1735 he initiated a process that led to his full break with the Established Church: first, even though himself only a priest, he ordained other men for sacramental ministry in the American colonies; second, never very comfortable with an excessive stress on justification over against the need for the justified sinner to pursue a life of holiness (tensions between justification and sanctification had always marked the Reformation), he unilaterally excised all of the articles of the Thirty-Nine Articles that, to Wesley, stressed justification at the expense of the necessary pursuit of holiness in the church.[21]

With the exception of his demurral of the descent-clause in the Apostles' Creed, Wesley's "innovations" did not touch on Christology *sensu stricto* (strictly considered).[22] But the question naturally arises whether he had a

---

outfitted with a secret compartment to hide his sensitive papers from her. These presumably must have included portions of his famous *Journal*, for in one bitter letter to her he explained that his indictment of her character was incomplete because he did not have his journal with him at the moment: "I have therefore only my memory to depend on; and that is not very retentive of evil." No surprise, then, that he did not attend her funeral, and of her own £5,000 legacy (holdings from her first husband, a wealthy Huguenot merchant), she bequeathed to him only a ring. Tomkins knows he is not the first biographer to see the connection between the bad marriage and Wesley's evangelical zeal, for he cites other contemporary witnesses who came to the same conclusion: "According to an early biographer, Wesley 'believed the Lord overruled [watched over] this painful business for good, and that, if Mrs. Wesley had been a better wife, he might have been unfaithful to the great work to which God had called him.' Whether or not their unhappiness was the work of God, there can be little doubt how greatly it benefited the Methodist movement, keeping him on the road while Charles [John's brother], a happy husband and father, was now virtually retired. As Berridge of Everton put it, 'Matrimony has quite maimed poor Charles and might have spoiled John and George [Whitefield], if a wise master had not graciously sent them a brace of ferrets'" (Tomkins, *John Wesley*, p. 167).

21. Wesley also omitted the Third Article, on Christ's descent into hell. One author speculates that "Wesley was loath to teach anything suggesting a second chance for those who resisted repentance in this life." See John Deschner, *Wesley's Christology: An Interpretation* (Dallas: Southern Methodist University Press, 1885), p. 51. The objection seems peculiar, however, since Christ would obviously have encountered only those who — having been born before Christ's advent on earth — had never heard of him to begin with. This issue will be treated more extensively in a later *excursus*.

22. I place "innovations" in scare quotes because some might regard his excisions of the Articles on justification as a return to the Great Tradition, which had never placed such an overwhelming stress on justification to begin with. That certainly was the view of his enemies back in England upon his return from America, who accused him of "papist" innova-

distinctive Christology, distinctive enough to serve as the catalyst for (or at least confirmation of) his break with the Church of England, for his evangelical zeal, and for his urgent desire that Christians become "perfect as [their] heavenly Father is perfect." In that regard it must be recalled that Wesley was not a systematic theologian by either training or inclination and never wrote the equivalent of Calvin's *Institutes*. Like Paul's, his writings are mostly occasional.[23] Nor was it ever part of his project to depart from the Chalcedonian framework that was the common legacy of the major Reformers. Perhaps the most balanced account of his Christology comes from John Deschner's classic study:

> Wesley's Christology is not, for the most part, unique. It is part of an ecumenical stream of Christological tradition. When his systematic statements are examined, they are seen to follow classical models: the Anglican Thirty-Nine Articles [at least the nonexcised ones dealing with the person and office of Christ], the ecumenical creeds, or the doctrinal formulas of Protestant orthodoxy: . . . the person, the two states [natures], the three offices of Christ.[24]

That said, a careful study of his writings shows that he does lay very strong emphasis on the divinity of Christ: "Wesley betrays a decided emphasis on the divine nature and a corresponding underemphasis on the human."[25] In his sermon on Jesus' Sermon on the Mount, for example, he speaks of the authority of the speaker (Christ) as "something more than human; more than can agree with any created being! It speaks the Creator of all! A God, a God appears! Yes, Ὁ Ὤv, the Being of beings, JEHOVAH, the self-existent, the Supreme, the God who is over all, blessed forever!"[26]

Given this extraordinarily "high" Christology, one can see why Wesley put so much stress on another line from the Sermon on the Mount: "Be per-

---

tions, the same charge that would face John Henry Newman when he published *Tract 90*. In Wesley's case, the accusation gained added plausibility when his nephew, Charles's son Samuel, became a Catholic.

23. In the literal sense of being prompted by specific occasions and crises, and obviously not in the wider sense of being written from time to time when the mood suited him — Wesley was too productive for that meaning to apply!

24. Deschner, *Wesley's Christology*, pp. 5-6.

25. Deschner, *Wesley's Christology*, p. 6.

26. John Wesley, Sermon 16, in *Wesley's Standard Sermons*, ed. Edward H. Sugden (London: Epworth Press, 1921), introduction, p. 9. Note again the quasi-modalist formulation, similar to Zinzendorf's.

fect, as your heavenly Father is perfect" (Matt. 5:48). Indeed, his emphasis on that line as coming from a divine oracle was his trump, so to speak, against all the naysayers in England who accused him of introducing works-righteousness into his Methodist reform.[27] It is difficult to tell which came first: a Christology that began with the divinity of Christ and thus saw the command of perfection as thereby coming from a divine oracle; or Wesley's prior pastoral drive to emphasize sanctification, one that needed the strongest support from a divine oracle in order to overcome both Puritan and Established opposition; and perhaps that question is not crucial.[28]

What can be said, however, is that on the basis of his high Christology Wesley very much falls in with the Scotist position that God both foresaw and above all foreordained the incarnation, independent of Adam's fall; and this Scotist position is directly related to Wesley's stress on sanctification, as Deschner rightly notes:

> God decrees, foresees, and permits the creation, fall and incarnation in order to effect His overriding purpose, that man should be made holier and happier than Adam before the fall! Man's freedom is no longer the fulcrum of the doctrine: man's freedom here serves God's supreme purpose of increasing holiness. God foresaw the fall, but knew that "it was best upon the whole not to prevent it," because abundantly more good than evil would accrue to the posterity of Adam by his fall. . . . Mankind in general have gained . . . a capacity of attaining more holiness and happiness on earth, than . . . would have been possible . . . if Adam had not fallen.[29]

This emphasis on holiness as God's supreme goal for his creatures affects Wesley's theology across the board. One aspect of the tension between justification and sanctification is the question of *growth*. Justification is a forensic concept drawn from the law courts and denotes an irrevocable verdict

---

27. Like the coinages "Shaker," "Quaker," and "Jesuit," the term "Methodism" first began as a term of abuse to refer to a small society of "enthusiastic" students at Oxford who met together between 1729 and 1735 for mutual edification. Because they took communion every week, fasted, abstained from card-playing and other amusements, and visited the sick and the poor, their "methodical" life attracted notice, itself a telling indication of the moribund life of most members of the Established Church, at least at Oxford.

28. One must certainly add that the linkage worked, for Wesley not only gave birth to Methodism but also, however indirectly, to all the "holiness churches" (including Pentecostalism) that are today's fastest-growing segment of world Christianity.

29. Deschner, *Wesley's Christology*, pp. 22-23, quoting Wesley's Sermon 59.

of acquittal;[30] but sanctification is more of a process, implying a goal not yet reached and attended by all the possibilities of backsliding and periodic breakthroughs that characterize any human biography.[31] Thus, for Wesley there is always another choice around each corner, which immediately places much greater value on the exercise of free will than countenanced by either Luther or Calvin.[32]

Not surprisingly, despite his heavy stress on Christ's divine nature, he sees Christ's life in terms of process too and frankly avowed that "Our Lord passed through and sanctified every stage of human life. Old age only did not become him."[33] Christ grows in bodily strength, and the powers of his

---

30. "The ruling metaphor of classical Protestant soteriology has always been the courtroom, together with a cluster of forensic concepts about a human offender arraigned before the divine judge who must, if justice is not to be mocked, convict and condemn the offender. What happens, then, in the case of the elect, however, is a juridical move in which the judge decides (or has already decided) to commute the sinner's sentence, on the basis of the imputed righteousness of Christ." Albert C. Outler, *Theology in the Wesleyan Spirit* (Nashville: Tidings, 1975), p. 51. If he were to go back on that verdict, in other words, God would have to indulge in a kind of double jeopardy. Hence justification implies a once-and-for-all decision that cannot be revoked. Hence the "once saved, always saved" motto of some evangelical churches, a position that Wesley would have rejected out of hand as presumptuous.

31. This was certainly true of Wesley's own life. Historians make much of his line, "I felt my heart strangely warmed," which referred to Wesley's hearing of Luther's preface to Paul's letter to the Romans read out loud at a Moravian meeting in Aldersgate Street in London on May 24, 1738. Scholars often refer to the event as a defining moment for the Methodist movement, and no doubt it was. But this event occurred *after* his return to England, after, that is, his sojourn in Georgia and long after 1725, when he began gathering fellow Oxfordians to study the Scriptures and make their Christian way of life more "methodical." Nor did Wesley cease to grow after the "strange warming" episode of 1738, which was, ironically enough, caused by hearing Luther read out loud. By 1741 he had read Luther's commentary on Galatians, to which he reacted negatively, repelled by what he thought was its irrationalism and antinomianism. Albert Outler picks up the story from there: "Thus it was that with respect to the relationships between law and gospel and also the specific mode of Christ's redemptive work, Wesley was closer to Calvin than to Luther. But then, after 1765 or thereabouts, under increasing pressure from the 'imputationists,' Wesley began to pull away from the Calvinists, too, and returned, more and more, to his native holy-living tradition. . . . From 1770 until his death, the breach with the Calvinists was open and bitter. They never forgave Wesley his synergism [fusing free will and predestination]; he never dropped his charge that their predestination theories were a charter for antinomianism." Outler, *Theology in the Wesleyan Spirit*, pp. 50-51.

32. "It may be observed that Wesley places no particular emphasis on the comfort or consolation to be derived from [predestination], a note which is prominent in Calvin, Luther, and the Thirty-nine Articles. Comfort and consolation are not built on so conditional a foundation" (Deschner, *Wesley's Christology*, p. 23).

33. Cited in Deschner, *Wesley's Christology*, p. 24.

mind daily improve. That said, the accusation is often made that Wesley did not give sufficient berth to Christ's human nature. For example, when Article II of the Thirty-Nine Articles says that the "Son, which is the Word of the Father, begotten from everlasting of the Father, the very and eternal God, and of one substance with the Father, took Man's nature in the womb of the blessed Virgin, of her substance," Wesley, in his excising mood, dropped the last phrase: "of her substance." When Jesus escapes from angry crowds, for Wesley he does so because he has become invisible. And Wesley's account of the sufferings of Christ in the passion carries a whiff of Apollinarian Logos-Sarx Christology, as if the soul of Christ did not — perhaps could not — *really* suffer, only his body, as we see in this telling passage from one of his sermons:

> He died . . . [but] in a way peculiar to himself. He alone, of all men that ever were, could have continued alive, even in the greatest tortures as long as He pleased, or have retired from the body whenever he had thought fit. And how does it illustrate that love which He manifested in His death! Inasmuch as He did not use His power to quit His body as soon as it was fastened to the cross, leaving only an insensible corpse to the cruelty of His murderers; but continued His abode in it, with a steady resolution, as long as it was proper. He then retired from it, with a majesty and dignity never known or to be known in any other death; dying, if one may so express it, like the Prince of Life.[34]

Such views obviously could not withstand the skeptical blasts from historical criticism in the nineteenth century, any more than the trend after Wesley for penning "lives of Christ," quasi-biographies of Jesus, could withstand the withering criticism of Albert Schweitzer. This trend, which would prove so popular in the next century, actually began with Wesley himself, who commented "freely on Christ's appearance, age, tempers, attitudes, His courage and intrepidity, and on His wise strategy in carrying through His ministry."[35] But the impact of historical criticism on mainline Methodism

---

34. Cited in Deschner, *Wesley's Christology*, p. 26, from Sermon 49, "The Lord Our Righteousness." Little wonder, then, that Wesley denied outright that Christ's human soul descended into hell. He never says exactly what happened to Christ's soul between his death and his resurrection, but surely Deschner is right in his guess here: "If not in hell, then, where was Christ's soul between Good Friday and Easter? It is very likely that Wesley held the view that it departed into paradise" (p. 51).

35. Deschner, *Wesley's Christology*, p. 27.

would ultimately prove quite devastating to these essential motifs in Wesley's Christology, nearly gutting Methodism of any theological substance, as many commentators have noted.[36]

But there are also internal flaws in Wesley's Christology. Besides the ones already noted, there is a deeper one, perhaps best summed up by Colin Williams in this shrewd observation:

> [Wesley's] concentration on Christ's work in reconciling us to God and making available to us pardon, assurance of God's favor and a knowledge of Christ's presence in us, leads to an underemphasis on Christ's struggle against the demonic forces and his resurrection victory over them. . . . [This myopia] leads, in Wesley's doctrine of sanctification, to an over-individualistic emphasis on conscious relationship to Christ with an underemphasis on the work of sanctification as bringing us to deeper awareness of the evil forces that grip our corporate life and call for Christ's conquest.[37]

Missing, at least in his theology, if not in the ultimate impact of his evangelizing and regenerating apostolate, is any notion of what it means for the church of believers to feel personally saved yet look with equanimity on the forces preventing *others* from feeling that same assurance. Wesley's evangelizing efforts always stressed individual responsibility and free choice (hence the attacks of the Calvinist churches on his theology, if not always on his work). But missing is much sense of human solidarity, which again shows up on his denial of the Apostles' Creed's clause on Christ's descent into hell.

In his encyclical *Spe Salvi*, promulgated on November 30, 2007, Pope Benedict XVI addressed this very issue of solidarity in salvation by quoting

---

36. For example, Colin Williams, a dean of Yale Divinity School in the 1950s: "An article in *Life* magazine some years ago concluded with the statement, 'Methodism is long on organization and short on theology.' If this is a just judgment of contemporary Methodism, it means that she has departed from her earliest tradition, for Methodism represented in her origins a revival of theology as well as a revival of life, and the former was inseparable from the latter." Colin W. Williams, *John Wesley's Theology Today* (Nashville: Abingdon, 1960), p. 5.

37. Williams, *Wesley's Theology Today*, p. 89. I would agree, but only as that pertains to Wesley's theology. The great irony here is that Wesley's stress on individual freedom and the pursuit of Christian perfection did more for the moral regeneration of nineteenth-century English *society* than all the "corporate" models of salvation have ever managed to achieve, including up to today.

the opening passage of Henri de Lubac's large book on just this issue, *Catholicism: Christ and the Common Destiny of Man:*

> Have I found joy? . . . No, but I have found *my* joy, and that is something wildly different. . . . The joy of Jesus can be personal. It can belong to a single man and he is saved. He is at peace, he is joyful now and for always, but he is alone. The isolation of this joy does not trouble him; on the contrary, he is the chosen one. In his blessedness he passes through the battlefields with a rose in his hand. . . . My joy will not be lasting unless it is the joy of all. I will not pass through the battlefields with a rose in my hand.[38]

To which the pope appends this commentary:

> Against this, drawing upon the vast range of patristic theology, de Lubac was able to demonstrate that salvation has always been considered a "social" reality. . . . Consistently with this view, sin is understood by the Fathers as the destruction of the unity of the human race, as fragmentation and division. Babel, the place where languages were confused, the place of separation, is seen to be an expression of what sin fundamentally is. Hence "redemption" appears as the re-establishment of unity, in which we come together once more in a union that begins to take shape in the world community of believers. . . . This real life, towards which we try to reach out again and again, is linked to a lived union with a "people," and for each individual it can only be attained within this "we." It presupposes that we escape from the prison of our "I," because only in the openness of this universal subject does our gaze open out to the source of joy, to love itself — to God. (*Spe Salvi* §14)

Catholic Devotion to the Sacred Heart

In 1673, on the feast of John the Evangelist (December 27), a Visitation nun by the name of Sr. Margaret Mary Alacoque received a vision of the risen Christ while she was praying before the Blessed Sacrament in the chapel of her convent in Paray-le-Monial in central France, in which she heard Jesus say these words: "My divine Heart is so impassioned with love for men that,

---

38. Henri de Lubac, *Catholicism: Christ and the Common Destiny of Man*, trans. Lancelot C. Sheppard and Sister Elizabeth Englund, OCD (San Francisco: Ignatius Press, 1988), p. 13, quoting Jean Giono, *Les vraies richesses* and cited by Pope Benedict, *Spe Salvi* §13.

no longer able to contain within itself the flames of its burning love, it must spread them abroad by means of you." She received another vision in the next calendar year, this time during the Octave of Corpus Christi (probably on the first Friday of June), which she described this way:

> Jesus Christ, my sweet Master, showed Himself to me resplendent in glory, His Five Wounds shining like five suns and flames darting from every part of His sacred humanity. . . . Then He showed me the inexplicable wonders of His pure love and to what extremes He had gone in loving men, from whom He received nothing but ingratitude. "This wounds me more than all I have suffered in My Passion."[39]

Finally, again within the Octave of Corpus Christi the next year (this time probably on Sunday, June 16, 1675), she received her last revelation, when her Lord enjoined upon her the task of getting the church to institute a special feast dedicated to the Sacred Heart, to be established on the first Friday after the Octave of Corpus Christi: "And I promise you that My Heart will pour the treasures of its love abundantly on all who render it this honor or will induce others to do so."

It took seventy-five years before the feast of the Sacred Heart received ecclesiastical approval, and even then the devotion did not really catch fire, so to speak, until the nineteenth century; and therein hangs a tale. For officially approved devotion to the Sacred Heart of Jesus faced two major obstacles: 1) opposition from the Jansenists, and 2) theological objections concerning the nature of Christ's *ongoing, present* sufferings, which were one aspect of Margaret Mary's revelations.

Jansenist Objections

Even on a surface level, Jansenist objections were incoherent. For Jansenists simultaneously accused advocates of the devotion of Nestorianism (by isolating the human heart of Jesus as the object of devotion) while simultaneously claiming that devotees of the Sacred Heart were worshiping a thing — an objection that itself divides Christ's humanity from his divine nature in the Nestorian manner. Clearly something else must have been at work. At a deeper level, they objected to the universal reach of the salvific love of the

---

39. These two visions, and the one related in the next paragraph, are recounted in Appendix A to Margaret Yeo, *These Three Hearts* (Milwaukee: Bruce, 1940), pp. 331-35.

Heart of Jesus. Jansenists gained their notoriety above all with their (again incoherent) doctrine that sufficient grace does not suffice. The logic of this peculiar view grew out of the views of Bishop Cornelius Jansen, or Jansenius (1585-1638), and his thoroughly Augustinian critique of Calvin's theory of predestination, a logic deftly summarized by Louis Dupré:

> According to Jansenius's interpretation, the human person was created in an original state of justice required by human nature itself. Through the fall humanity lost its original justice. Redemptive grace restored the human condition in all believers (here Jansenius differs from Baius), but this universal grace was no longer sufficient for salvation. Beyond the general offer of grace our fallen nature needs a special grace in order to overcome *efficaciously* its otherwise irresistible inclination toward evil. God does not grant this efficacious grace to all, but only to those whom he predestined in the death of Christ. Much in Jansenius's doctrine appears close to Calvin's theory of predestination. Yet, contrary to Calvin, Jansenius teaches that, in the predestined, faith alone does not suffice for justification; active cooperation through good works (assured through God's efficacious grace) is required as a separate condition.[40]

The difference with Calvin might seem arcane, but it only added to the gloom that a stress on predestination usually brings in its wake; for an inability to keep from sinning (or even simply not doing enough good works) inevitably leads to the conclusion that the believer has not been given that all-important efficacious grace and is thus predestined for hell. This disquiet in the believer's soul is what prompted Henri Bremond to accuse Jansenism of devouring "the heart of charity by which the Church lives. Before penetrating into the depths of the mind, it ruins peace, the condition of all true religion. Before making converts it makes partisans, sectarians, whom it fatally severs from the mystical currents of their time."[41]

At least as the accusation applies to Pascal — whose relationship to Jansenism (which was just getting started in his day) is far more ambivalent than is often recognized — the charge is unfair. Ironically, given his bitter polemics against the Jesuits (who later actively promoted devotion to the Sacred

---

40. Louis Dupré, "Jansenism and Quietism," in *Christian Spirituality: Post-Reformation and Modern*, ed. Louis Dupré and Don E. Saliers (New York: Crossroad, 1989), pp. 121-42; here 123.

41. Henri Bremond, *Histoire littéraire du sentiment religieux en France*, vol. 4, pp. 306-7, cited in Dupré, p. 125.

Heart), his own views anticipate in remarkable ways the distinctive theology of this devotion. Although we have already treated him in the previous chapter, where his affinities with Calvin's Christology were stressed, we should note here his doctrinal affinities with the devotees of the Sacred Heart:

> While ordinary knowledge, even philosophical knowledge, results in skepticism as its natural conclusion, the knowledge of the heart, the unified center of inner life, is the instinct that carries us upward. Through this natural instinct God touches his elect; without it religion remains an uncertain struggle. Those to whom God has given religious faith by moving their hearts are very fortunate, and feel quite legitimately convinced; but to those who do not have it, we can only give such faith through reasons, until God gives it by moving their heart.[42]

Such lines of course speak only of the *anthropology* of the later devotion: the heart is a better avenue to reach God than reason. More crucial for the christological side of the devotion to the Sacred Heart will be Pascal's insight into the ongoing sufferings of Christ in the members of his Body, the church. In a passage of extraordinary power, and one insufficiently cited by most Pascal scholars, he presents this meditation on the Agony in the Garden:

> Jesus suffers in his passion the torments inflicted upon him by men, but in his agony he [also] suffers the torments which he inflicts on himself: *He was troubled.*[43] This punishment is inflicted by no human, but by an almighty hand, and only he that is almighty can bear it. Jesus seeks some comfort at least from his three dearest friends, and they sleep: he asks them to bear with him a while, and they abandon him with complete indifference, and with so little pity that it did not keep them awake even for a single moment. And so Jesus was abandoned to face the wrath of God alone. Jesus is alone on earth, not merely with no one to feel and share his agony, but with no one even to know of it. Heaven and he are the only ones to know. Jesus is in a garden, not of delight, like the first Adam, who

42. Blaise Pascal, *Pensées*, trans. A. J. Krailsheimer (Harmondsworth: Penguin, 1966), p. 58, #110. Everyone is already familiar with his famous line that the heart has its reasons that reason knows nothing of, but Pascal varies that line throughout the *Pensées*, sometimes to the point of rejecting outright the scholastic fusion of faith and reason, as here: "It is the heart that perceives God and not the reason" (p. 154, #424).

43. John 11:33. The verb "was troubled" is reflexive ("he troubled himself") in the Latin Vulgate that Pascal is quoting here, which stresses Jesus' voluntary assumption of troubled emotions.

there fell and took with him all mankind, but of agony, where he has saved himself and all mankind. . . . *Jesus will be in agony until the end of the world. There must be no sleeping during that time.*[44]

Pascal also anticipates a motif that will recur throughout devotional literature on the Sacred Heart: the willingness to hear the voice of Christ speaking, in his agony, directly to the believer over the centuries, and without necessarily claiming (unlike Margaret Mary Alacoque) to be the recipient of an aural private revelation:

"Do you want it always to cost me the blood of my humanity while you do not even shed a tear?" [says Jesus to the soul of Pascal] . . . "I am a better friend to you than this man or that, for I have done more for you than they, and they would never endure what I have endured from you, and they would never die for you, while you were being faithless and cruel, as I did, and as I am ready to do, and *still do* in my elect, and in the Blessed Sacrament."[45]

Despite his services to the Jansenists' cause, Pascal's own theology of the heart did nothing to mitigate their opposition to the devotion to the Sacred Heart.[46] Their animating objection was, above all, the universal implications of Christ's love for all mankind in the revelations received by Margaret Mary, as pointed out by one historian of the devotion:

The Jansenists, in their effort to protect the divinity of Christ, were not merely angered that Christ's human nature was given divine worship. The cause of this opposition ran more deeply. It was that the heart of Christ symbolized his universal love for mankind. In their narrow vision of redemption (the few elect), they felt that the view which attributed to the divine nature universal merciful love for all mankind was the real evil of the devotion.[47]

44. Pascal, *Pensées*, pp. 312-13, #919; emphasis added.
45. Pascal, *Pensées*, p. 315, #919; emphasis added.
46. It is possible that toward the end of his life, Pascal began to reconsider his attachment to the Jansenists and his scathing attacks on the Jesuits, at least if these enigmatic lines from the *Pensées* are anything to go by (they immediately follow the meditation on the Agony in the Garden just quoted): "The Jansenists will pay the penalty. . . . The Society [of Jesus] is important to the Church. . . . I love all men as my brothers, because they are *all* redeemed" (pp. 316, 317, 321; #920, 931; emphasis added).
47. Timothy T. O'Donnell, *Heart of the Redeemer* (San Francisco: Ignatius Press, 1992), p. 153.

Even before Margaret Mary received her first revelation in 1673, Innocent X (r. 1644-55) condemned in 1653 the Jansenist teaching that the death of Jesus was not for all mankind.[48] Jansenists tried to wiggle out of this and later condemnations by claiming such condemned propositions did not in fact *(de fait)* occur in their writings; but this expedient was condemned by Clement XI (r. 1700-21) in 1705 as an untenable subterfuge (DH 2390). Opposition, though, continued unabated and culminated in the infamous Jansenist Synod of Pistoia of 1786, which condemned devotion to the Sacred Heart as giving worship to a creature. Pius VI (r. 1775-99) in turn condemned the entirety of the Synod in his Bull *Auctorem fidei* of August 28, 1794, the most relevant passage for our purposes being this:

> Likewise, devotees of the Sacred Heart of Jesus are reproached with paying no heed to the fact that neither the most sacred flesh of Christ, or any part of it, nor even the whole human nature if separate or apart from the Divinity, may be adored with the highest worship; as though the faithful adored the Heart of Jesus separate from the Divinity, whereas they adore it as the Heart *of Jesus,* that is, *as the Heart of the Person of the Word, with whom it is inseparably united.* . . . This doctrine is fallacious, injurious to the devout worshippers of the Heart of Christ. (DH 2663)

These added italicized emphases in the Bull point to the real doctrinal significance of the decree: by virtue of the communication of idioms, the human heart of Jesus is a divine heart, that is, the heart *of* the divine Person, who continues to suffer in his members. This point might seem controversial, but such ongoing suffering was already revealed to Paul on the road to Damascus, when he heard Jesus say, "Saul, Saul, why are you persecuting me?" (Acts 9:4). However much this insight might have receded into the background at various times in the history of the church, devotion to the Sacred Heart brings back to the foreground this important doctrinal point: Christ's ongoing *human* concern and involvement in his members, the church. Such indeed was the focus of Pope Pius XII's lengthy encyclical of 1956 on this devotion, *Haurietis aquas,* especially here:

---

48. "'It is semi-Pelagian to say that Christ died and poured out his blood for all men outright'. . . . This proposition we declare to be temerarious, scandalous, and — in the sense that Christ died only for the salvation of the predestined — impious, blasphemous, insulting, derogating to the divine mercy, and heretical." Heinrich Denzinger, *Enchiridion symbolorum definitionum et declarationum de rebus fidei et morum,* ed. Peter Hünermann (Freiburg im Breisgau: Herder, 2001), p. 615, #2005-6; abbreviated henceforth as DH.

Though it [the Heart of Jesus] is no longer subject to the varying emotions of this mortal life, yet it lives and beats and is united inseparably with the Person of the divine Word and, in Him and through Him, with the divine Will. Since then the Heart of Christ is overflowing with love *both human and divine* and rich with the treasure of all graces which our Redeemer acquired by His life, sufferings and death, it is therefore the enduring source of that charity which His Spirit pours forth on all the members of His Mystical Body. And so the Heart of our Savior reflects in some way the image of the divine Person of the Word and, at the same time, of His twofold nature, the human and the divine; in it we can consider not only the symbol but, in a sense, the summary of the whole mystery of our redemption. When we adore the Sacred Heart of Jesus Christ, we adore in it and through it both the uncreated love of the divine Word and also its human love *and its other emotions* and virtues, since both loves moved our Redeemer to sacrifice Himself for us and for His Spouse, the Universal Church. (§85, §86; emphasis added)

Given such consistently held papal approbation of the devotion and the theology behind it, the surprise is that it did not really become a widespread and popular devotion until the latter half of the nineteenth century. In 1765 Clement XIII (r. 1758-69) authorized a Mass and Office for the Visitation convent of Paray-le-Monial; but it was not extended to the universal church until 1856, when Pius IX (r. 1846-78) made it a universal feast; and Leo XIII (r. 1878-1903) dedicated the human race to the Sacred Heart in 1899. Moreover, the most controversial aspect of the devotion — the promise of the grace of final perseverance for those who make the nine First Friday devotions — did not catch on until 1882. In one of the odder byways of the church's christological development, the widespread fame of this promise was due to an American businessman from Dayton, Ohio — Philip Kemper by name — who distributed the list of promises throughout the world. On May 31, 1899, Pope Leo XIII congratulated Mr. Kemper in a document blessing his "pious" and "useful" work. Among the twelve promises are the following:

4. I will be their secure refuge during life, and above all, in death.

6. Sinners will find in my Heart the source and infinite ocean of mercy.

12. I promise you in the excessive mercy of my Heart that my all-powerful love will grant to all those who receive Holy Communion on the First Fri-

days in nine consecutive months the grace of final perseverance; they shall not die in my disgrace, nor without receiving the sacraments. My divine heart shall be their safe refuge in this last moment.[49]

This last promise especially has been attacked for its potential to lead to the sin of presumption. But besides the fact that the promises have long been approved by the Holy See, their beneficial effects must be seen against the lingering effects of Jansenism, with its *a priori* assumption that some souls are predestined to hell, shown most especially in moral failure, which the Jansenists took as *prima facie* evidence for the lack of efficacious grace. Despite condemnations of Jansenism spreading out over almost two centuries, the fear of God engendered by that heresy proved surprisingly tenacious, against which the twelfth promise served as a healing balm. As Karl Rahner rightly points out, the trust in Christ called for here is thoroughly biblical:

> In general with regard to these promises, it should be noted that, looked at as a whole, they do not affirm or promise any more than what was [already] promised to absolute faith by the Lord himself. . . . What is "new" therefore in these promises is not exactly what is promised, but the circumstances that what are basically already evangelically promised objects are also promised to devotion to the Sacred Heart.[50]

Despite its deep grounding in Scripture, its consistent approbation from the Holy See, the canonization of Margaret Mary Alacoque, and its widespread popularity from the late nineteenth century to the eve of Vatican II, this devotion has nonetheless fallen on hard times. Partly this is due to the heavy stress on the need for the devotee to make reparations for the ongoing pain to the Sacred Heart, which can seem both endless and joyless; partly it is due to an excessively lachrymose pumping up of the emotions, which itself can be draining. But the real reason must no doubt be due to its excessive individualism (the same flaw we saw afflicting German Pietism and English Methodism). The growing popularity of the liturgical movement,

---

49. The complete list can be found in O'Donnell, *Heart of the Redeemer,* pp. 139-40.

50. Karl Rahner, "Some Theses for a Theology of Devotion to the Sacred Heart," *Theological Investigations,* vol. 3, *The Theology of the Spiritual Life,* trans. Karl-Heinz and Boniface Kruger (Baltimore: Helicon Press, 1967), pp. 331-54; here 351. In the ellipsis Rahner cites several key passages from the Gospels to support his thesis, perhaps the most important of which is this one: "I tell you the truth, anyone who has faith in me will do what I have been doing. He will do even greater things than these, because I am going to the Father" (John 14:12).

coupled with its endorsement by the Second Vatican Council, led to a re-markably swift decline in the popularity of the devotion, as more than one commentator has seen, very much including Joseph Ratzinger:

> Although the encyclical *Haurietis aquas* was written at a time when devo-tion to the Sacred Heart was still alive in the forms of the nineteenth cen-tury, a crisis in this kind of devotion was already clearly detectable. More and more, the spirituality of the liturgical movement was dominating the church's spiritual climate in Central Europe; this spirituality, drawing its nourishment from the classical shape of the Roman liturgy, deliberately turned its back on the emotionalistic piety of the nineteenth century and its symbolism. It saw its model in the strict form of the Roman *orationes*, in which feeling is restrained and there is an extreme sobriety of expres-sion, free of all subjectivity. Along with this went a theological cast of mind which wanted to steer entirely by Scripture and the Fathers, fash-ioning itself equally strictly according to the objective structural laws of the Christian edifice. The more emotional emphases of modern times were to be subordinated once more within this objective form.[51]

Although eminently predictable (at least in retrospect), the diminution of fervor toward the Sacred Heart has not been without its costs, specifically theological costs. Whenever the specifically emotional side of Jesus' human soul recedes into the background, one notices either a bloodless rationalism taking its place (as in the Enlightenment, which considered Jesus at best a teacher of morality) or a lazy attribution of human emotions to God, seen most especially in Jürgen Moltmann but also in many others.[52] Again, only a devotion to the Sacred Heart will address this concern of the believer for an involved God in a way that is doctrinally sound, as again Ratzinger points out:

> The topic of the suffering God has become almost fashionable today, not without reason, as a result of the abandonment of a theology which was one-sidedly rationalist and as a result of the rejection of a portrait of Jesus and a concept of God which had been emasculated, where the love of God had degenerated into the cheap platitude of a God who was merely kind,

51. Joseph Cardinal Ratzinger, "The Mystery of Easter: Substance and Foundation of Devotion to the Sacred Heart," in *Behold the Pierced One: An Approach to a Spiritual Chris-tology*, trans. Graham Harrison (San Francisco: Ignatius Press, 1986), pp. 47-69; here 47.

52. The trends that led to this "suffering God" motif will be treated in the next three chapters.

and hence "harmless." Against such a backdrop Christianity is diminished to the level of philanthropic world improvement, and Eucharist becomes a brotherly meal. . . . The encyclical *Haurietis aquas* sees the passions of Jesus, which are summed up and set forth in the Heart, as the basis, as the reason why, the human heart, i.e., the capacity for feeling, the emotional side of love, must be drawn into man's relationship with God. Incarnational spirituality must be a spirituality of the passions, a spirituality of "heart to heart"; in that way, precisely it is an Easter spirituality, for the mystery of Easter, the mystery of suffering, is of its very nature a mystery of the heart.[53]

Indeed, one can go one step further and say with Aquinas that Christ's emotions are part of what makes his mission salvific. Commenting on the famous passage on the raising of Lazarus in the Gospel of John, where it says: "When Jesus saw her weeping, and the Jews who had come along with her also weeping, he was deeply moved in spirit and troubled" (John 11:33), a passage followed almost immediately by the verse "Jesus wept" (v. 35), Thomas points to Paul's admonition, "rejoice with those who rejoice; mourn with those who mourn" (Rom. 12:15) to explain this scene and thus concludes:

> We should note that Christ is truly divine and truly human. And so in his actions we find almost everywhere that the divine is mingled with the human, the human with the divine. . . . We have a similar situation here: for Christ experiences a certain weakness in his human affections, becoming disturbed over the death of Lazarus. . . . Note that Christ willed to be troubled for two reasons. *First, to show us a doctrine of faith.* . . . Second, he wanted to be an example for us. For if he had remained unmoved and had felt no emotions in his soul, he would not have been a satisfactory example of how we should face death. And so he willed to be troubled in order that when we are troubled at the prospect of death, we will not refuse to endure it, we will not run away: "For we have not a high priest who is unable to sympathize with our weakness, but one who in every respect has been tempted as we are, yet without sinning" (Heb. 4:15). . . . But some

53. Ratzinger, *Behold the Pierced One*, pp. 59-60. Sara Butler sees this book as the key for understanding the papacy of Benedict XVI: "Ratzinger makes the case that a 'devotion' that engages the emotions and passions of the human heart is the only worthy response to the passion of the heart of God revealed on the Cross." Sara Butler, M.S.B.T., "Benedict XVI: Apostle of the 'Pierced Heart of Jesus,'" in *The Pontificate of Benedict XVI: Its Premises and Promises,* ed. William G. Rusch (Grand Rapids: Eerdmans, 2009), pp. 144-67; here 154.

might have said to him: "Lord, you can calmly discuss and philosophize about death because you are above human emotions, and death does not trouble you." It was to counter this that he willed to be troubled. *This disturbance in Christ was natural: for just as the soul naturally loves union with its body, so it naturally shrinks from separation from it, especially since the reason of Christ allowed his soul and its inferior powers to act in their own proper way.* Again, when he said "Now is my soul troubled," he refuted the error of Arius and Apollinaris. For they said that Christ did not have a soul, and in place of his soul they substituted the Word.[54]

The revelations of the Sacred Heart came to Margaret Mary to make these insights come alive in the church once more.

54. Thomas Aquinas, *Commentary on the Gospel of St. John,* Part II (Petersham, MA: St. Bede's, 1999), pp. 181, 236-37; emphasis added. I wish to thank Fr. Richard Schenk, O.P. for drawing my attention to this passage. Another scholar points out the relevance of Christ's emotions for the Christian's specifically moral development and pleads that they become a part of Christian ethics: "The Gospels describe Jesus Christ as passionate and emotional. He wept over the death of a close friend (John 11:35) and shed tears over the fate of Jerusalem (Matt. 23:37); Luke 19:41). He rejoiced with his disciples (Luke 10:21) and expressed affection for particular people — men (Mark 10:21; John 13:23) and women, adults and children (Matt. 19:13-14; Mark 10:13-14). He was roused to anger (30 references: Mark 10:14; 11:15-19), but also to express compassion (25 references: Luke 7:13). He suffered physical hunger, thirst, pain, and death. These passages (and many others) demonstrate that the four canonical Gospels describe Jesus Christ as passionate, even spontaneous in the expression of his emotions. . . . Contemporary moral theologians, especially those [who] are interested in moral progress that seeks to imitate Christ, have reason to be attentive to the quality of his passions and emotions." Craig Steven Titus, "Passions in Christ: Spontaneity, Development, and Virtue," *The Thomist* 73 (2009): 53-87, here 53-54. Again, as mentioned in Chapter 5, the definitive study of this issue is Paul Gondreau, *The Passions of Christ's Soul in the Theology of St. Thomas Aquinas* (Münster: Aschendorff, 2002).

CHAPTER 8

German Idealism and Kenotic Christology

The insidious thing about the causal point of view is that it leads us to say: "Of course, it had to happen like that." Whereas we ought to think: it may have happened like that — and also in many other ways. . . . One of the most important methods I use is to imagine a historical development for our ideas different from what actually occurred. If we do this we see the problem from a completely new angle.

Ludwig Wittgenstein, *Culture and Value*

Whereas the previous chapter stressed the devotional and doctrinal implications of those "Christologies of the heart" that made German Pietism, English Methodism, and French Catholicism so influential, the Christologies of the nineteenth century became noticeably more technical. The problem faced by many nineteenth-century theologians, first German Lutherans and later English Anglicans, stemmed from a reopening of the question left unanswered by Chalcedon: the question of the historical consciousness of Jesus.

But this question was really part of a wider problem for the nineteenth century, which represents for European civilization a new insight into the essential historicity of all forms of human consciousness. With the nineteenth century, history comes into its own as the focus for philosophy, and then in its wake theology. This chapter will first trace how that problem came to the fore in the movement from Kant through Schleiermacher and terminating in Hegel, stressing always the specifically theological concerns of these authors. Then we will treat the specific Christologies of several authors who tried to address the problems left in the wake of these epochal German thinkers.

German Idealism

In an intriguing insight, the theologian Eugene TeSelle speaks of Kant, Schleiermacher, and Hegel as writers who each shifted the interpretation of the three major articles of the Apostles' Creed on Father, Son, and Holy Spirit:

> In Kant we find a "Christology of the first article," in the sense that he was concerned with the general relationship of man to God and linked his Christology with an ideal to which all are called. . . . In Schleiermacher we find a "Christology of the second article," in that he tried to give an account of the Christian consciousness as a specific feeling of dependence upon Jesus of Nazareth as the unique actualization of the idea and denied the possibility of ever going beyond this direct dependence on Jesus. In Hegel we find a "Christology of the third article," in that he emphasized, as against Kant, the transformation that can occur in human life, the real reconciliation with God and the real participation in the divine life that can come into being, and, as against Schleiermacher, the necessity of its occurring in each individual life and with a certain independence of the historical Jesus.[1]

This insight, as I say, is intriguing; but it should not obscure the commonalities that these three Germans share, at least in regard to Christology. For all three men subsumed Jesus Christ into some more overarching framework. Kant, to allude to the title of one of his most influential books, famously wanted to confine "religion within the limits of reason alone." Schleiermacher saw Jesus as the greatest exemplar of a feeling of absolute dependence. And Hegel, citing a Swabian tagline from his youth ("That's been true for so long it's no longer true"), saw the historical fact of Jesus of Nazareth as an ever-receding *datum* of history whose contemporary relevance could only be rescued if theology allowed itself to be subsumed *(aufgehoben)* into philosophy. Furthermore, unlike the Creed, each man treats the three main articles more or less in exclusion of the others: Kant really has no place for Jesus or the Holy Spirit in his philosophy; Schleiermacher never really developed a fully satisfactory philosophy or theology of God; and Hegel's Spirit *(Geist)* is so relentlessly all-subsuming that all the facts of historical revelation end up being taken up into the all-absorbing maw of his philosophy.

---

1. Eugene TeSelle, *Christ in Context: Divine Purpose and Human Possibility* (Philadelphia: Fortress Press, 1975), p. 48.

Immanuel Kant

Immanuel Kant (1724-1804) stands at the crossroads of modern philosophy. As the noted historian of philosophy James Collins says, "All highways in modern philosophy converge upon [Kant] and lead out from him again."[2] Nowhere is this more true than in his philosophy of religion, which gathered up all the Continental strains of rationalism from Descartes, Spinoza, and Leibniz, along with the prestige of Isaac Newton's thoroughly rational account for the law of gravity, and bequeathed to the world the notion that unless theology could justify its claims before the bar of reason it had no claim on the attentions of rational beings.

Although (or perhaps because) he was raised in a strict Pietist household, Kant had, even from his youth, rebelled against his upbringing. He objected to religious ceremonies in principle as self-degrading acts of ingratiation of the Deity, held that creeds were an imposition on man's inner freedom of thought, and considered petitionary prayer the "wheedling of God."[3] But far from thinking himself to be the forerunner of later freethinkers, Kant insisted, as he famously said at the beginning of the second edition of his *Critique of Pure Reason,* that "I had to do away with knowledge in order to make room for faith."[4] However, that is not the concession it might at first seem, for Kant resolutely maintained throughout his life that morality does not rest on religion, rather religion rests on morality. In fact he defines religion as "the cognition of all duties as divine commands."[5] Thus Kant's philosophy of religion is, as he openly avers, a "moral theology," which he contrasts with what he calls "theological morality," defined by him as the superstitious reliance on theological concepts to justify morality.

These views obviously put Kant on a collision course with the concept of revelation as traditionally understood, and gave to his view of religion a revolutionary cast, as one commentator shrewdly notes:

> In Kant's view, what unites people in a true religious community is not a
> common cult or creed, but a common devotion to the moral improve-

2. James Collins, *God in Modern Philosophy* (Chicago: Henry Regnery, 1959), p. 162.

3. Immanuel Kant, *Religion within the Limits of Reason Alone*, trans. Theodore M. Greene and Hoyt H. Hudson (New York: Harper & Row, 1960/1793), pp. 182-97; cited henceforth as *Religion.*

4. Kant, *Critique of Pure Reason*, trans. Norman Kemp Smith (New York: St. Martin's Press, 1965/1787), p. 29 (B xxx). The "B" refers to Kant's second and much revised version.

5. Kant, *Religion*, p. 142.

ment of humanity. Religion, the disposition to observe all duties as divine commands, can therefore exhibit itself in a wide variety of personal faiths. . . . Kant does not rule out the beliefs of traditional, revealed ecclesiastical faith, so long as they are presented in a spirit that is compatible with a genuine moral religion of reason. The point that matters most to him here is that acceptance of doctrines depending on revelation rather than reason should not be regarded as *morally required* for true religion. This is crucial, because true religion aspires to be a universal ethical community embracing all humanity, and this is something that no revealed religion can pretend to be.[6]

Again, however, we must stress that Kant does not explicitly *deny* the possibility of revelation, for that too would exceed the powers of reason to assert. In fact, at one point Kant seems to concede its necessity, albeit in a backhanded way: "Kant thinks that such (necessarily ungrounded) claims to divine revelation are just as necessary to the foundation of religion as ambition and violence are to the founding of states."[7] But just as it exceeds the powers of reason to deny that revelation occurred, it also exceeds the powers of a human being to authenticate, via publicly accessible norms, the claim that he has received a revelation from God: "For if God actually spoke to a human being," Kant says, "the latter could never *know* that it was God who spoke to him. It is absolutely impossible for a human being to grasp the Infinite through the senses, so as to distinguish him from sensible beings and become *acquainted* with him."[8]

For these reasons, Kant understandably rarely takes up the question of Jesus, although his remarks on the Founder of Christianity in *Religion within the Limits of Reason Alone* would prove decisive for later debate, especially in Germany. At first glance, it would seem impossible for Kant to find a place for Christ in his religion — unless he can show both that morality is the essence of Christianity and that the sole purpose of Christ's teaching on earth was to promote morality. This Kant attempts to do when he treats spe-

---

6. Allen W. Wood, "Rational Theology, Moral Faith, and Religion," in *The Cambridge Companion to Kant,* ed. Paul Guyer (Cambridge: Cambridge University Press, 1992), pp. 394-416; here 411; italics in the original.

7. Wood, "Rational Theology," pp. 412-13.

8. Kant, *Conflict of the Faculties,* trans. Mary J. Gregor (New York: Arabis Books, 1979/1798), p. 63; original emphases. This view hearkens back to Thomas Hobbes, who noted that when someone says "I met God in a dream," his listener can only report this news as "He had a dream of God."

cifically of Christianity in *Religion*. At one point he tellingly asserts that "we need no empirical example to make the idea of a person morally well pleasing to God our archetype; this idea, as an archetype, is already present in our reason."[9] Yet mankind also needs at least one example of someone who shows that it is possible to live up to this archetype of being morally well pleasing to God. In a remarkable anticipation of Schleiermacher, Kant holds Jesus up as the perfect exemplar of that archetype:

> This ideal of a humanity pleasing to God (and hence of such moral perfection as is possible to an *earthly* being who is subject to wants and inclinations), we can represent to ourselves only as the *idea* of a person who would be willing not merely to discharge all human duties and to spread about him goodness as widely as possible by precept and example, but, even though tempted by the greatest allurements, to take upon himself every affliction, up to the most ignominious death, for the good of the world, and even for his enemies.[10]

Friedrich Schleiermacher

The parallels with the Christology of Friedrich Schleiermacher (1768-1834) are more than obvious, made even more evident by the known fact that he studied Kant at the University of Halle, where he had matriculated in 1787. But Schleiermacher was no mere Kantian epigone, slavishly reproducing the master's thought. For far more than Kant, Schleiermacher stressed, in common with the budding Romanticism of the period, the role of *feeling* in religion.

Like Kant, he maintained that religion was an anthropological constant; but he saw the universality of religion as based in a more fundamental reality than morality. For he held that, from the time of his conception, man is utterly dependent on others, indeed on his whole environment, for his existence. But since everyone, however dimly, recognizes that even the universe as a whole cannot account for its own existence, man's consistent feeling of dependence — on the womb, on his parents, on air, water, food, society, and so forth — implicitly recognizes an *absolute* dependence, whence arises the feeling of the need for God. Polytheism refracts that feeling of absolute dependence through the prism of this multifaceted dependence by positing

---

9. Kant, *Religion*, p. 56.
10. Kant, *Religion*, p. 55. Kant's emphases.

many gods on which human society depends. But the great virtue of monotheism, for Schleiermacher, is that this feeling of absolute dependence comes to its purest expression in the recognition that, whereas the gods are born from the universe and thus in some sense dependent on it as well, monotheism recognizes the dependence of the universe as a whole on the absolutely independent God.

Doctrine, therefore, for Schleiermacher is but the second-order reflection on prior experience. Hence a theologian cannot claim for dogmatics a foundation in proofs; on the contrary, theology can only be pursued "by each man willing to have the experience [of being a Christian] for himself. . . . [It] can only be apprehended by the love that wills to perceive."[11] Even more explicitly, he tells us that Christian doctrines are but "accounts of the religious Christian affections set forth in speech" (*CF* §15). This assertion obviously implies that the starting point for his Christology will have to be the *experience* of redemption in Christ. Then, in a move directly reliant on Kant's transcendental method, Schleiermacher insists that a dogmatic Christology must ask: Given this experience, what are the conditions for its possibility?

He first begins negatively, with dogmatic positions (in traditional terms, heresies) that make the experience of redemption in Christ antecedently impossible, what he calls the "four natural heresies" (*CF* §22). These are "the Docetic and the Nazarean, the Manichean and the Pelagian" (*CF* §22).[12] The first two concern the person of Christ, while the second pair refers to the soteriological appropriation of the meaning of redemption. In a lucid essay Jacqueline Mariña sees exactly what this taxonomy means in Schleiermacher's Christology:

> If Jesus is to be the redeemer, two conditions must be met. First, he must be *like* us, that is, he must have a nature essentially like our own. Second, he must not himself stand in need of redemption, and he must have the requisite power to save those that need redemption. In this regard he must be *unlike* us. The first heresy, which Schleiermacher labels the Docetic, re-

11. Friedrich Daniel Ernst Schleiermacher, *The Christian Faith,* trans. H. R. Mackintosh and James Stuart Stewart (Edinburgh: T. & T. Clark, 1928/1999), §13.2; because of the variety of editions and translations, citations will not give the page numbers, but section numbers, which all German and English editions share. Further citations will be made in the body of the text, abbreviated as *CF.*

12. Subsequent remarks by Schleiermacher show that by docetic and "Nazarean" heresies he is referring to what later, more careful taxonomy calls monophysitism and Nestorianism, respectively.

sults from thinking of Jesus as so exalted above human nature that he does not partake of it. . . . The second heresy results from thinking of Jesus as so similar to other members of the human race that "no room is left for a distinctive superiority" (*CF* §22). In such a case he himself would stand in need of redemption, and would be powerless to effect the redemption of others.[13]

If this analysis shows how thinking about Jesus can go wrong, Schleiermacher also recognizes that a theologian must explain positively how "in Jesus Christ divine nature and human nature were combined into one person" (*CF* §96). No sooner has he formulated the problem in traditional Chalcedonian terms, however, than he immediately proceeds to reject the language of "two natures," insisting that "even pagans" realized that God cannot have a nature since God "is to be thought of as beyond all existence and being" (*CF* §96).[14] In other words, one cannot speak of God having a divine *nature*. Such a position might seem to undermine Chalcedon from the start; but for Schleiermacher the benefits outweigh the disadvantages. For him Chalcedon was correct in what it rejected and gains its validity from its rejection of impossible extremes. But the positive two-natures doctrine will not work, especially if the divine nature is defined purely negatively as the diametric opposite of human nature (infinite over against finite, impassible over against a suffering human nature, and so forth).

Schleiermacher finesses this problem by a move that will prove epochal for all later liberal Christologies: he says that the incarnation means that the ideal human nature (Plato again) becomes real for the first time in Jesus Christ. To justify that claim, he must first insist that sin is fundamentally adventitious (accidental) to the human essence. Thus he says that "it has always been assumed in Christian faith that a union with God is possible in terms of man's essence."[15] In one sense this is true, in that Adam and Eve

13. Jacqueline Mariña, "Christology and Anthropology," in *The Cambridge Companion to Friedrich Schleiermacher,* ed. Jacqueline Mariña (Cambridge: Cambridge University Press, 2005), p. 152.

14. Schleiermacher has often been called the "father of modern theology," which certainly holds true if one defines "modern" as "liberal." But he was also a philosopher of no mean talents, whose translations of Plato were so mellifluously accomplished that they still serve as the benchmark for all later German translations. I mention this because he was probably influenced in his rejection of two-natures language in Christology by Plato's doctrine that the Form of the Good exceeds even Being (Plato, *Republic* 509b).

15. Schleiermacher, *The Life of Jesus,* trans. S. Maclean Gilmour (Philadelphia: Fortress Press, 1975), p. 100.

were created sinless and only sinned out of free choice. But that's the point: once they did sin, man thereafter was born in a state of sin, as Paul clearly teaches throughout his letters: "Scripture makes no exception when it says that sin is master everywhere" (Gal. 3:22); "For I know that nothing good dwells within me, that is, in my flesh" (Rom. 7:17); and *that* is the flesh assumed by Christ: "For God has done what the law, weakened by the flesh, could not do: sending his own Son in the likeness of sinful flesh and as a sin offering, he condemned sin in the flesh" (Rom. 8:3). Thus Paul can say, in his most radical doctrine of soteriology, that God "made him who knew no sin to be sin" (2 Cor. 5:21).

In other words, besides jettisoning all talk of a divine nature, Schleiermacher also does not take seriously enough the depth of the *sinful* flesh Christ took on.[16] Even assuming that he is correct in asserting that the essence of human nature can be united with God, Schleiermacher cannot assume that Jesus is united to God in a way that allows him to be a redeemer *simply* through his human nature reaching the ideal of an already possible union with God. Perhaps if sin had never entered the world, then there would be no contradiction in thinking of Jesus as both fully human and as united with God. But that does not describe the real world Christ came to redeem. But such is his conclusion: "To ascribe to Christ an absolutely powerful God-consciousness, and to attribute to Him an existence of God in Him, are exactly the same thing" (*CF* §94).[17]

16. This point is made with great vigor by Thomas Weinandy: "Schleiermacher denied the traditional notion of the Incarnation, that the eternal Son of God came to exist as a man. In its place, Schleiermacher substituted a Christology of God-consciousness. Jesus' divinity consisted in his human consciousness being thoroughly centered upon and absorbed by the divine. Paradoxically, what happens in such a Christology is that, while it is proffered in order to make Jesus more like us, in actual fact, it makes him less like us for it makes his humanity so radically different from our own. There could have been no inner conflict, no true agony or struggle. The historical concrete, human Jesus, with his temptations and sufferings, would have been absorbed in the Buddha- or Hindu-like mystical and ethereal clouds of divine consciousness." Thomas Weinandy, O.F.M. Cap., *In the Likeness of Sinful Flesh: An Essay on the Humanity of Christ* (Edinburgh: T. & T. Clark, 1993), p. 55, note 2.

17. The irony is that such a move ends up downplaying Christ's humanity, which again Weinandy explains to devastating effect: "With this contemporary accent on the human subjectivity of Jesus and the often subsequent de-emphasis of his divine personhood, there has been, paradoxically, a defensive emphasis on the man Jesus' union or relationship with God/Son/Word so as not to be accused of some heresy, such as adoptionism. Despite the original intent, this tactical maneuver has shifted the christological focus to a demonstration of how the man Jesus significantly differed from us. . . . The lesson to be learned is that whenever the divine personhood of Christ is not accorded its proper standing, his authentic

Such a position leads Schleiermacher to a kind of monothelitism in reverse: instead of saying that Christ had only one divine will, now he has only one human will. Thus, instead of saying that the divine in Jesus is a real, discrete, personal consciousness, he says that Christ's God-consciousness is "something that lies at the *basis* of [his] total consciousness."[18] According to him, as soon as one posits a discrete divine consciousness in Jesus coexisting independently from his human will, "we clearly put an end to the unity of the personality."[19]

Schleiermacher thus bequeathed to liberal Christology its central presuppositions, which live on to this day: 1) Jesus' only true subjectivity is a human personality; 2) Jesus lives inside a God-consciousness that is but the pinnacle and culminating exemplar of what is already possible in human consciousness in human nature and in all the world religions without exception; 3) the legacy of the sin of Adam cannot therefore have impaired in any fundamental way a human being's God-consciousness; and 4) religious life is fundamentally a life of feeling, however evanescent. But as Karl Barth noted, not without a tone of biting sarcasm: if that is all Jesus represents in salvation history, then his coming is about as remarkable in mankind's religious history as "the formation of a new nebula" is for the cosmologist.[20]

A loss, no doubt. But for Schleiermacher the price was worth it, considering what he gained: a *publicly accessible and therefore academically respectable* Christology. Even if he did not share the presupposition of the roughly contemporaneous British utilitarians like Jeremy Bentham and John Stuart Mill that feelings could be measured along a pain/pleasure calculus ("the greatest happiness for the greatest number"), he did hold that all human beings had some inkling of the feeling of absolute dependence. Indeed, this for him was the anthropological basis for explaining the universality of religion in human societies. Furthermore, he believed he could show that, on strictly descriptive, phenomenological grounds, monotheism represents a more pristine expression of that feeling of absolute dependence and that, among the monotheistic religions, Christianity represents the most pristine expres-

---

humanity is consequently and immediately imperiled because it is then forced to bear the 'divine' weight left in its absence." Weinandy, *In the Likeness of Sinful Flesh*, pp. 54-55. On this distinction see Thomas Aquinas, *ST* III q.15 a.1 ad 4.

18. Weinandy, *In the Likeness of Sinful Flesh*, p. 97; emphasis added.

19. Weinandy, *In the Likeness of Sinful Flesh*, p. 96.

20. Karl Barth, *The Theology of Schleiermacher: Lectures at Göttingen, Winter Semester 1923/24*, ed. Dietrich Ritschl, trans. Geoffrey W. Bromiley (Grand Rapids: Eerdmans, 1982), p. 205.

sion of monotheism because Jesus was himself the one human being who most lived out — and showed us how to live out — that feeling.[21]

At first glance, this move seems to solve two problems at once: the problem of the public accessibility to academic study of the faith-claims of Christology, and the question of religious pluralism. But as subsequent history would show, the results did not live up to the promise. First, how can something as evanescent as feelings be measured, and against which standard? Second, as Friedrich Nietzsche would later point out, feelings are fundamentally biological reactions arising out of the struggle for life and thus are at root expressions of the "will to power," and thus do not lend themselves to the adjudication of a more rational schema. Seen from that point of view, Schleiermacher's assertion of the superiority of Jesus Christ is unveiled as the inner expression of Christianity's hegemonic drive to obliterate other cultures and religious worldviews.

The Nietzschean rejoinder obviously comes from the non-Christian side, but it does point out that the more the academy became influenced by post-Nietzschean relativism, the less Schleiermacher's version of Christology could gain a hearing from the Christian religion's "cultured despisers." But there is another, and a more telling, objection that came from within: that what Schleiermacher has in effect done is to subsume Jesus Christ into a more overarching framework (founder of a world religion on the analogue with other founders; prime exemplar of the feeling of absolute dependence which all other human beings share, albeit to a lesser degree, etc.), whereas the Christian kerygma proclaims Christ as the sole and definitive incarnation of God the Son "in whom the fullness of the deity was pleased to dwell" (Col. 1:19). Or as Barth put it, Schleiermacher has given us a quantitative Christology, but the New Testament bears witness to a qualitative Christology, and the former will always dissolve the latter. And since Paul says that no one can say "Jesus is Lord" except in the Holy Spirit (1 Cor. 12:3), which is

---

21. In a book written twenty-five years after his Göttingen lectures, Barth gives a more neutral description of what Schleiermacher is trying to do here (which of course he will also go on to criticize): "Schleiermacher's presentation of the faith . . . rests on the basis of a highest knowledge of human feeling or immediate self-awareness in its correlation to God, upon the basis of a highest knowledge of the nature and value of faith and the diversity of ways of believing altogether. It is not the Christian religion but the type to which this phenomenon belongs, religion as a necessary manifestation of human intellectual life, which is for Schleiermacher an object of speculative knowledge of an *a priori* kind." Karl Barth, *Protestant Theology in the Nineteenth Century: Its Background and History*, trans. Brian Cozens and John Bowden (Grand Rapids: Eerdmans, 1947/2001), p. 435.

the quintessential qualitative confession, this means — Barth does not hesitate to assert — that Schleiermacher is fashioning his Christology outside of the witness of the Holy Spirit:

> Schleiermacher's Christology has as its summit the indication of a quantitative superiority, dignity and significance in Christ in relation to our own Christianity. This is as much to say that . . . [Christ] has only an incomparably greater quantity of what we see in ourselves as *our* Christianity. . . . The Word is thereby not grounded here independently of faith as would be the case if [Schleiermacher's] theology of faith were a true theology of the Holy Spirit. In a proper theology of the Holy Spirit there would be no question of dissolving the Word.[22]

As is well known, Protestant divinity has never resolved this tension between Schleiermacher and Barth, and subsequent portions of this book will indicate a few key moments in that unfolding debate. For a while, Barth bestrode the world of Protestant theology like a colossus and completely overshadowed Schleiermacher. But after his death in 1968 the increased influence of post-Nietzschean relativism (which usually goes under the umbrella term "postmodernism") has led to a noticeable ebbing in Barth's influence outside of a few redoubts in Scotland and Princeton Theological Seminary. But Schleiermacher too has been caught in that same undertow and precisely because he claimed a neutral point of view for coming up with the (surely not coincidental) conclusion that Jesus is superior to all other "founders of world religions."

Furthermore, the pounding effects of the historical-critical study of the New Testament, which finally took flight in the nineteenth century and came to dominate all discussions of the historical Jesus, led to a view that we can know nothing, biographically considered, about the personal consciousness of Jesus. Thus the foundations so laboriously laid down by Schleiermacher rapidly crumbled. Clearly, the question of the relationship between history and faith had to be reopened: What is the relationship between the elusive facts dredged up by scientific historians and the universal truths of philosophy and theology? Which now brings us to Hegel's encounter with this now unavoidable problem and whose answer forms one of the essential steppingstones in that journey leading to the decline of Christocentrism in Protestant theology.

---

22. Barth, *Protestant Theology in the Nineteenth Century,* p. 457; emphasis added and translation silently emended.

Georg W. F. Hegel

In a famous sneer Nietzsche once described German Idealism as nothing but *hinterlistige Theologie* ("insidious theology"). Obviously he means that Hegel's Lutheran upbringing vitiated his philosophy, but theologians who claim his philosophy did damage to theology perhaps have a greater claim to the remark. As we saw at the outset of this chapter, Hegel was fond of the Swabian dismissive apothegm: "That's been true for so long it's stopped being true." This is the trouble with Christianity, he felt: it is too rooted in the ever-receding positivity of history, too reliant on facts that will eventually lose their grip on later generations — thus for him it is not the historical Good Friday that saves but only what he called a *speculative* Good Friday.[23]

Schleiermacher's near contemporary, Georg Wilhelm Friedrich Hegel (1770-1831) was born in Stuttgart and entered a Protestant seminary (called a *Stift*) in Tübingen in 1788, ostensibly to study for the Lutheran ministry. He stayed there until 1793, when he took up a three-year stint as a private tutor to a wealthy family in Switzerland, where he wrote two tracts clearly showing his theological interests: a *Life of Jesus* expounding Jesus as an exemplar of Kantian ethics;[24] and *The Positivity of the Christian Religion,* which adumbrated his concern with the ability of history to teach timeless truth, a book that also condemned Christian legalism in contrast to the alleged "spontaneity" of Jesus.

It is difficult to know how much these ideas had already taken shape in

---

23. One can of course take a more appreciative tack and see how much fruit can be harvested from Hegel's attempt to wrestle with the philosophical implications of the Christian message, a strategy adopted by James Yerkes, *The Christology of Hegel* (Albany: State University of New York Press, 1983), from which I will be drawing throughout this section. The book's opening paragraph sets the tone right away: "This essay is an attempt to demonstrate that Hegel's mature speculative philosophy of the Absolute as Spirit may best be understood as an explicit function of distinctly religious presuppositions — presuppositions which ultimately are rooted in his convictions about the decisive revelatory and redemptive importance of the Christ event in human history. It is in connection with these presuppositions that I think it is proper to speak about Hegel's 'christology,' for christological interpretation in the theology of the Christian church has always revolved round the question of the universal religious significance of the historical Christ event. It is this question, and the speculative answer which Hegel assayed to put forth about it, that makes his thought for me a matter of theological interest" (p. 1).

24. His rough contemporary Thomas Jefferson published an expurgated version of the gospels in which accounts of the miracles were excised, leaving only Jesus' moral teachings intact.

his mind in his seminary days. Certainly he must have read Kant intensively in Tübingen, and it was there also that he learned to regard the culture of Greece as the pinnacle of human achievement, which would have such important effects on his view of Christianity. But his life at the *Stift* cannot have been so traumatic as to make him abjure his religious upbringing, for he later insisted that the Christian doctrine of the incarnation was the "speculative central point"[25] of his system. Furthermore, in a manner redolent of Schleiermacher he claimed that, in contrast to all other religious worldviews, the Christ event was "absolutely adequate" for revealing the truth about God.[26] Finally, Hegel never denied his Lutheran faith and indeed on one occasion later in his life spoke of himself as belonging to the confessional circle of "we Lutherans" and then added: "I am and intend to remain one."[27]

That said, his reaction to the Lutheran orthodoxy of the Tübingen *Stift* must have been neuralgic, for the writings during his Swiss stint as a tutor betray an intense intellectual pain about the place of Christianity in a post-Kantian world — and his own place as a Christian in that same world.[28] These young writings, cited usually even in English by their German name, the *Jugendschriften,* never resolved the tension between his enthusiasm for Kant and his religious upbringing; but they did launch him on a six-year intellectual journey during his years at Jena that culminated in his epochal *Phenomenology of Spirit,* which he wrote, he said, "to reach the stage of genuine knowledge," for which "a long and laborious journey must be undertaken," a "road [that] can be looked on as the path of doubt, or more properly, a highway of despair."[29]

Part of Hegel's torment was clearly due to the incompatibility of the Tübingen version of Christianity with Kant's version of the Enlightenment, which Hegel entirely accepted.[30] But he was also growing increasingly dissat-

---

25. G. W. F. Hegel, *Lectures on the Philosophy of Religion,* trans. E. B. Spiers and J. B. Sanderson, 3 vols. (New York: Humanities Press, 1962), vol. 1, p. 151.

26. Hegel, *Lectures on the Philosophy of Religion,* vol. 1, p. 113.

27. *Hegel's Lectures on the History of Philosophy,* trans. E. S. Haldane and F. H. Simpson, 3 vols. (New York: Humanities Press, 1963), vol. 1, p. 63.

28. Nor can it have helped that Hegel had originally hoped to enter the study of law but was forced into the study of dogmatic theology by his father (exactly the reverse of what happened to Calvin, whose father forced his son to drop theology for law). Also, at the time Tübingen was dominated by a now-forgotten conservative Lutheran by the name of G. C. Storr.

29. Hegel, *Phenomenology of Mind,* trans. J. B. Baillie (New York: Harper, 1964), pp. 88, 135.

30. As he says in the *Phenomenology,* "It is not hard to see that our time is a time of

isfied with Kant as well. This growing unease probably accounts, at least in part, for his glowing views on the culture of Greece, especially of Periclean Athens, which he felt had discovered the ideal relation between religion and state, and between reason and feeling.[31] This enthusiasm for Greece resulted in several departures from the Kantian worldview: first, it gave him a vision of the social dimension of alienation and the possibility *in history* for its ultimate amelioration; second, it gave him a new appreciation for feeling and "heart" versus the bloodless abstractions of the Kantian system; third (and fatefully), it provided him with the contrast between the humane "light" of Hellas and the legalistic "dreariness" of Jewish legalism, which would tinge his Christology from then on out. As to that Christology, Yerkes rightly says:

> Hegel's final estimate of Jesus' religious significance in history, as understood by the witness of the Christian community in doctrine and cult, was the accumulated result of his early moves in these essays [of the *Jugendschriften*] away from what he called the purely "formal" and "abstract" interpretation of religion developed under Kant's Enlightenment ideal of "critical philosophy," towards the more "concrete" interpretation of religion under the Graeco-Romantic ideal of living intuition rooted in imagination and heart.[32]

As everyone knows, the result of all these tensions led Hegel to produce a remarkable system of philosophy, whose impact on world history can hardly be exaggerated. It can of course be no part of this book to follow him along the highways and byways of his extremely intricate thought, which pertains more to the history of philosophy than of Christology. I am thinking especially of his way of narrating history as a ceaseless movement of thesis met by its contradictory antithesis, the clash between which results in a higher synthesis, which both supersedes [*aufhebt*] the past clash and constitutes its own new thesis, ready to meet the next antithesis, resulting in a new synthesis, and so on. But at least this must be mentioned because of its effect

birth and the transition to a new period. The spirit [of man] has broken with the former world's manner of existing and expressing itself, and is at the point of letting it sink into the depths of the past and of working toward its own transformation" (p. 75).

31. "The impact of this Hellenic ideal on the young Hegel can hardly be overestimated — an idea glorified in the poetic works of his friend Hölderlin and those great writers Goethe and Schiller" (Yerkes, *Christology of Hegel*, p. 11). Hölderlin and Hegel were roommates at the *Stift*, which must have made for some remarkable late-night dorm-room conversations.

32. Yerkes, *Christology of Hegel*, p. 9; author's emphasis removed and his technical German terms translated into English.

both on Hegel's Christology and on later theology: *Hegel has subsumed history under the rubric of a necessary process of reason.*

Second, Hegel works back from contingent beings to God but in a way that quite inverts Thomas Aquinas's apparently similar *a posteriori* method; but in contrast to Thomas, Hegel sees the contingent creature as essentially a *negative* being:

> In an ordinary inference, the being of the finite appears as the ground of the absolute: the absolute *is* because the finite *is*. The truth, however, is that the absolute *is* just because the finite is self-contradictory opposition — just because, in other words, it [the finite] *is not*. . . . Not because the contingent *is,* but rather because it is a *non*being, only appearance (meaning, its being *not* veritable actuality), absolute necessity is. This is [contingency's only] being and its truth.[33]

This passage is undoubtedly murky, but it can be made clearer when Hegel combines these two insights together (that is, history-as-dialectic and God-as-the-posited-positive to the creature's negativity) in this telling passage:

> Thus the despotism of the Roman emperors had chased the human spirit from the earth and spread a misery which compelled men to seek and expect happiness in heaven. Now robbed of freedom, their spirit, their eternal and absolute element, was forced to take flight to the deity. God's objectivity is thus a counterpart to the corruption and slavery of man, and it is strictly speaking only a revelation, a manifestation, of the spirit of the age. . . . God was put into another world where we had no part, to which we contributed nothing by our activity, but into which, at best, we could beg or conjure our way.[34]

In other words, Hegel is the originator — well before Ludwig Feuerbach or Sigmund Freud — of the view that religions are essentially historical forms of projection that respond to social conditions of alienation by imagining a better world beyond this vale of tears (the "pie in the sky" theory, as it is popularly known).[35] How this projection-theory born out of social alien-

33. Hegel, *Science of Logic,* trans. W. H. Johnston and I. G. Struthers, 2 vols. (New York: Macmillan, 1929), vol. 2, p. 70; emphases in the original.

34. Hegel, "The Positivity of the Christian Religion," in *Early Theological Writings,* trans. T. M. Knox and R. Kroner (Chicago: University of Chicago Press, 1948), pp. 162-63.

35. Hegel often returns to this point, as in his preface to the *Phenomenology:* "Formerly

ation affected his Christology we shall get to in a moment. But there is another side to the story that must be treated first.

As is well known, Hegel's system gave rise to two contradictory schools of response, the so-called left and right Hegelians, with Feuerbach and Marx on the left, whose fame and later influence eclipsed the long-forgotten Hegelian epigones on the right — except for Hegel himself, who clearly would have sided with the right Hegelians. To be sure, in his days as a student at the Tübingen *Stift* and as a tutor in Bern, he spoke of dogma as alienation, but the trauma of the French Revolution noticeably altered his outlook. Contemporary neoconservatives are often described, in a famous quip, as liberals who have been mugged by reality, and that description fits Hegel too, at least to some extent. Not only did he grow increasingly appalled by the horrors of the French Revolution, but its issuance into the military dictatorship of Napoleon Bonaparte almost led to Hegel getting literally mugged: as he was finishing the *Phenomenology* and trying to get the text ready for the typesetters and an increasingly frantic publisher, Napoleon's armies were besieging Jena, and the traumatic effect it had on him emerges in the Preface, which was being written as Napoleon's army was marching through the city:

> Now the opposite need meets the eye: meaning [*Sinn*] seems to be so firmly rooted in what is worldly that it takes an equal force to raise it higher. The spirit [of man] appears so poor that, like a wanderer in the desert who languishes for a simple drink of water, it seems to crave for its refreshment merely the bare feeling of the divine in general. Simply by considering what the spirit needs and what suffices it, we can measure the extent of its loss.[36]

Hegel had always asserted that the doctrine of the incarnation stood as the "speculative midpoint" of his system, and the point must surely be granted.[37] His fear of the lasting effects of the French Revolution devolving

---

[otherworldly types of metaphysics] had a heaven furnished with abundant riches of thoughts and images. The significance of all that used to lie in the thread of light that tied it to the heavens; and, following this thread, the eye, instead of abiding in the present, rose above all that to the divine essence. . . . The eye of the spirit [thus] had to be directed *forcibly* to the things of the earth and kept there." In *Hegel: Reinterpretation, Texts, and Commentary*, trans. Walter Kaufmann (Garden City, NY: Doubleday, 1965), p. 15; emphasis added.

36. Kaufmann, trans., *Hegel: Reinterpretation, Texts, and Commentary*, p. 16; this passage goes far to explain the rise of fundamentalism as a response to a desiccated modernity.

37. A negative proof of that claim would be the disappointment that left Hegelians expressed about his reconciliation of Christianity and philosophy, from Nietzsche's accusation

into Napoleonic tyranny really reflects his fear for the future of Germany, which for him could only be avoided through a renewed understanding of God intimately related to the processes — above all, the negative processes — of history: "The specter of the political and social terrors of the French Revolution never ceased to haunt Hegel as what lay ahead for Germany if its inner spiritual substance was not disciplined by careful reflection and by a renewal of religious confidence in the living God as the ground and guarantor of *all* creative history."[38]

No wonder, then, that Hegel was drawn to the Christian doctrine of the incarnation, for he saw it as the way of justifying, indeed of *guaranteeing,* a speculative concept of God as always inherently a God immanently present to and *in relation with* man and his world. Only such a concept, he felt, could make God meaningful. No longer would God be dwelling in an inaccessible heaven "out there," in the manner of the English deists. To be sure, Hegel was not a theologian in the professional sense (he spends little time on the technicalities of Chalcedonian Christology, for example), but his views had immense influence on later theologians.[39] For example, George Rupp claims that "variables in Christology are correlative with differences in approaches to and interpretations of personal, social, and cultural life,"[40] a claim that could never be made except in Hegel's wake.

Not that Hegel's attention to the pathos of modern man as the touchstone of his Christology is without problems, as the dilemmas of liberation theology will prove, which hitched its wagon to a Marxian social analysis just a few years before the collapse of the Soviet Union. Plus, when theology gets

---

of "insidious theology" to Walter Kaufmann. But that's their problem, not Hegel's: "Though Kaufmann and others have bemoaned the eventual reconciliation of Hegel with Christian religion in the speculative thrust of his final philosophical system, Hegel himself, during the most productive years of his career as a philosopher, never left any question as to the fact that that very system owed its primary speculative inspiration to a more profound understanding of the Christian religion" (Yerkes, *The Christology of Hegel,* p. 7).

38. Yerkes, *Christology of Hegel,* pp. 213-14; Yerkes's emphasis.

39. In fact Hegel insisted he had no intention of poaching on the theologians' preserve: "Philosophy sets itself merely above the form of faith, the content is the same in both cases. . . . In faith, the true content is certainly already found [without the midwifery of philosophy]." Hegel, *Lectures on the Philosophy of Religion,* vol. 1, p. 80. On this see William C. Shepherd, "Hegel as a Theologian," *Harvard Theological Review* 61 (1968): 583-602: "If nothing else, Hegel has been set forth [here] as a much more subtle theological theorist than is ordinarily supposed, especially by those who automatically castigate him for making philosophy master over the handmaiden theology" (p. 602).

40. George Rupp, *Christologies and Cultures* (The Hague: Mouton, 1974), p. 1.

politicized, debate gets polarized; and technical issues that can only be resolved by careful scientific reasoning never even get addressed, lest they distract us from changing "sinful social structures." Indeed, that very program begs a question that Nietzsche was the first to see: by seeking redemption in ordinary grubby politics, life rapidly devolves into what he called "Great Politics." That is, politics pursued as an eschatological drama that only leads to disaster:

> Then the concept of politics will be completely dissolved in a war between spirits, all authority structures of the old society will be blown into the air — one and all, they rest upon a lie. There will be wars the likes of which have never existed on earth. From my time forward earth will see Great Politics.[41]

But even if history has refuted Hegel's hopes, and even though theologians ranging from traditional Thomists to Karl Barth, Eric Voegelin, and Hans Urs von Balthasar leveled extremely heavy artillery at Hegel's over-immanentizing of God's relation to the world, his legacy still lives on, even among those who most object to his influence, a point nicely captured by Yerkes:

> Kant, Schleiermacher and Hegel all share the concern to articulate . . . an "archetype christology." . . . That is to say, the overriding concern of these three thinkers, christologically speaking, was to try to show in what sense Jesus has a *personal* and *present* religious significance for human self-understanding in the ongoing economy of God's redemptive work in the world. The emphasis was not on the Jesus of the past, but on the Jesus who, religiously speaking, remains decisively significant by coming to us in the present. For these thinkers who lived after the rise of the historical-critical method in the eighteenth century, the idea that historiographical science can ever produce absolute "certainty" about who the Jesus of the past "really was" in his inner self-consciousness, or that the "objective" results of such a science could ever provide an adequate basis of faith, was clearly unthinkable.[42]

---

41. Friedrich Nietzsche, *Ecce Homo*, in *Sämtliche Werke*, ed. Giorgio Colli and Mazzino Montinari (Berlin: De Gruyter, 1988), vol. 6, p. 365; my translation.

42. Yerkes, *Christology of Hegel*, p. 215.

Kenotic Christology: Thomasius, Gess, Mackintosh

The names of Gottfried Thomasius (1802-75), Wolfgang Friedrich Gess (1819-91), and Hugh Ross Mackintosh (1870-1936) are not exactly household names, even among professional theologians. Their neglected status testifies not just to the esoteric nature of the questions they set for themselves but also to the fact that the answers they developed eventually came to be rejected by a wide spectrum of theologians. To be sure, that rejection had different, even opposite reasons: some rejected these three for their alleged unorthodoxy, while others scored them for their alleged pusillanimity before the challenge of historical criticism. Their inclusion in this work might therefore seem eccentric, except for two facts: their failure is itself instructive, and later theologians would claim to have learned from their mistakes and would then seek to revive a more orthodox version of kenotic Christology.

For that is the name of their school of Christological thought: kenotic. At first glance, it might seem surprising that any such school would run into trouble, grounded as it is in Paul's line that Christ "emptied" *(ekenōsen)* himself to take on the form of a slave (Phil. 2:7). For as Thomas Thompson points out:

> Every Christology of Incarnational tack celebrates a kenotic motif. Only the most docetic of Christological models depreciate the deigning grace of God the Son, who though rich became poor for our sakes. Such impugn the gospel witness: that the wisdom of God is uniquely cruciform, and therefore humble and meek — a refinement in the doctrine of God that many Greeks found unpalatably foolish. At the heart of its confession, the catholic church has long affirmed the humbling, self-accommodating, lisping humanity of God. In this broad thematic sense a "kenotic Christology" is rather a tautology, much like a "theology of hope."[43]

The situation is made even odder by the professed claims of the kenotic theologians that they were being faithful to the central pillars of Chalcedonian dogma: the true deity, the true humanity, and the true unity of these two in the single personhood of Christ. As Thomasius said in his most influ-

---

43. Thomas R. Thompson, "Nineteenth-Century Kenotic Christology: The Waxing, Waning, and Weighing of a Quest for a Coherent Orthodoxy," in *Exploring Kenotic Christology: The Self-Emptying of God,* ed. C. Stephan Evans (Oxford: Oxford University Press, 2006), pp. 74-111; here 74; cited henceforth as *Exploring.* I shall be relying throughout this section on Thompson's remarkably lucid chapter.

ential work, *Christi Person und Werk,* his dogmatic textbook using Christology as its organizing central focus: "Accordingly, for the treatment of Christology, we can set down the canon that every conception of the person of the mediator that endangers either the reality of his deity, or the truth of his humanity, or the unity of his person is an erroneous one."[44]

So far, so Chalcedonian; but patristic Christology also had another axiom that became problematic for the nineteenth century: the immutability and impassibility of God *(apatheia).* Because of that axiom, whenever Scripture speaks of the Word *becoming* flesh, the early fathers almost universally interpreted that becoming not as *metamorphosis* (genuine transformation, being-turned-into) but as *krypsis* (a voluntary hiding of the divine attributes during the earthly life of Jesus). Because of the divine changelessness, the *Logos asarkos* (that is, the Word before the incarnation) had to remain immutable, so that when he "emptied" himself he would do so by concealing his divine powers in his status as the *Logos ensarkos* (the historical Christ), rather than divesting himself of them.[45]

Speaking very broadly for a moment, the nineteenth-century kenoticists felt that concealment was insufficient to do justice to the New Testament's kenotic theme; rather, for them the incarnation had to entail a *suppression* of the divine qualities (or at least some of them, and which ones were suppressed became the focus of intra-kenotic debate). Part of the reason for this conclusion came from the growing influence of Hegel, whose thesis that the absolute Spirit finitized itself in the process of history by an act of self-divestment can be characterized as ultimately a kenotic *theo*logy (that is, as opposed to a kenotic *Christ*ology). But such Hegelian influences should not be exaggerated, because most kenoticists took pains to distance themselves from Hegel's implication that God's self-divestment in history was necessary in order for God to be God — always the crux for attempts by orthodox theologians to appropriate Hegel for their own purposes.[46]

44. Gottfried Thomasius, *Christi Person und Werk: Darstellung der evangelisch-lutherischen Dogmatik vom Mittelpunkte der Christologie aus,* 3rd edition, revised by F. Winter (Erlangen, 1886-88); there is a partial translation of this work by Claude Welch in *God and Incarnation in Mid-Nineteenth-Century German Theology* (New York: Oxford University Press, 1965), p. 37; cited henceforth as Thomasius, *Incarnation.*

45. "The truth is that no theologian of any standing in the early church ever adopted such a theory of the *kenosis* of the Logos as would involve an actual suppression of His divine form of existence by the human — a real 'becoming man,' that is, a transformation on the part of the Logos." Friedrich Loofs, "Kenosis," *Encyclopedia of Religion and Ethics,* p. 683.

46. So Thomasius: "God is the absolute personality and as such is complete in himself,

More telling for them was the influence of a burgeoning historical criticism. There were undoubtedly destructive elements to this criticism, but for the kenoticists there were also benefits, above all a new appreciation for the place of Jesus Christ as an essentially historical figure, a perspective that altered christological debate considerably.[47] This more appreciative tack led to what was in effect a new axiom to add to the Chalcedonian ones: *now the person of Christ had to be construed in its full historical integrity,* and that rendered the *krypsis* model problematic.

The chief difference between patristic Christology and that of the kenoticists, at least for Thomasius, comes down to this: for most of the patristic writers, the incarnate Son of God *concealed* his divine attributes, while for Thomasius the Son *divested* himself of them, or at least of some of them. To avoid the implication that the Son was divesting himself of his divinity *tout court* (which would make the doctrine of the incarnation meaningless), Thomasius drew two distinctions: that between God's potentiality and his actuality, and between "immanent" and "relative" divine attributes. Thus, in the incarnation, the Logos relinquished the actuality of his divine glory while maintaining it potentially, "in reserve," as it were. Further, Thomasius distinguished divine properties inherent in the godhead, such as truth, holiness, and love, from attributes that appertain (in his opinion) only to God's relation to creation, such as omnipotence, omniscience, and ubiquity, which for him get their meaning only vis-à-vis God's relation with the world.

Both distinctions were adopted by most later kenoticists, and not surprisingly were the focus of many of the attacks of those who doubted kenoticism's orthodoxy. Nor were they at all assuaged by Thomasius' attack on the notion of God's immutability, which even on his own account would

---

and humanity is his creature and as such is no element of the concept of God. Humanity is not one in essence with God, but is rather the product of his will, the work of his hands, destined to represent the absolute personality as a likeness within the limits of finitude" (Thomasius, *Incarnation,* p. 32). As Thompson rightly points out, "For Thomasius the Incarnation is no absolute necessity of the historical process, but a gracious response by God to remedy a world torn by sin" (Thompson, *Exploring,* p. 79). In a way, this debate hearkens back to the issue of "why God became man" among the medievals, although Duns Scotus would never have carried the reason for the Incarnation to the extent that Hegel did: for the Scot, God always intended to become man independent of sin, but he didn't *need* to do so.

47. As one minor figure in the movement (not otherwise treated here), A. M. Fairbairn, said: "But we feel Him more in our theology because we know Him better in history. His historical reality and significance have broken upon us with something of the surprise of a discovery, and He has, as it were, become to us a new and more actual Being." A. M. Fairbairn, *The Place of Christ in Modern Theology* (New York: Charles Scribner's Sons, 1916), p. 3.

have to rank as one of God's "inherent" attributes. But he felt he could give no ground here, as Thompson concisely summarizes:

> Besides a radical paring down of essential attributes, Thomasius' construct also takes to task the traditional understanding of divine immutability. There is no question that from Patristic and Chalcedonian times the insistence upon the strict ontological unchangeableness of the divine nature played a very important role in positing and maintaining the full actuality of divine attributes in the Incarnate Christ. To this tradition Thomasius rejoins that any strict view of divine immutability can actually constitute a "divine imperfection," since it would severely restrict God in determining what God wills; moreover this axiom, if logically pushed, would even preclude the sheer possibility of Incarnation, since "such a God will certainly also be incapable of becoming man."[48]

In other words, Thomasius caught (or felt he caught) orthodoxy in a bind: either maintain with Aristotle that God as "pure act" means that God cannot be affected by any potentiality whatever (thus making a doctrine of divine providence and being affected by prayer impossible), or go with Hegel and say that absolute necessity in the godhead requires the incarnation for God to be God. But while the problem is well drawn, his answer proved to be unworkable, even on its own terms. First, for historical and confessional reasons, the metaphysical insights of Thomas Aquinas were neglected, who went far to resolve these dilemmas.[49] Thomasius, however, was writing not just as a Lutheran but also at a time when Aquinas's influence was nugatory even in the Roman universities.

But another development arose to show that, left on its own terms, Thomasius' way of formulating the problem would inevitably lead to difficulties of its own — for another Lutheran theologian, Wolfgang Friedrich Gess, ran "the kenosis all the way empty," to use Thompson's lapidary phrase:

> In order to effect the Incarnation the Logos relinquishes all divine attributes, powers, prerogatives, and glory. The pre-existent Word *becomes*

---

48. Thompson, *Exploring*, p. 84; with an internal quote from Thomasius, *Incarnation*, p. 100.

49. Above all in the *Summa contra Gentiles* I, chapters 81-88, especially here: "It is necessary that God know other things, but not necessary that He will them. Hence, neither does God will all the things that can have an order to His goodness; but He knows all things that have any order whatever to His essence, by which He understands" (*Summa contra Gentiles* I, 81, 7).

flesh, literally. Having been transformed into a human soul, the Son gains consciousness of his divine identity and mission only in the gradual course of human development, a life of faith lived in complete dependence on God the Father in the power and energies of the Spirit, a life which also included the possibility of a fall into sin. Gess is recognized as the most consistent of the nineteenth-century kenoticists. He is also routinely cited for his vulnerability in securing the *vere Deus*.[50]

As well he might. The problem with Gess's rigorously consistent kenoticism is that it ends up resolving the fundamental christological paradox by dissolving it, as happened with all the failed attempts of the docetists, adoptionists, subordinationists, monophysites, Nestorians, and monothelites in the patristic period.[51] Clearly if kenotic Christology was going to live up to its promise of taking account of historical criticism while remaining faithful to Chalcedonian orthodoxy without falling into the Aristotle-Hegel vise, it would have to be rescued of its untenable axioms, the same ones that led to Gess's extreme conclusions, a task that fell to Hugh Ross Mackintosh.

In my opinion, Mackintosh is much the best of the kenoticists, not least because he comes at the end of the line of this school of Christology and is thus able both to sum up its achievements so far and yet to see the manifest dilemmas it had in no way resolved. As he says with admirable honesty, "The difficulties of a Kenotic view are no doubt extremely grave."[52] But he was not for that reason willing to abandon the project because for him (and this is key) the difficulties were *au fond* a legacy of Chalcedon itself. According to Mackintosh the root of the Chalcedonian dilemma stems from its assumption that natures are abstract, so that, in Thompson's words, if "the Logos is the person-forming principle of the man Jesus, whose human nature is thus anhypostatic [nonpersonal]," this will result in "a depreciation of his humanity."[53] Or as Mackintosh puts it:

> This dilemma, then — the Scylla of a duplex personality and the Charybdis of an impersonal manhood — has invariably proved fatal to the doctrine of two natures. If it takes Jesus' manhood seriously, as the New Tes-

50. Thompson, *Exploring*, p. 87; Thompson's emphasis.

51. One author rightly calls Gess's model the *absolute metamorphic* type: A. R. Bruce, *The Humiliation of Christ* (Edinburgh: T. & T. Clark, 1900), pp. 394-400.

52. H. R. Mackintosh, *The Doctrine of the Person of Jesus Christ,* 2nd edition (Edinburgh: T. & T. Clark, 1913, reprinted 1978), p. 466; quoted internally throughout this section.

53. Thompson, *Exploring*, pp. 90-91.

tament of course does by instinct, it makes shipwreck on the notion of a double Self. If, on the other hand, it insists on the unity of the person, the unavoidable result is to abridge the integrity of the manhood and present a Figure whom it is difficult to identify with the Jesus of the Synoptic Gospels. (pp. 296-97)

In other words, for the kenoticists, very much including Mackintosh here, Alexandria represents an unresolved monophysitism while Antioch never dealt with the implications of its posited duplicity, and this was the obstacle they felt duty-bound to overcome. Mackintosh's own contribution here was to eschew (for the most part) the *a priori* "metaphysical" formulation of the problem by the German Lutherans in favor a more *a posteriori* "moral" approach.[54] In that regard Mackintosh is the first, and virtually the only, kenotic christologian who links kenoticism with theodicy: "How shall we assure men in their agony that God veritably is love? For my part, I find the one completely satisfying solution in the certainty that Christ, the Son of God, has indeed suffered on our behalf."[55]

That said, Mackintosh will also concede that a "moral" approach to the kenosis of Christ does not render the issue of the metaphysics of his person otiose: "Between the ethical and the metaphysical view of Christ, then, there is no final antagonism" (p. 304). From that entirely legitimate perspective he goes on to level some quite devastating objections to Thomasius' attempt to distinguish the divine attributes that appertain to God *in se* and those that arise only in virtue of creation. For once the world is in place, he says, "the Divine relations of omnipotence, omniscience, and the like are as really essential as righteousness or grace" (p. 476). Thus, if Christ became incarnate *in* creation, how can God give up his *essential* difference from creation and still be God? Even if one concedes (and this would indeed be a big "if") that some divine attributes only pertain to

54. "Much has been made of the non-speculative character of English kenotic Christology, that compared with the rigor of Continental thought, the Isles offer a thinner theological gruel. Mackintosh himself notes this shift in tenor: 'There are obvious differences between the older Kenotic theories and the new. For the Christian thinker of today is more reserved and proportionally less vulnerable on points of speculation' (p. 468). . . . Thus moral and personalistic categories of thought will edge out philosophical ones in Mackintosh's model, whose treatment everywhere betrays a careful tentativeness." Thompson, *Exploring*, p. 88.

55. Mackintosh, *The Person of Jesus Christ* (London: Student Christian Movement, 1912), pp. 90-91; these are popular lectures that attempt to show the pastoral and practical application of kenotic Christology for the ordinary believer.

God's relation to the world *ad extra*, how can they be done away with in the incarnation without dismantling the very God-world relationship that is the presupposition *of* the incarnation?

These are the very objections that theologians from the time of Thomasius down to the present have raised as the central problem with the whole kenotic project. So why did Mackintosh come to praise, not to bury, the kenotic school? Here's the rub: yes, omniscience *is* essential to divinity (and whether *per se* or only in God's relation to the world is immaterial to this debate). The trouble is, he points out, the Gospels give no indication that Jesus possessed such omniscience (Mark 13:32). So how does Mackintosh solve this dilemma? Basically, by accepting Thomasius' distinction between God's actuality and potentiality while rejecting the distinction between God's absolute and relative attributes:

> Still, though not parted with, the attributes [of omniscience and the like] may be transposed. They may come to function in new ways, to assume new forms of activity, readjusted to the new condition of the Subject. It is possible to conceive the Son, who has entered at love's behest on the region of growth and progress, as now possessing all the qualities of Godhead in the form of concentrated potency rather than of full actuality, *dunamei* [potential power] rather than *energeia* [power exercised]. (p. 477)

Whether this proposal will work depends, as with Thomasius, on the viability of the proposal to abandon the classical definition of God's immutability by introducing the concept of potentiality into the godhead. But this means he has returned willy-nilly to the Thomasian dilemma: "elevating one attribute of God to be supreme, an attribute which then alone defines God's unchangeableness."[56] And that attribute — not surprisingly, given Mackintosh's moralistic twist to the kenotic program — is love: "What is immutable in God is the holy love which makes His essence" (p. 473). And this stress on love is what marks his advance on Thomasius' more speculative kenoticism, as Thompson deftly describes:

> Whereas for Thomasius divine love was the motive for the Incarnation and God's will or self-determination the immutable essence that allowed for such a self-limitation, for Mackintosh love is both the motive and the unchangeable divine essence that makes kenosis possible. Since the

56. Thompson, *Exploring*, p. 93.

kenosis is an expression — better, the supreme expression — of divine love, it is wholly consistent with who God is and therefore no violation of divine immutability.[57]

This passage has often struck readers in our age as eminently plausible (does not love *want* to do all in its power to conform itself to the needs of the beloved, even to the most extreme abasement?), but theologians more attuned to the patristic controversies, hammered out at such length in the first centuries of the church, immediately spotted the old specter of Arianism implicit in these perorations and panegyrics to love, and they were by far in the majority. One of the most vigorous critics was Francis Hall, who threw down the gauntlet with this by-no-means rhetorical question: "Was He God or not? If He possessed the fullness of the Godhead — i.e., all Divine attributes — He was God. But, if He was lacking in any of these attributes, He certainly was not God."[58] Karl Barth, too, was not shy in his criticism. Explicitly drawing on Athanasius' central polemic against Arius — that a lesser God brings a lesser salvation — Barth went for the jugular and in doing so concisely formulated the central orthodox objection to kenotic Christology *tout court*:

> God is always God even in His humiliation. The divine being does not suffer any change, any diminution, any transformation into something else, any admixture with something else, let alone any cessation. The deity of Christ is the one unaltered — because unalterable — deity of God. Any subtraction or weakening of it would at once throw doubt upon the atonement made in Him. . . . [For] if in Christ — even in the humiliated

57. Thompson, *Exploring*, p. 93.

58. Francis J. Hall, *The Kenotic Theory* (New York: Longmans, Green and Co., 1898), pp. 221-22. And again: "Moreover, the doctrine of the Trinity is violated by Kenoticism. Whatever the Trinity is, It is eternally. The three Persons are co-eternal and co-equal. But if the Son of God was at any time lacking in Divine attributes He was not then coequal with the Father and the Holy Spirit" (pp. 234-35). This objection is clearly the gravamen of Pius XII's condemnation of this movement in his 1951 encyclical *Sempiternus Rex:* "Likewise entirely opposed to Chalcedon's profession of faith is the erroneous opinion, rather widespread among non-Catholics, which imagines that in Christ the divinity of the Word is lost. Called the 'kenotic theory,' it finds a specious foundation in a rash misinterpretation of the text of the letter of the apostle Paul to the Philippians. It is truly a blasphemous theory, and, like the doctrine of Docetism directly opposed to it, it makes the mystery of the incarnation and redemption a lifeless and meaningless illusion." In *The Christian Faith in the Doctrinal Documents of the Catholic Church*, ed. J. Neuner, S.J. and J. Depuis, S.J., 7th edition (New York: Alba House, 2001), p. 262.

Christ born in a manger at Bethlehem and crucified on the cross of Golgotha — God is not unchanged and wholly God, then everything that we may say about the reconciliation of the world made by God in his humiliated One is left hanging in the air.[59]

Of course that still leaves the question hanging in the air: What does it mean, then, for the Word to *become* flesh? Although the next chapter will take up Barth's Christology on its own terms, nonetheless his exegesis of the "becoming" issue forms the basis of his critique of the kenotic-Christology movement, and since that critique brought an end to that movement, I shall cite him here:

> But can or will the Word of God *become* at all? Does He not surrender thereby His divinity? Or, if He does not surrender it, what does becoming mean? By what figures of speech or concepts is this becoming of the Word of God to be properly described? "The Word became" — if that is true, and true in such a way that a real becoming is thereby expressed without the slightest surrender of the divinity of the Word, its truth is that of a miraculous act, an act of mercy on the part of God. . . . If we paraphrase the statement "the Word became flesh" by "the Word assumed flesh," we guard against the misinterpretation already mentioned, that in the incarnation the Word ceases to be entirely Himself and equal to Himself, i.e., in the full sense of Word of God. God cannot cease to be God. *The incarna-*

---

59. Karl Barth, *Church Dogmatics* IV/1: *The Doctrine of Reconciliation,* trans. G. W. Bromiley (Edinburgh: T. & T. Clark, 1956), pp. 179-80, 183. I should add that I agree with Barth here. This agreement gives me the occasion to clarify a sentence in my chapter for *Exploring Kenotic Christology* bearing the title "'He descended into hell': The Depths of God's Self-Emptying Love on Holy Saturday in the Thought of Hans Urs von Balthasar" (pp. 218-45), where I said: "Christianity must continue to maintain that the infinite *remains* infinite while becoming (turning into) something finite" (at p. 219; emphasis in the original). As Ivor Davidson rightly points out: "Oakes begins his chapter on Balthasar with the supposition that the 'becoming' spoken of in the incarnation of the Word must mean that the infinite was 'turned into' the finite — a construal that might be news to a lot of orthodox Christologists," *Ars Disputandi* 7 (2007): paragraph 9; at http://www.ArsDisputandi.org). Although Davidson neglects to mention that I also insisted that the infinite *remain* infinite, he is still right that, when speaking of the incarnation, "becoming" cannot mean "being turned into," for that implies no remainder is left over from the previous state prior to the change, as Barth rightly sees. Of course, that still leaves the problem of how to interpret the "becoming" of the Word into flesh, since we are still using the most basic verb for change of the immutable Word. On this point Barth again I think gets it right, as the next citation from him will show. (See also the fuller treatment of Barth's Christology in the next chapter.)

tion is inconceivable, but it is not absurd, and it must not be explained as an absurdity. The inconceivable fact in it is that without ceasing to be God the Word of God is among us in such a way that He takes over human being, which is His creature, into His own being, and to that extent makes it His own being.[60]

But if *become* must be translated as *assumed,* does that not make the human nature something adventitious, "stuck on" or appended to the divinity, merely to preserve the immutability of the Word? No, and this is precisely Barth's point:

As His own predicate along with His original predicate of divinity, He takes over human being into unity with Himself. And it is by the paraphrase "the Word assumed flesh" that the second misunderstanding is also guarded against, that in the incarnation, by means of a union of divine and human being and nature, a third is supposed to arise. Jesus Christ as the Mediator between God and man is not a third, midway between the two. In that case God has at once ceased to be God and likewise He is not a man like us. But Jesus is the Mediator, the God-Man, in such a way that He is God and Man. *This "and" is the inconceivable act of the "becoming" in the incarnation.*[61]

But the kenotic-Christology movement ran into trouble long before Barth took up arms against it. Early in the twentieth century some critics raised the specter of modalism. Readers will recall that one of the central objections to modalism (or Sabellianism) was the problem that if the entirety of the godhead is in the crib in Bethlehem, who is governing the universe? The kenoticists were hardly modalists — just the opposite — but they paradoxically fell prey to the same objection, made most devastatingly by William Temple:

What was happening to the rest of the universe during the period of our Lord's earthly life? To say that the Infant Jesus was from His cradle exercis-

60. Karl Barth, *Church Dogmatics* I/2: *The Doctrine of the Word of God,* trans. G. T. Thompson and Harold Knight (Edinburgh: T. & T. Clark, 1956), pp. 159, 160-61; emphases added.

61. Barth, *Church Dogmatics* I/2, p. 161; emphasis added. Barth continues: "The unity of God and man in Christ is, then, the act of the Logos in assuming human being. His becoming, and therefore the thing that human being encounters in this becoming of the Logos, is an act of God in the person of the Word" (p. 162).

ing providential care over it all is certainly monstrous [the implication of modalism]; but to deny this, and yet say the Creative Word was so self-emptied as to have no being except in the Infant Jesus [the claim of the kenoticists], is to assert that for a certain period of history the world was let loose from the control of the Creative Word.[62]

These objections soon proved the undoing of the kenotic movement. But at least Thomasius had his own reply to make when objections were too vigorously made from the side of defenders of divine immutability: when divine immutability is too strictly defined, said Thomasius, then the very notion of incarnation becomes dubious. After all, John says that the Word *became* flesh. If that word is to be taken seriously, then something has to give. Otherwise, the word "became" takes on only a metaphorical hue, which makes Christology either docetic or adoptionist, but not orthodox.

Liberal theologians, who willingly eavesdropped on this debate, were more than happy to jettison orthodoxy in favor of a (vaguely defined) adoptionism — another point that counted against nineteenth-century kenoticism in the eyes of the orthodox. But the failure of that kenoticism was for the liberals precisely the point and gave them the initial launching point for advocating a simple and exclusive focus on the historical Jesus. For some this *might* lead to an orthodox confession of Jesus as the incarnate Son of God; but if it did so, it would only come at the end of a long process of historical reconstruction and justification, a view that culminated in Wolfhart Pannenberg's famous and (let's be blunt) nearly hegemonic distinction between "low" and "high" Christology. In Chapter 3 we have already seen the inadequacies of this distinction in handling the historical evidence of the New Testament, but the motivation of that approach arising from the failure of kenotic Christology in the nineteenth century should at least be briefly noted. Thompson again:

> With the modern turn to anthropology, subjectivity, and history came a shift in Christological method from "above" to "below," from an Incarnational approach to an emphasis on Jesuology that begins its reflections with Jesus of Nazareth and only allows the question of his divinity (as distinguished from deity) to emerge at inquiry's end.[63]

62. William Temple, *Christus Veritas* (1924), cited in Thompson, *Exploring*, p. 97; this point also recalls the disputes over the so-called extra-Calvinisticum between Lutherans and Calvinists discussed in Chapter 6.

63. Thompson, *Exploring*, p. 101.

So what came of this debate? One stream certainly led to a rephrasing of the question, to what might be called a "Christology of relation." This school refused to countenance a confession of Jesus as God but did display a (tempered) willingness to admit that God is *in* Jesus "in some sense." This position of course then inevitably issued into the dread specter of relativism of confessional claims and pluralism in savior-figures (the subject of the next two chapters). Those who shrank from that prospect in horror (Karl Barth, Joseph Ratzinger, Walter Kasper, Hans Urs von Balthasar) also saw that a mere republication of Chalcedonian orthodoxy without taking into account the failure of kenoticism would itself result in failure, if not in outright obscurantism and mere incantation of old formulae without due regard for the post-Hegelian situation. *This* at least they all recognized:

> If Jesus of Nazareth is identical in person with the eternally existent Son of God, one hypostasis of three in the Christian conception of God, that is, if God's presence in Christ is a "substantial presence" of the Logos, then there must be *some* description of his transition in status from an exclusively divine mode of being to a human mode of being.[64]

It would later be seen that such a transition could only be guaranteed by revisiting Athanasius' doctrine of the Trinity and radicalizing his view that, when the Father bestows his divine nature on the Son in the eternal act of generation, the Father gives of himself *without stint*. A convergence of twentieth-century theologians, Catholics especially (the motif is noticeably absent in Barth), would see that what Athanasius was essentially referring to was an intra-trinitarian kenosis. How that could be conceived without undermining the divine immutability (which they all claimed they were able to do) shall be the subject of Chapter 10. But first we must look at the issue of Christology and pluralism, which became ever dominant in the twentieth century and against which these later Catholic "Athanasian kenoticists" would struggle so vigorously.

---

64. Thompson, *Exploring*, p. 108; Thompson's emphasis.

CHAPTER 9

Christology and Pluralism: Protestant Theologians

But still this world (so fitted for the knave)
Contents us not. A better shall we have?
A kingdom of the Just then let it be:
But first consider how those Just agree.
The good must merit God's peculiar care!
But who but God can tell us who they are?
One thinks, on Calvin Heav'n's own spirit fell,
Another deems him instrument of hell;
If Calvin feel Heaven's blessing, or its rod,
This cries there is, and that, there is no God.
What shocks one part will edify the rest,
Nor with one system can they all be blest.

Alexander Pope, Essay on Man

In a very real sense, the question of Christology and pluralism arose at the very dawn of the Christian religion itself. The nineteenth century was hardly the first era of the church to ask how a particular itinerant rabbi from Galilee could be confessed as savior of the whole world, including all the souls who passed away long before his birth. The second-century pagan philosopher Celsus (exact dates unknown) raised just this objection, which stung Origen enough to prompt him to write a prodigiously long refutation, his famous *Contra Celsum*. But the problem was hardly mooted first with Celsus. In a way, Paul's Letter to the Romans also had to face that same question. For what Paul realized when he met Christ on the road to Damascus was that the atoning death of Christ was not only *all*-sufficient but *exclusively* sufficient for salvation: "Then, as one man's trespass led to condemnation for all men, so *one* man's act of righteousness leads to acquittal and life for *all* men" (Rom. 5:18; see too 3:21-26; 5:15-17). With that insight came a retrospective realization that the dialectic of law and sin functioned in a way discrepant from what Paul had previously assumed. Now he saw sin as universal (3:9-18), with the law (whether Mosaic or natural) serving only to check, but otherwise incapable of staunching, let alone conquering, sin (3:20). These were universal facts, against which the usual distinction between Jew and Gentile faded into insignificance against the overpowering love of God in Christ, who "has consigned all men to disobedience that he might have mercy upon all" (11:32).

That said, the question of the universal reach of God's saving will as mediated through the one Savior (the so-called "scandal of particularity") became much more burning in the nineteenth century; for at this point in history, the question of world religions had become all that more pressing. The nineteenth century witnessed an enormous flood of texts from past civilizations: some were discovered at this time and then translated by an increasing body of trained experts; others were long known but finally were brought into the consciousness of the educated West by new translations. Whether it was through *The Epic of Gilgamesh, Hammurabi's Code,* the Egyptian *Book of the Dead,* or the *Upanishads* and Confucius' *Analects,* theologians confronted in a new and more intense way the question of *pluralism:* How did the single Savior of the Christians relate to the plurality of religions, with different founders and different systems of belief?

Intimately related to the question of pluralism is that of *relativism:* Is each religion true relative to the society that gave it birth, or is there some way of adjudicating their differences via some more transcendental norm? This question was asked not only "synchronically," that is, across the contemporary spectrum of world civilizations, but also "diachronically," that is, across the historical strata of succeeding civilizations. We have already seen an earlier attempt to solve this problem in christological terms in Friedrich Schleiermacher, with his notion of the feeling of absolute dependence as the gold standard of religious value best exemplified by Jesus.

The increasing historical consciousness of the West, however, made that solution ever more problematic. Hegel was an early anticipator of the challenge of history and relativism, although his narrative of progress ran into immediate difficulties, as we saw in the last chapter. But even if those could have been resolved and his philosophy given new plausibility, his schema really only worked for the West (where Hegel claimed to see progress at work). But when Confucianism, Buddhism, Islam, Hinduism all continue to live as contemporary realities, when they all jostle for attention by Western scholars, and when they all seep into the consciousness of ordinary citizens of the West, of what help could Hegel be? Where is the concern for progress there?

The second half of the nineteenth century also saw the full efflorescence of historical scholarship on the Bible, which tended to relativize these texts as the product of the historical situation that gave them birth rather than as the timeless truth of God; and the challenge was severe, as Peter Berger notes:

> It was historical scholarship, especially as it developed in the nineteenth century, that first threatened to undermine theology at its very roots. Its challenge, too, began with details that could more or less plausibly be dismissed as trivial — the discovery of different sources for biblical books that had been canonized as unities, or of inconsistencies in the several accounts of the life of Jesus. All these details, however, came to add up to something much more serious — a pervasive sense of the historical character of *all* elements of the tradition, which significantly weakened the latter's claims to uniqueness and authority. Put simply, historical scholarship led to a perspective in which even the most sacrosanct elements of religious traditions came to be seen as *human products.*[1]

So significant were these issues as they began to be raised in the nineteenth century that they perforce remained unresolved and continued to preoccupy theologians in the twentieth. The problems bequeathed by the nineteenth century became the challenge of the twentieth; and how various theologians met that challenge will be the focus of this chapter and the next.

Protestants were the first to take up the issue of pluralism, the first to notice that it must move to the forefront of christological reflection. Because he straddled both the nineteenth and twentieth centuries and because he worked so intensively on all aspects of this problem, we will concentrate above all on Ernst Troeltsch, who both dominated the discussion and set the

---

1. Peter L. Berger, *A Rumor of Angels: Modern Sociology and the Rediscovery of the Supernatural* (New York: Doubleday, 1969), pp. 34-35. Because the results of this historical scholarship on Jesus have such obvious relevance for Christology, that question had to be treated in Chapter 3 of this book; so nothing more will be said about that here, except to point out its implications for relativism and pluralism.

terms of the debate for his successors, especially in Lutheran Germany; and so we will treat his predecessors, Albrecht Ritschl and Adolf von Harnack, only in terms of their influence on him, at which point we will hear Karl Barth's loud No to the entire project of liberal, pluralist Protestantism.

Albrecht Ritschl

Albrecht Ritschl (1822-89) was in many ways the true founder of liberal Protestantism, even more than Friedrich Schleiermacher. He built on Schleiermacher's notion that Jesus was unique only insofar as he represented the highest form of human religiosity; but Ritschl purged Schleiermacher's exemplarism of any lingering idealism, whether Platonic or Hegelian.[2] Like Schleiermacher, he insisted on the irreducibility of religious experience but went further by defining faith not as the *feeling* of absolute dependence but as a matter of making *judgments,* specifically *value* judgments *(Werturteile).* Thus, the divinity of Christ must be understood not as a statement of fact grounded in the independent revelation of God but as an expression of the revelational *value (Offenbarungswert)* of Christ for the community that trusts in him as God. Such a view obviously entails the rejection of philosophical idealism in any form.[3] Furthermore, the stress on the community as the locus of revelation led Ritschl to the conclusion that the classical Reformers, Luther especially, misunderstood Paul's doctrine of justification;

2. "The somewhat elusive Hegelian thesis of the manifestation of the Absolute and Infinite in the finite and relative conditions of human history appeared chimerical in the light of the concrete, empirical and verifiable knowledge deriving from the natural [and, we may add, historical] sciences. The origins of liberal theology may be seen in this growing disillusionment with Hegelian idealism, which left an ideological vacuum at a critical phase in German intellectual history. It was within this vacuum that the highly influential liberal theology of Albrecht Ritschl developed." Alister E. McGrath, *The Making of Modern German Christology: From the Enlightenment to Pannenberg* (Oxford: Blackwell, 1986), p. 55.

3. In his stress on the practical effects of justification in the life of the Church, Ritschl was to some extent hearkening back to Kant's stress on the practical effects of belief in God as the only justifiable way to ground religion. But even here the Kant to which Ritschl made appeal was a very anemic Kant, as Barth noticed: "[Ritschl] went back to Kant, but Kant quite definitely interpreted as an antimetaphysical moralist, by means of whom he thought he could understand Christianity as that which grandly and inevitably made possible, or realized, a practical ideal of life." Karl Barth, *Protestant Thought in the Nineteenth Century: Its Background and History,* trans. Brian Cozens and John Bowden (Grand Rapids: Eerdmans, 2002/1952), p. 641.

for Luther stressed too much the benefits of justification for the individual, whereas it was primarily the community that was forgiven and saved, and the individual only by being incorporated in the church.

Such a stress on the corporate nature of salvation is defensible as far as it goes, but with Ritschl at least, it cannot go very far. In fact, by purging himself of Schleiermacher's idealism, Ritschl brings Schleiermacher's legacy to its predetermined dead end, as Alister McGrath rightly notes:

> [For Ritschl] Christ's "uniqueness" is primarily to be articulated in terms of his being *the founder of the Christian community,* thus possessing temporal priority over those who followed him. Ritschl argues that, although it is conceivable that another individual could [later] arise, equal in his religious and ethical status to Christ, "he would stand in historical dependence upon Christ, and would therefore be distinguishable from him." This concession, however, is significant, in that it indicates that Christ's "uniqueness" is understood *historically* rather than *ontologically,* a *primus inter pares* whose primacy arises through the historical accident of his being the unique founder of the Christian church.[4]

German has two words for "unique," and they carry different connotations: *einzigartig* and *einmalig.* The first means unique for its type or kind *(Art),* as in "exemplary" (or, as we say idiomatically in English, "*kind* of" unique); the second term refers to unique in the unprecedented sense and is rooted in the German expression for "once and for all" *(ein für allemal).* Clearly for Ritschl, as for nearly all versions of liberal Christianity, Christ can only be unique in the first sense: the divinity of Christ is thus not true in any objective sense of the term but rests on a value judgment arising from within the community of faith, hearing and responding to the proclamation of the gospel (a proclamation which is itself of course a product of the community).

Adolf von Harnack

Even for those schooled in Ritschl's liberalism, massive amounts of New Testament data cried out in seeming rebuke of his theories, above all that pertaining to Jesus' relation to his Father, which, if it is an accurate portrayal of

---

4. McGrath, *Modern German Christology,* p. 57; emphases in the original. The quotation from Ritschl comes from *Die christliche Lehre von der Rechtfertigung und Versöhnung* (Bonn, 1870-1874), vol. 3, p. 438.

Jesus' piety, had to antedate the Christian community on which Ritschl set such store. Into that breach sprang Adolf von Harnack (1851-1930) with his stress on Jesus' preaching of the fatherhood of God. In fact, for Harnack that is *all* that Christianity is: "The Gospel is no theoretical system of doctrine or philosophy of the universe; it is doctrine only in so far as it proclaims the reality of God the Father."[5]

Harnack was a prodigiously industrious scholar of the dogmatic history of the early Christian church; but such Stakhanovite labors were also harnessed to a resolutely anti-dogmatic, indeed anti-metaphysical agenda. The Harvard process philosopher Alfred North Whitehead once remarked that Christianity is a religion searching for a metaphysics. For Harnack that was precisely the problem, and he meant for his historical labors to demonstrate the incompatibility of primitive (that is, "real") Christianity over against all subsequent developments:

> The gospel entered into the world, not as a doctrine, but as a joyful message and as a power of the Spirit of God, originally in the form of Judaism. [Soon, however,] it stripped off these forms with amazing rapidity, and united and amalgamated itself with Greek science, the Roman Empire and ancient culture, developing, as a counterpoise to this, renunciation of the world and the striving after supernatural life and deification. All this was summed up in the old dogma and in dogmatic Christianity.[6]

Out of this thesis comes Harnack's extraordinary hostility to christological dogma:

> In the course of this controversy men put an end to brotherly fellowship for the sake of a *nuance;* thousands were cast out, condemned, loaded with chains and done to death. It is a gruesome story. On the question of "Christology" men beat their religious doctrines into terrible weapons and spread fear and intimidation everywhere. This attitude still continues: Christology is treated as though the Gospel had no other problem to offer, and the accompanying fanaticism is still rampant in our own day.[7]

---

5. Adolf von Harnack, *What Is Christianity?* trans. Thomas Bailey Saunders (Philadelphia: Fortress Press, 1986/1900), p. 146.

6. Adolf von Harnack, *History of Dogma,* 7 vols. (Edinburgh: Williams & Norgate, 1894-99), vol. 7, p. 272.

7. Harnack, *What Is Christianity?* p. 12; Harnack's emphasis. Note the scare quotes around "Christology."

Since in his view the truth of the identity of Christ is meaningless for him, Harnack will out-Schleiermacher Schleiermacher by saying a page earlier that the "forces of the Gospel appeal to the deepest foundations of human existence and to them only; it is there alone that their leverage is applied." Nor can he fill in the lacunae in Ritschl's Christology with his stress on the fatherhood of God, for that turns out to be, at best, merely a *message* of Jesus and, at worst, an empty one at that:

> To our modern way of thinking and feeling, Christ's message appears in the clearest and most direct light when grasped in connection with the idea of God the Father and the infinite value of the human soul. . . . But the fact that the whole of Jesus' message may be reduced to these two heads — God as the Father, and the human soul so ennobled that it can and does unite with him — shows us that the Gospel is in nowise a positive religion like the rest; that it contains no statutory or particularistic elements; *that it is, therefore, religion itself.*[8]

In other words, no religion worthy of the name can have any dogmatic content whatever; and all do except Christianity. Except that, with "amazing rapidity," as Harnack puts it, Christianity *did* become dogmatic, and remains so to this day, indeed the most dogmatically elaborate of all the religions of the world — saving of course the "Christianity" born out of Harnack's liberal imagination.

Ernst Troeltsch

One can at least say this of Ernst Troeltsch (1865-1923): here the opponent of all relativizing trends in Christology has finally met his match.[9] Here is a representative of a de-absolutized Christology who must be taken seriously and whose legacy is not so easily dispatched as Ritschl's and Harnack's.[10]

---

8. Harnack, *What Is Christianity?* p. 63; Harnack's emphasis. He seems to be saying that no religion with particular doctrines can claim the name of being truly religious. No wonder later postmodern thinkers will accuse Enlightenment reason of being hegemonic!

9. For one thing, he could draw on a prodigious set of competences. In Sarah Coakley's words, he "was a polymathic figure: philosopher, historian, sociologist, politician, and theologian." Sarah Coakley, *Christ Without Absolutes: A Study of the Christology of Ernst Troeltsch* (Oxford: Clarendon Press, 1988), p. 1.

10. Not that Troeltsch was ever very critical of Harnack. As he said in tribute to his two mentors in a *Festschrift* dedicated to Harnack on the occasion of his seventieth birthday:

While originally respectful of Ritschl,[11] Troeltsch had broken with his teacher by 1898 in an article he wrote renouncing metaphysics in favor of history.[12] In this long essay he accused Ritschl of relying on a discredited supernaturalism, whereas he saw a consistently maintained historicism as the only option after the demise of Hegel and the growth of historical criticism. Ritschlians, according to Troeltsch, were willing to wrestle with specific historical problems raised by the historical-critical method, but they never came to terms with the underlying anti-metaphysics of that method. So by 1900 he threw down the gauntlet against any theologian who thought Christology could avoid the challenge of historical criticism with its attendant critique of metaphysics.[13]

For Troeltsch historical criticism is marked by three key methodological principles: 1) the principle of *criticism,* which for him meant that all historical judgments are mere matters of probability, and thus open to correction or refinement; 2) the principle of *analogy,* which says that events of the past must be similar to those of the present if they are to be understood, which automatically excludes the supernatural from any interpretation of the historical Jesus; and 3) the principle of *correlation,* that all historical events are caught in a complex cause-effect nexus, meaning that they must be inter-

---

"Baur and Harnack: they represent the aristocracy of scholarship; they combined strictest observance of method with a choice sensitivity of spirit and a kindly readiness for communication, and scholarly nobility with a humanitarian concern for all practical affairs of their fellow men. Today the current of events pulls us away from such intellectual nobility and such objective dependability." Harnack reciprocated and indeed spoke at Troeltsch's funeral in these effusive tones: "He was indisputably *the* German philosopher of history of our time. Indeed, after Hegel he was the first great philosopher of history whom Germany has produced." Both texts have been translated by Wilhelm Pauck in his monograph *Harnack and Troeltsch: Two Historical Theologians* (New York: Oxford University Press, 1968), pp. 95-127; here 99 and 122.

11. "Troeltsch, speaking as a representative of the 'younger generation' of Ritschlians, argued that the original success of the Ritschlian theology was a direct consequence of the cultural situation in the 1850s, in the aftermath of the collapse of the Hegelian speculative systems which had dominated the first half of the century. . . . In the meantime, however, culture had not remained unchanged: intellectual interest, in the universities and elsewhere, had shifted away from speculative philosophy to historical analysis, thus highlighting the deficiencies of the older Ritschlian analysis." McGrath, *Modern German Christology,* p. 82.

12. Ernst Troeltsch, "Geschichte und Metaphysik," *Zeitschrift für Theologie und Kirche* 8 (1898): 1-69.

13. Ernst Troeltsch, "Über historische und dogmatische Methode in der Theologie," *Theologische Arbeiten aus dem rheinischen wissenschaftlichen Predigerverein,* New Series 4 (1900): 81-108.

preted in terms of the antecedents and consequences. Failure to take seriously the historical method being applied and using it only piecemeal merely results in a "hybrid" *(Mischform)* portrait of Jesus.[14]

Out of these principles came the inevitable conclusions, ones he explicitly drew in his most influential work, *The Absoluteness of Christianity*,[15] where he avers that religions make claims that cannot be admitted except in terms made *inside* each religion, since acceptance of those claims constitutes, at least in part, membership in that religion. Correlatively, rejection of those claims is precisely what marks the outsider to that religion as an outsider. As Thomas Hobbes pointed out as early as the seventeenth century, when a man says he met God in a dream, the outsider can reply that the man had a dream of God; and Troeltsch himself frequently cited with approval Jean-Jacques Rousseau's maxim that religion is *une affaire de géographie.*

For that reason, Troeltsch argued, Christocentrism is to theology what geocentrism is to astronomy.[16] So how did Christocentrism arise historically? For Troeltsch the only answer could be: *to meet a social need.*[17] Where Schleiermacher explained Christ's significance for the Christian community as a personal religious experience, Troeltsch explained it sociologically. But

---

14. See Ernst Troeltsch, "The Significance of the Historical Existence of Jesus for Faith," in *Ernst Troeltsch: Writings on Theology and Religion,* trans. Robert Morgan and Michael Pye (Atlanta: John Knox Press, 1977), pp. 182-209; abbreviated hereafter as Troeltsch, "Significance."

15. Ernst Troeltsch, *The Absoluteness of Christianity and the History of Religions,* introduction by James Luther Adams, trans. David Reid (Richmond, VA: John Knox Press, 1971/1902); abbreviated hereafter as Troeltsch, *Absoluteness.*

16. "[Historical contingency] also seems to make this consequence impossible — calling the Christian community the eternal absolute center of salvation for the whole span of humanity. . . . Man's age upon earth amounts to several hundred thousand years or more. His future may come to still more. It is hard to imagine a single point of history along this line — and, as it just so happens, the midpoint of our own religious history — as the sole center of all humanity. That looks far too much like the absolutizing of our own contingent area of life. That would be in religion what geocentrism and anthropocentrism are in cosmology and metaphysics. The whole logic of Christocentrism places it with these other centrisms." Troeltsch, "Significance," p. 189 (translation slightly emended). Of course if one asks how a radical historicist and relativist like Troeltsch can get the wherewithal to make such an "absolutist" statement, ruling out Christ as the midpoint of history from the outset, Troeltsch would grant the point, since all historical judgments (including his) are always statements of probability: "Of course nothing certain can be said here; but it [Christocentrism] is not probable" (p. 189).

17. Not surprisingly, he went on to publish a highly regarded study of the social doctrines of the church: see Ernst Troeltsch, *The Social Teaching of the Christian Churches,* trans. Olive Wyon (London: Macmillan, 1930/1912).

without an adequate theory of value, what makes that social significance "truer" than another? To show how sharp this dilemma is, James Luther Adams recounts this fascinating anecdote as his lead-in to explaining Troeltsch's dilemma:

> Sometime during the course of World War II the United States War Department brought together a selected group of cultural anthropologists in order to secure their counsel regarding the management of psychological warfare in [the] face of German National Socialism. After the group had assembled in Washington one of their number asked what the War Department really expected of these men. He explained that in his work the cultural anthropologist for the sake of scientific objectivity presupposes the point of view of cultural relativism, and that therefore he entertains no biases or ethical preferences, in short, that he is not accustomed to making value judgments regarding the various cultures he studies. He went on to say that if the Germans preferred Nazism, they were entitled to that preference, just as democratic Americans are entitled to their own different preference. In either case, he said, the preference is simply an expression of a cultural milieu.[18]

Of course Adams is not holding Troeltsch responsible for this *reductio ad Hitlerum* of social-studies relativism. But having thrown out Ritschl's stress on faith as a value judgment, how could Troeltsch respond to these cultural anthropologists? In other words, later history must have something to say on the thoroughgoing inadequacy of Troeltsch's relentless historicism, as Adams notes:

> Troeltsch would have seen in the colloquy in Washington a sign of a major modern revolution that has affected all spheres of life — the arts, law, and religion as well as the sciences. In his view this revolution has come about as a consequence of the appearance of a new historical consciousness that recognizes the contingent and singular character of the events of history. Out of this new historical consciousness has developed the modern historical method.[19]

Clearly, liberal theology in its entire genealogy was headed for crisis, but one provoked not by World War II but by World War I. Farsighted theolo-

---

18. James Luther Adams, "Introduction," *Absoluteness*, p. 7.
19. Adams, "Introduction," *Absoluteness*, p. 8.

gians already saw that liberal Christology had reached a dead end: the apocalyptic approach of Albert Schweitzer (see Chapter 3) had given the theological public a portrait of Jesus as a strange and distant figure: Harnack's liberal portrait of Jesus began to look preposterously bourgeois, and Troeltsch's skeptical approach was pushing all dogmatic claims about the Person of Christ into catatonic silence. Who knows how long the crisis would have festered on its own? But history broke in like an interloper on the scholar's study and trashed the place: On August 1, 1914, the First World War broke out.

Karl Barth

It did not require any supernatural gift of perspicuity to see the connection between liberal theology and the outbreak of war: German liberal theologians had already made that connection clear when Harnack drafted an appeal, later signed by him and ninety-two of his colleagues, to the German people on behalf of the Kaiser and in support of the war effort. In a stroke, Karl Barth (1886-1968) saw what this pro-war manifesto meant: liberal theology was simply, totally, and utterly dead, at least for him.[20] Working at the time as pastor of a Calvinist congregation in Safenwil, a small village in Switzerland, he spent the war years brooding over the Bible and what it could say to a devastated Europe. The answer he found in Paul's letter to the Romans, his commentary of which stunned the theological world, which could scarcely believe what it was reading: not a commentary on an ancient and notoriously convoluted text requiring the decoding labors of philologists and experts in ancient religions, both Jewish and pagan, but an exposition of the words of an apostle who had been *sent* and whose mission was to preach a message of revelation, *God's* revelation.[21]

20. This passage is often quoted, but bears citing again here: "For me personally, one day in the beginning of August of that year stands out as *dies ater* [a black day], on which ninety-three German intellectuals, among whom I was horrified to discover almost all of my hitherto revered theological teachers, published a profession of support for the war policy of Kaiser Wilhelm II and his counselors. Amazed by their attitude, I realized that I could no longer follow their ethics and dogmatics, or their understandings of the Bible and history, and that the theology of the nineteenth century no longer had any future for me." Quoted in McGrath, *Modern German Christology*, p. 94.

21. Barth vividly described how he came to write this most famous of all commentaries on Romans and why it had such an impact: "As I look back upon my course, I see myself as one who, ascending the dark staircase of a church-tower and trying to steady himself,

Barth adamantly denied that he was being obscurantist or putting words into God's mouth or assuming that his views were God's. Quite the opposite, in fact; for nothing more characterizes his commentary than the Kierkegaardian theme of the infinite qualitative difference between God and man, drummed into the reader's ears with a constant beat. Furthermore, he resolutely denied that he was importing anything into the text that was not already there, plain as day. Far from using some sort of theological scrim that distorted the (ancient) meaning of the text, he was only pointing to what it was saying:

> I have, moreover, no desire to conceal the fact that my "Biblicist" method — which means in the end no more than "consider well" — is applicable also to the study of Lao-Tse or of Goethe. When I am named "Biblicist" all that can rightly be proved against me is that I am prejudiced in supposing the Bible to be a good book, and that I hold it to be profitable for men to take its conceptions at least as seriously as they take their own.[22]

But that was precisely the revolution in his outlook! "I entirely fail to see why parallels drawn from the ancient world . . . should be of more value for an understanding of the Epistle than the situation in which we find ourselves and to which we therefore can bear witness."[23]

---

reached for the banister but got hold of the bell-rope instead. To his horror, he had then to listen to what the great bell had resounded over him, and not over him alone." Karl Barth, *Die christliche Dogmatik im Entwurf* (Munich: Kaiser Verlag, 1927), p. ix.

22. Karl Barth, *The Epistle to the Romans,* trans. Edwyn C. Hoskins (London: Oxford University Press, 1933/1928), p. 12; abbreviated hereafter as Barth, *Romans.*

23. Barth, *Romans,* p. 11. One example will suffice to show Barth's total rejection of Troeltsch's historicism (not to mention Harnack's and all his predecessors' and epigones'). Commenting on the opening line of Romans ("Paul, a servant of Jesus Christ, called to be an apostle"), Barth explicates: "Here is no 'genius rejoicing in his own creative ability.' The man who is now speaking is an emissary, bound to perform his duty; the minister of his King; a servant, not a master. However great and important a man Paul may have been, the essential theme of his mission is not within him but above him — unapproachably distant and unutterably strange. His call to apostleship is not a familiar episode in his own personal history. . . . Paul, it is true, is always himself, and moves essentially on the same plane as all other men. But, in contradiction to himself and in distinction from all others, he is — called by God and sent forth. . . . Fashioned of the same stuff as all other men, a stone differing in no way from other stones, yet in his relation to God — and in this only — he is unique. As an apostle — and only as an apostle — he stands in no organic relationship with human society as it exists in history: seen from the point of view of human society, he can be regarded only as an exception, nay, rather, as an impossibility. Paul's position can be justified only as rest-

Admittedly, this revolution in theological thinking did not at first lead to a full-fledged Christology, which was partly due to the fact that Paul's Christology in Romans stresses more the soteriological effects of Christ's death, whereas his famous kenosis hymn in Philippians and the hymn to Christ as the firstborn of all creation in Colossians proved much more influential in the classic debates of patristic times (note that the resurrection is scarcely touched upon in Romans). But the real reason for Barth's neglect of the christological theme came from his stress on the infinite qualitative difference between God and man, which created such a gulf as to make sustained reflection on the incarnation well-nigh impossible. This exaggerated stress led to a method (called "dialectical theology") that felt compelled to take back any positive assertion that had just been made with its opposite, lest God get caught in the human net of words. Thus, in commenting on Romans 2:1 ("You, therefore, have no excuse, you who pass judgment on someone else, for at whatever point you judge the other, you are condemning yourself, because you do the same things"), Barth draws this startling conclusion:

> There is no fragment or epoch of history that can be pronounced divine. The whole history of the Church and of all religion takes place in this world. There are no saints in the midst of a company of sinners; for where men have claimed to be saints, they are thereby marked as not-saints. . . . This is as true of Paul, the prophet and apostle of the kingdom of God, and of Jeremiah, as it is of Luther, Kierkegaard and St. Francis, who far surpassed Jesus in "love," childlikeness and austerity. . . . Since power only belongs to God, it is the tragic story of every man of God that he has to contend for the right by placing himself in the wrong.[24]

Obviously anyone who thinks along these lines cannot construct a useful Christology. Fortunately, Barth came to see that a constant fireworks display of dialectics obscured the sheer positivity of revelation.[25] Thus he grad-

---

ing in God, and so only in this way can his words be regarded as at all credible, for they are as incapable of direct apprehension as is God Himself. For this reason he dares to approach others and to demand a hearing without fear either of exalting himself or of approximating too closely to his audience. He appeals only to the authority of God. This is the ground of his authority. There is no other." Barth, *Romans,* pp. 27-28.

24. Barth, *Romans,* p. 57. Passages similar to this one abound in *Romans,* which makes the reader feel as if he is reading the book under a stroboscope.

25. Not to mention the fact that it made a hash of Barth's own commentary, as his Swiss Catholic interlocutor Hans Urs von Balthasar was not slow to point out: "*The Epistle to the Romans* is the very thing against which it itself raged and thundered: a pinnacle of human

ually saw that theology, to be true to itself, must not be the version of Christianity thought up by one individual but has to be an account of what Christ's church as *constituted by God* truly believes on the basis of Scripture and tradition. (Yes, tradition: Barth believed that listening to all the great theologians of the past and incorporating them into his work was simply obedience to the commandment "Honor thy father and thy mother.") Not that such a move lessened his revolutionary impact, as William Nicholls rightly notes:

> Again Barth scandalized the theological public. Not only would he write dogmatics, he would now write *ecclesiastical* dogmatics, dogmatics linked to the church and to its confession, instead of to the academic community and to free inquiry. . . . But this repudiation of [outside norms] should not mislead us. Barth now intends to speak *more* rationally than before, not less so. Theology is defined as science, in the sense that it has an object by which it is determined, and a discipline which renders it critical in its attempts to conform its own utterance to the given nature of its object.[26]

Finally, Barth can now construct a truly *scientific* Christology, defined in Anselmian terms: once inside the faith, the believer can come to see the full rationality of what he believes. To be sure, since the *Church Dogmatics* covers fourteen volumes (including a full one-volume index), and since Barth's thought is nothing if not Christocentric from start to finish, an account of his Christology could never be encompassed even in a monograph, let alone this short section of one chapter. So only those features that are most re-markable can here be stressed.[27]

The Barth scholar George Hunsinger notes that, first and foremost, Barth's Christology is resolutely Chalcedonian through and through.[28] Of

---

religiosity. Its insistent cry of 'Not I! Rather God!' actually directs all eyes on itself instead of on God. Its cry for distance gives no room for distance." Hans Urs von Balthasar, *The Theology of Karl Barth: Exposition and Interpretation,* trans. Edward T. Oakes, S.J. (San Francisco: Ignatius Press, 1992), p. 84.

26. William Nicholls, *The Pelican Guide to Theology,* vol. 1: *Systematic and Philosophical Theology* (Harmondsworth: Penguin Books, 1969), pp. 108-19; emphasis added.

27. The English translation of the *Church Dogmatics* was published in Edinburgh by T. & T. Clark (various translators) from 1936 to 1977 (a new translation of I/1 appeared in 1975); abbreviated hereafter as *CD* followed by Volume number in Roman numerals, Tome number in Arabic numerals.

28. George Hunsinger, "Karl Barth's Christology: Its Basic Chalcedonian Character," in his book *Disruptive Grace: Studies in the Theology of Karl Barth* (Grand Rapids: Eerdmans,

course his Christology was not a mere republication of Chalcedon as if nothing had happened in doctrinal development since that Fourth Ecumenical Council. Far from it. For one thing Barth made sure that his Christology, however thoroughly orthodox in its roots and intent, did not just sit there, isolated as a treatise, to be absorbed until the time comes to move on to another topic. The very fact that one may quote significant passages relating to his Christology throughout *all* the volumes of the *Church Dogmatics* proves otherwise; and, as every commentator notes, Barth revolutionized key Reformation (and Augustinian) doctrines about predestination, free will, God's universal will to save, the nature-grace problem, and so on, based on his central christological insights. But here, we shall concentrate almost solely on his christological teaching as such, with only the barest indication of its implications for other areas of the Christian faith.

The first point to be noted is that Barth's appropriation of Chalcedon is "dialectical," but now in a different sense than was present in his commentary on Romans, where his very book undercut and contradicted itself. Now he takes the Chalcedonian pairing (as the tradition does) as a careful synthesis of two hard-to-reconcile Christologies, known conveniently (with a certain violence to history, to be sure) as Alexandrine and Antiochene. As we saw in Chapter 4, the two viewpoints are not easy to reconcile, and perhaps for conceptual thought never can be reconciled. Thus, for the patient reader of the vast volumes of the *Church Dogmatics,* one will detect an Alexandrine stress here and an Antiochene stress there. As Hunsinger notes, "Barth is probably the first theologian in the history of Christian doctrine who alternates back and forth, deliberately, between an 'Alexandrian' and an 'Antiochian' idiom."[29]

The adverb "deliberately" is crucial. As we saw in Chapter 4, post-Chalcedonian debate in the East often refused to take Chalcedon as the starting point for a consideration of the *conceptual breakdown* entailed in christological doctrine, from which arose monophysitism and monothelitism and from which Nestorianism continued to exist. Reading through a Barthian lens, we retrospectively see why the Chalcedonian decree devolved (among those who rejected that council) into two irreconcilable camps: be-

---

2000), pp. 131-47; abbreviated hereafter as Hunsinger, *Disruptive Grace.* A shorter version of this chapter (under the same title) may be found in *The Cambridge Companion to Karl Barth,* ed. John Webster (Cambridge: Cambridge University Press, 2000), pp. 127-42. I shall be citing from the longer version throughout.

29. Hunsinger, *Disruptive Grace,* p. 135.

cause both sides refused to let concepts yield to mystery. "The point of Christology, Barth believed, is to comprehend the incomprehensibility of the incarnation precisely in its incomprehensibility."[30]

A good sign that Barth was successful in fulfilling that admittedly difficult program can be seen by noting how often he was accused by his critics either of monophysitism or Nestorianism. Not surprisingly, given Barth's firm rejection of liberal Christologies in all forms and his explicit avowal of Chalcedon,[31] the charge most often made is that his Christology is too Alexandrian, always a false option for those who can countenance only a "low" Christology.[32] But one occasionally encounters accusations that Barth's Christology is too Nestorian, meaning that in Barth Christ's humanity is too externally juxtaposed, not united, to God.[33] Probably a good sign that Barth is doing something right. As Hunsinger rightly points out, "What makes Barth's Christology different from Alexandrian and Antiochian Christologies is mainly that these two alternatives, each in its own way, tend to re-

30. Hunsinger, *Disruptive Grace*, p. 135; Hunsinger continues: "The New Testament, he suggested, directs us to this incomprehensibility by the very way it juxtaposes two different modes of depiction. On the one hand, Jesus of Nazareth is depicted as the Son of God; and on the other, the Son of God is depicted as Jesus of Nazareth. The one mode is [largely] illustrated by the synoptic tradition; the other, by the Johannine tradition. The conclusion Barth drew is significant: 'It is impossible to listen at one and the same time to the two statements that Jesus of Nazareth is the Son of God, and that the Son of God is Jesus of Nazareth. One hears either the one or the other or one hears nothing. When one is heard, the other can be heard only indirectly, in faith.' [*CD* I/1, p. 180]." Hunsinger, p. 135. Note that this quotation is drawn from the very first tome of the *CD*.

31. Even to the point of adopting its vocabulary as his own: "God is himself this man Jesus Christ, very God and very man, both of them unconfused and unmixed, but also unseparated and undivided, in the one person of this Messiah and Savior" (*CD* II/1, p. 486).

32. Most prominently in the controversial book by Charles T. Waldrop, *Karl Barth's Christology: Its Basic Alexandrian Character* (Berlin: De Gruyter, 1984): "Barth assigns to 'Jesus Christ' predicates which appear startling, confusing, and even contradictory. Following the lead of analytic philosophers, I wanted to determine whether Barth's christological propositions are meaningful, and if they are, what factors prove the foundation for their meaning. It soon became evident to me, however, that *the principles which govern Barth's christological language are theological principles, not simply linguistic or philosophical principles*" (p. vii; emphasis added). Telling too is Waldrop's other admission: "At one stage of my research, I believed that Barth was an Antiochian theologian" (p. vii).

33. This accusation is admittedly much rarer but occurs in Regin Prenter, "Karl Barths Umbildung der traditionellen Zweinaturlehre in lutherischer Beleuchtung," *Studia Theologia* 11 (1958): 1-88, especially 10-43. As the title implies, this accusation hearkens back to former Lutheran-Calvinist disputes in Christology. See also John McIntyre, *The Shape of Christology* (Philadelphia: Westminster, 1966), pp. 153-55.

solve the incarnation mystery into something more nearly conceivable on the basis of ordinary experience and history."[34]

Of course, as we saw earlier, Barth did not merely republish Chalcedon without further ado.[35] The very fact that his Christology is entissued throughout the *Church Dogmatics* shows that it affects all the other topics he takes up. Although he rejected, for obvious reasons, Harnack's charge that Hellenistic philosophical categories represented a false admixture into the Semitic simplicity of the gospel message, he also insisted with equal force that we only learn what divine and human natures mean when we look at them in Christ.[36]

From that axiom Barth insisted that the hypostatic union is not so much an abstract state of being as the central fact of history. In other words Jesus Christ is an *actor* on the stage of world history, and thus by virtue of the hypostatic union he is *God* acting in history: "He acts as God when He acts as a human being, and as a human being when He acts as God" (*CD* IV/2, p. 115). For this reason Barth prefers to define the hypostatic union not as tradition did with the term *communicatio idiomatum* (interchange of attributes) but as the *communicatio operationum* (interchange of actions or operations). And thus he concludes:

34. Hunsinger, *Disruptive Grace*, p. 136.

35. He certainly has absorbed the lessons gleaned from the condemnation of monothelitism in the seventh century and perhaps did so more radically than even Maximus the Confessor: "The New Testament has . . . treated the *vere homo* with such seriousness that it has portrayed the obedience of Jesus throughout as a genuine struggle for obedience. . . . The temptation narrative of Matt. 4:1ff obviously describes the very opposite of a mock battle, and it would be wrong to conceive it as merely 'external molestation by Satan'. . . . The point, however, is that, in the state and situation of fallen humanity before God, Jesus did not take flight. Rather, he took it upon himself, lived it and bore it himself as the eternal Son of God. How could he have done so, if in his human existence, he had not been exposed to real inward temptation and trial? If like other men, he had not trodden an inner path? If he had not cried out to God, and wrestled with God, in real inward need? [But] even in this wrestling, in which he was in solidarity with us to the last, there was done that which is not done by us, the will of God" (*CD* I/2, p. 158). On this theme see Paul Dafydd Jones, *The Humanity of Christ: Christology in Karl Barth's Church Dogmatics* (London: T. & T. Clark, 2008).

36. "No general idea of the 'Godhead' developed abstractly from such concepts must be allowed to intrude at this point. How the freedom of God is constituted, in what character He is the Creator and Lord of all things, distinct from and superior to them, in short, what is to be understood by 'Godhead,' is something . . . we must always learn from Jesus Christ" (*CD* IV/1, p. 129). Correlatively: "What [Christ's] manhood is, and therefore true manhood, we cannot read into Him from elsewhere, but must be told by Him" (*CD* IV/1, p. 131).

Nor are abstractions possible to the one who knows Jesus Christ. There is no place for a dualistic thinking which divides the divine and human, but only for a historical [thinking], which at every point, in and with the humiliation and exaltation of the one Son of God and Son of Man, in and with His being as servant and Lord, is ready to accompany the event of the union of His divine and human essence. (*CD* IV/2, p. 115)

Since his death Barth's influence in the Protestant churches and divinity schools has waned, itself no doubt a sign of the tremendous difficulty in maintaining the primacy of Christ in our contemporary pluralistic setting. Why that should be the case can perhaps best be seen in the case of subsequent Catholic thinking on this issue, to which we now turn.

CHAPTER 10

Christology and Pluralism: Catholic Theologians

The horrors of hell can be experienced within a single day; that's plenty of time.

Ludwig Wittgenstein, *Culture and Value*

Speaking very generally, and at the risk of considerable oversimplification, trends in Catholic Christology in the second half of the twentieth century follow the "trajectory arc" that was taken in Protestant Christology from Schleiermacher to Barth. To be sure, the parallels are only formal, and even there very rough. Nonetheless, for purposes of the schema of this chapter I shall be arranging four significant Catholic theologians according to this rubric: just as Schleiermacher sought a common ground of discourse between the secular academy and Christian theology under the overarching concept of the feeling of absolute dependence, Rahner did something roughly similar with his concept of the supernatural existential; similarly, just as Troeltsch saw the "payoff" of Christology in the social teaching of the church, Sobrino interprets Christology according to its liberating potential to free victims of social oppression from their burdens; and finally, just as Barth said a loud No to the entire trend of liberal Protestant Christology because it led to a relativization of the claims of Christ, so too did Balthasar and Ratzinger.[1]

---

1. I am fully conscious that I am neglecting a number of important Catholic christologians, whom I must omit for reasons of space and because of my focus on the question of pluralism. However, a few more will be treated in Chapter 11, especially when their Christologies have met with specific responses from the church's magisterium.

Karl Rahner

Known above all for his technical prowess and extraordinary speculative gifts (and often murky style), Karl Rahner (1904-84) was, like Schleiermacher before him, passionately concerned to establish the credibility of the Christian message to the "cultured despisers" of his day; and like Schleiermacher, he saw only one possible program for apologetics in the modern setting: *start with the issue of what makes for credibility in general terms and then fit Jesus Christ within that framework.* As the acute critic Bruce Marshall notes: "Rahner's theology, and centrally his Christology, is like many others since the early eighteenth century in one distinctive respect: he supposes that in order to believe in Jesus Christ as the unique redeemer it is necessary to show how that belief is possible and credible, and to do so by an appeal to general criteria of religious and moral meaningfulness."[2] The assumption of course is that those norms of the "possible and credible" are to be established *first,* in order *then* to present the person of Jesus Christ in these now-made-credible terms; and on this program Rahner is admirably (some would say startlingly) explicit: "How can he [Jesus], the concrete one, in his historical-concrete reality, *which is not at all generally valid,* be a norm for me?"[3]

Clearly, if he is to succeed in his task of making the Christian message credible (including to himself), Rahner has to meet his own challenge of making Christ "generally valid" for all, especially under the self-imposed burden of assuming at the outset that the concrete, historical reality of Jesus somehow seems *not* to be generally valid. The key both to the problem and to the solution of general validity in Rahner's thought can be located in the crucial term "[Christ's] historical-concrete reality." Like so many other Enlightenment-influenced Protestant theologians, this is always the rub: How can one particular individual in history, who appears on the stage of history at one time and leaves it shortly thereafter, claim validity for all times and places?

To address this always-burning question Rahner adopted his famous "transcendental" method, a term he applied in its technical Kantian sense, which asked what the "conditions for the possibility" are for any act of human cognition. In Kant's case, the question was asked epistemologically:

---

2. Bruce Marshall, *Christologies in Conflict: The Identity of a Saviour in Rahner and Barth* (Oxford: Blackwell, 1987), p. 15; cited hereafter as Marshall, *Conflict.*

3. Karl Rahner, *Schriften zur Theologie,* vol. 15, p. 234; emphasis added: "wie kann er, der Konkrete, in seiner gar nicht allgemeingültigen, sondern in seiner geschichtlich-konkreten Wirklichkeit für mich eine Norm sein?"

since we in fact know things, what structure must the human mind have that enables us to have such knowledge? Even more crucially, how is the human mind so constituted not just to know things but also, and perhaps above all, to know its limits beyond which it may not stray? In his doctoral dissertation, *Spirit in the World,* Rahner answered that Kantian question in his own quasi-Thomist way: he said that when the human mind knows any particular thing, it is implicitly operating within a horizon of being whose ultimate determinant is God.[4]

Rahner then applied this method to revelation in *Hearer of the Word:* assuming that revelation has occurred (which all Christians do), this must mean that man is so constituted that he can hear it if and when it does come. And so, in true Kantian manner, the task for Rahner is then to analyze man's spiritual constitution to detect this aural capacity to recognize revelation if it should reach his ears. Here's the dilemma (note how redolent this passage is of Troeltsch):

> Revelation is essentially a historical process. That and how it took place depends strictly on a unique combination of historical events, in which God's work has authentically spoken to humanity. The philosophy of religion, on the other hand, seems to be essentially "supratemporal," "transhistorical," exactly like metaphysics with which it is supposed to coincide. Hence *the philosophy of religion seems to establish a religion that is basically independent of any historical event,* a religion which is equally available to everyone, at every moment of one's existence in history, a religion that may be ever founded again, for which every land is the holy land and every time the fullness of time. For the human spirit can always and everywhere reach the "eternal ideas" of the True, the Good and the Beautiful.[5]

Of course Rahner never denied that the definitive revelation in Jesus Christ had in fact taken place, but that concession did nothing, by his lights, to obviate the problem: "Revelation has in fact occurred. Because of our overall duty of obedience to God we have the duty to obey God's commands, hence, in our case, to accept the divine revelation with faith. However, logically speaking, the metaphysical justification of our duty to listen, to take a

---

4. In support of the Thomist provenance of this view, Rahner regularly cited Aquinas's line: "All knowing beings implicitly know God in everything they know" (*De veritate* 22, 1 ad 1).

5. Karl Rahner, *Hearer of the Word,* trans. Joseph Donceel (New York: Continuum, 1994/1941), p. 7; emphasis added; abbreviated hereafter as Rahner, *Hearer.*

possible revelation into account, is previous to the actual occurrence of it."[6] What is so fascinating about this opening axiom is Rahner's frank avowal of the difficulties he has created for himself — like a Houdini artist who ties himself in some elaborate knot just to show the public how skilled he is in extricating himself from it:

> If we start from ourselves, God's revelation cannot be validated either in its actuality, or in its necessity, or in its inner nature. . . . It remains questionable (at least for the time being) whether and in what sense we can discover in ourselves something like a "power of hearing" for an eventual revelation of God, *before* we have in fact heard it, and have thus found out that we are capable of hearing it.[7]

The dangers of this approach are obvious, and Rahner makes no attempt to deny them: "We must even expect in our work that, as far as our mere ideas are concerned, we shall construct a receptacle that is too narrow to receive the treasure of the divine faith."[8] No wonder, then, that when he gets to the end of the book he has to concede the nugatory results of the method: "It might seem that we had not achieved much."[9]

Despite these openly avowed difficulties, Rahner never abandoned his method, as can be seen by his constant invocation of his technical terms "transcendental" and "categorial."[10] The former term we have already defined (in its theological aspects) as the answer to this question: What must be true about the human person for a possible revelation to be recognized as such and received? Unfortunately, as Marshall rightly notes, Rahner never carefully defined what he meant by the latter term.[11]

---

6. Rahner, *Hearer,* p. 14. This view, it should be added in passing, has not found favor among postmodern philosophers of whatever stripe. As the late American pragmatist Richard Rorty once quipped: "Time will tell, but epistemology won't."

7. Rahner, *Hearer,* p. 5; Rahner's emphasis.

8. Rahner, *Hearer,* p. 21.

9. Rahner, *Hearer,* p. 154.

10. As in his last book, *Foundations of Christian Faith,* trans. William V. Dyke, S.J. (New York: Continuum, 1978/1976); abbreviated hereafter as Rahner, *Foundations.* In this book, he says that only a transcendental Christology can ensure that the claim of Jesus to be the absolute savior not become "simply a mythological (in the pejorative sense) overlay on historical events" (p. 207). Again note the Troeltschian formulation of the problem.

11. "By contrast with his occasional explicit sketches of the 'transcendental' aspect of theology, Rahner virtually never pauses to give a general characterization of the 'categorial' aspect." But from its contrast with "transcendental" one may at least come to this provi-

But this much is clear: what is categorial is always problematic; what is transcendental is the ground on which the problems of the categorial are resolved. Unfortunately, this opening gambit hobbles Rahner's Christology from the outset. For once we have answered what man must be like to be able to hear revelation (should it come), the very answer to that question makes the categorial, *historical* revelation (when it does come) opaque and problematic. In other words, no sooner has the categorial revelation occurred, than it must retreat back into the transcendental if it is to be meaningful both to the believer and to the potential believer.[12]

Clearly, the only way out of this dilemma is to show that in Jesus Christ the transcendental and categorial perfectly meet and coincide. But can such a coincidence ever be possible, even of Jesus Christ, given Rahner's formulation of the problem? Take the case of the resurrection of Jesus. For that event to be true "for us" we must gain access to it through our transcendentally necessary hope for our own resurrection; but how do we know Jesus was raised except in categorial terms (the New Testament, after all, uses human words to proclaim its message)? In Rahner's own words: "Hence if the testimony of the apostles about the resurrection were to be judged *only* according to the secular model of a witness's statement, it would have to be rejected as incredible."[13]

---

sional conclusion: "The basic import of what one could call 'categorial theology' is clear enough from what has been said about its contrast term. 'Categorial' simply means 'what can be put into categories'. . . . More precisely (since for Rahner the transcendental too can, at least indirectly, be evoked in language), the 'categorial' is circumscribed in space and time; in this sense human words, the sacraments, the church and Scripture can all be called 'something categorial.' Rahner is especially given to contrasting transcendental with 'historical,' where 'historical' has the broad meaning of 'spatio-temporal,' and so is equivalent to categorial." Marshall, *Conflict*, pp. 17-18. Marshall also notes that Rahner never defines "mythological" either, even though he uses the term almost invariably in its pejorative meaning (following Rudolf Bultmann here). The unusual neologism "categorial" is chosen over the more normal term "categorical," because that latter word usually means "unconditioned" or "absolute" — as in a categorical No or the categorical imperative (the same holds true of the German equivalents). That of course means nearly the opposite of what Rahner wishes to mean by "categorial."

12. "The 'kinds of things' Christians say about salvation [or revelation] are taken by Rahner to constitute a class or genus of claims, the credibility of which must be established before they can be predicated of a particular subject. Or, more precisely, the credibility of this class of claims as such must be established in order for its attribution to a particular subject to result in a credible proposition." Marshall, *Conflict*, p. 23.

13. Rahner, *Foundations*, p. 275. Of course, Rahner fully admits that faith is required for assent to the resurrection and that that faith is our link with the faith of the apostles; but to

The same problem crops up in confessing Jesus as "absolute Savior." Rahner claims on transcendental grounds that man's plight is so obvious to him that he longs for an absolute Savior. True enough, but what are the grounds for confessing an itinerant teacher from Galilee in the first century as that Savior? Here is Rahner's answer:

> But if this is the essence of man [to strive for God and find an absolute Savior], he attains his supreme fulfillment, the gratuitous fulfillment of his essence to which through his own ways of perfection he is always tending, only when he adoringly believes that *somewhere* there is a being whose existence steps so much out of itself into God that [this being] simply *is* the question [note: and not the answer!] about the mystery utterly given over to the mystery. . . . The rest of us are all farther from God, because we always have to think that we are the only ones who understand ourselves. But he [Jesus of Nazareth] *knew* that only the Father knows this mystery, and so he knew that only he knows the Father.[14]

And how does Rahner know this? Only in terms that can be called transcendental Schleiermacherianism: "The incarnation of God is therefore the unique, *supreme,* case of the total actualization of human reality, which consists of the fact that man *is* in so far as he surrenders himself."[15] But people

---

say that the reality of the resurrection is wholly *in*credible on the secular model is tantamount to saying more than that the historical-critical method cannot prove the resurrection (which no believer denies). He also seems to be saying that the historical-critical method must regard the resurrection as impossible from the outset. At all events, Marshall is certainly right to say that "no particular, that is, no specific object, is logically indispensable to the transcendental conditions in the human subject . . . which allow it to be experienced and known" (Marshall, *Conflict,* p. 80), which would seem to make the resurrection dispensable for the Christian. For what the historical-critical method can and cannot say about the resurrection, see Chapter 3.

14. Karl Rahner, "On the Theology of the Incarnation," *Theological Investigations,* vol. 4, trans. Kevin Smyth (Baltimore: Helicon Press, 1966), p. 111; cited hereafter as *TI.* As if worried that this passage sounds too much like Schleiermacher, Rahner adds: "To avoid misunderstanding, we must note that the Christology outlined above is not a 'Christology of consciousness' in contrast to an ontological Christology affirming the substantial unity of the Logos with his human nature. It is based on the metaphysical insight, derived from a strict ontology, that true being is the spirit as such itself" (p. 111). But if that spirit knows itself more surely via the transcendental method, and if we know that Jesus is the absolute Savior only categorially, how does that solve the problem?

15. Rahner, "On the Theology of the Incarnation," p. 110; Rahner's emphases; translation slightly altered.

can surrender themselves to all kinds of causes that later prove demonic; and like Troeltsch's relativism, Rahner's transcendental method offers no way to distinguish one version of surrender over another. Telling in this regard is Rahner's conclusion to *Hearer of the Word*:

> Because it [revelation] reaches us precisely *as* revelation of God in human historicity, it carries with it all that in historical phenomena is fortuitous and unclear; that might have been different and is likely to be criticized. Now, when somebody is ready, from the start, to consider the possibility of such a religion, is it hard for such a person to acknowledge the Holy Roman Catholic Church as the place of the real revelation of the living God?[16]

No doubt Rahner thought this final move in his argument (which is really nothing other than a rhetorical question) was obvious, given his thoroughly Catholic soul and his upbringing in Catholic Bavaria. But he wrote this book in 1941 in post-*Anschluss* Austria, where so many of his countrymen were not finding Rahner's option in the least obvious or easy.[17]

As noted in the previous chapter, Schleiermacher launched an entire way of doing Christology that resulted in the unresolved dilemmas of Troeltsch, whose contradictions then led to Barth. So, not surprisingly, Catholic theologians influenced by Barth found much to object to in Rahner, especially the Barth-influenced Hans Urs von Balthasar, who insisted that the revelation of God's glory needs no justification but itself. And this means that there will be no question in his theology, as Aidan Nichols rightly points out, "of dismembering the divine self-manifestation into, on the one hand, 'categorial' and on the other 'transcendental' aspects, such that . . . Christian truth becomes at best a key to, and at worst simply an illustration of, what is in any case already given in the universal God-world relationship."[18]

---

16. Rahner, *Hearer*, p. 155.

17. Nor did Rahner seem able to wiggle out of his self-made knot later: "When *in* the redeemed destiny of one human being and in that destiny experienced *as* redeemed, a person grasps God's promise of salvation to himself, he is practicing Christology explicitly or implicitly. . . . And, since a person can really only culpably suppress the question of his own salvation, such an explicitly or implicitly *questing* Christology involves in every human being today also the presence in transcendence and grace of the prerequisite that he is seeking and will eventually find *his own private Christology*." Karl Rahner, *TI*, vol. 18, trans. Edward Quinn (London: Darton, Longman & Todd, 1984), pp. 147-48; emphases added.

18. Aidan Nichols, O.P., *Say It Is Pentecost: A Guide Through Balthasar's Logic* (Washington, DC: Catholic University of America Press, 2001), p. 5. This is why Rahner often begins

But these remarks anticipate what only gradually became apparent toward the very end of the twentieth century. During the time of Rahner's greatest influence, however, and before Balthasar's theology began to gain an audience, another school of theology was emerging with important christological teachings — liberation theology — and to that we shall now turn.

Jon Sobrino

Jon Sobrino (1938-) was born of a Basque family in Barcelona, Spain, and entered the Society of Jesus at the age of eighteen. He was later sent by his Order to El Salvador as part of his training, after which he studied engineering at St. Louis University and then theology at the Jesuit-run theologate in Frankfurt, Germany. After that he was assigned to teach at the University of Central America (which indeed he helped to found) in San Salvador, the capital of El Salvador. Because he happened to be out of the country at the time, he escaped the assassination of six of his brother Jesuits, their housekeeper, and her daughter on November 16, 1989, by a rightwing paramilitary death squad — an act that had been carried out with clear connivance of the government, or at least of leading figures inside the regime. (This took place during a brutal civil war between leftist guerillas and the rightwing government, and Jesuit efforts to mediate the conflict by addressing the causes of the war so enraged the rightists that they ordered the assassinations.[19])

I have chosen Sobrino for treatment here not only because he is one of the most prominent exponents of liberation theology but also because he is

---

his essays on Christology with an opening premise that for him almost serves as a kind of Euclidian axiom: the universal possibility of salvation *within which* he presents his Christology, rather than, as Paul, did, beginning with Christ's work. See, for example, his essay "The One Christ and the Universality of Salvation": "[T]he theological truth of the universal possibility of salvation may be taken without reserve to possess binding dogmatic force. It may be that it has not been defined but there is no doubt that it belongs to the contemporary understanding of faith and may be considered as the explicit and official teaching of the Church. As such it is to be regarded as absolutely binding." Karl Rahner, *TI*, vol. 16, trans. David Morland, O.S.B. (London: Darton, Longman & Todd, 1979), p. 202. But Paul knew of God's universal saving will only through Christ.

19. Sobrino's portrait of his fellow Jesuits may be found in his *Companions of Jesus: The Jesuit Martyrs of El Salvador* (Maryknoll, NY: Orbis Books, 1990), pp. 3-56; an account of the crime and its aftermath by Stan Granot Duncan forms the Introduction to that volume, p. xxviii.

so explicitly christological in his theology.[20] That said, he certainly joins other liberation theologians in placing his theology in a certain specific context — the church of the poor, which, at least in certain senses, has priority over the institutional church: "This [institutional church], though fundamental, is not the most fundamental aspect of the church as a real setting for christology, since here we are still on the level of what we may call *secondary ecclesiality*."[21] In contrast, "primary ecclesiality" refers to the church where real faith, hope, and love are put into practice — in christological terms, where believers become disciples of Christ, and nowhere are disciples more faithful to Christ than where the poor follow Christ; and because Latin America is so pockmarked by poverty, Christology must be done in this setting:

> Latin American christology — and specifically as christology — identifies its setting, in the sense of a real situation, as the poor of the world, and this situation is what must be present in and permeate any particular setting in which christology is done. . . . Because they are God's preferred, and because of the difference between their faith and the faith of the nonpoor, the poor, within the faith community, question christological faith and give it its fundamental direction. . . . [This] social setting is thus the most crucial to faith, and most crucial in shaping the thought pattern of christology, and [is] what requires and encourages the epistemological break.[22]

Thus the two fissures, between the primary church of discipleship and the secondary institutional church, and between the poor and nonpoor (and not just between the poor and the *rich*), intersect to create what Sobrino calls the *epistemological break,* by which he means that a great gulf separates us from the ecumenical councils of the early church that defined classical christological doctrine. But that break is rooted in a more fundamental one: the break between New Testament Christology and that of the patristic councils. So severe for Sobrino is this rupture that appeal to the early coun-

---

20. As Kevin Burke rightly notes, Sobrino was by far the most systematic of the Jesuit liberation theologians in Latin America and the only one whose doctoral training was in systematic theology; see Kevin Burke, S.J., *The Ground Beneath the Cross: The Theology of Ignacio Ellacuría* (Washington, DC: Georgetown University Press, 2000), p. 23.

21. Jon Sobrino, *Jesus the Liberator: A Historical-Theological Reading of Jesus of Nazareth,* trans. Paul Burns and Francis McDonough (Maryknoll, NY: Orbis Books, 1994/1991), p. 29; Sobrino's emphasis; abbreviated hereafter as Sobrino, *Jesus.*

22. Sobrino, *Jesus,* pp. 28, 30, 31.

cils is deeply problematic, even perilous: "While these [conciliar] texts are useful theologically, besides being normative, they are also limited and even dangerous, as is widely recognized today."[23]

He does not cite the people — either experts in historical theology or ordinary lay folk, especially the poor — who have so widely recognized the "dangers" of christological doctrine. Nor does he ever get around to defining what he means by "dangerous," although one could say it emerges readily enough from the context: these conciliar texts are simultaneously normative and filled with peril, it seems, because they are time-bound, valid for the cultural setting in which they were formulated but dangerous if made normative today, except as a kind of nod to a setting different from our own. (The fact that radical historical critics like Albert Schweitzer say the same about the New Testament, which makes it just as strange to us as the Fathers, is an irony never addressed by Sobrino.)

To be sure, this break for Sobrino is not total; for at least the author concedes a modest continuity: "The New Testament . . . contains . . . the seed of what will produce confessions of the divinity of Christ in the strict sense."[24] That concession, though, does not really control Sobrino's analysis, for he does not take this metaphor in the organic sense it usually implies, as in Jesus' parable of the kingdom likened to a mustard seed that grows into a full tree (Mark 4:26-29) or in John Henry Newman's use of the image of seed and tree to establish the continuity of Christ's church over the centuries. For much earlier in the book he quite explicitly insists on *discontinuity:* "at the outset Jesus was not spoken of as *God,* nor was *divinity* a term applied to him; this happened only after a considerable interval of believing explication, almost certainly after the fall of Jerusalem."[25]

23. Jon Sobrino, *Christ the Liberator: A View from the Victims,* trans. Paul Burns (Maryknoll, NY: Orbis Books, 2001/1999), p. 221; abbreviated hereafter as Sobrino, *Christ.*

24. Sobrino, *Christ,* p. 257.

25. Sobrino, *Christ,* p. 114; emphases in the original. At least the author did not attribute all the "dangers" entailed in divinizing Jesus as having begun with the Council of Nicea in the manner of Dan Brown's *The Da Vinci Code.* Presumably, he is referring to the usual dating of Matthew, Luke, and John having been written after the destruction of the Temple in A.D. 70, so that any attribution of divinity to Jesus in these Gospels must be attributed to a later Christian "overlay." Chapter 3 of this book already tried to show, on exegetical grounds alone, the impossibility of this thesis. But in any case we already have the witness of Paul, all of whose letters were written before Rome destroyed the Temple, to refute this thesis. As the premier New Testament exegete in the English-speaking world, N. T. Wright, put it in a citation already adduced in Chapter 4, "Faced with that astonishing statement [1 Cor. 8:6], one would have to say that if the early Fathers of the church hadn't existed it would be necessary

Given the gulf that obtains (Sobrino alleges) between the New Testament's band of disciples and the institutional church of the patristic councils, and between those councils and today's "primary" church of the poor, one is not surprised that he does not really engage patristic Christology in all its complexities. (Why bother, if it is so dangerous?) This neglect is unfortunate, because it leads to some remarkably incautious formulations on Sobrino's part, including, ironically enough, statements that skirt close to saying that the orthodox councils *approved* the Logos-Sarx Christology of Apollinaris, in which the divinity of the Logos virtually takes over the humanity of Jesus:

> From a dogmatic point of view, we have to say, without any reservation, that the Son (the second person of the Trinity) took on the whole reality of Jesus and, although the dogmatic formula never explains the manner of this being affected by the human dimension, the thesis is radical. The *Son experienced Jesus' humanity,* existence in history, life, destiny, and death.[26]

Equally confused is his interpretation of the *communicatio idiomatum,* which in his reading does not work both ways: "the limited human is predicated of God, but the unlimited divine is not predicated of Jesus."[27] Sobrino seems here (although it is hard to tell) to be confusing attributes *(idiomata)* with substance *(hypostasis).* But what really seems to be at work here is a concern to make sure that Jesus' divinity not be interpreted in such a way that he no longer seems to be "one of us." Thus, despite his apparent endorsement of Apollinarianism above, the gravamen of both his books on Christology is to establish Jesus' solidarity with us in our plight — a laudable goal certainly,

---

to invent them." N. T. Wright, *What Paul Really Said: Was Paul of Tarsus the Real Founder of Christianity?* (Grand Rapids: Eerdmans, 1997), p. 66.

26. Sobrino, *Jesus,* p. 242; emphasis added. Having misinterpreted the councils so radically, the author then has to assume the orthodoxy of this allegedly conciliar position, which he can only do by absorbing God into Jesus and then into the poor: "However this statement may be used or manipulated, whether to promote resignation or to inspire action for liberation, whether to try [to] explain suffering or, on the contrary, to raise it to the status of an ultimate mystery — that is, of what cannot be explained — *it still holds good.* And this, undoubtedly, was the first great difficulty in the way of accepting the divinity of Christ at Nicea, the first council of the universal church, because it presents a Son — who is divine — taking on unreservedly every dimension of humanity" (p. 242; emphasis added).

27. Sobrino, *Christ,* p. 223; see also: "What happens in reality is that the *communicatio idiomatum* works only in one direction" (p. 333).

provided Sobrino can show that that solidarity is not so total that Jesus can no longer pluck us out of our desperation. Thus he says, with typical vagueness, "So one can, and in my view must, say that '*Jesus was an extraordinary believer* and had faith. Faith was Jesus' mode of being.'"[28] There is, of course, an enormous literature on the meaning of Hebrews 12:2, which describes Jesus as the "author and pioneer of our faith." But however the attribution of faith to Jesus is to be understood, the dogmatic theologian at least must pair that verse with John 6:46 ("No one has seen the Father except the one who is from God; only he has seen the Father"). Otherwise Jesus' "faith" becomes merely the same kind of faith as ours (albeit more intensely felt). Our faith holds that God will one day rescue us from our plight, and Jesus shows consistent awareness that he was *sent* by the Father to do the rescuing.

By omitting that dimension from Jesus' "faith," Sobrino ends up subordinating Jesus to the kingdom he preached, perhaps the most problematic aspect of his Christology. Yes, Jesus mediates the kingdom through his teaching, Sobrino concedes, but the kingdom has priority over the herald of the kingdom, so that to absolutize the messenger is to undermine the message: "[W]hen Christ the mediator is made absolute . . . there is no sense of his constitutive relatedness to what is mediated, the Kingdom of God."[29]

But this entirely ignores the central New Testament doctrine that we are not saved by Jesus' teaching but by his person. The whole point of the doctrine of the incarnation is to testify to the indispensability of the person of Christ to his mission. If Plato had never been born, something like Platonism (albeit under a different name) would have arisen anyway, given the sheer plausibility of that philosophy; also Jesus' proclamation of the Golden Rule is not unknown in other religions, so that his indispensability can hardly be located in his teaching alone. But in Sobrino's view, to absolutize Christ is to eclipse the teaching. (Why? Does the teaching become *less* true because a divine Jesus taught it, yet did so by drawing on the rabbinic tradition?) Sobrino even goes so far as to set up this analogy: "Mediation and mediator are, then, essentially related, but they are not the same thing. There is always a Moses and a promised land, an Archbishop Romero and a dream of justice."[30]

28. Sobrino, *Jesus*, p. 154, citing, with obvious approval, the *obiter dictum* of Leonardo Boff, *Jesucristo y la liberación del hombre* (Madrid, 1987), p. 137; emphasis added.

29. Sobrino, *Jesus*, p. 16. "This criticism may seem shocking, since it is obvious that, for Christian faith, Christ is an absolute, and it may also seem unjust, since the faith itself . . . has always presented Christ essentially 'in relation' to the Father and the Spirit within the Trinity" (p. 16). But having admitted that his views are shocking, he never goes on to mitigate the shock.

30. Sobrino, *Jesus*, p. 108. The author seems to take away the radicality of this analogy

Given Sobrino's precedence of the message over the messenger, the specifically saving activity of Christ recedes; in fact, for him it is not part of his message at all! Speaking in extraordinarily apodictic tones (something at least Troeltsch never did), he even goes so far as to make this claim:

> Let it be said from the start that the historical Jesus did not interpret his death in terms of salvation, in terms of soteriological models later developed by the New Testament such as expiatory sacrifice or vicarious satisfaction. . . . In other words, there are no grounds for thinking that Jesus attributed an absolute transcendent meaning to his own death, as the New Testament did later. This does not mean, however, that Jesus did not look for a meaning for his own death, that he did not see it in continuity with and supporting his own cause. All prophets, *religious or not,* have done this, because it is not possible to accept dying completely, and no prophet wants to accept that his cause will die completely.[31]

In making these extraordinary claims, and in phrasing them so infallibly, Sobrino does not even bother to consult the vast exegetical commentary on Mark 10:45 ("the Son of Man did not come to be served but to serve, and to give his life as a ransom for the many"); and he completely ignores the implications of this view for the historicity of one of the most pervasively attested episodes of the Gospels, Christ's institution of the Eucharist ("This is my blood of the covenant, which is poured out for many" [Mark 14:24]).

So, is the allegedly later attribution of saving significance to Jesus' death on the cross by subsequent New Testament writers wrong, or at least dispensable? Not quite, but Sobrino has a hard time admitting any efficacious saving power to the cross outside of its utility for illustrating how we should behave in the face of social oppression: "This saving efficacy [of the cross] is shown more in the form of an exemplary cause than of an efficient cause. But this does not mean that it is not effective. . . . [But] it is not efficient causality, but symbolic causality."[32]

---

by approving of Origen's definition of Christ as the *autobasileia* of God, meaning "the kingdom of God in person." But he has already undermined that appropriation by claiming that making Christ an absolute mediator eclipses the message of the kingdom. In any event, just after approving of Origen's coinage, he goes on to say: "important words that well describe the finality of the personal mediator of the Kingdom, but dangerous [that word again!] if they equate Christ with the reality of the Kingdom" (p. 108). The next section on Balthasar will show how this view can be refuted.

31. Sobrino, *Jesus,* pp. 201-2; emphasis added.

32. Sobrino, *Jesus,* p. 230. To be fair, the author mitigates these views with some strong

Left unaddressed here is how any of this is supposed to benefit the poor. Other authors have questioned whether liberation theology really liberates.[33] Clearly though, Sobrino is operating under a kind of Troeltschian assumption that the social payoff of the gospel message must in some way entail the relativization of christological claims — although Troeltsch is more concerned with the challenge of world religions than is Sobrino, who relativizes Jesus in terms of the kingdom he came to bring. But the tensions in the theology of both men carry obvious formal parallels, just as the responses to the latter's relativizing Christology by Hans Urs von Balthasar and Joseph Ratzinger have obvious parallels to the Christology of Karl Barth. For all three will insist, in their different ways of course, on giving primacy to the person of Christ in all interpretations of Christ, and so it is to these Christocentric Catholics that we now turn.

Hans Urs von Balthasar

No one tries to describe the Christology of Hans Urs von Balthasar (1905-88) in the space of one section of one chapter without trepidation. His output

---

statements on God's involvement in Jesus' cross: "there is no room for doubt that the initiative came from God himself. Jesus did not make God change. Jesus is the historical sacrament in which God expresses his irrevocable saving change toward us. Jesus' cross is the expression of God's love, and the novel and unexpected nature of this affirmation makes it a better confirmation than anything else of the initiative and credibility of God's love. Christ did not just die for a just person — something that is rare, but does happen — but 'died for the ungodly' (Rom. 5:6). This is the New Testament's fundamental affirmation. This affirmation does not 'explain' anything, but it says everything" (pp. 230-31). But how are these statements to be reconciled with the others cited above? Reading Sobrino often strikes this reader, at least, as like looking on Penelope unraveling at night the shawl she was working on the day before. For a more sympathetic view, in which Sobrino's more classical views are made to govern the interpretation of his more radical statements, see Walter Scott Hebden, *Christ Existing as Community and the Crucified People: Human Solidarity and Salvation in the Theology of Dietrich Bonhoeffer and Jon Sobrino* (Rome: Angelicum University, 2006).

33. See Michael Novak, *Will It Liberate? Questions About Liberation Theology* (New York: Paulist Press, 1986). One might add that Barth was a socialist, which at least proves that one may be thoroughly Chalcedonian, yet committed to the economic betterment of the poor. (I am not arguing for socialism here; merely pointing out that if one is convinced that socialism provides a better political economy for mankind, Chalcedonian Christology does not stand in the way. Whether socialism bears out the hopes placed in it, however, is the real question, one posed in Novak's book, but never by Sobrino, who takes a Marxian social analysis as axiomatic.)

was huge, gargantuanly so, and the sheer amount of the tradition — patristic, scholastic, and modern — on which he drew to fashion his theology was itself intimidating. For purposes of this chapter, therefore, attention will concentrate almost entirely on the implications of his Christology for answering the question of pluralism and its related issue of relativization.

Let us begin on a purely phenomenological level, prescinding from faith. What can we say about the various founders of the religions of the world? Recall the remark above about Plato: had he never existed, what now goes by the name of Platonism would surely have been mooted anyway, by somebody else.[34] Similarly in religion: theoretically, Aaron could have received the Tablets of Sinai as well as Moses; the Koran could have been revealed a generation earlier or later to a different prophet designated by God;[35] some other man could have come to the teachings of Confucius or the Buddha; Abraham's father Terah could just as well have been told to leave Ur as his son Abraham was (Gen. 11:31–12:2). As a Buddhist *koan* has it, "The finger that points to the moon is not the moon."

But it is otherwise with Jesus. Here we find a different kind of "founder," one who identifies his teaching with his person: "I am the Way, the Truth, and the Life" (John 14:6). Again it must be stressed that for the moment we are not asking whether the statement is true but what it means. We therefore can also provisionally ignore the knotty question of the historicity of the figure of Jesus presented in this most theological of the Gospels or whether this line records the actual words of the historical Jesus. By taking this claim purely on the phenomenological level, Balthasar asks us first and above all to concentrate on what the statement is actually saying, logically. How can a human being not

---

34. In fact Platonism *did* arise before Plato: "It was fairly widely believed in antiquity that Plato was not the first Platonist, as we might put it. Aristotle tells us that Plato 'followed the Italians (i.e., the Pythagoreans) in most things.' Plotinus tells us that Plato was not the first to say the things that in fact we today widely identify as elements of 'Platonism,' but he said them best. . . . In trying to understand what Platonism is, we must, therefore, recognize that Platonism is, in a sense, bigger than Plato." Lloyd P. Gerson, "What Is Platonism?" *Journal of the History of Philosophy* 43, no. 3 (July 2005): 253-76; here, 256, 257.

35. This, one gathers, is part of the reason for the storm of violence unleashed by the Danish cartoons of Mohammed; not only were the caricatures themselves offensive (as caricatures are meant to be); but according to Sunni majority doctrine, *any* pictorial depiction of the Prophet is forbidden, lest the pious believer be led into "idolatry," that is, into confusing the spokesman with the God who is speaking through him. Undoubtedly, the prohibition on depicting Mohammed can lead in the popular Muslim mind to his increased sacralization; but Muslim belief is clear: the Koran is *God's* message, not Mohammed's, who merely took down the "dictations" or "recitations" (the Arabic meaning of "koran").

just point *to* the truth but *be* the Truth? Against this other "koanic" background, the provocation represented in these words of Jesus to *be* the Truth becomes even more unsettling, as Balthasar explains in this key passage:

> The Greek mind found it absurd that one of the products of the all-pervasive *physis* should equate itself with the generative matrix. Jewish thought found it even more incredible that a created man should predicate of himself the attributes proper to the Creator of the world and the Covenant-Lord of Israel. It is still nonsense, but now to a modern evolutionary worldview of any persuasion, to assert that one wave in the river that has flowed on for millions of years and will continue to flow on unthinkably for yet more millions once the wave is no more, can be identified with the river. Nonsense, too, to assert that this wave has already comprehended all of that future and enclosed within itself the fullness of time and the end of time. On attempting to estimate the degree of provocation in such fantastic claims, we see clearly that *any school of religious or philosophic thought* must be surprised and further shocked by another statement in the same context: "They hated me without cause" (John 15:25).[36]

Christians, in other words, have their own *koan.* Instead of "The finger that points to the moon is not the moon," they have "The wave *is* the sea."

So the first question is not whether the claim is true (that comes next) but whether it is meaningful at all, as it seems at first glance not to be, no matter what worldview is involved. To address that difficulty, Balthasar shows that Jesus' claim to "absolute singularity" has at least three formal parallels in human life, that is, what he calls "relative singularities," and these are: falling in love, great works of art, and death. What any singularity, whether relative or absolute, does is to concentrate meaning (the sea) into one passing phenomenon (the wave). Thus the lover sees in the beloved a quasi-absolute value for whom he is willing to give up his life; Shakespeare encompasses the vast variety of human nature in his thirty-seven plays; and for all of us, whatever meaning the world has, it only has it through and for us, so that, after "we waves" foam up for a while and then return at death to the sea whence we came, the world dies *for us.*[37]

---

36. *Two Say Why:* "Why I Am Still a Christian," by Hans Urs von Balthasar and "Why I Am Still in the Church," by Joseph Ratzinger, trans. John Griffiths (Chicago: Franciscan Herald Press, 1973), p. 18. These two essays were originally lectures delivered to the Catholic Bavarian Academy in 1971; abbreviated henceforth as *2SW;* emphasis added.

37. This perspective also explains idolatry: the attempt to make the relative singularity absolute, such as when Juliet calls her Romeo "the god of my idolatry," Kurt Fürtwangler

Because of Balthasar's strongly aesthetic slant on theology, his example of great works of art, Shakespeare's especially, merits special attention for its illuminating power:

> Great works of art appear like inexplicable miracles and spontaneous ir-ruptions on the stage of history. Sociologists are as unable to calculate the precise day of their origin as they are to explain in retrospect why they ap-peared when they did. Of course, works of art are subject to certain pre-conditions without which they cannot come into being; such conditions may be effective stimuli but do not provide a full explanation of the work itself. Shakespeare had his predecessors, contemporaries and models; he was surrounded by the atmosphere of the theater of his time. He could only have emerged within that context. Yet who would dare offer to prove that his emergence was inevitable? At most we can point to or guess at the propitious moment — the *kairos* — but never what it is that flows into it and gives it that lasting form which, as soon as it emerges, takes control. *It speaks the word....* For a moment the contemporary world is taken aback, then people begin to absorb the work and to speak in the newly minted language (hence such terms as "the age of Goethe," or "age of Shake-speare," and so forth) with a taken-for-granted ease as though they had invented it themselves. The unique word, however, makes itself compre-hensible through its own self; and the greater a work of art, the more ex-tensive the cultural sphere it dominates will be.[38]

The advantages of this aesthetic approach to Christology, I think, should be clear. For one thing, it helps to solve the problem of Old Testa-ment prophecy thrown up by historical criticism. Previously, Christian apol-ogists like Pascal saw a remarkable symmetry between the messianic prophe-cies of Isaiah, Ezekiel, Jeremiah, and others, and their fulfillment by Jesus. But under the impact of historical criticism, scholars came to see the prophe-cies of the Hebrew Bible as taking place within a contemporary horizon alone. Moreover, it came increasingly to be seen that the evangelists couched their narratives retrospectively, that is, with these prophecies already in mind as they shaped their gospels.[39] But by using Shakespeare (among oth-

---

(the German orchestra conductor) says "Music is my goddess and I worship at her altar," and the narcissist sees everything in terms of his needs — all these are examples of the idola-try of the relatively singular.

38. *2SW*, pp. 20-21.

39. See Chapter 3 for an account of this process.

ers) as his model, Balthasar shows that, just as Shakespeare needed his predecessors yet transcended them, so too the salvation-history of Israel formed the necessary presuppositions for the event of Jesus but was transcended by him and remains truncated and jejune without his retrospective activity. And since *it* (the event of Jesus) determines *them* (the events of Israel's experience of God), just as Shakespeare brought retrospective fulfillment to the efforts of his lesser predecessors (Christopher Marlowe, Thomas Kyd, the medieval mystery plays, and so forth), it thus becomes understandable why and how the Evangelists would be justified in shaping their narratives retrospectively: this is what all history does in the light of definitive fulfillments (no one living during the reigns of Elizabeth I and James I thought at the time that he was living in the "age of Shakespeare," but we from our perspective are justified in saying so).

So far, my analysis has been phenomenological and aesthetic; and the analogies Balthasar draws only work after one has accepted Jesus' claim to absolute singularity. But how are we to make the crucial transition from the relative singularities of death, love, and great works of art to the absolute singularity of Jesus? In other words, how can we possibly accept his claim as true? How do we avoid the seeming arbitrariness in this choice that seems to be entailed in the approach of Troeltsch and Rahner?

At this point, Balthasar alters the image of wave and sea slightly and speaks of how each human life in history affects all others. He compares the mutual jostling of each life to a stone dropped into the sea, whose ripple effects radiate outward for the rest of historical time. With each human life, except for that of Jesus, effects always work forward in time (Charlemagne might still influence us, however distantly, but he had no influence at all on Cicero). Moreover, influence ineluctably fades (Napoleon's impact on contemporary history feels greater than does that of, say, Julius Caesar). But for Jesus to be the effective savior of the world, his stone must drop into history in such a way that *his* ripples go backward and forward. Furthermore, his ripples must reach us with such immediate directness that he remains ever-contemporary to us (this is the work of the Holy Spirit in the sacraments), without the fading away that characterizes all other events of world-historical time. This requirement is, for Balthasar, the reasoning behind that enigmatic line from the First Letter of Peter — which has often puzzled theologians down through the ages — that, after his death, Jesus descended into the underworld "to rescue those spirits in prison who disobeyed God *long ago*" (1 Pet. 3:19-20).

This doctrine of Christ's descent into hell surely constitutes the center of Balthasar's theology (coupled, of course, with the cross and resurrection) and is that part of his teaching for which he is most famously known (and criticized). It is, however, not the radical innovation it is often taken to be. By placing it in the context of his aesthetic Christology, I hope I have shown how its logic flows inexorably from the requirements of his distinction between relative and absolute singularities: Christ's claim to be *the* Truth is so provocative that it leads to his execution (an attempt to refute the claim, as it were), and was a claim so absurd and radical that only God can validate it and countermand the refutation by raising Jesus from the dead. But far from being merely an *ex post facto* confirmation by an outsider-God to the antecedent truth of the claim, God's validation of Jesus' claim *becomes* much more radically true by virtue of what happened during Christ's descent into hell:

> If the claim is to stand, the whole truth [of Jesus] must also possess a ballast, an absolute counterweight [*Schwergewicht*], that can be counterbalanced by nothing else; and because it is a question of truth, it must be able to show that it is so. The stone in the one pan of the scales must be so heavy that one can place in the other pan all the truth there is in the world, every religion, every philosophy, every complaint against God, *without counterbalancing it.* Only if that is true, is it worthwhile remaining a Christian today.[40]

In German the word *Schwergewicht* can mean "center of gravity" but more often means "counterweight," like the counterweight of an elevator attached to the cables holding it up, to make it easier for the pulleys to move the cab up and down. This image, I think, helps to explain how Jesus can be the savior of all, for if he is to lift up humanity (indeed the whole cosmos) and draw it back to the Father, he must be able to sink to the bottom with such a reverberating "thud" that he will be able to lift up the world into heaven. Moreover, he must do so in such a way that he will land at the bottom so heavily that he will continue to radiate outward in both directions so that his ripple effects will never fade. And this requires that the entire process, from incarnation and earthly ministry all the way to his death, descent into hell, and resurrection, be *a trinitarian event*: "What is at stake in theodrama is this: that God acts so as to take upon himself and make his own the tragedy of human existence even to the depths of that abyss, and thus conquering it, without at the same time robbing it of its

40. *2SW*, p. 29; emphasis added.

sting or going around this tragedy externally, as if he could overtake it by avoiding it."[41]

This requirement that the Trinity be actively and fully involved in the death of Jesus and above all in his descent into hell leads to two other conclusions, equally controversial in contemporary theology: a very strong (and perhaps dark?) theology of the atonement and a quasi-Origenist (and perhaps overly optimistic?) vision of the possible redemption of all humans at the end of time. As to the first, Balthasar quite fiercely rejects more modest exemplarist theories of the atonement, like those of Rahner and Sobrino, which held that what we see in the Cross is Jesus' (and God's?) "unconditional love," and this example of unconditional love inspires us to redouble our efforts to show similar solidarity with the lost and broken in our midst. (Needless to say, Balthasar would have even less truck with those liberal theologians who accuse the New Testament doctrine of the atonement of portraying God as a patriarchal child-abuser.)

Balthasar, in contrast, wishes to take much more radically Paul's statement that God "made him to *be* sin who knew no sin, so that we might become the righteousness of God" (2 Cor. 5:21). For Balthasar this passage can mean nothing else but what it explicitly says: that the Redeemer so identifies himself with sinners that, like a lightning rod, he draws the judgment of God onto himself: "Christ redeemed us from the curse of the law by becoming a curse for us" (Gal. 3:13). In other words, there is absolutely no concession whatsoever in Balthasar to the diffidence of contemporary Christians when they shy away from what such a hard doctrine of the atonement says about the image of God: "Let no one object that the notion of an angry God is archaic and obsolete since a loving Father has given his Son for the world's sake.... If, in his 'hour,' Jesus comes to experience the nature of sin from the inside, the center of the Passion lies not only in his perfect death (Anselm, Karl Rahner), but equally in his experience of mortal anguish and of being forsaken by God."[42]

To be fair, Rahner has his own rejoinder: he charges that Balthasar's theology of Christ's descent into hell, together with the Trinity's full engagement in that mystery, means that Balthasar has been influenced too much by the early German Idealists, Schelling especially, since he introduces into the Godhead too radical a division of Persons:

41. *Theo-Drama: Theological Dramatic Theory,* vol. 2: *Dramatis Personae,* trans. Graham Harrison (San Francisco: Ignatius Press, 1990), p. 54.

42. Hans Urs von Balthasar, *Does Jesus Know Us? Do We Know Him?* trans. Graham Harrison (San Francisco: Ignatius Press, 1983), pp. 32-33.

It is to me a source of consolation to realize that God, when and insofar as he entered into this history as into his own, did it in a different way than I did. From the beginning I am locked into this horror while God — if this word is to continue to have any meaning at all — is in a true and authentic sense the God who does not suffer, the immutable God, and so on. [In Balthasar, Moltmann, and others] I sense a theology of absolute paradox, of Patripassianism, perhaps even of a Schelling-esque projection into God of division, conflict, godlessness and death.[43]

I happen to believe these challenges can be answered, but the technicalities of this issue require that it be treated in the *Excursus* to this chapter. Here, however, I am more concerned with the implications of Balthasar's Christology for the issue of pluralism. Note first that, if his view is correct, one can no longer use the strategy adopted by C. S. Lewis, his famous "trilemma": granted that Jesus made the claim to be the absolute savior, Lewis said, that means that Jesus was either mad, lying, or telling the truth. The trouble with that exclusive trilemma is that it ignores a fourth possibility, one adopted, for example, by Sobrino: maybe these claims were put into the mouth of Jesus by the early church. Balthasar's answer to both Lewis and Sobrino is to point to two crucial statements embedded in the earliest strata of the New Testament proclamation: that *God* is the one who validates the claim of Jesus by raising him from the dead, and that *that* is what makes the claim true. Thus Peter says on Pentecost in his first "sermon": "God has raised this Jesus to life. . . . Therefore, let all Israel be assured of this: God *has made* this Jesus, whom you crucified, both Lord and Christ" (Acts 2:32, 36). And in the opening of Romans Paul says that Jesus Christ was "*declared with power* to be the Son of God by his resurrection from the dead" (Rom. 1:4).

Further, God did not merely raise Jesus from the dead immediately, but did so only after he preached to those spirits in prison who *dis*obeyed God long ago, which means that he was applying the results of his saving death to all who came before him, as the *Catechism of the Catholic Church* teaches: "The descent into hell brings the Gospel message of salvation to *complete* fulfillment. This is the last phase of Jesus' messianic mission, a phase which is condensed in time but vast in its real significance: the spread of Christ's redemptive work to *all* men of *all* times and *all* places,

---

43. Karl Rahner, *Karl Rahner in Dialogue: Conversations and Interviews, 1965-1982*, ed. Paul Imhoff and Hubert Biallowons, trans. Harvey D. Egan (New York: Crossroad, 1986), pp. 126-27.

for all who are saved have been made sharers in the redemption" (*CCC* §
634; emphases added).[44]

In other words, the solution to the question of pluralism can only be
found in the Eschaton. I owe this insight to J. A. DiNoia, who criticizes the
unlikely idea that non-Christians who never heard the gospel can have an
implicit faith in it.[45] As to Balthasar, it is true that he did not spill much of
his ink (large though his inkwell must have been) on the question of world
religions. But he did see interreligious dialogue, on the Christian's part, as an
aspect of the Christian's participation in the life of the Trinity.

Here is how it works: One "vestige" of the Trinity for Balthasar was the
"circumincession" (mutual interplay) of the Beautiful, the Good, and the
True in the world, under which rubric he wrote a trilogy, starting with a
theological aesthetics, then writing a theology of the drama of the Christian
life, and concluding with the theo-logic. But that same "circumincession"
also holds true for the ordinary believer, whose life is marked by three key
moments: the contemplative (a loving gaze on the beauty of revelation), the
kerygmatic (the dramatic proclamation of God's mighty deeds of salvation),

---

44. Walter Kasper says that for "the future of the faith, much depends upon our capacity to coordinate the biblical idea of representation with the modern idea of solidarity." Walter Kasper, *Jesus the Christ,* trans. Margaret Kohl (New York: Crossroad, 1989), p. 300. Unless
the two (vicarious atonement and solidarity) go together, theology will fall back into the
danger of liberal Christology once again, as Balthasar shows here: "It is a mistake to propose
that classical concepts are no longer intelligible, [and] can be replaced by other concepts that
are clearer to modern man. . . . Unfortunately, [this position] easily slides into misuse at the
ends of a liberal Christianity that puts emphasis on Jesus' solidarity — expressed in his life
and teaching — with the poor, sinners, and the marginalized and sees the Cross as nothing
more than the ultimate consequence of this 'social' solidarity." Hans Urs von Balthasar,
Theo-Drama, vol. 4: *The Action,* trans. Graham Harrison (San Francisco: Ignatius Press,
1994), pp. 266, 268.

45. J. A. DiNoia, O.P., *The Diversity of Religions: A Christian Perspective* (Washington,
DC: Catholic University of America Press, 1992), p. 105; cited later as DiNoia, *Diversity.* Notice how DiNoia's eschatology (albeit of the purgatorial variety) manages to reconcile both
prongs of the pluralist dilemma: "It by no means follows from the particular and unique
role ascribed to Jesus Christ in central Christian doctrines that those who do not *now* acknowledge him will be permanently excluded from sharing in the salvation he both signifies
and effects. Rather than attributing an implausible implicit faith in Christ to the members of
other religious communities, theology of religions in a prospective [that is, eschatological]
vein contends that non-Christians will have the opportunity to acknowledge Christ in the
future. This opportunity may come to them in the course of their lives here on earth or in
the course of their entrance into the life to come. Certainly such a view accords well with the
specific doctrines about the nature and agency of Jesus Christ and with the distinctive doctrines of other communities" (p. 107).

and the dialogic (the investigation of the truth of the gospel in its relation to the truth of the world).

Here is an illustration (my own) of how this works in practice in the life of a member of the clergy preaching to his congregation: in order to preach the Word, the minister must first have heard it and taken it to heart (Rom. 10:14-15); this is the *contemplative* moment, when the believer is lovingly enraptured by the message he has heard. So enrapturing is this message that the hearer/contemplator can do no other than proclaim to others the glorious and joyous message that has come to him; this is the *kerygmatic* moment. Finally, the proclamation of that message will elicit a variety of responses from the preacher's hearers, just as Paul's preaching to the Athenians on the Areopagus generated a variety of responses (Acts 17:23-34). What does the preacher do then? Perforce, he gets to know the mental worldview(s) of his listeners to see how their already-held presuppositions govern their responses. (Luke makes clear that the response to Paul's preaching on the Areopagus was determined by the philosophical doctrines already held by those who went to hear Paul preach; see Acts 17:16-21: "A group of Epicurean and Stoic philosophers began to dispute with him.") And this effort to engage listeners on their own terms is what Balthasar calls the *dialogic* moment.

Almost every preacher of any Christian denomination, I suspect, will understand Balthasar here: first comes homily preparation, which entails prayer and reflection, then comes the sermon, and finally comes the tricky task of dealing with the varied responses that will come from the congregation — often right after the service! But this example can be extended to all of theology, indeed to the life of the church as a whole: first prayer, then proclamation of the Good News, and finally dialogue with the world — not necessarily in that chronological order, but always each one in mutual dependence on the other two.

At all points, however, based on his belief in God's validation of the claims of Jesus in the resurrection, the preacher must hold fast to the victory already won by Jesus Christ and not seek the accommodationist model, by which the world determines the categories of truth in which the gospel is to be accepted. And the preacher can be confident of that victory precisely because his gaze is always on the Eschaton. As Paul said, in one of Balthasar's favorite quotes: "I capture every thought and make it obedient to Christ" (2 Cor. 10:5). Here, at least in broad outline, is how Balthasar would approach interreligious dialogue, even if he did not engage in it much himself.

Without any doubt, however, Joseph Ratzinger was much more concerned with the nuts and bolts of interreligious dialogue, particularly with the task of making sure Christian interlocutors (or Catholics ones, anyway) did not lift the counterweight of the gospel even slightly from the Christian pan of the scales of dialogue; because of his affinity with Balthasar's theology, we may perhaps see his career as a more explicit outworking of the Balthasarian vision, and so to him we now turn.

Joseph Ratzinger

In 1968 a professor of theology at the University of Regensburg wrote a modestly sized treatise on the Apostles' Creed called *Introduction to Christianity*. Its impact, however, was anything but modest, for the book so captivated Pope Paul VI that he made its author Archbishop of Munich (and later Cardinal, one of his last appointments to the College); and just a few years later, the new Pope, John Paul II, summoned the same man to Rome to head the Congregation for the Doctrine of the Faith (CDF). After a long career in this position he himself was elected pope in April 2005. His name of course is Joseph Ratzinger (1927-). Not many books have changed history, but this one certainly did, not just for the author personally, but also for the wider church. (*Introduction to Christianity* became an immediate bestseller in Germany when it first appeared.) What made this book itself so remarkable was not just its deft use of the Apostles' Creed to explain Christianity to the lay reader or its acute analysis of unbelief and the secular mind. An even greater virtue of the book was the future Pope's keen analysis of why the promising spirit of Vatican II failed to bring about a reunited Christianity and a re-Christianized Europe: a weak and less than full-bodied Christology.

According to his analysis, post-Enlightenment Christianity in Europe had been conned into adopting an evangelical strategy too superficial in its approach and too intimidated by Enlightened objections to Christian doctrine, a strategy that usually goes under the name of "accommodationism." Of course at the time that strategy carried considerable plausibility, which Ratzinger illustrated with a parable, one that Søren Kierkegaard once used, about a fire that breaks out backstage right before a circus is set to perform. In panic the stage manager sends out one of the performers — a clown as it happens, and naturally already in costume — to warn the audience to leave immediately. But the spectators take the clown's desperate pleas as part of his schtick; and the more he gesticulates the more they laugh, until fire engulfs the whole theater. This, said Kierkegaard, is the situation of Christians: the more they gesticulate with their creeds, the more laughable they seem to their skeptical neighbors, until the world becomes engulfed in the flames of war and mutual hatred: a hell on earth as prelude to the hell after death. If only these Christian clowns had first thought to change out of their goofy costumes, he implied, the theatergoing world might have been spared.

Now Kierkegaard did not explicitly say just what kind of funny clothes he thought Christians should now strip off to make their message of impending doom more credible. But whatever costume this Danish philosopher felt Christians should doff, his parable, at least for the professor from Regensburg, does not really get at the real dilemma of preaching the gospel to a secular culture. For the very news that a fire is on the way — and, above all, that we can be spared by the simple expedient of a *belief* in a transworldly message (why not just leave the theater?) — strikes the contemporary secular spectator as much more incredible than any costumed language in which it might be couched. Changing the rites of the Mass from Latin to the vernacular, calling on nuns to modernize their habits, introducing guitars and folk music in the church's worship, addressing the modern world in tones of respect and hope, praising modernity for its achievements: the *core* of the message will still seem absurd to the secular mind.

So maybe Kierkegaard misled us with his famous parable. Perhaps another story is more appropriate. For that reason, the future Cardinal and Pope began his book with an even more somber narrative, one of the fairy tales from the Brothers Grimm: Once upon a time, a poor widow sends her young son Hans into the village to fetch a simple meal, but along the way he discovers a lump of gold. Thrilled, he heads back home to show his mother his amazing good luck. But no sooner has he started back than he meets a knight who persuades him to exchange the gold for the knight's steed. "The better for plowing!" the knight assures the boy. Then a farmer farther along the way explains that the widow can't eat a horse, so why not exchange the horse for the farmer's cow? After making this seemingly reasonable bargain, the boy continues home but then meets up with a neighbor carrying a goose under his arm. Of course the widow wants a meal today, says the neighbor, so why not exchange cow for goose? Done. Finally, nearly home, he meets up with a boy who tells him that if he exchanges the goose for a whetstone he can keep his knife sharpened for slaughtering any number of geese in the future. Done again. But when he gets home he notices this clumsy stone in his pocket and, puzzled at its presence, throws it away before crossing the threshold of his home, none the sadder and certainly none the wiser.

Anyone who has followed the path taken by Protestant theology in the past two centuries as outlined in Chapters 8 and 9 and by Catholic theology in the past five decades as outlined in this chapter already knows the point of this story: *not all the costume changes in the world will matter if the messenger has squandered his treasure by altering his message to suit the convenience of the audience.* For the future Cardinal and now Pope, creeds matter only if what they proclaim is true, and if Christians deep down don't really believe it so, then all the translation strategies in the world will mean nothing:

> The worried Christian of today is often bothered by questions like these: has our theology in the last few years not taken in many ways a similar path? Has it not gradually watered down the demands of faith, which had been found all too demanding, always only so little that nothing important seemed to be lost, yet always so much that it was soon possible to venture on to the next step? And will poor Hans, the Christian who trustfully let himself be led from exchange to exchange, from interpretation to interpretation, not really soon hold in his hand, instead of the gold with which he began, only a whetstone, which he can be confidently recommended to throw away?[46]

For anyone remotely familiar with the career of this remarkable man, this paragraph will be recognized as his personal manifesto. Obviously in his role as cardinal enforcer of the church's orthodoxy, his efforts to arrest this unsettling trend have aroused controversy, intense controversy.[47] The question before us here concentrates solely on his personal theology out of which he acted as head of the CDF and is currently acting as pope.

The first place where Ratzinger takes up the question of Christology in his career in a fully systematic way is in *Introduction to Christianity*.[48] Commenting on the line in the Apostles' Creed "and I believe in Jesus Christ, His only Son, our Lord," he gets right to the scandal of particularity and begs the reader to notice how sheerly astonishing is this profession of faith:

46. Joseph Ratzinger, *Introduction to Christianity*, trans. J. R. Foster (San Francisco: Ignatius Press, 2004/1968), p. 31; cited hereafter as Ratzinger, *Introduction*.

47. Documents promulgated under his official role will be taken up in the next chapter; only those views which he has expressed as a private theologian *in propria persona* will be treated here.

48. For an account of his theology as a whole, see Aidan Nichols, O.P., *The Thought of Benedict XVI: An Introduction to the Theology of Joseph Ratzinger* (London: Burns & Oates, 2005), an unchanged republication of his *The Theology of Joseph Ratzinger* (Edinburgh: T. & T. Clark, 1988); and Tracey Rowland, *Ratzinger's Faith: The Theology of Pope Benedict XVI* (Oxford: Oxford University Press, 2008).

It is only in the second section of the Creed that we come up against the real difficulty . . . about Christianity: the profession of faith that the man Jesus, an individual executed in Palestine about the year 30, the *Christus* (anointed, chosen) of God, indeed God's own Son, is the central and decisive point of all human history. It seems both presumptuous and foolish to assert that one single figure who is bound to disappear farther and farther into the mists of the past is the authoritative center of all history. Although faith in the *logos,* the meaningfulness of being, corresponds perfectly with a tendency in the human reason, this second article of the Creed proclaims the absolutely staggering alliance of *logos* and *sarx,* of meaning and a single historical figure. *The meaning that sustains all being has become flesh;* that is, it has entered history and become one individual in it; it is no longer simply what encompasses and sustains history but is a point *in* it.[49]

To accept this claim (in Balthasarian terms, to assert that the wave is the sea) entails an important methodological consideration, one that must overthrow the usual philosophical approach to reality:

Accordingly the meaning of all being is first of all no longer to be found in the sweep of mind that rises above the individual, the limited, into the universal; it is no longer simply given in the world of ideas, which transcends the individual and is reflected in it only in a fragmentary fashion; it is to be found in the midst of time, in the countenance of one man.[50]

In his commentary on the first section of the Creed ("I believe in God") Ratzinger stressed a key motif that runs through all his writings: the harmony between faith and reason, between the God of faith and the God of the philosophers and the dangers to the faith when they are divorced. But here he tempers that theme with another point: a union of faith and history for him is based on the union of word and flesh, which, the author concedes, is much harder for the human intellect to grasp and then to accept:

Perhaps it is already clear at this point that even in the paradox of word and flesh we are faced with something meaningful and in accordance with the

---

49. Ratzinger, *Introduction,* p. 193; Latin and Greek terms italicized by Ratzinger (or at least the translator); other emphases added.

50. Ratzinger, *Introduction,* pp. 193-94. Cardinal Ratzinger once mentioned that when he read Karl Rahner, he felt he, Ratzinger, was dwelling on a different theological planet. This passage explains why.

logos. Yet at first this article of faith represents a stumbling block for human thinking. In this have we not fallen victim to an absolutely staggering kind of positivism? Can we cling at all to the straw of one single historical event? Can we dare to base our whole existence, indeed the whole of history, on the straw of one happening in the great sea of history?[51]

Moreover, as we have seen in Troeltsch, "history" now means for so many in the West what is accessible through the historical-critical method. The results of that method, as we have already seen, can be nugatory indeed, and can then tempt the theologian once again to abandon the particular for the universal and thus to find meaning exclusively there. Positivist historians can see only the facts of history, Hegelians only the universal meaning that those facts illustrate or exemplify: "The dilemma of the two courses — on the one hand, that of transposing or reducing Christology to history and, on the other, that of escaping history completely and abandoning it, as irrelevant to faith — could be quite accurately summarized in the two alternatives by which modern theology is vexed: Jesus or Christ?"[52]

For his own schematic purposes, Ratzinger takes Harnack and Bultmann as the two representatives of each fork of the dilemma: Harnack wanted to strip Christianity of any philosophical overlay to reach the Jesus of history, but his failure[53] led, perhaps inevitably, to Bultmann's insistence that the only historically important fact about Jesus is that he existed and died on the cross; everything else comes from faith in the preached Christ. In each case, the move seemed liberating. In Harnack's case (who said, as we have seen in the previous chapter, that only the Father belongs to the message of Jesus, not the Son), the liberation was from religious division: "Where faith in the Son had divided people — Christians from non-Christians, Christians of different denominations from one another — knowledge of the Father can unite."[54] In Bultmann's case, faith is now immune to the ups and downs of historical re-

---

51. Ratzinger, *Introduction*, p. 194. Note also the resonance with Balthasar's imagery in this passage: "Such a notion, which even in itself is an adventurous one and seemed equally improbable to both ancient and Asiatic thought, is rendered still more difficult in the intellectual climate of modern times" (p. 194).

52. Ratzinger, *Introduction*, p. 198.

53. "While Harnack was still proclaiming his optimistic message about Jesus, those who were to bury his work were already knocking at the door. At the very same time, proof was produced that the plain Jesus of whom he spoke was a romantic dream, a *Fata Morgana* of the historian, a mirage induced by thirst and longing which dissolved as he approached it" (*Introduction*, pp. 199-200).

54. Ratzinger, *Introduction*, p. 193, paraphrasing Harnack.

search, which is endlessly revising its conclusions based on new evidence or new considerations of old evidence.

But as the later history of theology proved, neither approach worked: Harnack saw only his own bourgeois image in Jesus, and Bultmann tied the believer not to Jesus but to a verbal event coming from the pulpit. But this shuttlecock movement from Jesus to Christ and back to Jesus again (Bultmann's own students came to reject his radical skepticism and launched the so-called Second Quest for the historical Jesus[55]) can itself be illuminating for Christology (just as the tension between Antiochene and Alexandrian Christologies illustrates the same point): "I believe that [this example of Harnack and Bultmann] can become a very useful pointer to something," says the Bavarian theologian, "namely, to the fact that the one (Jesus) cannot exist without the other (Christ), that, on the contrary, one is bound to be continually pushed from one to the other because in reality Jesus only subsists as the Christ and the Christ only subsists in the shape of Jesus."[56]

History of course cannot prove this mutual interplay and internal subsistence; it can only show the consequences of its denial. Again, like Balthasar, Ratzinger insists that it must be *made* true by the action of God, specifically God's involvement in the cross. In a fascinating passage, he admits that Jesus never called himself Messiah (Christ, King) in any unequivocal way; the title was explicitly *imposed* on him (during his life) by, ironically, Pontius Pilate. But by virtue of Jesus' mission from his Father, God made him the *true* King and in doing so overthrew all our worldly categories of kingship:

> Jesus did not call himself unequivocally the Messiah (Christ); the man who gave him this name was Pilate. . . . This execution notice ["Jesus of

55. Details of that and the Third Quest may be found in Chapter 3 of this work.

56. Ratzinger, *Introduction*, p. 201; at this point the author cites Balthasar to fuse the function of Jesus (to save) with his being as the preexistent Logos (p. 204, note 11). On this point, see the wise remarks of Peter Steinfels: "One might expect that the Jesus of history would be a flesh-and-blood person, and the Christ of faith the more theoretical product of belief and doctrine. Instead, the Jesus of history turns out to be one (or several) of an array of scholarly constructs, whose shelf life may be quite limited — hardly an individual to be personally and intimately known, loved, worshiped, and followed. By contrast, it is the Christ of faith who is concrete and enfleshed, embodied in centuries of saints and experienced in family, sacraments, and a lifetime of gestures, stories, and prayers. For many Catholics like myself, moments of intimate friendship or personal relationship with Jesus are more likely to occur in returning from Communion than in encountering Scripture." Peter Steinfels, "The Face of God: What Benedict's *Jesus* Offers," *Commonweal* 134, no. 14 (August 17, 2007).

Nazareth, King of the Jews"], the death sentence of history, became *with paradoxical unity* the "profession of faith," the real starting point and tap-root of the Christian faith, which holds Jesus to be the Christ: as the cruci-fied criminal, this Jesus is the Christ, the King. His crucifixion is his coro-nation, his kingship is his surrender of himself to men, the identification of word, mission, and existence in the yielding up of this very existence. His existence is thus his word. He *is* word because he is love. From the Cross faith understands in increasing measure that this Jesus did not just do and say something; that *in him message and person are identical,* that he is all along what he says.[57]

Of course Ratzinger does not make these assertions about the meaning of the cross in isolation. They must be theologically established by looking at God's involvement in Christ's descent into hell and in raising him from the dead. Like Balthasar he will have important things to say about Holy Satur-day, that notoriously difficult theologoumenon, a difficulty he fully con-cedes: "Probably no article of the Creed is so far from present-day attitudes of mind as this one. Together with the belief in the birth of Jesus from the Virgin Mary and that in the Ascension of the Lord, it seems to call most of all for 'demythologization,' a process that in this case looks devoid of danger and unlikely to provoke opposition."[58]

Ratzinger, however, disagrees. He counters this neglect by pointing out that the mystery of Christ's descent into hell has perhaps never become more meaningful than today and calls it "particularly close" to the experience of the twentieth century:

On Good Friday our gaze remains fixed on the crucified Christ, but Holy Saturday is the day of the "death of God," the day that expresses the un-paralleled experience of our age, anticipating the fact that God is simply absent, that the grave hides him, that he no longer awakes, no longer speaks, so that one no longer needs to deny him but can simply ignore him. "God is dead and we have killed him." This saying of Nietzsche's be-longs linguistically to the tradition of Christian Passiontide piety; it ex-presses the content of Holy Saturday, "descended into hell."[59]

---

57. Ratzinger, *Introduction*, p. 206; emphases added.

58. Ratzinger, *Introduction*, pp. 293-94.

59. Ratzinger, *Introduction*, p. 294; translation slightly emended. In a sense for Ratzinger, this silence, at least for man, even has primacy over the speech that is the *logos* (which in Greek means both reason and speech): "God is not only the comprehensible word

Ratzinger even joins Lutheran exegete Ernst Käsemann in describing Jesus' cry on the cross, "My God, my God, why have you forsaken me?" (Mark 15:34) as a prayer sent up from hell, and draws this meaning from that exegesis: "After this, do we still need to ask what worship must be in our hour of darkness? Can it be anything else but the cry from the depths in company with the Lord who 'has descended into hell' and who has established the nearness of God in the midst of abandonment by God?"[60] In other words, Ratzinger is quite explicit in linking the mystery of Holy Saturday with the atonement, and this is true throughout his entire career. For example in his manual on eschatology he speaks even more explicitly than in *Introduction to Christianity*:

> The true Bodhisattva, Christ, descends into Hell and *suffers it in all its emptiness*. . . . While the real quality of evil and its consequences become quite palpable here, the question arises . . . whether in this event we are not in touch with a divine response able to draw freedom precisely as freedom to itself. The answer lies hidden in Jesus' descent into Sheol, in the night of the soul which he suffered, a night which no one can observe except by entering this darkness in suffering faith. Thus . . . in John of the Cross, in Carmelite piety in general, and in that of Thérèse of Lisieux in particular, "Hell" has taken on a completely new meaning and form. For the saints, "Hell" is not so much a threat to be hurled at other people but a challenge to oneself. It is a challenge to suffer in the dark night of faith, to experience communion with Christ in solidarity with his descent into the Night. *One draws near to the Lord's radiance by sharing his darkness.* One serves the salvation of the world by leaving one's own salvation behind for the sake of the others.[61]

A further implication of this approach is that hell, as traditionally understood as the place of eternal damnation for the reprobate, only comes

---

that comes to us; he is also the silent, inaccessible, uncomprehended, and incomprehensible ground that eludes us. To be sure, in Christianity there is a primacy of the *logos*, of the word, over silence; God *has* spoken. God *is* word. But this does not entitle us to forget the truth of God's abiding concealment. Only when we have experienced him as silence may we hope to hear his speech, too, which proceeds in silence" (p. 296).

60. Ratzinger, *Introduction*, p. 297.

61. Joseph Ratzinger, *Eschatology: Death and Eternal Life*, trans. Michael Waldstein (Washington, DC: Catholic University of America Press, 1988/1977), pp. 216-18; emphases added. How and why these views became such common currency in Catholic theology in the past few decades will be taken up in the *Excursus* immediately following this chapter.

into being by Christ's descent into the underworld. On the basis of both exegesis of the Bible and a philological study of the Latin of the Apostles' Creed, Ratzinger comes to this conclusion:

> In reality, the *"inferi"* [lower regions] of the Creed, [which] in German was first translated by *hell* [*Hölle*] and more recently by *kingdom of the dead* [*das Reich des Todes*], is simply the Latin equivalent of the Hebrew word *sheol*, which indicates a realm of the dead that can be imagined as a kind of shadowy existence, existence and non-existence at the same time. It is very similar to the image of *hades* we have inherited from Homer that coincides rather with the view of the dead of the Ancient Near East.[62]

In other words, until Christ got there, the underworld was more or less undifferentiated, both vaguely conceived and hovering in uncertainty and darkness. This changes with Christ's descent into that underworld, for only in reaction to him can a definitive yes or no be made to God. Such, at any rate, is Ratzinger's exegesis. But he does not stop at exegesis, needless to say.[63] In fact, he is one of the first theologians to see how the question of religious pluralism must be solved from an eschatological viewpoint, whereas the more "horizontal" solutions sought on the level of interreligious dialogue will never bear the fruit it expects without the contribution of the new perspective on eschatology offered up by recent theology. In a book written just two years before his election to the papacy, he explains how the Christian concept of salvation forms the basis for authentic interreligious dialogue, the common ground that all can agree on without abandoning the particulars of their respective faiths:

> When people talk about the significance of religions for salvation, it is quite astonishing that they for the most part think only that all of them make eternal life possible; and when they think like that, the concept of eternal life is neutralized, since everyone gets there in any case. But that sells the question of salvation short, in [a] most inappropriate fashion. Heaven begins on earth. . . . We have to ask what heaven is and how it comes upon earth. Future salvation must make its mark in a way of life

62. Joseph Ratzinger, *The Sabbath of History*, trans. Susan Scott Cesaritti (the Italian Preface here quoted) and John Rock, S.J. (the German main text) (Washington, DC: The William G. Congdon Foundation, 2000), pp. 21-22; emphases in the original translation.

63. "Since I had always had great respect for the exegetes, I assumed that this statement was as such correct, but saw too that it was not thought through to the end" (Ratzinger, *The Sabbath of History*, p. 22).

that makes a person "human" here and thus capable of relating to God. That in turn means that when we are concerned with the question of salvation, we must look beyond religions themselves and that this involves standards of right living that one cannot just relativize at will. . . . That means that salvation does not lie in religions as such, but it is connected to them, inasmuch as, and to the extent that, they lead man toward the one good, toward the search for God, for truth, and for love. The question of salvation therefore always carries within it an element of the criticism of religion, just as, contrariwise, it can build a positive relationship to religions. It has in any case to do with the unity of the good, with the unity of what is true — with the unity of God and man.[64]

In other words, unless the teaching on the unity of God and man — most splendidly realized in Jesus Christ, incarnate Son of God — is maintained, the very coherence of the one world we live in will be threatened. These are the views out of which the Cardinal Prefect of the Congregation for the Doctrine of the Faith operated. They formed his outlook as he guided the *Catechism of the Catholic Church* through its various drafting stages and to its final promulgation; and they clearly still shape his views as universal Shepherd of the Catholic Church. We are thus nearing the threshold where we must consider, not just the private voices of professional theologians, but the teaching of the church, the topic of the next chapter.

64. Joseph Cardinal Ratzinger, *Truth and Tolerance: Christian Belief and World Religions,* trans. Henry Taylor (San Francisco: Ignatius Press, 2004/German edition 2003), p. 205.

Christ's Descent into Hell

The place of Christ's descent into hell in the theology of Joseph Ratzinger/ Pope Benedict, with which we concluded the main body of the chapter immediately above, requires an *Excursus* on the technicalities involved in coming to terms with Christ's descent and makes this the natural site for its placement. To put it mildly, the event of Christ's descent into hell remains to this day one of the most obscure points of revelation. For one thing, it is rarely preached. How could it be? There is a place for a homily during the Good Friday services, which for obvious reasons concentrates on Christ's passion and his gruesome death on a cross; the next opportunity for a sermon occurs late on Saturday night, on the Feast of the Vigil of Easter, where the homily takes place *after* the gospel reading on the resurrection. There is, in short, no liturgical space for a specific "celebration" of the descent: while Christ is sojourning in the underworld, the church on earth keeps silent vigil in that dark and mysterious time between his death and resurrection. *Wovon man nicht sprechen kann, darüber muss man schweigen:* where revelation does not speak, the church keeps her silence as well.

That conceded, and although by no means a motif of the preaching of the early church that overshadowed all other themes, there are unmistakable references in the New Testament to *some* sort of journey of Christ to the underworld after his death, the primary ones being these (the added italics stress the phrases where Christ's descent to the realm of the dead is most clearly indicated):

> "How can anyone enter a strong man's house and carry off his possessions unless he first ties up the strong man? Then he can rob his house." (Matt. 12:29, Jesus speaking)

"For as Jonah was three days and three nights in the belly of the whale, so the Son of Man will be three days and three nights in the heart of the earth." (Matt. 12:40, Jesus speaking)

"But God raised him from the dead, *freeing him from the pangs of Hades, because it was impossible for death to keep its hold on him.*" (Acts 2:24, Peter speaking)[65]

For Christ died for sins once for all, the righteous for the unrighteous, to bring you to God. He was put to death in the body but made alive by the Spirit, through whom he also *went and preached to the spirits in prison who disobeyed God long ago.* (1 Pet. 3:18-20)

But they [sinners] will have to give account to him who is ready to judge the living and the dead. For this is the reason the gospel was preached *even to those who are now dead,* so that they might be judged according to men in regard to the body, but live according to God in regard to the spirit. (1 Pet. 4:5-6)

Do not say in your heart, "Who will ascend into heaven?" (that is, to bring Christ down) or "Who will descend into the abyss?" (that is, to bring Christ up from the dead). (Rom. 10:6-7)

So then, whether we live or whether we die, we are the Lord's. For to this end Christ died and lived again, *that he might be the Lord both of the dead and of the living.* (Rom. 14:8-9)

But to each one of us grace has been given as Christ apportioned it. This is why it says: "When he ascended on high, he led captives in his train and gave gifts to men" [Psalm 68:18]. But what does "he ascended" mean except that *he also descended to the depths of the earth?* He who is descended is the very one who ascended higher than all the heavens, *in order to fill all things.* (Eph. 4:7-10)

---

65. Be it noted that the italicized portion of this passage comes from the Western textual tradition. Acts of the Apostles has the most divergent textual variants of all of the books of the New Testament; and most of these variants share enough similarities and come from the western half of the Roman Empire to have been given their own name. I use this textual variant not to make any statement one way or the other on which tradition might embody the "inspired" (that is, canonical) text, but simply to highlight that the prevalence of this textual variant points to a similar prevalence of belief in Christ's descent into Hades.

Therefore God exalted him to the highest place and gave him the name that is above every name, so that at the name of Jesus every knee should bend, in heaven and on earth and *under the earth* and every tongue confess that Jesus Christ is Lord, to the glory of God the Father. (Phil. 2:9-11)

When taken together, these passages not only speak of a journey to the underworld,[66] but they also attribute a saving, soteriological significance to that descent. Thus the focus of the debate in the early church was not so much over the event itself or its place, but on the *range* of Christ's saving presence there. Interpretations varied wildly, with some authors insisting that Christ went to Hades to empty it entirely, while others claimed he went only to save the "just," however defined. Cyril of Alexandria, for one, claimed that Christ quite emptied hell,[67] whereas Origen (ironically, given his later reputation) held to a limited emptying of hell.[68] Augustine stands somewhat in the middle of this debate: baffled by the doctrine and by no means as confident as Cyril of Christ's total vastation of hell, still the bishop of Hippo was not willing with Origen to specify a pre-descent Gehenna to which Christ did not descend but went only to Hades. In a letter to his fellow bishop Evodius, who queried him on just this point, he says:

66. "The belief that Christ spent the interval between His expiry on the cross and His resurrection in the underworld was a commonplace of Christian teaching from the earliest times." J. N. D. Kelly, *Early Christian Creeds*, 3rd ed. (New York: David McKay, 1972), p. 379.

67. The New Testament scholar W. J. Dalton provides a fine history of the interpretation of this theme in 1 Peter, where he says of Cyril: "In his commentary on John 16:16 [at *PG* 74, 456A], [Cyril says] that Christ saved not merely those on earth but proclaimed the liberation of the dead. In his commentary on Luke 4:18 [at *PG* 72, 537D] he . . . implies the conversion of these sinners. . . . In another passage dealing with the descent of Christ [*Homilia Paschalis* 8, *PG* 77, 552A] . . . he describes dramatically how Christ threw open the gates of hell, understood as the abode of the devil, and *emptied it completely.*" William Joseph Dalton, *Christ's Proclamation to the Spirits: A Study of 1 Peter 3:18–4:6*, Analecta Biblica 23 (Rome: Pontifical Biblical Institute, 1989), p. 30; emphasis added.

68. Origen, *Contra Celsum* 2, 43 (*PG* 11, 865). The historical Origen was no Origenist, as Lawrence Hennessey rightly sees: "By His descent [according to Origen], Christ destroys the Devil's dominion over captured humanity. . . . [But] if the saints and repentant sinners eventually dwell in the heavens, . . . the wicked — unrepentant and hardened sinners — are damned to Gehenna, the place of fire." Lawrence R. Hennessey, "The Place of Saints and Sinners After Death," in *Origen of Alexandria: His World and His Legacy*, ed. Charles Kannengiesser and William L. Petersen (Notre Dame: University of Notre Dame Press, 1988), pp. 295-312; here 299, 306. Another author with roughly similar views would be Irenaeus, *Adversus Haereses* IV, 22 and 27, 1 (*PG* 7, 1047 and 1056-58). For a full overview of patristic opinion on this perennially enigmatic motif, see Hans Urs von Balthasar, *Mysterium*

Consequently, if holy Scripture had said that Christ after death came into that bosom of Abraham, without naming hell and its sorrows, I wonder if anyone would dare to affirm that He descended into hell. But, because this clear testimony mentions both hell *and its sorrows,* I can think of no reason for believing that the Savior went there except to save souls from its sorrows. I am still uncertain whether He saved all those whom He found there or certain ones whom He deemed worthy of that boon. I do not doubt, however, that He was in hell, and that He granted this favor to those *entangled in its sorrows.*[69]

On Augustine's *dubium* about the soteriological range of Christ's descent Cyril of Alexandria, as we saw above, had no doubts. In one of his Easter homilies he says that as a consequence of Christ's descent, the devil was left all alone with a devastated hell, sulking in a corner like a pouty schoolboy: "For having destroyed hell and opened the impassable gates for the departed spirits, He left the devil there abandoned and lonely."[70]

In all this range of opinion about the soteriological range of the descent, what remains common to the tradition is that because Christ's descent among the dead was regarded as in some hard-to-specify way *salvific,* the descent must have been, also in some hard-to-specify way, *expiatory,* precisely because until Christ's atonement for sin on the Cross, the sins of those in the underworld needed to have that atonement *applied* to them. True, at first that application will not be seen as necessarily entailing Christ suffering in the underworld, an insight that will only come in medieval theology in the wake of a style of piety that stressed the saving nature of Christ's intense sufferings during his passion and death on a cross. Initially, however, the stress was on the connection of the descent with atonement in a more abstract sense.

Such a connection flows naturally out of a trope commonly used in early Christian literature to explain the atonement, the fishhook that Satan swallows: the bait is Christ's human nature, the hook is his divinity, and the devil is the deceived Leviathan whose innards are ripped apart when he ingests the hook. This piscine imagery has been much derided by later theolo-

---

Paschale: The Mystery of Easter, trans. Aidan Nichols, O.P. (Grand Rapids: Eerdmans, 1990), pp. 160-88, especially 187, note 155.

69. *Saint Augustine: Letters,* vol. 3 (131-64), trans. Sister Wilfrid Parsons, S.N.D. (New York: Fathers of the Church, Inc., 1953), p. 386; emphases added. Also: "Who, then, but an unbeliever will deny that Christ was in hell?" (p. 383).

70. Cyril of Alexandria, *Homilia Paschalis* 7.2 (*PG* 77, 552 A; also 657).

gians, as we saw in Chapters 4 and 5, for its implication that Satan had a "right" to all the other "bait" (the rest of us) and needed to be "deceived" in order to be induced to swallow Christ's divinity. Perhaps so, but to concentrate on the folksy naïveté of the imagery is to miss its real point: that Satan's kingdom could only be destroyed (this image of swallowing implies) when God's power breaks into the underworld and destroys it *from within*.

This motif of conquest from within is surely the point of Jesus' prediction of his death and descent when he compares his fate with that of Jonah in "the belly of the beast" (Matt. 12:40) and insists that no one can despoil a strong man's house unless he first overpowers and ties up the owner of the house (Matt. 12:29); so that after he has accomplished this task on Holy Saturday, he can say in his risen state: "I am the Living One; I was dead, and behold I am alive for ever and ever. I hold the keys of death and Hades" (Rev. 1:18).

But the question that will preoccupy the tradition is not so much the fact of the descent or its saving purposes, but *how* Christ overcame the "strong man" of evil. Here one notices a definite development, especially in the West, where the connection between suffering and atonement was especially strong. But that connection was also made, however embryonically in the East as well, as deftly summarized by Jaroslav Pelikan:

> The words of Jesus in Matthew 12:29 meant that Satan would be bound with the very chains with which he had bound man and would be led captive. Paraphrasing the passage, Irenaeus said: "He [Christ] fought and was victorious; for he was man doing battle for the fathers, and by his obedience utterly abolishing disobedience. For he bound the strong man, liberated the weak, and by destroying sin endowed his creation with salvation." From [this statement of Irenaeus] it is evident that not only the resurrection of Christ, but especially his passion and death belonged to the description of salvation as the victory of Christ over the enemies of man. Another event sometimes associated with that victory was the descent into hell. . . . [which in the West] acquired creedal status with its incorporation into the final text of the Apostles' Creed, no earlier than 370. By that time, however, Western theology was [already] interpreting the atonement as a sacrifice and increasingly as an act of satisfaction offered by the death of Christ. . . . As "the harrowing of hell," the descent played a significant part in the arts as well as in the church's teaching, but it was not until the Middle Ages and the Reformation that it became an issue of dogmatic debate.[71]

71. Jaroslav Pelikan, *The Christian Tradition: A History of the Development of Doctrine*,

In that debate Thomas Aquinas strikes an important note, one that will become increasingly dominant later, especially in the mystical tradition. In his *Exposition of the Apostles' Creed* (written in the last year of his life), Thomas explains this Creed's famous descent clause thus: "There are four reasons why Christ descended in his [human] soul to hell. The first was to take on the entire punishment of sin and thereby to atone [*expiaret*] wholly for its guilt."[72] Once Thomas had made that link explicit between atoning suffering and the descent, certain mystics begin to speak ever more frequently of their own souls' experiences of hell (*"cum animis eorum,"* as it were), most prominently of course St. John of the Cross but also Blessed Angela of Foligno[73] and St. Rose of Lima.[74]

With the Reformers, however, one detects a noticeable shying away from the expiatory interpretation of Holy Saturday. It comes as no surprise that

---

vol. 1: *The Emergence of the Catholic Tradition (100-600)* (Chicago: University of Chicago Press, 1971), pp. 150-51.

72. "Sunt autem quatuor rationes quare Christus cum anima ad infernum descendit. Prima ut sustineret totam poenam peccati, ut sic totam culpam expiaret." Thomas Aquinas, *In Symbolum Apostolorum Expositio*, art. 5, 926, in *Opuscula Theologica*, vol. 2, ed. Raimund Spiazzi, O.P. (Turin/Rome: Marietti, 1954), p. 204.

73. "I perceive that demons hold my soul in a state of suspension; just as a hanged man has nothing to support him, so my soul does not seem to have any supports left. . . . While I am in this most horrible darkness caused by demons, it seems to me that there is nothing I can hope for. . . . When I am in that darkness I think I would prefer to be burned than to suffer such afflictions. I even cry out for death to come in whatever form God would grant it. I beseech him to send me to hell without delay. 'Since you have abandoned me,' I tell him, 'make an end to it now and completely submerge me.'" Angela of Foligno, *Memorial*, Chapter VIII, a and b, in *Angela of Foligno: Complete Works*, trans. Paul Lachance, O.F.M. (New York: Paulist Press, 1993), pp. 197, 198. See also Paul Lachance, O.F.M., *The Spiritual Journey of Blessed Angela of Foligno According to the Memorial of Frater A.* (Rome: Pontificium Athenaeum Antonianum, 1984), especially here: "'Surrounded on all sides by demons,' she feels trapped in a kind of hell, even damned to its lowest depths. Not only is all hope lost, . . . her soul is reduced to a complete blankness about God's presence (and the memory of it), and is brimming over with that of the evil one" (pp. 312-13).

74. "She was daily visited by the most frightful nights of the soul which . . . for hours caused her such anxiety that she knew not if she were in hell. . . . Her will wanted to tend to love, but was paralyzed as if petrified in ice. . . . Terror and anguish took possession of her totally, and her heart, overwhelmed, cried out: 'My God, my God, why have you forsaken me?' But no one replied. . . . Yet what was worst of all in her sufferings was that these ills presented themselves as having to last eternally; that no glimpse was given of an end to the distress; and that, since a wall of bronze made all escape impossible, no exit from the labyrinth could be found." Quoted in Hans Urs von Balthasar, *Mysterium Paschale: The Mystery of Easter*, trans. Aidan Nichols, O.P. (Grand Rapids: Eerdmans, 1990), p. 87, note 77.

the former Augustinian monk Luther subscribed, at least at times, to Augustine's view that Christ went to the depths of hell.[75] Thus he openly avers a very concrete hell of God-abandonment that Jesus experienced: "He descended into the deepest of *all* depths," says Luther, "under the law, under the devil, death, sin and hell; and that, I think, is verily the last and lowest depth."[76]

Calvin, however, as we have seen in Chapter 6, is less extreme in painting contrasts between law and gospel, Old and New Testaments, and the reprobation Christ experienced on the cross versus his sinlessness. Thus he mitigates the descent-doctrine by attributing Christ's experiences of godforsakenness only *as death approached* — on earth, that is, and not in any locatable, postmortem "hell." Even so, at least the Geneva theologian insists that the descent into hell does refer to Christ's spiritual sufferings in his relation to God his Father, sufferings that go far beyond those of bodily death, for in approaching death Jesus had to "grapple hand to hand with the armies of hell and the dread of everlasting death."[77] Nonetheless, these were for Calvin clearly sufferings that Jesus underwent *in the course of* his passion and death, not after death: "He paid a greater and more excellent price in suffering in his soul the terrible torments of a condemned and forsaken man."[78]

---

75. In his influential letter to Evodius that we have already cited, Augustine distinguished between two separate realms in Hades, one a lower *infernum*, where the rich man Dives was sent to suffer eternally, and a higher one where Lazarus dwelt "in the bosom of Abraham" until Christ's descent, between which a "great gulf" *(chaos magnum)* prevented communication. Despite that gulf, Augustine insisted that Christ went to the *lower* region. This seems to contradict Augustine's view of double predestination and the *massa damnata*. It is the judgment of Brian Daley, however, that Augustine never really resolved the tension in his thought: On the one hand, "Throughout his life, Augustine remained convinced that the souls of some of the dead, who are condemned to punishment immediately after death because of their sins, will be released from that punishment before God's sentence of judgment is passed. . . . Augustine frequently insists, however, that not all the dead are capable of receiving God's mercy through the prayers and meritorious actions of the Church done in their name." Brian E. Daley, S.J., *The Hope of the Early Church: A Handbook of Patristic Eschatology* (Cambridge: Cambridge University Press, 1991), pp. 138, 139. Yet Augustine will also seem to indicate that "hell is not a permanent state . . . until the common passage of all creatures from time into eternity" (p. 139).

76. Martin Luther, *Sermon* on Ephesians 4:8-10.

77. John Calvin, *Institutes of the Christian Religion*, ed. J. T. McNeill, trans. F. L. Battles (Philadelphia: Westminster Press, 1960), vol. 2, xvi. #10 (p. 515).

78. Calvin, *Institutes*, vol. 2, xvi. #10 (p. 516): Calvin immediately continues: "No wonder, then, if he is said to have descended into hell, for he suffered the death that God in his wrath had inflicted upon the wicked!" We know that this passage clearly refers to Jesus' ex-

Calvin's views mark a crucial moment when theologians, both Catholic and Protestant, begin to mitigate the common patristic (and biblical) assumption of the soteriological significance of Christ's descent into hell. For example, the Methodist version of the Apostles' Creed omitted outright the line "and he descended into hell," due to John Wesley's consistent opposition to the doctrine:

> Wesley's resistance to this doctrine is well known and documented. He omitted reference to it from his Twenty-Five Articles, and the American Methodist Conference of 1786 followed his lead and deleted the article from the Apostles' Creed as used in Sunday services. In handling the classical texts, Wesley uniformly opposes the doctrine . . . [His] note on Acts 2:27 makes the flat statement: "It doth not appear that ever our Lord went into hell."[79]

What can account for this outright denial of a clause of the Apostles' Creed, especially when viewed against the consistent (if controverted) doctrine of the church? One can only speculate here, but John Deschner must surely be at least partly right when he says that "the practical Wesley considered the doctrine too controversial — there had been a violent controversy about it in Elizabeth's reign."[80] But surely there was more:

> Could there also be a theological reason: that Wesley was loath to teach anything suggesting a second chance for those who resisted repentance in this life? The saints who die before Christ will indeed be reconciled by Christ's blood. But Wesley regards every man's final state as determined by the moment of death. The perfecting which Wesley occasionally allows to be possible in paradise can be assumed to apply only to the saints. If not in hell, then, where was Christ's soul between Good Friday

---

perience of suffering before and in death because Calvin addresses an objection here that the descent is mentioned as occurring *after* the burial of Jesus: "Those who — on the ground that it is absurd to put after his burial what preceded it — say that the order is reversed in this way are making a very trifling and ridiculous objection" (p. 516). Perhaps, but Calvin seems to be arguing entirely *ipse dixit* here. For his insouciant dismissal of this objection does seem to leave a big question unaddressed: *Why* does Scripture "put after [Christ's] burial what preceded it" if the only soteriologically significant sufferings of Jesus were those he underwent in and at death?

79. John Deschner, *Wesley's Christology: An Interpretation* (Dallas: Southern Methodist University Press, 1985), pp. 50-51.

80. Deschner, *Wesley's Christology*, p. 51.

and Easter? It is very likely that Wesley held the view that it departed into paradise.[81]

At all events, Methodists dropped the line about the descent in their version of the Apostles' Creed, at least in their Sunday services (it was restored in 1968 for ecumenical reasons).[82]

Meanwhile, in Catholic theology, development of this doctrine continued apace, largely, to be sure, among the mystics rather than the theologians, some of whom we have already cited above. This mystical tradition becomes most evident, and reaches a new culmination, in the remarkable autobiography of St. Thérèse de Lisieux, *The Story of a Soul,* where the author recounts how she came to *volunteer* for hell:

> One night, not knowing how to tell Jesus that I loved Him and how much I desired that He be everywhere loved and glorified, I was thinking with

---

81. Deschner, *Wesley's Christology,* p. 51.

82. The story of how this happened is actually rather complicated. See Karen Westerfield Tucker, *American Methodist Worship* (New York: Oxford University Press, 2001), pp. 39-41: "Another clause from the Apostles' Creed, not found in the oldest forms of the symbol of faith but understood by later Christians to be part of the received text, was short-lived in Methodist usage. It appeared in the 1784 *Sunday Service,* but was deleted at one of the creed's three appearances in the 1786 edition, an omission that some scholars contend did not originate with Wesley. In the 1786 formulation, 'he went down into hell' disappeared from the adult baptismal rite while 'he descended into hell' was retained in the orders for morning and evening prayer. The discrepancy may be explained as an oversight, but by 1792 it made no practical difference since, with the dropping of morning and evening prayer, the baptismal formulation was the only version to remain. The omission of the phrase may be explained as an effort to remove a theologically volatile subject: the thirty-ninth Anglican Article affirming Christ's descent into hell had prompted debate within the Puritan wing and also among the founders of the Protestant Episcopal Church in America; *it had not been included in Wesley's revision of the Articles.* Only in the late twentieth century would United Methodists reintroduce the phrase, and then as part of the stated 'ecumenical' version of the creed produced by the English Language Liturgical Consultation" (p. 40); emphasis added. I owe this reference to the Methodist theologian Geoffrey Wainwright. See also John Wesley's own remarks on 1 Peter 3:19 in his *Explanatory Notes on the New Testament* (London: Epworth Press, 1976), p. 882: "*To the spirits in prison* — [this verse refers to] the unholy men before the Flood, who were then reserved by the justice of God, as in a prison, till He executed the sentences upon them all; and are now also reserved to the judgement of the great day." This gloss by Wesley seems to imply that for him the salvific effects of Christ's descent into hell will have no ultimate bearing on the verdict delivered at the Last Judgment. Similarly, when St. Paul says "he descended to the lowest parts of the earth" (Eph. 4:9), Wesley interprets that as meaning the Virgin's womb, not to the underworld (p. 713), a desperate exegesis whose only justification is Wesley's need to deny the descent article in the Apostles' Creed.

sorrow that He could never receive in hell a single act of love. So I told God that to please Him I would willingly consent to find myself plunged into hell, so that He might be eternally loved in that place of blasphemy.[83]

It was left to several twentieth-century theologians to realize that the Persons of the Trinity could hardly be less generous in their desire to find love in the underworld of rejected love than was a pious, doted-on adolescent raised in the hothouse atmosphere of nineteenth-century bourgeois French Catholicism. The most obvious proponent of this view that the Trinity is fully engaged in the event of Christ's descent into hell is of course Hans Urs von Balthasar (treated already above in the main body of this chapter), who draws on all the authors so far cited and then adds four key motifs from the tradition to forge his own account of the descent: Pauline soteriology, patristic accounts (above all Cyril's) of Christ's vastation of hell, the Christology of Maximus the Confessor, and the medieval distinction between the immanent and economic Trinity.

But as to the specific link, already made by Aquinas, between atoning suffering and Christ's descent, Balthasar is hardly alone among his contemporaries. He himself cites Jean Daniélou, Maurice Blondel, and numerous French exegetes who agree with him (and Thomas) here.[84] Among this cloud of witnesses, obviously his most important ally on this theologoumenon is surely Joseph Ratzinger, whose career shows a remarkable consistency, as we saw above, when he comes to discuss the connection between Christ's vicarious, atoning suffering and his descent into hell. In addition to what was said there, we may add this passage:

> After this, do we still need to ask what worship must be in our hour of darkness? Can it be anything else but the cry from the depths in company with the Lord who "has descended into hell" and who has established the nearness of God *in the midst of abandonment by God?* . . . This brings us back to our starting point, the article of the Creed that speaks of the descent into hell. This article thus asserts that Christ strode through the gate of our final loneliness, that in his Passion he went down into the abyss of our abandonment. Where no voice can reach us any longer, there is he.

83. St. Thérèse of Lisieux, *The Story of a Soul,* trans. Robert J. Edmonson, C.J. (Brewster, MA: Paraclete Press, 2006), p. 122. This passage occurs where the saint is describing her experiences roughly a year before she entered Carmel.

84. Hans Urs von Balthasar, *Theo-Drama,* vol. 4: *The Action,* trans. Graham Harrison (San Francisco: Ignatius Press, 1994), pp. 296-97.

Hell is thereby overcome, or, to be more accurate, death, which was previously hell, is hell no longer. Neither is the same any longer because there is life in the midst of death, because love dwells in it. *Now only deliberate self-enclosure is hell* or, as the Bible calls it, the second death (Revelation 20:14, for example). But death is no longer the path into icy solitude, the gates of *sheol* have been opened.[85]

In his 1977 book *Eschatology* the professor of dogmatic theology (as he still was at the time) makes the link between Christ's suffering in hell, the experiences of the mystics, and a renewed *theology* of the descent even more explicit. Although a shorter portion of this passage was already quoted in the section devoted specifically to his theology, the longer version bears quoting here:

> The answer [to the mystery of evil] lies hidden in Jesus' descent into Sheol, in the *night of the soul which he suffered,* a night which no one can observe except by entering this darkness in suffering faith. Thus, in the history of holiness which hagiology offers us, and notably in the course of recent centuries, in John of the Cross, in Carmelite piety in general, and in that of Thérèse of Lisieux in particular, "Hell" has taken on a completely new meaning and form. *For the saints, "Hell" is not so much a threat to be hurled at other people but a challenge to oneself.* It is a challenge to suffer in the dark night of faith, to experience communion with Christ in solidarity with his descent into the Night. One draws near to the Lord's radiance by sharing *his darkness.* One serves the salvation of the world by leaving one's own salvation behind for the sake of others. In such piety, nothing of the dreadful reality of Hell is denied. Hell is so real that it reaches right into the existence of the saints. Hope can take it on, only if one shares in the suffering of Hell's night by the side of the One who came to transform our night *by his suffering.*[86]

Finally, there is his most recent book, written entirely during his tenure on the Chair of Peter, *Jesus of Nazareth,* which draws on a traditional patristic theme that interprets Jesus' descent into the river Jordan at his baptism as an anticipation of his descent into hell:

---

85. Ratzinger, *Introduction,* pp. 297, 301; emphases added.

86. Joseph Ratzinger, *Eschatology: Death and Eternal Life,* trans. Michael Waldstein and Aidan Nichols, O.P. (Washington, DC: Catholic University of America Press, 1988), pp. 217-18; emphases added.

Jesus' Baptism, then, is understood as a repetition of the whole of history, which both recapitulates the past and anticipates the future. His entering into the sin of others is a descent into the "inferno." But he does not descend merely in the role of a spectator, as in Dante's *Inferno.* Rather, he goes down in the role of one *whose suffering-with-others is a transforming suffering that turns the underworld around,* knocking down and flinging open the gates of the abyss. His Baptism is a descent into the house of the evil one, combat with the "strong man" (cf. Luke 11:22) who holds men captive (and the truth is that we are all very much captive to powers that anonymously manipulate us!). Throughout all its history, the world is powerless to defeat the "strong man"; he is overcome and bound by one yet stronger, who, because of his equality with God, can take upon himself all the sin of the world and then *suffers it through to the end — omitting nothing on the downward path into identity with the fallen.* This struggle is the "conversion" of being that brings it into a new condition, that prepares a new heaven and a new earth. Looked at from this angle, the sacrament of Baptism appears as the gift of participation in Jesus' world-transforming struggle in the conversion of life that took place in his descent and ascent.[87]

An expiatory Holy Saturday is thus clearly the consensus of Catholic theologians, and contemporary Protestant too, at least if Karl Barth can be taken as indicative:

> It is a serious matter to be threatened by hell, sentenced to hell, worthy of hell, and already on the road to hell. On the other hand, we must not minimize the fact that we actually know of only one certain triumph of hell — the handing-over of Jesus — and that this triumph of hell took place in order that it would never again be able to triumph over anyone. We must not deny that Jesus gave Himself up into the depths of hell not only with many others but on their behalf, in their place, in the place of all who believe in Him.[88]

---

87. Joseph Ratzinger/Pope Benedict XVI, *Jesus of Nazareth: From the Baptism in the Jordan to the Transfiguration,* trans. Adrian J. Walker (New York: Doubleday, 2007), p. 20; emphases added.

88. Karl Barth, *Church Dogmatics* II/2: *The Doctrine of God,* ed. G. W. Bromiley and T. F. Torrance (Edinburgh: T. & T. Clark, 1957), p. 496. On the role of this theologoumenon see David Lauber, *Barth on the Descent into Hell: God, Atonement and the Christian Life* (Burlington, VT: Ashgate, 2004).

CHAPTER 11

Recent Magisterial Christology

Only something supernatural can express the supernatural.

Ludwig Wittgenstein, *Culture and Value*

Throughout this book we have seen a constant interplay between individual genius and collective wisdom, between suggestions proposed coupled with official adoption or rejection of those suggestions. As we saw in Chapter 4, this interplay was part of the development of the church's christological doctrine from the outset. Nor was this interplay between individual theologian and teaching office a matter of historical accident, contingent upon the growth of early Christianity in the Roman Empire. As Cardinal Newman observed, the very concept of revelation directly entails an infallible interpreter of that revelation:

> The most obvious answer, then, to the question, why we yield to the authority of the Church in the questions and developments of faith, is, that some authority there must be if there is a revelation given, and other authority there is none but she. A revelation is not given if there be no authority to decide what it is that is given. . . . If Christianity is both social and dogmatic, and intended for all ages, it must humanly speaking have an infallible expounder. Else you will secure unity of form at the loss of unity of doctrine, or unity of doctrine at the loss of unity of form; you will have to choose between a comprehension of opinions and a resolution into parties, between latitudinarian and sectarian error. You may be tolerant or intolerant of contrarieties of thought, but contrarieties you

will have. By the Church of England a hollow uniformity is preferred to an infallible chair; and by the sects of England an interminable division. Germany and Geneva began with persecution and have ended in scepticism. The doctrine of infallibility is a less violent hypothesis than this sacrifice either of faith or of charity. It secures the object, while it gives definiteness and force to the matter, of the Revelation.[1]

There is no need in this chapter to repeat what was said of earlier magisterial teachings on Christology, that having already been covered. But after experiencing a certain quietus after Chalcedon (at least in Catholic theology and without in any way disparaging the achievements of medieval Christology), developments in Catholic Christology have been remarkably turbulent in the last half of the twentieth century, requiring the intervention of the church's teaching office (magisterium) at a number of points and at numerous levels of authority. The result of these interventions has been to give, in the midst of this turbulence, a fairly clear picture of what the Catholic Church confesses regarding the identity and mission of her Lord.

The church has long recognized that she speaks with different levels of authority and addresses issues of greater and lesser moment. Indeed the very truths she seeks both to propound and to defend are themselves arranged according to a certain hierarchy, with some doctrines of greater significance (among which would of course include Christology) and others not so much of lesser significance but ones that *gain their force,* so to speak, by their relation to the truths of greater moment. Of course, truths that are implications of "higher" truths are not *less* true; rather, they gain their truth-value from their relation (as implications) to more fundamental doctrines.

Accordingly, this chapter will move from the highest instances of the church's magisterial authority — the twenty-first Ecumenical Council, called Vatican II, and the teachings of recent popes — to such "lower" instances as the documents of the Congregation for the Doctrine of the Faith (CDF), the *Catechism of the Catholic Church (CCC),* the International Theological Commission (ITC), and the Pontifical Biblical Commission (PBC). Again, as with the hierarchy of truths, this does not imply that teachings that come from lower instances have for that reason lesser truth-value; only that truths expounded by a council or pope are more definitively defined than those that issue from Vatican congregations and commissions.

1. John Henry Newman, *An Essay on the Development of Christian Doctrine,* in *Conscience, Consensus, and the Development of Doctrine,* ed. James Gaffney (New York: Doubleday, 1992/1845), pp. 111-12.

Vatican II

At first glance, the Second Vatican Council seems to offer nothing specific, or at least nothing new, to the church's treasury of teachings about the person and work of Christ. As John XXIII himself acknowledged in his address opening the council, its salient purpose would not be to discuss "one article or another of the fundamental doctrine of the Church . . . which is presumed to be well known and familiar to all."[2] But what was assumed to be known (and accepted!) by all was by no means for that reason not proclaimed or taught, as becomes evident in a statement that the council fathers issued nine days after John XXIII opened this sacred synod (and two days before the Cuban missile crisis became public):

> We believe that the Father so loved the world that He gave His own Son to save it. Indeed, through this same Son of His He freed us from bondage to sin, reconciling all things unto Himself through Him, "making peace through the blood of his cross" (Col. 1:20) so that "we might be called sons of God, and truly be such."[3]

In other words, whatever the council taught, it did so out of the fundamental trinitarian and christological doctrines that form the very summit of the hierarchy of revealed truths that it was the task of this council to expound. To be sure, the developments in doctrine for which the council became most famous were primarily in the area of ecclesiology, ecumenism, and the relation of the church to the modern world (including of course non-Christian religions). But these teachings would have made no sense outside of the trinitarian/christological vision that animated all of the teachings of Vatican II without exception.

2. "Pope John's Opening Speech to the Council," in *The Documents of Vatican II*, ed. Walter M. Abbott, S.J. (New York: Guild Press, 1966), pp. 710-19; here 715. One of the unexpected effects of Vatican II was the vast loss of the knowledge that John XXIII thought he could take for granted, which is another reason the CDF had to intervene so often in the past fifty years. Because most Vatican documents are available on the Vatican's website and because printed versions are found in many different formats and page numbers, most documents of this council cited in this chapter will give only the section/paragraph number for ease of consultation, using the standard abbreviations: *LG* for *Lumen gentium,* the Dogmatic Constitution on the Church, *DV* for *Dei verbum,* the Dogmatic Constitution on Sacred Scripture, *GS* for *Gaudium et spes,* the Pastoral Constitution on the Church in the Modern World, and *UR* for *Unitatis redintegratio,* the Decree on Ecumenism.

3. "Message to Humanity," Abbott, p. 4.

The reception-history of this epochal council shows that this trinitar-ian/christological priority was sometimes obscured. For example, it is widely known that the Dogmatic Constitution on the Church, *Lumen gentium (LG)*, spoke of the church as the People of God before discussing her hierar-chical structure, which led to some misunderstandings later. It is true that priests (and thus bishops and deacons) are, as the Bible says, called from among men (Heb. 5:1), and are baptized members of the church long before they are ordained to the episcopacy, presbyterate, or diaconate. But it is im-portant to realize that, while the council treated the church as the People of God before it treated the hierarchy, it did not *begin* with a chapter on the church as the People of God but rather with one first on the church as *mys-tery,* the mystery of the church as Christ's sacrament: "Christ is the light of all nations. . . . By her relationship with Christ, the Church is a kind of sacra-ment or sign of intimate union with God, and of the unity of all mankind" (*LG* §1). The point is crucial, and when it is lost sight of, a theological distor-tion is bound to set in, as Hans Urs von Balthasar noted as early as 1969:

> Things already get murky if we start out by ignoring the specifically New Testament element in the constitution of the Church. ("The People of God" is primarily an Old Testament concept and is thus unsuited, when taken alone for its own sake, to bring the decisively christological element into view.) It is not even sufficient to say that the "People of God" is the kind of concept that needs only to be supplemented with the *differentia specifica* of the New Testament. For first of all, the Old and New Cove-nants are not two different types of the same species. God's covenant is single and supersedes the Old Covenant as fulfillment does promise. . . . Secondly, the concept of "the People" is ordered to the Old Testament and appears in the New Testament only in quotes from the Old. If the Second Vatican Council tried to replace a certainly insufficient concept of the Church (as that of the "perfect society," or *societas completa,* a society that was completely separated between hierarchy and laity) with the concept of the People of God, it is none the less a concept that hides opposite dan-gers within itself when taken abstractly and absolutely. Concepts are our fate. One cannot emphasize enough that Vatican II's decree on the Church, *Lumen gentium,* introduces the concept of the People of God only *after* it has treated the Church as Mystery.[4]

---

4. Hans Urs von Balthasar, "Christology and Ecclesial Obedience," *Explorations in Theology,* vol. 4, *Spirit and Institution,* trans. Edward T. Oakes, S.J. (San Francisco: Ignatius Press, 1995), p. 139; the article originally appeared in German in *Geist und Leben* 42 (1969):

Other aspects of the council's Christocentrism were, however, better received in the postconciliar church, especially the Dogmatic Constitution on Divine Revelation, *Dei verbum (DV),* which brilliantly cut the Gordian knot in the debate over the relative weight to be given to the "two founts" of revelation: Scripture and tradition. It had long been recognized that crucial Catholic doctrines such as the Immaculate Conception of Mary and papal infallibility were not located (at least in so many words) in the Bible yet had to belong, in some sense, to the truths revealed by God. Hence the thesis that God's revelation could not be exclusively contained in the Christian Scriptures but had also been transmitted by oral tradition. The trouble with that thesis was its implication that there was a set of truths known to the apostles that, for whatever reason, were not put down in the New Testament but were handed on orally. But historical studies could find no evidence for a reified and fully intact tradition handed down in that manner.

Take, for example, the case of the Immaculate Conception, a doctrine that Thomas Aquinas, for one, denied and Duns Scotus accepted. Did that mean that the immensely learned Thomas was unaware of a consistently handed-down oral tradition yet Scotus did know of it? Hardly. A solution to this problem was first adumbrated by Newman's *Essay on Development,* which showed that doctrines have an internal logic that naturally grows throughout time. In the twentieth century, historical critics of the Bible showed that the New Testament itself grew out of an oral tradition and was, so to speak, its precipitate, its distillation. Moreover, this tradition continued on after the canon of the New Testament reached its final stage (infant baptism being a case in point).

Vatican II accepted these findings but went further by locating both Scripture and tradition in the ultimate source of revelation, Jesus Christ, because he is both mediator and plenitude of revelation:

> In His goodness and wisdom, God chose to reveal Himself and to make known to us the hidden purpose of His will by which through Christ, the Word made flesh, man has access to the Father in the Holy Spirit and comes to share in the divine nature.... By this revelation, then, the deepest truth about God and the salvation of man is made clear to us in Christ, who is the Mediator and at the same time the fullness of all revelation. (*DV* §2)

185-203. And of course for Balthasar that mystery is primarily a christological mystery, for as *Lumen gentium* says in its opening line: "*Christ* is the light of nations."

The council also resolved, again through its christological focus, the Gordian knot of the tangled debate between nature and grace. For the past several centuries (going all the way back to the Renaissance in fact), theologians had debated whether postlapsarian man (after the fall of Adam) had a natural desire for God that could be sated independently of grace. The council, relying on Paul's letter to the Colossians ("For by him all things were created; . . . all things were created by him and for him": Col. 1:16), taught that all creatures "in heaven and on earth, visible and invisible, whether thrones or powers or rulers or authorities" are oriented to Christ:

> Human dignity rests above all on the fact that humanity is called to communion with God. . . . Since Christ died for all, and since all are in fact called to one and the same destiny, which is divine, we must hold that the Holy Spirit offers to all the possibility of being made partners, in a way known to God, in the paschal mystery. (*GS*, §§19, 22)[5]

Finally, the council was so confident of the church's grounding in the revelation of Christ that it was able to encourage Catholics to rejoice whenever the Lordship of Christ was proclaimed and lived out in other churches and denominations. So, in its Decree on Ecumenism, *Unitatis redintegratio* *(UR)*, it boldly proclaimed:

> Catholics must joyfully acknowledge and esteem the truly Christian endowments from our common heritage which are to be found among our separated brethren. It is right and salutary to recognize the riches of Christ and virtuous works in the lives of others who are bearing witness to Christ, sometimes even to the shedding of their blood. For God is always wonderful in His works and worthy of admiration. Nor should we forget that whatever is wrought by the grace of the Holy Spirit in the hearts of our separated brethren can contribute to our own edification. Whatever is truly Christian never conflicts with the genuine interests of the faith; indeed, it can always result in a more ample realization of the very mystery of Christ and the Church. (*UR* §4)[6]

5. This Pastoral Constitution on the Church in the Modern World, the longest of the council's documents, has often been faulted by some commentators for its lack of robust christological teaching; but these two passages, in my opinion, belie that charge. In fact, these lines have served as the basis of later magisterial teaching on the person and work of Christ in the contemporary world, as we shall see later in this chapter.

6. This vision, I hope it can now go without saying, has animated the presentation of

Pope John Paul II

In a revealing article he wrote during his papacy, John Paul II claimed that *Gaudium et spes* was the touchstone and charter of his papacy — not least because of the role he played in its drafting committee:

> I must confess that *Gaudium et spes* is particularly dear to me, not only for the themes it develops, but also because of my direct involvement in its drafting. In fact, as the young Archbishop of Krakow, I was a member of the subcommission responsible for studying "the signs of the times" and, from November 1964, I was asked to be part of the central subcommission in charge of the origin of the text. It is precisely my intimate knowledge of the origins of *Gaudium et spes* that has enabled me fully to appreciate its prophetic value and to make wide use of it in my magisterium, starting with my first encyclical, *Redemptor hominis*. In it I took up the legacy of the conciliar Constitution and wished to confirm that the nature and destiny of humanity and of the world can be definitively revealed only in the light of the crucified and risen Christ.[7]

The passage in that first encyclical where he takes up that famous line from *GS* §22 expands that teaching in fascinating ways:

> When we penetrate by means of the continually and rapidly increasing experience of the human family into the mystery of Jesus Christ, we understand with greater clarity that there is at the basis of all these ways the path that the Church of our time must follow. . . . Christ the Lord indicated this way especially, when, as the Council teaches, "by his Incarnation, he, the Son of God, in a certain way *united himself with each man*" [*GS* §22]. The Church therefore sees its fundamental task in enabling that union to be brought about and renewed continually. The Church wishes to serve *this single end:* that each person may be able to find Christ, in order that Christ may walk with each person the path of life, with the power of the truth about man and the world that is contained in the mystery of

---

Christology of this book; as its subtitle indicates, there is nothing inherently contradictory in a Christology that is both Catholic and evangelical.

7. John Paul II, "Only Christ can fulfill man's hopes," *Communio: International Catholic Review* 13 (Spring 1996): 122-23. Again, papal encyclicals will be cited by section number only, although there is a good collection of this pope's encyclicals in book form in *The Encyclicals of John Paul II*, ed. J. Michael Miller, C.S.B. (Huntington, IN: Our Sunday Visitor, 1996).

the Incarnation and the Redemption and with the power of the love that is radiated by that truth. . . . Jesus Christ becomes, in a way, *newly present, in spite of all his apparent absences,* in spite of all the limitations of the presence and of the institutional activity of the Church. Jesus Christ becomes present with the power of the truth and the love that are expressed in him with unique, unrepeatable fullness in spite of the shortness of his life on earth and the even greater shortness of his public activity. (*Redemptor hominis* §13; emphases added, except the quotation from *GS* §22, which is the pope's)

In other words, if *Gaudium et spes* functioned as John Paul II's *magna carta* for his papacy, then its famous line in *GS* §22 was for the pope the lodestar of that document; which perhaps should not surprise us, since he apparently was the one, along with Henri de Lubac, who was chiefly responsible for its inclusion.[8] What makes this line from *GS* so important — something that emerged throughout John Paul II's remarkably lengthy papacy — is that it finally managed to unite Christocentrism with universalism. The opening line of *Redemptor hominis* reads: "The Redeemer of man, Jesus Christ, is the center of the universe and of history" (*RH* §1), about the most lapidary formulation of Christocentrism ever penned. But precisely because Christ is the center of the universe and of history, *no one finds himself on the periphery.* The pope explains how this can be in his encyclical *Dominum et vivificantem (DViv):*

The Incarnation of God the Son signifies the taking up into unity with God not only of human nature, but in this human nature, in a sense, of everything that is "flesh"; the whole of humanity, the entire visible and

8. On the one hand, the affinities of *GS* §22 with de Lubac are more than evident, as Paul McPartlan rightly sees: "These words [in *GS* §22] remarkably reflect what Henri de Lubac had already said, as long ago as 1938, in his first book *Catholicism,* 'By revealing the Father and by being revealed by him, Christ completes the revelation of man to himself.'" Paul McPartlan, "Henri de Lubac: Evangeliser," *Priests and People* (August-September 1992): 343-46; here at 344, citing de Lubac in the Ignatius Press translation at 339. This of course does not obviate Wojtyla's influence, as de Lubac himself freely concedes: "I had known Bishop Wojtyla in Rome, at the time of the Council. We worked side by side at the time of the arduous birth of the famous Schema 13, which, after a number of hasty modifications, became the Constitution *Gaudium et spes.*" Henri de Lubac, *At the Service of the Church: Henri de Lubac Reflects on the Circumstances That Occasioned His Writings,* trans. Anne Elizabeth Englund (San Francisco: Ignatius Press, 1993), p. 171. On this relationship, see as well David L. Schindler, "Christology and the *Imago Dei:* Interpreting *Gaudium et spes,*" *Communio: International Catholic Review* 23 (Spring 1996): 156-84, esp. 168.

material world. The Incarnation, then, also has a cosmic significance, a cosmic dimension. The "firstborn of all creation" (Col. 1:15), becoming incarnate in the individual humanity of Christ, unites Himself in some way with the entire reality of man, which is also "flesh" (cf. Gen. 9:11, etc.) — and in this reality with all "flesh," with the whole creation. (*DViv* §7)

Only a proper stress on the humanity of Christ, the pope is in effect saying, can show how Christocentrism is truly universal. In an earlier chapter, we saw how Ernst Troeltsch compared Christocentrism with geocentrism in astronomy; but the analogy breaks down if one takes seriously the human nature that Christ assumed at the incarnation, a point shrewdly observed by John Saward:

The history of heresy is a saga of false oppositions: unity of essence without distinction of persons (Sabellianism), distinction of persons without unity of essence (Arianism), freedom without grace (Pelagianism), grace without freedom (Calvinism). To demand a choice between Creation-Christocentricity and a Redemption-Christocentricity would only add to the catalogue of wrong-headed alternatives. Pope John Paul II makes no such mistake. He teaches that the Son of God becomes man for the purpose of redemption, but he is also insistent that Christ, in His humanity as well as in His divinity, is "the center of the universe and of history."[9]

It has admittedly proven difficult to join, at one and the same time, Christocentrism with openness to the truth of other religions, but for John Paul II that problem only arises when Christians are not radically Christocentric enough. Perhaps the place where one can best discover how the pope personally fused these two aspects of his papacy can be found in an address he gave to followers of various religions in Los Angeles during his 1987 visit to the United States, where he gave this manifesto:

Throughout my Pontificate it has been my constant concern to fulfill this twofold task of proclamation and dialogue. On my pastoral visits around

9. John Saward, *Christ Is the Answer: The Christ-Centered Teaching of Pope John Paul II* (New York: Alba House, 1995), p. 55. This book is the best analysis in English of this pope's Christology. Avery Dulles also notes that the pope's serene and confident faith in the universal reach of Christ as center of revelation, history, and the world accounts for his style of teaching: "While he is firm, he is never polemical. He believes that a serene exposition of the truth is its best defense." Avery Dulles, S.J., *The Splendor of Faith: The Theological Vision of Pope John Paul II* (New York: Crossroad, 1999), p. vii.

the world I have sought to encourage and strengthen the faith of Catholic people and other Christians as well. At the same time, I have been pleased to meet leaders of all religions in the hope of promoting greater interreligious understanding and cooperation for the good of the human family. . . . To the Buddhist community, which reflects numerous Asian traditions as well as American, I wish respectfully to acknowledge your way of life, based upon compassion and loving kindness. . . . To the Islamic community: I share your belief that mankind owes its existence to the one, compassionate God who created heaven and earth. . . . To the Hindu community: I hold in esteem your concern for inner peace and for the peace of the world, based not on purely mechanical or materialistic political considerations, but on self-purification, unselfishness, love and sympathy for all. . . . To the Jewish community: I repeat the Second Vatican Council's conviction that the Church "cannot forget that she received the revelation of the Old Testament through the people with whom God in his mercy established the Ancient Covenant. Nor can she forget that she draws sustenance from the root of that good olive tree onto which has been grafted the wild olive branches of the Gentiles" (cf. *Nostra aetate* §4).[10]

These remarks of course do not remotely imply a slackening of missionary fervor, a point the pope obviously felt had to be made when he promulgated his encyclical of December 7, 1990, *Redemptoris missio (RM)*, where he reaffirmed this central teaching of Vatican II:

Christ is the one mediator between God and mankind. . . . No one, therefore, can enter into communion with God except through Christ, by the working of the Holy Spirit. Christ's one, universal mediation, far from being an obstacle on the journey toward God, is the way established by God himself, a fact of which Christ is fully aware. Although participated forms of mediation of different kinds and degrees are not excluded, they acquire meaning and value only from Christ's own mediation, and they cannot be understood as parallel or complementary to his. (*RM* §5.4)

But far from representing any backtracking on what he said in Los Angeles, this encyclical explicitly reaffirms it:

10. John Paul II, "Address to Followers of Various Religions in the United States," in *John Paul II and Interreligious Dialogue*, ed. Byron L. Sherwin and Harold Kasimow (Maryknoll, NY: Orbis Books, 1999), pp. 44-47; here 45-46.

The universality of salvation means that it is granted not only to those who explicitly believe in Christ and have entered the Church. Since salvation is offered to all, it must be made concretely available to all. But it is clear that today, as in the past, many people do not have an opportunity to come to know or accept the Gospel revelation or to enter the Church. The social and cultural conditions in which they live do not permit this, and frequently they have been brought up in other religious traditions. For such people salvation in Christ is accessible by virtue of a grace which, while having a mysterious relationship to the Church, does not make them formally part of the Church but enlightens them in a way which is accommodated to their spiritual and material situation. This grace comes from Christ: it is the result of his Sacrifice and is communicated by the Holy Spirit. It enables each person to attain salvation through his or her free cooperation. (*RM* §10.1)[11]

That not every Catholic theologian sees things in the same way goes without saying: some assert that Christ cannot be the center unless other religions on the supposed "periphery" of that center were correlatively rejected (such say the followers of the schismatic Archbishop Lefebvre), while others aver that members of other religions (and ideologies) cannot be saved unless their founders are conceded equal status with Christ as fellow founders of their respective religions. Far and away the latter group is the more numerous (despite the attention of the press on the Lefebvrists), and they have become the concern of the Congregation for the Doctrine of the Faith, to whose interventions we now turn.

---

11. In his doctoral dissertation on the concept of faith in John of the Cross, the future pope showed that he was already distancing himself from the manual Thomism of the Roman universities, where ecumenism and interreligious dialogue were not popular at the time. Wojtyla's director during those years was the famous neo-Thomist Reginald Garrigou-Lagrange, who had this problem with the dissertation, as recounted by the pope's best biographer: "In his review of the dissertation, Garrigou criticized Wojtyla for not using the phrase 'divine object' of God. One assumes that this was an issue between dissertation director and student during the preparation of the dissertation and that Garrigou did not persuade Wojtyla of his point. Whatever the process involved, the fact remains that, in his insistence on not treating God as a divine 'object,' even by way of analogy, Wojtyla was moving beyond the vocabulary, formulas, and intellectual categories that dominated the Angelicum during his two years there." George Weigel, *Witness to Hope: The Biography of Pope John Paul II* (New York: HarperCollins, 1999), pp. 86-87. Thus, the freedom he established for himself *vis-à-vis* the various schools of theology before Vatican II would stand him in good stead both during the council itself and during his pontificate.

The Congregation for the Doctrine of the Faith

Because it is the specific task of the Congregation for the Doctrine of the Faith (CDF) to ensure that Catholic theologians teach the Catholic faith and none other, and because Joseph Cardinal Ratzinger served as head of that congregation from 1983 to his election to the papacy in April 2005, his interventions often, perforce, had to take on the task of disciplining wayward theologians, leading many journalists to see the relationship between John Paul II and Cardinal Ratzinger as a kind of "good cop, bad cop" routine. The charge is quite unfair, since they had different roles. As we have already seen, both Vatican II and John Paul II felt called by the Holy Spirit to be open to members of other religions precisely *because* of their mutually held Christocentrism, the collapse of which inevitably entails the disappearance of the faith itself, which has no other task but to proclaim the Lordship of Christ, as events would prove.

Evangelical theologians occasionally took worried notice of a strong postconciliar trend among some liberal Catholic theologians to abandon Christocentrism. For example, a Dutch evangelical by the name of Klaas Runia saw an arc of diminished confessional commitment to the Lordship of Christ in the Dutch Catholic theologians Piet Schoonenberg and Edward Schillebeeckx. Chalcedonian orthodoxy holds that Christ's human nature does not have its own hypostasis (this is the doctrine of the *anhypostasis*) but from the moment of Jesus' conception had its hypostasis in the Logos, the Second Person of the Trinity (the doctrine of the *enhypostasis*). Schoonenberg reversed this solution by claiming that the Word of God is in itself impersonal (that is, is *anhypostatic*) and only takes on individuality in the substantial man Jesus (which is thus *enhypostatic*): "[I]t is primarily not the human nature which is enhypostatic in the divine person, but the divine nature in the human person."[12] But as Runia points out, this solution, however attractive it might at first seem, raises a host of ancillary problems:

> But is this enough? Does the New Testament not speak of Jesus Christ in terms of pre-existence, that is, of the Word that was with God before the incarnation and that became flesh? Schoonenberg believes that we should not take the texts about pre-existence literally, but should re-interpret

12. Piet Schoonenberg, *The Christ: A Study of the God-Man Relationship in the Whole of Creation and in Jesus Christ,* trans. Della Couling (New York: Seabury Press, 1971), p. 87.

them. . . . In other words, we should not take our starting-point in a divine person who subsequently becomes man, but we should start from the man Jesus concerning whom pre-existence is predicated.[13]

Edward Schillebeeckx, in two large volumes titled *Jesus*[14] and *Christ*,[15] began a trend in Catholic Christology that has lasted down to this day: the use of historical criticism not just to determine what can be reliably said about the historical Jesus but, above all, to use that constructed portrait as the norm for judging all later dogmatic statements about the identity of Christ — very much including the dogmatic statements found in the New Testament itself. For him the earliest layer shows that Jesus understood himself as an eschatological prophet *out of which* developed later titles such as Christ, Lord, and Son of God.[16] This means that all the later titles must be interpreted functionally, not ontologically. The title "Son of God," for example, says: "The final prophet is Son of God because, initiated into God's wisdom, he speaks of and for God to men."[17]

As we saw in Chapter 9, Protestants had already gone down that road, until Karl Barth blocked the way. (Catholic Christology after Vatican II, at least among the most famous theologians of the time, recapitulated in forty years what it had taken two centuries for Protestant theology to discover, and rarely by learning from its mistakes and dead ends.) Here is how the evangelical Runia assesses the matter:

> But this historical Jesus whom Schillebeeckx claims to have found is the result of his own research; and that, in turn, is determined by his own starting-point, namely, that we have to see Jesus' historical manifestation within the quite specific ongoing tradition in which he and his contemporaries were set [which would be Second Temple Judaism]. . . . But this means that from start to finish Schillebeeckx's historical Jesus is interpreted in categories of Jewish-functional theology. And since this historical Jesus is the final norm and criterion by which all later interpretations must be tested and checked, it is not surprising to see that the

13. Klaas Runia, *The Present-Day Christological Debate* (Downers Grove, IL: InterVarsity Press, 1984), p. 49.

14. Edward Schillebeeckx, *Jesus: An Experiment in Christology,* trans. John Bowden (New York: Seabury Press, 1979).

15. Edward Schillebeeckx, *Christ: The Christian Experience in the Modern World,* trans. John Bowden (New York: Seabury Press, 1980).

16. Schillebeeckx, *Jesus,* p. 480.

17. Schillebeeckx, *Jesus,* p. 498.

whole New Testament itself is also interpreted in functional categories. Concepts such as Son of God and pre-existence cannot be essential categories any more. So the road to Nicea and Chalcedon is automatically blocked.[18]

The nadir of these trends was reached in 1999 with Roger Haight's book *Jesus: Symbol of God*, where the priority is no longer given even to the historical Jesus but merely to his message, and the resurrection is entirely functionalized as merely the disciples' vivid memory of Jesus' extraordinarily uplifting teaching:

> Resurrection faith today is not belief in an external miracle, an empirical historical event testified to by disciples, which we take as a fact on the basis of their word. Although that may describe in fact the belief of many Christians, it is no ideal. A reflective faith-hope today will affirm Jesus risen on the basis of a conviction that Jesus' *message* is true; because God is the way Jesus revealed God to be, Jesus is alive. . . . Because it was Jesus whom people experienced as risen, *and not someone else,* one must assume that *Jesus had a forceful religious impact on people.* . . . In the view proposed here, the external event that helped mediate a consciousness of Jesus risen was Jesus himself *during his ministry.* Or, to be more exact, after his death, the disciples' *memory* of Jesus filled this role. . . . My understanding of the resurrection does not support the necessity of an empty tomb *in principle.*[19]

These increasingly *recherché* views need to be rehearsed here to show why the CDF had to act as it did: by rebuking these views (many others of course could be cited too), it necessarily had to come across as "negative," for that is its role — not to speak its own positive proposals but to correct erroneous ones. Moreover, because it was not a small group of theologians who

18. Runia, *Christological Debate,* pp. 57-58.

19. Roger Haight, *Jesus: Symbol of God* (Maryknoll, NY: Orbis Books, 1999), pp. 150, 143, 141, 134; all emphases added. A teacher of mine once told me that the New Testament is hard to believe but easy to understand: everyone knows what it *means* for God to raise an itinerant Galilean rabbi from the dead, but to believe it involves an immense overthrow of one's worldview (and behavior). But modernist theologians, he claimed, panic at these faith-demands and so reverse the line: in their hands the New Testament becomes easy to believe but hard to understand. That is, if all the resurrection means is that Jesus' message is still true, well, *that* is certainly easy to believe; but to understand how so complicated a text could yield such nugatory results — well, that takes effort to understand!

held these views but was a position that could be found throughout the guild, the CDF finally addressed the issue itself in its famous document dated August 6, 2000 (but promulgated on September 5), *Dominus Iesus (DI)*. Not since Paul VI's encyclical *Humanae vitae* has a Vatican document provoked such a controversy, which its authors seem to have anticipated. At all events, its indictment of the majority trend in professional Catholic theology is quite comprehensive and shows, by the way, a thorough knowledge of the worldview of liberal theology *tout court:*

> The roots of these problems are to be found in certain presuppositions of both a philosophical and theological nature, which hinder the understanding and acceptance of the revealed truth. Some of these can be mentioned: the conviction of the elusiveness and inexpressibility of divine truth, even by Christian revelation; relativistic attitudes toward truth itself, according to which what is true for some would not be true for others; the radical opposition posited between the logical mentality of the West and the symbolic mentality of the East; the subjectivism which, by regarding reason as the only source of knowledge, becomes incapable of raising its "gaze to the heights, not daring to rise to the truth of being"; the difficulty in understanding and accepting the presence of definitive and eschatological events in history; the metaphysical emptying of the historical incarnation of the Eternal Logos, reduced to a mere appearing of God in history; the eclecticism of those who, in theological research, uncritically absorb ideas from a variety of philosophical and theological contexts without regard for consistency, systematic connection, or compatibility with Christian truth; finally, the tendency to read and to interpret Sacred Scripture outside the Tradition and Magisterium of the Church. (*DI* §4)

Obviously, the heated reaction to the document was itself both sign and proof of the truth of these observations. By insisting on the salvific *uniqueness* of Jesus Christ, the document was not saying, as so many assumed, that salvation is *exclusive* to Christians. In fact the subtitle of the document reads: "On the Unicity and Salvific *Universality* of Jesus Christ and the Church." Not only was the document based on *GS* §22, it quoted it (at *DI* §12). As Paul Griffiths rightly notes:

> *DI* is for the most part a deeply traditional document. It says nothing substantively new, and nothing that had not already been said by recent curial and consultative documents. This fact makes the overheated expressions

of surprise at *DI* a bit puzzling: no one of serious interest in the recent history of magisterial thinking about religious diversity should have been surprised by the central emphases of *DI*.[20]

Perhaps the most intriguing phrase in *DI* §4 is the reference to philosophical errors. For implicit in many of the heated reactions against the document seems to be the presupposition inherited from German Idealism that the particular cannot reveal the universal unless it is subsumed *(aufgehoben)* into the universal categories of philosophy. But John Henry Newman had already refuted that view in one of his early sermons:

> Mercies given to multitudes are not less mercies because they are made to flow from particular sources. Indeed, most of the great appointments of Divine goodness are marked by this very character of what men call *exclusiveness*. God distributes numberless benefits to all men, but He does so through a few select instruments. The few are favored for the good of the many. Wealth, power, gifts of mind, learning, all tend towards the welfare of the community; yet, for all that, they are not given at once to all, but channeled out to the many through the few. And so the blessings of the Gospel are open to the whole world, as freely given as light or fire; yet even light has had its own receptacle since the fourth day of creation; and fire has been hidden in the flinty rock, as if to show us that the light and fire of our souls are not gained without the use of means, nor except from special sources.[21]

Tellingly, the sermon from which these observations are drawn Newman called "Submission to Church Authority," and it reads almost as a commentary both on *DI* itself and on the pained reactions it elicited: "[I]t is more tolerable to be called narrow-minded by man, than to be pronounced self-wise and self-sufficient by God; it is happier to be thought overscrupulous, with the Bible, than to have the world's praise for liberality without it."[22] A world that is already relativistic is bound to take scandal at the exclusive claims of Christ, but in seeking to have the church follow the world's lead, liberal theology is but asking the church to dispense with some-

---

20. Paul J. Griffiths, "On *Dominus Iesus:* Complementarity Can Be Claimed," in *Concilium: Learning from Other Faiths,* ed. Hermann Häring, Janet Martin Soskice, and Felix Wilfred (London: SCM Press, 2003), p. 22.

21. John Henry Newman, "Submission to Church Authority," in *Parochial and Plain Sermons* (San Francisco: Ignatius Press, 1997), pp. 604-13; here 606-7; Newman's emphasis.

22. Newman, "Submission to Church Authority," p. 606.

thing *the world* has already shed: "Such persons, then, however well they mean it, yet, in fact, ask us to give up something, while they give up nothing themselves; for that is not much to give up which a man sets no value upon."[23] Liberal theologians call for the church to sacrifice her claims, but they "cannot make such a sacrifice, because they have made it already, or their fathers before them, when they left the Church."[24]

So *DI*, or something very like it, was bound to be issued, again as Newman anticipated with remarkable prescience: "[T]eachers have been bound to teach in one way, not in another, as well as hearers to hear."[25] This again does not mean exclusiveness toward others of other religions: "We are bound to love them and pray for them, not to be harsh with them, or revile or despise them, but to be gentle, patient, apt to teach, merciful, to make allowance, to interpret their conduct for the best."[26] But that same openness must go hand in hand with firmness in protecting what God has given the church as his revelation. If Catholics had heeded these next lines, the controversy over *DI* would never have arisen:

> We desire to meet together, but it must be in the Church, not on neutral ground, or rather an enemy's, the open inhospitality, the waste of this world, but within that sheltered heritage whose landmarks have long since been set up. If Christ has constituted one Holy Society (which He has done); if His Apostles have set it in order (which they did), and have expressly bidden us (as they have in Scripture) not to undo what they have begun; and if (in matter of fact) their Work, so set in order and so blessed, is among us this very day (as it is), and we partakers of it, it were a traitor's act in us to abandon it, an unthankful slight on those who have preserved it for so many ages, a cruel disregard of those who are to come after us, nay of those now alive who are external to it and might otherwise be brought into it. We must transmit as we have received. We did not make the Church, we may not unmake it.[27]

In that Newmanian light, there should be nothing controversial (at least for confessing Christians, still less for Catholic theologians, who were after all the main target of the document) in these affirmations:

23. Newman, "Submission to Church Authority," p. 608.
24. Newman, "Submission to Church Authority," p. 608.
25. Newman, "Submission to Church Authority," p. 609.
26. Newman, "Submission to Church Authority," p. 611.
27. Newman, "Submission to Church Authority," p. 611.

Jesus Christ has a significance and a value for the human race and its history, which are unique and singular, proper to him alone, exclusive, universal, and absolute. (*DI* §15)

Therefore, the theory of the limited, incomplete, or imperfect character of the revelation of Jesus Christ, which would be complementary to that found in other religions, is contrary to the Church's faith. Such a position would claim to be based on the notion that the truth about God cannot be grasped and manifested in its globality and completeness by any historical religion, neither by Christianity nor by Jesus Christ. (*DI* §5)

It is likewise contrary to the Catholic faith to introduce a separation between the salvific actions of the Word as such and that of the Word made man. With the incarnation, all the salvific actions of the Word of God are always done in unity with the human nature that he has assumed for the salvation of all people. The one subject which operates in the two natures, human and divine, is the single person of the Word.

Therefore, the theory which would attribute, after the incarnation as well, a salvific activity to the Logos as such in his divinity, exercised "in addition to" or "beyond" the humanity of Christ, is not compatible with the Catholic faith. (*DI* §10)

This last cited §10, especially the last paragraph, seems on the surface to deny the *extra Calvinisticum,* which as we saw should really be called the *extra Catholicum,* since it is well grounded in patristic and medieval texts. However, in the wake of a fascinating exchange between the Jesuit Belgian theologian Jacques Dupuis and the CDF that took place after the promulgation of *DI,* the CDF changed the wording of this paragraph.

Both before and after the promulgation of *DI,* Dupuis had published several books that tried to do justice both to the uniqueness and to the universal reach of Christ's salvific effects by extending a distinction already known in the patristic era between the *Logos asarkos* (that is, the Logos prior to the incarnation) and the *Logos ensarkos* (the incarnate Logos). In the course of his writings, Dupuis eventually came to hold that this distinction could be maintained after the incarnation as well. In his first book on this theme, he began with a distinction between the explicit and implicit presence of Christ in other religions:

Since Christ is God in a personal relationship with human beings, or personally present to them, salvation always involves an encounter with the mystery of Christ. The members of the other religious traditions who are saved have been and are personally confronted with his mystery. Their Christic experience, however, is an implicit one. As long as the human Jesus has not been revealed to them, they cannot recognize the mystery of Christ in his humanity. An implicit experience of the Christic mystery is one thing; its explicit discovery in Jesus of Nazareth is something else again. The former is a necessary condition of salvation; the latter is the privilege of Christians.[28]

In his next book Dupuis began to see that such a solution had problems of its own, at least if we are to judge by the following rhetorical questions posed toward the end of the book:

That one particular culture could have received, nearly exclusively, the legacy of a solitary salvation event, an event occurring in a particular religious tradition, seems to constitute a belittling of humanity's other religious traditions and cultures. . . . Is the claim of universality that Christianity makes for the Jesus Christ event still possible to sustain? Is it enough, in order to defend it today, to call it "not exclusive but inclusive"? And what is the actual purpose of such distinctions? In the last analysis, does the traditional Christocentrism of Christian theology stand up to the shock of the current encounter of cultures and religious traditions? These questions will have to be answered.[29]

Dupuis's provisional answer was to look toward the cosmic dimension of Christ's presence and work of redemption.[30] But with his *magnum opus* on this knotty question of religious pluralism, *Toward a Christian Theology of Religious Pluralism,* he brought to a boil his vague disquiets with previous solutions (including his own) and then introduced his latest solution:

28. Jacques Dupuis, S.J., *Jesus Christ at the Encounter of World Religions,* trans. Robert R. Barr (New York: Orbis Books, 1991), p. 145.

29. Jacques Dupuis, S.J., *Who Do You Say I Am? An Introduction to Christology* (New York: Orbis Books, 1994), p. 149.

30. "Meanwhile, let us observe, with Karl Rahner, that the most urgent christological task today surely consists in demonstrating the universal significance and cosmic dimension of the Jesus Christ event, with Christ as the pinnacle of salvation history and Christology as that history's sharpest formulation. A cosmic Christology would, in the first place, have to show the cosmic dimension of the Incarnation, that is, the significance of Jesus Christ not only for the salvation of human beings and their history, but for the whole universe" (Dupuis, *Who Do You Say I Am?,* p. 149).

Admittedly, in the mystery of Jesus-the-Christ, the Word cannot be separated from the flesh it has assumed. But, inseparable as the divine Word and Jesus' human existence may be, they nevertheless remain distinct. While, then, the human action of the Logos *ensarkos* is the universal sacrament of God's saving action, it does not exhaust the action of the Logos. A distinct action of the Logos *asarkos* endures [after the incarnation] — not, to be sure, as constituting a distinct economy of salvation, parallel to that realized in the flesh of Christ, but as the expression of God's superabundant graciousness and absolute freedom.[31]

It was clearly this passage, and the reasoning behind it, that *DI* §10 had in mind, as emerged during the conversations the CDF had with Dupuis both leading up to the promulgation of *DI* and after. Although these conversations were not technically a "trial," since Dupuis pledged his cooperation with the proceedings, it did lead to an official *Notification* roughly three months after the promulgation of *DI,* which Dupuis signed.[32] This document affirms all that *DI* had to say about the unicity and universality of the salvation effected by Christ — with one significant variant. Specifically referring to *RM* §6.1 ("To introduce any sort of separation between the Word and Jesus Christ is contrary to the Christian faith") and to *DI* §10, it said the following: "It is therefore contrary to the Catholic faith not only to posit a separation between the Word and Jesus, or between the Word's salvific activity and that of Jesus, but also to maintain that there is a salvific activity of the Word as such in his divinity, *independent of* the humanity of the Incarnate Word" (*NJP* §I.2; emphasis added).

The earlier formulation had condemned any theory that would distinguish, in its words, "a salvific activity to the Logos as such in his divinity, exercised *'in addition to'* or *'beyond'* the humanity of Christ," saying that such a distinction "is not compatible with the Catholic faith" (*DI* §10). But now those prepositional phrases are altered to say *independent of* the humanity of

31. Jacques Dupuis, S.J., *Toward a Christian Theology of Religious Pluralism* (New York: Orbis Books, 1997), p. 299.

32. "This *Notification,* approved by the Holy Father in the Audience of November 24, 2000, was presented to Father Jacques Dupuis and was accepted by him. By signing the text, the author committed himself to assent to the stated theses and, in his future theological activity and publications, to hold the doctrinal contents indicated in the *Notification,* the text of which must be included in any reprinting or further editions of his book, as well as in all translations." *Notification on the book* Toward a Christian Theology of Religions *by Jacques Dupuis,* Preface; abbreviated as *NJP;* available at the Vatican website here: http://www.vatican.va/roman_curia/congregations/cfaith/documents/rc_con_cfaith_doc_20010124_dupuis_en.html.

Christ. The change must surely be significant, for a number of reasons. First, one gathers that it enabled Dupuis to sign the document.

On the one hand, he no longer talked about the *Logos asarkos* and *ensarkos,* which some saw as referring to two different *subjects;* now he spoke of the Word *as such* and the Word *incarnate,* or the *Verbum incarnandum* and the *Verbum incarnatum.*[33] On the other hand, Dupuis was able in his last book to continue to affirm some kind of "beyond" or "in addition to" in the salvific activity of Christ, since the *Notification* now condemned only hypotheses that spoke of the Word acting *independently* but not *beyond* the humanity of Christ:

> The personal identity between the Word of God and Jesus Christ . . . must always be maintained. . . . This is not to say that it is not possible to speak of an action of the Word as such, distinct from his working through the humanity of Jesus, even in his risen and glorified state. It is necessary, however, to understand correctly this action of the Word as such. It must be well understood that the Word of God with whom we are dealing is not different from the one who became incarnate in Jesus Christ. . . . But, while the mystery of the incarnation of the Word is an historic event and therefore particular in time and space, the Word as such exists in the eternity of the divine mystery. He also exists and is present and working throughout the history of the world and humanity — which in fact be-

33. Some might charge that Dupuis is indulging in a subterfuge here, but a denial of that distinction would surely leave difficulties of its own, as one of his ablest defenders points out: "Dupuis [earlier] distinguished the Logos *asarkos* (the Word of God *in himself* and not, or not yet incarnated) from the Logos *ensarkos* (the Word of God precisely as incarnated). Dupuis was surprised to find this distinction leading a few readers to conclude that he was 'doubling' the Logos, as if he were holding that there were four persons in God! To avoid such odd misunderstandings, he has dropped the terms *asarkos* and *ensarkos.* However, he continues to distinguish between the Word of God *in se* and to be incarnated . . . and the Word of God precisely as incarnated. We must make such terminological distinctions. Otherwise we will finish up joining some critics in such a strange statement as 'the Word of God *as such* is the Word incarnate.' Those who fail 'to watch their language' and use such an expression seem to attribute an eternal, real (and not just an intentional) existence to the humanity created and assumed by the Word of God at a certain point in the history of the world, as well as appearing to cast doubt upon the loving freedom of the Word of God in becoming incarnate for our salvation." Gerald O'Collins, S.J., "Jacques Dupuis: His Person and Work," in *In Many and Diverse Ways: In Honor of Jacques Dupuis,* ed. Daniel Kendall and Gerald O'Collins (New York: Orbis Books, 2003), pp. 18-29; here 25. Readers of Chapter 7 might be reminded of Joanna Petersen here: unless something like the distinctions Dupuis is trying to make are admitted, one will suddenly find oneself holding to the preexistence of the celestial flesh of Christ.

comes the history of salvation in as much as it comprehends the totality of self-manifestations of God to humanity through his Word. The Word of God is therefore operative through the whole of history, both before and after the mystery of the incarnation.[34]

That Dupuis finds himself on safer ground here can be seen not just in the fact that his last book was never condemned (or even investigated) but also in two remarks that Cardinal Ratzinger/Pope Benedict made about the issue. First, alluding specifically to the conversations between Dupuis and the CDF, Cardinal Ratzinger has this to say:

> But above all we must mention J. Dupuis as eminent advocate of an attempt at reconciliation. . . . The Congregation for the Doctrine of the Faith also concerned itself with his work, since the average reader — in all loyalty to the uniqueness of Jesus Christ — would nevertheless get an impression of a leaning toward pluralist positions. The dialogue with the author led to a "Notification," in which all the theological points important to Fr. Dupuis were clarified by mutual agreement, and the boundary in the direction of pluralism was thus also clearly marked out.[35]

In other words, the Cardinal Prefect of the CDF now says that his chief worry about Dupuis's work is that it might have led to pluralism rather than inclusivism.[36] Notice also that Cardinal Ratzinger nowhere denies or retracts the change in wording from *DI* to the *Notification*. But more telling in that regard is a remark he made as Pope Benedict in his book on Jesus:

> We have said that in Jesus' filial communion with the Father, *his human soul is also taken up into the act of praying.* He who sees Jesus sees the Fa-

---

34. Jacques Dupuis, *Christianity and the Religions: From Confrontation to Dialogue,* trans. Phillip Berryman (Maryknoll, NY: Orbis Books, 2002), p. 140.

35. Joseph Cardinal Ratzinger, *Truth and Tolerance: Christian Belief and World Religions,* trans. Henry Taylor (San Francisco: Ignatius Press, 2004), pp. 51-52.

36. In ecumenical and interreligious theology, there are three terms that are commonly used: "exclusivism," "inclusivism," and "pluralism." *Exclusivism* refers to the uniqueness of Jesus Christ as entailing that only those who explicitly confess his Lordship and are baptized (at least *in voto,* by desire) are saved. *Inclusivism* holds that Jesus is the unique Savior but has saved all mankind (at least potentially), which is the teaching of Vatican II, as we saw. *Pluralism* starts with the fact that all are (potentially) saved and works back from there to insist that the channels of salvation must be plural as well, which it was the burden of *DI* to reject. On the ramifications of this terminology see J. A. DiNoia, O.P., *The Diversity of Religions: A Christian Perspective* (Washington, DC: Catholic University of America Press, 1992).

ther (cf. Jn 14:9). The disciple who walks with Jesus is thus caught up *with him* into communion with God. And that is what redemption means: this stepping *beyond the limits of human nature,* which has been there as a possibility and an expectation in man, God's image and likeness, since the moment of creation.[37]

Of course these are only passing remarks, but they do hint at the Catholic orthodoxy of the *extra Calvinisticum.* Of greater doctrinal weight, however, is the logic of the *extra Calvinisticum* that seems to be operative in *Lumen gentium,* in the famous passage that asserts that the fullness of the church "subsists in" the Catholic Church "although many elements of sanctification and of truth can be found outside of her visible structure" (*LG* §8). To explain the reality of this relation the council uses this analogy:

> For this reason, by an excellent analogy, this reality is compared to the mystery of the incarnate Word. Just as the assumed nature inseparably united to the divine Word serves Him as a living instrument of salvation, so, in a similar way, does the communal structure of the Church serve Christ's Spirit, who vivifies her by way of building up the body (cf. Eph. 4:16). (*LG* §8)

In other words, if the relationship between the Word of God and the human nature of Christ is analogous to the relationship between the Spirit of Christ and the visible structures of the church (which fully inhabits those structures yet somehow goes beyond them), then the council is implying that the Word of God is active, too, beyond the human nature of Christ — *beyond* but not *independent of* that nature. For as the council goes on to teach about the ultimate teleology of those elements "beyond" the boundaries of the Catholic Church: "These elements, however, as gifts belonging to the Church of Christ, possess an inner dynamism toward Catholic unity" (*LG* §8). So too with the other religions: whatever is truthful in them — and recall that the "Catholic Church rejects nothing which is true and holy in these religions" (*Nostra aetate* §2) — will ultimately lead to unity in Christ.

Finally one may add internal doctrinal considerations. To assert otherwise, that is, to deny any activity of the Word beyond the human nature of Christ would be to attribute whatever truth can be found in other religions to

---

37. Pope Benedict XVI/Joseph Ratzinger, *Jesus of Nazareth: From the Baptism in the Jordan to the Transfiguration,* trans. Adrian J. Walker (New York: Doubleday, 2007), pp. 7-8; emphases added.

the Holy Spirit alone, which would undermine the Augustinian axiom *opera omnia Trinitatis ad extra indivisa sunt* (all the actions of the Trinity toward the world are indivisible). True, in the economy of salvation distinctions must be made (to avoid modalism), but that only holds true in and by virtue of the human nature of Christ, as Thomas teaches: "It is clear that the human operation [of Christ], in which the Father and the Holy Spirit do not share, except by their merciful consent, is distinct from his operation as the Word of God, in which the Father and Holy Spirit share" (*ST* III q.19 a.19 ad 1).

Hence I conclude that Fr. Dupuis performed a useful service for the church in his conversations with the CDF, which came to a more precise view of how the human activity and nature of Christ relate to his divinity. *Beyond*, in other words, is not the same thing as *independent of*.[38]

The *Catechism of the Catholic Church*

The first point to make about the *Catechism of the Catholic Church (CCC)* is that it has no independent authority of its own. Its level of authority (technically known as an "instance") derives solely from the various magisterial statements on which it draws. This we know not only from the nature of what a catechism is meant to do and how it is meant to function (to provide, in the words of John Paul II promulgating this Catechism, a "sure norm for instruction in the faith"[39]) but also from the words of Cardinal Ratzinger himself: "The individual doctrines which the Catechism presents receive no other weight than that which they already possess."[40] For that reason, we should not expect to find anything startlingly new or deviant in the Catechism. Thus, to present a full-scale summary of its christological teachings would necessarily involve certain redundancies and repetitions of what has already been said in previous chapters and above all in this one.

That said, there is a serenity of style and a firmness of conviction in this version of the Catechism that can help bring all of the previous summaries to a deft conclusion; and so we will treat, however briefly, the main tenets of its teaching.

---

38. I owe these insights regarding the CDF's dialogue with Jacques Dupuis and the relationship of that dialogue with the *extra Calvinisticum* to my student Andrew Liaugminas.

39. *Fidei depositum*, the papal bull promulgating the *CCC* on October 11, 1992, exactly thirty years to the day after the opening of Vatican II.

40. Joseph Cardinal Ratzinger and Christoph Schönborn, *Introduction to the Catechism of the Catholic Church* (San Francisco: Ignatius Press, 1994), p. 26.

The first point to stress is that the *CCC* insists that the incarnation has but one purpose: salvation. "The Word became flesh for us *in order to save us by reconciling us with God*" (§457; emphasis in the original). Only from the perspective of our plight does the incarnation make sense, prompting the Catechism at this point to cite Gregory of Nyssa:

> Sick, our nature demanded to be healed; fallen, to be raised up; dead, to rise again. We had lost the possession of the good; it was necessary for it to be given back to us. Closed in the darkness, it was necessary to bring us the light; captives, we awaited a Savior; prisoners, help; slaves, a liberator. Are these things minor or insignificant? Did they not move God to descend to human nature and visit it, since humanity was in so miserable and unhappy a state? (§457)

That explains the *why* of the incarnation; to explain the *what* of the incarnation, the Catechism draws on one of the loveliest passages in *Gaudium et spes:*

> For by his incarnation the Son of God has united himself in some fashion with every man. He worked with human hands; he thought with a human mind. He acted with a human will, and with a human heart he loved. Born of the Virgin Mary, he has truly been made one of us, like to us in all things but sin. (§470, quoting *GS* §22)

These phrases "he thought with a human mind" and "with a human heart he loved" obviously raise the question of the human consciousness of Christ and his beatific vision, on which the Catechism pronounces most carefully:

> The human soul that the Son of God assumed is endowed with a true human knowledge. As such, *this knowledge could not in itself be unlimited:* it was exercised in the historical conditions of his existence in space and time. This is why the Son of God could, when he became man, "increase in wisdom and in stature, and in favor with God and man" (Luke 2:52), and would even *have to* inquire for himself about what one in the human condition can learn only from experience (cf. Mark 6:38; 8:27; John 11:34, etc.). This corresponds to the reality of his voluntary emptying of himself, taking "the form of a slave" (Phil. 2:7). (§472; emphases added)

This passage is noteworthy in not taking scandal at the notion of ignorance in the empirical knowledge of Jesus and seems to agree with those church fathers, Athanasius for example, who interpreted passages like Mark 6:38, 8:27, and John 11:34 as referring to genuine ignorance. Moreover, in a remarkable passage outside the sections on Christology and Mariology, the Catechism teaches that Jesus even *learned to pray* from his mother:

> The Son of God who became Son of the Virgin also learned to pray, according to his human heart. He learns the formulas of prayer from his mother, who kept in her heart and meditated upon all the "great things" done by the Almighty (cf. Luke 1:49, 2:19, 2:51). He learns to pray in the words and rhythms of the prayer of his people, in the synagogue at Nazareth and the Temple at Jerusalem. (§2599)

To be sure, this is not the whole story, for the Gospels clearly portray something unique about Jesus' prayer, which could never be learned:

> But his prayer springs from an otherwise secret source, as he intimates at the age of twelve: "I must be in my Father's house" (Luke 2:49). Here the newness of prayer in the fullness of time begins to be revealed: his *filial prayer*, which the Father awaits from his children, is finally going to be lived out by the only Son in his humanity, with and for men. (§2599; emphasis in the original)

So too in a passage immediately following §472, the one cited above, which grants the need of the human mind of Christ to acquire empirical knowledge, the Catechism affirms something unique in his knowledge by virtue of the hypostatic union:

> But at the same time, this truly human knowledge of God's Son expressed the divine life of his person. The human nature of God's Son, *not by itself but by its union with the Word*, knew and showed forth in itself everything that pertains to God. Such is first of all the case with the intimate and immediate knowledge that the Son of God made man has of his Father (cf. Mark 14:36; Matt. 11:27; John 1:18; 8:55, etc.). The Son in his human knowledge also showed the divine penetration he had into the secret thoughts of the human heart (cf. Mark 2:8; John 2:25; 6:61, etc.). (§473; emphasis in the original)

> By its union to the divine wisdom in the person of the Word incarnate, Christ enjoyed in his human knowledge the fullness of understanding of the eternal plans he had come to reveal. What he admitted not knowing in

this area, he elsewhere declared himself not sent to reveal (cf. Mark 13:32; Acts 1:7). (§474)

Noteworthy in all these carefully weighed and balanced passages is the absence of the term "beatific vision," perhaps because of the shift in meaning of the term "beatific" from medieval Latin to contemporary usage in most languages. There is of course no denial of what the term means to say: that Jesus enjoyed a special knowledge of his mission by virtue of his identity as the Son of God, which is nonetheless a human knowledge, precisely because it is a saving knowledge: "Jesus knew and loved us each and all during his life, his agony, and his Passion and gave himself up for each one of us" (§478).[41] But this knowledge could only be a saving knowledge because Jesus in his very person is the Son of God: "After the Council of Chalcedon, some made of Christ's human nature a kind of personal subject. Against them, the fifth ecumenical council of Constantinople in 553 confessed that 'there is but one *hypostasis* [or person] which is our Lord Jesus Christ, one of the Trinity'" (§468). Hence all that is human about Jesus has his divine person for its subject: "Thus everything in Christ's human nature is to be attributed to his divine person as its proper subject, not only his miracles but also his sufferings and even his death" (§468).

The International Theological Commission

If the *Catechism of the Catholic Church* has no independent magisterial authority of its own but depends entirely on previously promulgated decrees of the magisterium, it goes without saying that, *a fortiori*, the International Theological Commission (ITC) enjoys even less magisterial weight. Where the *CCC* means to sum up past teaching and be cast in a form suitable for instruction in the Catholic faith, the ITC is a papal creation meant to help the pope in his divinely appointed task of addressing new questions, both dogmatic and moral. Thus the various statements and documents issued by the ITC, when later approved by the pope *in forma specifica*, can give theologians a reliable indication of where theological development is likely to be headed.[42] Moreover, the influence of some of these documents, when they

41. This personal love of Jesus for each human being is the dogmatic foundation, as we saw in Chapter 7, for the devotion to the Sacred Heart of Jesus.

42. Documents of the ITC are issued either *in forma specifica* or *in forma generica*. The former means that everything in the document was approved by the entirety of the ITC (and

preceded the drafting of the *CCC*, can be detected in the Catechism itself, which raises, perhaps, the status of the documents.

The Commission itself was born from a recommendation made by the Synod of Bishops (itself called for by Vatican II) that met in 1967. Cardinal Ratzinger picks up the story from there:

> Also uppermost in the minds of the bishops who proposed the commission was the thought that a rapprochement of scholarly reflection and pastoral responsibility was not the least urgent need of a period when intellectual problems were becoming ever more complex, and scholarship was leaving its impress on the lives of men in modern society, whether at a sophisticated or a simple level. Pope Paul VI at once took up the idea, so that as early as autumn 1969 the Commission's members were getting together for the first time. It consisted of thirty theologians, selected on the basis of advice from episcopal conferences in different parts of the world. In this way, the Commission would not just represent different theological disciplines, diverse language groups with their attendant cultural specificities and varying approaches to theological method. In addition, this procedure would also entail collaboration between the universal primate and the world episcopate as well as a *commercium* between pastors and teachers. For, although admittedly an individual theologian could only represent his own scholarly competence, yet he would be aware that he brought with him the confidence of his own bishop and that his labors were serving the bonds that should hold between bishops and theologians. . . . Thus it was hoped that a balance could be struck between continuity and renewal. The Commission is not an organ of the Curia but an autonomous body. However, it is linked with the Church's organizational leadership in that the Prefect of the Congregation for the Doctrine of the Faith is its president.[43]

---

then later by the pope, otherwise the document would never have been published), including the text, ideas, wording, and presentation; the latter term means that the ITC accepts the principal ideas of the text but that the individual authors take responsibility for their own section of the text. Documents given approval *in forma generica* usually consist of a set of contributions on a particular theme on which each author has his or her particular say. On this see *International Theological Commission: Texts and Documents, 1969-1985*, Foreword by Joseph Cardinal Ratzinger, ed. Rev. Michael Sharkey (San Francisco: Ignatius Press, 1989). All citations of ITC documents will come from this edition, abbreviated as *ITC:TD*.

43. Joseph Cardinal Ratzinger, "Foreword," *ITC:TD*, vii. It is on the basis of these remarks that the documents of the ITC belong in this chapter on magisterial Christology.

Over the years, the ITC took up the specific issue of Christology on three separate occasions, which led to the promulgation of these three documents: "Select Questions on Christology" (1979), "Theology, Christology, Anthropology" (1981), and "The Consciousness of Christ Concerning Himself and His Mission" (1985). All three documents were also approved *in forma specifica.*

The concern of the 1979 document was both to acknowledge the difficulties some contemporary Christians have in understanding terms like "nature" and "person" used in the Council of Chalcedon and to defend simultaneously its definitive decree on the hypostatic union. Similarly, it both saluted the validity of the historical-critical method ("The great value of scholarly inquiries on the Jesus of history is beyond doubt") and yet warned against using that method to divide the Jesus of history from the Christ of faith ("At the same time, a truly Christian knowledge of Jesus cannot rest content with these limited perspectives. . . . We cannot secure a full knowledge of Jesus unless we take into account the living Faith of the Christian community, which sustains this vision of the facts").[44]

Similarly, the Commission both insists that "the dogma defined at the Council of Chalcedon most especially retain[s] a definitive value" and concedes that its teachings "must always be actualized in the consciousness and preaching of the Church, under the guidance of the Holy Spirit."[45] This latter task entails that theologians first of all must "construct a synthesis in which are underlined all the aspects and all the values of the mystery of Christ." These would include "the authentic findings of biblical exegesis, and of the research on the history of salvation," a synthesis that "cannot but enrich the formula of Chalcedon through more soteriological perspectives" so that believers see the connection with the incarnation and the full meaning of the phrase "Christ died for us."[46]

Striking in that regard is the ITC's insistence that the connection between soteriology and Chalcedon cannot be secured unless we can affirm that Jesus knew, as part of his knowledge of his mission, that his death would be a saving death, while not excluding the idea that Jesus could grow in that knowledge: "Although Jesus was entirely open to God's will, he had the capacity to perceive questions that emerged."[47] That said, his growth in such

44. *ITC:TD*, pp. 186, 187.
45. *ITC:TD*, pp. 194, 195.
46. *ITC:TD*, p. 195.
47. *ITC:TD*, p. 198.

knowledge only occurred because of his prior unlearned (that is, infused) knowledge of his mission. So how does infused knowledge relate to the growth of Jesus' knowledge of his saving mission? According to the ITC, by asking himself these (at times no doubt painful) questions:

> Would God bestow full and total success to [his] proclamations of the Kingdom? Would Israel prove incapable of clinging to [its] eschatological salvation? . . . Would the Father want to establish his reign, if Jesus should meet with failure, with death, nay, with the cruel death of martyrdom? Would the Father, in the end, ensure the saving efficacy of what Jesus would have suffered by "dying for others"? Jesus *gathered* affirmative answers to these questions from his awareness of *being* the eschatological mediator of salvation, the reign of God come to presence. Hence, he was able to arrive in all confidence at the solution to the problems that arose.[48]

Two years later the Commission took up a different set of issues dealing with what now goes under the name of fundamental theology, such as: What is the relationship of Christology to Theology? ("Theology" is being used here in the strict sense of that word: referring to reflection on the nature of God — hence the capital T, to mark it off from the generic study of Christian revelation in all its ramifications.) Such questions would include how the sufferings of Christ relate to God's impassibility and whether Theocentrism stands in conflict — or at least is in tension — with Christocentrism. As to the latter question, the ITC rejects (at least by implication) Karl Barth's view that the only knowledge man can gain of God comes through Jesus Christ exclusively.[49]

As to the former question, the Commission had to balance two difficult-to-reconcile aspects of the tradition: on the one hand, it rejected any Hegelian notion that the idea of God must include "the suffering of the negative" or that God needs the world; on the other, the ITC recognized that the impassibility of God "is not to be understood as though God remained indifferent to human events.[50] It reconciled this tension between impassibility and compassion by grounding the incarnation in the prior being of God:

---

48. *ITC:TD*, p. 198; emphases added.

49. Hans Urs von Balthasar was a member of the ITC for two separate terms, 1974-1979 and 1980-1985, thus had a hand in the drafting of all three documents here considered. I mention this because one is reminded of his famous charge that Barth had created a kind of "christological bottleneck" by disallowing any role for natural theology.

50. *ITC:TD*, p. 220 (against Hegel), 221 (God is compassionate).

The eternal generation of the Son and his role as the immaculate Lamb who would pour out his precious blood are equally eternal and precede the free creation of the world (cf. 1 Peter 1:19ff; Eph. 1:7). In this sense, there is a very close correspondence between the gift of divinity that the Father gives to the Son and the gift by which the Father consigns his Son to the abandonment of the Cross. Since, however, the Resurrection is also present in the eternal plan of God, the suffering of "separation" is always overcome by the joy of union; the compassion of the Trinitarian God for the suffering *of the Word* is properly understood as the work of most perfect love, which is normally a source of joy. As for the Hegelian concept of "negativity," this is radically excluded from our idea of God.[51]

In 1985 the ITC took up, for the last time (so far), a matter pertaining to Christology, here specifically once again the question of the consciousness of Christ. The focus of the document is actually quite narrow. The question of the beatific vision, for example, is never raised.[52] Rather, the issue it treats centers on the relation between historical criticism and the human consciousness of Jesus. The problem is obviously crucial for the church's evangelizing mission, as the Commission notes:

> The use of the historical-critical method in Gospel study gives rise to questions about Jesus Christ, his consciousness of his own divinity, of his life and redemptive death, of his mission, of his teaching, and above all of his project of founding the Church. The scholars in the field have given various answers, at times one contradicting the other. . . . These are obviously questions of importance for many different kinds of people, and particularly for Christians. The latter indeed often find it difficult to answer those who ask them the reasons for their hope (1 Peter 3:15). In fact, who would trust a Savior who may not have known who he was or was willing to be what he was?[53]

Note that that last rhetorical question presupposes a dogmatic rather than a historical logic: *since* the church already confesses Jesus as Savior and *since* it would make no sense to suppose such a Savior would be unaware of his mission, *therefore* the church already knows that, in a sense yet to be de-

---

51. *ITC:TD*, p. 222; emphasis added.

52. Thomas Aquinas's *Commentary on the Sentences of Peter Lombard* is cited (but not quoted), not on the beatific vision, however, but on the mission of Jesus in time as a prolongation of his eternal procession from the Father, at *ITC:TD*, p. 322, note 9.

53. *ITC:TD*, p. 306.

fined, he knew his identity. But with the presupposition already granted, the Commission does not see its role to validate or condemn one theological account of that consciousness over another: "[We] expressly avoid theological elaborations calculated to give an account of this datum of faith. There is, then, no reference to attempt [in what follows] to give theological formulation as to how such a consciousness could have been articulated within the humanity of Christ."[54]

The ITC then sets out four propositions that it insists all Catholic theologians must hold concerning the consciousness of Christ: 1) The life of Jesus itself in its totality testifies to his consciousness of a filial relationship with the Father from which he drew his incomparable authority; 2) Jesus recognized that his mission to announce the kingdom of God was made present in his own person and thus knew that it was his Father's will to give his own life for the salvation of all mankind; 3) with this end in mind, he did certain acts that, if taken altogether, can only be explained as a preparation for the church, which would be definitively constituted at the time of Easter and Pentecost: "It is therefore to be affirmed of necessity that Jesus willed the foundation of the Church"[55]; and 4) finally, in a passage directly relevant to the question of Christ's beatific vision: "The consciousness that Christ had of being the Father's emissary to save the world . . . involves in a mysterious way, a love for all mankind so much so that we may all say: 'The Son of God loved me and gave himself up for me' (Gal. 2:20)."[56]

The Pontifical Biblical Commission

If the ITC carries no independent doctrinal authority of its own, the same applies of course to the Pontifical Biblical Commission (PBC). The origins of the PBC go back much further than the ITC; for it was established by Pope Leo XIII in 1902 in his Apostolic Letter *Vigilantiae*, renewed by Pius X in his *motu proprio* of 1907, *Praestantia sacrae Scripturae*. Although Pius X said its decrees were not to be understood as infallibly issued but were "useful for the proper progress and the guidance of biblical scholarship along safe paths," nevertheless "all are obliged to submit to past and future decisions of the Biblical Commission in the same way as to the decrees . . . issued

54. *ITC:TD*, p. 307.
55. *ITC:TD*, p. 311.
56. *ITC:TD*, p. 314.

by [other] Sacred Congregations approved by the Pope."[57] In 1943 Pius XII issued his famous encyclical *Divino afflante Spiritu* promoting a more independent Catholic scriptural scholarship, after which the PBC began to issue "responses" *(responsa)* rather than "decrees." Finally Paul VI issued his own *motu proprio* on the PBC in 1971 *Sedula cura,* in which he revamped the Commission by making it a counterpart to the ITC and staffing it with scholars but no cardinals. It thus became, like the ITC, purely advisory, having been "demoted," so to speak, from its prior magisterial status.

The point is rather ironic, because its first statement under its new constitution on Christology was its 1964 "Instruction on the Historical Truth of the Gospels,"[58] which proved to have enormous influence on Vatican II's decree on revelation, *Dei verbum,* especially this passage:

> Holy Mother Church has firmly and with utmost constancy held, and continues to hold, that the four gospels just named, whose historical character the Church unhesitatingly asserts, faithfully hand on what Jesus the Son of God, while living among men, really did and taught for their eternal salvation. . . . The sacred authors, however, wrote the four Gospels, selecting some things from the many which had been handed on either by word of mouth or in writing, reducing some of them to a synthesis, explicating some things in view of the situation of their churches, and preserving the form of proclamation but always in such fashion that they recounted to us the honest truth about Jesus [*vera et sincera Jesu*]. (*DV* §19)

Dei verbum was promulgated in the last session of Vatican II in 1965, and the PBC "Instruction" came out in 1964, which means that the influence of the latter on the former can be easily detected by the remarkable similarity of wording between the two documents:

> This primitive instruction, which was at first passed on by word of mouth and then in writing — for it soon happened that many tried "to compile a narrative of these things" (Luke 1:1) which concerned the Lord Jesus, was then committed to writing by the sacred authors in four gospels for the benefit of the churches, with a method suited to the peculiar purpose which each [author] set for himself. From the many things handed down

---

57. Pope Pius X, *Praestantia sacrae Scripturae,* in *Acta Sanctae Sedis* 40 (1907): 723-26.

58. An English translation of the text can be found in Joseph Fitzmyer, S.J., *A Christological Catechism: New Testament Answers,* 2nd ed. (New York: Paulist Press, 1991), pp. 153-62.

they selected some things, reduced others to a synthesis, [still] others they explicated as they kept in mind the situation of the churches.[59]

In 1984 the PBC issued another document, "Scripture and Christol-ogy."[60] As the title implies, the focus of this document ranges much more widely than its 1964 counterpart. Given the provenance of the document — composed entirely by biblical scholars — the document is resolutely empiri-cal, although it must be immediately conceded that its authors display no *a priori* hostility to a speculative or systematic Christology: "Studies in specu-lative theology about Christ take as a principle, *and not without reason,* the refusal to depend on critical hypotheses that are always subject to revi-sion. . . . All attempts to unite a Christology 'from below' with a Christology 'from above' are on the right track."[61] That said, it pleads for an openness to the results of historical research:

> In the area of exegetical studies many problems remain to be resolved, in particular critical questions about the Gospels: the way the sayings of Je-sus have come to be formulated in them; the more or less "historical" character (in the strict sense) of the narratives that concern Jesus; the date and authorship of individual books; the modes and stages of their com-position; and the development of christological doctrine. This area of studies lies open to investigation; it is not only legitimate but even neces-sary and capable of bearing fruit for systematic Christology itself.[62]

Given this resolutely empirical approach, it might surprise some readers (and will relieve others) to learn that the PBC grants full biblical legitimacy to systematic investigations into the consciousness of Jesus. Indeed, it comes to roughly the same conclusion reached by the ITC and its more deductive conclusions:

> With such considerations, exegetes and theologians approach the ques-tion of the individual personality of Jesus. This individual personality was cultivated and formed by a Jewish education, the positive values of which Jesus took fully to himself. But it was also endowed with a quite singular

59. Fitzmyer, *A Christological Catechism,* p. 157; this passage comes from §9 of the In-struction.

60. *Scripture and Christology: A Statement of the Biblical Commission with a Commen-tary,* trans. Joseph A. Fitzmyer, S.J. (New York: Paulist Press, 1985).

61. *Scripture and Christology,* p. 29; emphasis added.

62. *Scripture and Christology,* p. 30.

consciousness of himself, as far as his relation to God was concerned as well as the mission he was to carry out for human beings.[63]

This convergence of conclusions between the ITC and the PBC serves as an admirable example of the possibilities of fruitful dialogue between exegetes and theologians, especially when conducted under the aegis of the See of Rome.

63. *Scripture and Christology*, p. 18.

CHAPTER 12

Conclusion: The Victory of Christ

*Within Christianity it's as though God says to men: Don't act out a
tragedy, that is to say, don't enact heaven and hell on earth. Heaven
and hell are* my *affair.*

Ludwig Wittgenstein, *Culture and Value*

It would be pointless to speak of the current state of the church's
christological reflection without first treating the place of the Christian religion in contemporary civilization, for the two are intimately related. Cardinal Ratzinger saw this with uncommon perspicuity in his famous interview
with Vittorio Messori published as *The Ratzinger Report*:

> It is surely no secret [opines Messori] that missionaries are suffering from
> a very tangible identity crisis and even a lack of motivation. [The cardi-
> nal's] answer manifests a considerable concern: "It is part of the Church's
> ancient, traditional teaching that every man is called to salvation and de
> facto can be saved if he sincerely follows the precepts of his own con-
> science, even without being a visible member of the Catholic Church.
> This teaching, however, which (I repeat) was already accepted [as] beyond
> dispute, has been put forward in an extreme form since the Council, on
> the basis of theories like that of 'anonymous Christians.' Ultimately it has
> been proposed that grace is always given provided that a person — believ-
> ing in no religion at all or subscribing to any religion whatsoever — ac-
> cepts himself as a human being. That is all that is necessary. According to
> these theories the Christian's 'plus' is only that he is *aware* of this grace,

which inheres actually in all people, whether baptized or not. Hand in hand, then, with the weakening of the necessity of baptism, went the overemphasis on the values of the non-Christian religions, which many theologians saw not as *extraordinary* paths of salvation but precisely as *ordinary* ones."[1]

And what, Messori asks, are the results — both for the church and for missionary endeavor — of this kind of theology? The cardinal responds:

"Naturally, hypotheses of this kind caused the missionary zeal of many to slacken. Many a one began to wonder, 'Why should we disturb non-Christians, urging them to accept baptism and faith in Christ, if their religion is *their* way to salvation in their culture, in their part of the world?' These people surrendered, among other things, the connection which the New Testament creates between *salvation* and *truth,* for as Jesus explicitly affirms, it is knowledge of the truth that liberates and hence saves. Or as St. Paul says: 'God our Savior . . . desires all men to be saved and to come to the knowledge of the truth.' And this truth, the Apostle goes on, consists in the knowledge that 'there is one God, and there is one mediator between God and men, the man Christ Jesus, who gave himself as a ransom for all' (1 Tim. 2:4-7). This is what we must proclaim to the modern world, with humility but also with power, in response to the challenging example of the generations who have gone before us in faith."[2]

In other words, a faulty Christology lurks as the fundamental reason the Second Vatican Council did not lead to the fruits expected of it. What the council called for was a new Catholic unity, "and instead," the cardinal ruefully noted, "one has encountered a dissension which . . . seems to have passed over from self-criticism to self-destruction." Instead of a new Pentecost, boredom and discouragement have become the lot of the church: "There had been the expectation of a step forward, and instead one found oneself facing a progressive process of decadence that to a large measure has been unfolding under the sign of a summons to a presumed 'spirit of the Council' and by so doing has actually increasingly discredited it."[3]

This dolorous situation has led many to regard Vatican II as, at best, a

1. Joseph Cardinal Ratzinger with Vittorio Messori, *The Ratzinger Report: An Exclusive Interview on the State of the Church,* trans. Salvator Attanasio and Graham Harrison (San Francisco: Ignatius Press, 1985), pp. 196-97; emphases in the original.

2. *The Ratzinger Report,* p. 197; emphasis in the original.

3. *The Ratzinger Report,* pp. 29, 30.

mistake (or among the Lefebvrist schismatics, heretical). But the cardinal sees the problem not as due to the council itself, "but to the unleashing *within* the Church of latent polemical and centrifugal forces; and *outside* the Church it is due to the confrontation with a cultural revolution in the West . . . with its liberal-radical ideology of individualistic, rationalistic and hedonistic stamp."[4]

In a strange way, one might even say that these dynamics (at least the latter one) were provoked by the entrance of Christ onto the stage of history, as Hans Urs von Balthasar pointed out on numerous occasions, as here:

> A man who asserts about himself "I am the way, and the truth, and the life" (John 14:6) is simply intolerable in the world as it is. This was so once before and has remained so ever since. It is entirely clear that such a one, who concentrates all religions of mankind to himself — "I am the door; whoever comes in by any other way is a thief and a robber" (John 10:7-8) — provokes atheism. Very rightly did atheism appear in the world [only] after Christ, because it was precisely the word of God that was unbearable for it. Occasionally it shows itself openly as anti-Christian; and its program could be nothing else than to replace the claim, the crazy assertion of Christ, with something more meaningful and effective. "He has claimed to free mankind: What is going on here? Now, we will show him how one does that."[5]

Given this provocation that leads the world to make its ever louder No to Christ's claim about himself, one might be surprised that Catholics felt so optimistic right after Vatican II; in which case the shock of dissension and bourgeois, secular rebellion has served as a salutary reminder of the real nature of the victory Christ won over the world. Pope Leo I (r. 440-61) described that victory in one of his sermons on the Ascension that exactly captures this dilemma of Christians — knowing they are saved through the victory of Christ yet living in a world that denies that victory in every aspect of its being:

> Whatever in our Redeemer had been visible, has now passed into mysteries [at his Ascension]; and so in order that faith might be nobler and firmer, sight was succeeded by doctrine, the authority of which might be

---

4. *The Ratzinger Report,* p. 30; emphases in the original.

5. Hans Urs von Balthasar, "Holy Scripture," trans. Jeremy Holmes in *Nova et Vetera* 5, no. 4 (Fall 2007): 707-24; here 723-24.

accepted by believing hearts, illuminated by rays from on high. This faith, increased by Our Lord's Ascension, and strengthened by the gift of the Holy Spirit, has not been overawed by chains, or imprisonments, or banishments, or famine, or the sword, or the teeth of wild beasts, or punishments invented by the cruelty of persecutors. . . . Hence the reason why even the blessed Apostles themselves — who, although they had been confirmed by so many miracles and instructed by so many discourses, had still been terrified by the horror of the Lord's Passion and had not yet received without hesitation the truth of his resurrection — profited so greatly by the Lord's Ascension, so that whatever before had caused them to fear was turned into joy. . . . Accordingly, it was then, dearly beloved, that the Son of Man, the Son of God, became known in a more transcendent and sacred way, when he betook himself to the glory of the Father's Majesty, and in an ineffable manner began to be more present in his divinity when he became further off in his humanity.[6]

Behind and beyond all the christological controversies treated in this book, there always lurks a hidden or not-so-hidden anxiety among Christians: that the victory won by Christ does not *look* like much of a victory. This fact is not so much a "problem" as part of the very essence of revelation. Often this fact is couched in terms of the "already/not yet" aspect of redemption: the kingdom is both here among us now but yet to come. Although he does not use that exact terminology, Paul is clearly operating out of that same logic when he speaks of the victory of Christ in these terms:

I consider that the sufferings of this present time are not worth comparing with the glory that is to be revealed to us. For creation waits with eager longing for the revealing of the sons of God. For creation was subject to futility, not of its own will but by the will of him who subjected it in hope, because creation itself will be set free from its bondage to decay and obtain the glorious liberty of the children of God. We know that the whole of creation has been groaning in travail together until now, not only creation but we ourselves, who have the first fruits of the Spirit, groan inwardly as we wait for adoption as sons, the redemption of our bodies. For in this hope we were saved. Now hope that is seen is not hope. For who hopes for what he sees? But if we hope for what we do not see, we wait for it with patience. (Rom. 8:18-25)

6. Leo the Great, *Sermo 84*, PL 54.

A more abstract way of putting this same point would be to speak of the quality versus the quantity of Christ's victory. Such was the strategy of Abbot Vonier, who speaks very illuminatingly under that rubric:

> It is clear that a victory so-called may have a double perfection, that of quantity and that of quality. A victory of quantity would only be complete when every individual being who had been an opponent was brought into subjection by the victorious power. A victory of quality would be so complete a conquest of all opposing forces that it might be truthfully said that all hostilities were over, that all the resources of the enemy had passed into the hands of the victor, that there was no chance of a reaction, and that it would be a mere matter of time for the numerical results to appear.[7]

Phrased in that way, one sees why the believer should *want* a qualitative victory over a merely quantitative one:

> Christ's victory has both these features, but not simultaneously. The victory of quality precedes the victory of numbers; the latter is delayed until a moment, which is one of the Father's unrevealed secrets; the former is dated in a most precise fashion from the hour in which the Son of God rose from the dead; it is with us now, and will be with us forever, to be supplemented in due time by the second victory, that of quantity. The Catholic mind is not indifferent to the numerical extent of Christ's achievement, but, in comparison with the qualitative intensity of the influence of Christ's work, quantitative extension holds a secondary place.[8]

We already saw in Chapter 3 Oscar Cullmann's analogy of D-Day as the final moment in World War II when the outcome of the war leading to V-E Day was now determined, despite later setbacks like the Battle of the Bulge. In that regard, what ultimate good would it do to have rounded up any number of Nazis and German soldiers but left Nazism intact? Vonier wrote his book *The Victory of Christ* in 1934, but one reads the same kind of logic at work:

> Is there any kind of evil which Christ has left unconquered; or, if He has overcome it once, has the dark power a chance of rising again? It is precisely that unrestricted universality of victory that appeals to the Catholic

---

7. Abbot Vonier, *The Victory of Christ,* in *The Collected Works of Abbot Vonier,* vol. 1: *The Incarnation and Redemption* (Westminster, MD: Newman Press, no date but originally published in 1934), pp. 242-43.

8. Vonier, *Victory of Christ,* p. 243.

mind and makes the universality of mere numbers a matter of less importance. If all men were *de facto* saved by Christ, but were not saved in a supreme and irrevocable fashion from all evil, such salvation would be as
nothing compared with the condition of those, many or few, who are delivered from evil *überhaupt* [entirely], with no possible or imaginable limitation to their deliverance. It is therefore entirely in accordance with
Christian sentiment to say that Christ would have labored in vain had He
left one single enemy unchallenged and unconquered.[9]

"In hope were we saved," says St. Paul (Rom. 8:24), the very line that
both began and gave the title to Pope Benedict XVI's encyclical *Spe salvi*. If
we are *justified* by faith, then we are *saved* by hope. Here is the perspective by
which all Christologies can be judged; and here is the reason why the health
of the church depends on a healthy (that is, true) Christology. One might
even, if only in a rough and ready way, look at the major eras of the church
under this rubric, as Abbot Vonier does in this fascinating passage:

> On the whole the Christian ages have thought more of Christ's absolute
> triumph, with the result that their faith has suffered no scandal either
> from the sins of believers or from the great numbers of unbelievers. The
> Middle Ages were certainly ages of faith through this very feature, the
> universal sense of Christ's supremacy. . . . The period we call the Renais-
> sance is a great assertion of the final victory of Christ in the plan of the
> universe, and this assertion is made by Catholics and by Protestants alike,
> though in different ways. Protestantism narrowed down the triumph of
> Christ to the redemptive mission of the Son of God, and to the unshaken
> confidence on the part of man that Christ's supremely efficacious Re-
> demption was applied to individuals. Catholicism, on the other hand,
> went on, as it had done through the ages, giving a much wider interpre-
> tation to Christ's victory.[10]

However fair (or not) Vonier is in his analysis here, there can be no
question that the era of modern Christianity, in contrast to past eras, seems
much more intimidated by the discrepancy between the world and the gospel. Have modern Christians kept to that same confident sense of victory

9. Vonier, *Victory of Christ*, p. 243.
10. Vonier, *Victory of Christ*, p. 245. This schema is of course a bit too, well, schematic. I
think a fairer assessment would hold that, through Augustine, western Christianity as a
whole was more focused on individual salvation than was the East. Not for nothing were Luther and Calvin thoroughgoing Augustinians.

known to past Christians almost as a matter of course? Christians in their worship constantly hear the good news of the gospel, and hymns of praise are ever on their lips when they join the official prayer of the church. But is that only, as the expression goes, mere "lip service"? If the believer knows not the shadow of the glory of Christ, how can there be exultation in his victory? Such is the real challenge of Christology today. For as Vonier says:

> The denial of Christ's position in the affairs of mankind is a comparatively recent phenomenon: we may assign to the eighteenth century the beginning of that hostile movement against the supremacy of the Redeemer. The whole of the nineteenth century and after has been the glorification of a civilization that boasts its independence of Christ, its complete self-sufficiency; in no wise will it acknowledge indebtedness to the Son of God for any of its achievements. This almost universal self-sufficiency of the political world has become a grave temptation for believers themselves. So we find everywhere instances of the apologetic attitude of Christians, of the feeling of inferiority at least in sentiment and imagination, which takes many forms, from the speculative to the devotional.[11]

Signs of such Christian querulousness can be found everywhere. One would be the loss of a sense of Christ's *glory,* the sheer *splendor* of his victory.[12] Another would be the obsession with politics as a necessary reflection of Christ's victory, the kind of victory that theocrats seek, despite the fact that Christianity was born in, of all places, the Roman Empire. Another would be any obsession with the end times, as if Christian hope cannot bear to look with equanimity at the idea that human history just *might* actually continue for many millennia to come. Why not assume the attitude of that great Christian of hope, Pope John Paul II, who told a group of scientists and theologians gathered by papal invitation at the Vatican Observatory outside Rome to "be not afraid." Here is how to approach the future in confidence:

> If the cosmologies of the ancient Near Eastern world could be purified and assimilated into the first chapters of Genesis, might contemporary cosmology have something to offer to our reflections upon creation? Does an evolutionary perspective bring any light to bear upon theological

---

11. Vonier, *Victory of Christ*, p. 246.

12. One sign of how much theological labor would be entailed in trying to overcome that insensitivity to Christ's glory — and how much can be gained by recovering it — can be found in the attempt at a restoration of that sense in Hans Urs von Balthasar's seven-volume *The Glory of the Lord.*

anthropology, the meaning of the human person as the *imago Dei*, the problem of Christology — and even upon the development of doctrine itself? What, if any, are the eschatological implications of contemporary cosmology, *especially in light of the vast future of our universe?* Can theological method fruitfully appropriate insights from scientific methodology and the philosophy of science?[13]

A final sign of that same querulousness can be found in the way the question of world religions is being debated, both on the right and the left. The former group worries, often rightly, that any allowance made to the possibility of salvation outside the Church will lead to a watering down of the gospel; the latter group, often rightly, objects to the idea of the Church as a private salvation club when set against the clear statements of Scripture that God intends his salvation for all mankind. We have already seen in the previous three chapters how convoluted that debate can become; but what is often missing is *confidence* that the victory has already been won, the kind of confidence so radiantly on display in this passage from Cardinal Ratzinger:

> We cannot start to set limits on God's behalf. The very heart of the faith has been lost to anyone who supposes that it is only worthwhile, if it is, so to say, made worthwhile by the damnation of others. Such a way of thinking, which finds the punishment of other people necessary, springs from not having inwardly accepted the faith; from loving only oneself and not God the Creator, to whom his creatures belong. That way of thinking would be like the attitude of those people who could not bear the workers who came last being paid a denarius like the rest; like the attitude of people who feel properly rewarded only if others have received less. This would be the attitude of the son who stayed at home, who could not bear the reconciling kindness of his father. It would be a hardening of our hearts, in which it would become clear that we were only looking out for ourselves and not looking for God; in which it would be clear that we did not love our faith, but merely bore it like a burden. . . . It is a basic element of the biblical message that the Lord died for all — being jealous of salvation is not Christian.[14]

---

13. John Paul II, "Message to the Director of the Vatican Observatory," in *Physics, Philosophy and Theology: A Quest for Common Understanding,* ed. Robert J. Russell, William R. Stoeger, S.J., and George V. Coyne, S.J. (Vatican City: Libreria Editrice Vaticana, 1988), p. M11; emphasis added.

14. Joseph Cardinal Ratzinger, *God Is Near Us: The Eucharist, the Heart of Life,* trans. Henry Taylor (San Francisco: Ignatius Press, 2003), pp. 35-36.

But as we have already seen in Chapter 11, that confidence in salvation already won must be balanced out by a firm conviction that such confidence stems from a radiant faith in the victory won *by Christ alone,* which puts the problem into a perspective often missing in this discussion, as Chapters 9 and 10 have shown. Consider how Abbot Vonier takes up this issue, decades before the issue of pluralism became such a burning topic of discussion among Catholic theologians in postconciliar debate:

> We have become unduly worried by the conclusions of the so-called science of comparative religion. We make of the problem of the salvation of infidels an acute theological question, much to the detriment of the doctrine of the salvation of the faithful through Christ. We too readily admire the works of the modern world, and we become unjust towards Christianity in our judgments of the Christian past. In politics we readily become the prey of slogans and we are led astray like sheep that have not Christ for their Shepherd. Not infrequently our devotional life reveals a lamentable ignorance or forgetfulness of the essential doctrines of the supernatural order as it is in Christ. The diminution of the spirit of worship in the world may be taken as the most evident sign of the decay of faith in Christ's supremacy. It is at the same time a cause and an effect. When men cease to praise Christ and to adore Him as their Lord and Master, their feelings become more and more secularized; as, on the other hand, practical worldliness becomes increasingly impatient with all the duties of public and private worship.[15]

It cannot be stressed often enough how much the duties of public and private worship are directed to a thanksgiving on the part of the believer for the victory of Christ already won and how much that linkage is tied to the believer's sense of glory, another point made by Cardinal Ratzinger in his interview:

> The only really effective apologia for Christianity comes down to two arguments, namely, the *saints* the Church has produced and the *art* which has grown in her womb. Better witness is borne to the Lord by the splendor of holiness and art which have arisen in the community of believers than by the clever excuses which apologetics has come up with to justify the dark sides which, sadly, are so frequent in the Church's human history. If the Church is to continue to transform and humanize the world, how

---

15. Vonier, *The Victory of Christ,* pp. 246-47.

can she dispense with beauty in her liturgies, that beauty which is so closely linked with love and with the radiance of the Resurrection? No, Christians must not be too easily satisfied. They must make their Church into a place where beauty — and truth — is at home. Without this the world will become the first circle of hell. . . . A theologian who does not love art, poetry, music and nature can be dangerous. Blindness and deafness toward the beautiful are not incidental: they necessarily are reflected in his theology.[16]

Fortunately, there has been a noticeable shift in recent theology toward a Christocentric affirmation of glory and beauty, as seen in the increasing attention being paid to the theology of Hans Urs von Balthasar and in the election of Pope Benedict XVI. A similar trend can be detected in the guild of theologians, at least if the reception accorded to Robert Barron's appropriately titled book *The Priority of Christ* is anything to go by. He begins one of his chapters by recalling Luke's account of the calling of the first apostles:

One day as Jesus was by the Lake of Gennesaret, with the people crowding around him and listening to the word of God, he saw at the water's edge two boats, left there by the fishermen, who were washing their nets. He got into one of the boats, the one belonging to Simon, and asked him to put out a little from shore. Then he sat down and taught the people from the boat. When he had finished speaking, he said to Simon, "Put out into deep water and let down the nets for a catch." Simon answered: "Master, we have worked hard all night and have nothing. But because you say so, I will let down the nets." When they had done so, they caught such a large number of fish that their nets began to break. So they signaled their partners in the other boat to come and help them, and they came and filled both boats so full that they began to sink. When Simon Peter saw this, he fell at Jesus' knees and said, "Depart from me, Lord; I am a sinful man." For he and all his companions were astonished at the catch of fish they had taken in, and so were James and John, the sons of Zebedee, Simon's partners. Then Jesus said to Simon, "Do not be afraid; from now on you will be fishers of men." So they pulled their boats up on shore, left everything and followed him. (Luke 5:1-11)

On this deftly written scene, Barron draws these conclusions for how Christ establishes his priority in the Church:

16. Joseph Cardinal Ratzinger, *Ratzinger Report*, pp. 129-30; italics in the original.

For a Galilean fisherman, his boat was everything. It was his livelihood, his work, the means by which he supported his family and put food on the table. Recent archeological and anthropological research has shown that first-century Galilean fishermen sent their product not only around the towns of Palestine but also to distant cities within the Roman Empire. So Peter's humble vessel represented his contact with the wider world and functioned, if I may put it this way, as an instrument of his professional creativity. As such, it serves as a symbol of all that Peter can accomplish spiritually and morally through his own power, using his gifts, energy and creativity.[17]

But note how Jesus never asks permission to use Peter's boat but simply boards it without further ado:

He doesn't seek Peter's approval nor does he solicit his permission. He simply commandeers this vessel that is central to the fisherman's life and commences to give orders. This represents something of enormous moment: the invasion of grace. Though God respects our relative independence and smiles on the work that we can accomplish on our own, he is not the least bit content to leave us in a "natural" state. Instead, he wants to live in us, to become the Lord of our lives, moving into our minds, wills, bodies, imaginations, nerves, and bones.[18]

To give priority to Christ in Christology, then, is but the smallest part of letting him have the priority in our lives. "I have told you these things," he told his disciples, "so that in me you may have peace. In this world you will suffer tribulation. But take heart! I have overcome the world" (John 16:33).

17. Robert Barron, *The Priority of Christ: Toward a Postliberal Catholicism* (Grand Rapids: Brazos Press, 2007), pp. 274-75.
18. Barron, *The Priority of Christ* p. 275.

The First Seven Ecumenical Councils

All quotations from the following councils come from *Decrees of the Ecumenical Councils*, vol. 1: *Nicaea I to Lateran V*, ed. Norman P. Tanner, S.J. (Washington, DC: Georgetown University Press, 1990)

The First Ecumenical Council

Nicea I (325). Summoned by the newly converted (but not yet baptized) emperor Constantine I (r. 312-37) to resolve the Arian heresy, which held that Christ was in some sense a lesser god. Against this view Athanasius (c. 296-373), who attended the council as a deacon representing his bishop, the patriarch of Alexandria, held that only someone who was fully God could fully save. Therefore, Christ had to be *homoousios* (of the same substance) as the Father. The italicized phrases from the decree are aimed at Arianism:

> We believe in one God the Father all-powerful, maker of all things both seen and unseen. And in one Lord Jesus Christ, the Son of God, the *only-begotten* from the Father, *who is from the substance of the Father,* God from God, light from light, *true God from true God, begotten not made, of the same substance with the Father* through whom all things came to be, both those in heaven and those on earth. For us and for our salvation he came down and became incarnate, became man, suffered and rose up on the third day, ascended into the heavens and is coming to judge the living and the dead. And in the Holy Spirit.
> *And those who say "there once was when he was not" and "before he was*

begotten he was not," and that he came to be from things that were not, or from another hypostasis or substance, affirming that the Son of God is subject to change or alteration — these the Catholic and Apostolic Church anathematizes. (Tanner, p. 5)

The Second Ecumenical Council

Constantinople I (381). Summoned by the emperor Theodosius I (r. 379-95) to condemn two heresies, one that held the Holy Spirit was not fully divine (maintained by the so-called Pneumatomachians), and the other that said that Christ did not have a fully human soul (maintained by the Apollinarians). In other words, just as Nicea I affirmed the full divinity of the divine nature of Christ, Constantinople I affirmed the full humanity of Christ's human nature. The creed promulgated by this council is actually the form used today under the name of the Nicene Creed and hence is more accurately described as the Nicene-Constantinopolitan Creed. The phrases "*born* of the Virgin Mary" and "*suffered* under Pontius Pilate" were aimed at the Apollinarians, and the added line "We believe in the Holy Spirit, the *Lord* and Giver of life, proceeding from the Father, who is *worshipped and glorified with Father and Son*" (Tanner, p. 24) was aimed at the Pneumatomachians.

The Third Ecumenical Council

Ephesus (431). Summoned by the emperor Theodosius II (r. 408-50) to combat Nestorianism, the heresy that said Mary could only be called the Mother of Christ but not Mother of God because she could only give birth to a human being, not God. This position of course denied the substantial unity of Christ, who is both God and man, against which this council affirmed Mary as Mother of God (*Theotokos,* "God-bearer"):

> We confess, then, our Lord Jesus Christ, the only-begotten Son of God, perfect God and perfect man of a rational soul and a body, begotten before all ages from the Father in his godhead, the same in the last days, for us and for our salvation, born of the Virgin Mary according to his humanity, one and the same consubstantial with the Father in godhead and consubstantial with us in humanity, for a union of two natures took place. Therefore we confess one Christ, one Son, one Lord. According to this un-

derstanding of the unconfused union, *we confess the holy Virgin to be the Mother of God because God the Word took flesh and became man and from his very conception united to himself the temple he took from her.* (Tanner, pp. 69-70)

The Fourth Ecumenical Council

Chalcedon (451). Summoned by the emperor Marcian (r. 450-57) to refute the monophysitism of Eutyches (c. 378-454), who so opposed Nestorianism that he fell into the opposite error of claiming that Christ had only one nature, divine. In condemning Eutyches, Chalcedon gave proper allowance to the orthodox residue in Nestorius's two-natures Christology while of course still condemning Nestorianism itself. In fact, several letters of Cyril of Alexandria (died 444) were entered into the record, along with the *Tome* of Pope Leo I (r. 440-61). The need to balance a condemnation of both Nestorianism and Eutyches led to the most carefully formulated of all conciliar decrees on Christology and became the touchstone for all later orthodox Christologies:

> So, following the saintly fathers [of past councils], we all with one voice teach the confession of one and the same Son, our Lord Jesus Christ: the same perfect in divinity and perfect in humanity, the same truly God and truly man, of a rational soul and a body, consubstantial with us as regards his humanity; like us in all respects except for sin; begotten before the ages from the Father as regards his divinity, and in the last days the same for us and for our salvation from Mary, the Virgin God-bearer, as regards his humanity, one and the same Christ, Son, Lord, only begotten, acknowledged *in two natures* [against Eutyches' monophysitism] which undergo *no confusion, no change* [against Eutyches], no division, *no separation* [against Nestorius]; *at no point was the difference between the natures taken away through the union* [against Eutyches], but rather *the property of both natures is preserved* [against Eutyches] and comes together into *a single person and a single subsistent being* [against Nestorius]; *he is not parted or divided into two persons, but is one and the same only begotten Son, God, Word, Lord Jesus Christ* [against Nestorius], just as the prophets taught from the beginning about him, and as the Lord Jesus Christ himself instructed us, and as the creed of the fathers handed it down to us. (Tanner, pp. 86-87)

The Fifth Ecumenical Council

Constantinople II (553). Summoned by the emperor Justinian I (r. 527-65) to reconcile monophysites to Chalcedon, which they continued to reject. To accomplish this goal, Justinian condemned fourteen specific propositions in the writings of Theodore of Mopsuestia (c. 350-428) and two other long-dead bishops of the Nestorian party (the so-called "Three Chapters"). Pope Vigilius (r. 537-55) opposed this unilateral move by Justinian on the grounds that prior councils had only condemned living heretics and, anyway, neither Ephesus nor Chalcedon had singled out the three men during their lifetimes. Moreover, the pope suspected that Justinian's real goal was to undermine Chalcedon for the sake of reconciling the monophysites. Prompted by this papal opposition, Justinian summoned Vigilius to Constantinople, forcing him to repudiate the Three Chapters, which papal move met with such opposition in the West that the pope then repudiated his repudiation of the Three Chapters. At which point, Justinian summoned this council, which Vigilius naturally refused to attend, hiding from the emperor in Chalcedon. The council condemned the Three Chapters, though taking care to reaffirm Chalcedon. Justinian would not allow Vigilius to return to Rome unless he accepted Constantinople II. After six months' consideration, he consented and departed for Italy in 555 but died before he reached Rome. Obviously, this council had nothing new to propound regarding Christology but only rehashed old condemnations, albeit only of the Nestorians. If the intent of these condemnations was to reconcile the monophysites (and it was), it failed, as proved by the controversy of monothelitism, the subject of the next council.

The Sixth Ecumenical Council

Constantinople III (680-81). Summoned by the emperor Constantine IV to condemn monothelitism, the doctrine that Christ had only one will, a divine will. Once again, monothelitism was an attempt to reconcile the monophysites to Chalcedon and had the initial plausibility of claiming that the orthodox dyothelites (who held that Christ had two wills, human and divine) were positing a kind of schizophrenia in Christ and thereby lapsing back into Nestorianism. But under the tenacious opposition of Maximus the Confessor (c. 580-662) dyothelitism won the day by again invoking the patristic axiom that what has not been assumed has not been saved; and since the human will was the seat and origin of sin, to say that Christ did not have a human will meant that our will has not been saved, the very faculty most in need of redemption. Moreover, for that same reason, this council said that the union of the two wills *(thelēmata)* of Christ was not natural (meaning inherent) but only "moral" *(katallēlōs suntrechonta/ convenienter in eo concurrentes)* which ensured that Christ's human will had its own "operation" *(energeia),* making it a truly human will with the freedom to obey the will of his Father:

> We proclaim equally *two natural volitions or wills in him and two natural principles of action* which undergo no division, no change, no partition, no confusion, in accordance with the teachings of the fathers; and the two natural wills not in opposition. And we hold there to be *two natural principles of action* in the same Jesus Christ our Lord and true God, which undergo no division, no change, no partition, no confusion, that is, a divine principle of action and a human principle of action, according to the godly-speaking Leo, who says most clearly: "For each form does in a communion with the other that activity which it possesses as its own: the Word working that which is the Word's and the body accomplishing the things that are the body's." . . . Believing our Lord Jesus Christ, even after his incarnation, to be one of the holy Trinity and our true God, we say that he has two natures shining forth, in his one subsistence in which he demonstrated the miracles and the sufferings throughout his entire providential dwelling here, not in appearance but in truth, the difference of the natures being made known in the same one subsistence in that *each nature wills and performs the things that are proper to it in a communion with the other;* then in accord with this reasoning we hold that *the two natural wills and principles of action meet in correspondence (katallēlōs suntrechonta)* for the salvation of the human race. (Tanner, pp. 128-30)

The Seventh Ecumenical Council

Nicea II (787). Summoned by the empress Irena acting on behalf of her son Constantine VI (780-97; the dates of his life coincide with his reign) to put an end to iconoclasm, which condemned the veneration of images as idolatry, which was forbidden by the Old Testament (Exod. 20:4; Deut. 5:8). While not technically a christological heresy, iconoclasm in effect denied the reality of the flesh of Christ, or so said the iconodules (defenders of the veneration of icons), and thus the condemnation of iconoclasm had christological implications. Hence the decree:

> If anyone does not confess that *Christ our God can be represented in his humanity,* let him be anathema. If anyone does not accept representation of art in evangelical scenes, let him be anathema. (Tanner, p. 137)

GLOSSARY

Terms in **bold** inside the definitions are defined more exactly under their own entry. Terms are bolded only once inside each entry. With only a few exceptions, terms defined here mostly come from the patristic era, when many of these words were first used in their technical and here specifically dogmatic sense, which often differed from their usage in the prior philosophical literature and in ordinary language, then or today.

adoptionism. A heresy that says Jesus was born entirely and solely human but raised to divine status at his baptism by a kind of legal fiction. Often called **psilanthropism**, from the Greek for "mere man."

anhypostasis/anhypostasia. See **hypostasis** and **hypostatic union**.

Apollinarianism. See **Logos-sarx Christology**.

Arianism. The heretical form of **subordinationism**.

communicatio idiomatum. A Latin term meaning "interchange of attributes or properties," itself an implication of the **hypostatic union**. Because the unity of Christ's Person to his divine and human natures is a *substantial* one, the attributes of the human nature can be attributed to the divine Person of the Son, so that it is possible to say with Cyril that "God suffered" and that Mary was the Mother of God.

docetism. A heresy claiming that Jesus only seemed to be human but was in fact a divine being "in disguise" in the manner of ancient myths, or in modern terms a kind of celestial hologram.

446

dyophysitism (also spelled **duophysitism**). The orthodox doctrine that says Christ had two natures, divine and human. See **monophysitism**.

dyothelitism (also spelled **duothelitism**). The orthodox doctrine that Christ had two wills, divine and human. See **monothelitism**.

Ebionitism (also spelled **Ebionism**). A heresy among some early Jewish Christians (exactly how many is unknown) in the late first and early second century that held that Jesus was entirely and exclusively the human son of Joseph and Mary. It is in effect the Jewish-Christian version of **adoptionism**.

economic and immanent Trinity. These terms in their adjectival forms did not gain currency until the nineteenth century. In the patristic era the nouns "economy" (meaning God in his manifestation in salvation history) and "theology" (meaning God "in himself") were used; but in modern times "theology" generally refers to an academic discipline, so that it would be eccentric to speak of "God in theology." At all events, the distinction became crucial with the condemnation of **Arianism**. Now that the full equality of the Son to the Father was established within the Trinity itself, a way had to be found to account for the obedience of Christ to the Father (which clearly implies **subordinationism**) not just in Christ's earthly life but also in the trinitarian decision to become man, for Paul speaks of Christ "who, though in the form of God, did not count *equality* with God [no subordinationism there] something to be grasped but emptied himself, taking on the form of a *slave* [extreme subordination there], being born in the likeness of men. And being found in human form *he humbled himself* and *became obedient* unto death, even death on a cross" (Phil. 2:6-8). The only way to reconcile these statements while avoiding both Arianism and **modalism** was through some kind of distinction between God in himself and his activities in salvation history, a distinction nowadays that mostly goes under the adjectives immanent and economic.

enhypostasis/enhypostasia. See **hypostasis** and **hypostatic union**.

extra Calvinisticum. An implication of the Calvinist principle that the finite cannot contain the infinite *(finitum non capax infiniti)*. In essence, the teaching holds that the Logos must still reign in heaven during the earthly life of Jesus. The term started off as an accusation by Lutheran theologians (as if the Calvinists were introducing something "extra" in the tradition), but it became a neutral term when it began to refer to the transcendence of the Word to the human nature of Christ. In other words, the Reformed theologians argued that the Word is certainly fully *united* to but is never totally *contained* within the human nature of Christ; and therefore the Word is to be conceived of as still outside or beyond *(extra)* the human nature. Lutherans countered that this doctrine undermines Paul's teaching that "the fullness of the godhead was pleased to dwell in him [Christ]" (Col. 1:19) and "In Christ all the fullness of the godhead dwells in bodily form" (Col. 2:9). Calvinists responded by saying that the Lutheran counter-doctrine of *Logos non extra carnem* (the Logos is not beyond the flesh) leads not only to **modalism** but to the absurdity of saying that wherever the Logos is (which is of course everywhere), so too is the human nature, which is impossible. The Catholic magisterium has never ruled on the matter, but something like this doctrine did come into play in the Notice issued by the Congregation for the Doctrine of the Faith regarding the theology of the Jesuit theologian Jacques Dupuis (see Chapter 11 for details).

homoousios. A Greek adjective meaning, literally, "of the same essence" but translated into Latin as *consubstantialis* ("of the same substance"). Made famous by the Council of Nicea to define the oneness in being of the Son with the Father. To be distinguished from . . .

homoiousios. A Greek term meaning "of *similar* substance," a term favored by advocates of **Arianism** because of the distinction they wanted to draw between the being of the Father (fully divine) and that of the Son (less so, but still "sort of" divine).

hypostasis. The Greek word literally meaning "substance," that which "stands under." In Aristotle, the term was used to denote that which perdures or "stands under" accidental changes in a substance. Thus one does not change one's substance as a human being by getting a tan or growing old. In this regard, the term could be used interchangeably both with **physis** ("nature") and with **ousia** ("essence"); but under the pressure of christological reflection, fifth-century theologians saw that the terms had to refer to separate realities. For once it was agreed that the Son or Logos was one in substance, or **homoousios**, with the Father, there had to be a way of saying that Jesus was still one in substance *with us too*. Which meant that he had *two natures* but not *two substances* or *essences*. For that reason, *hypostasis* was translated into Latin not as *substantia* but as **persona**.

hypostatic union. The core doctrine of all varieties of orthodox Christology which teaches the full union of the divine and human natures in the *one being* or *subsistence* (**hypostasis**) of Christ. The doctrine of the hypostatic union, which can of course just as easily be translated as *substantial union,* condemns the notion of a merely moral union of the two natures (**Nestorianism**) and validates the **communicatio idiomatum** ("interchange of attributes"): *since* the two natures are *substantially* united, both the divine and human attributes are predicated of one and the same Son, as Chalcedon teaches. In other words, the hypostatic union is a substantial union in that the human nature is substantially united to the person of the Son so that the Son substantially exists as man. The term *hypostatic* ensures that the substantial union is in the Person/Hypostasis of the Son. It must be stressed that the attributes of the divine nature are not predicated of the human nature, nor are the human attributes predicated of the divine nature, which would be conceptually self-contradictory, like claiming the attributes of red are really blue. Thus, if the attributes are predicated of the natures, the result would be the mixing and confusion forbidden by Chalcedon. It is one and the same Son who exists in two natures, and thus the attributes of each nature are predicated of that one and same Son, the *hypostasis* of the Second Person of the Trinity. This doctrine leads to two ancillary doctrines:

> **anhypostasis/anhypostasia.** Greek terms meaning "non-hypostasis" or "non-hypostatic," that is, not personal (the *a* in both words is an alpha-privative). The latter term *anhypostasia* is an abstract noun referring to the doctrine meant by the former term *anhypostasis* (the early fathers never used the abstract form *anhypostasia,* but it has become common). It is important to note that neither term, despite first appearances, means to deny the hypostatic union. Rather it denies that Christ's human nature had its own subsistence or **hypostasis**. This does not mean that Christ was not a man, or even a lesser man than the rest of the members of the human race, which would be **Apollinarianism**. Rather it ensures the **communicatio idiomatum**; for if Christ had his own human hypostasis, then what pertains to his humanity could be ascribed only to his human hypostasis and not to his divine hypostasis.

> **enhypostasis/enhypostasia.** Greek terms that literally mean "in-hypostasis" or "in-hypostatic." Again the latter term is a later coinage referring to the abstract doctrine itself. The former seems to have been coined by Leontius of Byzantium but brought into general use by John of Damascus to avoid any implication that Jesus was less a man because of the hypostatic union. The term also safeguards the union of the two natures *in* the oneness of the divine Person by holding that Jesus' human personhood was derived from the divine **hypostasis**. In other

words, while there is no independent human *person* in Jesus, nonetheless his human nature became fully personal in the incarnation. Karl Barth defends both terms as complementary to each other:

Anhypostasis asserts the negative. Since in virtue of the *egeneto* ["he became"], that is, in virtue of the *assumptio,* Christ's human nature has its existence — the ancients said its subsistence — in the existence of God, meaning in the mode of being (*hypostasis,* "person") of the Word; it does not possess it in and for itself, *in abstracto.* . . . *Enhypostasis* asserts the positive. In virtue of the *egeneto,* that is, in virtue of the *assumptio,* the human nature acquires existence (subsistence) in the existence of God. . . . We have seen earlier that what the eternal Word made His own, giving it thereby His own existence, was not a man, but man's nature, man's being, and so not a second existence but a second possibility of existence, that of a man. (*Church Dogmatics* I/2, p. 163).

kenōsis. The Greek word for "emptying." This word in its nominal form does not occur in the New Testament but is used to refer to Paul's doctrine that Christ "emptied himself" to become incarnate (Phil. 2:7a). But of what did he empty himself? Clearly it could not be of his divinity as such; otherwise he would not be true God and true man. Generally speaking, the Church fathers held to the doctrine of **krypsis** (hiding), but this was attacked by some nineteenth-century Lutheran and Anglican theologians for mitigating Paul's teaching; but these views collapsed under the strong attacks of Karl Barth.

krypsis. The Greek word for "hiding," referring here to the doctrine that Christ's divinity could not be so overwhelmingly obvious that faith was rendered unnecessary. To the extent that this term was used to explain Paul's doctrine of **kenōsis,** it was attacked as not so much explaining the doctrine as explaining it away.

Logos asarkos. The Word or Logos considered apart from the flesh of Christ, a term used to distinguish the Second Person of the Trinity in his pre-incarnate role in contrast to the **Logos ensarkos,** meaning the enfleshed Word, the incarnate Word.

Logos-sarx Christology. Literally "Word-flesh" Christology. Because of its roots in John 1:14 ("The Word became flesh"), this style of Christology can be orthodox but rarely is. For it most often refers to the heresy of **Apollinarianism,** which says that the Logos *replaced* what would have been the human soul of Christ and assumed only flesh, not mind or soul. This heresy collapsed for two reasons: first, it would mean that our souls too were not redeemed, since what was not assumed was not saved. Second, it brought back the dread specter of **Arianism**: since Christ clearly suffered, got angry, felt hunger, and so on, he had to have a human soul to feel these woes; otherwise one would be ascribing human emotions and feelings to the divinity, an impossibility — and a heresy, **patripassianism**.

modalism. Technically, a trinitarian heresy that says that God is only One but "comes across" in salvation history in three "modes" or aspects: in the Old Testament God appears as Father, in the New Testament as Son, and in the Church after Pentecost as Spirit. Because of the name of one of its chief proponents, this heresy also goes under the name of Sabellianism. The terms **monarchianism** and **patripassianism** are also used. Despite its status as a trinitarian heresy, it was refuted on christological grounds, by using the example of Jesus in the Gospels: If Jesus was God in his totality, then whom was he praying to during his life? This refutation is obviously so probative that the modalist proposal had a very short life indeed. But its condemnation was important because it opened up the way to a more full-bodied trinitarian theology, meaning that the distinctions between the **persons** of the Trinity were eternal distinctions within the divine life of God.

monarchianism. Another name for **modalism**, so called because its advocates denied the distinction of **persons** in the Trinity.

monophysitism. The heresy that said that Christ had only one nature, divine. The orthodox doctrine said that Christ had two natures, called **dyophysitism** (sometimes spelled **duophysitism**).

monothelitism. The heresy that said Christ had only one will. The orthodox counterpart is **dyothelitism** (sometimes spelled **duothelitism**).

nature. That which is inherent to something, "innate," as we say. The word has an extraordinary range of meanings (some incompatible with other usages) in ethics ("natural law"), psychology ("natural character," "nature vs. nurture"), anthropology (human "nature"), metaphysics ("essence") and theology (see **physis**). Here I shall rely on Thomas Aquinas's definition:

> We should note that the word *nature* is derived from *nascendo* [being born]; hence the nativity of living beings, that is, animals and plants, was first called *natura*, as though the word were *nascitura*. Then the term "na-

ture" was extended to the principle of this nativity. And because the principle of such nativity is internal, the name "nature" was further employed to designate the interior principle of movement. . . . And because natural motion, especially in procreation and generation, has as its term the essence of a species, that essence of a species — signified by its definition — is called nature. (*Quaestio disputata de unione Verbi incarnati,* article 1)

Nestorianism. The heretical version of **two-natures Christology,** which so stressed the impassibility of God that only Jesus' human nature suffered at the cross because the Logos (by definition impassible) could not, although Christ's human nature was received into heaven by virtue of *its* (not *his*!) obedience and union with the divine nature. Nestorius, in other words, turned two-natures Christology into a "two-sons" Christology.

ousia. The Greek word for "essence." Normally, the word for essence can be used as the equivalent of "nature," in the sense that if it is man's nature to be a rational animal, it is also his essence. Therefore, just as **physis** might have been used interchangeably with **hypostasis,** so could *ousia.* But just as pressure from **Nestorianism** forced the orthodox party to distinguish *physis* from *hypostasis,* so **Arianism** forced the orthodox party (primarily the Cappadocians) to distinguish *ousia* from *hypostasis* in trinitarian theology. Thus Nicea defined God as one in essence (hence **homoousios**) but three in *hypostases.* Unfortunately for students first trying to get a handle on this terminology, the Latins usually translated *ousia* with *substantia* ("substance"), which is the literal meaning of *hypostasis.* For that term they used **persona** ("person"), which originally meant "mask" and thus was a much weaker term than *hypostasis,* which obviously connoted something more, well, substantial. At all events, in matters trinitarian, one must never equate *ousia* with *hypostasis,* and in Christology *hypostasis* must not be equated with *physis,* even if such important distinctions were not present in the philosophical literature prior to the advent of Christianity.

patripassianism. Literally a doctrine that asserted that the Father suffered when Christ suffered. When used as a synonym for **modalism,** the term is somewhat of a misnomer, since the modalists held that the entirety of the godhead was in Christ (this view supposedly then preserved monotheism), although one modalist did assert that the Father suffered, since Christ really is only the Father; and from the notoriety of that position came the name *patripassianism.* Since patripassianism makes no distinction between the **persons** of the Trinity, it is also called **monarchianism.** Outside of patristic controversies, the term can also be used generally to refer to contemporary views in which God is held to take on the sufferings of the world.

persona/prosōpon. Latin and Greek terms for **person**, respectively. The term originally meant "mask" or "countenance" and thus was favored by Nestorians for describing the unity of Christ's being, since they tended to downplay the substantial unity of Christ lest they fall into what was for them the absurdity of saying things like "God suffered." But an overstress on **hypostasis** could end up downplaying the humanity of Christ, as the career of **monophysitism** showed. Therefore Chalcedon, which wanted to give due credit to what was valuable in **two-natures Christology** used both terms, to the evident displeasure of the monophysites. The Latin word *persona* was used by Tertullian in the second century to describe the three Persons of the Trinity. Although, taken literally, such a term could smack of **modalism**, it was accepted since *substantia* was already used to translate **hypostasis** and was thus unavailable. One other detail: the word "person" now means quite the opposite of mask, the exterior presentation of someone ("role" fills that function now). Currently, it denotes that which is most interior and intimate; and that largely occurred under the influence of trinitarian theology.

physis. The Greek word for "nature," that which is inherent to something. Though in many contexts, especially outside of theology, it can mean much the same as "essence" or "substance," theologians were forced to distinguish it from its semantic relatives, **ousia** and **hypostasis**.

psilanthropism. The heresy usually known as **adoptionism** that says Jesus was only a man, from the Greek *psilos anthrōpos* meaning "mere man."

Sabellianism. See **modalism**.

subordinationism. Technically an aspect of trinitarian theology, it was almost universally held by theologians in the third century because of Jesus' statement that "the Father is greater than I" (John 14:28c), and Paul's statement that "Christ was the firstborn of *creation*" (Col. 1:15b). But Arius radicalized this subordinationism by making it, so to speak, ontological. That is, he claimed that Jesus was truly a lesser god by asserting that "there was once when he was not." But for Athanasius a lesser god (and a changeable one at that) could only bring a lesser salvation, in effect no salvation at all. The Nicene Council (325) condemned Arianism (but not Arius by name). This of course left open the question of how to interpret John 14:28c, which eventually led to the distinction between the **economic and immanent Trinity**.

two-natures Christology. The doctrine that says Jesus Christ has two complete natures, divine and human, lacking in nothing that is essential to either nature. When the two natures are seen as too much juxtaposed and separated, it then takes the heretical form called **Nestorianism**. When the two natures are seen as too fused, with the divine nature absorbing the human, **monophysitism** results.

INDEX

The authors of the epigraphs at the start of each chapter and the terms defined in the Glossary are not listed in this Index. The pages in **bold** indicate the major treatment of that theologian or topic.

Bornkamm, Günther, 97n.51
Boyle, John F., 67-69, 198n.64
Bremond, Henri, 292
Brown, David, 176n.12, 179n.19, 181
Brown, Raymond E., 89n.35
Bucer, Martin, 247
Bultmann, Rudolf, 94-95, 376-77
Burke, Kevin, 357n.20
Butterfield, Herbert, 105n.65

Calvin, John, 19, **245-58**, 259, 265-67,
  388-89
Cappadocians, **133-35**
Carol, Juniper, 205n.3
*Catechism of the Catholic Church
  (CCC)*, **417-20**
Cavadini, John, 126n.24, 170n.2
Celsus, 6, 331
Chalcedon, Council of, **149-53**
Chenu, M. D., 193n.54, 198n.64
Chesterton, G. K., 12, 19-20, 135n.45,
  143n.61, 203, 261
Chiasmus, 183, 242
Christology: Antiochene vs. Alexan-
  drine, 138; high vs. low, 77-80;
  kenotic, 319-30; paradoxical language
  of, **9-23** 202-4, 262n.78. *See also*
  Barth, Karl: on kenotic Christology;
  Jesus: Christology of; John, Christol-
  ogy of; Logos-Sarx Christology;
  Luke: Christology of; Mark, Christol-
  ogy of; Matthew, Christology of; Old
  Testament Christology; Paul, Chris-
  tology of; Sacred Heart of Jesus;
  Two-Natures Christology
Clement XI, 295
Coakley, Sarah, 337n.9
Collins, James, 303
Congregation of the Doctrine of the
  Faith (CDF), 269, **405-17**
Cullmann, Oscar, 28-35, 46-48, 51n.36,
  54, 56-60
Cyril of Alexandria, 16-17, **141-48**, 152-
  53, 156, 217n.93, 385

Daley, Brian, 117

Dalton, W. J., 384n.67
Daniélou, Jean, 391
De Jonge, M., 98
De Lubac, Henri, 115, 260n.75, 290,
  401n.8
Delio, Ilia, 184n.34, 187n.40, 188n.41
Descent into Hell, Christ's, 366-70, 378-
  80, **382-93**; Aquinas on, 387; Augus-
  tine on, 384-85, 388n.75; Balthasar on,
  366-70; Barth on, 277-78, 393; Calvin
  on, 388-89; *Catechism of the Catholic
  Church* on, 369-70; Ratzinger/Pope
  Benedict XVI on, 378-80, 391-93;
  Thérèse of Lisieux on, 390-91; Wesley
  on, 389-90
Deschner, John, 284n.21, 285, 287n.32,
  288, 389-90
Diachronic analysis, 26-27, 63-67
DiNoia, J. A., 370n.45
Dioscorus, 148
Dodd, C. H., 39, 73-74, 79n.80, 91n.38
Dominus Iesus (DI: 2000 decree of the
  CDF), 408-9, 411, 413
Dulles, Avery Cardinal, 106, 402n.9
Dupré, Louis, 292
Dupuis, Jacques, 269, **411-15**

Earman, John, 100n.57
Epanados, 183n.28
Evennett, H. Outram, 222n.1
Euthyphro, 273n.2
Eutyches/Eutychianism, 148, 196
Extra Calvinisticum, 252-53, **265-70**, 411,
  416-17; Barth on, 268-69

Fairbairn, A. M., 321n.47
Fee, Gordon D., 79n.20
Fitzmyer, Joseph, 25n.3
Fredriksen, Paula, 71, 87-88, 90n.37, 91,
  103n.63

Galot, Jean, 210-11
Gavrilyuk, Paul L., 18, 132n.38, 133n.39,
  147
Geach, Peter, 12-13
Gerrish, B. A., 254-55, 257-58